Double Cross

Double Cross

The Code of the Catholic Church

David Ranan

Theo Press

Published by Theo Press Ltd.
Suite 229, 19-21 Crawford Street
London W1H 1PJ

ISBN 978-0-9554133-0-8

Cover design and typsetting by Mark Lee.

A catalogue record for this book is available from the British Library.

For Germaine Davys
1915 – 1944

Contents

Contents

Introduction

The renowned Catholic theologian and dissenter Hans Küng asserts that even though 'Rome has recently been asking "for forgiveness" for the monstrous errors and atrocities of the past … the present-day church administration and inquisition are producing still more victims'.[1]

People who live in countries in which the Catholic Church is powerful are rarely indifferent to her. Religion tends to bring out strong reactions. It may be its absoluteness, the underlying issues of life and death it deals with, or the history of its power which cause most people to have not only a view about religion but very often an emotional one. The Catholic Church is a worldwide organisation that offers its members spiritual and moral guidance and support. Her message is love and hope. Based on the teachings of Jesus, a power structure was built which has outlived any other political structure in the world. In addition to her religious services, the Church operates a wide range of social, educational and medical institutions throughout the world. There are countries in which the entire medical or educational infrastructures were first established by the Church and in some of them they are still run by her. Thousands of Catholic priests, monks, nuns and lay members dedicate their lives to good work inspired and encouraged by the Church. And yet, not only outsiders but also insiders believe that the Church must change and reform herself. Küng speaks of an organisation which 'deals in a despicable way with critics … discriminate[s] so much against women … polarises society'.[2] The Catholic writer and professor, Garry Wills, writes about 'Papal Sin' and 'Structures of Deceit'.[3] Whereas some Catholics who are unhappy with their Church hope that she will indeed reform, outsiders sometimes attack the Church with blind hostility that almost nears religious fervour. The Church herself tries to reject writers who attack her by attempting to de-legitimise them or their motives. Insiders are described as 'bitter "ex-priests", or jaundiced "ex-seminarians"' or even worse as 'fraudulent Catholics'.[4] Outsiders are discarded as those who do not understand the Church and simply wish to harm her.

This book deals with the Church as a power structure and not with her beliefs. It is not about Catholicism. It does not question Catholic theological dogma. Nor does it investigate spiritual aspects of the Catholic religion. It does not doubt the many benefits which religious people derive from their religion, nor does it doubt that many of the Catholic clergy are honest, true and loving. I am definitely an outsider. My interest in the potency of power, its use, abuse and manipulation have inspired me in my research and writing. The trigger for this work, which covers a range of issues from the Catholic Church's history, was the revelations concerning Church policy to cover up the sexual abuse of minors by her clergy. My intention in writing this book is to reflect on whether there is systemic fault inherent in the Church. Where and why is it going wrong? What in her structure and her culture causes the Church to act as she does? Is it possible to repair the defect? To this end, I set out with a wide angle which enables me to take an across-the-board approach and consider a fuller context of the Church's history, dogma and strategies. It is based on the assumption that abuse is not a single issue problem but systemic and that in order to understand it her structures and decision-making have to be examined. Unlike the faithful insiders who promote reform within the Church – because they would not consider the dismantling of the Church – I question the ability of the Church to change.

Recent fundamentalist politicians, US presidents Ronald Reagan and George W. Bush, have introduced the religious faith-weighted term *evil* into our political jargon. Ronald Reagan famously included the phrase *evil empire* in the 1983 speech he gave before the National Association of Evangelicals Convention. Here he sought to recruit religious leaders to his campaign against the Soviet Union, to which the phrase referred.[5] Right after suicide bombers attacked the Twin Towers in New York and the Pentagon in Washington on 11 September 2001, President George W. Bush adopted the *evil* terminology. At the time, the US and most of the Western world, were still in shock from the attack by *Al Quaeda*, a fundamentalist Muslim group, which with its successful missions had managed to question the world's general status quo. As an adjective, evil is popularly synonymous with foul, nasty and malicious. However, Bush has left us in no doubt that he was using the word as a noun, as he soon defined three countries as an *axis of evil* and then proceeded to wage war against Iraq, one of the three. As a noun, evil has definite religious connotations. Indeed, in an off-the-cuff remark, Bush even referred to his war as a crusade, reminding his public of Church-generated wars to liberate the Holy Land from Muslim control.

As the notion of organisational structures encompassing evil was introduced by politicians appealing to the religious voter, we might attempt to turn the tables and ask ourselves whether what is normally perceived to be the opposite of evil, a religious organisation such as the Catholic Church, could, in actual fact, be institutionally evil. At first, this would almost seem to be a contradiction in terms. How could the

Catholic Church, which is founded on Jesus' teachings of faith, hope and love, be evil? Abusive husbands, in all likelihood, truly believe and honestly undertake to 'love and to cherish till death do us part'. The ideas espoused by Jesus were indeed all about love, faith and hope. Very soon, however, like the abusive husbands, the Church, the structure which was established around Jesus' teaching, became nasty and abusive. The nineteenth-century German philosopher Friedrich Nietzsche suggested that 'The Christian resolve to find the world evil and ugly, has made the world evil and ugly.'[6] Was Nietzsche right? Has the Church made the world evil and ugly?

Religion, the belief in a superhuman controlling power, serves as a powerful medium which attempts to lay to rest or, at least, respond to some of the existential *angsts* of mankind. The magician who was able to convince his audience that, by following his recipe, his rules, and ultimately him, the eclipsed sun would return and thus not leave them in darkness and in the cold forever, became a powerful person in his community. The man who maintains that he has the formula which will prevent his adherents from burning in the fires of hell, will place them in heaven and, eventually bring them back to life, continues to have a following, is still able to command respect and even to discipline his followers. Religions are adept at exploiting human anxiety, human weaknesses and the centrality of the non-rational in human life. Many institutions, not only religious ones, are established to be power bases geared to bring under their control certain aspects of human behaviour as defined by their objectives. Some lobbies against the use of animals in research laboratories or against hunting are examples of such institutions. Crucial in the assessment of them is the means they employ to realise their objectives.

The use of force by agencies other than state ones is not usually tolerated by secular power holders. Force does not necessarily have to be physical. Psychological manipulation can be very powerful. The means used by religious organisations to attain and to hold on to power are sophisticated and potent: a storyline based on faith rather than facts combined with ceremonies which are designed to strike awe and instil respect in the congregation for the relevant god and, importantly also, for the human medium purporting to speak in that god's name. These are rounded off with threats of punishment unless rules – as set out by the hierarchy of the religious organisation – are followed.

The Catholic Church draws her strength from her claim to be God's vehicle, in fact God's unique vehicle. From early on, the Church was tremendously successful in her marketing efforts, eventually persuading most of the Western world to become members. Although schisms at various stages in her history brought about the establishment of competing Christian Churches, she is still considered a leading force in matters of

3

spiritual and moral guidance. The Church's success and her seminal impact would not have been possible if human nature was not receptive, even susceptible, to decisiveness on one hand, and to the proffering of hope on the other. Human frailty is the basis of the Church's prosperity and she is adept at spreading *angst* and deepening guilt. Having instilled fear, the Church proceeds to offer love and hope.

To deepen her hold and further her interests, the Catholic Church has developed political mass. Initially, heads of state were targeted and either personally caught by religion, or made to understand that there was enough of a Church-bound population in their countries that they could not afford to disregard the Church. This enabled the Church to infiltrate her own teachings into states' legislation. In return, Christianity taught that obedience to the ruler was a duty imposed by God.[7]

The Catholic Church enjoys a special status around the world. In addition to the political power she has gained in many countries, thereby influencing state legislation, the Church runs the State of Vatican City which, as an independent state, enjoys all the trappings of statehood. These include diplomatic immunity for those it nominates as diplomats, tax advantages and membership of various international organisations (such as observer status at the United Nations and membership of the Bank for International Settlements). The pope doubles as head of the Church and head of State. This status is unique to the Catholic Church. No other religion benefits from having the powers of a sovereign state. In addition to this exceptional status, many countries have granted the Church special rights including exemption from tax, exemption from army service to her priests and the right to keep information, revealed in confession, confidential, even where reporting that information would prevent a crime. Although some countries have granted rights to other religious organisations too, the Catholic Church is the largest global and centralised religious structure.

The close juxtaposition of 'vice' and 'vicar' in the dictionary is almost emblematic of the allegations of sexual abuse by Catholic priests in positions of trust and authority, which have hounded the Church for many years. The increasing number of disclosures about sexual abuse within the Catholic Church snowballed in the first months of 2002. The developing freedom of the press in the Western world in the last decades of the twentieth century has brought issues to the public domain which, for many years, had been kept hidden by the powerful Church. The decline in the power of the Church has enabled questions, which previously had only been whispered, to be openly discussed. And the questions asked were not solely about the Church's sex scandals.

This book investigates various areas in which the Catholic Church has been, and still is, active and reveals that the Church has used her power sometimes illegally, often immorally and always undemocratically and without any transparency. It further demonstrates that such conduct is inherent in the culture and the structure of the Church. None of the situations described are one-offs. There is continuity in the misbehaviour and similarity in the cover-up which have not changed over centuries.

Manipulation and distortion are notoriously employed by the 'wicked'.[8] Religion exploits such means too. Without indulging in the question of whether religion is, as Marx suggested, opium for the masses, there is no doubt that religious leaders are often able to exert strong influence over their followers. The Catholic Church, which has a history of urging her flock to blind obedience, has made proficient use of propaganda devices which were geared to impress the senses. Catholic ceremonies involve a high level of theatricality, music, incense, and often within powerful architecture. As a result, Church members are sometimes damaged and act in ways which are harmful to themselves and to others. In such situations, the matter becomes a public concern. Police officers around the world collaborated with the Catholic Church in hushing up sexual assaults by Catholic clergy. Time after time, at the request of local bishops, police would 'let the Church deal with the matter', and even keep paedophile assaults out of the police files. Every police officer who colluded with the Church in such hush-ups was not only acting illegally, he was also directly responsible for the suffering of additional victims of the abusive priest he had shielded. The likely explanation for such deviation from their role and general commitment to values of law and order is the informal power of the Church, the awe in which she is held and the psychological subordination *vis-à-vis* the Church hierarchy. This also explains the refusal of Massachusetts lawmakers, seventy-five per cent of whom were members of the Catholic Church, to include clergy in a 1983 bill requiring a very wide and inclusive list of professions (police officers, teachers, doctors, social workers etc.) to report suspected child abuse. The Church objected and her members obliged.[9]

Even at the price of curtailing free choice, society sometimes protects itself from activities and organisations which it considers contrary to the public interest. Laws which make the wearing of seat-belts compulsory or prohibit various drugs are examples of attempts to protect us from ourselves. Speed limits and the setting of noise levels and of pollution levels which may not be exceeded are imposed to protect us from each other. There is a growing tendency to legislate in various areas of consumer protection, to safeguard us from unwittingly being taken advantage of by commercial enterprises. Much of that is concerned with ensuring the availability of information about the products and services we are being sold. Attention is also drawn to the possible abuse through environmental conditioning at decision-making points. There is a view that we should be safeguarded from buying products we would otherwise not have bought, when shops surround us with music and scent which alter our state of mind. There is an awareness and a wariness of psychological manipulation. We tend to be more vigilant nowadays, in regulating advertising, to ensure that it does not exert undue influence over its target population. Such regulation is liable to touch on issues of free speech and general liberal concepts.

We may have to consider legislation which will safeguard society from undue influence by the Church. It sometimes takes substantial traumatic experiences to bring about change. In some US states, under present legislation a policeman who sees two men in the street, one holding an open beer can, the other holding a pistol, will let the man with the pistol walk on and arrest the man with the open beer can. The alcohol lobby in the USA has not yet succeeded in doing away with the remnants of the alcohol prohibition years (1919 to 1933). The gun lobby, on the other hand, has been successful in preventing anti-gun laws from being passed, although calls for such legislation regularly arise whenever some brutal murders make the national news in the US. The clerical sex abuse and Church cover-up scandals have changed the attitude of some legislators with regard to the extra-territoriality of the Church.

How evil must a structure be before we decide to close it down? Should the fact that occasional popes have moved in positive directions be enough to save the Church? Jonah Goldhagen is not alone in considering the Church to bear responsibility for the deaths of many Jews throughout much of her history. However, Goldhagen suggests that 'the Church though populous, is weak … and is politically incapable of enforcing its wishes on its members and those over whom it would like to gain suzerainty'. He concludes that 'these limiting features reduce the likelihood of physical danger resulting from the Church's doctrines, the parallel organisational structure that embodies them and its practices'.[10] He may be mistaken in his assessment. Catholic doctrine concerning contraception, for example, contributes directly to the spread of AIDS and the deaths of people who to this very day continue to be instructed, convinced and prevented by the Church from using condoms. Thousands of women continue to die each year from botched back-street abortions in countries where, due to Church influence and pressure, abortions are not made legally available. The Church may no longer have armies at her disposal, but she still is very powerful in playing with the minds of the faithful. Especially vulnerable are the uneducated, the poor and those living in less developed countries.

As a structure which cultivates political and other power bases, the Catholic Church has compromised her original values and is considered by some to have lost the purity of commitment exemplified by Jesus, whose teaching and whose life, after all, form the basis of the truth which the Catholic Church purports to proclaim. She could have been wonderful. She could have promoted values of love and respect, been at the forefront of the bettering of human rights, of racial equality, sexual equality, democracy, freedom, liberalism, equal opportunities regardless of sex, sexuality, race, religion, social strata or wealth. Social norms, political norms and human rights in many Western countries have undergone substantial advancement. It would be wrong to pass judgement on previous generations solely on the basis of present-day standards. Yet, would one not have expected the Church to be and to have been at the forefront of positive change, at the forefront of the struggle to abolish slavery, the forefront of the opposition to colonialism, the forefront of enlightenment, and the forefront of the move towards democracy? Instead, at the time when there were slaves, the Church actually owned slaves. When Spain and Portugal sent their respective navies to capture new lands, subdue their populations and steal their riches, the Pope determined which areas should be conquered by Spain and which should be colonised by Portugal. To stop people from reading any new ideas which might enlighten them, the Church compiled a list of prohibited books.[11] In 1864, Pope Pius IX (1846–1878) condemned the notion that the Roman Pontiff ought to 'come to terms with progress, liberalism and modern civilization'.[12]

Indeed, more often than not the Church was a bulwark against progress. Although now pro-democracy, the Church was, historically, a regular bed-fellow of dictators and still collaborates with questionable regimes, provided they are Church-friendly. The Church was at best a follower, never a leader of enlightenment. Whilst the Church still had temporal power, and as late as the 1830s, she executed people who tried to revolt against the ever-higher taxation which the Holy See demanded,[13] whereas, in the 1970s, the Vatican transferred its assets outside Italy to avoid paying Italian withholding tax.[14] The fact is that new progressive ideas were conceived and did get promoted, often at great risk to their initiators, but progress came from other corners of society and not from the Catholic Church. Instead she participated in wars and ran her own torture chambers to persecute those who would not accept her authority. She locked Jews in ghettos and deprived them of their most basic human rights. She still objects to the freedom to use contraceptives, to women's rights to end unwanted pregnancies and to equal rights for homosexuals. When smallpox inoculations were first developed, the Church prohibited their use,[15] just as she now prohibits HIV-infected persons from using condoms.

With that track record, the Catholic Church still expects to be considered by the whole world as a symbol of and spokesman for ethical principles. She demands and has been given rights to participate in various United Nations forums, and energetically attempts to influence political life in Europe, the United States and wherever else she can because, it is maintained, the pope is the spiritual leader of more than a billion Catholics and a moral spokesman for the entire world. Indeed, millions of Catholics were brought up to look up to the pope as their moral guide. And yet, how dismal is the Church's record. Should we allow the holders of this record to continue wielding influence? Should we let those who so easily sink to evil continue to cause suffering?

This book investigates topics which are central to assessing the question 'is the Church inherently evil?' The Church's attitude to non-Catholics is examined, starting from her missionary and evangelising activities by means which often could – at best – be defined as 'not-Christian'. In this context the use of the crusades and of the Inquisition as instruments to combat heresy are also explored. Other wars which the Church instigated or was party to, often had purely materialistic motives. Many of these wars took place in the most corrupt periods in the Church's history. The book also examines other forms of corruption in the Church up to twentieth-century financial scandals. The relationship of the Church with Jews and her responsibility for the Holocaust are evaluated in separate chapters. Two areas of major significance, the Church's attitude to sex and sexual abuse within the Church, are each investigated.

This book is not about the Church's culpability, shame or scandal in any one particular area. It focuses on the Catholic Church as a structure that has failed. It has failed its own ideals, it has failed its hierarchy, it has failed its members and it has failed the rest of humanity. Significantly it is a dangerous structure. If she is evil, what is it in the structure of the Catholic Church which causes her to be so? Why has it caused so much alienation? Why has a Church which is supposed to be about life caused so much death? Where has she gone wrong? Is there a way out?

Part One

The Church and Power

Chapter One
Structures and Power Base

The Catholic Church has succeeded – more than any other religious organisation – in integrating herself into the world's political power structures. Collaboration between religious leaders and secular leaders is a well-known and well-documented phenomenon. The Bible describes how thousands of years ago kings were anointed by the high priests. No longer anointed by priests, secular leaders continue to seek priestly approval. Thus, the secular government of Margaret Thatcher considered it useful to have a church service led by the head of the Church of England, the Archbishop of Canterbury, to mark the end of the 1982 Falklands War, and by the way, on a subconscious level, generate the impression that God was on 'our side'. This reflects the success of religion in imprinting on secular power holders that they need, or at least can benefit from, cooperation with the power brokers of the gods.

The Catholic Church is the largest religious organisation in the world with more than one billion members worldwide. She is unique among the big religions in her centralised structure. Judaism, Islam and various non-Catholic Christian churches operate without a centralised organisation. The Catholic Church is an ambitious organisation which wants the whole universe – every single living human being – to be a member, to accept her teaching, to adhere to her rules and to bow to her authority. The means she has employed have changed over the years but not the ends.

In the beginning, before she was well established, the Church depended on the backing of secular rulers. Support such as that of the Emperor Constantine, who legalised Christianity in 313, proved to be a breakthrough. With time, political power was achieved as a result of a two-pronged attack: kings, dukes and other heads of state were targeted and either personally caught by religion, or made to understand that there was enough of a Christian population in their countries that they could not afford to disregard the Church. Once the Church had achieved an influential position, she could make demands on the secular powers and could threaten the independent power of the secular heads of state.

Double Cross

The deal which the Church offered the secular rulers was the notion that they were chosen to their noble and high status by no less a being than God and therefore any disobedience to them would be tantamount to disrespect for God. Collaboration between religious and secular power bases serves both sides: the secular ruler benefits from the message given to the faithful that the almighty God supports his or her rule, thereby adding religious faith to force as a component of his or her power over the people; the religious leaders gain from status and material benefits which the state allows them to enjoy. History has shown that when religious and secular leaders clashed, the wealth and power of the religious were curtailed.

The Church and the state were often at loggerheads as to who was superior – the pope or the emperor. Popes considered that they were the appointing and anointing power, and hence the 'kingmakers', whereas emperors and kings considered that selecting and appointing bishops in their realm was their right and the pope had to keep out of it.[1] The history of the Church is also a history of the relationship between the Church and the state. The concept, known as 'The Two Swords', for what was also sometimes referred to as the *sacerdotium* and *imperium*, was developed by Pope Gelasius I (492–496). The underlying theory was that the source of everything and the origin of all power was God and that everybody in this world owed allegiance to God. There were two swords, an ecclesiastical one for spiritual matters and a temporal one for secular matters. The pope had the one sword and the emperor the other. Gelasius, in his letter to the Byzantine Emperor Anastasius, clarified the Church's view as to the supremacy of the Church over the Empire.[2] Gelasius also claimed jurisdiction, at least in spiritual matters, over all priests and teachers of Christian religion, who were 'out-of-bounds' for civil law and secular authorities. There were periods when the Church demanded more: control of both swords; at other times, she tried to accommodate to a changing world which would not accept such ideas. The power struggle produced ideological rifts which developed in tandem with the other ideological and philosophical developments in the West. And yet, with all the ups and downs in the standing of the Church, we should not forget that what Gelasius said fifteen hundred years ago is what the Church still believes to be right.

In the Middle Ages, the struggle over clerical investiture was a major conflict between the state and the Church. Lay investiture is the ceremony in which a layman such as a king or an emperor transfers a clerical office, nominating a priest or a bishop. Even if the spiritual power did not stem from the secular ruler, the nomination of the cleric in a lay investiture was that of the lay power. The tenth century saw a great decline in the papacy, a period in which powerful Roman families considered the papacy an asset to bargain with. In the eleventh century, the movement to reform the Church considered it vital to have Church control over the nomination of bishops. One of the better known episodes in the struggle took place between Pope Gregory VII (1073–1085) and the Holy Roman Emperor Henry IV. In 1075, Gregory forbade lay investiture. The idea that anyone but the pope should be able to create or depose bishops, or have any right whatsoever in the running of the Church, was totally unthinkable to this Pope. Henry IV disobeyed Gregory, who in turn excommunicated him, and nobles in Germany were encouraged by the Church to disobey the excommunicated king. In this dramatic confrontation, the Pope absolved the king's subjects from their allegiance to the king; whereas, Henry denounced the Pope and got the bishops of Lombardy to confirm his sentence deposing the Pope. Henry, whose own father had deposed three popes, was however unable to get away with his rebellion against the Church. The Pope excommunicated all the bishops who had collaborated with the king and released all Christians from allegiance to him. Henry was handed an ultimatum by the German princes: not only did they demand that he swear obedience to the Pope, they also demanded that he obtain absolution within a year of his excommunication. Henry was forced to go grovelling and the Pope indeed made him grovel. In January 1077, in Canossa, high in the snowy mountains, Pope Gregory VII made Holy Roman Emperor Henry IV, who barefoot in the snow was begging for forgiveness, prostrate himself before he granted him absolution. Confrontations between the two continued and the Pope's views on secular leaders included such utterances as: 'kings and rulers are sprung from men who were ignorant of God, who by pride, robbery, perfidy, murders, ... have striven with blind cupidity and intolerable presumption, to dominate over their equals, that is over mankind'.[3] In 1080, Gregory spoke to a council in Rome about the role of the Church in running the world. In what sounds like a call to arms he said:

> So act, I beg you, holy fathers and princes, that all the world may know that, if you have power to bind and loose in Heaven, you have power on earth to take away or grant empires, kingdoms, principalities, dukedoms, marches, counties and the possessions of all men according to their merits. ... Let kings and all the princes of the world learn how great you are and what power you have and let these small men fear to disobey the command of your church.[4]

A hundred years later, Pope Innocent III (1198–1216), who considered that the pope 'was lower than God but higher than man: one who judges all, and is judged by no one',[5] was hoping to regain territories which the Papal

States[i] had previously lost. The Pope entered into a German succession wrangle, aiming to negotiate a deal on Sicily, which the Church claimed was her fief. Innocent's attitude, stated in his 1202 bull, *Venerabilem*, was that not only did the pope have a right to adjudicate in disputed or irregular elections, but that the papal decision should and would favour the candidate whom he considered to have the Church's interests at heart. This is an unusual concept to anyone who expects courts, judges and arbitrators to make their decisions on the merits of a case rather than on which of the sides to the conflict would best serve the arbitrator's interests. Indeed, thirteenth-century popes considered themselves not only morally superior, but also jurisdictional overlords. Innocent III claimed for the papacy a general power of review over virtually any decision made by a secular leader. In 1212, Innocent chose to support Frederick II and in 1215 the Fourth Lateran Council elected Frederick Holy Roman Emperor. Frederick would soon renege on the agreements made with the Church but would eventually have to pay the price for crossing the popes. Innocent's successor, Honorius III (1216–1227), elicited a promise from Frederick to undertake a crusade, a promise the Emperor did not keep. The next pope, Gregory IX (1227–1241) actually excommunicated Frederick for not keeping his pledge.[ii] Gregory, a nephew of the pope who had first established the relationship with Frederick, was in constant confrontation with the Emperor, a battle of both fiery language and fiery acts: in 1241, to prevent bishops from attending a Council which the Pope had called, Frederick kidnapped one hundred bishops by seizing their boats. It took one more pope to break the emperor's might and thereby draw that German dynasty to an end. Pope Innocent IV (1243–1254) summoned a council in Lyons in 1245, which excommunicated Frederick, deposed him and encouraged disobedience amongst the German princes. Innocent defined his power, *plenitude potestatis*:

> Though there are many offices and governments in the world, there can always be an appeal to the pope when necessary, whether the need arises from the law, because the judge is uncertain what decision he ought legally to give, or from fact, because there is no higher judge, or because inferior judges cannot execute their judgements, or are not willing to do justice as they ought.[6]

This papal claim to authority stemmed from the contention that the pope was the successor of Peter and the Vicar of Christ. Another Pope who had

---

[i] For more than a thousand years popes were not only spiritual heads of the Catholic world but also secular rulers of territories, sometimes referred to as *Patrimonium Sancti Petri*, and better known as the Papal States. These were lands which were partly granted to her by kings and partly seized by the Church in wars until finally in 1870 she lost them to the newly united Kingdom of Italy.

[ii] Frederick did eventually embark on a crusade, the Sixth, in 1228.

strong views about the supremacy of the Church over secular leaders and who was willing to go into battle for his opinions was Boniface VIII (1294–1303). In *Unam Sanctam*, his papal bull of 1302, Boniface maintained that both swords were, in fact, his and that the princes only had use of the secular sword, granted to them by the pope, for the good of the Church. To avoid any misunderstanding, the bull states: 'it is altogether necessary for salvation for every human creature to be subject to the Roman Pontiff'.[7] Boniface decided to stand up against Philip IV (Philip the Fair), the King of France, whose ambition was to be the head of an empire which would include the Papal States. The Pope stood no chance and in 1303 the French King responded by sending French forces to attack the Pope in his own palace in Anagni. They did not kill the Pope, but – a broken man – he died a month later. This extreme papal doctrine, promulgated at a time of great papal weakness, did not deliver the goods the Pope must have hoped for. Several years later, the papacy itself was compelled to move from Rome to Avignon and would stay there until 1377. The so-called 'Avignon papacy' is sometimes also referred to as the 'Babylonian captivity' – a period in which popes became a tool of the French monarchy. Soon after its return in 1377 to Rome, the papacy fell into a schism, out of which it did not emerge until 1417. For forty years there were two contemporaneous popes and, for a while, even three.[8]

The period of an ever-sinking reputation of the Church produced revulsion and rebels, leading to Martin Luther (1483–1546). Luther, a theology professor in Wittenberg in Germany was so disgusted by the Church's practice of selling indulgences[iii] that he decided to act. The starting date for the Reformation, the movement which broke the monopoly of the Catholic Church in Western Christianity, is normally thought of as 1517, the year that Luther famously nailed a sheet with ninety-five theses (arguments against the sale of indulgences), to the door of the Wittenberg castle church. However, it did not start with Luther as dissent had been brewing for almost a century. Nor did it end with Luther; it continued evolving with people like John Calvin, a contemporary of Luther, down to the eighteenth-century founder of the Methodist Church, John Wesley. The Church often declared dissenters, heretics, persecuted them and sometimes handed over them to the state authorities for punishment. As opposition to the Church grew, rulers became more and more reluctant to do the Church's 'dirty work'. Luther's rebellion gained momentum with the support of German princes who pushed Emperor Charles V for *cuius regio, eius religio*. This formula was agreed in the 1555 Peace of Augsburg, giving rulers the right to decide the religion in their country. The idea that a secular ruler should be able to choose the religion of his people and whether his country would be

---

iii   Indulgences were documents releasing the holder from punishment in Purgatory and they were sold to fill the coffers of the Vatican.

Catholic or Protestant was anathema to the Church. This was a very long way from the old Church concept that the secular rulers owed their power and their authority to the popes and had definitely no say in matters of faith. In post-Lutheran Europe the position of the Catholic Church was substantially eroded. The state–Church relationship may have reached a different balance, but these two power structures continued to be intertwined.

The decline of the papacy in the fifteenth and sixteenth centuries and the rise of nation states changed the rules of engagement between the Church and the states. The Church could no longer command heads of state to prostrate themselves in the snow in the hope of receiving absolution, but her objectives did not change. The means had to be modified. She continued to be a very powerful organisation, skilful in furthering her interests.

The Church continued to fight secular rulers, but mainly co-existed with them. In the Inquisition, her campaigns to persecute those she considered heretics, the Church utilised the arrangements and treaties she had with various states in which she operated. It involved imprisonment and torture, internment without trial, confiscation of property and even death. Death sentences were carried out by secular powers at the behest of the Catholic Church. Another area of symbiosis between the Church and the state were the missionary activities in the colonies. European powers sent armies forcefully to colonise countries in Africa, Asia and South America to extract their gold and silver and whatever else they could lay their hands on. The Church gave her blessing and in return Christian missionaries were allowed to convert the local population. In these two realms of Church–state collaboration violence was employed in the name of God and of the Church, as a result of which many suffered and many died.[iv]

In the eighteenth century, the erosion of Church power continued. Catholic monarchs whittled away the power of the popes. The rulers of France, the Holy Roman Empire, Spain and Portugal understood the power of religion and therefore wanted to control the Church themselves. Basic conflicts of interest, which turned into serious clashes, were sometimes supported by theological argumentation. European monarchs backed theologies, such as *Gallicanism* or *Febronianism*, which wanted to transfer power from the papacy to the bishops, and as bishops were appointed by the kings, to move power from the popes to the monarchs. In 1768 the Duke of Parma issued an edict forbidding appeals to Rome by anyone in his duchy, unless the appeal had his prior approval. The irritated Pope, Clement XIII (1758–1769), issued a declaration nullifying the Duke's edict. European rulers no longer allowed a pope to cross a secular head

---

iv   They are dealt with in more detail in Chapter 4.

of state and their reaction was immediate: the Pope had based his action on the old papal bull *In Coena Domini*, which two hundred years earlier had caused much tension between Church and state. Consequently, Portugal, Naples, Parma, Monaco, Genoa, Venice and Austria declared it treason to print, sell or distribute the bull. France used the opportunity to occupy Avignon and Naples occupied Benevento, both of which were papal territories.

As papal power declined and more states emancipated themselves from the hold of the Church, the Church sought to formalise and secure her interests by negotiating concordats – treaties between states and the Holy See regulating the civil status of the Church. Monarchs were willing to pay a certain price, both monetary and political, for a peaceful agreement with the Church. Thus, for example, rather than unilaterally annulling the Church's rights without an agreement, Spain paid compensation for the transfer of virtually all the benefices from the Church to the Spanish crown in the framework of the 1753 concordat.

In the mid-nineteenth century concordats were signed with many Latin American countries. Among other provisions these concordats agreed that: the Catholic religion was declared the state religion; unrestricted communication with the pope was guaranteed to clergy and laity; education was placed under the supervision of the bishops, as was the censorship of books. Tithes were abolished and the expenses of worship were to be defrayed by the State; the ecclesiastical courts were recognised only for purely spiritual matters, temporal matters were to be subject to the civil jurisdiction; the right to acquire and possess property was guaranteed to the Church. Varying arrangements were made with regard to the nomination of bishops. A prayer for the republic was granted by the Church and in some concordats the Church agreed that the name of the local ruler be inserted in the Canon.

'Monopoly Catholicism' is the term coined by sociologist David Martin to describe the Catholic Church's politics in countries in which the population is predominantly Catholic. In such countries the Church offers her educational, social and sometimes medical services to the state in return for a special status granting her religious monopoly and a certain control over the population. In these countries, whatever their political system (monarchy, democracy or dictatorship), the Church preaches loyalty to the government, which, grateful for the Church's delivery of God as a supporter of the regime, gives the Church full control over the faith and moral values of the population.

The historical base of the Church's power was Europe. Enlightenment and democratisation weakened the Church's hold over political state-structures in Europe. It is therefore not surprising that the Church objected to these new concepts when they first appeared. As the head of the Catholic Church, no pope could be expected to have sympathy for religious freedom, and as monarchs themselves, popes rightly feared republicanism. In his 1832 encyclical *Mirari vos*, Pope Gregory XVI (1831–1846) attacked the 'absurd and erroneous doctrine or rather delirium, that freedom of conscience is to be claimed and defended for all men'. The Pope also made it clear that upsetting the 'rights of rulers' was a 'detestable and insolent malice'.[9] Papal objections did not stop democratisation or religious freedom.

In reply to a suggestion by French Foreign Minister, Pierre Laval, in 1935, that the Soviet Union should encourage Catholicism in order to propitiate the Pope, the Soviet leader, Joseph Stalin, reportedly asked: 'The Pope? How many divisions has he got?' The Catholic Church would not have been so successful had she not had some kind of divisions, different from those referred to by Stalin, but still powerful. The answer to Stalin's question lies in the loyalty of the Catholics to their spiritual leader and to their Church. The greater the Catholic population of a country, the more powerful is the Church in her dealings with that country. Napoleon, for one, understood this. He even put a number on it: he explained that the moral authority of the Pope was the equivalent of an army of two hundred thousand soldiers.[10] Less than fifty years after Stalin had asked his rhetorical question, Leonid Brezhnev and the Soviet leadership had to face the successful deployment in Poland of the pope's divisions, the importance of which Stalin had belittled. Indeed, former Deputy CIA Director and President Reagan's Ambassador-at-Large, General Vernon Walters, described the Pope as 'powerful jet fuel'.[11]

The Church opposed Socialism and Communism from very early on, preceding Soviet abuse of populations under their power. In 1849, less than a year after the publication of the Communist Manifesto, Pope Pius IX (1846–1878) referred to the 'pernicious fictions of Socialism and Communism'.[12] The Catholic Church did not object to dictatorship, secret police power, mass imprisonment of political opponents and other infringements of human rights. The Church, after all, collaborated with right-wing dictatorships. What the Catholic Church objected to was an ideology which competed with her in offering a world view and a set of values by which people were called to live. Moreover, it was an ideology which totally negated religion. An 1878 papal encyclical which referred to Socialism as a 'deadly plague that is creeping into the very fibres of human society', strongly objected to the concept of the equality of all men. It also offered the Church's support to the rulers even if they trampled on their subjects: Pope Leo XIII (1878–1903) instructed that 'if at any time it happen that the power of the State is rashly and tyrannically wielded by princes, the teaching of the Catholic church does not allow an insurrection on private authority against them'.

... We speak of that sect of men who, under various and almost barbarous names, are called socialists, communists, or nihilists, and who, spread over all the world ... strive to bring to a head what they have long been planning-the overthrow of all civil society whatsoever.

... they proclaim the absolute equality of all men in rights and duties. They debase the natural union of man and woman, which is held sacred even among barbarous peoples; and its bond, by which the family is chiefly held together, they weaken, or even deliver up to lust. ... they assail the right of property sanctioned by natural law;

... For, He who created and governs all things has, in His wise providence, appointed that the things which are lowest should attain their ends by those which are intermediate, and these again by the highest. ... He appointed that there should be various orders in civil society, differing indignity, rights, and power, whereby the State, like the Church, should be one body, consisting of many members, some nobler than others, but all necessary to each other and solicitous for the common good.

... For, while the socialists would destroy the 'right' of property, alleging it to be a human invention altogether opposed to the inborn equality of man, and, claiming a community of goods, argue that poverty should not be peaceably endured, and that the property and privileges of the rich may be rightly invaded, the Church, with much greater wisdom and good sense, recognizes the inequality among men, who are born with different powers of body and mind, inequality in actual possession, also, and holds that the right of property and of ownership, which springs from nature itself, must not be touched and stands inviolate.

... our holy Mother [does] not neglect the care of the poor or omit to provide for their necessities; ... She does all she can to help them; she provides homes and hospitals where they may be received, nourished, and cared for all the world over and watches over these. She is constantly pressing on the rich that most grave precept to give what remains to the poor; and she holds over their heads the divine sentence that unless they succor the needy they will be repaid by eternal torments. In fine, she does all she can to relieve and comfort the poor...

But you, venerable brethren, ... labour hard that the children of the Catholic Church neither join nor favour in any way whatsoever this abominable sect; ... as the recruits of socialism are especially sought among artisans and workmen, who, tired, perhaps, of labour, are more easily allured by the hope of riches and the promise of wealth, it is well to encourage societies of artisans and workmen which, constituted under the guardianship of religion, may tend to make all associates contented with their lot and move them to a quiet and peaceful life.[13]

The Church's anti-Communist policy has never wavered. In pre-War Germany, the Church preferred the Nazis to the Communists and in post-

War Italy, in the 1948 elections, she co-financed the Christian Democrats against the Communists. Giuseppe Siri, the Archbishop of Genoa, told his diocese that 'voting Communist was not reconcilable with being a Catholic' and that confessors 'should withdraw absolution from any who have failed to heed his instructions'.[14] Bishops all over Italy acted similarly. Thirty year later, a pope would undertake an even more adventurous task: Pope John Paul II was instrumental in the overthrow of the Communist regime in Poland. In addition to the moral support which he gave the Solidarity movement, the Pope is said to have transferred funds estimated at US $100 million to Solidarity in Poland.[15]

While the Church remained resolutely opposed to Communism, she showed a willingness to do business with Fascist regimes. The most famous concordats of the twentieth century are those the Church signed with Fascist Italy and with Nazi Germany. The Church defends herself against criticism of her willingness to do such deals by maintaining that doing deals with a dictator does not mean approving of his regime. And yet, a major reason for Mussolini's agreeing the 1929 Lateran Accords or Hitler's signing the 1933 concordat, was just that – the public perception of moral approval granted by the pope. The Church, a seasoned actor in the international political sphere, can claim neither ignorance nor naiveté. The Vatican knew that the return for concessions such as exemption from military service for Catholic clergy in the concordat with Nazi Germany was not only the Vatican's agreement to the abolition of the Catholic Centre Party of Germany – it was the implied approval by the Vatican of the Nazi regime.[16] Four years earlier, when Pius XI signed the Lateran Accords, he offered Mussolini, whom he referred to as 'a man sent by Providence', the prestige of settling the 'Roman Question'.[v] The Lateran Accords recognised the property rights and exclusive sovereignty of the Vatican, which the Holy See maintains it needs to be able to govern the worldwide Catholic Church. The treaties also agreed a financial settlement paid to the Church for the loss of their states and granted Roman Catholicism special status in Italy. The concordat included clauses which ensured that priests who commit crimes were to be treated according to their hierarchical grade and punished separately from lay people or that apostate priests were to be prevented from being given any job which would give them contact with the public.[17]

In Ireland, a country in which the Church was involved in all aspects of national life and the bishops' fingers were in every pie, the Catholic Church was defined by the constitution as 'guardian of the faith professed by the great majority of the citizens'.[18] The Irish state surrendered certain educational and social functions to the Church, under the roof of which, it turned out, the most vulnerable people were severely abused. A well-

---

[v]   The 'Roman Question' was the unresolved relationship between the Vatican and Italy, ever since the 1870 unification of Italy, when the Church lost her temporal power over the Papal States.

known example is the *Magdalene Asylums*, which were run by Catholic nuns to house girls who got pregnant outside marriage, or who were considered too sexual, too flirtatious or just too attractive. In collusion with the Irish state and the girls' families, they were sent to these asylums, which were little more than slave-labour outfits, for life. Thanks to the Catholic Church, Ireland has the toughest abortion laws in Europe, which have produced heartbreak, tragedy and outrage.[vi]

In Spain, the Church supported the 1923 to 1930 military dictatorship of General Miguel Primo de Rivera, and actively participated in efforts to bring down the Second Republic established in 1931. In 1935, as the Fascists were already in power in Italy and Germany and were on their offensive in Spain, Cardinal Hinsley of Westminster said 'If fascism goes under, God's cause goes under with it'.[19] In Spain, God's cause was not only ideology, but also wealth. The Catholic Church in Spain was rich: she controlled banks and industries and she was a major landowner in a country in which peasants were starving. The support of Catholic clergy for the 1936 military revolt was followed by their support of the Fascist regime of Generalissimo Franco. The Spanish dictator, who ruled for almost thirty years (1936–1975) re-established Catholicism as the state religion – after several years in which Spain was a secular state – and bestowed important privileges on the Church. The list of dictators who had the backing of the Catholic Church is long and includes such twentieth-century figures as: Antonio Salazar of Portugal, Francisco Franco of Spain, Engelbert Dollfuss of Austria, Nicolas Horthy of Hungary, Ion Antonescu of Romania and Henri Petain of France.

During his long papacy, Pope John Paul II systematically appointed conservative bishops. Through his nominations, the Pope sent a clear message of support to some rather nasty regimes. This was especially noticeable in the countries of Latin America, where part of the hierarchy in the years after the Second Vatican Council (Vatican II, 1962-65) had focused on concern for the poor and thus came into conflict with their military regimes. In Peru, the country where 'Liberation Theology'[vii] had first emerged, John Paul chose to promote the Bishop of Ayacucho who was criticised by the Truth Commission – which looked at human rights abuses in Peru – for having done 'nothing to improve the human rights situation'. The Pope made Juan Luis Cipriani, a member of the ultra-conservative and elitist *Opus Dei*, Archbishop of Lima and Cardinal.[20]

One regime, with which the Church had a dismal record of collaboration, was the blood-stained dictatorship of Somoza in Nicaragua.

---

vi   Described in more detail in Chapter 8.
vii   Liberation Theology is a social justice oriented movement within Christianity which emerged in the late 1960s, in which struggle against political and economic exploitation were made the focus of action. Latin American liberation theologians interpreted Scripture 'with a bias towards the poor'.

For a short while after the Second Vatican Council, the Church distanced herself from the Somoza regime, which she had supported since its establishment in 1937. In the first year of the *Sandinistas*, Nicaraguan bishops even supported them. Their support did not last and in 1982, Pope John Paul II instructed Nicaraguan Catholics to take up an anti-*Sandinista* stance. The Church fully supported the *Contras*, the militant US-sponsored opposition to the Nicaraguan government. A Nicaraguan archbishop, Archbishop Obando, actually travelled to Washington in 1986 to help the US administration pass a US $100 million aid bid to the *Contras*. The Church was worried about the regime's Marxism, which she felt might endanger her status, and she was therefore willing to accept any right-wing alternative, provided that her hold over religion in the country was assured.

Mexico, in which Church and State were firmly separate, which had no diplomatic ties with the Holy See and whose government was anticlerical, was the first Latin American country Pope John Paul II visited. The Mexican government totally failed in its attempt to keep the Pope's visit low key. There were neither flags nor honour guards at the airport of Mexico City as the Mexican President greeted him simply with 'Welcome, señor, to Mexico'. The Church had other ideas. As the Pope landed, all the Church bells started ringing and the streets from the airport into the centre of the city throbbed with millions of the faithful waving Vatican flags. The country was swamped with welcome posters bearing the Pope's picture. The Church's success in orchestrating a popular welcome overwhelmed Mexico. Several days later, having finished his business at the Latin American Bishops' Conference in Puebla, the Pope arrived by helicopter to meet native Indians. Again, in a well-orchestrated production, twenty-five thousand Indians, who had been waiting in an open field for hours, could gawp as the Pope came down from the skies to talk to them. On a throne under a canopy, the anti-Marxist and anti-Liberation Theology Pope spoke with great fervour against the injustice done to the destitute, suggesting that, if necessary, expropriation of land might have to be undertaken.[21] Would the Pope have spoken with such intensity in a country the government of which was more Church-friendly?

In 1987, the Pope visited Chile. He did not speak out against General Pinochet's regime. Instead, the Pope joined the brutal dictator, under whose rule thousands were killed and thousands 'disappeared', on the balcony of the presidential residence waving to the people who were bussed there by the police. So sure of himself was Pinochet, that he had a demonstration which took place during an outdoor papal mass violently suppressed. The actions of the police were condemned by the Socialist and Communist Parties, but not by the Church. Instead of attacking the brutal police, Cardinal Fresno and the Chilean bishops criticised the demonstrators.

In democratic Argentina, the Pope was less restrained. Whilst the country was under military dictatorships, the Church was deeply involved with the government. Now, it appeared, with a newly elected democratic government, the Church considered that the time had come to preach to the president, who was instructed that 'Human rights had to be guaranteed even in extremely tense situations'. Where was the Church in the days of torture? In the main, she looked the other way. One of her bishops, Bishop Medina, head chaplain of the armed forces, had actually justified torture. The 'Mothers of May Square', women who were demanding a public enquiry into the kidnapping by the military and disappearance of their relatives, asked to meet the Pope. He refused to meet them.[22]

Although much weakened, the Church continues to operate directly through the faithful and indirectly through political lobbying for the political preservation of her doctrines. In 2000, because of the Pope's objection, the Rome city council withdrew its backing and financial support for a gay rights festival.

The Church uses her power over people and expects her members, as soldiers in the pope's divisions, to agitate on her behalf. The Catechism of the Catholic Church[viii] instructs the faithful:

> The initiative of lay Christians is necessary especially when the matter involves discovering or inventing the means for permeating social, political, and economic realities with the demands of Christian doctrine and life. This initiative is a normal element of the life of the Church: Lay believers are in the front line of Church life; for them the Church is the animating principle of human society.[23]

Sometimes, in her endeavour to force civil legislation to adhere to religious directives, the Church acts directly and not through the laity. Such was, for instance, the case in December 2002, when Roman Catholic bishops in New York sued the state to overturn a new law requiring insurers to include birth control in their cover.

A recent example of the way in which the Church acts to instruct her members on how to use their political power is the 'Doctrinal Note on Some Questions Regarding the Participation of Catholics in Political Life' produced in November 2002 by the Vatican's Congregation for the Doctrine of the Faith. In this document the Vatican instructs that 'those who are directly involved in lawmaking bodies have a *grave and clear obligation to oppose* any law that attacks human life. For them, as for every Catholic, it is impossible to promote such laws or to vote for them.'[24] It then clarifies the particular areas which it considered acute at the time and

---

[viii]   The Catechism is the official exposition of the teachings of the Catholic Church.

which it expected Catholics and specifically politically active Catholics and Catholic lawmakers to oppose: homosexual unions, cohabitation, divorce, contraception, abortion and euthanasia. Published at the height of the US priests sexual abuse scandal, this document does not suggest any punitive action against Catholics who covered up the abuse. Catholic bishops, who for years had been in charge and gave cover to sexually abusive priests, had no difficulty in preaching morality to politicians.

Towards the 2004 elections in the USA, President Bush lobbied the Vatican for help. A week after Bush's visit to the Pope, Cardinal Ratzinger sent a letter to the US bishops, stressing that Catholics who were pro-choice on abortion were committing a grave sin and were to be denied communion.[25] Soon thereafter, bishops up and down the country began issuing their guidance to the faithful. Bishop Michael Sheridan from Colorado Springs published a pastoral letter in which he stated that Catholic politicians who supported abortion, embryonic stem-cell research, euthanasia, or same-sex marriage, as well as any Catholics who voted for such politicians, jeopardised their salvation. Although Ratzinger gave some leeway to vote for a pro-abortion candidate, if there were 'proportionate reasons' to do so, US bishops made it clear that no 'possible good or collection of goods could ever outweigh the destruction of human lives wrought by legalised abortion'. Archbishop John Myers of Newark, N.J., left no doubt: 'Certainly policies on welfare, national security, the war in Iraq, Social Security or taxes, taken singly or in combination, do not provide a proportionate reason to vote for a pro-abortion candidate.'[26] The guidance given by the bishops was sometimes covered by a fig leaf to the effect that the bishop does not instruct his flock who to vote for, but in truth, the message was loud and clear: if you voted for Kerry you would go to hell.

The State of Vatican City

The Roman Catholic religion is the only religion in the world which has the status of a fully fledged state for its headquarters. The State of Vatican City was established in 1929 as part of the Lateran treaties signed between Italy and the Catholic Church. These agreements:

- created a sovereign state of the Vatican City, recognised by Italy;
- defined the relations between the Italian government and the Catholic Church in Italy; and
- provided financial compensation to the Holy See for the loss of the Papal States in 1870.

Considering the size of the State of the Vatican City this could be deemed insignificant. However, the advantages sovereign status confers, including banking unsupervised by any banking authority,[ix] the ability to issue

---

ix   This is covered in more detail in Chapter 3.

passports, the granting of diplomatic immunity and membership of international organisations at state-level, should not be underestimated.

In 1870, the Church lost the remainder of the Papal States to the newly united Kingdom of Italy. The Law of Guarantees which was passed by Italy in 1871 designated the area of the Holy See, the supreme Authority of the Catholic Church, without ceding it any territorial sovereignty. The popes on the other hand considered that they had never lost their sovereignty and that it was not up to the Italian State to grant them any rights. Under this law, Italy agreed: that the pope's person was sacred and inviolable, that insult or injury to the pope be treated on a par with insult or injury to the Italian king and that an annual endowment would be paid to the pope to cover the needs of the Holy See. The Vatican, the Lateran palaces as well as the Villa of *Castel Gandolfo* were to remain the property of the pope. The pope of the day, Pius IX (1846–1878), and his successors were offended by the seizure of their lands and refused to recognise the Italian government's right to legislate concessions or otherwise in connection with their person or the Church and in fact never made use of their entitlement to an annual endowment. They regularly protested that their ability to exercise their authority independently was hampered. They hoped that at least the 'occupation' of Rome would be temporary and that what was referred to as the 'Roman Question' would be concluded – that the city would be returned to them. But, to no avail. For almost sixty years, popes regarded themselves as 'prisoners' in the Vatican.

International representation is, in fact, the realm of the Holy See and not that of the State of Vatican City. Between 1870 and 1929, when the State of Vatican City did not exist, the Holy See, which considers itself to be the juridical equivalent of a state, maintained diplomatic relations with many states. The State of Vatican City, which does not receive or send diplomatic representatives, does, however, enter into international agreements. It also issues passports, which the Holy See does not. Vatican, the State of Vatican City, Holy See, are used by many interchangeably, especially as both the State of Vatican City and the Holy See, as the sovereign organ of the Catholic Church, have obtained international recognition and are members of and participate in international organisations. Through shrewd political manoeuvring the Catholic Church has optimised the benefits she derives from this dual structure.

This state, which has fewer than six hundred citizens, of which less than half actually live in the Vatican, and which also occupies buildings outside the Vatican City area, exempt from taxation and expropriation, is an instrument of the Catholic Church. In this monarchy, the pope enjoys full legislative, executive and judicial power. The Vatican refers to the State and the Holy See as 'indissolubly united in the person of the Supreme Pontiff, as Head of State, who possesses full legislative, judicial and executive powers'.[27] Although the pope shares legislative power with a commission of cardinals, the cardinals with whom he shares power are nominated by him for a period of five years. The state law guarantees the pope's independence.

The State has its own force, the Swiss Guards, a radio station (Radio Vatican) and a daily newspaper (*L'Osservatore Romano*). It issues stamps and coins, it also runs its own bank and owns and manages properties and investments. The body running the state on behalf of the pope is the Pontifical Commission for the State of the Vatican City. The Holy See maintains diplomatic relations with over a hundred and seventy states and participates in scores of international and regional intergovernmental organisations and bodies, either as member or as observer. It has observer status at the United Nations (UN), the Council of Europe and other similar bodies. In other international bodies, such as the UN Conference on Trade and Development and the Arab League, it is a fully fledged member.[28] It is clear that the Vatican tries to get its foot into every organisation it can, be it as a full member or, if that is unacceptable, at least as an observer. This enables the Church to further her agenda in a way which is not open to any other religious organisation in the world. Where she is a fully fledged member she has voting power, and where she is an observer she is able to lobby from within, having access to all internal papers and decision-making processes.

The Church's ability to lobby from within was demonstrated at the 1994 UN Conference on Population and Development in Cairo. In a joint effort with fundamentalist Muslim countries the Church attempted to scupper the conference's decision to launch a programme which would empower women, giving them the right to determine the size of their family, and pledging to make family planning available worldwide. At a European level, Pope John Paul II lobbied hard, but failed in his endeavours to get the European Union (EU) to include a 'Christian clause' in the EU's constitution. The Pope called for a 'clear reference to God and the Christian faith' to be included in the constitution 'to cement the extraordinary religious, cultural and civic heritage that has made Europe great down the centuries'.[29] Although much was made of the Pope's anger at the EU's refusal, a spokesman for Europe's Catholic bishops confirmed that 'in reality, what you have is not so bad'.[30] The constitution allows established religion EU recognition and thereby a platform for dialogue. In his attempt to keep Europe a Christian affair, the Pope also made clear his objection to the accession to the EU of Turkey, a predominantly Muslim country.

Hierarchy and Authority

The starting point for understanding the hierarchical structure of the Catholic Church and its internal rules of authority is Jesus Christ.[x]

---

[x]   The Hebrew name *Yehoshua*, from which the name Jesus stems, means God saves. The Greek word *christos* means the anointed.

According to the Gospel of Matthew in the New Testament, Jesus chose one of his twelve apostles, Simon Bar-Jona, whom he named *Petros* (from *petra* meaning 'rock', and translated into English as 'Peter'), as the rock upon which he would build his church.[31] Peter thus became the first Vicar of Christ and, as such, is considered to have been the first pope. 'Vice', the Latin ablative form of 'vix', means 'in the place of' or 'in succession to'. A vicar is someone who has been deputed to act for another person and whose authority derives from such delegation. As Jesus clearly appointed one man (rather than all twelve apostles), the Catholic Church considers that it is one man who becomes the Vicar of Christ, the Supreme Head of the Catholic Church – the pope. This point is crucial in understanding the absolute status a pope has in the Church. Once elected by the cardinals to his supreme office, the pope no longer depends on them, nor does he share his power with them.[32] His authority henceforth is derived from God. The powers of the Vicar of Christ are, to a believer, pretty much all-embracing. He is given the keys to heaven and his decisions as to what is permitted and what is forbidden on earth, shall be what is permitted and what is forbidden in heaven.[33]

In 1870, with the unification of Italy, and as he was losing the last vestige of his secular power, Pope Pius IX (1846–1878) had the issue of papal infallibility brought to a convention of all Catholic bishops held in Rome. This council, Vatican I, discussed the question of the possibility of papal error and concluded that in matters of dogma and morals, the pope is incapable of making a mistake, as he is, in such situations, guided by the Holy Spirit. At that low point in the Church's history, the Pope's eagerness for such an affirmation, which was meant to define the pope's special elevated and unique status, is not surprising. The Church instructs that infallible teachings 'must be adhered to with the obedience of faith'; this is 'to submit freely to the word that has been heard, because its truth is guaranteed by God, who is Truth itself'.[34] Opposition to this newly established infallibility was not well received. Views, such as those of German Catholic historian and theologian Ignaz von Döllinger, who was excommunicated for his dissent, have not lessened papal resolve to hold on to absolute power.[35] Abraham, who was willing to sacrifice his own son, is considered by the Catholic Church to be the model of such obedience.[36] The Church also demands that the faithful adhere to ordinary teachings which, although not defined as infallible, lead, due to 'divine assistance ... given to the successors of the apostles', to 'better understanding of Revelation in matters of faith and morals' with 'religious assent' defined as an extension of assent of faith.[37] To date, popes have made very little use of their licence to define specific teaching infallible, but even with regard to teaching which does not fall under this rule, popes rarely cancel a previous pope's ruling and never publicly condemn or criticise a previous pope's decision. It would be quite confusing for the faithful who are called upon to adhere to papal teachings 'with religious assent', even when not defined infallible, to find out that a new pope had nullified that teaching.[38]

The Catholic Church is not a democratic system. However, popes cannot bequeath their throne nor nominate their successor. Popes get elected for life and when a pope dies it is the College of Cardinals which elects the next pope.[39] The College of Cardinals is the group encompassing all the cardinals of the Catholic Church. Ever since the election of John Paul I (1978), according to the instruction of Pope Paul VI, cardinals who are older than eighty do not participate in the vote. After the pope, the rank of cardinal is the most senior rank in the Catholic Church. Heads of important archdioceses and heads of important departments of the Vatican government, the Roman Curia, or of other Vatican bodies are created cardinals by the pope. Thus, the power to appoint cardinals is not only the power to influence the running of the Church during a pope's lifetime, it is significantly the power to influence the decision on the election of the next pope. A conservative pope will not wish his successor to undo his work and by ensuring a conservative majority within the College of Cardinals can have an impact on the choice of his heir. John Paul II, who died in 2005, appointed all but three of the cardinals who elected his successor. Obviously, liberal popes may want to ensure that changes they have introduced will not be lost through the election of a conservative pope. Interestingly, the number of cardinals dramatically increased in the second half of the twentieth century. Their number grew from sixty to seventy in 1958, to eighty under John XXIII and then to one hundred and twenty after Paul VI's reform of the College of Cardinals in 1979. Under Pope John Paul II the number increased further and by 2006 there were one hundred and ninety cardinals.[xi]

There are two kinds of meetings of the Church's cardinals: a conclave, in which the College of Cardinals elects a new pope; and a consistory, where the College of Cardinals meets for other purposes. Consistories had not been held since the sixteenth century but have been re-introduced by Pope John Paul II. Soon after his election, the new pope began to hold meetings with the College of Cardinals, thereby widening his decision-making circle with non-curial cardinals. Extraordinary consistories are meetings of the cardinals to which all cardinals are invited. Ordinary consistories are often ceremonial affairs for the purpose of canonisation or the conferral of the pallium[xii] on archbishops. The Pope has brought structural and organisational issues, as well as those of dogma, to the consistories. In the aftermath of the financial scandals of Michael Sindona and Roberto Calvi, the finances of the Holy See and Vatican

---

[xi]   Seventy four of which were over the age of eighty.
[xii] Pallium is a shoulder-band given by the pope to an archbishop as a symbol of authority.

Bank were, at least twice, the subject of a consistory.[xiii] The consistories dealing with dogma tend to be less of a consultative exercise and more of an educational and promotional one in areas which the pope wishes to advance.

The next level in the hierarchy of the Church is the bishops, of whom there are over four thousand. Most bishops are residential, in charge of and chief pastors of a diocese entrusted to them by the Vatican. Dioceses are geographical administrative units of the Church, normally consisting of several parishes. Bishops are considered successors of the apostles and are appointed directly by the pope, who, upon his election, also becomes the Bishop of Rome. Archdioceses, which cover very large areas, are run by archbishops and those responsible for the important archdioceses may be made cardinals. There is also a number of bishops who work in the Vatican and have no pastoral responsibilities. Most countries have a structure known as a National Episcopal Conference, which serves as a forum for all bishops, archbishops and cardinals. Such episcopal conferences will discuss common problems (such as sexual abuse) and sometimes agree common policies. These conferences, do not, however, have a formal standing in the Church hierarchy. The bishops are not only appointed by the pope, they also report to him. Once every five years, every bishop must visit the pope for what is known as an *ad limina* visit, at which he has to report at length and in detail about his diocese.

An Ecumenical Council is an episcopal council convened by the pope and presided by the pope or by his legate.[xiv] For decisions of an Ecumenical Council to become binding they require papal approval and promulgation. Councils to which all Catholic bishops are invited are very expensive and difficult to manage. As a result, they are held at long intervals. The First Vatican Council (Vatican I) was held in 1870 and the Second (Vatican II), the last Ecumenical Council to be held, took place between the years 1962 and 1965. Two thousand eight hundred and sixty of the world's bishops participated in meetings which took place in four phases over a thirty-eight-month span. Vatican I is noteworthy for having introduced the concepts of papal infallibility and papal primacy, whereas Vatican II softened these concepts and brought in the idea of collegiality to give bishops greater prominence in the governing of the Church.

To maintain the mood of 'bishop power' versus the power of the well-ensconced Roman Curia, participants in Vatican II tried to create some sort of continuity. A synod of bishops was to be created. But the suggestion that the synod of bishops should have executive and decision-making powers for the whole Church was quickly seen off by Pope Paul VI. Instead, the synod is no more than a representative institution

---

[xiii] See chapter 3.
[xiv] The term ecumenical means representing the whole of the Christian world, or seeking to promote Christian unity.

with delegates from episcopal conferences around the world, which the pope, if he wishes, convenes and consults. An ordinary synod will comprise two hundred to two hundred and fifty delegates, elected by national episcopal conferences, and by other Church organisations (such as religious orders), but whose election has to be ratified by the pope. Evidently the pope and the Vatican administration do not even trust the bishops and their conferences to elect the 'right' delegates for a synod. Moreover, all the heads of curia congregations, councils and other Vatican bodies are ex-officio members of the bishops' synod. In the excitement and elevated mood of Vatican II a body was created to maintain the influence of bishops on Vatican policy and decision-making, but it was without teeth. The pope convenes the meetings, decides who participates, sets the agenda and then decides whether to accept the recommendations. A variety of bodies has been created around these synods, such as The Council of the Synod Secretariat, which deals with the post-synod work and documents produced. But none of this can change the fact that Vatican II has not transferred power to the bishops. The pope continues to have full authority in the Catholic Church; he may consult his bishops, but doesn't have to, and, if he does, he doesn't have to follow their advice.

There is a plethora of titles for office-holders serving under a bishop. Senior titles include vicar-general, who may be an ordained bishop himself and monsignor. The basic unit of the Church, a parish, is normally run on behalf of the diocesan bishop by a parish priest. Priests, sometimes known as pastors, are appointed by a bishop. Other functionaries are parochial vicars (sometimes known as curates) and deacons. Some priests are diocesan and some belong to a religious order (such as the *Franciscans, Jesuits* or *Benedictines*).[40]

Bureaucracy

The Roman Curia, the bureaucracy which helps popes run the Catholic Church, at present, consists of nine congregations and eleven councils. Congregations rank higher than councils. They have both jurisdictional and promotional authority, although most councils are mainly promotional. Congregations are committees of cardinals and, since 1967, and as a result of Vatican II, also bishops. Councils may also have lay members. Members of both congregations and councils are appointed by the pope for five-year renewable terms and must retire at the age of eighty. Many, and especially, the curial cardinals, will sit on quite a few congregations and councils. This ensures coordination and should lead to more streamlined work and policy. And yet, a group of American canonists visiting the Vatican was struck by how little communication there was between the congregations and councils.[41] Of course, membership of important congregations does also reflect the degree of power a cardinal holds. In practice, the power of curial cardinals is even greater, though, than that of other cardinals as officials who have to travel from afar are prevented, by distance, from attending many meetings.

In charge of this bureaucracy is the Secretary of State. The role of the closest person to the pope was, until the seventeenth century, often held by the 'cardinal nephew'. To ensure total loyalty, the pope would appoint a nephew or another relative to this position of confidence and power. This practice died out and the Secretary of State became the main adviser to the pope and head of the administration. Although the congregations and councils report to the pope, it is the Secretariat of State which coordinates their work. As such, traditionally the Secretary of State is the most important cardinal. The Secretariat of State is divided into two sections: one deals with general affairs, including the pope's correspondence, and is headed by the *Sostituto* (Substitute); and the other deals with relations with states. The *Sostituto*, who controls an important and even crucial junction in the Vatican apparatus, is more influential and powerful than many of the church's cardinals; he himself is normally an archbishop.

The *Universal Inquisition* was the first permanent congregation. It was established in 1542, in response to the Reformation, to deal with matters of faith and heresy. It later became the *Holy Office* and is now called the *Congregation for the Doctrine of the Faith* (CDF). The CDF determines the official teaching of the Catholic Church and is in charge of the investigation of theologians who deviate from Catholic teaching. This congregation also handles cases of grave offences by priests, and as such is also the body which deals with sexual abuse cases. As this most important and powerful congregation has the responsibility of defending the existing doctrine, it will, by definition, be a conservative force in the Church. Although all congregations are considered equal, the body which can decide that an issue, document, opinion, person, book or institution is not in keeping with Catholic doctrine has patently more power than any of the other congregations. In fact, many of the other congregations have to pass their documents for vetting to the CDF. Hence, in any matter which can have a doctrinal angle, the congregation's prefect is, next to the pope, the most important person in the Church.[42]

The *Congregation for the Eastern Churches* deals with almost all matters[xv] pertaining to the twenty Eastern-Rite (also known as 'Oriental') Churches, most of which are in Eastern Europe and the Middle East. These Churches, although no longer part of the Latin Church, still consider the pope to be their head and remain part of the Catholic Church. The Oriental Churches have their own rites and procedures for the election of bishops and the details of candidates put forward are sent to Rome for approval.

[xv] Excluding matters of doctrine and the making of saints.

All of the Oriental Churches, however, allow Rome much less say in the election of bishops than those using the Latin rite. The congregation has its own endowment and distributes moneys to its member Churches. It does not hold plenary sessions at all. Its work is prepared by congregation staff, and disseminated for input to its members.

The *Congregation for Divine Worship and the Discipline of the Sacraments* is an amalgamation of two former congregations. It is organised in two main sections; one deals with liturgy and the other is concerned with canonical issues relating to the sacraments. This congregation not only encourages liturgical worship, but also has the authority to approve liturgical texts. One notable area for which this congregation is responsible and for which no other congregation wished to acquire responsibility, concerns the petitions of priests who have left the ministry for dispensation from celibacy.

The *Congregation for the Causes of Saints* processes work connected with beatifications and canonisations.

The *Congregation for Bishops* is in charge of all personal matters of bishops in the Latin non-mission dioceses. Their main work is connected with the appointment of new bishops. This entails reviewing and investigating the recommendations and reports received from the papal nuncio in the country of the diocese and preparing the recommendation for the pope's decision. The vetting process, which checks that nothing untoward is in the files of the *Congregation for the Clergy,* also ensures that the main power players in the Vatican (i.e. the *Secretariat of State* and the CDF) have no objection to the appointment. Loyalty to the pope, Church doctrine and her institutions is paramount and this is especially important as removing a bishop from office can be extremely difficult. A bishop cannot be defrocked. Ideally, in a situation in which the Vatican wants to remove a bishop, the individual concerned is persuaded to resign. From time to time, cases arise which come to the attention of the media, exposing bishops whose sexual entanglements (some have even fathered children) have become public knowledge and who have therefore had to resign. A bishop can be removed from a diocese, even excommunicated, but he will continue to be a bishop and, as such, he will continue to have the power to ordain priests. Sometimes the Vatican can remove a bishop from the area in which he is causing trouble and 'bring him in'. In such cases, a title is bestowed, or a meaningless job is defined and the troublemaker is 'lost' in the Vatican.[43]

Popes, understandably, try to ensure that only totally reliable men are appointed as bishops. However, the emphasis on loyalty can come at a price in that bishops can appear and become alienated from their own pastoral communities. Particularly difficult issues that contribute to this isolation are the Church's strong views about birth control, which are widely flaunted by Catholics all over the world, or its attitude to active homosexual behaviour, which is not only not adhered to by Catholic laity, but also by some Catholic clergy. In such areas, it is considered vital by the pope that local bishops should not dissent from the teaching of the Church.

The *Congregation for the Clergy* was established in 1564 as the *Congregation of the Council* to implement the reforms of the Council of Trent. These were mostly matters to do with the clergy, catechetics and local church finances and have remained in the realm of this congregation. Only seminaries were moved to the *Congregation for Catholic Education*. This congregation handles personal issues of priests, including any disputes or possible removals of a priest and can overrule bishops when they violate canon law in dealing with their clergy. It also promotes activities for the betterment of the spiritual lives of priests.

The *Congregation for the Evangelisation of Peoples*, formerly known as the *Congregation for the Propagation of the Faith* (*Propaganda Fide*), is the main address for bishops from missionary territories and handles issues of clergy and bishops in missionary dioceses. In collaboration with the *Congregation for Catholic Education* it handles education matters in mission territories. It also has a say in the nomination of papal nuncios (the archbishop representing the Holy See) to countries in its jurisdiction. The procedure for the appointment of bishops in missionary territories is the same as that of the *Congregation for Bishops*. The congregation has a substantial budget and its own endowment and investments (including real estate) which are managed separately. This is an important source of money for the missionary dioceses, although these often also get money directly from the pope from monies coming in as *Peter's Pence*. The congregation has a number of mission societies, which fundraise independently and which finance projects and activities in missionary dioceses.

The *Congregation for Institutes of Consecrated Life and for Societies for Apostolic Life* is in charge of the nature of life in religious communities and is divided into two sections; the religious and the secular institutes. The spiritual life of such communities, even in missionary territories is dealt with by this congregation, whereas the apostolic work of the missionaries comes under the jurisdiction of the *Congregation for the Evangelisation of the People*. Matters of discipline within religious communities and religious constitutions of the various orders and communities come under their authority. Questions regarding relationships and matters of authority between lay members and clerics are also the responsibility of this congregation.

The *Congregation for Catholic Education* deals with ecclesiastical faculties, universities, seminaries and schools. It is in charge of education programmes and the promotion and training of seminarians. This congregation is a vetting authority for the approval of professors in ecclesiastical faculties chartered by the Holy See. Before granting its *nihil obstat* (literally 'no objection') the files of the CDF are checked. Anything untoward can bring the appointment to a standstill or even abort it. Here the old inquisitional traits come into play, and the candidate may be asked to answer a written questionnaire devised by the CDF before a decision is made. This way the Vatican holds very tight control of what is taught as Catholic theology. Not only are theologians such as Hans Küng, who challenged papal infallibility, denied approval, but minor dissents of theologians such as Father Michael Buckley, president of the Catholic Theological Society of America, or David Hollenbach, who was highly regarded by the US bishops, have also led to denial of *nihil obstat* and consequently to their leaving to teach at non-Catholic universities. The bestowing of honorary degrees also requires the Congregation's consent. As usual in most systems, it helps when you go to the top. As usual in most systems, it helps when you go to the top. When *Opus Dei* came up against the Congregation's (and those of the rest of the curial bureaucracy) objections to their request for an *Opus Dei* ecclesiastical university in Rome they worked their way through to the Pope and by his decree approval was granted.

Both congregations and councils are referred to as dicasteries. The eleven councils are not as well established as the congregations. They are structurally quite similar but lower in the Vatican pecking order. The councils are: Council for the Laity; Council for Promoting Christian Unity; Council for the Family; Council for Justice and Peace; Council *Cor Unum* (responsible for charitable work); Council for the Pastoral Care of Migrants and Travellers; Council for Pastoral Assistance for Health Care Workers; Council for the Interpretation of Legislative Texts; Council for Inter-religious Dialogue; Council for Culture; and Council for Social Communications.

As is often the case in bureaucracies and power structures, anomalies abound and complex divisions of responsibility, which reflect power struggles, can sometimes only be explained by the personal ambitions of the present and past players in the Vatican government. One such anomaly is the fact that the *Commission for Religious Relations with Jews* is coordinated by the *Council for Promoting Christian Unity* and not, as one would have thought, the *Council for Inter-religious Dialogue*.

Power and Religion

Before exploring various areas in which the Church has used and abused her power, it is useful to understand why and how the Church was able to amass such power.

Religions did not need the sword to attain their might. Although once they had power, most of them did not shy away from using the sword to further their interests. What is it in religion that makes an organisation such as the Catholic Church so powerful? What enables religion to gain such a hold over mankind? 'The belief in a superhuman controlling power, especially in a personal God or gods entitled to obedience and worship' is the Concise Oxford Dictionary's definition of religion.[44] Sir James George Frazer in his classic *The Golden Bough: A Study in Magic and Religion* defines religion as 'a propitiation or conciliation of powers superior to man which are believed to direct and control the course of nature and of human life'.[45] *Religio*, the Latin source of the word religion, stands for a greater-than-human power that requires a person to respond in a certain way to avoid some dire consequence or the feeling that is present in persons who vividly conceive of and observe such power.[46]

The first obstacle men of religion would have had to overcome would have been the natural scepticism thrown at any man claiming to have special powers. If one goes back to pre-monotheistic religions, one can find an abundance of examples in which the living 'representatives' of a higher power found ways of impressing their public with their 'supernatural' craft. Moses, according to the Bible, asked God for proof to satisfy (probably) his own disbelief and that of the Israelites whom he was instructed by God to lead out of Egypt and into the Land of Israel. God understood and supplied the necessary proof.[47] When Pharaoh would not agree to Moses' demand to let his people go, a set of plagues was brought down on the land of Egypt to make him change his mind.[48] Jesus also sought to prove to his followers that he had extraordinary powers.

Frazer suggests that the Age of Religion was preceded by an Age of Magic.[49] In the Age of Magic, men believed that there were those among them who had the capacity to control nature. The magicians were meant to be able to control especially those elements which were either very frightening (such as the disappearance of the sun) or which had grave consequences (such as weather conditions). Ensuring that rain would fall in time to enable the crops to grow and replenish the reservoirs to quench the thirst of men and cattle, was – and still is – vital; without it people die. Of similar importance was the act of averting rains to prevent flooding. Charismatic men were able to convince their tribes and communities that they actually had control over the rain, that it was in their power, through a ceremony or ritual, to which only they were privy, to bring the rain when it was needed and to clear the skies when there was enough. Compared to the issues at stake, the price paid for such services was not high: some social standing and respect and, of course, material reward for the magician.

It is likely that the shift from magic to religion started to take place at that stage of human development when people became sceptical of the magician's authority. It was no longer the local magician who had to be pacified, but rather, some external power. Such change would not have been an abrupt one and the magicians were replaced by priests, intermediaries to the new powers. Priests knew what was expected of them; they instructed their people about the rules, interpreted them, and, of course, accepted both the honours and the remuneration which reflected their importance in securing a safe voyage through life.

To smooth the transformation from magic to religion, some rituals were retained and some beliefs were not lost. Mircea Eliade proposed the term *hierophany* for the act of manifestation of the sacred, 'a mysterious act, something of a wholly different order, a reality that does not belong to our world'.[50] Eliade makes the point that the history of religions is constituted by a great number of hierophanies. It is against this backdrop of magical power that Jesus, his followers and the Church had to compete to attract the attention of the people they were, and still are, trying to attract.

Symbols and sacramentals have been established in all religions and have been used generously in pagan cultures. The early leaders of the Church must have understood the value of co-opting pre-Christian and even pre-Jewish symbols which have served as common currency in human society. Indeed, Catholic worship makes use of an abundance of symbols in its rituals. Such, for example, is the power of water, symbolising cleanliness, purification and regeneration – a new beginning. Likewise, the burning of incense – already known in some societies as an aid in exorcising harmful influences, dispelling the powers of evil or expelling witches – has smoothly passed into Christian rituals. Gold and silver ornaments and religious processions are some of the other religious aids and rituals that the Catholic Church took over from both Jewish and pagan practices. The use of incense and adornment with gold and silver ornaments serve to make the experience in church, the participation in the religious ceremony, more pleasant. Religious processions have a theological explanation: they remind the faithful that they are still on their journey, the final goal of which is heaven. Grouping people and marching them in one direction in a uniform tempo, with rhythmic or contemplative music, and leading them to an end station, often a church, psychologically instils in them a feeling of belonging and a strong sense of group identity: a common rhythm with a common purpose. Even watching processions is enjoyable for many. The physical commotion and togetherness is exhilarating and generates feelings of joy and other emotional reactions. Catholic tradition includes regular processions on Good Friday, Palm Sunday and *Corpus Christi*.[51] The Church may try to distance her rites from pagan ones but the impact they have on the faithful is the same. A considerable part of their pre-Christian religious heritage, the cosmic religion inherited from prehistoric times, has been retained.[52] Especially in rural, agricultural communities, Christianity has incorporated the mystery of nature's participation in religious traditions.

The theologian and philosopher, Rudolf Otto (1869–1937), uses the term *numinous* for the non-rational factor in the idea of the divine; that is, the non-rational aspect of the term 'holy'. Otto suggests that numinous consciousness can be induced or awakened with the indirect aid of media such as architecture or music.[53] Religious practices and rituals are designed to appeal to the senses: music to the ears, incense to the nose, paintings and sculptures to the eyes, the Eucharist to the tongue. Active bodily participation – such as kneeling, genuflecting, prostrating, dancing, standing and sitting, singing, reciting prayers – can all be effective in affecting participants. Sometimes such practices are meant to over-stimulate and bring about a feeling of ecstasy. The direct appeal to the senses and the sensations produced by active bodily participation in turn become associated with the religious ideas being promulgated.

Most people are especially prone to suggestibility and to religious experiences during periods of low self-esteem and helplessness.[54] Fear-inducing procedures may increase the body's production of endorphins which have a soothing and sometimes a euphoric effect. Not only frightening witchcraft rituals but also ultra-aggressive preaching may be fear-inducing and thus have a similar effect. The manipulation of people's states of consciousness can be realised through physical means, be they kinetic or sensory. Such manipulation can lead to ecstatic and even hallucinatory states. Sensory stimulation and increased bodily movement, especially in a group, are known to bring about trances. Sleep deprivation, fasting, physical pain (such as self-flagellation), seclusion and breath control can all bring about changes to one's state of mind and make one pliable. All these are known to have been effectively used in the questioning of prisoners. Sleep and food are important resources necessary for our well-being. Physiological processes, such as fasting, can play an important role in religion. Fasting is meant to purify the soul by controlling the desires of the body. Judaism has several days of fasting per year. Islam has the month of Ramadan, in which Muslims eat and drink only after sundown and fast during the day. Up to the Vatican II, Catholics were expected to abstain from eating meat on Fridays. This rule was changed and now it suffices if abstention from meat is maintained on Fridays during Lent.[55]

Sex is an activity which can substantially contribute to one's well-being. By taking control of this activity the discipline in command gains in effectiveness. The persons who can, with their charisma, draw and fascinate others into giving up or limiting their intake of such vital resources, reap even more devotion as a result of the self-inflicted deprivation. Ascetic practices, that is self-denial of bodily pleasures or even self-imposition of displeasure as a means of attaining a higher spiritual state, are sometimes used as an act of penitence to pacify an authority of some sort.

Religious rituals often incorporate techniques for the purpose of inducing a specific mental state in the worshipper by triggering physiological processes in them. The most extreme and obvious are states of religious ecstasy in which people manifest bodily changes and in which they often are more vulnerable than normal. The ability to take advantage of such vulnerability in moulding behaviour of both individuals and whole groups is well documented. Subjecting people to plays of light and dark, quiet and noise, aerobic activation such as standing, sitting and prostrating, can be very effective in stirring and manipulating them, creating a state of mind in which they are most receptive to the message addressed to them. Thus the architecture of churches can serve to accentuate the feeling of the 'sublime'. Mystical experience may be generated by dimly lit cathedrals and by the use of candles or with the help of subdued music. Aesthetes may be grateful for the very rich artistic depiction of Jesus, the Virgin Mary, apostles and saints in various biblical scenes. Even the Holy Ghost appears in the paintings of old masters. One cannot, however, escape the fact that the Church, her popes, cardinals and bishops have commissioned such art for a purpose: the celebration of Christ and of Christianity. A visual depiction of biblical scenes and of Church 'heroes' serves to further the awe and admiration for Christ and Christianity and deepen the bond of the viewers with the Church. Similar effect can be achieved with glorious and glorifying music. The Church commissioned liturgical music to produce the elation which the playing or singing of music brings. Music can also be used effectively in religious processions. There have been suggestions and some supporting research that religious feelings can be generated or at least helped along by music, including the sub-auditory elements of music. Rhythmic music has been proven to affect neural functioning and it is even argued that repetitive sounds 'can transform our sensibility, our way of thinking, the state of our soul, and even our moral character'.[56] Catholic worship regularly uses music, especially organ music and choirs.

Similarly, active participation in prayer and the repetition of prayer-formulae is not only a communion with God, it also serves as a reminder to the praying person of the order of the world, the order which the Church wishes to maintain. Public prayer additionally serves to give the participants mutual reinforcement in their 'way'. Prayers, usually taught in childhood, are an activity for which children are praised and which connect to the satisfaction of food and sleep. This conditioning in itself provides for a soothing feeling. The wording of prayers which offer comfort and fantasy to the faithful who struggle with daily hardships, can sometimes even induce a certain level of autohypnosis.

Early History

It all started with Jesus, who lived in Palestine some two thousand years ago. Although Palestine was not part of the Roman Empire (it had its own king, Herod), it was part of the Roman sphere of influence. Real power, in fact, was in the hands of Pontius Pilate, an appointee of Caesar as governor of Judea. The population of Palestine was predominantly Jewish, with various groups and sects vying for influence and differing in their orthodoxy. Jesus, who in today's world would be considered a political activist or agitator, was like an Old Testament prophet, warning the rulers of his day to mend their ways or else be punished by God's wrath. He objected to the corruption in the establishment, to the deterioration of morals and to the hypocrisy in the norms and behaviour he encountered in society. His Sermon on the Mount[57] had great attraction for the deprived and the destitute. In a society which respected material success, Jesus maintained that the rich were – in fact – at a disadvantage compared to the poor.[58] He had a group of close followers, his disciples.

Up to this point, matters are straightforward and politically not unusual. Two important phenomena happened after Jesus' crucifixion. One, which is only accepted by the believers, is that three days after his execution, Jesus rose from the dead. The Jews have a concept of a Messiah, the 'anointed one', a descendant of King David whom God would raise and anoint in the last days of the Earth and who would lead the people of Israel. Especially during periods of oppression, such mystical hopes would abound. Various Jewish sects during the lifetime of Jesus were actively preparing for the arrival of the Messiah. To his followers, who were called Christians, Jesus was this Messiah. Unacceptable, in fact blasphemous, to the Jews was the fact that Jesus referred to himself as the son of God. The second important phenomenon was the success in converting both Jews, but mainly pagans, to Christianity. Jesus and his twelve closest followers, the apostles, were practicing Jews and his call for his listeners to follow him was not a call to move away from Judaism, neither in faith, nor in tradition, religious rituals and laws. This only happened in the post-Jesus period.

During Jesus' lifetime and immediately after his death, Christianity was a small sect whose members were Jews. The beginning of the breakthrough for Christianity was the conversion of Paul (whose name in Hebrew was 'Saul') on the way to Damascus. Once converted, Paul started spreading the gospel to non-Jewish communities, thereby widening the scope of influence beyond the Jewish world. Before Paul, the Christian community in Jerusalem accepted a dualistic approach. Jews who turned to Christianity would continue obeying the Jewish commandments, laws and rituals, whereas non-Jewish converts would be exempt from the Jewish laws. Paul took this one important step further. Christians were no longer to follow the Jewish laws. The more successful Christianity was in proselytising to the pagans, the less Jewish it became. Paul maintained that the arrival of the Messiah had moved the world to the period of grace and it was no longer necessary automatically to follow the religious laws, other than those of a basic moral code. Most important of all was the proposition that the way to salvation was through the belief in Christ. It was, according to Paul, every Christian's duty to offer salvation to the whole world.

The Jewish religion has six hundred and thirteen laws, which religious Jews are obliged to follow. Paul's doing away with these laws, doing away with circumcision, must have dramatically eased the acceptance of his message. In approaching the pagan world, Paul would have been less likely to make converts, had the 'welcome party' included circumcision. Instead, there were very few laws to follow and a promise of salvation. Moreover, the story of a god that died and was resurrected is not exclusively Christian. Similar myths abounded in the ancient world and that would have made the story of Jesus' resurrection more understandable for pagan society. Although Paul made great strides in preaching Christianity outside the Jewish world, it was an uphill struggle. Christianity was by no means accepted by the Roman rulers. There were periods of persecution, such as in AD64, when Nero sentenced both Peter and Paul, leaders of the Christian community in Rome, to death. Yet, except for not-very-long periods of hardship, the community was left to lead its life without too much disturbance.

It was not until the year 313 that Christianity was legalised. In the Edict of Milan, Emperor Constantine brought to an end the period in which Christianity and Christians had been maltreated by Rome. Some seventy years later, in 380, Christianity was made the official state religion. So often in history, the move from ideological splinter to hegemony and might brings with it not only a loss of innocence but also carelessness and even abandonment of the original ideology. Christianity would grow and become more and more powerful. It went upwards in power, wealth and influence and downwards in moral standing.

For the marketing of Christianity by the Church to succeed it had to be simplified. Pagans were told that their gods were in reality devils and that the only road to heaven was through Jesus Christ and the Catholic Church. Unless they converted to Christianity through the act of Baptism they would end up in hell. Only Christians could reach heaven. A simple act, they were told, would give them a better chance of not burning in the fires of hell. In the meantime, because pagans were used to worshiping a variety of gods, who had specific functions in people's personal lives and in the life of their communities, the Church offered them saints instead. With a bit of imagination, saint and relic worship developed to take the place of pagan worship of gods. Even some of the rituals were adopted. Not all, however. Human sacrifice, for example, was out, but other forms of sacrifice could be adjusted. It is said that Pope Gregory I (590–604), decided to evangelise Britain after he saw fair-haired Anglo-Saxon boys in the slave market in Rome and commented *Non Angli, sed angeli* (not Angles, but angels). Whatever, his inspiration, Pope Gregory I showed great pragmatism when he instructed his emissary as follows:

> We have come to the conclusion that the temples of idols ... should on no account be destroyed. He is to destroy the idols, but the temples themselves are to be aspersed with holy water, altars set up, and relics enclosed in them ... In this way, we hope that the people may abandon idolatry ... and resort to these places as before ... And since they have a custom of sacrificing many oxen to devils, let other solemnity be substituted in its place ... They are no longer to sacrifice beasts to the Devil, but they may kill them for food to the praise of God ... If the people are allowed some worldly pleasures ... they will come more readily to desire the joys of the spirit. For it is impossible to eradicate all errors from obstinate minds at a stroke; and whoever wishes to climb to a mountain climbs step by step.[59]

Well, this is a sixth-century religious marketing manual, written by no less a person than the Pope himself. The marketing efforts were successful and by the end of the tenth century the whole of Western Europe was Catholic. Some of those who felt uncomfortable with 'Christianity light' and what they considered to be compromises, sought purity and asceticism in monastic life.

Miracles

Miracles – defined as wonders performed by supernatural power, as signs of some special mission or gift and explicitly ascribed to God – play an essential role in Catholicism. The Gospels, telling the story of Christ, are awash with them. Miracles were, according to these books, a core component of the work of Jesus. The Church contends that miracles are signs of the supernatural world and our connection with it and that the prime or supreme end of every miracle is the glory of God and the good of mankind. Miracles are also proof of divine missions such as that of Jesus and his apostles or a confirmation of the truth of a doctrine. The Gospels show that Jesus used miracles regularly as a technique to prove that he was sent by God and that he was the son of God. He argued, speaking to the Jews: 'accept the evidence of my deeds, even if you do not believe me, so that you may recognise and know that the Father is in me, and I in the Father'.[60] The Gospels bring many examples of miracles: the man who had been crippled for thirty-eight years and was told by Jesus 'Rise to your feet, take up your bed and walk. The man recovered instantly, took up his stretcher, and began to walk.'[61] The blind man for whom

Jesus 'spat on the ground and made a paste with the spittle; he spread it on the man's eyes, and said to him "Go and wash in the pool of Siloam." The man went away and washed and when he came back he could see.'[62] Jesus actually explained to his disciples that the man was born blind so 'that God's power might be displayed in curing him.'[63] The Gospel of John speaks of 'signs that Jesus performed in the presence of his disciples', that 'have been recorded in order that you may hold the faith that Jesus is the Christ, the Son of God, and that through this faith you may possess eternal life by his name'.[64] Mark who also 'attested' that Jesus walked on water[65] describes how Jesus fed five thousand people with five loaves of bread and two fish, having 'looked up to heaven, said the blessing. ... They all ate to their hearts content; and twelve great basketfuls of scraps were picked up, with what was left of the fish.'[66] Sometimes the symbolism is spelled out, such as in the draught of fishes. Luke described how Simon, the fisherman who had come back with empty nets, was sent out by Jesus to try again and came back with a big haul of fish, almost splitting the nets. Simon fell at Jesus' knees and Jesus said to him 'Do not be afraid ... from now on you will be a fisher of men.'[67]

In addition to such 'theatrical' miracles, Jesus is supposed to have regularly healed the sick as 'he laid hands on them one by one and cured them'.[68] Jesus promised that the faithful would continue to benefit from miracles: 'Faith will bring with it these miracles: believers will cast out devils in my name and speak strange tongues; if they handle snakes or drink any deadly poison, they will come to no harm; and the sick on whom they lay their hands will recover.'[69] The Gospels also claim that Jesus authorised the apostles and the disciples to use miracles to further their work. They should preach Christ's miracles and perform their own. Disciples, sent out to heal the sick and preach, were told by Jesus that 'whoever rejects you rejects me. And whoever rejects me rejects the One who sent me.'[70] Apostles were sent to 'Heal the sick, raise the dead, cleanse lepers, cast out devils.'[71] Paul in his Second Letter to the Corinthians mentions the miracles as a proof of his apostleship.[72]

The most spectacular miracle of all is, of course, the Resurrection. It is suggested by the Gospels and considered to be true and central to the teachings of the Church that three days after Jesus died, he came back to the Earth before going up to heaven. In the interim period, he ate and drank with his apostles, appeared to other groups of 'witnesses whom God had chosen in advance' and commanded them 'to proclaim him to the people, and affirm that he is the one that is designated by God as judge of the living and the dead'.[73] After Christ's death, his apostles busily travelled about to make souls for Jesus. Convincing the listeners of the Resurrection would not have been easy. In Paul's First Letter to the Corinthians, he writes:

how can some of you say there is no resurrection of the dead? If there be no resurrection, then Christ was not raised; and if Christ was not raised, then our gospel is null and void, and so is your faith; and we turn out to be lying witnesses for God ... And if Christ was not raised, your faith has nothing in it and you are still in your old state of sin. It follows also that those who have died within Christ's fellowship are utterly lost. ... But the truth is, Christ was raised to life.[74]

Here is the problem of the Catholic Church: if you don't believe in the Resurrection then the witnesses, on whom the whole Church is founded, are liars. To avoid this becoming the accepted view, Paul makes it clear to his readers that it is also in their interest to believe in the Resurrection. If they won't, they will still be in their old state of sin and those believers who have died would be utterly lost (i.e. burn in hell). It is therefore not possible to accept the teaching about sin without accepting the Resurrection story.

The Church had constantly to stave off rational explanations of the 'miracles' themselves and attitudes of philosophers such as Spinoza, Locke, Kant and others who argued that 'miracles' were just events which we are unable to explain by other events familiar to our experience. Not only did that pose a threat to the Church's concept of her hold over the faithful and her ability to continue evangelising, such rational thinking was considered dangerous on the grounds that miracles might be seen to be an appeal to ignorance. Similarly, the Church will not accept any suggestion that anything in the Gospels is not 'the gospel truth'. It is testimony and fact. Theories suggesting that perhaps the apostles were in an excited state of mind, or may have exaggerated what they saw are, according to the Catholic Encyclopaedia, 'far more improbable than the miracles themselves'.[75]

The Catholic Church contends that she continues to have the power to work miracles. Church history has many instances of such miracles which she maintains – on the basis of testimonies she considers to be true – to be facts. The Church keeps records of such miracle workers, many of whom are canonised and are now known as saints. Society's need for magic or miracles of the kind which will produce rain or stop it has not died with the transition from magic to religion.[76] Such practices do not disappear. Religious ceremonies and rituals to procure rain are still customary in Catholic countries. Sacramentals, such as consecrated candles, are burned, processions of men carrying crucifixes parade and all the saints with a 'proven' track record of bringing about rain are recruited to 'do their thing'. Statues of such saints are carried around, taken to the fields and to gardens which need water. Local priests lead their congregations in prayers and Holy Masses are said in order to bring the needed rain.[77] Occasionally, when none of these measures is effective, farmers have been known to show their disrespect towards the saints. Statues have been disrobed, threatened with drowning or hanging and sometimes even dumped. It may be that having a level of saints under the top level of God or of the Holy Trinity serves as a safety valve, a kind of buffer which ensures that angry mobs vent their frustration and disappointment against a saint rather than against God. As long as God is not faulted, the teachings of the Church are intact and the standing of the Church leaders is not at risk.

The process of canonisation, in which the Church names saints, is managed by the Vatican bureaucracy. It requires evidence of miracles as proof that the person to be canonised can intercede for us with God. The Church lists more than ten thousand saints. Many are patrons of at least one (but often several) causes, places or organisations. They are meant to be protectors of a certain area of life, be it a country or a church, an occupation, a cause or even an illness. They cover all one's needs from skin diseases through to sick horses and skating. Not only are there saints for and against rain, there is a saint (St Barbara) to be utilised against mine collapses, and another (St Ulric) is meant to be effective against moles. There is even a saint against oversleeping (St Vitus).

Saints and their worship are central to the life of the Catholic Church. The extent to which the Catholic Church still considers saints an integral and practical part of everyday life can be seen from the suggestion to name a patron saint of internet users made by a US Catholic internet publication.[78]

The adoration of saints in the Catholic Church includes the veneration of relics. The most sought-after relics are the body parts of saints. Any personal article is also considered holy and venerable. Catholics even consider a card which touched the body part of a saint to be holy. A holy card is a classical Catholic get-well present, with the hope that the saint in question will intercede with God and have the sick person healed.

To ensure that worshipping saints does not become idolatry, the pagan worship of deities, the Church emphasises that one prays *with* a saint who is asked to 'pray for us' rather than *to* a saint. Those who turn to a patron saint, supposedly, also follow the example given by the patron saint's holy life. The common understanding of a person asking a saint for his or her intervention is that the saint is capable of intervening with God and in reality is being prayed *to*, rather than prayed *with*.[xvi]

As miracles play such an important part in the Catholic faith, the Church supports events which promulgate the idea that miracles demonstrating the existence of a Christian supernatural power continue to take place. To non-believers such episodes are explicable as fraud, hysterics or just coincidence. The Church refers to them as facts. One such phenomenon

---

[xvi] Indeed, the Church teaches that every human being is capable of intervening with God.

is stigmata. Stigmata are marks corresponding to those allegedly left on Christ's body by the Crucifixion, which are said to appear on certain individuals as a result of intense piety or suffering. There has been a number of such people. The first person known to bear stigmata was St Francis of Assisi (1186–1226). Sixty-two men and women, including twentieth-century St Pio of Pietreicina (1887–1968), who have produced stigmata, have been canonised or beatified by the Church.[79]

Shrines and apparitions form part of Catholic tradition and are handled as important by the Church. Some reports of apparitions are rejected as fraudulent or as occurrences which have a natural explanation. Occasionally the Church will conclude that she has no explanation for an occurrence but that there is not enough evidence to prove a supernatural situation. Supernatural events are divided by the Catholic Church into those which are the work of the devil and those which are of heavenly origin.

Once an apparition has been confirmed by the Church to have been real and divine, and therefore worthy of belief, the locality of the occurrence soon becomes a pilgrimage site. It strengthens the Church-woven web of assumptions about a God who continues to produce miracles and to demand devotion and adherence to the rules laid out by his Church. *Our Lady of Fatima* in Portugal and *Our Lady of Lourdes* in France are two of the most vivid and active shrines. An average of five million believers a year make pilgrimages to the French village of Lourdes where, in 1858, a local girl, Bernadette Soubirous, maintained that she saw an apparition of Mary in a cave. Pilgrims arrive in train-loads, many of them sick believers, who leave proclaiming that the miraculous water has healed them. Every night mass prayer sessions, candlelight processions and healing festivities take place in Lourdes. If nothing else, they are big business.[80]

Fatima does not have the healing power of Lourdes and therefore does not get the numbers of pilgrims Lourdes gets. The Church maintains that between the months of May and October 1917, Mary appeared to three shepherd children near the Portuguese village of Fatima. There were six monthly visitations, always on the thirteenth of the month. Mary asked the children to pray the Rosary for the conversion of sinners. She also predicted the Second World War and the expansion of Communism.[81] For the believers, the Second World War happened because Russia was not consecrated to Mary's Immaculate Heart. Moreover, they believe that when Communism fell in 1990, it happened because Pope John Paul II in 1982, with the world's bishops, did consecrate Russia to the Immaculate Heart of Mary.[82] Fatima has become a pilgrimage site with thousands coming to see the place and to participate in mass prayers and outdoor Masses. Promoted and encouraged by the Pope, Catholics come to venerate and celebrate seven-, eight- and nine-year-old children who they believe sat in Fatima, wept for the sins of the world and bewailed the sins of the flesh. The Vatican kept a 'third secret of Fatima' confidential for half a century and revealed it in 2000. In keeping with the apocalyptic style of the first two secrets, the third secret warns of the most terrible fate for the world.

The Power of Sin

Religion comprises a belief, a set of values, rules of behaviour, ritual and in certain cases an organisational structure. Judaism introduced into the pagan world the concept of monotheism. There is but one God and He created all. It also introduced a set of values, which, together with its belief, are defined in the ten commandments. Judaism began with Moses, a leader who prepared his people to re-conquer their land and set up their state. It was, therefore, of importance to set out rules and to create communal institutions. To cement the group further, rituals were introduced.

The Christian Church added three tenets to the belief in one God. The first tenet it added was that the man Jesus was the son of God. To avoid the slippery slope of pantheism, it defined Christ as God's 'one, perfect and unsurpassable Word',[83] rather than as an additional god. In addition to God and his Son, Christianity also believed in the Holy Spirit by the power of which the man Jesus was born to a virgin, a married woman named Mary. The trinity of God, his Son and the Holy Spirit could not be explained. Christian theology accepts it as a *mysterium absolutum*. One might discuss it but could not fully understand it. This was, of course, a convenient tool for authoritarian leaders who demanded acceptance without question. The more intelligent believers philosophised about the issue of a god who had three personas but the majority of the believers just repeated what they were taught. To prevent competition from future usurpers, the Catholic Church stated that in Jesus, God 'has said everything; there will be no other word than this one'.[84]

The second tenet introduced by the Christian Church was that of original sin. Adam and Eve's disobedience for which they were ejected from the Garden of Eden was, according to the Christian faith, inherited by the whole human race and was defined as the original sin. The Church maintained that this sin was passed on, as it were genetically, to all of us as we all stem from Adam and Eve. Having implicated and tainted the whole of mankind in Adam's sin, and taught that 'the overwhelming misery which oppresses men and their inclination towards evil and death cannot be understood apart from their connection with Adam's sin and the fact that he has transmitted to us a sin with which we are all born afflicted', the Church concludes that the whole world is born with 'dead souls'.[85] To uphold this doctrine the Catechism of the Catholic Church adds that 'the transmission of original sin is a mystery that we cannot fully understand'.[86] Because of the inherited original sin and further sins perpetrated by us we are all sent to hell. For mysterious reasons almighty God was unable to prevent the original sin, or any further sinning activity. Moreover, his only solution to rescue us from Satan was to give us his only son. Not only did God send us his only son to do good and to preach good, God had to make an offering of his innocent son to Satan. His son had to suffer, be crucified and die. This is heavenly grace in action. The faithful cannot question it. If, indeed, Jesus had to suffer and to die – why has the Church throughout her history vilified the Jews for their role in bringing Jesus to his trial? Were the Jews not God's instrument for the very purpose of bringing salvation?

The third tenet was the Church's solution to the problem she defined in the second tenet. The Church now waits for Jesus to come back from heaven for the final battle between the forces of God and the forces of Satan. The battle will be won by God and after Satan's defeat, Judgement Day will come. God will judge the dead and the living. The righteous will go to the 'reactivated' paradise and the evil will be sent to hell. This will be the end of time and the world will revert to its original state. The timing of the next stage is unknown. Until that stage is reached the Church's role is to guide mankind according to the teachings of Jesus, following the rituals which the Church maintains were instituted by Jesus. This will enable the faithful to achieve salvation. Having established that all need salvation, the Church maintains that Jesus 'suffered to atone for our sins and to purchase for us eternal life. ... His precious blood is the price by which we were ransomed.'[87] Salvation is thereby available to all through Christ, the Saviour of all men.[88] The instrument for this is the Catholic Church. It is God's will and 'arrangement' that:

> Sacred Tradition, Sacred Scripture and the Magisterium of the Church are so connected and associated that one of them cannot stand without the others. ... they all contribute effectively to the salvation of souls. ...The task of interpreting the Word of God authentically has been entrusted solely to the Magisterium of the Church, that is to the Pope and to the bishops in communion with him.[89]

Original sin is the Catholic Church's device which ensures that as many newborn babies as possible are caught in her web. Having inflicted Adam's sin upon us all, the Church warns that anyone who dies in a state of sin will never reach heaven and will instead suffer in hell. The Church's remedy is to baptise the child and absolve the sin.

In most cases the baptised are infants, but they could also be adults who have not been baptised before. The person baptised is asked to answer some questions, such as 'Do you renounce Satan? And all his works? And all his empty promises?', 'Do you believe in Jesus Christ' or 'Do you believe in the Holy Spirit?' These questions are answered by parents and godparents on behalf of baptised infants. Only once these questions have been satisfactorily answered, does the sprinkling of the water take place, followed by the anointing of the head with Chrism Oil.[xvii]

The Catholic Church teaches that those who are baptised have their sins forgiven them, become united with Christ and receive salvation.[90] The Church promises that all sins, both original and personal, are forgiven through Baptism and the door to the Kingdom of God is thereby opened.[91] The Church believes that 'sanctifying grace' enables humans to enter heaven and that 'sanctifying grace' is imparted to the newly baptised through the specific mentioning of their name in the ceremony of Baptism. As the Church teaches that babies are born with original sin, and if they die un-baptised, their souls would perish, it is of great importance to have newborn infants baptised. A person undergoing Baptism is meant to consciously accept Christianity and reject Satan, at a ceremony believed by Christians to leave a mystical indelible mark (*character indelibilis*) on the baptised. Babies, are clearly unable to make such conscious decisions, let alone pronounce them. In their stead, the undertaking is made by the godparents of the baby. The trend to baptise babies, rather than older and more informed individuals, began in the fourth century. At a time when infant mortality was still high, parents were in a panic that unless their children were baptised they might die in a state of sin and go to hell. From the Church's point of view it had the advantage of bringing in the masses caught at a point of great emotional vulnerability.[xviii]

The Church considers herself gateway and gatekeeper to God and to heaven. In her double-pronged function, the Church also is the emotional support system of her members. The Catholic Church, like many other religious organisations, has positioned herself at all critical junctions of life: birth, marriage, divorce and death. This is where human emotions reach their peak: happiness, thankfulness, worry, sadness and grief. The Church has made herself party to these peaks in an individual's life.

By defining a wide variety of sexual activities, even if they are not enacted but only imagined, as mortal sins, the Church has tried to maintain a regular flow of repenting adults who would come to her for absolution to avoid the fires of hell. Sex is a primal urge, it is central

---

[xvii] Chrism Oil is olive oil, suffused with balsam, which has been blessed by a bishop during Holy Week.

[xviii] Confirmation, the third Sacrament of Initiation, completes the initiation into the Catholic community. Most Catholics are confirmed between the ages of eight and eighteen, at which time, the young person accepts responsibility for his or her faith. The ritual, which is usually led by a bishop, and which 'imprints on the soul an indelible spiritual mark, the 'character', which is the sign that Jesus Christ has marked a Christian with the seal of his Spirit' (Catechism of the Catholic Church, 1304) includes the anointing of the confirmands with Chrism oil.

to life, driving most people's conduct through a greater part of their lives. The sexual urge, which is implanted in us in order to bring about procreation, is central to human existence. The Church claims to set the rules and to punish severely anyone who strays from her rules. She has positioned herself as a regulator of sexual activity. There is nothing in sex which the Catholic Church does not order. She instructs who can have sex with whom, who is prohibited from having sex, what sexual activities are permitted and what is forbidden. The Church then sets out punishments for any deviation.

Similarly, the Church has latched on to the centrality of death in the human psyche. Death, an unknown state, often appears to be inexplicable. Is it final? Is there a way back? Theories of an afterlife have abounded since early times and in most cultures. Death is not only a source of sadness and loss, it is also worrying and frightening. Not only has the Church placed herself as the organisation which runs the burial and funeral ceremonies, she also promises an afterlife to the faithful.

The following is an excerpt from an old English version of the Catechism of the Catholic Church:

> After night prayers ... observe due modesty in going to bed; occupy myself with the thoughts of death and endeavour to compose myself to rest at the foot of the cross, and give my last thoughts to my crucified Saviour.[92]

The Catholic Church instructed her members to refrain from any cheerfulness when they go to bed. Whether they are on their own, or with their spouse, they may not take joy in their bodies, and every night they must prepare for death and think of the crucified Jesus. After a long day, the majority of the Church's members, the hard-working poor, might want to enjoy the physical closeness of their husband or wife, their love and sex. But the Church will not have any of that. Instead, they must prepare for death.

Through such instructions, the Church is in a win–win situation. If the directives are followed, the Church adds to the portion of the believer's life she controls and enhances their acceptance of the Church's control. If the believer has strayed, he or she will have to confess, and confession is yet another control mechanism of the Church, a mechanism which has taught the faithful that unless they confess their sins to their Catholic priest, they will burn in hell. A mechanism which should ensure the binding of the faithful to their priests and keep the Church in business.

The Holy Sacrifice of the Mass, usually referred to as just 'Mass', is Catholicism's central act of worship. The Mass incorporates readings from the Bible, prayers, singing of hymns, a sermon and the 'Penitential Rite', which is a proclamation of guilt and shame and a public acknowledgment that everyone is a sinner. What makes the Mass so very central, however, is Holy Eucharist. The word Eucharist comes from the Greek *eukharistia*, which means thanksgiving, and the sacrament commemorates the Last Supper. At this stage, the priest holds the Host (bread to be consecrated) and, using the words of Jesus at the Last Supper, says 'This is My body which will be given up for you.' Similarly, with the chalice of wine in his hands, the priest says 'This is the cup of My blood, the blood of the new and everlasting covenant. It shall be shed for you and for all so that sins may be forgiven. Do this in memory of Me.' Whereas Baptism is the first sacrament in a person's life, the Holy Eucharist is considered the most significant sacrament, the 'heart and summit of the Church's life'.[93] It goes back to a Gospel report about an incident in a synagogue in Capernaum, according to which Jesus said 'I am the living bread that came down from heaven; if any one eats of this bread, he will live forever; … he who eats my flesh and drinks my blood has eternal life … abides in me, and I in him.'[94] The Catholic Church maintains that through a miracle which regularly takes place in Catholic churches throughout the world, the bread and wine undergo 'transubstantiation' and become the body and blood of Jesus. It should be made clear that, according to the teaching of the Catholic Church, the consecrated bread and wine are not just symbols, they actually are the body and the blood of Christ.[95]

Finally, Catholics who are not aware of any mortal sins they have not confessed to and had absolved and who do not publicly dissent from Church teaching, can 'receive Christ in Eucharistic communion', that is, participate in Holy Communion, in which they are given a consecrated Host, either laid on their tongue or in their hand. Often, Holy Communion will also include a sip of the consecrated wine. Yet, it is not necessary, as the entirety of Christ is in every part of the consecrated Host or in one drop of consecrated wine. Participating in Holy Communion with the Body and Blood of Christ forgives venial sins and preserves those participating from grave sins.[xix]

The Catholic Mass, at which bread and wine are transformed into the body and blood of Christ, is an example of a ritual made to stir. By including transubstantiation in the Catholic Mass, the Church provides her members with a remnant of the old magic and can thereby satisfy the human need for miracles to happen and to be demonstrated. To a much lesser extent, the power of a priest to turn an ordinary item into a holy one is also brought into play in the oil blessed by bishops during

---

[xix] Whereas mortal sins are so evil that they kill the soul, and those in state of grave sin have lost their baptismal grace and wounded ecclesial communion, venial sins are less serious and only wound the soul. (Catechism of the Catholic Church, 1446)

Holy Week. As *oleum infirmorum*, it is used to anoint the sick;[xx] as *oleum catechumenorum*, it is used to bless people prior to their Baptism, and as *sacrum chrisma* which has added *balsam* to give it a nice scent, it is used at Baptism and when administering sacraments of Confirmation or of Holy Orders. Chrism Oil is also used to consecrate churches, altars and to bless church bells.

Conclusion

Religion is adept at exploiting human anxiety, human weaknesses and the centrality of the non-rational in human life. Indeed, people who feel vulnerable or anxious are more likely to seek shelter or emotional relief through the irrational. To the unsure and susceptible, religions offer clear-cut answers and solutions. Religions, and especially the mutually exclusive ones, such as the monotheistic religions, have cultivated and promoted intolerance of any competing institution or structure. This intolerance has levied and still levies a very high toll. Many institutions, including religious institutions, are designed to be power bases created to achieve certain ends, by controlling behaviour which is relevant to these ends. This is true of a wide variety of institutions, be they a local wild-life preservation trust, a political party or a religious institution. One of the crucial questions in assessing such institutions is the means used to achieve control. Most people consider use of force unacceptable for a political party in its endeavour to attain power. If one considers the means used by religious organisations to attain and to hold on to power one finds that they use a different, more sophisticated kind of force. It combines a fictitious storyline with threats of punishment unless rules – as set out by the hierarchy of the organisation – are obeyed.

Based on the hold which religion has over many and the specific devices of power integrated in Christian dogma and in Church tradition, the Catholic Church has been able to build up an extensive power base worldwide. The Church has infiltrated political institutions and has for a long time been at the centre of power, at first in most Western countries and later in many other countries. The power of the Church has oscillated over her history. It has done so, however, within a broad downward spiral. The Church, which had originally opposed democracy and with time learned to accept it, has not become democratic herself. Democratisation and general enlightenment have reduced the Church's

---

[xx] The Anointing of the Sick used to be referred to as the Last Anointing (*Extreme Unction*), otherwise known as the 'Last Rites'. In this sacrament, in which a priest prays over the sick person and anoints them with the Oil of the Sick, all hitherto unconfessed sins can be confessed and absolved. If the person is unconscious or otherwise unable to confess, then those sins which the person would have confessed to, had he or she been able to, are forgiven.

authority. In her *realpolitik*, the Church has simply perfected the art of operating in democracies to further her agenda.

The Catholic Church has historically been an ideological bedfellow of many right-wing and conservative governments. As an undemocratic structure the Church had no qualms about doing business with undemocratic political structures, which, moreover, can be easier to deal with. These regimes were not only anti-Communist but often also anti-Semitic. The Church did not shirk from partnership with and support of regimes with very poor human rights records, provided they gave the Catholic Church a monopoly over matters of faith and religion.

She has had a somewhat schizophrenic attitude to dictatorships. In Poland, a country especially near to the then Pope's heart, the Church was very active in bringing about the downfall of the regime. Not only was the Pope Polish, the Church had opposed Communism from its very early days and had fought this atheistic philosophy of life. Under John Paul II, the Church used Church funds and clandestinely co-funded the revolutionary *Solidarity* movement, coordinating her Polish activities with the CIA.[96] The population in South America was not so fortunate: the Church collaborated with right-wing military regimes in several Latin-American countries. Right-wing dictators, who accepted the Church as a partner, offered not only a role for the Church, but also an anti-Marxist attitude. The Church was too often willing to overlook atrocities carried out by these regimes against their own population. Whereas the Church's involvement in Poland may have freed the Polish people from the yoke of an oppressive regime, we should not forget that the Church was fighting Communism, a competing world system, and not oppression.

In recent history, the Church has been able to take advantage of the sovereign status of Vatican City, the independence of her secretive financial institutions, which are not subject to any external control, her membership and observer status in almost all international organisations and her direct influence over the faithful to further her interests.

The Church continues to use whatever means she has at her disposal to influence legislation in areas such as: prevention of divorce, discrimination against homosexuals, prohibition of same-sex marriage, prevention of legal abortion or availability of contraception and access to family-planning education. The Church continues to wield much influence, often to lethal effect. Her impact is most damaging in the poorer and needier societies, which have less access to other sources of information.

Chapter Two
Truth and the Policing of Thought

Christianity is the story of certain events which are said to have taken place two thousand years ago. Even though there is no way of proving that all the events mentioned in Christian Scripture did indeed take place, Christianity believes these events to be true. The Catholic Church claims to be the sole authority for interpreting these events. The Church has successfully established for herself substantial power, ostensibly in order to offer her teaching to as many as possible. She has required the subordination of populations to her teaching and the enforcement of her beliefs. As a result, there have been many instances where the acquired power has been used more to abuse and cause harm than to promote love and hope.

The Catechism of the Catholic Church gives us the principles on which the Church bases her beliefs. The Apostles' Credo, a statement of Christian belief, contains the following points: God created heaven and earth; Jesus was God's only son whose mother was Mary, a virgin; Jesus was crucified, died, was buried and joined the other dead in purgatory;[i] on the third day Jesus came back to life and after some time ascended into heaven, where he is seated at the right hand of God the Father.[1] The information on which Christianity bases her teaching appears in the four Gospels of Matthew, Mark, Luke and John. The Church has declared that she 'holds firmly that the four Gospels, whose historicity she unhesitatingly affirms, faithfully hand on what Jesus, the Son of God, while he lived among men, really did and taught for their eternal salvation, until the day when he was taken up'.[2] Rather than leaving God as an idea, Christianity has entangled itself with material features such as father, mother, birth, death and virginity. Unlike the transcendental concept of God – these are features most of us have personal experience with. The idea of God's existence is not so difficult to 'market'. We have no scientific knowledge as to why the world exists or how it was created and many find the idea, which is proffered by various religions, that there is a God who created the world, perhaps even a good God, quite reassuring.

---

[i] Purgatory is not hell. It is a place of temporary punishment in which souls destined for heaven cleanse their sins.

Christianity's further assertions in areas which are scientifically accessible, such as loss of virginity, or resurrection, necessitate stronger willingness to accept the Church's authority as a source of truth.

By employing terminology which, in its daily use, reflects a factual situation, one which can be tested and verified, whilst referring to a matter of faith, for which there can be no proof, the Church misleads the person she addresses and exploits the high value which truth generally enjoys. The Church offered explanations which believers accept, such as: 'as soon as Christ was dead His blessed Soul went into that part of hell called Limbo. ... a place of rest, where the souls of the just who died before Christ were detained. ... because they could not go up to the Kingdom of Heaven till Christ had opened it for them'.[3] This account, which explains hell almost in estate-agent's terminology, is presented to be as true as the verifiable fact that the vicar was bald.

The Church maintains that Christianity has not only superseded Judaism, but also that with Christ, God has said his last word: Christ 'is the Father's one, perfect and unsurpassable Word. In him he has said everything; there will be no other word than this one.'[4] The claim of uniqueness and exclusivity and the rubbishing of competition is a sensible strategy, suggesting that the Catholic Church was the 'only show in town'. No doubt is left as to the fact that the Bible – both the Old and New Testaments – is 'the speech of God as it is put down in writing under the breath of the Holy Spirit', and to the inquisitive mind the Church offers the explanation:

> To compose the sacred books, God chose certain men who, all the while he employed them in this task, made full use of their own faculties and powers so that, though he acted in them and by them, it was as true authors that they consigned to writing whatever he wanted written, and no more.[5]

As if there could be any doubt with this august authorship, the Catechism adds that 'The inspired books teach the truth.' Through Tradition, which 'transmits in its entirety the Word of God which has been entrusted to the apostles by Christ the Lord and the Holy Spirit', the Church enters the picture. Tradition, we are told, is transmitted 'to the successors of the apostles so that, enlightened by the Spirit of truth, they may faithfully preserve, expound and spread it abroad by their preaching'. Hence, the Bible and also Tradition are defined as true, and both 'must be accepted and honoured with equal sentiments of devotion and reverence'.[6] The Church also claims that her Magisterium[ii] holds its authority 'from Christ to the fullest extent when it defines dogmas, that is, when it proposes truths contained in divine Revelation or also when it proposes in a definitive

---

ii   The teaching authority of the Church.

way truths having a necessary connection with them'.[7] Virtually every papal encyclical is strewn with quotations from predecessors' assertions, declarations and decrees. The concept that every pope is a successor of Peter and Vicar of Christ would, to an outsider, seem particularly difficult to fathom, as there can be no doubt that the history of the Church is dotted with quite a few decadent, immoral and corrupt popes. There is no mechanism at the Church's disposal which would enable her to define such obvious aberrations from the ideal as anything but legally nominated and instituted Vicars of Christ.

Having established the sources of truth, the Church makes a further claim and defines herself as the unique franchise holder: 'The task of interpreting the Word of God authentically has been entrusted solely to the Magisterium of the Church, that is, to the Pope and to the bishops in communion with him.'[8] This authority is widened to cover the 'interpretation of the Word of God, whether in its written form or in the form of Tradition'.[9] To allay any possible questioning, this arrangement is defined by the Church as God's own arrangement, which is necessary for the salvation of souls:

> It is clear therefore that, in the supremely wise arrangement of God, Sacred Tradition, Sacred Scripture and the Magisterium of the Church are so connected and associated that one of them cannot stand without the others. Working together, each in its own way, under the action of the one Holy Spirit, they all contribute effectively to the salvation of souls.[10]

The philosopher Professor Richard Blackwell speaks of the 'logic of centralised authority', which, according to Catholic tradition, is required 'by the scripturally based revelation that serves as the source of religion'.[11] The intertwining of Tradition and her own teaching with Sacred Scriptures, serve to give substantial weighting and importance to all that has been laid down by previous popes and, of course, by important Church teachers such as St Augustine or Thomas Aquinas. These are instruments which have enabled the Church to lay down the law and to define what is true and what is not true. Considered without the benefit of faith, the Church's concept of truth is most open to challenge. Not only is one expected to accept various miracles described in the Scriptures as true, it is also proposed to us, for example, that bread and wine regularly turn into the actual flesh and blood of Christ in the service of the Eucharist. This is meant to happen regularly at every Mass.

The sixteenth-century Dominican, Melchior Cano, maintained that in the Bible 'not only the words but even every comma has been supplied by the Holy Spirit'.[12] With the surfacing of ever more serious theological questioning of the Church's inflexible teaching, Pope Pius X (1903–1914) reminded his flock in his encyclical *Pascendi* (1907): 'We hold that the Sacred Books [which were] written under the inspiration of the Holy Ghost have God for their author.' In his encyclical, the Pope launched an across-the-board attack on the 'modernists' who suggest that the Scriptures really dealt with religion and morals and should not be considered as a source and basis for science and history. The Pope quotes St Augustine's warning of the slippery slope one would risk:

'In an authority so high, admit but one officious lie, and there will not remain a single passage of those apparently difficult to practice or to believe, which on the same most pernicious rule may not be explained as a lie uttered by the author wilfully and to serve a purpose.' And thus it will come about, the holy Doctor continues, that 'everybody will believe and refuse to believe what he likes or dislikes in them,' namely, the Scriptures.[13]

By considering herself but a trusted guardian and not the author of her teaching, the Church leaves herself very little room for manoeuvre. Instead of being a source of values, the Church is a source of interpretation of a fixed set of God-given unchangeable texts. The Church does not make do with a claim that whatever Jesus is meant to have said and done corresponds with values which she considers worthy. She defines the words and the deeds as true and a set of early Christian interpretations as binding. Pope Pius IX (1846–1878) instructed that: 'In matters of religion it is the duty of philosophy … not to scrutinize the depths of the mysteries of God, but to venerate them devoutly and humbly.' And the First Vatican Council of 1870 declared: 'The doctrine of the faith which God has revealed has not been proposed to human intelligence to be perfected by them as if it were a philosophical system, but as a divine deposit entrusted to the Spouse of Christ to be faithfully guarded and infallibly interpreted.'[14]

Casting doubt on Church truths was tantamount to suggesting that the Church, Church Fathers, popes and the Magisterium of the Church were defining something which was false as the truth. These were serious allegations and would have serious consequences. The Church used whatever means she had at her disposal to punish those who doubted her word. The Church went further and considered it her right and her duty to prevent the dissemination of ideas which contradicted her truth. One such contradiction that had to be dealt with was raised by Galileo.

The Galileo Affair

From the Galileo affair we can learn a lesson which remains valid in relation to similar situations which occur today and which may occur in the future.[15]

Galileo is a thorn in the Catholic Church's side. The Church would not continue to be so uncomfortable about the Galileo affair had Galileo not been such an important and celebrated scientist, even to this very day.[16] After all, the Church does not regularly deal with the tens of thousands of other victims of the Inquisition.

The trial of Galileo Galilei (1564–1642) in 1633 by the Catholic Church and his subsequent imprisonment constitute the most famous example of the Church attempting to use violent means in order to prevent the teaching of views with which she does not agree. It took the Church three hundred and fifty-nine years to concede that she was wrong in her judgement about Galileo. In his allocution to the Pontifical Academy of Sciences in 1992, Pope John Paul II said so. However, he did not concede that it was wrong to try someone and imprison him for his views or for his scientific findings. In fact, he never even mentioned the abuse of Galileo at the hands of the Church.

It all started with Mikolaj Kopernik, better known as Copernicus (1473–1543) who established that the Sun lay at the centre of the solar system. The prevailing belief had always been that it was the Earth which lay at the centre of the world. It was based on Aristotelian (384–322 BC) physical laws, the concept of the Earth as immovable, and on Ptolemy's[iii] picture of the Earth being the centre of a universe around which all heavenly bodies, including the Sun, would rotate. This view complemented the Church's own understanding which was based on scripture: 'The earth is firmly fixed; it shall not be moved.'[17] How, then, can anyone suggest otherwise? Copernicus kept his findings quiet for some thirty years and only published his conclusions, which were based on detailed experiments and measurements, towards the end of his life. Osiander, the editor of Copernicus' opus *De revolutionibus orbium coelestium*, which Copernicus had dedicated to Pope Paul III and which was published in 1543, was so worried about its ramifications that he replaced Copernicus' introduction with a misleading preface of his own.[18] In his preface, Osiander explained that Copernicus had only meant his work to be a mathematical expedient.

For a while Copernicus' findings were not taken up. They only became explosive when Galileo, almost a hundred years after Copernicus had made his observations, came out in his support. Before Galileo, Giordano Bruno (1548–1600), a former Dominican monk, had published in one of his books, *Cena de le Ceneri*, a defence of Copernicus' heliocentric theory. As this contained various heterodoxical views, Bruno was considered problematic by the Inquisition and had to flee first Naples and then Rome to avoid prosecution. He was finally arrested and tried by the Inquisition in Venice in 1591. A year later, Bruno, who did not stick to his recanting,

---

iii   A second-century astronomer.

was sent to Rome for another trial. For eight years he was kept imprisoned and was interrogated by the Inquisition. Defiant and refusing to recant, he was burned at the stake as a heretic in 1600. As Bruno's Inquisition file is missing, we do not know exactly what the Church wanted Bruno to recant and what he refused. We do know that he was imprisoned and interrogated by the Catholic Church and finally burned for holding and not retracting views of which the Church did not approve. Ten years later, Galileo published his book *Sidereus Nuncius* (The Starry Messenger) in which he contradicted Ptolemy and thereby implied that Copernicus was right. In 1616, the Jesuit Cardinal Robert Bellarmine issued a decree that declared Copernicus wrong, thereby also declaring Galileo to be wrong. On the instructions of Pope Paul V (1605–1621) Galileo was summoned by Bellarmine to a Church procedure at which he was duly admonished. According to a transcribed copy in the Inquisition file, the veracity of which is not clear, Galileo was:

> commanded and enjoined, in the name of His Holiness the Pope and the whole Congregation of the Holy Office, to relinquish altogether the said opinion that the Sun is the centre of the world and immovable and that the Earth moves; nor further to hold, teach, or defend it in any way whatsoever, verbally or in writing; otherwise proceedings would be taken against him by the Holy Office; which injunction the said Galileo acquiesced in and promised to obey.[19]

Galileo, one of the world's most important scientific inventors and thinkers, started out as a lecturer in Florence and then became professor of Mathematics at the University of Padua. He was well known as an inventor and was respected for his work. Contemporary Aristotelians, unsurprisingly, were unhappy about this mould-breaking interpretation of the world. Although Galileo was on friendly terms with Pope Urban VIII (1623–1644), who in fact had even written an ode in Latin to celebrate Galileo's discovery of sun spots, the Pope was not willing to allow him total freedom. He was granted permission by the papal court to publish his views (that is the Copernican concept) only if he presented a balanced case for both heliocentric and geocentric systems. In 1632, Galileo's *Dialogo sopra due massimi sistemi del mondo* (Dialogue on the Two Chief World Systems) was published. It did indeed present both Ptolemaic and Copernican views. There was, however, no question about the author's bias and as a direct result the seventy-year-old and sick Galileo was charged with heresy and taken to the dungeons of the Inquisition. Having been shown the instruments of torture that the Inquisition used to 'induce' those who fell into their hands, Galileo agreed to retract and renounce all he had said. In return, he was punished with 'only' house arrest. He died eight years later.

The Galileo affair has been a *cause célèbre* ever since his trial. It became a symbol of an assumed anti-scientific stance by the Church. This, however, is an oversimplification. The Church did not and does not hold an anti-science policy. Galileo made certain scientific statements which contradicted the long-held beliefs about the Earth and the Sun, beliefs which in turn went hand-in-hand with the prevailing interpretation of the Scriptures. Galileo also made certain theological statements in which he apparently rejected the role of the Scriptures in those areas where science offered answers. In a letter Galileo wrote in 1615, he explained:

> the Holy Spirit did not want to teach us whether heaven moves or stands still, nor whether its shape is spherical or like a discus or extended along a plane, nor whether the earth is located at its centre or on one side ... But if the Holy Spirit deliberately avoided teaching us such propositions, inasmuch as they are of no relevance to His intention (that is, to our salvation), how can one now say that to hold this rather than that proposition on this topic is so important that one is a principle of faith and the other erroneous?

> ...I would say that the authority of the Holy Scripture aims chiefly at persuading men about those articles and propositions which, surpassing all human reason, could not be discovered by scientific research or by any other means than through the mouth of the Holy Spirit.

> ...I should think it would be very prudent not to allow anyone to commit and in a way oblige scriptural passages to have to maintain the truth of any physical conclusions whose contrary could ever be proved to us by the senses and demonstrative and necessary reasons.[20]

In making these statements about the jurisdiction of the Bible, albeit to support his underlying scientific interest, Galileo trod into even more dangerous grounds. He will have angered not only the conservative scientists but also those in the Church who may not have been that bothered by the purely scientific points that Galileo was making. That presented the Church with a problem which she attempted to deal with in two ways: by stating that Galileo's scientific statements were false; and by forbidding Galileo from teaching or even discussing those scientific statements. Galileo's sentence makes interesting reading as it so clearly demonstrates how narrow minded the Church was compared to the unprejudiced thinking of some scientists of the day.

For defying the Church's order in his book, in which he introduced the Copernican system and 'labelled it as probable', Galileo was tried by the Church in 1633. His sentence reiterated that 'The proposition that the Sun is the centre of the world and does not move from its place is absurd and false philosophically and formally heretical, because it is expressly contrary to Holy Scripture.' The Church was worried as, 'with the printing of this book the false opinion of the earth's motion and the sun's stability was being disseminated and taking hold more and more every day'. In thinking which is shared even today by fundamentalists of different religions, the sentence explains that 'there is no way an opinion declared and defined contrary to divine Scripture may be probable'.[21]

In order to escape imprisonment and be allowed the more comfortable house arrest, Galileo was forced to sign a recantation.[22] To avoid prison, the old and sick Galileo had not only to deny his scientific findings, he was also made to promise to act as an informer of the Inquisition and report others to the Church's secret police and torture operation.

In 1992, 359 years later, Pope John Paul II had the following to say about the case of the Catholic Church vs. Galileo:

> A twofold question is at the heart of the debate of which Galileo was the centre. …
>
> In the first place, like most of his adversaries, Galileo made no distinction between the scientific approach to natural phenomena and a reflection on nature, of the philosophical order, which that approach generally calls for. That is why *he rejected the suggestion made to him* to present the Copernican system as a hypothesis, inasmuch as it had not been confirmed by irrefutable proof. Such, however, was *an exigency of the experimental method* of which he was the inspired founder.
>
> … The *problem posed by the theologians* of that age was, therefore, that of the compatibility between heliocentrism and Scripture. Thus the new science … obliged the theologians to examine their own criteria of scriptural interpretation. *Most of them did not know how to do so.*
>
> … the cultural horizon of Galileo's age was uniform and carried the imprint of a particular philosophical formation. This unitary character of culture, which in itself is positive and desirable even in our own day, was one of the reasons for Galileo's condemnation. *The majority of theologians did not recognize* the formal distinction between Sacred Scripture and its interpretation, and this led them unduly to transpose into the realm of the doctrine of the faith a question which in fact pertained to scientific investigation.
>
> … From the beginning of the Age of Enlightenment down to our own day, the Galileo case has been a sort of 'myth', in which *the image fabricated out of the events was quite far removed from reality.* In this perspective, the Galileo case was the symbol of *the Church's supposed rejection of scientific progress,* or of 'dogmatic' obscurantism opposed to the free search for truth. This myth has played a considerable cultural role. It has helped to anchor a number of scientists of good faith in the idea that there was an incompatibility between the spirit of science and its rules of research on the one hand and the Christian faith on the other. A *tragic mutual*

incomprehension has been interpreted as the reflection of a fundamental opposition between science and faith.

> ... In Galileo's time, to depict the world as lacking an absolute physical reference point was, so to speak, inconceivable. And since the cosmos, as it was then known, was contained within the solar system alone, this reference point could only be situated in the Earth or in the Sun. Today, after Einstein and within the perspective of contemporary cosmology, neither of these two reference points has the importance they once had. This observation, it goes without saying, is not directed against the validity of Galileo's position in the debate; it is only meant to show that often, beyond two partial and contrasting perceptions, there exists a wider perception which includes them and goes beyond both of them.[23] [emphasis added]

Thus, in what the world may have expected to be a *mea culpa* for the abuse of Galileo and for the attempts to scare other free thinkers from uttering ideas contradicting Church dogma, we instead received a lukewarm papal explanation about the difficulties of 'the theologians' in Galileo's days. The Pope refers to a 'debate', apparently forgetting that it was more an interrogation by the policing arm of his own Church. Galileo's 'debate' was with the dreaded Inquisition and not in a scientific colloquium. Not once does the Pope find fault with any popes or cardinals. He does not mention Pope Paul V, under whose authority Galileo was taken to task in 1616, nor does he mention Pope Urban VIII under whose authority Galileo was interrogated and tried in 1633. He does not mention the cardinals in charge of the Congregation of the Holy Office which ran the Inquisition, nor the Congregation of the Index, which was in charge of the Index of prohibited books. They all had names, titles, offices and Church authority. Instead John Paul talks only about theologians. It seems that in this centrist institution, rather atypically, the proverbial buck stopped with the theologians. There may indeed have been an intellectual inability on the part of theologians to deal with what Professor Ernan McMullin referred to as 'a perceived threat to the authority of Scripture as well as to their own authority as its licensed interpreters'.[24] Would the Church have permitted the theologians any alternative? She continues to hold that she has a monopoly in certain matters, which include the interpretation of Scripture. Gregory IX (1227–1241) was quite direct when he addressed some theologians of his time:

> Some among you, puffed up like bladders with the spirit of vanity strive by profane novelties to cross the boundaries fixed by the Fathers, twisting the meaning of the sacred text ... to the philosophical teaching of the rationalists, not for the profit of their hearer but to make a show of science ... these men, led away by various and strange doctrines, turn the head into the tail and force the queen to serve the handmaid.[25]

The language of discipline may have changed since the thirteenth century, but the fervour of the present-day Congregation for the Doctrine of the Faith (CDF) is just as strong. Present-day theologians are still being censured by the CDF if they dare to veer from the approved path.

The Pope treats the whole matter as a 'myth' blown out of all proportion. Moreover, he adds that today 'neither of these two reference points has the importance they once had', implying that the Church was right not to form too quick an opinion. He even intimates that there was contributory negligence on Galileo's part; Galileo had rejected the suggestion of presenting the Copernican system simply as a hypothesis which, as the 'founder' of the 'experimental method', he should have done. Had he done so, the Pope insinuates, Galileo would have stayed out of trouble and would have, moreover, followed the correct scientific professional procedure. By describing the matter as a 'tragic mutual incomprehension', the Pope further pushes the blame onto Galileo and some theologians who 'did not know how to' examine their own criteria of scriptural interpretation. Evidently, the Vatican decided to give as little as possible. When, in 1979, Pope John Paul II first spoke about Galileo to the Pontifical Academy of Sciences, he did so at the Plenary Session to commemorate the centenary of the birth of Albert Einstein. On that occasion, the Pope did not mince his words:

> Mr President! You said, very rightly, in your address that Galileo and Einstein characterised an era. The greatness of Galileo is known to everyone, like that of Einstein; but unlike the latter, whom we are honouring today before the College of Cardinals in the apostolic palace, the former had to suffer a great deal – we cannot conceal the fact – at the hands of men and organisms of the Church.
>
> ... I hope that theologians, scholars and historians, animated by a spirit of sincere collaboration, will study the Galileo case more deeply and, in loyal recognition of wrongs from whatever side they come, will dispel the mistrust that still opposes, in many minds, a fruitful concord between science and faith, between the Church and the world.[26]

It took the pope a very long time, thirteen years to be exact, before he was able to produce a result from the study which he announced in 1979. The Galileo Commission, which was established by the Vatican in 1981, met seven times over seven years, and in 1990 their work was declared complete. Why did it take so long to deal with the simple fact that the Church investigated, tried and imprisoned a scientist for publishing his views? George V. Coyne, the Director of the Vatican Observatory, a member of the Galileo Commission, reported that the Commission had twice applied to the Pope to have the archives of the one-time Congregations of the Holy Office and of the Index opened, but ultimately without success.[27] Was the Vatican machinery ensuring that John Paul's instruction to come clean on the Galileo case did not get out of hand? Should not the outcome have been a straightforward apology for the policy and procedures under which the Church, her popes and cardinals and other office holders not only declared which scientific theories were true and which were not but also forbade free scientific research and free speech? Should not the outcome have been a clear-cut and frank apology for the fact which Pope John Paul II mentioned in 1979 but omitted in his 1992 conclusion, that Galileo 'had to suffer a great deal – we cannot conceal the fact – at the hands of men and organisms of the Church'? Unwittingly, in 1979, the Pope stated that the fact that Galileo suffered at the hands of the Church cannot be concealed. Little did he know that thirteen years later, he himself would seek to conceal it.

The issue, however, is a bigger one. As much as the Churchmen hated the idea, they were able to find a formula by which they conceded that the judgement of Galileo was a mistake. The real issue is not why this wonderful, exciting and innovative scientist was not understood by the Church, it is more a question of why the Church undertook such outrageous stifling of intellectual activities. However, if this question were asked, the uncomfortable answer would be that the Church continues to do so to this very day. This is the role of the Congregation for the Doctrine of the Faith which was founded in 1542 and was originally called the Sacred Congregation of the Universal Inquisition. In 1908 its name was changed to the Sacred Congregation of the Holy Office and in 1965 it received its current name. The Apostolic Constitution on the Roman Curia, *Pastor Bonus*, promulgated by John Paul II in 1988, defines that its duty is 'to promote and safeguard the doctrine on the faith and morals throughout the Catholic world', adding 'for this reason everything which in any way touches such matter falls within its competence'.[28] The titles have changed but the concept has not. The main difference between then and now is the extent of the power of the Church. Fortunately, the Catholic Church can no longer pick up people in the streets, haul them into the offices of the Inquisition, torture them into submission and punish them. The Church still has some power and uses it to muzzle those who choose to be her members, when they do not conform to dogma as set out and as policed by the CDF.

Censorship

In addition to the loss of personal liberty imposed by the Church on Galileo, the Inquisition added his *Dialogue* to the Index of Forbidden Books, the *Index liborum prohibitorum*, where it remained until 1835. Copernicus' writings had already been put on the Index in 1616:

in order that this opinion may not creep any further to the prejudice of Catholic truth, the Congregation has decided that the books by Nikolaus Copernicus (On the Revolutions of Spheres) and Diego de Zuñiga (On Job) be suspended until corrected.[29]

Censorship of books by the Church existed long before the Index was created in 1557. Professors at the University of Paris were forbidden by papal statutes issued in 1342 to hand over any text to the booksellers before the text had been examined by the professors of theology. The first Index of Forbidden Books was produced during the papacy of Paul IV (1555–1559), the Pope who, as Cardinal Caraffa, was the originator of the Roman Inquisition and one of the first Inquisitors General. The Pauline Index, which had banned numerous scientific texts only because their author was Protestant, was considered even by many in the Church hierarchy to be too restrictive and as a result of discussions at the Council of Trent, a Tridentine Index was published in 1564. From time to time new editions were published with additions and sometimes also deletions. The last Index to be published was the thirty-second edition which came out in 1948 and included four thousand titles. The Index of Forbidden Books was finally scrapped by Pope Paul VI (1963–1978) in 1966. However, the CDF hastened to clarify the fact that the Index still served as a 'moral guide in so far as it reminds the conscience of the faithful they must avoid writings which can be dangerous to faith and morals'.

The names on the Church's Index read like a veritable Who's Who. They include: Voltaire, Descartes, La Fontaine, Montaigne, Rabelais, Montesquieu, Jean-Jacques Rousseau, Diderot, Blaise Pascal, Erasmus, Machiavelli, John Calvin, John Milton, Spinoza, John Locke, David Hume, Emmanuel Kant, Jean Paul Sartre, John Stuart Mill, Thomas Hobbes, Francis Bacon, Edward Gibbon, Ernest Renan, Henri Bergson, Stendhal, Balzac, Victor Hugo, Flaubert, Dumas, Emile Zola, Anatole France, Daniel Defoe, Jonathan Swift, Heinrich Heine, George Sand, D'Annunzio, Alberto Moravia, Mme de Staël, Sade, Casanova and Andre Gide. It also included various Jewish books such as the Talmud, the authoritative record of rabbinic discussions on Jewish law, ethics, customs and legends and unauthorised translations of the Bible.

Up to 1870, the Church, as the secular ruler of the Papal States, still had executive and policing power, and in those territories control over publishing, selling, owning and reading of prohibited books was secured by the Church's instruments of state. Publishers and booksellers were shown the lists of books and authors that were prohibited by the Congregation of the Index and were made to sign the back of the list as an acknowledgement and pledge neither to publish nor to handle any of the listed books. Some printers, in the late sixteenth century, had to flee to

Switzerland to avoid incarceration. After 1870, obedience to Church rules could only be enforced through the instrument of excommunication.

The loss of the Papal States did not weaken the papal fervour. In his bull *Officiorum ac munerum* (1897), Pope Leo XIII (1878–1903) specified precise instructions regarding censorship, and the duty and 'concern of all Catholics and particularly of the educated to give notice of pernicious books to the bishops or the Apostolic See' is made clear. The Pope also assures denouncers of their anonymity, as those 'to whom information is given, have the sacred duty to keep private the names of informers'.[30] Worries about 'modernism' caused his successor, Pope Pius X (1903–1914), to issue additional instructions in his encyclical *Pascendi* (1907):

> It is also the duty of the Bishops to prevent writings of Modernists, or whatever savours of Modernism or promotes it, from being read when they have been published, and to hinder their publication when they have not.

> ... It is not enough to hinder the reading and the sale of bad books – it is also necessary to prevent them from being published. Hence, let the Bishops use the utmost strictness in granting permission to print. ... We have the highest esteem for this institution of censors, and ... In all Episcopal Curias, therefore, let censors be appointed for the revision of works intended for publication ... The censor shall give his verdict in writing. If it be favourable, the Bishop will give the permission for publication by the word Imprimatur, which must be preceded by the Nihil obstat and the name of the censor. ... The name of the censor shall never be made known to the authors until he shall have given a favourable decision, so that he may not have to suffer inconvenience either while he is engaged in the examination of a writing or in case he should withhold his approval. Censors shall never be chosen from the religious orders until the opinion of the Provincial, or in Rome, of the General, has been privately obtained, and the Provincial or the General must give a conscientious account of the character, knowledge, and orthodoxy of the candidate. We admonish religious superiors of their most solemn duty never to allow anything to be published by any of their subjects without permission from themselves and from the Ordinary.[31]

The Pope also saw fit to widen the scope of the Congregation of the Index to include pro-active 'fishing expeditions':

> Henceforth it will be the task of this Sacred Congregation not only to examine carefully the books denounced to it, to prohibit them if necessary, and to grant permission for reading forbidden books, but also to supervise, ex officio, books that are being published, and to pass sentence on such as deserve to be prohibited. Its further task is to remind the bishops of

their sacred duty to combat the publication of pernicious writings and give information about them to the Apostolic See, in accordance with the Constitution.[32]

The Church was not alone in her fight against books of which she disapproved. Censorship has historically been and still is a tool-in-trade of every totalitarian regime. In extreme cases censorship was enhanced by the burning of books. The Nazis burned Jewish books and others which they considered unacceptable. The Catholic Encyclopedia suggests that people's hatred of the Church instrument limiting freedom of speech is misplaced, stemming from the fact that 'in past centuries particularly the censorship of the State often made itself decidedly unpopular with the people, and that their hatred was but too easily, but without reason, transferred to the censorship of the Church'. It also feels that 'the Roman expurgation of books, so often unjustly held in ill repute … displayed wise moderation and true justice, since it intended only to keep faith and morals unpolluted'.[33] But the Church thinking behind the burning of books has apparently not changed. Only recently, a Catholic cardinal in Kenya led the public burning of safe-sex literature to prevent it being read by the people of his country. The Kenyan cardinal's actions have roots in those of his clerical ancestors: Pope Gregory IX (1227–1241) had all Jewish books confiscated and, in a bull issued in 1239, called for the burning of the Talmud. In response, the king of France delivered more than twenty thousand copies of the Talmud, seized from the Jews, which were burned in a fire at the Place de Grève in 1240. Sometimes, the burning of the Jewish books went hand in hand with the burning of synagogues. Church attempts to prevent people, including Jews, from reading the Talmud, by way of searching for clandestinely held copies and burning them, continued well into the eighteenth century.

The Vatican did not let the Second World War deflect it from its important work and in 1940 the Catholic Church produced yet another edition of the *Index librorum prohibitorum*. In the preface to this edition Cardinal Merry del Val explained 'Today we face a struggle which is led by the Devil himself; it is founded on something both insincere and destructive; malicious publications. No other danger is greater.' It is dumbfounding to think that the devil in question was not Adolf Hitler but 'malicious publications'. In fact neither Hitler's *Mein Kampf* nor any other Nazi books were included in the Index. The cardinal continues:

The Holy Church, which was appointed by God himself, could not proceed otherwise. It represents an infallible master who securely leads his believers. Thus, the Church is equipped with all necessary and useful means to prevent the infection of the herd of Jesus, by the erroneous and corrupt which will show itself irrespective of the mask it hides behind.

Consequently The Holy Church has the duty, and hence the right, to pursue this aim.

Irreligious and immoral books are written in a seductive manner, often with themes which deal with fleshly passion, or themes that deceive the pride of the soul. These books are carefully written to make an impression and aim at gaining ground in both the heart and mind of the incautious reader.

One must not claim that the condemnation of harmful books is a violation of freedom or a war against the Light of Truth, and that the index of forbidden books is a permanent attack against the progress of science and literature.[34]

The files of the Congregation of the Index have not yet been published, although the Church several years ago permitted a German Church historian access to her archives. The Church has chosen to open her secret archives to someone who is not only a historian but also a Catholic priest. Time will tell whether the planned indexing of all book censorship cases and the publication of a databank with all the relevant information will not itself be subject to censorship or even worse. Professor Richard Blackwell in his *Could there be another Galileo Case?* describes how the Pontifical Academy of Sciences had in 1942, the three-hundredth anniversary of Galileo's death, sponsored a new book about the great scientist. The Academy's president, Agostino Gemelli, who announced the project for which he had selected Monsignor Pio Paschini, in true 'scientific' form announced the results of the research before it had even begun. Gemelli said:

> The projected volume will be an effective proof that the Church did not persecute Galileo, but helped him considerably in his studies. It will not be an apologetic book, for that is not the task of scholars, but will be a historical and scholarly study of the documents.[35]

Paschini turned out not to be as safe as his Church masters had expected, and whilst Europe was burning in the fierce battles of the Second World War, the Church evidently considered that her reputation might be tarnished by publishing the truth about her persecution of Galileo. Thus, when Paschini completed his *Vita e Opere di Galileo Galilei* in 1944, the Vatican refused to grant permission to publish. Paschini objected to the censorship and refused to modify his manuscript, which was left untouched until after his death in 1962. Twenty years after Paschini's work was completed, and two years after his death, the Pontifical Academy of Sciences decided to take an adventurous step and publish. The Jesuit scholar Edmond Lamalle, in his introduction to what purported to be Paschini's book, explained that he had made a few very moderate changes in the text and in the footnotes. The truth, which only came out fifteen years later, was that Lamalle had made extensive changes. There were, in fact, hundreds of changes, additions and deletions, often producing a reversal of meaning. This academic fraud was a serious adulteration of the original text. It served to create a false picture of Galileo, the Church and the role of the Jesuits in the affair. Lamalle had finally produced what the Church had originally expected from Paschini. The Church has once again demonstrated how far she was willing to go to conceal the truth from seeing the light of day. In her intellectual dishonesty the step was made from simple censorship to outright forgery.

Truth and Freedom of Speech

Internal control from within the Church, especially when popes feel under siege from new ideas, can be uncomfortably strict, almost approaching the standards of a police state. In 1907, the Pope directed:

> We order that you do everything in your power to drive out of your dioceses, even by solemn interdict, any pernicious books that may be in circulation there. The Holy See neglects no means to remove writings of this kind, but their number has now grown to such an extent that it is hardly possible to subject them all to censure. ... Let no Bishop think that he fulfils his duty by denouncing to Us one or two books, while a great many others of the same kind are being published and circulated. ... in all cases it will be obligatory on Catholic booksellers not to put on sale books condemned by the Bishop.
>
> ... Bishops shall not permit congresses of priests except on very rare occasions. When they do permit them it shall only be on condition that matters appertaining to the Bishops or the Apostolic See be not treated in them, and that no resolutions or petitions be allowed that would imply a usurpation of sacred authority, and that absolutely nothing be said in them which savours of Modernism, Presbyterianism, or laicism. At congresses of this kind, which can only be held after permission in writing has been obtained in due time and for each case it shall not be lawful for priests of other dioceses to be present without the written permission of their Ordinary.
>
> ... We decree, therefore, that in every diocese ... a 'Council of Vigilance', be instituted without delay. The priests called to form part in it shall be chosen somewhat after the manner above prescribed for the censors, and they shall meet every two months on an appointed day in the presence of the Bishop. They shall be bound to secrecy as to their deliberations and decisions, and in their functions shall be included the following: they shall watch most carefully for every trace and sign of Modernism both in publications and in teaching, and to preserve the clergy and the young from it they shall take all prudent, prompt, and efficacious measures. Let

them combat novelties of words, ... Language of the kind here indicated is not to be tolerated either in books or in lectures ...We entrust to the Councils of Vigilance the duty of overlooking assiduously and diligently social institutions as well as writings on social questions so that they may harbour no trace of Modernism, but obey the prescriptions of the Roman Pontiffs.[36]

In her attitude to freedom of speech, the Church suffers from a remarkable split morality. She denies others the very freedom of speech she demands for herself. In 1996, the Catholic bishops of Mexico reacted energetically against the Mexican government's decision to prevent the Church by law from making public statements regarding 'political or economic issues, or any other linked to the country's situation'. One of the Mexican bishops explained: 'Those seeking to block the Catholic Church are truly interested in stopping the democratic progress of our country in order to keep our people in submission', adding 'we won't let anybody control our ability to fulfil our responsibility to the truth'.[37]

When, however, a Catholic priest or theologian develops ideas of which the Vatican does not approve, the Church mechanism comes down on him like a ton of bricks. The Vatican's attitude to dissent in recent times has surfaced in some well-publicised cases, such as those of Teilhard de Chardin, Yves Congar, Tissa Balasuriya and Hans Küng. Teilhard de Chardin (1881–1955), a French Jesuit, geologist and palaeontologist, developed a theory that man was evolving, mentally and socially, towards a final spiritual unity, maintaining that the acceptance of evolution did not entail the rejection of Christianity. His first book *The Phenomenon of Man* contained his expectations as to the course human evolution would take. His religious superiors were unconvinced and forbade him to publish any of his evolutionary ideas. In 1924, after he was appointed Professor of Geology at the Catholic Institute of Paris, he was forbidden to teach because his ideas about original sin and evolution were considered unorthodox by the Church. Teilhard then spent many years as a geologist and explorer, mainly in China. Back in France after the Second World War, he was informed by the Church that he was prohibited from writing about any philosophical subjects. Uncomfortable with his controversial ideas, the Church forbade Teilhard to put forth his candidacy as Professor at the College de France. In fact, the Catholic Church never gave him the permission to publish any of his books and they were only published after his death. As a Jesuit, Teilhard had made a vow of obedience to the Pope and, as chagrined as he was, he did not rebel and accepted the decision.

The Dominican theologian Cardinal Yves Congar (1904–1995), who was ruthlessly silenced by Rome, described his torture in a pre-Vatican II letter to the Holy Office:

> What has put me in the wrong (in their eyes) is not having said false things, but having said things that they do not like to have said. I have touched on problems without always aligning myself to the one point of view which [Rome] wants to impose on the comportment of the whole of the Christian world and which is: to think nothing, to say nothing, except what they propose.
>
> There is one pope who thinks everything, who says everything, and the whole quality of being Catholic consists in obeying him.
>
> ... Rome has never looked for and even now does not look for anything but the affirmation of its own authority ... the whole history of Rome is about insisting on its own authority and the destruction of everything that cannot be reduced to submission.
>
> ... They have not, of course, hurt my body; nor have they touched my soul or forced me to do anything. But a person is not limited to his skin and his soul ... he *is* his friendships, he *is* his relationships, he *is* his social outreach; they have taken all that away from me. ... I have been profoundly wounded. They have reduced me to nothing and so they have for all practical purposes destroyed me.[38]

The Church disapproved of Congar's ecumenism and of other proposals that he made. Restrictions were, therefore, imposed on him, beginning in 1946. He was no longer permitted to attend ecumenical meetings and public gatherings. A new edition of his book *Disunited Christians* (1937) was suspended and all of his writings were censured.

In 1954, Father Congar was informed by his superiors that he was no longer allowed to teach. His teaching post at *Le Saulchoir* theological centre was cancelled. Congar, who was interrogated by the Holy Office in Rome, confirms that he was only mentally, and not physically, tortured. Prevented from writing, teaching, meeting people he wanted to meet, the Church attempted to emasculate Congar of any intellectual influence. The move for change brought on by Pope John XXIII in convening the Second Vatican Council also brought Congar in from the cold. He was one of the more powerful advocates of the ecumenical movement and one of the great theologians of the Second Vatican Council.

In 1994, Pope John Paul II made him cardinal but Congar's pre-Vatican II words evidently continue to be pertinent in more recent times – in John Paul II's papacy. The same Pope who made Congar cardinal, excommunicated Tissa Balasuriya, a Sri-Lankan priest, member of the order of the *Oblates of Mary Immaculate*. Balasuriya was excommunicated in 1998, after the CDF concluded that his writings contained 'glaring errors', which it considered to be 'manifestly incompatible with the faith of the Church'. Balasuriya, who contends that his texts were misrepresented, distorted and falsified, describes his ordeal at the Congregation's hands:

My problem was with the CDF's methodology. ... nobody listens to you when you protest, nobody in authority is held accountable; the accused alone must explain themselves. ... I asked Cardinal Ratzinger to inquire into these grave misrepresentations and render justice to me ... I have had no response because everyone else involved in the process is presumed to be right. They also hide behind the mask of anonymity. ...

Right through this period the superior-general of the Oblates, Father Zago, kept telling me that I should conform and accept the decisions of the Church authorities. He advised me that submission was 'good for my spiritual development'.

... The whole thing seemed designed to force me into a corner, almost to give me a heart attack! In this situation I was faced with the question of personal stamina, because they trap you by a combination of forces, psychological, spiritual, theological, social, political and economic, the purpose of which is to bring you down. The old Inquisition brought the coercive power of Church and state to bear on an individual. Now they use a combination of other more subtle forces, as well as the media. In fact, it was through the BBC that I first heard about my own excommunication.

... They were imposing not only social and ecclesiastical ostracism, but also implicitly threatening eternal damnation.

... I had faced death threats from those who opposed our efforts for justice and human rights in Sri Lanka. Now it was a question of facing the threat of being cut off from the Christian community and all the services and activities of the Church to which I had given my life. ... I felt like I was being treated as a spiritual leper by people with whom I had lived my life.[39]

Balasuriya was the first theologian to be excommunicated in the post-Vatican II Church. This severe punitive action caused such a furore within the Catholic world that, a year later, a way was found to reconcile and repeal the excommunication. This, however, did not signal a new attitude to freedom of speech within the Catholic Church. The Church had for years been combating two Americans who concentrated their pastoral work in gay and lesbian Catholic communities; Sister Jeannine Gramick and Father Robert Nugent. More and more restrictions were put in their way to prevent them from carrying out their pastoral work with homosexuals who sought solace in the Catholic Church. Gramick and Nugent were put through Church enquiries and special commissions were set up to investigate their activities. In 1995 their 'case' was transferred to Rome, to the Vatican's Congregation for the Doctrine of the Faith. In 1999 they were both banned by the CDF from any pastoral work with homosexual persons. The following year, Gramick and Nugent were summoned to Rome and given further restrictions. The CDF and the Congregation for Institutes of Consecrated Life and Apostolic Life, in charge of religious orders to which both belonged, decided to shut them up totally. They were informed that they were not allowed to write or speak about their ordeal and anything in connection with the Church procedures that they underwent. The Church not only prevented them from conducting their pastoral work, she also wanted only her side of the story told. The prohibition included 'the 1999 Notification itself, the ecclesiastical processes that led to it, as well as the issue of homosexuality'.[40]

Hans Küng is a central figure in the ecumenical movement; he is personally engaged in dialogues with other world religions and continues to publish widely. Since 1979 Küng is no longer permitted to teach Catholic doctrine. The Church was not able to shut him up, but not for lack of trying. The noted and highly respected Küng, in his depiction of his trial by the CDF which took place between 1971 and 1975, describes the medieval procedures which the Vatican still maintains in the twentieth century:

> you cannot win by debating the substantial theological issues with the CDF. They are always right, and there is no other possibility. It is just like dealing with the Kremlin: what they ultimately want is for you to say exactly what they say.
>
> … I demanded to see my file … criticised the injustice of their processes, requested the right to know who my defence lawyer was, and asked for some type of appeal process. Occasionally you won a point with them, but they were always adamant that I would not be allowed to see my file, was not permitted to know who would defend me, and was given no right of appeal.[41]

The ruthlessness with which the Church acts reflects her power. The Church has historically employed the maximum power to implement her policies. In times and areas in which the Church had her own police, she physically seized books and imprisoned their authors. Elsewhere the popes operated through cooperative monarchs, whom they instructed to do their will. With her powers reduced, the Church can no longer physically harm those she disapproves of, although she does her utmost to discredit them and to prevent them from being heard. Unlike Galileo, Küng did not have to renounce his ideas to avoid imprisonment. The Catholic Church today can only call to task and discipline those who, of their own volition, choose to be members of the Church. There can be no doubt that the Church's attitude to freedom of speech and to the truth is as lacking now as it was in the darkest days of the Inquisition. The only difference is the enforcement ability at the Church's disposal.

Lies in the Battle Against Condoms

The Catholic Church does not permit the use of contraceptives. The arrival of the sexually transmittable Human Immuno-deficiency Virus

(HIV) which in most cases causes AIDS (Acquired Immune Deficiency Syndrome), has, in almost all countries, led to government efforts to educate the population in the use of condoms. Condoms are considered by doctors, scientists and by the World Health Organisation (WHO) an effective barrier which prevents the transmission of the virus during sexual intercourse. This is not the first time the Church has considered it preferable to allow the spread of a serious disease over the use of condoms and acted to stop information from reaching the population at risk. During the First World War, the Church blocked the distribution of US government-sponsored VD prevention films. Now, seventy years later, the Church has been unable to stop the condom education effort. The Church's teaching on contraception is clear – it is prohibited. The Church has very little freedom to act in this area because highly venerated Church fathers such as St Augustine or Thomas Aquinas have, for centuries, been quoted by popes and have been included in Church teaching with no doubt left as to the immorality of contraception. Never before did the Catholic Church have to come up against such sustained government propaganda and advocacy which openly discussed and widely disseminated teaching which was anathema to her.

This could have been an opportunity for the Church to come out with a message of love, care and responsibility. She could have explained that she continued to prohibit sex outside marriage and that contraceptives even within marriage were not permitted. She could have added that the preservation of life was the highest-ranking command and duty and, therefore, if the use of a condom was the only practical safe prevention from contracting AIDS, the Church not only permitted it but instructed that it be used. Instead, she embarked on a campaign of deceit and misinformation. Cunningly, the Church's effort was concentrated mainly in less developed countries; countries in which people respect the clergy and consider them to be a source of education and knowledge.

AIDS has already killed some twenty-five million people worldwide and the infection rate in third world countries continues to be very high. Although bishops' conferences in France, as early as 1989, and in Germany in 1993, suggested that information on condoms ought to be made available and should be considered even if the underlying behaviour was not condoned, the Vatican remained resolute in its opposition. The South African Catholic Bishops' Conference, in its meeting in July 2001, reiterated that 'The Bishops regard the widespread and indiscriminate promotion of condoms as an immoral and misguided weapon in our battle against HIV/AIDS ... condoms may even be one of the main reasons for the spread of HIV/AIDS'.[42] Bishop John Njue in Kenya spread false information, purporting to be scientific, claiming that condoms were responsible for the spread of AIDS. In 1997, Father Jacques Suaudeau wrote in the journal *Medicina e Morale*, 'using a condom to protect yourself against HIV amounts to playing Russian roulette'.[43] When, in 1996, health officials planned to distribute condoms at polling stations in AIDS-ridden Honduras, the Catholic Church in Tegucigalpa prevented the action. Their brothers-in-faith in Kenya, led by Cardinal Maurice Otunga, burned boxes of condoms and safe sex literature.[44] In other countries, such as Zambia, Brazil and the Philippines, Church officials actively and aggressively acted against any public condom education programme. In Kenya, the Catholic Church 'succeeded' in preventing the government from activating a comprehensive sexual education curriculum, which was developed to fight AIDS. Congo Kinshasa's Archbishop Dominique Bulamatari explained in 2003 that 'using condoms as a means of preventing AIDS can only lead to sexual promiscuity'.[45]

As outrageous as the Catholic Church stand on condoms is, the matter becomes criminal when the Church disseminates falsehoods which directly bring about the death of those who listen to her. In an interview, given on Vatican Radio in November 2003 by the president of the Pontifical Council for the Family, Cardinal Alfonso López Trujillo, said:

> One cannot really speak of 'safe sex', leading people to believe that the use of condoms is the formula to avoid the risk of HIV ... there is a percentage of grave risk, not only of AIDS, but also of the different sexually transmitted diseases, and ... the rate of failure is quite high.

> There are many published studies that give rise to well-founded doubts regarding the 'safety' of condom use.

> ... I simply wish to remind the public, seconding the opinion of a good number of experts, that when the condom is employed as a contraceptive, it is not totally dependable, and that the cases of pregnancy is not rare.

> In the case of the AIDS virus, which is around 450 times smaller than the sperm cell, the condom's latex material obviously gives much less security. Some studies reveal permeability of condoms in 15% or even up to 20%.

> Thus to talk of condom as 'safe sex' is a form of Russian roulette! And this is even without considering other possible reasons for condom failure, such as degradation of latex due to exposure to sunlight and heat, rupture and breakdown.

> ... I propose that the Ministries of Health require the inclusion in condom packages and advertisements, and in the apparatus or shelves where they are displayed, a warning, that the condom is not safe. This has been done since some time ago with cigarettes, saying that the filter does not guarantee protection.[46]

In an interesting development, the Church seems to have decided that it was not enough to repeat the Scripture- and Tradition-related prohibitions on contraception and that she should attempt and dissuade people from using condoms by proffering clinical and scientific arguments, albeit false arguments and flawed science. Unfortunately, due to the immense power of the Vatican, lies about the inefficacy of condoms are repeated by both senior hierarchy and lower clergy, especially in the less-developed countries, the very countries which bear the main burden of AIDS. A BBC Panorama programme about this issue, aired in October 2003, showed a Catholic nun advising her HIV-infected choir master not to use condoms with his wife because 'the virus can pass through'. In the same programme, the director of an AIDS testing station near Lake Victoria reported that 'some priests have even been saying that condoms are laced with HIV/AIDS'. Catholic bishops in Kenya produced a pamphlet which claims 'Latex rubber from which condoms are made does have pores through which viral sized particles can squeeze through during intercourse'.[47] The WHO has condemned the Vatican's 'incorrect statements about condoms and HIV [which] are dangerous when we are facing a pandemic which has already killed more than 20 million people, and currently affects at least 42 million'. Moreover, scientific research by the US National Institute of Health (NIH) and the WHO have found that 'intact condoms … are essentially impermeable to particles the size of STD pathogens including the smallest sexually transmitted virus … condoms provide a highly effective barrier to transmission of particles of similar size to those of the smallest STD viruses'.[48]

Instead of a health warning on condom packs, should not a health warning be displayed in this context over the Catholic Church and all her establishments? Can and do the falsehoods propagated by her hierarchy not kill?

The burning of condoms and of sex education literature at the end of the twentieth century must be seen in the light of an old Church tradition of preventing free speech and the use of violent means to enforce her dogma.

Do the popes and the cardinals lie intentionally or do they believe what they proclaim to be the truth? This is a much wider issue which an agnostic or an atheist will occasionally ask himself with regard to the more general questions of faith. When the Church categorically states that Jesus was born to a virgin and that three days after his death he came back to life before then going to heaven (i.e. dying again) such scientifically baseless and improbable statements do not cause direct harm. Therefore, the question of whether the Church hierarchy really believes in the virgin birth and in the resurrection may be an important ethical issue, but it does not kill. This, however, is not the case with Church declarations such as those stating that condoms are laced with

HIV or are so porous that the virus can get through. This kills. The willingness of the Catholic Church to lie in order to maintain her control in a way which directly harms others is where her actions are not only immoral, but should also be prohibited by society. The root lies in the coming together of the undying certainty of the Church in her dogma with her hold on power.

Is Cardinal Trujillo, who made the false claims about the inefficacy of condoms, a liar? Is he simply an ignoramus? Neither should be acceptable for a senior leader of a religious organisation. However, the statements the Cardinal made were similar to those made by senior members of the Catholic hierarchy in various countries all over the world. This was not some stupid utterance by an unimportant clergyman, it was part of a concerted effort of the Church to spread a lie. This lie is as pernicious as the AIDS virus. Both kill.

There has, however, been noteworthy internal opposition to the Church's merciless stubbornness. Indeed, some members of the clergy actively promote condoms to populations at risk, such as prostitutes, thereby risking disciplinary action by their superiors. Others, such as Jesuits working in AIDS-stricken Africa, openly advocate dropping the ban on condoms. Bishops' conferences in various European countries have for years been grappling with the issue of condom use in face of the AIDS pandemic. In January 2005, Bishop Juan Antonio Martinez Camino, spokesman for the Spanish Bishops' Conference, stated that 'condoms have a place in the global prevention of AIDS'. The statement caused such an uproar that the next day, the Bishops' Conference issued a backtracking clarification. Under pressure from the Vatican, they made the following statement: 'use of condoms implies immoral sexual conduct', adding that 'in accordance with these principles, it is not possible to recommend the use of condoms'.[49] In fact, the Bishops explained that sexual abstinence and monogamy are the only successful ways to prevent HIV transmission.[50] Thereby, the Spanish Bishops' Conference slipped back into the old position of a disseminator of falsehoods. This was not the last to be heard in the Church condom debacle. Several days after the Spanish reversal, Swiss Cardinal Georges Cottier, the theologian to the pontifical household, suggested in an interview which was reported in the Italian newspaper *Corriere della Sera*, that in certain cases the use of condoms 'could be considered legitimate'. Cottier stressed that he was not speaking for the Pope when he explained that, in his opinion, condom use was legitimate as a means to avoid transferring the HIV virus during sexual intercourse. 'The virus is transmitted during a sexual act; so at the same time as [bringing] life there is also a risk of transmitting death, and that is where the commandment "thou shalt not kill" is valid.'[51] The increased openness of senior clergymen stating that condoms could be used to prevent AIDS reflected, in all likelihood, the weakened health of Pope John Paul II, who was less able to exert his control over the Church.

Conclusion

In his incomplete exculpation of Galileo, Pope John Paul II explained why it was important to return to the Galileo case: 'the underlying problems of this case concern both the nature of science and the message of faith. It is therefore not to be excluded that one day we shall find ourselves in a similar situation, one which will require both sides to have an informed awareness of the field and of the limits of their competencies'. He added, 'it is a question of knowing how to judge a new scientific datum when it seems to contradict the truths of faith'. The Pope was right, the Church continues to be unable to deal with cases in which science contradicts faith. This inability stems from her definition of the Scriptures as truth. To the Church, the Bible is not a compilation of texts, written by different people at different times, reflecting the needs and interests of the day. It is revealed truth, that is, it is God-inspired and the Church is bound by it and by her own Tradition and interpretative doctrines. The consequence is an almost total inflexibility and resistance to change. To achieve her mission, without losing power, the Church succumbs to rather flexible means such as lies about condoms, or cover-ups of clerical abuse. The confident arrogance of the Church which forced Galileo to withdraw his scientific findings, because they did not suit her, is repeated three hundred and seventy years later when she produces alleged scientific facts about the inefficiency of condoms, simply because the truth does not suit her. The same Church which considered it appropriate to imprison a scientist for promoting a thesis which contradicted her teaching now considers it appropriate to spread a serious lie in support of one of her doctrines. Professor Blackwell, who believes that a recurrence of a Galileo case was rather unlikely, concludes, however, that 'should a new and sufficiently great threat to religion arise from science, the conditions for the recurrence may come into play'.[52]

The Catholic Church – as do other churches and religions – may choose to continue to believe that Scriptures should order our lives. Society must decide whether to allow the Church to use the significant power she still has, both directly over the faithful and indirectly via political structures, to cause death and suffering. Every day people die from AIDS because they refrained from using condoms. Some of them as a result of the Church's teaching. The Catholic Church is responsible and must be taken to task for their deaths.

The nineteenth-century Cardinal, John Henry Newman, one-time rector of the Catholic University in Dublin, once observed that 'piety and power make life difficult for truth'. The Church continues to prove him right. The pernicious fusion of deep faith, unquestioning subordination to revealed truth, haughtiness and power are at the root of this systemic problem – an inherent defect of the Catholic Church. The problem will not disappear – even if a new pope were to find a way to permit the use of condoms – just as the scrapping of the Index of Prohibited Books has not stopped the Church's attempts to prevent knowledge and information she disagrees with from reaching the people. Eventually, the defect will rear its head again in another, yet unknown, situation and again cause untold suffering. It is unlikely that any pope will be willing or able to break the mould. It is unlikely that the Church would allow him to.

Chapter Three
Corruption

The Catholic Church claims to be an instrument established by Jesus who died to bring salvation to mankind. She has been created and empowered to act as gatekeeper to heaven, and entrusted with the task of showing the way of Christ and, thereby, the way to heaven, leading mankind away from temptation and preventing evil. To fulfil what she considers to be her mission, the Church has, throughout history, striven for power. In this context, the Church has also demanded and continues to demand respect both for the institution and for those in office. Those in authority, who maintain that they are the direct followers and representatives of Jesus and of his apostles and yet lack the personal humility described in the gospels, expect to be addressed as Your Holiness, Excellency, Eminence, Your Grace and demand to be shown other forms of obedience, by both the faithful and by many others in society. This whole structure is based on the idea that the Church epitomises the good, that she is good.

The contemporary reader's first thought in connection with corruption within the Catholic Church is likely to be of the sexual scandals of recent years. Sexual misbehaviour by the clergy is not new and has been reported from early on. Keeping quiet about it, covering the offenders and helping them avoid justice and thereby also enabling them to carry on transgressing, adds an institutional culpability to the personal guilt. This subject is dealt with in greater detail in chapter 10.

Personal Corruption

When one speaks of corruption within the Catholic Church, there are two aspects to consider: institutional corruption and the personal corruption of popes and of other members of the Catholic hierarchy. The Church has been around for almost two thousand years and the norms of governing and of public conduct have undergone many changes during this time. Throughout her history, the Church – instead of being at the forefront of moral behaviour, a source of ethical illumination and an example for the rest of society to emulate – has been as corrupt as other centres of power. This is problematic for an organisation whose *raison d'être* is to lead morally and spiritually. Personal corruption itself is to be considered at two levels: the objective level at which murder, torture, rape and sexual abuse are wicked, immoral and illegal; and the subjective level at which a priest, who himself violates rules and principles regarding sex, preaches about the sins of masturbation, extra-marital sex, greed or lust, threatens his flock with the punishing fires of hell.

Simony and nepotism are central to the history of corruption in the Catholic Church. The term 'simony' stems from the New Testament story that recalls the magician, Simon Magus, approaching Peter and Paul and offering them money to buy the power of the Holy Spirit. Peter's response was 'Thy money perish with thee, because thou hast thought that the gift of God may be purchased with money.'[1] It appears that quite a few ecclesiastics had either not read their Bible or did not take its teaching seriously. It also appears that they were right not to take the story seriously. From time to time, a pope would speak out against simony, but it never took long until either he himself or his successor continued in the lucrative trade in Church offices. It was widespread in the Catholic Church for a long time. Everything was sold – including all levels of Church appointments, from benefices, which gave the holder property and income, up to the papacy itself.

Nepotism is the practice of showing favouritism or the granting of patronage to family members by people in power. The term[i] developed from the papal practice – prevalent until the start of the twentieth century – where popes placed their 'nephews', in some cases a euphemism for their illegitimate sons, in positions of power within the Church. For years, the Borgia Apartments at the Vatican were reserved lodgings for the 'cardinal nephew'. The last Pope who installed his nephews in positions of power was Pius XII (1939 –1958). His two nephews, who served as directors in the Vatican Bank, were asked to resign by his successor, Pope John XXIII.

The other divine grace which was available for money was pardon for sins. The sale of indulgences straddles both the personal and institutional areas of corruption. Catholic dogma maintains that sins are punishable on two levels: the spiritual and the temporal. Unlike Baptism, which remits both the guilt of sin and the penalties attached to sin, penance only removes the guilt of sin. This, in itself, is vital as eternal punishment (in hell), due for mortal sin, is thereby remitted. However, temporal punishment is still required and must be discharged either during one's lifetime or after one's death, in purgatory. The Church maintains that she has the power to relieve this indebtedness of the penitent through the granting of indulgences. The Catholic Church – having frightened her flock about the terrible suffering in purgatory – offered her members a way to alleviate their temporal punishment. Certain acts – such as

---

[i] *Nepos* means grandson as well as nephew in Latin.

participation in a crusade – could earn indulgences which in turn could be exchanged for time in purgatory. They were used as instruments to further causes which were important to the Church and, in addition to crusades, indulgences would be earned for the visiting of the tombs of the apostles and for pilgrimages to shrines (such as Compostela in Spain). Sometimes a whole community would be granted an indulgence at the dedication of a new church. Indulgences can be universal or local, they may be plenary and thereby remit the entire temporal punishment due to sin, or partial, defining the number of days or years of purgatorial punishment they cancel. The Church specified who was authorised to grant indulgences, on what occasions and for what periods. The risk with partial indulgences is that no one knows what penalties are due and how helpful a partial relief would turn out to be.

It was not long before commercial considerations within the Church took a hold and enabled indulgences to be bought simply for money. This led to widespread trafficking in the now sought-after indulgences. Abuse was rampant. It was indeed a licence to print money, employed by various Catholic organisations, religious orders and priests who took advantage of faithful followers to whom they promised anything from a clean slate and perpetual happiness to immediate release of their loved ones from purgatory. Moreover, the bookkeeping was so well developed in those pre-computer days that indulgences could not only release souls presently suffering in purgatory but they could also be saved up for possible future use. A kind of 'pay now – sin later' scheme. The most cynical trade in indulgences was developed during the papacy of Leo X (1513–1521). Leo X did not invent the sale of indulgences. He did, however, take it to an extreme which in turn triggered Luther's ninety-five theses, the firing shot which precipitated the great schism in Christianity and the establishment of the Protestant Church.

During the thousand years in which the Church was not only a spiritual organisation but also included the temporal structure of the Papal States, popes regularly considered that any means were justified to further the interests of their secular realm. In this, popes were no different to and, unfortunately, no better than other monarchs. They initiated wars, blackmailed, had people tortured and killed, financially squeezed their populace and stole the Church's wealth to enrich their own families. Although modern popes are not known to have enriched their own families, the willingness to act corruptly has not changed as a result of the loss of the Papal States in 1870. The Church has assiduously maintained total opaqueness in its financial dealings. From time to time, the scandals could not be kept secret and information oozed out.

Most popes, of course, never stood trial for their crimes. Some, however, did. One pope, whose true crime was that he belonged to a different faction than that of the pope who had him tried, was judged posthumously. The mummified cadaver of Pope Formosus (891–896) was exhumed by Pope Stephen VI (896–897) and tried by a special synod, *Synod horrenda*. Dressed in papal robes, the corpse was even assigned a defence attorney at the trial which was led by Pope Stephen. Formosus, who was found guilty of perjury, had the three fingers of benediction hacked off and his corpse was thrown into the Tiber. Later, justice for Pope Stephen was less theatrical, he was simply seized by the Roman crowds and strangled in prison.

Another pope who was tried was John XII (955–964). John was made pope at the ripe age of eighteen, as a result of a deal made between his father, Alberic, the secular ruler of Rome, and the Roman nobility. The twenty-seven-year-old Pope died of an apparent stroke whilst in bed with a married woman. Some have it that his death was brought about following an attack by the woman's husband. Before he died, Pope John managed to be deposed by a synod, convened at the behest of the Holy Roman Emperor, Otto of Saxony, a man he had crowned Emperor only two years before. The synod heard witnesses who confirmed various instances of adultery, murder by castration and the receiving of money for the ordination of bishops, as well as the ordination of a deacon in a stable. It was decided that the Pope should be deposed. John, who had left Rome whilst the Emperor was there, returned after Otto's departure and punished some of those who had spoken out against him; several had their hands amputated and one had his tongue cut off. John's successor, who was elected after he was deposed, fled Rome and assumed office only after his death.

Nepotism was rife in the Church. As well as the practice of appointing 'nephews' to important curial positions, in some instances, popes even delegated authority to their mistresses and children. Other appointments were just as morally questionable. Julius III (1550–1555) picked up a boy on the street in Parma and made him papal monkey-keeper. The Pope's attachment to the boy, Innocenzo, was no secret and he later had him adopted by his brother before making the teenager a cardinal.

The Papal attitude to the Church as a personal fiefdom, for popes to enjoy and enrich their families, resulted in the systematic appointment of family members as cardinals and the placing of their sons, daughters and nephews, through marriage pacts, into virtually all of the ruling houses of Europe. Intertwined in this embroidery of secular and non-secular positions was the regular milking of Church revenues into the private pockets of the Church hierarchy, which produced great wealth for the families in charge.

Boniface VIII (1294–1303) was so worried by the power of his predecessor, Celestine V, who had abdicated after only fifteen weeks as pope, that he had the eighty-five-year-old recluse, who was made pope because of a two-year deadlock in the conclave, locked up until he died. Having secured his seat, Boniface applied himself and his papacy to enrich his family. With funds acquired by selling Church offices, a substantial part of other Church income, Boniface acquired lands which were then handed over to his nephews and other family members as vassals. Throughout his tenure Boniface, who was of the Gaetani family, led bloody battles with a rival family, the Colonnas. In these wars, he employed the Church apparatus to totally rout the Colonnas: members of the rival family were excommunicated to the fourth generation. Anyone stealing from the Colonnas was absolved of sin and papal troops were dispatched to destroy towns which were connected to the Colonna family. Peasants and their families, who lived in lands owned by the Colonnas, were killed or sold as slaves.[2]

Pope Clement VI (1342–1352), kept various mistresses. His main mistress, the Countess of Turenne, wielded so much power in the papal court due to her position in the pope's bedroom, that she was able to become rich from bribes she collected and to improve, quite considerably, her own family's wealth.

Pope Callistus III (1455–1458) made two of his nephews cardinals and a third nephew was appointed commander in chief of the papal armies. His successor, Pius II (1458–1464), who, as Aeneas Silvio Piccolomini, was a well-known Humanist, historian and author of erotic plays, also made two of his nephews cardinals. Several years later, Sixtus IV (1471–1484) appointed no fewer than six nephews as cardinals.

Pope Innocent VIII (1484–1492) had so many illegitimate children that he didn't even bother calling them his 'nephews' and, instead, referred to them as his 'children'. One of his sons, Franceschetto, was especially well looked after: Innocent actually arranged his wedding to take place at the Vatican itself. The Pope's son also got a cut from the Vatican's revenues from the sale of offices and pardons. The first one hundred and fifty ducats from all fines levied by the Church went to Franceschetto and only then did the cardinals get their cut. A cardinal, who had made the mistake of winning fourteen thousand ducats at a Rome card game with the Pope's son, was instructed the following day by the Pope to repay his son.

Popes funded themselves by charging whoever they could for whatever they could. Uniquely, there was one who sold his own position as a pope to his godfather. Benedict IX was Pope for a long stretch from 1032 to 1044 (when he was deposed) but continued as Pope intermittently thereafter until he abdicated in 1048. Rather like John XII, Benedict, who was made pope in his twenties, was violent and debauched. He squandered Church funds in brothels and on banquets, and had acquired his office through his father's bribery. After he was deposed, he managed to regain power by using the private armies of his family. Finally, Benedict agreed to give up the papacy in return for a bribe paid to him by his godfather who, thereby, became Pope Gregory VI (1045–1046) – using the money to fund his marriage, Benedict became a husband.

Monasteries paid the popes for letters of papal protection against their local bishops! The number of such letters had risen from two hundred and seventy in the eleventh century to two thousand in the twelfth century. Archbishops paid popes for their pallium and cardinals for their nominations. Taxes (Peter's Pence) were levied on churches and kings paid feudal dues or special payments; Henry III paid Pope Alexander IV (1254–1261) to have his son made king of Sicily, at the time a papal fief.

The sale of benefices became an important source of income for popes and cardinals. It thus was not only a control, centralisation and power issue, but also a money interest for the popes to dominate as many appointments and benefices as possible. Towards the end of the thirteenth century, all newly appointed bishops and abbots had to pay a third of their first year's income to Rome – half of it to the pope and the other half to the cardinals.

Simony at the conclave was rampant during the Renaissance. Cardinals who had enough money and spent it wisely bought the votes they needed. Often, cardinals had amassed sufficient benefices and other sources of income, which were offered quite openly, to clinch a deal. For hundreds of years, cardinals were entitled to half the revenue (Peter's Pence, taxes, gifts) of the Holy See. Additionally, cardinals were regularly bribed and paid by monarchs who wanted to buy influence at the curia. In fact, for the 1492 conclave, both the king of France and the Republic of Genoa deposited substantial funds as a war chest to bribe participating cardinals and have their favourite candidates elected pope. It was expected that a newly elected pope should offer valuable gifts to the cardinals who had just elected him. It was therefore not unusual to actually find bags full of gold kept in cardinals' homes.

The conclave of 1492 elected a pope whose gifts to the cardinals were of a different sort. Alexander VI (1492–1503) was a danger to his own cardinals as he had a somewhat unusual habit for a pope: he had quite a few cardinals poisoned so that he could lay his hands on their property. Cardinal Rodrigo Borgia bought his papacy with hard cash. A deal he made with his main rival, Cardinal Sforza, gave Sforza not only the lucrative Vice-Chancellorship of the Catholic Church, but also four mule loads of gold bullion. Simony had always been considered a sin and this Pope, like so many of his predecessors and successors, thought nothing of preaching against simony whilst actively engaging in it. Alexander, who was made cardinal at the age of twenty-three by his uncle, Pope Calixtus III, had at least nine children, by three or more women. At the age of fifty-six, while still only a cardinal, he took a new mistress, sixteen-year-old Giulia Farnese, who was married to the son of his cousin, Madonna Adriana. Three years later, as soon as he became pope, Borgia made Alessandro Farnese, his mistress's brother, a cardinal. In time, Farnese would become Pope Paul III. Borgia made Cesare, his eighteen-year-old son, cardinal immediately after his elevation to the papacy. Other children were married off to ruling houses in Spain and in Italy. The Pope alienated substantial Church land and arranged to dispossess various landowners to endow his children with lucrative property and establish for them independent duchies. The wedding of Lucrezia Borgia, the Pope's daughter by his long-time mistress Vannozza de' Catanei, was celebrated with great pomp, a lavish banquet and dancing in the Sala Reale of the Vatican. The rule, that no women were allowed at papal banquets, was, of course, disregarded.

It went from bad to worse once Pope Alexander started lending his status and the power of the Church to the ambitions of his son, Cesare Borgia. In those years, the corruption of the Church reached depths of unthinkable depravity. At one feast, attended by both Lucrezia and Cesare, a competition was held at which fifty Roman prostitutes copulated with fifty servants. Prizes were presented by the Pope. Another family entertainment was for Cesare to shoot criminals who were released into the Vatican grounds. The family stood at the Vatican windows and Cesare aimed at and killed the men as they tried to run for their lives. Cesare Borgia had a free run as long as his father was Pope. After Alexander's death and with the election of Julius II, alliances and loyalties soon changed and Cesare had to flee the country.

An indication of the extent of the thievery, dishonesty and financial chaos in the Vatican can be grasped from the fact that when Pope Julius II (1503–1513) died – an unusually honest Pope for his time – he not only issued a deathbed bull making any simonical election invalid, but also had the treasure of the Vatican transferred to the castellan of Sant' Angelo with instructions that the treasure only be handed over to his successor, so little trust did he have in cardinals not plundering the Church's assets. Even this 'honest' Pope came into the papacy as a father of three illegitimate daughters whom he fathered whilst he was 'only' a cardinal.

After Julius' death, the cardinals, having suffered ten years under a strict Pope who forbade simony and enforced strict rules on them, voted for a Pope who 'understood' that the Church was a benefit, its purpose being to enrich and please popes and cardinals. The cardinal elected, Giovanni Medici, was thirty-seven when he became Pope Leo X (1513–1521). The other cardinals were aware of Giovanni's poor state of health and would otherwise not have elected so young a Pope. Giovanni, Lorenzo the Magnificent's son, had already been made abbot of Font Douce in France at the age of eight; by the age of eleven he had two more abbeys and when he was fourteen he was made cardinal. Leo X, in good papal tradition, set out to enrich his own family. The Pope's younger brother, Giuliano, was set up to marry a French princess and be invested with the title of a French duke. A bastard cousin, Giulio, was made cardinal, to which end documents were forged to wed his parents retroactively. (Canon law would have otherwise prevented the nomination.)[3] Leo was a heavy spender, not only on the dynastic wars in his endeavours to establish his own family, but also on his own lifestyle. Half of the income of the papal states was spent on papal banquets. To fund it all, Leo dramatically increased the number of curial positions which were for sale. He also founded a new order, the Order of St Peter, and collected payments from those who wanted to be knighted. Another funding source was the creation of thirty-one cardinals in one go – all of whom had to pay substantial amounts to the Pope for the benefit of their newly elevated positions. This Pope, whose greed seemed to know no end, also established a lucrative business in the sale of indulgences. A special joint venture was set up between the Pope and Albert, Prince of Hohenzollern. Albert's bankers pressed for the repayment of a loan originally made to the Prince to fund the payment he had made to the curia in Rome for being made Archbishop of Magdeburg. Under this joint venture, an eight-year indulgence was established purporting to collect money for the basilica of St Peter and for a new holy war against the Turks. The spoils were divided fifty-fifty and a German Dominican monk, Johann Tetzel, was placed in charge of this operation. Tetzel worked the indulgence market on a grand scale. He worked his way around Germany, moving from town to town with great fanfare selling chits of paper which granted their bearers indulgences. The bigger the amount paid, the more purgatory days' relief were granted. Wherever Tetzel went, the representatives of Prince Albert's bankers collected fifty per cent of the monies given. The bankers trusted neither the Church and her representatives, nor Prince Albert, and collected what was due to them at source.

It is truly astounding how, in the very years Lutheran disgust with Church corruption was bringing about the schism in Christianity, popes continued with acts of nepotism and theft. Paul III (1534–1549), the brother of a previous Pope's (Alexander VI) mistress, appointed two teenage grandsons (he had four children by his mistress) and various nephews as cardinals. Paul also transferred substantial tracts of Church land to his sons. Even Paul IV (1555–1559), who was extremely scrupulous, appointed his nephews to positions of power, which they promptly misused for their own benefit. Growing criticism of the private conduct of the Church hierarchy did not prevent the election of Pius IV (1559–1565), who had three illegitimate children.

Urban VIII (1623–1644) is best known for his patronage of the great Baroque sculptor Bernini and for his prosecution of Galileo Galilei. Urban, who had inherited debts from his predecessor, spent sizable amounts on grand artistic *oeuvres*, and even more on enriching his own family. His nepotism burdened the Church with even more debt, to such an extent that there was hardly any money left for the running of the organisation itself. Considerable sums were spent on running land-grabbing wars on behalf of his nephews. The wars were lost and, under the Urban papacy, the Church lost both money and stature.

Pius VI (1775–1799), the patron of many artists who embellished Rome during his pontificate, presided over the Church in the heady years of the guillotine, the nationalisation of Church assets, the massacre of clergy, and the de-Christianisation of France. Pius also looked after his nephews at the expense of the Church.

The trappings of power are hard to resist. Throughout the Church's history, popes have taken great pleasure from the joys of good living. Even today, the Pope inhabits a sumptuous palace at the Vatican and an even bigger summer residence at Castelgandolfo. Most cardinals reside in extravagant and costly mansions. In 2004, in an unusual and desperate step, the Cardinal of Boston had to sell his mansion and other Church property to raise funds needed to pay compensation to victims of sexual abuse by Boston clergy. The behaviour of some of these clerics was arrogant and personally corrupt. Not surprisingly, such corruption trickled down the hierarchy. This was a Church of sumptuous feasts, in which foods and wines were partaken by the pope and his cardinals, eaten from gold plates by prelates bedecked in jewels wearing the most expensive silk and damask. A corrupt Church which milked Europe for gold to pay for the earthly joys of her top clergy. Emulating and often surpassing the excesses of secular monarchs is not what one would expect of a spiritual and moral leadership and definitely not of those claiming to be the followers of Jesus, who lived modestly and preached poverty.

The examples given of papal corruption suggest a pattern, rather than a one-off accident. They are sometimes so appalling that they read like present-day tabloid press scandals and yet the Church is unable to distance herself from previous popes, however low their behaviour sank. The Catechism of the Catholic Church states that 'the Roman Pontiff, Peter's successor, and the bishops, the successors of the apostles, are related with and united to one another'. It also states 'The Pope, Bishop of Rome and Peter's successor, is the perpetual and visible source and foundation of the unity both of the bishops and of the whole company of the faithful.' And to be clear: 'The Pope enjoys, by divine institution, supreme, full, immediate, and universal power in the care of souls.'[4] All those corrupt popes were, according to the Catechism, St Peter's successors, had universal power in the care of souls, granted to them by God, and they are related to each other. The Church bases her claim on this continuity and closes her eyes to the significance of such continuity. Knowing the history of the Church, how can one automatically consider the pope 'Vicar of Christ and Pastor of the universal Church on earth' whose teaching are to be adhered to it with 'religious assent'?

Is the Church's history of corrupt popes and cardinals, hundreds of years ago, relevant to today's Church? It would perhaps only be of anecdotal importance, had the Church mended her ways. If the Church had publicly disassociated herself from the corrupt popes and corrupt Church structures and had she established transparent institutions and procedures, she would perhaps not have slipped into further shady and fraudulent dealings.

Institutional Corruption

The *Amministrazione del Patrimonio della Sede Apostolica* (Administration of the Patrimony of the Apostolic See, APSA) is the body set up by the Holy See in 1870 to manage its assets after the loss of the Papal States. In 1929, when the *Lateran Pacts* were signed, Italy paid the Holy See 750 million Lire in cash and 1 billion Lire in state bonds as payment for the papal states it lost.[ii] These funds were invested by the APSA and produce an important part of the Holy See's income. The first man to run the organisation was Bernardino Nogara, who accepted the job on condition that he would be free to invest wherever he wanted, without any geographical, ethical or doctrinal restrictions. And without restriction he did indeed run it! The man who was reluctant to take the job when it was first offered to him, remained in it for twenty-five years and continued to influence the Vatican's business and financial enterprise until his death in 1958. Nogara speculated in gold, currencies and shares, acquired control in industrial companies, property companies, insurance and finance companies. New York's Cardinal Spellman's epitaph to Nogara was 'Next to Jesus Christ the greatest thing that has happened to the Catholic Church is Bernardino Nogara.'[5] Is this what the Church was meant to be: an organisation in which the next best thing to Jesus Christ is the man who ran its finances?

Where does the Vatican get its funds from? Much of it comes from Roman Catholics all over the world who voluntarily send money to the Vatican. This is done in several ways. The best known is Peter's Pence. Established in 1860, Peter's Pence became especially important when the Holy See lost temporal power in 1871. In some countries, pictures portraying the Pope lying on a bed of straw in a dark dungeon were used to squeeze the emotions of simple believers into making donations. Although such images are no longer used, the collection continues. Catholic churches throughout the world send monies collected on one day

---

ii   This would roughly be worth US $ 2 billion in 2006 values.

a year (very often, it is 29 June, St Peter's day) to Rome. Typically, these are small amounts collected mainly in predominantly Catholic areas which, more often than not, means from the poor. The money is collected for the person of the Pope and sent to him. Heads of dioceses able to send substantial amounts to Rome can naturally create personal power bases for themselves. Cardinal John Patrick Cody, head of the archdiocese of Chicago, was for many years a thorn in the side of the Vatican. He was considered to be a racist, years of financial mismanagement by him culminated in a US Inland Revenue investigation into illegal diversion by Cody of US $1 million of Church funds to his life-long friend Helen Wilson and his own priests passed a motion publicly condemning him. Pope John Paul I (1978) was about to remove Cody when he died (or was murdered, as some believe). The next pope, Pope John Paul II (1978–2005) decided to leave Cody in place. Cody made an appropriate welcome gift to the new Pope. On his arrival in Chicago for a visit in October 1979, he was met by the cardinal at the airport, who placed a small box with $50,000 into the Pope's hands.[6] Thus the Pope becomes beholden to his funding sources.

The Vatican does not publish how much it collects through Peter's Pence, but it is said to run into tens of millions of US dollars a year. A pope such as John Paul II, who is constantly on the move, incurs substantial costs, but also produces a high income. The monies collected are managed directly by the State Secretariat of the Vatican in close coordination with the pope and not by any of the financial or economic bodies of the Holy See. In addition to Peter's Pence, some of the richer dioceses are asked to support Vatican activities out of their own surplus funds. Local religious orders are also a funding source. These are traditionally expected to pay the expenditure of Vatican diplomats accredited to their countries.[7] Another source of funding is special collections, such as the Mother Teresa Appeal which collected money in Calcutta and elsewhere. The more emotive these special collections are, the more money they bring in. How the monies are spent, who by and under whose control are unanswered questions.

An important source of funding for Vatican activities are its own investments and banking activities. During the Second World War, Pope Pius XII established a financial instrument with a somewhat misleading name. The Istituto per le Opere de Religione (the Institute for Religious Works, IOR) was set up in 1942, as a separate entity from the APSA. Why the Pope chose to establish his bank in the middle of the war is unclear. Ever since 1945 rumours have spread that the IOR had been instrumental in laundering Nazi financial transactions and that it was a safe-haven for money and gold which were looted by the Nazis and by some of their collaborators. The Vatican has been steadfast in its denials of these rumours. It has also been steadfast in denying access to its records. This would suggest that the Vatican Bank has something to hide and that some of its dealings might embarrass the Church. A 1948 US Treasury Department report said that the Vatican held on to Ustasha[iii] funds. Some reports suggested that these monies have since been transferred by the IOR to Nazis who had fled to Argentina.[8] According to the writers Aarons and Loftus 'the bulk of stolen Nazi money was laundered from Switzerland through the one bank that can never be audited. The trail of Nazi money leads to one financial institution with total diplomatic immunity: the Vatican Bank'.[9]

The IOR operates as a bank, although the APSA, rather than the IOR, is recognised by the World Bank, the Bank for International Settlements (BIS) and the International Monetary Fund (IMF) as a central bank. Neither of these institutions are formally defined as banks, but both act as banks and are considered by other banking institutions as banks. As they are under Vatican sovereignty, they are not subject to any banking legislation or supervision outside the Vatican. Like other off-shore banking centres, they benefit from the attractions of secrecy, no questions asked, no control – with the added bonus of the assumed reputation of the Church.

Even if the Church is not poor, should she not at least be ethical in her investments? Should she not put her money where her mouth is? Apparently not. A good example is the Vatican's investment in Serono. Whilst opposing the use of contraceptives, the Vatican owned shares in Istituto Farmacologico Serono, which produced the oral contraceptive *Luteolas*.[10] Surely they could not have been that devious, forbidding Catholics to use contraceptives but quite happy for non-Catholics to refrain from multiplying? Information about the Vatican's investment policy is not regularly made public. From time to time, mainly when things go wrong or for political convenience, information is forthcoming. Such was the case in the 1960s in Italy when a shift to the political left brought about pressures to do away with some of the tax exemptions enjoyed by the Vatican. Specifically, the exemption from paying tax on dividends that the Vatican received on shares that it held in Italian companies was targeted. In that period the Italian press would publish information about discoveries regarding the unethical investments of the Holy See. Amongst others, the Vatican, directly or indirectly, seems to have owned shares in arms manufacturers and even in a porn printing house. More than twenty years later, the Vatican's cavalier attitude to ethics in its investment policy could also be concluded from its substantial participation in bond issues for South African government entities. At a time when South Africa was still under white Apartheid rule, most of

---

iii   More detail in Chapter 4.

the world (including all US financial institutions) boycotted these issues. The Vatican obviously had no qualms about supporting the regime.

If she does not adhere to an ethical investment policy, the least that could be expected of the Church is that she choose her business partners with great care and, above all, never be involved in anything which is illegal. It appears that the Catholic Church has different ideas. Having no external controlling bodies gives the Vatican a lot of freedom. Right from the beginning, the Vatican allowed the IOR to be used as a convenient instrument for affluent Italians who wanted to spirit money out of Italy to safe-havens such as the US or Switzerland. In theory, the bank will only open accounts to residents of Vatican City State, diplomats accredited to the Holy See, members of the Curia and heads of religious orders or other religious institutions. However, 'a very few Italian citizens to whom the privilege was granted because of their business relations with the Vatican or their good work on behalf of the Church', were also permitted to open accounts at the IOR.[11] Details of some of these 'business relations' and of the 'good work on behalf of the Church' are described later in this chapter. In 1948, Monsignor Edoardo Cippino, a Curia Prelate, was arrested by the Italian authorities and later imprisoned for exchange control violations. The technique is fairly simple. There are no physical barriers between Italy and Vatican City and all one has to do is walk over to the IOR with a suitcase full of Italian Lire and arrange to have them transferred abroad. Alternatively, such money could be deposited in bank accounts that the IOR maintains with various Italian banks. The Vatican has always denied that it was involved in such smuggling but the activities of the IOR have proven beyond doubt that the Vatican had no reservations about participating in illegal financial dealings and transactions. The more illegal it was, the higher the cut they took. This was one of the sources with which the Holy See funded its expenditure. Laymen who were allowed to open accounts at the IOR were expected to leave ten per cent of their deposit (often as a stipulation in their wills) to the IOR.[12] A 1978 report prepared for Pope John Paul I showed that of the eleven thousand accounts held at the IOR, only one thousand six hundred and fifty were held by ecclesiastical bodies.[13] According to a report on worldwide fiscal havens, the Vatican is included in the list of top ten money-laundering destinations.[14]

Over the years, the Vatican, through its bank the IOR, has participated in some of the most outrageous business transactions Italy has known. Two of the most astonishing were the Sindona affair and the Calvi affair.

The Sicilian tax lawyer Michele Sindona is dead. He was found poisoned in his cell in an Italian jail in 1986. Before he was murdered, Sindona was a close financial adviser to the Pope and the Vatican was deeply involved in many of Sindona's businesses. He was sent to the

Italian jail from the US, having been sentenced to twenty-five years there for fraud and misappropriation of bank funds. How did the Vatican find itself in such close involvement with such an unsavoury character? Who was Sindona? Born 8 May 1920, educated by the Jesuits, he avoided conscription and, instead, worked the black market during the war. He studied law and, when he left Sicily for Milan in 1946, he, amongst others, obtained a letter of introduction from the Archbishop of Messina whom he had befriended. In Milan he set up as a tax consultant, soon thereafter gained the Mafia as a client and bought his first bank, Banca Privata Finanziaria. Within a few years he acquired his second bank, the Banca di Messina, which cannot have displeased his Mafia clients. He not only built up his Mafia base, but, creating a perfect union, he also nurtured his Vatican connections. According to the writer David Yallop, Sindona had been recycling proceeds from Mafia heroin sales through the Vatican Bank to his bank in Switzerland.[15]

Sindona, in his quest for networking, diligently worked three axes: the Vatican, the Mafia and the powerful Italian Freemasons' Lodge, P2. Sindona's first contact with the IOR was in 1958, when he met its senior lay officer, Prince Massimo Spada. Sindona knew how to nurture such relationships and a few years later, upon Spada's retirement, Sindona made him a director of one of his banks. His successor at the IOR, Luigi Mennini, was also made director in some of Sindona's banks. Sometimes it was more than diligence; Sindona must have considered it higher providence when Cardinal Montini, the archbishop of Milan, whom he had helped to raise substantial funds for an old-age home, subsequently (in 1963) was elected Pope (Paul VI). Montini greatly believed in Sindona and a few years later made him financial adviser to the Vatican. A 1969 papal document named Sindona *Mercator Senesis Romanam Curiam*, the leading banker of the Roman Curia.[16] Sindona's first assignment was to transfer out of Italy the major bulk of the Vatican's financial and investment assets, as a tax evasion exercise.[17] Until 1978, the year Pope Paul VI died, Sindona benefited both from the trust and from his closeness to the Pope.

Well ensconced, Sindona's new direct contact at the Vatican was an American bishop who was soon to be in charge of the IOR – Bishop Paul Marcinkus. As the Vatican's financial adviser, Sindona bought and sold companies; he bought from and sold to the Vatican, acting on his own behalf and in partnership with the Vatican. When the Vatican's investment arm, APSA, wanted to sell its substantial thirty-three per cent holding in the international property group, *Societa Generale Immobiliare*, the man for the job was Sindona, and he actually bought the shares himself. Before his fall, Sindona owned or controlled several banks, including Banca Privata Finanziaria and Banca Unione in Milan, Banque de Financement in Geneva, and the Franklin National Bank, at the time the twentieth largest bank in the US. The IOR not only deposited monies with Sindona's banks, it also acquired enough shares to become an important shareholder in the banks, and thereby became Sindona's partner. In 1974, a slump in the world economy which was triggered by OPEC's 1973 increase in oil prices, also brought about increased inflation and interest rates and caused massive fluctuations in exchange rates. Banks which did not have a first rate reputation were considered risky. One such bank was the Franklin National Bank, which collapsed in 1974. Ten days before Franklin's collapse, the Central Bank of Italy forced Sindona's Italian bank, Banca Privata Italiana,[iv] into liquidation. The Central Bank appointed a Milanese lawyer, Giorgio Ambrosoli, as liquidator. For his meticulous work for the public good, Ambrosoli paid with his life. In his 1979 report, Ambrosoli established that Sindona had purchased his shares in Franklin National Bank using clients' bank deposits from his Italian banks. Ambrosoli did not succumb to pressure from Sindona and his partners and shared his findings with the American officials who were investigating Sindona. He was assassinated in July 1979. In 1981 Sindona was charged with ordering Ambrosoli's murder.

After the collapse of his Italian empire and to avoid arrest in Italy, Sindona fled the country. A few years later, he was arrested in the US and indicted for fraud, perjury and misappropriation of bank funds, in connection with his running of the Franklin National Bank. In June 1980, Michele Sindona, the Vatican's financial adviser, intimate of cardinals and popes, was sentenced to twenty-five years in jail. In July 1982 he was one of twenty-six who were indicted by an Italian court on charges of fraudulent bankruptcy, violation of Italian banking rules and falsification of company accounts in connection with the collapse of his Banca Privata Italiana. One of the co-indicted with Sindona was none other than Luigi Mennini, the second-in-command at the IOR, the Vatican Bank.

The Vatican has never confirmed the magnitude of its losses in the Sindona Affair. Estimates as to the lost deposits, lost investment as a shareholder in the banks and lost participations in other businesses, fluctuated between US $30 and $300 million.

Another monumental financial scandal for the Vatican, in the second half of the twentieth century, was the Calvi affair. Like Sindona, Roberto Calvi is now dead. Like Sindona, he was murdered. Like Sindona, he was a close financial confidante of the Vatican and of its bank, the IOR. Roberto Calvi was Managing Director and, from 1975, also Chairman of

---

[iv] This was a new bank resulting from the merger of Banca Privata and Banca Unione, a last-minute attempt by the Italian government to rescue the bank, aided by a US $100 million loan from state-owned Banco di Roma.

Italy's largest private bank, Banco Ambrosiano. This bank, established in 1896 by Catholic businessmen in northern Italy, was based in Milan. To ensure its independence, the bank's statutes prevented any individual from holding more than five per cent of the shares. Ironically, this restriction, which enabled Calvi to run the bank without interference from any strong shareholders, would eventually lead to Ambrosiano's downfall. The bank was always close to the Catholic Church and was often referred to as 'the priests' bank'. Indeed, it was so Catholic that, to be able to exercise shareholder rights, or to work in the bank, shareholders and employees alike had to produce certificates of baptism and certificates of good conduct from their parish priest. Calvi and his friends at the IOR must have had their very own notions of 'good conduct' as they took that relationship to new and most surprising frontiers, ending with enormous losses, bankruptcies and murder.

The Calvi and Sindona affairs are intertwined. It was, in fact, Sindona who, in 1971, first introduced Calvi to the Vatican Bank and to its president, Archbishop Paul Marcinkus. In his book *In God's Name*, David Yallop claims that Calvi was a money launderer for the Mafia as well as the paymaster general of the notorious *Propaganda Due*, the P2 Freemasons' Lodge.[18] Through its members, who included cabinet ministers, judges, senior clergy, bankers and top military and secret service officers, the Lodge was a shadow state running and corrupting Italy. In blatant contradiction of Canon law, many senior members of the Church hierarchy were secretly also Freemasons and members of P2.[19]

In the years 1971 to 1982, using Banco Ambrosiano's funds and resources and those of its clients and shareholders, Calvi, on his own account, for the bank and for the Vatican, bought banks, stockbrokers, insurance companies, media companies and industrial holding companies, in addition to setting up overseas subsidiaries and a long line of secretly held off-shore companies. These included Banca Cattolica del Veneto and Credito Varesino, both in Italy, Banco del Gottardo in Switzerland, a large Italian insurance company, Toro Assicurazioni and the large Italian holding company La Centrale Finanziaria, which owned industrial, commercial, insurance and finance companies.[20]

One of Calvi's standard modes of operation was, first, to arrange for parcels of shares in the companies he acquired to be bought by off-shore companies that he controlled. He would later arrange for Banco Ambrosiano to purchase the shares from the off-shore companies at an inflated price. This operation had a double benefit to Calvi. He was able to transfer funds overseas, circumventing and contravening Italian exchange control regulations, and he was able fraudulently to inflate the value of the companies he controlled. That way, for instance, when the Vatican (through the IOR) sold its holding in Banca Cattolica del Veneto, the shares were first sold to a Lichtenstein-based company connected to Sindona. This company then sold the shares to yet another off-shore company, this time one controlled by Calvi. Giorgio Ambrosoli, the liquidator of Sindona's Banca Privata, in his 1979 report, stated that in this transaction alone, a 'commission' of US $6.5 million was divided between an American archbishop and a Milanese banker.

The IOR directly and indirectly (through off-shore companies, which it confirmed it owned) owned shares in Banco Ambrosiano and in its Swiss bank, Banca del Gottardo. Having sold Banca Cattolica del Veneto to Calvi, the IOR held on to five per cent of its shares and was represented on its board. It was also a shareholder in Banco Ambrosiano Overseas in the Bahamas. There the Vatican was represented by Archbishop Marcinkus, who apparently quite enjoyed his business trips to the Bahamas. This association of the IOR with Banco Ambrosiano did not remain unnoticed. Italy's central bank started to become concerned and its inspectors, according to their 1978 report, were troubled by the linkage between the IOR and the Ambrosiano group, especially because of their joint transactions of doubtful nature.

Two central questions are: 'what was Calvi doing?' and 'why was the Vatican involved with him?' There were very few people who had the full picture and who knew what was really happening. Most of them are dead; the others won't talk. Calvi was murdered in London and his secretary killed herself by jumping (or was pushed) from her office window in Milan; Sindona was poisoned in his Italian prison cell; Giorgio Ambrosoli, the liquidator of Sindona's Banca Privata, was assassinated in front of his home; Licio Gelli, Grandmaster of the P2 Freemasons' Lodge, who escaped from a Swiss jail in 1983, was next arrested in 1998; Umberto Ortolani, Gelli's closest associate in the P2, has died; Archbishop Marcinkus remained silent until his death in 2006.

What we do know is that in 1982, when Calvi's banks fell apart, there was a hole of US $1.3 billion in the Banco Ambrosiano's balance sheet. Banco Ambrosiano had made loans to other banks in its group, or to third party banks as fiduciary deposits[v] to be lent to Ambrosiano's off-shore banks. The borrowing banks were unable to repay Banco Ambrosiano because they had made loans to off-shore companies. These mainly Panamanian companies had spent the money they borrowed partly to purchase shares in Banco Ambrosiano and partly in payments to third parties for uses one can only guess. They may have included the lining of Calvi's own pockets, bribes to politicians and to political parties, payments to blackmailers and people who offered Calvi help and protection and payments to people such as Sindona and Gelli.[21]

---

[v]   By making fiduciary deposits, Ambrosiano was trying to hide from the Italian bank supervisory authorities the fact that it was lending so much money to its own companies.

Having established what Calvi was up to, the big question that arises is: 'why was the Vatican involved with Banco Ambrosiano and its activities?' Not only was the IOR a shareholder in most of the Ambrosiano group banks, but it even held directorships in them. Moreover, Payments were also made to a senior Vatican archbishop and were rumoured to have been for the use of covert political Vatican activities in South America and, nearer to Pope John Paul II's heart, Poland. As directors they were responsible for the activities of these banks. But that was not the end of the Vatican's involvement. It turned out that at least eleven of the off-shore companies that Calvi had established were actually owned by the Vatican.[22] In July 1982, after Calvi's body was found hanging under London's Blackfriars bridge, the Bank of Italy's commissioners, who took over the management of the bank, approached Archbishop Marcinkus demanding the Vatican repay the debt of its companies. The Vatican, legally, refused. The Vatican's ownership of the off-shore companies, which owed some US $1.4 billion, did not create any obligation on them.[23] Marcinkus, who denied any Vatican connection to the loans, explained that he had agreed to issue 'letters of comfort' on behalf of the IOR as a friend only in order to help Calvi.[24]

At first the Vatican tried to lie and flatly denied any connection with the off-shore companies, and went so far as to accuse the press of lying. After some time, it confirmed that it owned two of the companies. Several months later, and only after the press came out with proof that there were more Panamanian companies owned by the IOR, did the Vatican confirm ownership of all of the companies concerned. And yet the Vatican continued to issue further lies, some of which were, indeed, ridiculous. The Vatican's IOR owned an Italian construction company, Vianini, the deputy chairman of which was IOR's own deputy chairman, Pellegrino de Strobel. Shares in Vianini were held by one of the hitherto denied Panamanian companies and were used by it to secure a US $27.8 million loan it had received. Slowly, as the scandal became exposed, more and more facts about the Vatican's involvement came to light, such as the fact that, in 1978, the accounting firm Coopers & Lybrand, who were the auditors of Banco Ambrosiano Overseas in the Bahamas, had met with Marcinkus. The auditors were worried about the high exposure of the bank to the off-shore companies and Calvi arranged for them to meet the Archbishop. Marcinkus put their minds at ease, probably by confirming the IOR's standing behind the companies. So when, in 1982, Marcinkus said that he had issued the letters of comfort just to help a friend, he was lying as, four years before, he had already said enough to allay the apprehension of the bank's auditors. Clearly, the Vatican was lying in 1982 when it denied knowledge of these off-shore companies, as the loans to such companies had been discussed with the auditors in 1978.

In the end, the Vatican had to pay. They may not have been legally bound to do so, but the public uproar and the political pressure emanating from the Italian government for the Vatican to underwrite at least part of the loss, left them no alternative. In 1984 the Vatican paid US $250 million to Banco Ambrosiano's creditors.[25] In February 1987, Italian investigating magistrates concluded that the Vatican Bank had acted as an umbrella for Calvi's transactions and issued arrest warrants for Archbishop Paul Marcinkus and his associates Luigi Mennini and Pellegrino del Strobel.[26]

The Vatican did not limit itself to Italy in its illegal activities. In the US, the IOR was fined for an improperly documented acquisition of a company. It was also involved in a counterfeit stock deal which was organised by the Mafia. In 1973, the FBI investigated the involvement of the IOR and Archbishop Marcinkus in Mafia money-laundering. Between the years 1971 and 1973 the Vatican was negotiating with Mafia middlemen for the purchase of US $1 billion in nominal value of counterfeit stock certificates of top US corporates. The main Vatican contact with the Mafia intermediaries was Cardinal Eugene Tisserant. Tisserant, a close confidant of Pope Paul VI and a very senior man in the Roman Curia, by then already in his eighties, was the head of the Society for the Propagation of the Faith as well as dean of the College of Cardinals. The transaction was eventually aborted as trial specimens, which were paid into banks in Italy and Switzerland, were detected as forgeries. The first shipment of US $14 million, which was made as a trial shipment for the Vatican and which was apparently delivered, has never been located. According to the writer Richard Hammer, the Vatican thinking was that even if the forgery were to be found out, the US administration would never consider the Vatican to be complicit with the Mafia but rather assume that they had been duped. Moreover, because of the Vatican's standing, they expected the American government to keep the whole matter under wraps and even reimburse the Vatican for its losses. Evidently, Cardinal Tisserant and Bishop Marcinkus thought they were not only on to a winner, but that this was a win–win situation. Even if found out, they expected to be neither considered culpable nor left out of pocket.[27] When, in 1973, the FBI tried to get Vatican cooperation in its investigations of the matter, not surprisingly, they were stonewalled.[28]

On 31 August 1978, several days after Albino Luciani was elected Pope John Paul I and four weeks before he was found dead, some say murdered, the Italian economic periodical *Il Mondo* addressed an open letter to the Pope. In the letter *Your Holiness, Is It Right?* the Vatican's financial operations, management and partnerships are severely attacked, described as 'speculation in unhealthy waters' and immoral.[29] Apparently, the Pope had made it clear that he was about to undertake a cleansing of the Vatican, starting with the immediate removal of Marcinkus from the bank and including the removal of various other powerful cardinals, such as the Secretary of State Cardinal Villot.[30] Powerful people were pleased to get rid of this Pope, within a month of his election. It is not known whether John Paul I was indeed murdered, as the Vatican refused to permit an autopsy.

Evidently, none of these scandals brought doubts into John Paul I's successor's mind as to Marcinkus' integrity and suitability. Soon Marcinkus would become instrumental in transferring more than US $100 million from the Vatican to Poland and to the Polish Solidarity movement. To prevent Marcinkus' arrest, the Vatican invoked article 11 of the Lateran Treaty, according to which 'All central bodies of the Catholic Church shall be exempt from any interference on the part of the Italian State.'[31] The Pope was only held back from his wish to create Marcinkus a cardinal by Cardinal Casaroli's strong objection. Vatican secretary of state, Cardinal Casaroli, understood that elevating Marcinkus, who was central in the corrupt goings on of recent years, would create too much of an uproar.[32]

For seven years, Italian magistrates tried to investigate and possibly prosecute Marcinkus in connection with his involvement in the Calvi and Sindona affairs. Marcinkus hid in Vatican City, invoking sovereign immunity of the independent state of the Vatican City. In 1989, accepting the immunity claim, Italy finally gave up. The Vatican was now able to send its Archbishop back to the US without risking open discussions about their illegal activities in Italian courts. Marcinkus, from Chicago, was allowed to go back to America. To ensure that he would never have to answer anybody's questions, Pope John Paul II gave him diplomatic status. In 1993, a Swiss court tried to get a deposition from Marcinkus, who had retired and was living in Arizona, in connection with Vatican Bank transactions with one of Calvi's banks. A request was filed with the US District Court in Phoenix, Arizona. The Vatican produced documentation stating that Marcinkus was entitled to immunity and the case was closed. Pope John Paul II interfered in the proper legal proceedings of Italy, Switzerland and the US, preventing justice from being done and the truth from coming out. Why? What was the Pope hiding?

In 1993, the public investigation into the enormous bribes (amounting to hundreds of millions of US dollars) paid to Italian politicians by the Italian conglomerate Montedison, revealed that more than US $57 million of the funds were deposited with the IOR. Again, the question must be asked why this Institute for Religious Works – which exists, according to the attorney defending it against a 1999 lawsuit in California, 'to promote pious acts' – should be chosen as, and agree to be, the depository for bribery funds of this magnitude.

In recent years, an attempt to gain some insight into the IOR's activities was made in the case of Alperin v. Vatican Bank, filed in the District Court in San Francisco in 1999. The case is based on a US State Department document that implicates the Vatican in laundering Nazi gold and which claims that it was a depositary of monies stolen by the Ustasha regime in Croatia from Serbs, Gypsies and Jews killed by the Ustasha. This attempt was also quashed. The Vatican succeeded in using its sovereign immunity status to prevent a US court from judging a claim for restitution for assets allegedly stolen and then deposited with the Vatican Bank. Why did the Catholic Church and her institutions from the Pope downward not grab the opportunity to either prove that they were never involved in laundering Nazi and Ustasha funds, or to finally make good and return these funds?

Conclusion

It is remarkable how prominent dishonesty, crooked dealings and debauchery have been in the actions of so many successors of Peter; a string of popes have been guilty of simony, nepotism, murder, sexual debauchery and general depravity. It is no longer the norm for popes to divert Church property and funds to enrich their own families, but the twentieth-century Vatican Bank saw nothing wrong in colluding with the Mafia and in running money-laundering operations. Moreover, the Church has not formally condemned the corrupt popes.

New York's former archbishop, Cardinal John J. O'Connor, in a homily he gave in 1998, suggested that corrupt clergy was not a reason to discard the Catholic Church. He accepted that the Church had 'experienced corruption, ... [and] has at times demonstrated great arrogance through its bishops and priests and even through its popes'. And yet, the Cardinal maintained that Catholics had no right to say 'enough is enough'; they had no right to say that they believed in Christ, in Christian values and that the institution of the Church was too corrupt and must go. Christ, the Cardinal reminds us, said: 'Who hears you, hears me. Who despises you, despises me. Who despises me, despises him who sent me ... On you, Peter, I will build my church. Teach everyone what I have taught you.' Therefore, although, 'there have been so many sins in the Church, so much weakness in the Church, there have been so many corrupt popes in the Church, corrupt bishops, corrupt priests, corrupt Catholic lay persons', Catholics must continue in total adherence to the institution. It is Christ's Church and if one believes in Christ one has to believe in and respect the Catholic Church.[33]

This perpetuation of the myth of a holy Church – although historically proven to be far from holy – may be acceptable to some Catholics, yet, even those Catholics, as Christians, should have a problem with the notion of obedience to a corrupt Church. To non-Catholics, this reasoning is at best puzzling.

It would be wrong to reject the Catholic Church on account of the very many corrupt popes and corrupt administrations which have headed her. However, the goings on in the Church and in her financial institutions are still kept secret. Ignoring norms of public governance, the Catholic Church keeps a veil of secrecy over almost everything. Her archives, which would bring to light some of the scandalous deeds of previous popes and of the Church, are secret. Although the Church manages billions of US dollars of essentially other people's money, she does not issue audited information to the public.

Even the much-revered Pope John Paul II colluded in the cover up of financial corruption. There is no reason to believe that we have heard the last of financial corruption in the Catholic Church. How can one comply with Cardinal O'Connor's call to disregard it all and simply adhere and to respect the Church?

Chapter Four
Holy Violence

'It is from God's love for all men that the Church in every age receives both the obligation and the vigour of her missionary dynamism.'[1]

Throughout her history the Catholic Church has initiated, sponsored and condoned violence; she seems to have a skewed understanding of God's love.

In his message for the World Day of Peace of 1 January 2000, Pope John Paul II spoke of war as a 'defeat for humanity', as 'only in peace and through peace can respect for human dignity and its inalienable rights be guaranteed'. God, according to the Pope, 'loves all men and women on earth and gives them the hope of a new era, an era of peace'. It should, perhaps, not surprise us that in his explanations for the 'endless and horrifying sequence of wars, conflicts, genocides and "ethnic cleansings" which have caused unspeakable suffering' the Pope neglects to mention religion. They are apparently the result of 'a logic of supremacy fuelled by the desire to dominate and exploit others, by ideologies of power or totalitarian utopias, by crazed nationalisms or ancient tribal hatreds'.[2] No one suspects the Pope of condoning the violent acts carried out by the Irish Republican Army (IRA). It is, however, a fact that the Church has not spoken out loudly and clearly forbidden Catholics to participate in these acts. Nor has the Church publicly excommunicated any one for carrying them out.

The Catholic Church proclaims that she is a Church of peace. Indeed, in a world which professes to be peace-aspiring, the Church is no longer involved in wars. However, this was not always so. The Church has a long history of involvement in wars; preaching, planning and even participating in them. Since the beginning of history, wars have existed as a mechanism for settling economic disputes, enforcing rights over resources and establishing security. However, the addition of religious content, symbols and sentiment has produced in such conflicts a fervour of which material interest alone would not have been capable. As faith does not allow for compromise, it created inflexibility. Indeed, religion is absolute and hence was attractive to those secular rulers who took advantage of religious fanaticism to inspire their armies.

The Papal States

At the beginning of the eighth century, Arab armies overran Spain and set up Islamic strongholds. This offensive, which imperilled the Christianity of Europe, was brought to an end in 732 at Poitiers, where Charles Martel put a stop to the Muslim advance. Martel, the actual power holder in the Merovingian kingdom, was formally only Mayor to the palace of the King. This was a time in which the Byzantine Empire was weak and was made more vulnerable by Islamic attacks in Asia Minor. European power seekers, such as the Lombards, were thereby able to grab Byzantine territories. When the Lombard King, Liutprand, attacked Rome in 729, it was only due to the awe in which he held the papacy, that Liutprand left without harming St Peter's and Rome was saved. When the King came again ten years later, he must have changed his mind and lost his scruples, as he allowed his army to loot St Peter's. Pope Gregory III (731–741) needed help, knew it and had a deal in mind when he made advances to Martel asking for his support. In return for military aid, the Pope offered Martel connectivity to God. The Pope's emissaries were sent not only with a letter from the Pope but also with keys of the shrine of St Peter. In his plea, Gregory warned: 'Do not despise my appeal, that the Prince of the Apostles may not shut the kingdom of heaven against you.'3 Although the Pope suggested that he might prevent Martel from reaching Heaven unless Martel came to his aid, no deal was done at that stage. Where they failed, both their successors succeeded.

Pepin, Martel's son, wanted to be king in his own right and not just Mayor of the Palace to the Merovingian King. As his family already held actual power, they now wanted the crown. In 750, Pope Zacharias (741–752) supplied the necessary theological justification. Zacharias confirmed that those who had the reality of royal power should also hold the royal title. This enabled Pepin to depose the sovereign king and seize the throne of Francia.

In 754, Pope Stephen II (752–757), Zacharias' successor, under even more strain due to Lombard control over the duchy of Rome, travelled to Gaul and met King Pepin. The Pope now anointed the King, Queen and their sons and proclaimed that the kingdom of Francia was to remain with their family in perpetuity. In return, Pepin invaded Italy, defeated the Lombards and gifted the former Byzantine province, the Exarchate of Ravenna, the five cities (*Pentapolis*) of Riminia, Ancona, Fano, Pesaro and Senigallia, the duchy of Rome and the province of Emilia to the Pope. Byzantium demanded that Pepin return the territories seized from them by the Lombards. Neither Pepin nor the Pope heeded the protests of the Byzantine Emperor, who saw his lands freed from the Lombards only to be given to the Pope rather than returned to him. The gift of these provinces to the Church was considered by Byzantium as an anti-Byzantine act, and its acceptance by the Pope as abandonment of his allegiance to the Byzantine Emperor. Up to then, formally at least, the papal allegiance to the Byzantine Emperor provided the papacy with security. However, as the Emperor was less and less capable of offering that protection, a new power had to be found. The Pope found it in Francia.

Pepin's generosity was continued by Charlemagne, Pepin's son, in 774. At the time, the Church also produced – or rather, manufactured – the 'Donation of Constantine'. This document – which was later proven to be a Church forgery, a fact now even accepted by the Catholic Church – claimed that vast areas of land had been bequeathed by the fourth-century Emperor, Constantine, to Pope Sylvester I. In all likelihood, this document was forged by the Church in order to reinforce the 'Donation of Pepin'.

Twenty-five years later, on Christmas Day 800, Pope Leo III (795–816) crowned Charlemagne as Roman Emperor in return for his coming to Leo's help when he was under threat of being deposed by the Romans.[4] The axis forged by Stephen II and Pepin created the basis for the Papal States which gave the Church one thousand years of secular control over a substantial part of Italy.

Papal Wars

Popes were involved in wars not only as spiritual leaders of the Christian world but also as temporal heads of the Papal States. Land was acquired by the Catholic Church in a variety of ways: by way of endowments given to popes; in return for papal support which kings and other rulers wanted from the Church in various conflicts; and through outright acts of war. Some popes spent most of their revenue on warfare. For example, throughout the Avignon papacy (1309–1377), two-thirds of papal revenues were blown on mercenary armies and on deals with allies in their politicking in Italy.[5]

One of the Church's great warriors was a Franciscan theologian; perhaps one could have expected a greater humility and simplicity more commensurate with his Franciscan roots of the man who was to become Pope Sixtus IV (1471–1484). This pope, who was involved in a variety of wars, changing allegiances without any qualms, spent a third of the papacy's annual income just on his coronation tiara. Sixtus, who was a great patron of the arts, completed the picture of the ideal pope, as participant in a murder conspiracy which was to take place during High Mass in the Duomo of Florence.

The degree of papal control over his territories fluctuated and depended both on the ambitions and power of kings and nobility in those areas and on the ambitions and skills of different popes. It was only in the sixteenth century that the papacy began to have real power over its territories. The Renaissance papacy is well known for its corruption. Indeed, some of the wars undertaken by Renaissance popes (such as Leo X (1513–1521)), served mainly to enrich the pope's family, whereas Pope Julius II (1503–1513) went to war to win back some territories which papal families had 'acquired'. Julius, an active participant in the Italian Wars, personally led his troops to crush any defiance as he abolished local autonomies. In that period European powers were fighting for control over the independent states in Italy and popes played an active role in these wars. Pope Alexander VI (1492–1503) in coalition with Spain, the Holy Roman Emperor, Venice and Milan, fought Charles VIII of France who had seized Naples. Four years later, in 1499, the next French king, Louis XII, was able to occupy Naples in agreement with Spain and with the blessing of the Pope. In 1508, Julius II formed the League of Cambrai, a coalition with France, Spain and the Holy Roman Emperor against Venice. This war against Venice won back Ravenna, Rimini and Faenza for the Holy See. One year later, the same pope formed an alliance (the Holy League) with Venice, the Swiss cantons, Ferdinand II of Aragon, Henry VIII and the Holy Roman Emperor against his former coalition partner, France. The purpose of the new alliance was to push France out of Italy. Pope Clement VII (1523–1534) formed the League of Cognac with Francis I of France, Henry VIII, Venice and Florence which enabled Francis to repudiate his treaty with Spain (the 1526 Treaty of Madrid). This coalition of the Pope with France resulted in a swift act of punishment by Charles V, King of Spain and Holy Roman Emperor who, in 1527, sent his army to Italy to raid and plunder Rome. The French had to abandon their Italian holdings and the Spaniards gained complete supremacy in Italy.

The Papal States were finally lost when Victor Emmanuel seized Rome in 1870. The Holy See regained temporal sovereignty of the small area of the Vatican through the 1929 Lateran Accords.

Crusades

Nowadays, Christianity is not the first religion which springs to mind in connection with holy wars, and yet it has its own history of them. The crusades were not even the beginning. The concept of holy wars had already been employed by Christianity in the fight against the Muslim invasion of Spain in the eighth century. Some three hundred and sixty years later, the Church initiated her faith-imbued wars which were to last over a period of two hundred years; a series of wars which were embarked on by Christians with the declared goal of liberating the Holy Land from the Muslims. Not all of the crusades were instigated by the Church. However, the first five were very much the result of papal agitation. The Church was the active fermenting agent mustering the will and the energy of the faithful into participating in these crusades.

In 1095, Pope Urban II (1088–1099) made a speech at the Council of Clermont in which he urged all Christians to do their duty and recover the Holy Places epitomised by the Holy Sepulchre, the grave in which Christians believe Jesus was buried. To put the minds of the warriors-to-be at ease, the Pope promised that homes, properties and families of the absent crusaders would be protected by declaring a truce, a period during which any hostilities amongst Christians would cease. They were also given immunity from any action by secular courts for the period of the crusade. As a special incentive, in defining this war a pilgrimage, the Pope was able to promise that all participants would be granted full penance and all of their sins would be forgiven. These were times when penance entailed more than just ten Hail Marys. Sinners were expected to undergo personal hardship such as long periods of fasting to redeem their transgressions. This across-the-board remission of sins proved to be a great attraction and it fired the emotions and fantasies of Europe beyond papal expectations. The Pope thus combined practical advantages with spiritual promise to produce the First Crusade.

It was Urban II who coined the phrase *Deus lo Volt* (God wills it) which was to become the battle cry of the Christian crusaders. There are many explanations, beyond the promise of salvation and exemption from prosecution, for the unprecedented and incredible impact that the Pope's call to arms had. Europe had been through a period of increased prosperity and its trading classes were attracted by the promise of new markets and expanded trade. It was also a period in which Europe saw an increase in population; its nobility was itching for territorial gains and the lower classes were eager to gain more freedom. Moreover, the Peace of God movement, which was initiated by bishops who were trying to bring the local wars waged by the nobility to an end, had spread through France, Italy and northern Europe. Truce periods were established in which it was not permissible for a Christian to wage war against a fellow Christian. Thus, trigger-happy aristocrats were now glad to have a 'permissible' outlet for their bellicose temperaments.

The First Crusade began with hordes of German peasants robbing and massacring thousands of Jews who lived on their route. The power to murder was unleashed by the Pope and even local bishops, who were trying to protect Jews from death, were unable to stop the crusaders. They marched on and, with their French co-crusaders, pillaged Belgrade. However, they were defeated by the Turks in Asia Minor. It took further armies which were better organised, under the control of the Byzantine Emperor Alexius I, to defeat the Turks and take Antioch. Finally, in 1099, Jerusalem fell to the crusaders and tens of thousands of Muslims and Jews were massacred by the *Deus lo Volt* crusaders. The Church had its success with the creation of the Latin Kingdom of Jerusalem, with a Latin patriarch, at its head which lasted until 1291. In 1291, when Acre fell to the Muslims, there was no longer sufficient Christian zeal to drive them out.

The Second Crusade (1147–1149) did not end well. Cajoled into their holy mission by the influential monastic reformer, St Bernard of Clairvaux, who believed that the pope's task was 'to direct princes, to command bishops, to set kingdoms and empires in order',[6] the armies plundered properties on their way to the Holy Land. Led by the Holy Roman Emperor Conrad III and King Louis VII of France, the French and German armies were decimated by the Turks.

Pope Gregory VIII (1187) urged the kings of England and France and the Holy Roman Emperor to recapture Jerusalem, which had been taken by Saladin in 1187. However, the combined forces of Richard Cœur de Lion, Philippe Auguste and Frederick Barbarossa that comprised the Third Crusade, were unable to take Jerusalem. In 1192, their mission ended in failure. Six years later, Pope Innocent III (1198–1216) started preaching the Fourth Crusade which eventually took off in 1202. This Crusade was led by French and Flemish noblemen and over two years the army of crusaders were more akin to mercenaries than anything else. The Pope was so angered by his army's first campaign – recovering Zadar on the Dalmatian coast from the Hungarians as a service to the Doge of Venice, Enrico Dandolo – that he excommunicated the lot. The army then proceeded and, in return for money, aid in conquering Egypt and the union of the Eastern and the Roman Churches, helped Alexius (the future Alexius IV) to depose his uncle, the Byzantine Emperor Alexius III, savagely plundering Constantinople and massacring its inhabitants in the process. Several years later, the same pope, Innocent III, actively preached yet another crusade. By the time the Fifth Crusade (1217–1221) began, Innocent was dead and his successor, Honorius III (1216–1227), was in office. This expedition, which was led by the King of Hungary, Duke Leopold VI of Austria, campaigned as far as Egypt but returned home defeated. But this did not put off Pope Gregory IX (1227–1241), Honorius' successor, from demanding that the faithful undertake a new crusade. Gregory, in fact, excommunicated the Holy Roman Emperor Frederick II for causing delay. Frederick, who had already promised Honorius to go on a crusade, did not leave until 1228, when he undertook the Sixth Crusade.

Four more crusades were undertaken between 1228 and 1272 but the fall of Acre to the Muslims in 1291 put a stop to the launch of any further campaigns. For more than two hundred years the Church and her popes sent people to kill and to die so that Christian sovereignty be gained over land which the Church considered holy and hers. Popes continued to preach crusades for years thereafter but the excitement of the first crusades could not be reignited and the papal calls fell on deaf ears. The crusades gave birth to the *Knights Templar* and the *Knights Hospitaler,* Christian military orders which took it upon themselves to continue fighting to regain and retain the Holy Land in Christian hands. However, the Church was no longer able to produce the necessary forces to achieve an aim so close to her heart. Less than two hundred years after the last crusade, in 1453, Constantinople fell to the Turks. The Christian wish to roll-back Islam was reawakened and three popes, Nicholas V (1447–1455), Callistus III (1455–1458) and Pius II (1458–1464), attempted but failed in their concentrated endeavours to regain the city. Callistus sold Church property and taxed the clergy to finance the building of a fleet in shipyards on the Tiber. He sent envoys across Europe to persuade the faithful to lend their support and participate with the promise of Crusading Indulgences, but to no avail. Callistus' successor, Pope Pius II, sold offices in the Roman Curia to generate funds for a new crusade which he was hoping to participate in personally. Pius II hoped that by leading the crusade himself he would finally be able to mobilise an uninterested Europe into fighting the Turks and make Constantinople Christian again. He died before anything came of it.

Having established their willingness to apply violence to further what they considered was Church interest in the Holy Land, popes turned to violence within Europe. To combat heresy, popes gave their consent and even provided the impetus for fierce expeditions to subdue heathens and heretics inside Europe. Innocent III (1198–1216) had no reservations about the use of extreme measures in attempting to eradicate the Cathars, a movement in Spain and France which denied the concept of the Church's sacramental system. They were massacred. All participants in this Crusade, which ended with the massacre of the inhabitants of Beziers in 1209, were granted an Indulgence by the Pope.

Evangelising

Jesus' last words in St Mark's Gospel are: 'Go out to the whole world; proclaim the Good News to all creation.'[7] These inoffensive words of Jesus are the cause of a long history of much suffering for many to whom the 'Good News' was proclaimed. The Church has never ceased in her attempts to convert people to Catholicism and much of this was done by force. Ideas adopted by the Second Vatican Council (1963–1965) which have made the Church more open to the possibility of non-Catholic routes to salvation have resulted in some questioning the need to convert people to Catholicism. Questions as to what present-day evangelising should mean and might entail were studied in depth by the synod of bishops which Pope Paul VI had called in 1973 for that purpose. Based on their work, the Pope produced his Apostolic Letter, *Evangelii Nuntiandi*, in December 1975, which established the continued centrality of evangelism to Catholicism. The Pope states: 'The Church is born of the evangelizing activity of Jesus and the Twelve ... And it is above all His mission and His condition of being an evangelizer that she is called upon to continue.'[8]

The Church leaves us in no doubt as to the never-ending need to evangelise, to proclaim Jesus as the saviour of the world, to call on people to believe in Jesus, to convert to Catholicism and to become members of the Church. The growing secularisation of the Western world (excluding the United States) on one hand and the end of colonialism on the other hand have produced a redirection of the Church's missionary activities. No longer do Church missionaries have automatic access to indigenous populations on the back of colonial power. Missions continue to exist but they are now dependant on the willingness of the host countries to accept them and their activities are defined in terms of reference approved by their hosts. On the other hand, the Church faces the need to combat increased secularism. The Church is worried. Pope Pius VI explained that 'faith is nearly always today exposed to secularism, even to militant atheism. It is a faith exposed to trials and threats, and even more, a faith besieged and actively opposed. It runs the risk of perishing from suffocation or starvation.'[9] In fact the Church is so worried that senior members of the Catholic hierarchy have equated humanism with the beliefs of extreme regimes. For example, Archbishop Barry Hickey of Perth, Australia, has provocatively described 'secular humanism' as taking 'the place of other totalitarian regimes like Marxism or Freemasonry or Nazism in trying to suppress religion by relegating it to the private sphere where it has no say in public life'.[10] It takes some chutzpah to suggest that humanism in any way, just because it is secular, replaces Nazism.

Ten years after the Second Vatican Council (Vatican II), the Church clarified her position with regard to non-Christian religions. Unfortunately, the tone is rather condescending:

> The Church respects and esteems these non Christian religions because they are the living expression of the soul of vast groups of people. They carry within them the echo of thousands of years of searching for God, a quest which is incomplete but often made with great sincerity and righteousness of heart. They possess an impressive patrimony of deeply religious texts. They have taught generations of people how to pray. They are all impregnated with innumerable 'seeds of the Word' and can constitute a true 'preparation for the Gospel', to quote a felicitous term used by the Second Vatican Council and borrowed from Eusebius of Caesarea.[11]

The other religions get brownie points for trying. Reminiscent of the colonial attitudes towards the population in countries they conquered, the Church leaves no doubt that these other religions are just not enough, as 'our religion effectively establishes with God an authentic and living relationship which the other religions do not succeed in doing, even though they have, as it were, their arms stretched out towards heaven'. Therefore, 'the missionary proclamation never ceases' and the Church will not withhold 'from these non-Christians the proclamation of Jesus Christ'. Repeatedly, the Church refers to the 'most worthy esteem' in which she holds the other religions. Yet, in practice, she wants to take their place.

Setting up his stall in the marketplace of competing Christian churches, Paul VI states: 'There is thus a profound link between Christ, the Church and evangelization. During the period of the Church that we are living in, it is she who has the task of evangelizing. This mandate is not accomplished without her, and still less against her.'[12] Indeed, 'before all men can be brought together and restored to the grace of God our Father, communion must be re-established between those who by faith have acknowledged and accepted Jesus Christ as the Lord of mercy who sets men free and unites them in the Spirit of love and truth'.[13] Catholicism does not consider such communion to be anything other than under the headship of the Roman Church led by the pope.

In an act of Church acrobatics, the Catechism of the Catholic Church attempts to square the circle: 'How are we to understand this affirmation, [Outside the Church there is no salvation] often repeated by the Church Fathers?' On one hand 'the Church is the place where humanity must rediscover its unity and salvation'. But, on the other hand, although all must find salvation in the Catholic Church, 'Those who, through no fault of their own, do not know the Gospel of Christ or his Church, but who nevertheless seek God with a sincere heart, and, moved by grace, try in their actions to do his will as they know it through the dictates of their conscience – those too may achieve eternal salvation.' This, however, does not close the door, as 'the Church still has the obligation and also the sacred right to evangelize all men', and especially for the non-Christians, the warning is that 'Apart from the cross there is no other ladder by which we may get to heaven.'[14]

The acrobatics were necessary because many in the Church were extremely unhappy about the new Vatican II ideas of 'inclusivism'. The twentieth-century Catholic theologian Karl Rahner coined the term 'Anonymous Christianity'. Those who have a fundamentally correct orientation towards God, whatever their ignorance of Christ, can be viewed as 'anonymous Christians'.[15] To some Christians and to some followers of non-Christian religions the idea of such automatic membership may seem uncomfortable, unacceptable and even outrageous.

Pope Paul VI wrote that if 'it had to be expressed in one sentence the best way of stating it would be to say that the Church evangelizes when she seeks to convert, solely through the divine power of the message she proclaims, both the personal and collective consciences of people, the activities in which they engage, and the lives and concrete milieu which are theirs'.[16] This was not always the Catholic way of converting. The Church has a long history of various forms of aggressive evangelising and enforced conversions. Some of these activities involved physical abuse of those she considered to be heretics.

Combating Heresy: the Holy Inquisition

The Concise Oxford Dictionary defines heresy as 'belief or practice contrary to orthodox doctrine'. In 1199, Pope Innocent III (1198–1216) declared heresy to be 'treason against God'.[17] This opened the door for harsh treatment of heretics by the Church. Soon the willingness to kill in the name of the Lord spread from killing Muslims and Jews to killing Christians who had fallen into heresy.

The Inquisition had three main phases: the medieval, the Spanish and the Roman. Pope Lucius III (1181–1185), in league with Emperor Friedrich Barbarossa, was the pope who, in 1184, started the Church on this ugly road. The task itself was entrusted to bishops. Thirty years later, the Lateran Council of 1215 resolved to eliminate heresy which, according to Canon Law, is 'the obstinate post-baptismal denial of some truth, which must be believed with divine and Catholic faith'.[18] In his 1231 bull, *Excommunicamus*, Pope Gregory IX (1227–1241) set up roving ecclesiastical courts manned by Dominicans and Franciscans.[19] In 1252, Pope Innocent IV issued a decree permitting the use of torture by the inquisitors. A papal bull, to which the local ruler would add his authority, enabled the papal inquisitors to act with all the powers, force and violence of the state and to override local laws and report directly to the pope. By stipulating that the property of heretics be confiscated by the secular lords, the Church added an incentive for cooperation by the secular leaders.

The Inquisition's harshness varied at different periods and under different administrations. The process included physical searches, the summoning and questioning of those who were being accused and of witnesses. Often, the Inquisition's power to lock people up indefinitely sufficed and they confessed to crimes as demanded of them whether guilty or not in order to bring their ordeal to an end. At times, it took years to obtain such confessions. As considered 'necessary' the accused were locked up in the most dire conditions and tortured, sometimes employing the vilest sadistic methods to elicit confessions. Finally, the Inquisition apportioned justice. Punishment could range from an expression of regret and repentance through to the confiscation of property, imprisonment and burning at the stake. Only the latter was not carried out by the Church herself. The secular authority – the state

– acted as her agent for this purpose. Nicolas Eymerich's fourteenth-century document, *Directorium inquisitorum*, a handbook for inquisitors, instructed that under no circumstance must an accused be found innocent. In cases in which the court was unable to pass a guilty verdict, it was to leave the matter open, stating that nothing had been proven. Eymerich's handbook also classified the accused according to the severity of their 'obstinacy'. Relapsed penitents were those who had already been convicted as heretics, done penance and relapsed into heresy. Another group were 'first time offenders', those non-relapsed who, although found guilty, were impenitent. The most serious offenders were the relapsed impenitent. These were the accused who had been found guilty in the past and were found guilty yet again, unwilling to confess and repent. Recidivism brought the death penalty and the relapsed heretics had only death to look forward to. The Inquisition, however, stipulated that those who confessed would be strangled before being burned, whereas those who stuck to 'their' truth and denied that they were guilty, had to suffer the slow agony of being burned alive.

The medieval Inquisition is best known for its ruthless rooting-out of the Cathars and the Waldensians in the Languedoc region.[20] These heresies had become so widespread in the Languedoc area that Pope Innocent III (1198–1216) set out to eradicate them. As the Pope felt that the Languedocian princes were not supportive enough of his attempts to wipe out heresy, he decided to unseat them and called for a crusade. In June 1209, Languedoc was invaded by an army of twenty thousand led by a large number of nobles from the north of France. At least forty thousand Albigensians in the Languedoc region of France were murdered during this crusade, which only came to an end in 1229. As the crusade did not succeed in eliminating heresy, Pope Gregory IX established tribunals of inquisition to continue harassing the population in the Languedoc region. Bernard Gui, inquisitor of Toulouse, in his inquisition manual, *Practica inquisitionis*, explained his thinking:

> The end of the office of the inquisition is the destruction of heresy; this cannot be destroyed unless heretics are destroyed. Moreover, these cannot be destroyed unless their receivers, fauteurs [favourers] and defenders are destroyed. ... Heretics are destroyed in a double fashion: first, when they are converted from heresy to the true, Catholic faith. ... secondly, when they are surrendered to the secular jurisdiction to be corporeally burned.[21]

The historian Professor James B. Given, explains that the inquisition's penal system was 'designed to teach the masses a number of salutary lessons: the orthodox nature of the Roman Catholic Church, the damnable nature of dissent, and the terrible majesty of the church, together with its merciful and nurturing disposition'.[22] To that end, the sentencing

– unlike the trials, which were held in secret – was a big theatrical affair. Once the inquisition had concluded an adequate number of trials, they summoned the town's people to attend a public sermon, normally on a feast day and often at the local church. After delivering the sermon, the Inquisitor would receive oaths from the local leadership, including any royal representatives and any other power holders who would undertake to assist the inquisitors in their task. Only then were the sentences announced in a long and ceremonious manner.

The Church's power to limit freedom, both physical and mental, led to the perversion and manipulation of reality by the inquisitors. Of particular perfidy was the eliciting of confessions to deeds which never took place but which existed in certain public myths. The resulting scandal was that those very confessions extracted by force served further to implant absurd fantasies, public dread and vilification of certain groups. Thus Jews were accused, made to confess and 'found guilty' of ritual murder of Christian children, a blood libel which was rampant in Europe for centuries and still rears its ugly head in more primitive societies. Lepers in fourteenth-century France were accused and made to confess that they were planning to poison all the country's wells and rivers. Members of the order of the Knights Templar confessed to devil worship, homosexual practices and denial of the Church, leading to the suppression of the order. Through the Inquisition, the Catholic Church sought to and succeeded in imposing her moral order on significant groups which rejected her vision. It may be that the medieval Church's culpability in subjecting people, for no other reason than their belief, to torture, punishments and even death, extended beyond the subjects of her wrath. The Catholic Church did not invent unfair trials, unjust imprisonment or torture. The Church simply developed a concept of what the moral order of the world was and designed instruments which imposed this model of hers. Is the Inquisition not a blueprint for more recent absolutist regimes' actions to enforce their *weltanschauung* on citizens under their jurisdiction?

The Inquisition as a tool against heresy was only applicable to Catholics. However, as pressure from the Church forced many non-Christians to convert publicly whilst privately they retained their Jewish or Muslim faith, the Inquisition became the instrument for enforcing faithful adherence. Fifteenth-century Spain, under joint rulers Ferdinand and Isabella, produced a joint venture between the state and the Church which in contemporary terminology could be described as a franchise. The Spanish Kings applied to Pope Sixtus IV (1471–1484) for authorisation to set up an Inquisition. They evidently understood the power of a religious faith-based instrument of submission.

On 1 November 1478, Sixtus IV gave his assent to the request of the Spanish sovereigns and, in his bull *Exigit sincerae devotionis*, authorised them to appoint inquisitors. The Spanish Inquisition, which was administered by the Holy Office, had been in force for more than three hundred and fifty years when it was finally dismantled in 1834. Although it had no brief over Jews, only over Judaisers (those who had converted but continued to maintain their Jewish faith) the Inquisition led to the annihilation of Spanish Jewry: the option that the Jews were given was to convert or be deported. The Grand Inquisitor, the Dominican monk Tomás de Torquemada, who has since become a byword for torture in interrogation, considered the continued existence of Jews in Spain an encouragement for the *conversos* and he convinced the Spanish sovereigns to issue a decree in 1492 which brought about the expulsion of all the Jews who refused to convert.[i]

Inquisitors used to travel with companies of familiars, armed men who both protected the inquisitors and enforced their commands. Familiars were also spread all around the country as informal agents, who spied on their neighbours and denounced anyone they suspected of heresy. Property confiscated by the Spanish Inquisition produced income for the crown which, to a large extent, served as the source of funding for the apparatus of the Holy Office. The crown also benefited from the income it derived from composition fines. By paying a composition fine, those who were found guilty of heresy were able to buy back the status they had lost. Especially important was the ineligibility for various public posts of the victims and even their descendants. Another problem was the obligation to wear a *sambenito*, a tunic which publicly proclaimed their shame. Both of these could often be avoided by paying very hefty composition fines. It did not take long for inquisitors to target wealthy subjects only in order to find them guilty and confiscate their possessions. In other cases, wives and daughters of detainees were sexually abused by the inquisitors.

Inquisitorial processes began with a call to all to confess to any possible heresy and to denounce anyone they suspected of heresy. Those who were found guilty or who refused to confess were sentenced to death. Confessors were 'rewarded' with forced labour and confiscation of property. The accused were never told who their accusers were and they were not even allowed to know the 'rules of the game'; statutes and operational manuals of the Inquisition were all considered secret. Once jailed, a person was considered guilty. The purpose of the process was to elicit confessions. More than that, the Inquisition wanted to produce public confessions and public expressions of repentance. The role of the lawyer appointed for the accused was to persuade him to confess. If, however, the accused stubbornly refused to do this, he was tortured.[23]

The grand finale was the auto-da-fé, a public ceremony in which heresy was denounced and anyone found guilty of it was expected to

---

i   See also in Chapter 5.

confess, repent and receive punishment. The death penalty, however, was carried out by the civil authorities and not as part of the auto-da-fé. To that end, the Inquisition coordinated with the civil authority the setting up of scaffolds and the availability of executioners and their equipment including firewood and the garrotting machine. To prevent possible troublemakers from using the auto-da-fé as a stage to retract their previous confessions in public, some heretics had their tongues tied down. These grand Church–State co-productions were elaborate and pompous affairs which took place with the participation many public dignitaries. To terrorise as many people as possible, the public acts of faith were often held on Sundays to enable the entire local population to attend. Both Spain and Portugal exported the Inquisition to their colonies as an efficacious means of control. The last auto-da-fé took place in Mexico in 1850.

The State did not use the Church to deal with non-Church matters but the existence of a powerful law-enforcement agency in the form of the Inquisition, which in turn ran thousands of informants and created an atmosphere of doubt and uncertainty, served as a general control mechanism.

It is not surprising that the Church employed the mechanism of the Inquisition to deal with the most concerted and damning attack on her existence: the Protestant Reformation. Cardinal Caraffa convinced Pope Paul III (1534–1549) to set up a Roman Inquisition which would hunt down and eliminate heretics. Caraffa became one of six General Inquisitors with powers of arrest and interrogation covering the whole of Europe. A special prison was also constructed in Rome. Unlike the medieval Inquisition which was operated through many local independent inquisitors, the central tribunal, established by Paul III in 1542, was a centralised organ known as the 'Sacred Congregation of the Holy Roman and Universal Inquisition', or, in short, the 'Holy Office'. In 1555, the inquisitor, Cardinal Caraffa, became Pope Paul IV (1555–1559).

The Roman Inquisition is probably best known for its trial and burning of Giordano Bruno in 1600 and for its trial of Galileo in 1633. As pope, Paul utilised the Inquisition to harass the Jews under his jurisdiction. According to the Catholic Church, once a person was baptised it could not be undone. The Church did not care if baptism was enforced on babies snatched from their parents' arms: there was no way out. This was the basis upon which the Inquisition proceeded against Jews who had converted to Christianity under pressure and then continued to practice Jewish rituals in the privacy of their own homes.[24]

The Catholic Church established her instruments of investigation and torture. These were then adopted and adapted by several Catholic rulers for their own ends for a period of six hundred years from the end of the twelfth century to the end of the eighteenth century. In 2000, Pope John Paul II (1978–2005) apologised for the Inquisition, which he described as 'a sad chapter which Christians should ponder in an open spirit of repentance'. He asked for pardon 'for errors committed in the service of truth through use of methods that had nothing to do with the Gospel'. The Vatican, however, was eager to prove that the Inquisition was not as terrible as the general public believed it to have been. It commissioned research, which was published in June 2004, according to which 'only' one per cent of the one hundred and twenty-five thousand people tried by Church tribunals in Spain were actually executed. The Church also maintains that Church-initiated torture was hugely regulated and took place in the presence of a doctor for periods not exceeding fifteen minutes. Attempts – whatever their academic value is – to prove that the Inquisition was not as terrible as legend has portrayed it, may create more comfortable statistics but they cannot change the fact that the Church chose violence to further her cause.

Witches

Another shameful chapter in the Catholic Church's history is the hysteria surrounding witches. The Church may not have been alone in this but it certainly suited her overall plans: she wanted to control the supernatural and the miraculous. Her methods were nothing but efficient: anyone outside the Church who delved into these areas was likely to be tortured to elicit a confession, then executed. If people turned to witches for a good harvest, or for rain, they would not pray for them at Mass. The Church combated witches in the manner she combated heresy.

A special area of witchcraft which fascinated the Church was the witches' alleged power to induce impotence. Real and imagined remedies for impotence are still sought after today. It was a natural niche for witchcraft. The superstitious belief in witches and witchcraft was taken up by none other than the much-venerated St Thomas Aquinas. Thomas negated the thinking of sceptics of his time who suggested that there was no such thing as witchcraft. Unlike those who 'take the view that demons are only a delusion', Thomas stood on firm Catholic ground: 'The Catholic faith teaches us that demons are of consequence; that they can not only harm people but inhibit sexual intercourse'.[25]

Thirteenth- and fourteenth-century Church synods all over Europe issued condemnations of witchcraft and specifically condemned witches who induced impotence. Pope Innocent VIII (1484–1492) was clearly worried about witches' powers and in 1484 issued his *Summis desiderantes*, a papal bull encouraging witch-hunting.[26] In his bull he suggests that witches actually had sex with the devil and authorises the Inquisition to investigate and to punish them:

It has recently come to our ears, not without great pain to us, that … many persons of both sexes, heedless of their own salvation and forsaking the catholic faith, give themselves over to devils male and female, and by their incantations, charms, and conjurings, and by other abominable superstitions and sortileges, offences, crimes, and misdeeds, ruin and cause to perish the offspring of women, the foal of animals, the products of the earth, … and hinder men from begetting and women from conceiving, and prevent all consummation of marriage

… our beloved sons Henricus Institoris and Jacobus Sprenger, of the order of Friars Preachers, professors of theology, have been and still are deputed by our apostolic letters as inquisitors of heretical pravity, … we grant to the said inquisitors … or any other notary public who by them or by either of them shall have been temporarily delegated in the provinces, cities, dioceses, territories, and places aforesaid, [that they] may exercise against all persons, of whatsoever condition and rank, the said office of inquisition, correcting, imprisoning, punishing and chastising, according to their deserts, those persons whom they shall find guilty as aforesaid.[27]

In 1486, *Malleus Maleficarum* (The Hammer of the Magicians), a book which advocated the death penalty for witches, was published. The book's joint authors were the two Dominicans who, in 1484, were appointed by the Pope as inquisitors into heresy and witchcraft, Jacob Sprenger and Heinrich Institoris. These noble representatives of the Catholic Church introduced 'apportioned torture', endlessly protracted infliction of pain, to enable the inquisitors to extract the confessions and denunciations that they were after. Thomas Aquinas was one of this deadly duo's main theological sources.[28]

Colonialism

Often, missionaries were sent by the Church to baptise pagans with a sword in their hand. Such was the case when in 1200, Pope Innocent III proclaimed a crusade to enforce his religion on the pagan inhabitants of the Baltic area. The Teutonic Order was established in 1190 during the Third Crusade, which had failed to recapture Jerusalem from Saladin. Early in the thirteenth century, the Order was granted pagan Prussian lands. By this means, the secular ruler, Emperor Frederick II, and Pope Gregory IX who gave his blessing and approval, brought about the Christianisation of the Prussian tribes. Having successfully forced Christianity on these pagans, the Teutonic Order proceeded to wage their war of the Cross against the Lithuanians. Their wars, which started in 1283, lasted one hundred years. As is often the case, the war was not driven by religion but by political and economic interests. Religion, however, lent its fervour and intensified the campaign and thus Teutonic Knights went about killing and pillaging, burning farms and villages, taking the livestock and capturing those they did not kill.[29] As in other crusades, the papal blessing was the necessary lubricant which assisted in the recruitment of adventurous volunteers eager for plunder and grateful for the Church's indulgences. With the advent of colonial exploration and exploitation, collaboration in matters of conversion between the Church and secular leaders continued. When Spain and Portugal sent their respective navies to capture new lands, subdue their populations and steal their riches, the Pope determined which areas should be conquered by Spain and which should be colonised by Portugal. From the fifteenth century onwards, Portuguese and Spanish missionaries followed their countries' armies to Christianise the indigenous population of the newly conquered colonies.

Slavery was never considered unlawful, evil or immoral by the Catholic Church. She had to be dragged to condemn slavery in Second Vatican Council (1963–1965). As late as 1866, the Holy Office replied to a question that 'although the popes had left nothing untried by which slavery might be abolished, slavery per se was not repugnant to natural law or to divine law'.[30] To put this response in historical perspective, one should take into account that in 1814 Great Britain, in its endeavours to bring an end to slavery, had attempted to obtain a papal prohibition of the slave trade which the Pope (Pius VII) declined to issue. Judge John T. Noonan considers that it was 'British resolution and sea power that brought a stop to the business'.[31] The Pope did write letters disapproving of the trade to the monarchs of France, Portugal and Spain but continued to hold that slavery itself, which was approved of in the Old Testament, was not against the natural law. It continued to exist in the Papal States into the early nineteenth century. In 1907, the Congregation for the Propagation of the Faith issued a collection of rulings pertinent to Catholic missions, all of which 'had assumed that slavery in itself was a morally acceptable institution'.

Indeed, the Church, religious orders and even popes bought, sold and owned slaves. There are records which specify purchases of slaves made by Pope Gregory I (590–604), which indicate that the Pope took care to buy the slaves cheaply.[32] Detailed, itemised documents evidence the legality and care taken in the conveyance of slave contracts in a 'Christian Europe' well into the nineteenth century. And yet, in the thirteenth century, Bologna, Verona and several other Italian cities bought all the slaves within their cities and liberated them. Evidently, these cities considered slavery to be so abominable that they decided to abolish it within their jurisdiction. The values which guided these cities were Christian values but it was not the leadership of the Church which brought about the liberation of the slaves. The first time the Church clearly condemned slaveholding was seven hundred years after Bologna had legislated that 'no one bound by any slavery dare to dwell in the city and episcopate of Bologna, lest the mass of natural liberty ... could be again corrupted by any yeast of slavery'.[33]

Not only did religious orders own slaves but Church institutions even traded in them. In Portuguese Angola, the bishop, ecclesiastical officials and the Holy House of Mercy (*Santa Case de Misericórdia*) partook in the business. Elsewhere, squabbles about profits from the sale of slaves make clear that Catholic orders did not see anything wrong with the sale of slaves and their children, not even the separation of a mother and her four-year-old daughter. In a specific case which came up in Maryland in 1793, Jesuits who owned land and leased it to French Sulpicians argued whether revenue from the sale of slaves belonged to the landlord or to the lessees. A dispute in 1826, between the Archbishop of Baltimore and the Jesuits, provides documentary evidence of the substantial number of slaves Maryland Jesuits held at the time.[34]

Portuguese explorers first brought slaves to Europe as a 'souvenir' on their return from an early foray to Africa in 1441. Lacking a papal blessing, Prince Henry of Portugal sent emissaries to the Pope, who was so convinced by the importance of such exploratory wars that he granted complete forgiveness of sins to all of those who were engaged in the exploitation. The end of the fifteenth century and the early sixteenth century saw increased exploratory activity. Portugal established a presence in Brazil in 1500, reached India and China and established trading posts in Goa and Macau. Mauritius was taken in 1505 and Indonesia in 1511. The Spaniards concentrated their attack on the Americas, which they assailed with much energy. In 1511, they made Cuba a Spanish base for their campaigns. Mexico was conquered and subjugated in 1519–20 and in the decades that followed further areas in present-day Costa Rica, Honduras, Guatemala, Colombia, Venezuela and Peru were occupied. Soon the English, the Dutch and the French joined the fray. A long era of exploitation, which immensely enriched Europe, followed.

The colossal richness of raw materials found in the Americas meant that the local population, which was enslaved by the colonists, did not suffice for the massive task of bleeding the landscape of its natural resources. Slave-trading in Africa was not invented by the Europeans. The trade had long been in African and Muslim hands and was facilitated by greedy African chiefs who were paid by the slave-traders for the men they supplied. However, with the arrival of the colonial powers, this trade took an enormous leap. As a consequence, millions of Africans were transported as slaves directly from Africa to the Americas. Long after slave ownership was outlawed in Europe, it was still legal in the European-owned colonies. Slavery was finally abolished by the Christian world only in the nineteenth century. It is estimated that some fifteen million Africans had been seized for slavery in the Western hemisphere. Of these only eleven to twelve million actually landed alive.[35] Coffee, cocoa, sugar, tobacco, spices and various foods hitherto unknown in Europe, but above all massive quantities of gold and silver were looted by the colonial powers. Slaves were forced to work in the most atrocious conditions. Millions of Africans and millions of Indians died to produce wealth for Europe, a continent moulded by 'Christian values'.

Why was the Catholic Church involved? Why did the popes of the day endorse this violence? Not all did and, indeed, several popes did oppose slavery and the inhuman conditions under which the Christian kings and princes exploited the inhabitants of the newly found lands. Quite a few popes, however, gave their blessing to the exploitation. The Church's interests in approving the colonial exploits were twofold: the Catholic Portuguese and Spanish monarchs who approached popes and requested that they issue bulls granting them exploitation rights in the new lands, did so because of the perceived power of the papacy. Although the military and naval capacity was that of the secular powers, they respected the pope as an authority and at times as an adjudicator. It was naturally in the Church's interest to maintain that status. Had the Church been too demanding, making it too difficult for the colonisers to operate, the Church may have risked being sidelined. In addition to her interest in retention of power and status, the Church was doubtlessly attracted by the idea of converting the new populations to Christianity.

Spreading the Gospel is an important tenet of Christianity. Alexander VI, in a bull issued to the monarchs of Spain in 1493, wrote:

> Among other works well pleasing to the Divine Majesty and cherished of our heart, this assuredly ranks highest, that in our times especially the Catholic faith and the Christian religion be exalted and be everywhere increased and spread, that the health of souls be cared for and that barbarous nations be overthrown and brought to the faith itself.[36]

In the deal between the Church and the colonial powers, the Church gave her blessing to the conquests and granted permission to nominate cardinals, bishops and abbots; importantly the Church also granted permission to collect tithes, designate where missions were to be established and determine boundaries for Episcopal sees. In return, Spain and Portugal established churches and monasteries in the newly conquered territories and lent their military might to support the missionaries in their Christianising activities.

For the colonial administrations, a most significant advantage of the Church–colonial collaboration was the spiritual subjugation of the natives to the white man's rule. The missionaries acted as an additional long arm to the central colonial power base, both as points of authority and as providers of social services. As a result, Christianity became one of the main shapers of colonialism. The price in human rights which the Church was willing to pay for the conversion of the native populations was high.

Various papal bulls served as holy enablers of Portuguese and Spanish colonialism. In a typical papal license, the pope would grant the king the right to 'invade, search out, capture, vanquish and subdue all Saracens and pagans whatsoever, ... and the kingdoms, dukedoms ... dominions, possessions, and all movable and immovable goods whatsoever held and possessed by them and to reduce their persons to perpetual slavery'.[37] In 1452, Pope Nicholas V issued *Dum diversas*, which granted King Alfonso of Portugal generous rights to pillage and subdue populations. He was given indefinite powers to enslave all pagans and appropriate their lands and goods. This bull was followed in 1455 by *Romanus pontifex*, a papal bull which settled colonial boundaries dispute between Castile and Portugal. Nicholas was evidently not put off by the slaughter caused as long as it furthered the cause of evangelisation:

> We have lately heard, not without great joy and gratification how our beloved son, the noble personage Henry, infante of Portugal ... after many wars had been waged ... against the enemies and infidels aforesaid, not without the greatest labours and expense, and with dangers and loss of life and property, and the slaughter of very many of their natural subjects, ... growing more zealous in prosecuting this his so laudable and pious purpose, has peopled with orthodox Christians certain solitary islands in the ocean sea, and has caused churches and other pious places to be there founded and built, in which divine service is celebrated.[38]

Not only was the Portuguese king granted ownership of men and chattels in these overseas lands, the Pope virtually ceded his role in these colonies to the secular authority of the king who 'may send over to them any ecclesiastical persons whatsoever'. These men were authorised by the Pope to hear confessions, give absolutions and administer ecclesiastical sacraments. Above all, it is significant that the Pope, the spiritual head of the Christian world, handed out licenses to kill. Neither Portuguese, nor Spanish, nor any other head of state, asked the Church for permission to go to war but many of them considered it useful to have the Church's blessing. The Church, evidently, had no moral qualms in granting this.

One year later, in 1456, Nicholas' successor, Pope Calixtus III, issued *Inter caetera*, which reconfirmed the grants of *Romanus pontifex* and additionally granted spiritual rights in all lands acquired and to be acquired to the Portuguese military Order of Christ. In a typical move of *realpolitik* to prevent conflicts of interest, the grandmastership of the Order was permanently united with the crown of Portugal in 1551.[39]

In 1481, Pope Sixtus IV issued *Aeterni Regis* which re-enforced the previous bulls of 1455 and 1456, adding West African Portuguese interests to the list of lands and populations that Portugal was permitted to control. After several pro-Portuguese popes, the first pope to favour Spain was Alexander VI. Alexander issued a series of bulls at the behest of the Spanish monarchs Ferdinand and Isabella, including *Inter caetera* of 1493 which gave Spain virtually a free run. The Pope, who was delighted by Ferdinand and Isabella's colonial activities, granted them ownership of anything which had not been previously taken by other Christians. Non-Christians, evidently, had no right to own their own land.[40]

Several months later, the Pope further extended the rights of Spain in his bull *Dudum siquidern*. The Spanish monarchs were powerful enough to secure whatever papal document they wanted. The pope's role, in their eyes, was to facilitate their rule and serve their interests. Thus when Spain wanted fully to control religious activities in the newly acquired territories, a dutiful pope, Julius II, issued *Universalis ecclesiae*. In this bull of 1508, he granted the Spanish King the right to collect taxes in the Americas in perpetuity. He also decreed that no one had the right to build a church or a monastery in the new lands without authority from the Spanish monarchs, thereby transferring Church jurisdiction to the Spanish monarch.

Columbus returned from his first trip (which did not include priests) filled with a desire to convert the Indians to Christianity. In December 1492, he reported accordingly to the Kings of Spain: 'Your Highnesses may have great joy of them, for soon you will have made them into Christians.' This pious Christian sentiment was, however, inspired more by the plentiful supplies of gold and slaves than by any moral vision. The Spanish monarchs were promised that they would 'succeed in converting to our Holy Faith a multitude of peoples while gaining great domains and wealth', as Columbus promised 'there are in these lands great quantities of gold'. Several years later, Columbus wrote: 'from here one might send, in the name of the Holy Trinity, as many slaves as could be sold, as well as a quantity of Brazil [timber]'.[41] By his second expedition, he was accompanied by priests who immediately began to convert the local Indians.

Despite the priests' fervour, many locals objected and others only converted outwardly whilst still retaining their old beliefs inwardly. The Indians, however, were soon given a lesson in the loving nature of 'their' new religion. According to one report, after one conversion ceremony, the men left the chapel and 'flung the images on the ground, covered them with a heap of earth, and pissed upon it'. In punishment for desecrating Christian images, Bartholomé, Columbus's brother who was Viceroy and governor of the islands, had the Indians burned alive.[42] In many cases the Indians were obliged to attend a weekly service and their children were made to attend daily catechism classes. Adults in authority were obliged to be baptised. The teaching was concentrated on rituals and the repetitive reading of prayers which the Indians, of course, did not understand. In 1562, two Indian youths in a village in the province of Yucatan came across a cave containing idols and some human skulls. The Franciscan friars were furious when they heard about the cave. At first the Indians did not understand what all the fuss was about as they had, after all, attended all of the religious sessions required of them by the Franciscans. They freely admitted to their habit of worshipping the idols 'so that it would rain and that they would give them much corn and so that they would kill many deer'. The Franciscans reverted to good old Church inquisition methods. Hundreds of Indians were rounded up for questioning and under the supervision of the friars, they were subjected to the garrucha torture. An eye-witness reported:

> When the Indians confessed to having so many idols, the friars proceeded to string up many of the Indians, having tied their wrists together with cord, and thus hoisted them from the ground, telling them that they must confess all the idols they had, and where they were. The Indians continued saying they had no more ... and so the friars ordered great stones attached to their feet, and so they were left to hang ... they were flogged as they hung there, and had burning wax splashed on their bodies.[43]

The matter did not end there. The Church, together with the secular governor, produced an auto-da-fé. It was presided over by Don Diego Quijada, the head of the secular government of the province of Yucatan, who arrived for the occasion with an armed Spanish escort unit and Fr Diego de Landa, Bishop of Yucatan. The Indians, who were already wounded by the whipping and tortures during their questioning, were now tied to a whipping post and given two hundred lashes each. This punishment was also meted out to children who had not betrayed their parents and reported their idolatry to the priests. Many were punished with up to ten years of servitude to the friars or to others. All of the idols and jewelled skulls of the ancestors were burned.[44]

There was a natural conflict of interest between the new settlers and the missionaries. The settlers came from Europe to the new lands for one reason alone: the booty. Anything which could further this objective and enrich them was considered just. Enslaving the local population was a means to that end. The settlers, therefore, had no interest in convincing Indians to accept Christianity, if that would result in Indians thereby retaining their freedom. Indeed, it did not take long for additional conflicts to arise between missionaries and settlers. Missionaries, who were appalled at the way the local population was treated by their new masters, reported to Spain and attempted to put a stop to such brutal and inhuman exploitation. On the other hand, the missionaries thought nothing of flogging Indians to force them into their weekly church service and using violent means to impose Christian rituals upon them. The settlers who were not worried by the questionable morality of the missionaries were, however, annoyed at them for damage caused to their workforce. Moreover, many Indians simply fled from the tyranny of the friars and their workforce was lost to the settlers. Conflicts also arose between the different Christian orders. Some of the debates reflected plain struggles for power, domains and in certain cases wealth. Priests of one order, which had built a network of churches and monasteries, would not be eager to welcome regular priests or individuals from another order.

In 1622, Pope Gregory XV established the Congregation of Propaganda Fide,[ii] charged with exercising control over all Catholic missionary activities.

Modern Attitude to Colonialism and Slavery

In *In plurimis*, an encyclical on the abolition of slavery addressed to the Bishops of Brazil and promulgated in May 1888, Leo condemned slavery. In this encyclical, Leo wrote about leaders of expeditions which took place at the 'end of the fifteenth century, at which time ... States were ... anxious to increase their empire', who 'Christians though they were, were wickedly making use of their arms and ingenuity, for establishing and imposing slavery on these innocent nations'. The Pope was clearly well informed about the practicalities of the slave-trade.[45] He knew what Columbus and other explorers had done. By explaining the 'need' to extract precious metals, he seems to accept that the explorers had a reason for their enslavement of the Africans and the Indians. The Pope does not cast doubt on the right of the European Christians to invade new lands, to steal their gold and silver and to exploit the local population as a labour force. He is simply uncomfortable about slavery. As more than one of Leo's predecessors had already granted licenses to the kings of Spain and Portugal to embark on their missions, Leo could not very well have objected. The Pope pointed out in *In plurimis* that the Church

has deprecated any precipitate action in securing the manumission and liberation of the slaves, because that would have entailed tumults and wrought injury, as well as to the slaves themselves as to the commonwealth, but with singular wisdom she has seen that the minds of the slaves

---

ii   The Sacred Congregation for the Propagation of the Faith was renamed in 1967 and is now called The Sacred Congregation for the Evangelisation of Peoples.

should be instructed through her discipline in the Christian faith, and with baptism should acquire habits suitable to the Christian life.[46]

Safely tucked into this anti-slavery encyclical, the Pope instructs slaves to stay put lest they damage the Capitalist system. Moreover, he more than hints at the inferiority of the slaves who seemed to need additional tutoring before they reached the heights of 'Christian life'. In great humility, the Pope also pats the Church, himself and his predecessors on the back for their 'singular wisdom'. In fact, not only should slaves accept their own exploitation but, in his encyclical on Socialism (1878) the Pope instructs that the poor in general should not envy the rich but be contented with their lot.[47] Slavery was not yet totally eradicated and the Pope describes the Church's attitude to a possible rebellion by slaves. The slaves, so he instructed, should never set themselves against their lords or even consider disobedience to them.[48]

In 1890, in response to reports by missionaries and others about the atrocities which took place in Africa, Pope Leo XIII (1878–1903) issued a condemnation of slavery:

> We have taken every occasion to openly condemn this gloomy plague of slavery ... How horrible it is to recall that almost 400,000 Africans are forcefully taken away each year from their villages. Bound and beaten, they are transported to a foreign land and sold like cattle. ... We have delegated the task of going to the principal countries of Europe to ... Cardinal Lavigerie ... to show how shameful this base dealing is and to incline the leaders and citizens to assist this miserable race.[49]

This encyclical was addressed only to the Catholic Missionaries in Africa. It is more of an apologia aimed at proving to the missionaries that the Church and the Pope of the time were doing something for the suffering slaves. If the subject was so close to his heart, why did the Pope not address the encyclical to the bishops in the colonising countries? Why was it not read from all of the pulpits of Catholic churches worldwide? Was it not the Catholic population which the Pope should have mobilised against slavery? In this encyclical, Leo refers to meetings in Brussels and Paris. The Pope may have sent Cardinal Lavigerie to various European countries but he evidently was not tough enough with the Catholic king of Belgium. It was finally an international scandal which forced the Belgian king to give up his lucrative colony.[50] The Pope, who theoretically objected to slavery, could have threatened to excommunicate the king. He didn't. Maintaining that 'the Church has cut out and destroyed this dreadful curse of slavery', the Pope made sure that this very convenient and profitable boat was not rocked. The Vatican supported theoretical equality but it was, in truth, aligned with the ruling classes.

Only two years later, on the fourth centenary of Columbus's trip, Pope Leo XIII chose to celebrate colonial exploration. 'Columbus is ours', the Pope boasted and sang his praises.[51] Leo chose to disregard the shameful history of Columbus and in *Quarto abeunte saeculo* he depicts Columbus as almost flawless.[52] The Pope of 1892 was willing to overlook the abuse, exploitation, torture and death of millions of Africans and Indians because they were given access to Christianity. He actually describes the process as extending the 'Christian name and the benefits of Christian charity to the West'. What charity is the Pope talking about? Sounding more like a marketing executive the Pope explains how fortunate the Church was to obtain access to new members at a time when Luther caused the schism and the loss to the Church of those who became Protestants:

> Columbus threw open America at the time when a great storm was about to break over the Church. As far, therefore, as it is lawful for man to divine from events the ways of Divine Providence, he seemed to have truly been born, by a singular provision of God, to remedy those losses which were awaiting the Catholic Church on the side of Europe.[53]

The Pope was willing to accept the price which the Africans and Indians had paid. Worse, in this misleading encyclical, the Pope brazenly makes the false claim that popes had done 'the best for the slaves'. The truth is different. Eugene IV, in his *Sicut dudum* bull of 1435, did indeed condemn enslavement in the Canary Islands.[54] Eugene, however, referred to those slaves who had been converted to Catholicism or promised baptism and were then taken from their homes and enslaved. Apparently the Pope had no issue with the enslavement of blacks who did not accept Christianity. One hundred years later, Pope Paul III in his bull *Sublimis Deus* (1537) condemned the maltreatment of Indians – which he described as Satan's doing:

> the enemy of the human race ... has stirred up some of his allies who, desiring to satisfy their own avarice, are presuming to assert far and wide that the Indians of the West and South who have come to our notice in these times be reduced to our service like brute animals, under the pretext that they are lacking the Catholic faith. And they reduce them to slavery treating them with afflictions they would scarcely use with brute animals.[55]

And yet, that same pope did not denounce enslavement right under his nose, in Europe.

Leo maintains that 'Whoever compare the pagan and the Christian attitude toward slavery will easily come to the conclusion that the one was marked by great cruelty and wickedness, and the other by great gentleness and humanity'. Was this baseless papal statement meant to belittle the enormous suffering of those colonised and enslaved by the Christian world?

A curious attempt to explain abuse of Indians by their Christian colonisers was made by Leo's successor, Pope Pius X (1903–1914) in *Lacrimabili statu* (1912), an encyclical addressed to the Archbishops and Bishops of Latin America. In this encyclical Pius makes the following observation:

> For, as these places are subjected to burning southern sun, which casts a languor into the veins and as it were, destroys the vigour of virtue, and as they are far removed from the habits of religion and the vigilance of the State, and in measure even from civil society, it easily comes to pass that those who have not already come there with evil morals soon begin to be corrupted, and then, when all bonds of right and duty are broken, they fall away into hateful vices. Nor in this do they take any pity on the weakness of sex or age, so that we are ashamed to mention the crimes and outrages they commit in seeking out and selling women and children, wherein it may be truly said that they have surpassed the worst examples of pagan iniquity.[56]

Perhaps we must be grateful that the Pope did not declare this scientific observation regarding the impact of the sun on human morality to be infallible teaching. His faithful bishops were, however, so impressed that they repeated this dictum in their sermons. However he may have reached his conclusion, it is noteworthy that as late as 1912, a pope chose to seek mitigating circumstances when referring to the outrageous treatment of Indians resulting from colonial rule, which he himself defined as a 'grave crime'. In fact, this encyclical was issued by the Pope only after pressure from the Church in Latin America. The Church had known about the history of abuse of Indians for hundreds of years and yet the Pope writes that he 'hesitated for some time to give credence to such atrocities' and that he 'pondered long in this matter' before he issued his encyclical in which he congratulates the governments in South America which 'are making every endeavour to remove this outstanding disgrace'. He suggests that the Church might lend her hand in the campaign against slavery and urges the bishops to continue doing their best. The underlying values which brought about the abolition of slavery may be Judaeo-Christian values of love and charity, but the Catholic Church as an institution not only had a supporting role in the establishment of colonialism and slavery (its by-product) she also did not use her power to abolish slavery. In Mexico, in 1543, Bartolomé de las Casas refused the sacraments to colonists who did not liberate the Indians.[57] The Church could have multiplied the effect of this priest's action by instructing all of her priests to act similarly, by excommunicating anyone who was involved in slavery. She didn't.

Missionaries

Out of deep faith missionaries leave the comfort of their homes and the safety of their countries to preach the religion they believe in. In most cases they also undertake certain social, educational or medical work, often acting in difficult conditions. Thus, organised in different orders and structures, the various Christian Churches send missionaries to third-world countries. Some go for a limited tour of duty, but many spend most of their lives in their missions. Christians believe that it is their role to spread the gospel. The morality and ethics of such evangelising, especially where the military or state law force populations to receive catechetical instruction, is doubtful. Some Christians believe that the advantage of seeing the truth is so great that the means by which this is achieved are almost irrelevant. Most will disagree with this view. This, however, is what took place in the colonial missions.

Voluntary teaching or nursing are noble and positive acts and, as such, they are praiseworthy. The picture, however, is somewhat muddied when the population in the under-developed countries is given no choice: the only school on offer in the area is a Church school, with a Church curriculum and a Church programme. One is taught how to read but the book is the Bible or a prayer book or some other Church-approved text. Through the commendable act of teaching, the population, which has no access to other sources of information or scholarship, is being indoctrinated. Doubtless this is preferable to illiteracy. The missionaries' choice of texts can neither be held against them nor against those who send them. And yet, it must be clear that even the non-religious good work carried out by the missionaries has a religious agenda. The underlying message to the recipients of the missionaries' ministry is that everything which is good in their lives comes from the Church. It becomes even more complicated when one considers the history of the missionary network which developed as a by-product of the colonial drive. Missionaries were expected by both colonial administrators and settlers to be loyal to the white man's interests. Invariably this led to conflicts in the many cases of abuse, exploitation and outright cruelty by the white men. Indeed, missionaries were often the source of information received in Europe about the cruelty of the colonisers. Some, like the sixteenth-century Dominican friar las Casas, who started out as a wealthy settler and slave-owning friar, became militant advocates for the cause of the indigenous population. But the basic teaching of the Church, as has been shown, is that of obedience to the ruler and she categorically prohibits rebellion, whatever the suffering of the slaves or the abused. Such teaching was, understandably, suitable to the needs of the colonial administrators who were, therefore, willing to swallow some lobbying by the missionaries for better conditions for the oppressed and the exploited. According to Hanson, post-Revolution French governments 'even the most anticlerical, valued the Church principally for its rural clerics who could be sent forth as missionary shock troops for colonial expansion'.[58] Similarly, the contribution of the Catholic Church to the Belgian colonial success in Rwanda has been described: 'Belgium will not find more open, understanding collaborators, amongst the natives, than the 20,000 Neophytes, whose allegiance has been secured by the White Fathers'.[59]

Rwanda, which achieved its independence in 1962, was, until 1916, a German colony and was taken over by Belgium during the First World War. Both German and Belgian colonial administrations found it convenient to leave areas such as education to the Catholic missionaries. The Church, in return, preached obedience to the rulers – a service much appreciated by the colonial powers. Missionary activity in Rwanda began with Catholic stations established by the *Society of Our Lady of Africa*, also known as the *White Fathers*. A letter written in 1913 by Dr Kandt, the German colonial administrator to Monseigneur Hirth, the vicar in charge of the *Society of Our Lady of Africa*'s activities in Rwanda, is quite blunt about the military value of the missionaries' work:

> Sir,
>
> The missions that you have founded in the north of Rwanda contribute a good deal to the pacification of that district. They facilitate substantially the task of government. The influence of your missionaries has saved us the necessity of undertaking military expeditions.[60]

The missionaries' strategy was to concentrate their attention on converting the leadership and elites; once this had been achieved, the rest would have to follow. Such a policy, as a result, led to a Church which, rather than being on the side of the destitute and needy, was linked to the better off. When the *White Fathers* embarked on their conversion programme in Rwanda in 1931, and in order to obliterate the local *Kubandwa* religion, they built their missions on land sacred to the *Kubandwa* and organised the public burning of religious objects used in *Kubandwa* rituals. Public posters called for the denunciation of converts who had lapsed. The missionaries may not have punished the lapsed as their predecessors had, but the Church did not shirk from encouraging people to betray their friends and family members. In Burundi, the Catholic missions arranged for the colonial administration to put a stop to the *Muganuro*, the local religious festival. In their quest to spread the gospel, the Catholic missionaries even attempted to fight off other Christian Churches. They succeeded in converting the son of Rwanda's King Musinga and then used their influence on the Belgian colonial administration to have the king deposed and his newly Catholic son, Rudahigwa, installed instead. To prevent the deposed king from reclaiming power, the missionaries arranged to have Musinga exiled. Similar policies that ensured that only converts to Catholicism received powerful positions, resulted in the conversion of many chiefs who only wanted to retain their power. A Belgian administrative inquiry held in 1929 in Burundi concluded that 'belonging to or leaning toward the Roman Catholic faith is a sufficient criterion to remain a chief'.[61]

Before the Church developed the concept of ethnicity in Rwanda, Tutsi and Hutu co-existed in peace, inter-married and shared a language and religion. Church schools developed the categorisation of the Rwandan people into racial classes, building up the Tutsi as a natural ruling class over the Hutu. Such concepts of ethnicity not only suited European ideas of racial differentiation, but they also suited the colonial powers who found such classification useful for their control of the population. They developed the feeling of superiority in the Tutsis on one hand and resentment of the Tutsi by the Hutu on the other.

In 1994, one million Tutsis were massacred by the Rwandan army and militia, largely Hutus. Timothy Longman, professor of political science and former consultant for 'Human Rights Watch on Rwanda, Burundi and Congo', speaks of clergy turning in parishioners in hiding, even participating in death squads. The Catholic archbishop himself, a close friend of the president, is said to have turned people (nuns and priests) who were gathered at the cathedral at Kabgayi over to a death squad. Longman maintains that the Churches were complicit because

> they helped to create and maintain the authoritarian and divided society that made genocide possible and because the entanglement of the Churches with the state made the Churches partners in state policy.[62]

Similarly, the French researcher, Charles de Lespinay, concluded that:

> it still appears, at first blush, that religious officials, backed by their respective Churches, were directly involved, either through complicity or incompetence, in the promotion of criminal ideologies. A clear cut, overt condemnation of all the massacres, regardless of their classification, and without the usual confusion between assassins and victims, is still awaited from the Christian Churches, especially the Catholic Church.[63]

Although Catholic missions were not the only active missions in Rwanda, others were not as widespread. As a result, Rwanda is now predominantly Catholic. Neither the policy of the missionaries in befriending the ruler, rather than the people, nor the building up of the Tutsi as a ruling class and then changing sides to the Hutu, could have taken place without the knowledge of the Vatican. Even in the sixteenth century, when communication and travel were less easy than they are today, systematic information about atrocities in the colonies reached Europe.

All this happened in order to spread the gospel. Undoubtedly, the Vatican had no interest in anyone's massacre. The Vatican's representatives, however, created the setting and the Vatican's local partners did the deeds. Why was the Archbishop of Rwanda not called to order by his Church superiors? Why did the Vatican not use all its political clout and its media management to put an end to the deteriorating situation and eventually to the killings? Is the Church responsible for the actions of Father Wenceslas Munyeshyaka, who 'was seen separating Tutsi from Hutu and, day after day, turning the former over to death squads'? There are numerous testimonies according to which Munyeshyaka left people to starve to death and demanded sex in return for sparing people from slaughter.[64] Should the Catholic Church in France have shielded this priest who fled there attempting to escape justice? The Church has an odd willingness to accept evil, mixed with a policy of long-term support for evil-doers.

Croatia

Catholic willingness to use force to further the cause of evangelisation was no more apparent than during the Second World War in Croatia. In the years 1941 to 1945, twenty-seven thousand Gypsies and thirty thousand Jews were exterminated in the Independent State of Croatia; four hundred and eighty-seven thousand Orthodox Serbs were massacred and hundreds of thousands were forcefully converted to Catholicism.[65] What did the Pope know? Did he approve? Did he do anything to stop it from happening? How has the Vatican dealt with the culpability in the post-War period?

The Treaty of Versailles, which established the post-First World War division and arrangements in Europe, created the Kingdom of Yugoslavia. The new state contained substantial Catholic Croatian and Orthodox Serb populations, and additionally other religious and ethnic groups. These national, ethnic and religious distinctions fed strong emotions and in the years leading to the Second World War, the Serb majority in Yugoslavia treated the Croat minority as second-rate citizens. They were discriminated against in education and the professions. The Ustasha, established by former Austrian officer Slavko Kvaternik and Ante Pavelic, was a movement whose aim was to oppose the newly established State of Yugoslavia by any means, peaceful or other. Ustati means 'to rise', 'to leap to one's feet' and the Ustasha had been fighting to make a stand for an independent Croat state since 1919. Pavelic found the Fascist Italian leader Mussolini sympathetic to his cause and in 1929 concluded a cooperation agreement with him. The Ustasha were provided by Italy with training camps for sabotage and disruption agents and were permitted to use Radio Bari for propaganda broadcasts. After the murder of the king of Yugoslavia, Alexander, in 1934, Pavelic was tried in absentia and found guilty for his role in plotting the murder by both French and Yugoslav courts. Neither countries managed to lay a hand on Pavelic and he thus escaped the death to which he had been sentenced.

From its foundation the Ustasha organisation, which spread Fascist propaganda and called for the extermination of Jews and the conversion of Serbs, had close ties with Roman Catholic clergy. Practical execution of their plans was often channelled through *Catholic Action*, the lay network, defined by Pope Pius XI in 1927 as 'the participation of the laity in the apostolate of the hierarchy'. Catholic monasteries were used as clandestine headquarters for the Ustasha movement. Some of the priests even boasted publicly about their close connections with the group. In 1938, on a trip to the Vatican, the Archbishop of Sarajevo, Dr Ivan Saric, met the fugitive from justice, Pavelic, in the Basilica of St Peter's. This clergyman was so enamoured by the Ustasha leader that three years later he would publish a poem, 'Ode to the Chieftain', about this encounter.[66]

In April 1941 Yugoslavia was attacked by Germany, which divided the country and enabled the Ustasha movement in Croatia, headed by Pavelic, to create the Independent state of Croatia (Nezavisna Drzava Hrvatska or NDH), a Nazi sympathising and collaborating state. The new state encompassed Croatia, Slovenia, Bosnia, Herzegovina and part of Dalmatia. Some areas on the Dalmatian coast were, under pressure from Germany, transferred to Italy by Croatia in May 1942. The new Ustasha regime immediately set to its tasks, central to which was their wish to rid Croatia of non-Catholic elements, as their Minister of Education and Culture, Mile Budak, succinctly put it:

> The basis for the Ustasha movement is religion. For minorities such as the Serbs, Jews, and Gypsies, we have three million bullets. We will kill a part of the Serbs. Others we will deport, and the rest we will force to accept the Roman Catholic Religion. Thus the new Croatia will be rid of all Serbs in its midst in order to be 100% Catholic within 10 years.[67]

The main religion of the Serbs was also Christianity, but they belonged to the Eastern Orthodox Church. Croatia at that time had a population of 6.7 million, of which 3.3 million were Catholics, 2.2 million Orthodox Serbs, seven hundred and fifty thousand Muslims and forty-five thousand Jews. Whereas the general attitude of the Croatian Government was that Croatian equals Catholic, they made an exception for the Muslims. Taking advantage of this, the Nazis were able to establish Muslim Waffen

SS units.[iii] The Catholic Croats wanted to get rid of the Orthodox Church and the Jews. A special government department, headed by Franciscan priest Dionizije Juric, devised the conversion plan. In November 1941, the Catholic Bishops, in a conference chaired by Archbishop Alojzije Stepinac, decided on the forcible conversion of Serbs. Catholic bishops and priests competed in converting large numbers of Serbs and in looting property of the Orthodox Church. A committee comprising Archbishop Stepinac, the Bishop of Senj and the Apostolic Administrator, was in charge. The official Bishopric paper published the Apostolic Administrator's directive, according to which:

> Special offices and Church committees must be created immediately for those to be converted. … Our universal mission, the salvation of souls and the greatest glory of our Lord Jesus Christ, is involved in this issue. Our work is legal because it is in accord with official Vatican policy, with the directives of the Saintly Congregation of the Cardinals for the Eastern Church … and with the circular of the Government of the Independent State of Croatia of July 30, 1941, which desires that members of the Eastern Orthodox Church be converted to the Catholic faith.[68]

Less than three years later, in May 1944, Stepinac was able to report his success to the Pope – the conversion of two hundred and forty thousand Eastern Orthodox Christians to the Roman Catholic Church.[69] As is evident from internal Nazi documentation, the Croat methods managed to shock even the Nazis, who considered them too sadistic. Nazi Germany was also aware of the fact that the issue to the Ustasha was Catholicism and not Serb ethnicity. Serbs who converted were left in peace.[70] Fifty-six years later, on 3 October 1998, Pope John Paul II travelled to the Republic of Croatia and beatified Alojzije Stepinac. This was not the first honour bestowed on him for services to the Catholic Church: in 1953, whilst serving a sixteen-year prison term set by a Yugoslav war crimes tribunal, Pope Pius XII made Stepinac a Cardinal. Stepinac, Archbishop of Zagreb, military vicar to the armed forces and the Ustasha, was the most powerful Catholic in Croatia. A diary note made on 28 March 1941, two weeks before the new Croatia was established, gives insight into Stepinac's thinking:

> All in all, Croats and Serbs are of two worlds, north pole and south pole; they will never be able to get together unless by a miracle of God. The schism [Eastern Orthodoxy] is the greatest curse in Europe, almost greater

---

iii   In Yugoslavia the Nazis recruited Muslims into two dedicated SS divisions: the Bosnian 13th Waffen Hanjar (Sword) SS division, and the Albanian Skanderbeg 21st Waffen SS division. More than twenty thousand Muslims members of the Hanjar SS Division fought against Yugoslav partisans led by General Tito, and carried out police and security details in Fascist Hungary.

than Protestantism. Here there is no moral, no principles, no truth, no justice, no honesty.[71]

Now, with the power of the state behind him, the Archbishop was able to realise his dreams. And, indeed, the Catholic Church set out energetically to force Serbs to convert to Catholicism. The 'gentle' approach promised Serbs a better life as Catholics. Not only would their souls be saved, but they would also be allowed to keep their houses and even to prosper. The alternative was obvious: resisting conversion would result in losing one's home. In 1941, the Bishop of Djakovo published a leaflet to that effect:

A FRIENDLY SUGGESTION

The Lord Jesus Christ said that there shall be one pasture and one shepherd. This unity must be carried out in the Independent State of Croatia. Inhabitants of the Greek-Eastern faith, hear this friendly advice! The Bishop of Djakovo has already received thousands of citizens in the Holy Catholic Church, and these citizens received certificates of honesty from the State authorities. Follow these brothers of yours, and report as soon as possible for rechristening into the Catholic Church. As Catholics, you will be allowed to remain in your homes. You may increase your property in peace and rear your children for God and for the Independent State of Croatia. In the Catholic Church you will ensure the saving of your immortal souls.[72]

It is well documented that many of the clergy not only incited but actually participated in atrocities against the Serb non-Catholic population. According to Italian historian, Carlo Falconi, 'it is almost impossible to imagine a Ustasha punitive expedition without a priest at its head spurring it on, and usually a Franciscan'.[73] The Yugoslav State Commission for Investigating War Crimes has collated testimonies in hundreds and hundreds of files. What is evident is that Catholic priests were instrumental in both forceful conversions of Serbs and even more shockingly in the brutal torture of Serbs. One of them was a priest by the name of Ante Djuric who imprisoned Serbs in his stable and barn where he tortured them with hunger and whipping until they accepted Catholicism. He ordered slaughter and plunder and sent hundreds of Serbs to the concentration camp in Kostajnica.

In village after village, Serbs were assembled by the Catholic priests, accompanied by Ustasha soldiers, and were told by the priests that unless they converted to Catholicism they would be taken to concentration camps to be killed. Where 'necessary', they would be killed on the spot.[74] The Independent State of Croatia maintained several concentration camps. The largest concentration camp, *Jasenovac*, was for some time run by a former Franciscan friar, Miroslav Filipovic, who confessed in his trial to having personally supervised the murders of thousands of Serbs, Jews and Gypsies. When Filipovic was replaced in 1943, the next concentration camp commandant was another former priest, Ivica Brkljacic. Not only Franciscans were involved. A Jesuit priest, Dr Dragutin Kamber, ordered the killing of three hundred Orthodox Serbs in Doboj and the court-martial of two hundred and fifty others, most of whom were shot.[75] The archive of the Italian Foreign Ministry has photographic records of such atrocities; photographs of the victims and their remains along with pictures of the knives, axes and meat hooks which were used by the perpetrators.

There were also financial benefits. Property of the Eastern Orthodox Church was confiscated and transferred to the Catholic Church; a substantial share went to the Order of the Franciscans who were instrumental in the enforcement of conversion and in the extermination of Serbs. After the liberation of Zagreb, thirty-six boxes of gold (including bracelets, earrings and gold teeth), stolen by the Ustasha, were found under the crypt of the Franciscan monastery.

Throughout those years, in which the Independent State of Croatia murdered hundreds of thousands of people and forced others to convert to Catholicism, its partner in crime was the Catholic Church. The Primate of Croatia during those years, Archbishop Alojzije Stepinac, did not participate in any of the outrageous actions. However, he and his bishops, by showering support and admiration on the Ustasha and its leader and by not standing up for the rights of non-Catholics, share the responsibility for what was done in the name of Catholicism. Although Stepinac welcomed the Ustasha, was instrumental in their rule and supported them throughout, he began to feel uncomfortable with events, as more and more people were being converted at gun-point. He boasted about the success in his reports to the Vatican, but some of his sermons contained veiled protests against the extreme methods used by the Ustasha. He did not, however, instruct the clergy to refrain from their terrorising actions. Although Pavelic was annoyed by some of Stepinac's protests and at one point wanted him removed, he continued to consider him to be a safe pair of hands. When, at the end of the War, Pavelic himself had to flee Croatia, he suggested that Stepinac take over from him. Stepinac refused the offer.

The pope at the time was Pius XII. It is highly unlikely that he was comfortable with the means and with what was done in the name of his Church, but approving of the ends, he did not object. An important blow to the Eastern Orthodox Church, for many years a thorn in the side of the Vatican, and the conversion of hundreds of thousands to Catholicism, had the Pope's support. In November 1939, the Pope addressed a group of Croat pilgrims headed by the Croat primate, Stepinac, and spoke of Croatia as 'the outpost of Christianity'. The Pope seems thereby to define

Christians who are not members of his Church, those who are members of the schismatic Orthodox Church, as not Christian. This would have tragic impact in the years to come. Throughout the War, and during the time when, in the name of Catholicism, hundreds of thousands were massacred, the Pope did not once publicly mention Croatia.

Is it at all feasible that the Vatican was not informed? Croatia bordered with Italy and messengers were able to move with little difficulty, even during the War, between Croatia and the Vatican. The Pope had a personal representative in Croatia, Monsignor Ramiro Marcone, who liaised with the Croatian government.[76] Moreover, on two occasions during those years, Pope Pius XII met with Archbishop Stepinac. The Pope also regularly received reports from Pavelic's ambassador to the Vatican. Croatian bishops came for visits to Rome and met various members of the Roman Curia. Regular meetings were held with the three cardinals, the Secretary of State and his two assistants. Cardinal Eugène Tisserant, head of the Holy Congregation of Eastern Churches, the Vatican department in charge of missionary work in the East, received detailed reports from Croatia and, in fact, found some of the Franciscan behaviour unacceptable.[77] Tisserant would have informed the Pope and the Pope could have instructed the Catholic Hierarchy in Croatia to stop their atrocities immediately or he could have acted through the Franciscan Order. He didn't. Instead, he systematically sent positive signals to the Ustasha leadership of Croatia. Prince Erwin Lobkowicz, the Croatian representative at the Vatican, reports that as late as January 1943, at an audience granted to him, 'The Holy Father, was very amiable, and expressed his pleasure at the personal letter he had received from our Poglavnik [leader] … the Holy Father told me he was disappointed that, in spite of everything, no one wants to acknowledge the one, real and principal enemy of Europe; no true, communal military crusade against Bolshevism has been initiated'.[78]

After all the atrocities carried out by them, the message the Pope had for the Croat government was one of partnership. The Ustasha regime was still a partner in the fight against Bolshevism 'the principal enemy of Europe'. The Pope was actually calling for a new war, this time against the Soviet Union. Tisserant thought otherwise. In May 1940, he already said: 'I fear that history will reproach the Holy See for having practiced a policy of selfish convenience and little else.'[79]

After the war, the newly re-established Yugoslavia requested the Vatican to remove Stepinac. The Vatican refused. Stepinac was then tried for war crimes by Yugoslavia and sentenced to sixteen years imprisonment. Stepinac's only defence at his trial was that his conscience was clear. Following the conviction of Stepinac, the Vatican excommunicated all persons who had taken part in or were considered responsible for the prosecution of the Archbishop on the grounds that no member of the

Catholic clergy could be prosecuted without consent of the Vatican. The Church herself did not bring any of the perpetrators to her own ecclesiastical courts.

The Vatican's attitude in the 1998 beatification of Stepinac is not surprising. In beatifying Stepinac, Pope John Paul II was sending a very clear message. The Church will support its emissaries, who are relentless in furthering Catholic dogma and who are 'successful' in converting non-Catholics, and will overlook 'unattractive' aspects of their regimes such as torture and killings. It is not surprising because the Vatican has done nothing to punish its priests, bishops and other members for their proven atrocities. The Vatican, which was very quick to excommunicate all those involved in the trial of Stepinac, has not excommunicated the Franciscan monks and priests who were so active in the Ustasha. Vatican support continued even after the War. The College of San Girolamo degli Illirici, home of Croatian priests studying in Rome, became the headquarters of the Ustasha underground where Croatian war criminals were provided with protection, passports and fake identities and escape routes. This operation was run by Father Draganović, a Croatian priest, who was allowed to stay at the college as long as Pope Pius XII lived (he was expelled a few days after the pope's death). Franciscan monasteries in Klagenfurt (Austria), Modena (Italy) and in France took in members of the Ustasha who were fleeing from justice, trying to avoid prosecution for their murderous activities. They concealed the war criminal Ante Pavelic within the walls of the Vatican. Pavelic was later helped by the Church, which supplied him with false documents and a safe passage to the Nazi-friendly Argentine, at that time ruled by Peron.[iv] In 1959, as Pavelic lay dying as a guest of Spain's Franco, another Fascist dictator, Pope John XXIII gave him his personal benediction.

Conclusion

There is probably no other area where there is such a contrast between Christian preaching and the Catholic Church's practice as in her association with violence. In various forms and on various levels, the Church was involved in acts of physical violence which she either instigated or tacitly approved of in others. Sometimes, violence was directly carried out by the Church herself. When she had her own armies, she sent them to wars; when she was able to convince secular rulers to use force in furtherance of her interests, she did so. There were periods in which Church violence was aimed at furthering her material interests but in the main the Church employed violence to give power to her evangelical mission.

[iv] See Chapter 7.

Crusades did not stop because the Church concluded that they were immoral or that it was just plain wrong to send people to kill and be killed. Crusades only stopped when the Church failed to persuade people to take part in them. Although, right from the First Crusade, the most terrible atrocities were carried out by their participants, the popes did not cease preaching further crusades and from pressuring kings and aristocracy to get on the road. The popes used their power to militarise Christianity. Europe had serious problems such as overpopulation and famine; it was also troubled by local wars. Instead of developing a peace-furthering and humanity-loving institution, which would convert human proclivity to aggression and violence to harmony and mutual respect, the Church harnessed those very traits of violent behaviour which were carried out in her name.

Popes no longer have armies at their command, nor are they likely in the present geopolitical structures to invest, as their predecessors did, in mercenary armies. Some may view the involvement of the Catholic Church under Pope John Paul II in activities to destabilise the Communist government in Poland as questionable. Whatever one's view about the evil of a regime, one should consider whether it is indeed the role of the Church to change governments of countries, other than her own. After all, the Catholic Church continues to be run as an autocratic regime, totally untransparent, which uses its considerable power according to the personal views, morality, wisdom and whims of the pope of the day.

It may be the nature of religion, so certain of its own truth and lacking in self-doubt and humility, which has brought out the more malignant forms of evangelisation. Evangelisation would turn out to be most harmful when it had the backing of secular power structures. The religious wish to save souls and open the door to salvation very quickly became secondary to the Inquisition's and the Church's desire to hold on to power. This turned into a significant factor energising the Catholic Church's secret police operation. However, even if it had only been the devout effort to save souls, could that have justified torture and the use of the death penalty to enforce the Christian message of love and hope? Thousands of men and women were torched to death on the basis of indictments by messengers of the Church. The 'Bride of Christ', as the Church likes to refer to herself, the same Christ who stopped the stoning of an adulteress with the famous words with which he challenged those without sin to cast the first stone, created elaborate, mean and cruel apparatuses to do their version of stoning.

Even by acquiescence, defined by Michael Winter as 'a form of sinful collaboration by passive alliance with wickedness',[80] the Church is guilty. Popes knew about the horrendous conduct of colonisers who, 'under license' and with the authority of the Church, captured and exploited far-off lands using slaves. Popes also knew about forced conversions and other atrocities and did nothing. The Church gave her blessing to the monarchs who conquered, killed, pillaged and forcibly converted indigenous populations to Catholicism. The language used by popes, permitting invasions and wishing for spoils and triumphs, leaves no doubt that they understood what was happening in the colonial wars. Moreover, during the colonial period there were quite a few popes who objected to the slavery and maltreatment of natives by their colonisers, indicating an awareness of the atrocities being committed. However, the initiative and leadership of the actions for the abolition of slavery had nothing to do with the Catholic Church. Only after anti-slavery laws were introduced in the western world, did the Church toe the line.

The Catholic Church, as we all know, was not the originator of the phrase, 'Make Love Not War'. How could she have been? This was coined by the generation that embraced the introduction of the pregnancy-risk-free contraceptive but that revolted against the American military involvement and war in Vietnam. In principle, at least, the Church opposes war and various popes have, over the years, made their views clear on this matter. And yet, the Church has always been willing to go out to war to prevent the making of love, which cannot be said about her actions to prevent war, so decried by the Pope. During the First World War, the Church blocked the distribution of US government-sponsored VD prevention films. There was no similar Church attempt to block the manufacture of bombs. In a similar vein, the Catholic Church supported George W. Bush against John Kerry in the 2004 US Presidential elections. Bush was the man who took America into the Iraq war and the man who, practicing what he preached with regard to the death penalty, signed more than 150 death warrants whilst he was Governor of Texas. The Church had opposed the Iraq war, which she considered illegal, and maintains her stated policy against the death penalty. And yet, when it came to the crunch, the Church supported Bush, because of his fundamentalist pro-family, anti-gay marriage, anti-abortion campaign. Incidentally, much to the worry of the Muslim world, President George W. Bush has, after the September 11 attack in the US, ignorantly or perhaps unwittingly called his war against terror a crusade. For Muslims, crusades are, not surprisingly, a byword for faith and Church-driven slaughter of Muslims by Christians.

What are the values of this Church which believes that it is right to torture and kill? Some of the papal activities are truly hair-raising, especially if one considers that they were undertaken by a supposedly 'spiritual leadership'. The Church likes to link every pope through his predecessor to Peter and thereby to Jesus.[81] We must therefore accept that Jews, heretics, witches and others were tortured, deprived of liberty and often of their life, even burned to death by the messengers of Jesus himself. The Catholic Church has a history of wicked leaders who instigated murderous crusades, waged wars and partook in political manipulation often as evil as any other political actors of their time. Instead of general apologies, should the Church not at least 'name and shame' them and apologise for their deeds? As it stands, wicked popes continue to be considered by the Church as 'Vicars of Christ', forming a chain from Jesus to the present pope.

The driving force is the Church's central doctrine of evangelism. The Church believes that it is her duty to evangelise and to convert. This doctrine has historically led to use of violence to enforce conversion, to subdue unwilling populations, to discriminate and even to eliminate those who resisted. The Church nowadays has less power to implement her doctrine, but it is still in place and the Church has not given up on it.

Part Two

The Church and the Jews

Chapter Five
A History of Anti-Semitism

The attitude of the Catholic Church to Jews has been complicated right from the beginning. It has known the most shameful lows. There was never a high. The history of the Church's approach can be learned from both theory and practice. Catholic theology has dealt with the 'Jewish question' leading to anti-Jewish actions by the Church directly or by others acting on the Church's behalf, or at least with her blessing. These have blighted Jewish life and anti-Semitic acts, the inevitable consequence of anti-Semitism fuelled by the Church's stance, culminated in the holocaust.

The Catholic Church is based on the belief that the life and death of Jesus took place exactly as described in the Gospels. The Church further believes that she has been entrusted by Jesus to spread his message and was given by him the keys to the gates of heaven. The Church considers the conversion of mankind to Roman Catholicism a central role and duty. Fundamental to the Church are her belief that Jesus was not just a prophet but that he is God, and that the Jews rejected him and caused his crucifixion. Furthermore, that as a result, the covenant of God with the Jews has been superseded by a new covenant with those who accept the way of Jesus and the authority of the Catholic Church.

For almost two thousand years the Church has developed and distributed this theory. She has also initiated theological deliberation which defined the role that Jews were allowed to play in a Christian world. This, in turn, resulted in papal bulls setting out the rights of Jews and limitations to be imposed on them. With time and for a while, they deteriorated to direct enacting of torture and to sanctioning their murder. The Church has recognised her history but does not accept her culpability. Even the limited recognition has only come about as a result of a post-Holocaust feeling of guilt in many Christian circles.

In the beginning there was the word. Indeed, the New Testament is strewn with strong invective against the Jews. The holiest book of the Christian world refers to Jews as dogs,[1] snakes and a vipers' brood who cannot escape being condemned to hell. [2]

Jews, on whom God had brought 'a numbness of spirit; he gave them blind eyes and deaf ears',[3] are described as 'stubborn … heathen at heart and deaf to the truth'[4] and as hypocrites.[5] Jesus is quoted as telling Jews who reject him: 'Your father is the devil and you choose to carry out your father's desires. He was a murderer from the beginning, and is not rooted in the truth.'[6] The Pharisees were told 'inside you there is nothing but greed and wickedness'.[7]

Although the Gospels clearly state that the Roman governor, Pontius Pilate had Jesus flogged and sentenced to death and that Romans carried out the crucifixion, the Gospels do their utmost to malign the Jews and to blame them for the death of Jesus. The disciples quite systematically disseminate hatred of the Jews:

> I send you therefore prophets, sages, and teachers; some of them you will kill and crucify, others you will flog in your synagogues and hound from city to city.[8]

> … the Pharisees, on leaving the synagogue, began plotting against him with the partisans of Herod to see how they could make away with him.[9]

> … The chief priests and the whole Council tried to find some evidence against Jesus to warrant a death-sentence, but failed to find any. Many gave false evidence against him.[10]

> … the Jews, who killed the Lord Jesus and the prophets and drove us out, the Jews who are heedless of God's will and enemies of their fellow-men, hindering us from speaking to the Gentiles to lead them to salvation. All this time they have been making up the full measure of their guilt, and now retribution has overtaken them for good and all.[11]

The New Testament also accuses the Jews of hatching a plot against Paul's life.[12] They 'banned together and took an oath not to eat or drink until they had killed Paul … Jews from Antioch and Iconium … stoned Paul, and dragged him out of the city, thinking him dead.'[13]

A question which begs to be asked is, considering Christian dogma, according to which the death of Jesus was necessary for the salvation of mankind and he was in fact sent to the world by God for this very purpose, why are those who caused his death to be punished?[14] A second question is: Why have the followers of Jesus been so assiduous in shifting the blame from the Romans to the Jews? The most obvious explanation is expediency. Why blame the Romans who were the rulers and had the power? Could it not be useful to transfer the guilt to someone else? Diverting the blame could avert a collision course with the powerful empire. It might even act to bring Roman sentiment to favour Christianity over Judaism. It would definitely make it easier to recruit new adherents to Christianity, who might be worried about joining a sect whose leader had just been tried, sentenced to death and crucified by the [Roman] government. The Catholic theologian Rosemary Radford Ruether suggests that there is more to it than that. Ruether maintains that it was important to the Gospel writers to place the blame for the deaths of Jesus and his disciples 'specifically on the head of the Jewish *religious* tradition and its authority. ... the purpose of this shift was not merely one of apologetics towards the Gentiles, but one, first of all, of polemic toward the Jewish religious tradition.'[15] Blaming the Jews for the death of Jesus was the culmination of the anti-Jewish message, the purpose of which was to gain converts to Christianity and to decimate Judaism.

The battle for the hearts and minds of Jews and Gentiles was on.[16] And it seems that all is fair also in religious wars. The followers of Jesus propagated not only the stories of Jesus' miracles, but they also spread the concept of Jewish responsibility for the death of Jesus and their conclusion that Jews abandoned God and had as punishment been abandoned by God. According to Matthew, Jesus condemned the Jews who had 'shut the door of the kingdom of Heaven in men's faces; you do not enter yourselves, and when others are entering, you stop them'.[17] John has Jesus telling the Jews 'Why do you not understand my language? It is because my revelation is beyond your grasp. ...You are not God's children; that is why you do not listen.'[18]

In his Letter to the Romans, Paul describes the Jews who 'ignore God's way of righteousness, and try to set up their own, and therefore they have not submitted themselves to God's righteousness'.[19] Paul, who calls Jews 'dogs', writes in his Letter to the Philippians that 'we are the circumcised, we whose worship is spiritual, whose pride is in Jesus Christ'. Hence, according to Paul, circumcision, which symbolises the covenant of God with his Chosen People, is in truth a spiritual circumcision and not the physical act, which he warns is 'mutilation – circumcision I will not call it'. Paul, having converted to Christianity, tells the Philippians that he has thrown all the Jewish 'garbage' behind him 'for the sake of gaining Christ'.[20]

In an enlightening metaphor, which likens Jews to old olive branches which have been lopped off and are no longer connected to the roots of the tree, and Christians to newly grafted branches, which are now connected to the roots, Paul tells the Christians that the Jews, 'were lopped off for lack of faith, and by faith you hold your place'.[21]

It was important to show that they knew what they were doing:

> Paul devoted himself entirely to preaching, affirming before the Jews that the Messiah was Jesus. But when they opposed him and resorted to abuse, he shook out the skirts of his cloak and said to them 'Your blood be on your own heads! My conscience is clear.'[22]

The pinnacle of the New Testament's vilification was demonstrating that the Jews accepted their responsibility. This was made clear by the inclusion of 'with one voice the people cried, 'His blood be on us, and on our children''[23] in the Gospels. Did the Gospel writers, between forty and sixty years after the event, really know exactly what happened, and who said what? And yet, how often was this very sentence used to justify the murder of Jews by Christians, up to the twentieth century.

If the Church believes that the anti-Jewish teachings which appear in the New Testament were indeed given by Jesus and by his disciples, she can either agree with them or not. If the Church agrees with this diatribe she should say so. Her view would be clear. If the Church does not agree with these utterances, she should clearly distance herself from them. Professor Daniel Jonah Goldhagen, in his *A Moral Reckoning*, developed the idea that such texts should actually be changed.[24] In this case and, of course, also if the Church actually does not believe that the language of hatred was truly used, as it appears in the New Testament, the Church should act to have them excluded.

The Church Fathers Speak

Is it surprising that the Church Fathers, various popes, Christian theologians and others followed in the footsteps of their holy, biblical models? The list of Fathers of the Church is long and their importance to the tradition-bound Church is in giving testimony to what the Christians believed in the early ages of the Church. From very early days, Church sermons and Christian theological writing almost invariably included passionate anti-Jewish incitement. Twenty-seven of the thirty-two surviving works of Tertullian (160–225), a priest from Carthage who is considered the first theologian of the West, contain anti-Jewish discourse. In *De Oratione*, he wrote that 'though Israel may wash all its members every day, it is never clean. Its hands . . . are always stained, covered forever with the blood of the prophets and of our Lord himself.'[25] His *Adversus Iudaeos* ('Against the Jews') is the earliest such anti-Jewish treatise on record. Such *Adversus Iudaeos*, penned by the Church Fathers, have impregnated the Christian mind in disinheriting the Jews from their God, their laws and their belief in a Messiah. They vilified the Jews with devastating effect. The Alexandrian theologian, Origen (182–251) preached that 'the blood of Jesus falls not only on the Jews of that time, but on all generations of Jews up to the end of the world'. This state of endless and timeless culpability, says Origen, ensures that the Jews, whose 'rejection of Jesus has resulted in their present calamity and exile ... will never be restored to their former condition'.[26] Saint Cyprian (200–258), Bishop of Carthage, in his three books of Testimonies Against the Jews, cites quotation after quotation from the Old Testament attempting to 'prove' that the case of Christianity against Judaism had been foreseen in that work.[27] This became the norm in Christian anti-Jewish writing. Attacks on the Jews were based on the idea that they are Christ killers and were embellished with scriptural passages (mainly out of context) defaming and besmirching Jews. Any Old Testament prophet's condemnation of events in his time would serve as proof that present-day Jews were hypocrites, villains, evil, haters of and rejected by God. Cyprian, who speaks of the Jews as a 'sinful nation, people weighed down with guilt, breed of evil-doers, lawless children', maintains that the only way open to them to atone for their sin is converting to Christianity. There was no salvation for Jews outside the Church. This notion was relaxed only after the Holocaust, in the framework of the Second Vatican Council (Vatican II).

Saint Ephraem Syrus (306–373) calls the Jews the 'circumcised dogs' and 'circumcised vagabonds', and refers to Judaism as a worthless vineyard which cannot bear fruit. In his writing, Ephraem refers to God's punishment for the Jews. Because they reviled Jesus, the Lord has banished them from their land, and now they are condemned to wander over the whole face of the earth.[28] St Gregory of Nyssa (c. 331–396), with wanton eloquence, describes the Jews as 'slayers of the Lord, murderers of the prophets, enemies of God, haters of God, adversaries of grace, enemies of their fathers' faith, advocates of the devil, brood of vipers, slanderers, scoffers, men of darkened minds, leaven of the Pharisees, congregation of demons, sinners, wicked men, stoners, and haters of goodness'[29] – a veritable catalogue for future anti-Semites to pick from.

The fourth century was of critical importance to Jewish–Christian relations. Christianity had become the state Church and Judaism was fast losing its independent status in the Roman Empire. The writing of Christian theologians exerted a dominant influence on political life. The persecution Jews suffered during the fourth century was largely the result of Christian propaganda by the Church Fathers and religious fanatics who deliberately stirred up both popular resentment and official repression of the Jews. There was a close connection between the writings of the Church fathers and anti-Jewish legislation by contemporary Roman emperors. In this hour of triumph for the Church, 'the pens of Sts. Jerome, Gregory of Nyssa, John Chrysostom, Ambrose, and Augustine brought the patristic age to full flower; the Councils of Nicaea and Constantinople canonized the essentials of Catholic belief.'[30] Unfortunately, these pens were dipped in poison where Jews and Judaism were concerned. Crucial to this process was the conversion of Roman Emperor Constantine in 313 and the elevation of Christianity to be the state religion for the whole of the Roman Empire, in 380. Christian bishops and priests who had been pounding anti-Jewish propaganda to bring in the flocks, now used state legislation to promote their own agenda. To this end, every trick in the book was acceptable.

The producer of arguably the vilest early anti-Jewish sermons was Saint John Chrysostom (347–407), Bishop of Antioch and later Archbishop of Constantinople. He is considered one of the major Church Fathers and is still admired for the beauty of his sermons. Eight of these sermons, which appear as *Eight Homilies Against the Jews*, are, as their name suggests, violently anti-Jewish. He is so loved by some of the faithful that they try to mitigate the shame. They suggest that Chrysostom did not mean the Jews, he was only attacking the 'judaisers', a term used to describe those who had already undertaken Christianity but still kept some Jewish laws or practices, as if that would make such language of hatred acceptable! They also ask that one read these sermons 'in context'. Interestingly, they do not draw the most obvious conclusion that the rest of these old documents, including the Gospels, should also be read in context.

Chrysostom came out with his venomous attack at a time when Christianity was already the state religion of the Roman Empire. It was no longer fighting for recognition. He is one of fewer than forty ecclesiastical writers who have received the title *Doctor of the Church*, a title conferred by the Church on a teacher of the Faith, outstanding for holiness as well as learning (*eximia scientia et eximia sanctitas*), on account of the great advantage the whole Church has derived from their doctrine. Chrysostom is generally considered the most prominent doctor of the Greek Church and the greatest preacher ever heard in a Christian pulpit. In 1909, Pope Pius X declared him patron of preachers. Chrysostom's fanatical hatred of the Jews was clearly not considered to be detrimental.

Chrysostom's eight long sermons deal with only one subject: the despicable nature of Judaism and of 'the Jewish people [who] were driven by their drunkenness and plumpness to the ultimate evil'. Chrysostom compared Jews to brutish animals that had grown plump and obstinate and were hard to hold in check: 'Although such beasts are unfit for work, they are fit for killing. And this is what happened to the Jews: while they were making themselves unfit for work, they grew fit for slaughter'. What Christian morality allows for such licence to kill? Chrysostom has the answer: 'This is why Christ said: "But as for these my enemies, who did not want me to be king over them, bring them here and slay them."'[31]

Christians are warned not to come into contact with Jews, the people in whose souls 'demons dwell'.[32] In fact, the demons also inhabit the synagogues, which Chrysostom describes as 'not only a brothel and a theatre; it also is a den of robbers and a lodging for wild beasts'.[33] Is it then surprising that these terrible Jews have altars in their synagogues, in which they sacrifice the souls of men?[34] How long will it take from the use of this rhetoric to the accusations that Jews actually sacrifice Christian children and not 'only' the souls of men? After all, what else is there to expect from these Jews, a people whose 'mothers ate their own children'?[35] The directive is clear – the Jews are, at best, untouchable:

Do you not shudder to come into the same place with men possessed, who have so many unclean spirits, who have been reared amid slaughter and bloodshed? Must you share a greeting with them and exchange a bare word? Must you not turn away from them since they are the common disgrace and infection of the whole world?[36]

Addressing the Jews, Chrysostom tells them that their case is lost. God has deserted them, they can forget about any possibility of atonement. 'Your mad rage against Christ, the Anointed One,' he tells them 'left no way for anyone to surpass your sin.'[37] Adding salt to the wound, he adds: 'If God had not abandoned you, the ruin of desolation would not have lasted so long a time, nor would your frequent efforts to rebuild the temple have been in vain.'[38]

The *Adversus Judaeos* sermons at which Chrysostom (which is Greek for golden mouth) excelled, led to assaults on Jews and the burning of synagogues. In fact the immediate result of Chrysostom's sermons was the destruction of the great synagogue of Antioch.[39] It was also there that the first charge regarding 'ritual murder' was brought against Jews.[40] This did not stop the Church from considering him to be a saint. Nor did it prevent the twentieth-century Church from declaring Chrysostom the patron saint of all Catholic preachers. Chrysostom's sermons continued to be taught up to the twentieth century in Church seminaries.

Saint Ambrose (339–397), who like Chrysostom was pronounced Doctor of the Church, was bishop of Milan. According to Saint Augustine's autobiography, *Confessions*, Ambrose was a highly cultured, learned and intelligent man who introduced him to his own understanding of the existence of a spiritual world and converted him to Christianity. Saint Ambrose, a virulent hater of Judaism, stated that he was ready to burn any number of synagogues, 'haunts of infidels, homes of the impious, hiding places of madmen'.[41]

Saint Ambrose, who was and still is held in high esteem by the Church, is credited as being a bishop who courageously and unyieldingly fought the Church's case. She was proud of his successful intervention with Roman Emperor Theodosius to achieve a volte-face in his decision to do justice. Ambrose did not object to justice itself, he just objected to justice for the Jews. In a riot which took place in 388, in the city of Callinicum on the Euphrates, Christian mobs, incited by the local bishop, first plundered and then burned down a synagogue. The local governor sought not only to punish the perpetrators, but also imposed the cost of rebuilding the synagogue upon the local bishop. Ambrose, the Bishop of Milan, came to his colleague's help. He wrote a long letter to the Emperor.

This letter is a masterpiece. It preaches anti-Semitism to the Emperor, denigrating the Jews and the synagogue. It advises the Emperor that he may not use his imperial powers to give instructions which could result in apostasy. Ambrose quotes Jeremiah, an Old Testament prophet, out of context to 'prove' that God forbids the Emperor's intercession. Although he expects the Emperor to revoke his edict, just in case he does not and to ensure that the Emperor understands what is at stake for him, Saint Ambrose warns him of the personal consequences of non-acquiescence. The Emperor's own salvation would be at risk. Moreover, the Emperor is warned that whereas this letter is private, unless he acts on it, he will have to listen to Ambrose in Church.[42] And, indeed, he did hear from the bishop in Church. It did not suffice that Theodosius rescind the punishment of the perpetrators and no longer demand that the bishop of Callinicum or the Church pay for the rebuilding of the synagogue, because the Emperor still wanted to have the synagogue rebuilt for the Jews, at state expense. To force his views on the Emperor, Ambrose gave him an ultimatum: he stopped the service and would not continue the liturgy until the quest to punish the Christians of Callinicum was dropped. Theodosius caved in and Ambrose, the saint, bishop of Milan, one of the important Fathers of the Church, legitimising violence in pursuit of a religious cause, actively and successfully promoted the riotous persecution of Jews.

Some in the Catholic Church who consider Vatican II to have turned 'the clear doctrines into the sewage of ecumenism, humanism, pluralism and modernism' still yearn for the likes of Ambrose, who had 'brought the clear waters of truth to Italy'.[43]

Saint Jerome (341–420), Church Father and Doctor of the Church, identified all Jews with Judas, the apostle who betrayed Jesus in return for thirty pieces of silver:

> Who do you suppose are the sons of Judas? The Jews. The Jews take their name, not from Juda who was a holy man, but from the betrayer. … Synagogue was divorced by the Saviour and became the wife of Judas, the betrayer.[44]

He added, 'If it is expedient to hate any men and to loathe any race I have a strange dislike for those of the circumcision. For up to the present day, they persecute our Lord Jesus Christ in the synagogues of Satan.' Jerome introduces deceit and sexual depravity as metaphors for Jewish behaviour[45] and describes the synagogue:

> if you call it a brothel, a den of vice, the devil's refuge, Satan's fortress, a place to deprave the soul, an abyss of every conceivable disaster or whatever else you will, you are still saying less than it deserves.[46]

Saint Augustine (354–430), bishop of the North African city of Hippo, was a prolific and inventive writer of sermons, letters and books. He was one of the most revered authors of the patristic period with nearly a hundred books to his name, and as such was influential throughout Christian history. Augustine's fundamental attitude was that the human condition was flawed and that the Church was the forum for Christians to confess their sins before God. His theology of original sin has forged Christian thinking and Church teaching, which is obsessed with sin and is uncomfortable with and repulsed by flesh.

Towards the end of his life, Augustine considered the use of force acceptable for the purpose of theological 'correction'. In 'The Correction of Donatists', he wrote 'For many have found advantage (as we have proved, and are daily proving by actual experiment), in being first compelled by fear or pain, so that they might afterwards be influenced by teaching.'[47] Augustine only reluctantly came to the conclusion that it was right to inflict punishment in order to improve the spiritual welfare of heretics. However, his espousal of coercion to enforce faith was to become Church doctrine.

Considered by many to be the father of Christian theology and of the Western Church, Augustine is also considered by some as a saviour of the Jews. His defence of the Jews was not only ambivalent but was soon perverted. Moses Mendelssohn, the eighteenth-century German-Jewish philosopher of the Age of Enlightenment, wrote about Augustine, 'Blessed be the ashes of that humane theologian, who was the first to declare that God was preserving us as a visible proof of the Nazarene religion. But for this lovely brainwave, we would have been exterminated long ago.'[48] As grateful as one can be to Augustine for developing a theology according to which Jews should be allowed to live and should not be killed, one cannot overlook the fact that Augustine's underlying belief and teaching was that the Jews were contemptible because they had rejected Christ: they, not the Romans, had killed Jesus; they had been cast off by God; and Jesus had considered the Jews to be his enemies. Unlike Chrysostom, whose contemporary he was and who considered Jews fit for slaughter, Augustine wanted them to survive, believing that at the end of time 'suffering humiliation like dogs and joining the ranks of the uncircumcised' they would come to the Church. Unlike Saint Ambrose, his teacher, who urged violence as the proper response to the Jews, Augustine taught that Jews should survive as witnesses of prophesies given in the Old Testament, which the Christians believed pertained to Jesus.[49]

The approach which was developed on the basis of Augustine's 'witness protection scheme' was as follows: Jews had to be kept in a state of perpetual punishment; punishment should make them suffer and be seen to make them suffer but should not annihilate them; and they should continue existing in Christian society to give future generations of Christians their service as 'witnesses' to the veracity of the Gospel.

Augustinian theology instructed the Church and the whole Christian world that Jews should be despised and punished, but kept alive. Generations of Christian preachers taught their congregations the vile and loathsome nature of the Jews. Is it surprising that the Jews were hated and that this hatred produced pogroms? The Augustinian doctrine that preaches the dispersal of Jews all over the world away from Jerusalem has not died. It has unquestionably informed the systematic and unyielding anti-Zionist stance of the Church.

Repressive Laws

The anti-Jewish orations and writing by zealous Christian priests and bishops yielded results. On a popular level they resulted in the burning of synagogues and pogroms and, at administrative and government level, they resulted in repressive laws against the Jews. The hatred of Jews and the abusive language used in the New Testament and by the Church Fathers in connection with Jews soon turned into down-to-earth anti-Jewish decisions and legislation by Church synods and councils.

The Church Fathers' invective resulted in direct Christian action: attacks on synagogues increased. Although laws against such attacks were enacted, the fact that from 373 to 423 six such laws had to be passed demonstrates how grave the problem had become and how powerful the Christian anti-Jewish masses had become. Mobs were giving vent to their Church-driven anti-Semitism. Popular attacks on synagogues continued and synagogues were often destroyed under Church supervision. In some cases synagogues were seized and turned into churches. The first recorded serious large-scale Christian pogrom of Jews took place in Alexandria in Egypt in 414. This organised assault totally wiped out the thriving Jewish community of that city.

The importance of the fourth century for the continued humiliation and persecution of Jews in an ever more Christian world – a world in which the Church took it upon herself to define morality and to dictate moral norms to society – cannot be exaggerated. The fanatical and obsessive anti-Jewish writings of the Church Fathers were repeated and quoted by Christians from pope downwards as a basis and justification for economic extortion, physical torture, expulsion and murder of Jews up to the twentieth century. The extent to which fourth century Augustine is not only an exception but unique, in the two thousand years of Church history, can be gathered from James Carroll's contemplative remark 'Are we reduced to gratitude for the day when one of us found a way, through a jury-rigged theology if there ever was one, to justify the cry "Do not slay them!"? Yes, we are.'[50] The Church, which until 1966 maintained a register of forbidden books, never included any of these anti-Semitic ravings in this Index. She has still not distanced herself from any of these writings. The fact that the fulminations of St Jerome, St Ambrose,

St Chrysostom and others were directly followed by pogroms in which Jews were killed was apparently no reason to forbid their dissemination.

In the following centuries, Church councils and synods continued to pass anti-Jewish rulings. The language used and the myths ascribed to the Jews in the New Testament and in the sermons and writings of the Church Fathers came to dominate the Christian perception of Jews. To a large extent these are still ingrained in Christian minds.

What we have is an extreme form of marketing. The new religion, Christianity, in an attempt to wipe out an existing and 'competitive' religion preached hatred of its competitor, and was not afraid to murder to achieve its ends. The authors of the New Testament and the Church Fathers devised their strategies and sharpened their tactics to annihilate totally the competition, and they almost succeeded. In their strategy, everything which they liked in the old religion was hijacked and defined as Christian: starting with God and ending with Jesus, who after all was a practicing Jew, as were his apostles. The Church, which took from Judaism what it wanted, turned those who would not follow her into figures of hate. Jewish concepts of their God, of their being a chosen people which had a covenant with God, were simply denied. By sheer misrepresentation and falsification of biblical texts, Judaism's credibility was eroded. God was no longer the God of the Jews, he was rejected by them and no longer wanted them. The original covenant with the Jews was superseded by a new covenant with Christians. Circumcision, a mark of the covenant of the Jews, was defined as a mark of Cain – the mark of a murderer. The Promised Land, which played a central role in the Jewish concept of its relationship with God, was never again to be theirs. The creative talents of Christianity's first centuries produced material which was utilised by the Church even up to the twentieth century. A successful marketing campaign, but at what price?

The earliest Church synod to mention Jews is the Synod of Elvira, which took place in 306. This synod passed resolutions forbidding Christians to have sex with Jews, to marry Jews, or even to have a joint meal with Jews. Curiously the Church prohibition referred only to Jewish men taking Christian women. They did not seem to be worried about Christian men who might fancy a Jewish woman, unless these Christian men were married, in which case the synod forbade fornication specifically with Jewish women. Less than twenty years later, at the Council of Nicea, in 325, Christian clergy were prohibited from fellowship with Jews or just from holding conversations with Jews. By then, Christianity had been recognised by Emperor Constantine, who in the *Edict of Milan* in 313, extended religious tolerance to Christians whilst curtailing the rights of Jews.

The Church had gained authority and prestige. The ever growing influence of Christianity on the laws of the land is evident in the *Codex Theodosianus*, the compilation of all laws enacted from the reign of

Constantine until its eventual composition in 438. It includes numerous statutes which deal with Judaism. The Christianisation of the Roman Empire resulted in an anti-Jewish government with anti-Jewish policies and anti-Jewish laws. The gist of these laws was to turn the Jews into an underclass which deserved and got less protection than the Christians. Restrictions were imposed on economic as well as on other activities of the Jews. They were not allowed to participate in government and were driven out of the administrative, military and legal professions. The religious abuse of fiery Christian preachers became the terminology of the state laws. The Church succeeded in turning the theology of triumph, with which she conditioned the Emperor, into secular law.

To make converting to Judaism difficult, converts were rendered intestate, whereas Jews were forbidden to disinherit children who converted to Christianity and proselytising by Jews was made illegal. Already in 329, it became a criminal offence to become a Jew. This was repeated in a 409 law.[51]

Decisions of Church Councils, such as the Council of Elvira in Spain in 306, prohibiting marriage of Christians with Jews, were made state law. Such marriages were punishable by exile, expropriation or death. By 388, Theodosius I made intermarriage both ways equal to fornication and punishable by death.[52] The imperial Roman law defined marriages to Jews as 'shameful' and 'adulterous' unions. This denigratory language, emanating from the Church Fathers, made its way into the secular codex. Judaism is referred to as a 'wicked sect', a 'superstition', its congregation, as a 'sacrilegious assembly'; and Jews are termed 'abominable'. Christianity, by contrast, is designated as the 'venerable religion'. From 398, Jewish tribunals were denied competence over any matters which were not purely religious and in 429 the Jewish patriarchate was abolished.

The sixth-century document, *Codex Justinianus* (a compilation of anti-Jewish laws promulgated in 528 by Emperor Justinian), repeated previous laws and hardened the state's attitude towards Jews. Jews were now told how to interpret the Bible and the *Talmud*[i] was prohibited. Adding insult to injury, Justinian gave the Church full authority to administer laws pertaining to Jews.

The Elvira prohibition on joint meals with Jews, punishable by ostracism, was repeated at various other synods of the Church, such as Vannes in 465, Agde in 506, Epaon in 517, Orleans in 538, Macon in 589, Clichy in 626, Reims in 630, Metz in 888 and Coyaca in 1050. The 535 Synod of Claremont ruled that Jews could not hold public office or have authority over Christians.

---

[i] A fundamental source of Jewish legislation, case histories and moral exhortations, constitutes Judaism's oral tradition and is considered an authoritative record of rabbinic discussions on Jewish law, ethics, customs and legends.

More than a thousand years before the Church concluded that slavery was evil, she decided that Jewish ownership of Christian slaves was unacceptable. The Third Synod of Orleans in 538, passed a ruling forbidding Jews from possessing Christian slaves or even employing Christian servants. Obediently the Roman emperors passed the requisite laws.

The Third and the Fourth Synods of Toledo in 589 and 633, as well as many other synods, reiterated the ban on Jews holding public office. Some referred to specific positions such as judges or tax collectors. The Fourth Lateran Council (1215) repeated the bans, explaining that 'it is absurd that a blasphemer of Christ exercise authority over Christians'.[53]

Not only did the Church Council forbid granting any public office to Jews, it made the appointment of Jews to such offices punishable under Church law. It also instructed all Christians not to have any contact with any Jew in public office. Thus, if government, disregarding the Church ban, did appoint a Jew to a public office, it could expect the Christian population to boycott him. Innocent III (1198–1216) who probably drafted the decree himself during his papacy, actively put pressure on Christian rulers to have Jews removed from public offices in their countries. When Count Raymond VI of Toulouse disregarded papal instructions regarding Jews in public positions, he was threatened by this pope in 1207 with boycott and even with rectification by force through a crusade. Two years earlier, the Pope, who is described in the Catholic Encyclopaedia as 'one of the greatest popes of the Middle Ages', instructed the Count of Nevers:

> The Jews, like the fratricide Cain, are doomed to wander through the earth as fugitives and vagabonds, and their faces must be covered with shame. They are under no circumstances to be protected by Christian princes; but are, on the contrary, to be condemned to serfdom.[54]

Innocent III did not invent new modes of hatred. He adopted many of the anti-Jewish ideas and concepts of the Church Fathers and turned them into practice. He issued more than thirty-two bulls dealing with Jews. His authoritative status, at a time when the papacy was the most powerful force in Christian Europe, enabled him to bully secular rulers into submission. In many instances his views are reminiscent of those of Chrysostom and his anti-Jewish ravings, whilst at the same time keeping to the Augustine formula that Jews should be held low but kept alive. In one of his earlier documents in the *Sicut Judeis* format the Pope wrote:

> Although in many ways the perfidy of the Jews must be reproved, since nevertheless through them our own faith is truly proved, they must not be oppressed grievously by the faithful as the prophet says: 'Do not slay them, lest these be forgetful of Thy Law,' [Ps. 58 (59):12] as if he were

155

saying more openly: 'Do not wipe out the Jews completely, lest perhaps Christians might be able to forget Thy Law, which the former, although not understanding it, present in their books to those who do understand it.'[55]

The dichotomy is revealing: 'Do not wipe out the Jews completely', which would signify that it is alright to partially wipe them out. However, 'since they wish to go on in their own hardness rather than … to come to a knowledge of the Christian faith, … since they beseech the help of Our defence, We, out of the meekness proper to Christian piety, … grant them the buckler of Our protection'.[56] Such dichotomy is typical of papal 'protection' documents. Jews were allowed to stay alive but should be hated, humiliated and punished. Indeed, the same Innocent, throughout his papacy, encouraged hatred and demanded limitations be imposed on Jews. These came to an apex in his important Fourth Lateran Council, which in addition to the already mentioned prohibition on Jews holding public offices, is notorious for its decree that Jews and Muslims wear distinctive clothing. Other decisions included a tax which each Jewish family had to pay at Easter, the levy of a tithe to the Church on property held by Jews and the ordinance that three days before Easter Jews be quarantined in their homes. The Lateran Council of 1215 also ruled that Jews who had received baptism were to be restrained by the prelates from returning to Judaism: 'having given themselves of their own free will to the Christian religion salutary coercive action may preserve them in its observance'.[57]

The opening paragraph of Innocent's *Sicut Judeis* is the standard first set by Gregory I (590–604) when he wrote to the bishop of Palermo setting out Augustine's ambivalent concept. Future popes would regularly be called upon by harassed Jews begging them to remind the Christian world of Augustine's 'Do not Slay them'. Many popes did issue similar *Sicut Judeis* instructing local Church hierarchies that Jews should not be baptised by force and that they should be left to live in their misery. Often, the only way for Jewish communities to obtain a renewed *Sicut Judeis* was through bribery. Money had passed hands before bulls were issued. In one particular case, Pope Callistus III (455–458) threatened the Jewish community that unless they made a substantial donation to the papal coffers, he would issue a bull which would significantly limit their rights. Callistus was in need of funds to finance his war against the Turks so blackmailing the Jews was an easy way to raise the money and, so it seems, was neither against any Church law nor contrary to her ethical values. Central to these letters of protection is the concept that keeping Jews within Christian society is of theological benefit to that society; more than killing them, expelling them or forcing their baptism. There is no true piety involved. Training hunting dogs to catch and then preventing them from biting is not easy. Regularly teaching contempt and hatred, calling Jews by the vilest names, accusing them of deicide, and then preventing acts of violence against them is equally difficult. Indeed, the Church has not succeeded, notwithstanding her *Sicut Judeis*.

The decree of the Fourth Lateran Council that Jews were to wear distinctive clothing was subsequently reiterated, added to and embellished by Church synods and councils. In 1227, the Council of Narbonne ordered Jews to wear a round patch, in 1234 the Council of Arles took the same decision, as did the Council of Albi in 1254. The Church Council of Breslau, convened in 1266, ordered that Jews wear 'a peculiarly shaped hat, with a horn-like shield and that any Jew showing himself on the street without this headgear shall be subject to punishment'. Nimes came in 1284 and Vienna, having in 1267 decided on horned hats for Jews, added a round patch in 1289. In 1434, Jewish men in Augsburg were made to sew yellow buttons to their clothes. Throughout Europe, Jews were forced to wear humiliating clothes such as long undergarments, bells and tall pointed yellow hats with large buttons on them. In 1555 Pope Paul IV decreed distinctive headgear for Jews: women had to wear a yellow veil or scarf and men had to wear a piece of yellow cloth on their hat. Some four hundred years later, the Nazis would adopt this insistence on distinctive clothing for Jews with the introduction of the yellow Star of David.

In 1050, the Synod of Narbonne forbade Christians to live in Jewish homes. The Third Lateran Council in 1179 strictly forbade Christians to act as servants to Jews. This prohibition was evidently often disregarded as it was regularly repeated by Church councils. In 1456, Pope Callistus III (1455–1458), banned all social communication between Christians and Jews. In 1465, Pope Paul II (1464–1471), a patron of the arts who was so proud of his good looks that he considered naming himself *Formosus II* ('beautiful'), issued instructions regarding slave trade. He did not mind the capture of the Africans by slave traders, their sale to Europeans or their enslavement for life. Their suffering was not the issue of the Pope's directive. Instead, the Pope ordered that slaves who had been baptised were not to be sold to Jews or to other non-Christians. Any such deal would result in the buyer and the vendor losing both money and slaves.

As with other limitations that the Church imposed on Jews, forbidding Jewish physicians from treating Christians served two ends: the wish to humiliate and shame the Jews and to hold them as an underclass in a constant state of servility; and the wish to instil in Christians the belief that being Jewish was almost contagious. Indeed, in the seventeenth century, objecting to a licence to practice medicine given to a Jew, the clergy in the city of Halle (Württemberg) delivered the statement 'it were better to die with Christ than to be cured by a Jew doctor aided by the devil'.[58] The Synod of Constantinople in 692 forbade Christians from receiving treatment from Jewish physicians. A number of other synods issued similar decrees: the 1227 council in Trieste instructed the secular rulers to prevent Jews from handling Christian patients or from prescribing drugs to them. In 1255, the Synod of Albi threatened Christians with boycott if they saw Jewish physicians. Benedict XIII (1394–1417) issued a bull, *Etsi doctoris gentium*, which barred Jewish physicians, pharmacists or midwives from treating Christians. This was restated by similar bulls issued by other fifteenth-century popes. However, the wish of influential Christians to receive medical treatment was often stronger than the power of the ban. Doctorates in medicine were introduced by universities in the thirteenth century; prior to this, a physician was described as 'surgeon' or *'magister'*. The ban on granting doctorates to Jews was first broken by popes who granted special permits to their personal physicians. With time, at the behest of kings who wanted their physicians released from the ban, additional licences to practice medicine and to grant doctorates in medicine were given by fifteenth- and sixteenth-century popes. With more such licences given, some Christian doctors, who were unhappy about the competition, lobbied the pope for additional limitations on Jewish doctors. Eugenius IV (1431–1447) was the first pope to introduce the additional hurdle for Christian patients who wanted to be treated by an approved Jewish physician: prior to seeing the doctor, the patient would have to go to confession, receive the last rites and write their wills. With time, the number of approvals became so high that the ban on Jewish doctors became meaningless. The idea that Jewish doctors might contaminate their non-Jewish patients resurfaced when the Nazis, in 1938, passed a law forbidding Jews to treat non-Jewish patients.

Decrees keeping Jews out of public service were passed by Church synods and councils as early as the sixth century and regularly reiterated and widened. A seventh-century decree forbade Jews from farming. More laws preventing Jews from practicing medicine, owning land and farming, setting up industry, or sometimes even selling new goods (1592 in Avignon, or the papal bull *Ex injuncto nobis* issued by Pope Innocent XIII in 1724 followed by a similar bull by Benoit XIV in 1729) were added. The 1555 *Cum Nimis Absurdum*, Paul IV's bull, allowed Jews two professions only: money lending and trade in second hand clothing. There seemed to be no limit to the restrictions that the Church created to beleaguer and to humiliate Jews. Eventually, Jews were despised for carrying out the only professions which the Church allowed them.

Hatred of Jews was often intertwined with public mockery. During carnival time in papal Rome, for example, one of the amusements in festivities sponsored by the pope involved making fun of Jews. A description from 1466 portrays how Jews were made to run naked through the streets of Rome:

Races were run on each of the eight days of the Carnival by horses, asses and buffaloes, old men, lads, children, and Jews. Before they were to run, the Jews were richly fed, so as to make the race more difficult for them and at the same time more amusing for the spectators. They ran ... amid Rome's taunting shrieks of encouragement and peals of laughter, while the Holy Father stood upon a richly ornamented balcony and laughed heartily.[59]

In the seventeenth century, Jews were no longer required to run naked in the streets, however, rabbis were still forced to wear clownish costumes and march through them. Additionally, Jews were now forced to fund the carnival through a special heavy tax levied on them by the pope. In 1836, the Jews pleaded with the Vatican to put an end to a rite in which Jewish officials were made to wear peculiar dress and, in a public piazza, to the joy of the rowdy mob, pay homage to Rome's governors. The Vatican's response was 'It is not opportune to make any innovation.'[60]

Ghettos

The Church's policy to single out the Jews, discriminate against them and debase them reached a new peak with the ruling that Jews had to live in prescribed zones. With time, these became known as *Ghettos*, after the sixteenth-century Jewish quarter in Venice. The first attempts to ostracise the Jews came when the Church threatened to boycott Christians who lived with them (Third Lateran Council in 1179), or ate with them (1267 in Breslau). The Breslau synod took up the issue raised at the Fourth Lateran Council which decreed that Jews should reside in confined areas. To 'protect' the neophytes from Jewish influence, the synod instructed that Jews in the province of Gnesen were to live in houses separated from the dwellings of Christians by a fence. In 1340, Pope Benedict XII (1334–1342) wrote to the king of Aragon, Pedro IV and implored him to bring an end to the co-habitation of Jews and Muslims in Christian areas. Similarly, Urban V (1362–1370) acted to prevent 'scandalous' situations of Jews and Christians living in too great a proximity. Benedict XIII (1394–1417) issued a bull in which he urged princes and other secular rulers to define boundaries outside of which Jews would not be permitted to live. Limiting Jews to specified neighbourhoods soon became the norm throughout the empire. Pope after pope in the fifteenth century dealt with the Church's wish to keep Jews and Christians apart, often going into fine detail as to what was and was not permissible. Special permits were given to those who had connection with the centres of power such as personal physicians or bankers. Slowly the next step established itself. Jews were being forced to move into closed areas. Frankfurt established a closed Jewish quarter in 1460, Krakow in 1496 and Venice in 1516.

When the man who oversaw the burning of a Franciscan monk and others for converting to Judaism, the former grand inquisitor Cardinal Gian Pietro Caraffa, became pope, matters grew worse. As Pope Paul IV (1555–1559), his bull, *Cum Nimis Absurdum* created *inter alia* the Roman ghetto. In this bull, which literally means 'when too much is absurd', the Pope specified that Jewish males were to wear a yellow hat and females a yellow kerchief. Owning property or practicing medicine on Christians was forbidden. Taxes on Jews were increased. Jews were not to be adressed as 'sir' by Christians, were not to attend any Christian university and were not to hire Christian servants. It also decreed the confiscation and later the public burning of the Talmud. All this was due to to the Pope's anger that:

> It has come to our notice that in Rome and in other cities their [Jews'] shamefulness is carried so far that they not only make bold to dwell among Christians, even near their churches, and without any distinction in their dress, but even rent houses in the distinguished streets and squares of these cities, villages and localities, acquire and possess landed property, keep Christian nurses, maids, and other servants, and do much else that is in disgrace to the Christian name.[61]

The Pope decreed that the one street in which the Jews would be permitted to live would have only two gates. Yet even in that street Jews were not permitted to own the property, only rent it. On exiting the ghetto, Jews were confronted by an anti-Jewish inscription on the facade of the Church of San Gregorio alla Divina Pietà, which stood directly opposite those gates.[62] Jews had already been forced into ghettos before this papal bull but these were always initiated by local Church hierarchies. *Cum Nimis Absurdum* was the first instance of papal instructions specifically setting up a ghetto, followed by strict papal controls to ensure the implementation of his bull. Things under this pope moved very fast: less than two weeks after his bull was promulgated, Jews were rounded up and brought into the enclosure.

Pope Sixtus V (1585–1590), a Franciscan friar, was a ruthless ruler who introduced tough legislation to curb violence in Rome and throughout the papal states. A great moraliser, he executed any member of a religious order who broke their vow of chastity and he also attempted to introduce the death penalty for adultery within the general population. Sixtus, who in 1589 enlarged the Roman ghetto, was however not that moral himself. Cardinal Santa Croce, his chief administrator, was the owner of almost thirty per cent of the additional land that in 1589 was to be enclosed within ghetto walls. Jews who were forced to live in such enclosures were easy prey to landlords who could and did squeeze extortionate rents from people who had nowhere else to go. The Cardinal was not the only beneficiary of the papal decree. The Pope's own sister, Camilla Peretti, also owned property in the newly created enclosure. Moreover, the property which was in the name of Peretti, was in fact originally purchased by the Pope himself. The building contract for the walls and gates surrounding the ghetto was granted to a papal contact and friend, the architect Domenico Fontana. Fontana's contract stipulated that remuneration was to be paid to him and to his heirs forever.

In 1593, Pope Clement VIII limited the Jews of the Papal States to the ghettos of Rome and Ancona. Jews who lived in other cities were to be expelled and sent to one of these two ghettos. In 1775, Pius VI (1775–1799) issued *Editto Sopra Gli Ebrei*, his Edict Over the Jews. This comprised forty-four clauses restricting the lives of Jews and remained in effect until the arrival of Napoleon's army twenty-five years later. The edict, which instructed that Jews were not allowed to spend even one night outside the ghetto without special permission, also stipulated that, if such permission were granted, the Jew was not permitted to live in the same house with Christians nor 'speak familiarly with them'. Other highlights of this late eighteenth-century papal document, which was issued as part of the Church's anti-Liberal and anti-Reformation attempts, forbade Jews from riding in carriages and from having any inscriptions on their tombstones. It also reinforced the compulsory Catholic sermons which Jews were required to attend.[63]

In 1798, Napoleon's army marched on Rome. Pius VI fled and the ghettos were opened. His successor, Pius VII, was elected in 1800 as the French were retreating. In 1809, however, Napoleon was back. This time the occupation lasted longer and the Pope lived in exile in France until 1814. The Congress of Vienna (1815–1822), the international conference which restructured post-Napoleonic Europe, reinstated almost all of the papal lands. For the Jews, it meant a return to the old anti-Jewish regime of the Church. The gates of the ghettos were closed again and the mighty Inquisition revived.

In 1826, Pope Leo XII (1823–1829) re-established walled ghettos which were kept locked at night throughout the Papal States. Jews were forbidden to own property or to transact business with Christians. The Jewish community had to deliver three hundred Jews a week to attend Christian sermons. Gregory XVI (1831–1846), decreed that a heavy fine was payable by any Jew failing to attend the forced sermons. The Church rewarded informers with a third of the fine collected.

Revolts in the Papal States in 1848 made Pius IX (1846–1878) flee Rome, dressed as a simple priest and concealed in the carriage of the Bavarian Ambassador. The newly established Roman Republic lasted until the armies of Catholic France and Austria came to the Pope's rescue.

The Pope, however, was in need of funding to finance his return and was unable to find a bank which would lend him any money. He approached the Rothschilds for a loan, which they were willing to make provided he abolished the ghetto and some of the restrictions which were still in force under papal laws. The Pope indicated to Rothschild that he would publish an edict to that effect. Based on that understanding, the loan was made and in 1850 the Pope was able to return to Rome and resume power. The Pope did not keep his word. The restrictions on Jews were retained and Jews had to continue living in the ghetto until 1870. As a result of the Church's loss of the Papal States at this time, Jews were finally liberated from their imprisonment in the Vatican-created ghetto in the very centre of Rome. Incidentally, only then did the payments to architect Fontana's heirs also come to an end. By then, the Jewish community in Rome had been decimated and totally impoverished.

Attempts to Convert

With all these restrictions, the degradation and Church-induced bullying, life as a Jew was quite unbearable. Many took the easy way out and converted to Christianity. In fact, it is surprising that they did not all take that route – although Martin Luther, in his hatred for the Catholic Church, said that if he were a Jew he would rather become a pig than a Catholic. Later, angry that Jews did not see 'the light' in the new Protestant Church and 'stubbornly' remained Jewish, Catholic-educated Luther referred to Jews as 'liars and bloodhounds ... The sun never did shine on a more bloodthirsty and revengeful people.'[64]

Since Augustine's 'witness' concept, popes regularly preached against forced baptism. The theory required the maintenance of a certain Jewish existence in Christian society. That did not prevent local hierarchy from attempting to convert Jews. Such was, for instance, the decision by the Church Council of Basel in 1431 which required that Jews attend Church sermons. In 1565, the synod of Milan issued a similar decree, forcing Jews to attend Church sessions and listen to sermons for their conversion. Dominicans and Franciscans were important Church instruments for the enforcement of this policy. These friars would force their way into synagogues and use violence to impose debates on the Jews in the synagogues. This papal army was out, some believe, 'to eliminate the Jewish presence in Christendom – both by inducing the Jews to convert and by destroying all remnants of Judaism even after no Jews remained'.[65] The Church policy of frontal attacks on Judaism was also apparent in public debates enforced by the Church, sometimes by the pope himself, on other occasions by the secular rulers at the Church's behest. In such debates, senior rabbinical authorities were instructed to debate with a Dominican or other Christian scholar on whether Jewish belief is superseded by Christianity and, thus, terminated. Whatever the

Jewish scholar uttered was defined as blasphemy and caused even more harassment of the Jewish community. Often, the reluctant Jewish debater would have to flee the town after the debate. The failure to convince the Jews, through this means, frustrated the proselytisers and made them even more vicious.

For a long while the Church followed the teaching of St Augustine and did not coerce Jews to convert to Christianity. Missionaries tried to bring about conversions made by the free will of Jews but it was not to be done by force. On a local level, there were many instances where bishops and members of religious orders initiated forced conversions but this was not Church policy.

Paul IV, the grand inquisitor turned pope, abandoned that view. Luther's *Ninety-Five Theses*, which he posted on the door of the Wittenberg church in 1517, divided the Church. The Council of Trent, which was convened by Pope Paul III (1534–1549), sat over issues of Church reform and doctrine in three separate sessions (1545–1548, 1551–1552, 1562–1563). Paul, whose notion of what was right and wrong did not prevent him fathering children and appointing his two teenage grandsons cardinals, had already, in 1542, established the Roman Inquisition which was to pursue agents of doctrinal impurity in the Church. He chose Gian Pietro Caraffa, former papal nuncio in Spain, to head the Inquisition. He wanted Jews to convert, and containing them in ghettos was a means to that end. The delicate balancing act of the Church which combined hatred with protection was thereby disturbed. The attack on the Catholic Church by the Reformation and the onset of Protestantism brought about the excesses of the Roman Inquisition and the election of an inquisitor as pope. This Pope apparently believed that it was his role to bring back order to the world and that to this end force could and should be used. Violence was to be employed in the name of the Church in fighting the Protestants and once and for all in getting rid of the Jewish problem – by converting the Jews. By different means, Paul's successors continued with the same ideas. Pius V (1566–1572) expelled the 'obstinate' Jews from most of the papal states and his successor, Gregory XIII (1572–1585) forced the Jews in the Roman ghetto to listen to Christian missionaries whom he sent to preach conversion in the one and only synagogue Jews were allowed to have there. After years in which the Jews in Rome were left in peace, the Church snatched Jews, and especially Jewish children, and baptised them. Once these children were baptised, the Church ruled that they were no longer permitted to be in touch with their parents. A House of Catechumens for those 'waiting' for their conversion was established which the Church forced the Jewish community to finance. As long as the pope had secular control over Rome, abduction of children and women from their Jewish families and forced baptism continued to take place.

A 1703 Vatican document set out the regulations governing catechumens. The House of Catechumens, which was established by Pope Paul III in 1543, was located in Rome's *via Madonna dei Monti*.[66] Once inside, no-one was allowed to leave the building without permission. Anyone who was found out at night was subject to one month in prison locked in shackles with a diet of bread and water.

The number of Jews actually held and converted in the House of Catechumens was not great. Very few went there of their own volition, although were they to do so they would automatically subject their families to pressure to also convert. Many Jewish families were broken up through this Catholic institution. Cases are recorded of families where small children were baptised and kept by the Church, even when parents would not convert. The 'obstinate' parents were sent back to the ghetto and their babies held by force. In any civilised society, such activities would be considered criminal. Indeed, in the 1809 to 1814 interval during which the French occupied Rome, and during which the Pope was exiled, the rector of the House of Catechumens, Don Filippo, was deported to Corsica. Unfortunately, he came back after the French defeat in 1814.

The Church lamented the fact that the majority of those who came to the House of Catechumens were the destitute, who only came to better their material life. So eager was the Church to grab souls that anyone, whatever their mental state, who walked in was made to sign a document 'offering' his family to the Church, whereupon she would send the police to bring them in. So outraged was the Church by refusals that she made the Jewish community pay her expenses whenever members of the community were unwilling to convert to Christianity. Cases are recorded of people who had signed and changed their mind, but to no avail. Wives and babies were kidnapped by the papal police and locked in the House of Catechumens. In one recorded case, a pregnant woman was seized and, although she would not convert, the Church ruled that the unborn baby belonged to them. The House of Catechumens wanted to retain the woman until she gave birth but as the woman became ill, they agreed to let her return to the ghetto, provided the *fattori*, the leaders of the Jewish community, undertook to inform the Church a soon as she went into labour. When labour commenced, the Church sent a midwife who delivered the baby and immediately took it with her to the House of Catechumens. The family was sent an invoice for the midwife's services. There were cases of children who left home after an argument with their parents and knocked at the doors of the House on *via Madonna dei Monti*. No pleading of the family or second thoughts of the children would help. They were there and that was that. There was even a case of a Jewish family which was brought in after their senile eighty-year-old grandfather had signed his agreement.

In 1858, Pope Pius IX kidnapped a six-year-old Jewish boy, Edgardo Mortara, from his parental home in Bologna and had him installed in the House of Catechumens. The Pope, who took personal interest in the education of the boy, 'succeeded' with his endeavour – the boy became a Catholic priest. His parents tried to get him back, and were allowed to see him, but not to take him home. Delegations from the Jewish community pleaded with the Pope to return the child and were sent away with a rebuke for 'stirring up a storm all over Europe about this Mortara case'.[67] The Pope was right; the whole of Europe was indeed in a storm over this affair. The world media caught on to the story and reported every detail. It turned out that the world in 1858 was no longer willing to accept such abuse of power by the Church. France tried to pressurise the Pope into relenting and returning the child to his parents. He did not give in. The Pope's justification was that Edgardo had, according to a report, been baptised as a baby by a maid in the Mortara household who had secretly sprinkled water on the child pronouncing the baptismal formula. That, in the Church's eyes, made the infant a Christian and therefore under no circumstances permitted to be brought up by Jews.

Expulsion and Murder

In 561 the bishop of Uzes, in France, expelled all the Jews who lived in his diocese. In 937, Pope Leo VII encouraged the archbishop of Mainz to expel all Jews who refused to be baptised. In 1182, Jews were expelled from France, their property was confiscated and debts to Jews by Christians were cancelled against a twenty per cent payment to the state. Pope Innocent IV (1243–1254) approved the plan of St Louis, King of France, to drive the Jews beyond the boundaries of his kingdom: 'since We strive with all Our heart for the salvation of souls, We grant you full power by the authority of this letter to expel the Jews, particularly since We have learned that they do not obey statutes issued by the Holy See against them'.[68] In 1283, Jews who were allowed back to France were forbidden to live in the countryside to prevent Jews from 'leading simple country people astray' and, in 1294, they were restricted to special quarters within the cities. Further expulsions recorded include: from Bern in 1294; again from France in 1306; from many parts of Germany in 1350; from Hungary in 1367; from Strasbourg in 1381; from Mainz in 1420; and from Austria in 1421. In 1424 Jews were expelled from Fribourg and Zurich; in 1426 from Cologne; in 1432 from Saxony; in 1439 from Augsburg; and in 1453 from Würzburg. In 1485, Warsaw and Krakow expelled the Jews; and in 1492, three hundred thousand Jews were expelled from Spain.

Often Jews were allowed back to their homes if they paid a large ransom to the local authorities; this was soon recognised as a good source of revenue. A few years later, a new decision to expel the Jews would be promulgated and more ransom would be collected from them.

The hatred which led to expulsions sometimes ended with murder and massacres in the name of Christ and the Church. In Rouen, Orleans, Limoges and Mainz, Jews were massacred in a frenzy of enforced conversions, expulsions and outright murder in the years 1010 to 1020. Eighty years later, on their way to liberate Jerusalem from Muslims and Jews, crusaders in the First Crusade decided to begin by killing the local Jews. Under the slogan 'Christ-killers, embrace the Cross or die', twelve thousand Jews were killed in the Rhine Valley alone. The only ones saved were those who accepted baptism. In Jerusalem, the crusaders forced all the Jews into a synagogue and set it on fire. Those who tried to escape were forced back into the fire. In 1298, the whole Jewish community of Röttingen was accused of profaning the Host and were all massacred and burned. The Shepherds Crusade, in 1320, has been described as follows: 'The shepherds laid siege to all the Jews who had come from all sides to take refuge ... the Jews defended themselves heroically ... but their resistance served no purpose, for the shepherds slaughtered a great number of the besieged Jews by smoke and fire'.[69]

The Holy Inquisition

The Inquisition was originally instituted by the Church to combat heresy and should not have touched anyone who was not a member of the Church. Why were Jews affected? Pope Gregory IX, who wrote the imperial legislation which decreed the burning of convicted heretics into Canon Law, demanded juridical authority in matters of apostasy against Judaism. This enabled the Church, through the Inquisition, to interfere in Jewish life. Although the Church did not consider the Talmud to be heretical, it was included in the domain of the Inquisition. Bernardus Guidonis, whose title was 'Inquisitor of depraved heresy and apostasy of the Jews in the kingdom of France appointed by the Apostolic See',[ii] called for the burning of all copies of the Talmud and of certain other rabbinical books, and for their owners to be punished. The Inquisitions' main anti-Jewish activity was to prevent those who had converted to Christianity from lapsing to Judaism. From their point of view, these people were Christians and any apostasy was punishable. The fact that in the majority of cases the conversions to Christianity took place under duress was not considered by the Church to be relevant. Once converted, they were caught. In 1267, Clement IV (1265–1268) issued *Turbato Corde* which instructed the Inquisition to deal harshly with any Christians who joined 'the Jewish ritual' and to use all the apostolic powers to

---

ii   *Inquisitor heretice pravitatis ac perfidie Judaeorum in regno Francie per sedem apostolicam deputatus.*

eradicate such behaviour. Jews who had or who were planning to convert Christians to 'their filthy ritual' were to be punished. Adversaries, the Pope instructed, had to be thwarted by means of ecclesiastical punitive measures without the right of appeal and, if necessary, with the help of the secular authority.

The Inquisition's zeal in its anti-Jewish activities was such that Jews sometimes successfully appealed for papal defence against his own inquisitors. The intense anti-Jewish activities of the Church, the hatred, the Blood Libel, slander and general harassment, resulted, especially in periods of pogroms or heightened anti-Jewish activity, in mass conversions. Thousands of Jews were baptised to avoid expulsion or confiscation of property. These conversions, under duress, had nothing to do with true conversion or with these Jews accepting Christ as the Messiah and rejecting Judaism. In their hearts, within their homes, many continued to be Jewish. When the troubles abated, many wanted to return to Judaism, their own and their forefathers' faith. Many Jews who fled France to escape the long arm of the inquisitors, found to their horror that the Catholic Church, a truly global operator, hounded them wherever they went. Pope Innocent VI (1352–1362) directed the Franciscan, Bernard Dupuy, to search for converts to Christianity who had gone back to Judaism, wherever they were. The Pope specifically requested the kings of Aragon and of Castile to lend their help to the Inquisitor. Secret procedures, confiscation of property, torture and confinement in filthy dungeons, were all part of the routine. Adding insult to injury, Alexander V (1409–1410) instructed the papal legate in Provence to tax the Jews of Avignon and Venaissin in order to fund the growing apparatus of his appointee, Pons Feugeyron. This notion of taxing the persecuted to fund the persecution, would, five hundred years later, be adopted by the Nazis with relish.

Inflammatory preaching in various centres in Spain, towards the end of the fourteenth century, brought about anti-Jewish riots in Seville, Valencia, Barcelona and in other centres of Jewish population. Preachers called for the massacre of Jews and for the conversion of synagogues to churches. The Jewish community in Barcelona was decimated and thousands were killed in other towns. Many Jews died and many preferred suicide to conversion. Many, however, were baptised. It is estimated that up to half of Spain's Jews were baptised during the first twenty-five years of the fifteenth century.[70] These Jews, who converted to Christianity to save their lives, were called *conversos*. Many of the *conversos* continued to maintain their Jewish lifestyle and uphold Jewish rituals. Mass conversions on a truly large scale, such as those which took place in Spain after the 1391 pogroms, did little to improve the social conditions for these Jews: the converted continued to live within their own community; and Christian society was unable to absorb such numbers and unwilling to accept people who up until then had been unacceptable. Neophytes who actually wanted to assimilate and be integrated in Christian society found that as newcomers, they were treated by the 'old' Christians with disdain. Soon, laws were passed which closed public, judicial and other important positions to the *conversos*, who thus found themselves in a social limbo. They were not considered by Christian society to be 'real' Christians and became the subject of derision of Jews who pointed out to them that baptism had not helped them. Popes tried, without much success, to act against this discrimination. From the point of view of the Church it was counter-productive, as it reduced Jewish willingness to convert and the conversion of Jews was an important task of the Church. The status of Jews as pariahs was, however, convenient and ingrained in Christian society.

Aragon and Castile, which through the marriage of Ferdinand and Isabella were united in 1469, had a strong central government. Tensions between *conversos* and the Church, the establishment and the veteran Christians resulted in civil unrest, which Ferdinand and Isabella repressed with severe measures. In 1478, in response to their demand, Pope Sixtus IV (1471–1484) approved a Spanish Inquisition. This consisted of royal inquisitors who were appointed in addition to the special inquisitors appointed by the pope and to the Inquisition held by the local bishops. In his bull, *Exigit sincere devotionis* he gave Ferdinand and Isabella a licence to kill. The royal Inquisition was to a large extent greed-driven and many complaints reached the Pope about the terror and the unfair trials in which people were unjustly accused of apostasy and executed only in order to confiscate their assets. The Pope's response was to send more of his own inquisitors to Spain and to instruct the royal Inquisition to work in conjunction with the bishops. One of the new papal envoys was Thomas Torquemada. This Dominican Prior of the Monastery of the Holy Cross in Segovia was personal confessor to Ferdinand and Isabella, and, at their request, was appointed Inquisitor General, responsible for all inquisitors in Spain. The Holy Inquisition, for all intents and purposes, became the Spanish Inquisition. Although formally appointed by the Pope, Torquemada was soon an independent operator. Popes tried, but failed, to rein him in. Tens of thousands of *conversos* were tried by Torquemada's Inquisition and thousands were killed at the notorious auto-da-fé (act of faith) stakes at which heretics who would not recant were burned to death.

In 1492, Ferdinand and Isabella ordered the expulsion from Spain of all Jews who had not converted. Torquemada had for some time contended that *conversos* had to live in a *judenrein* environment. According to Torquemada, the proximity of Jews, reminding them of their ancestral faith, was a constant danger and resulted in high incidence of heresy amongst the *conversos*. Once the royal couple, who would later be bestowed the honorific title 'Catholic Monarchs' by Pope Alexander VI (1492–1503), were won over by that hypothesis, the road was clear for the grand expulsion. The Jews were given three months to make up their minds: convert or leave. It is estimated that about half of Spain's three hundred thousand Jews chose to leave.[71] Some made the mistake of leaving for Portugal where, five years later, they were forcefully baptised, without even the option of expulsion. Many of the Spanish Jews left for the Papal States.

The abundance of *conversos* in Spain continued to cause tensions between the new and the old Christians. Remarkably, they were even rejected by the very people whose vocation it was to convert them to Christianity. Religious orders refused neophytes. In fact, purity of blood, a notion which the Nazis would develop in their extermination of the Jews, and which the Church so very much objected to, was used by the Church herself in sixteenth-century Spain. In 1525, under pressure from the Franciscans, Pope Clement VII (1523–1534) closed the observant wing of the order to Christians who were unable to prove at least four generations of Christian ancestors. Similar instructions were approved by the Dominicans and by certain Spanish bishoprics. The Archbishop of Seville issued a decree preventing any position in the Seville church to first- and second-generation new Christians. In 1546, Pope Paul III (1534–1549) extended the decree to the third generation. Similar decrees were proclaimed in other Spanish bishoprics. This was Church generated racism and no longer theological anti-Judaism.

Book Burning

In 681 the synod of Toledo ordered the burning of the Talmud and other Jewish books. Various charges were brought – time after time – against the Talmud; it was considered to be objectionable, heretical and contain anti-Christian ideas; it prevented Jews from seeing the light and converting to Christianity. Considering the powerful status of the Church, it is surprising that she was so worried about what these Jewish scriptures did or did not include. However, the Church became obsessed with the Talmud. Jewish synagogues and homes were invaded under the Holy Inquisition and copies of these 'forbidden books' seized and burned. Every so often, popes would initiate public disputations between Christian and Jews, as a sort of a public trial of the text.

In a bull issued in 1239, Gregory IX (1227–1241) encouraged the burning of the Talmud everywhere. In 1240, Gregory instructed all prelates and monarchs in Europe to enable Franciscan and Dominican friars to seize all copies of it. In Paris, the king of France delivered more than twenty thousand copies seized from the Jews which were burned in a fire at the Place de Grève. Similar papal orders were sent to Church hierarchy in England, France, Portugal and Spain. In 1264, Pope Urban

IV (1261–1264) ordered the removal of certain passages in the Talmud reprehensible from a Christian point of view. In 1319, a further burning was ordered by the Inquisitor in Toulouse and in Perpignan.

In 1411, Pope Martin V issued a bull forbidding the Jews to read the text, and ordering the destruction of all copies of it. In 1443, Pope Eugenius IV re-issued a bull prohibiting Jews from studying it. On Jewish New Year's Day in 1553, the copies of the Talmud which had been confiscated in compliance with a decree of the Inquisition were burned at the Campo dei Fiori in Rome. Similar burnings took place in other Italian cities. Pope Pius IV decreed, in 1565, that the Talmud be deprived of its name. Pope Clement VIII (1592–1605) included all Jewish books in the Index of Forbidden Books. In 1757, a Polish bishop, Dembowski, convened a public disputation and ordered all copies of the work found in his bishopric to be confiscated and burned by the hangman. One thousand copies of the Talmud were thrown into a pit at Kamenets-Podolski and burned.

Blood Libel

The first recorded incident of Blood Libel took place in Norwich, England, in 1144. Blood Libel was a false charge against Jews which maintained that for Jewish religious ritual purposes, they would kidnap, kill and bleed a Christian male – in most cases a boy. Often the accusation was that Jews needed the blood of a Christian for the preparation of Matzoth, the unleavened bread eaten by Jews during Passover week. Hence, Holy Week regularly became the time of year in which any murder or disappearance of a boy would be blamed on the local Jewish community. Logical defences – such as the fifth commandment, Thou shalt not kill, or the Jewish Kashrus laws, the dietary restrictions, which forbid them to consume any food which contains animal blood, let alone human blood – were not listened to. A pattern soon developed of turning the graves of dead children, whose death was libellously ascribed to Jews, into holy shrines. William in Norwich (1144), Harold in Gloucester (1164), and others in Bristol, Bury St. Edmunds, Gloucester and Winchester were all buried in their respective cathedrals next to the archbishop's altar. The faithful came to worship their tombs and 'miracles' were soon produced by these shrines. From England the hysteria moved to France. In 1171, Blood Libels appeared in both Pontoise and Blois. The immediate reaction of Thibaud, the Count of Blois, was to burn all thirty-two local Jews. In Fulda, in Germany, Jews were accused of killing all five children and burning the house of a miller. Under terrible torture, two Jews 'confessed' to the crime and to the fact that Jews needed the blood of a non-Jewish child to bake Matzoth – thirty-four Jews were executed. The following year, Jewish communities in Lauda and in Pforzheim underwent similar ordeals.

The Libel and subsequent arrests and trials were often co-productions of the local rulers and local monks or clergy. Popes regularly objected; more often than not, after Jews had already been put to death. In 1247, two Franciscans accused the Jews of Valréas of killing a child (whose body was found in the canal) and using the blood for ritual purposes. The ruler of Montauban, Draconet, arrested a number of Jews. The Jews were tortured – some were quartered, some men were castrated, and women had their breasts amputated – until they agreed to sign the confessions dictated by the monks. Personal greed played a role in this affair: Draconet confiscated the property of all the arrested Jews. The local bishop was party not only to the burning of Jews at the stake but also to the benefits of receiving confiscated property. Finally, an appeal to Pope Innocent IV, who issued two bulls to bring an end to the situation in Valréas, produced a strong papal condemnation: 'whenever a corpse is found somewhere, it is to the Jews that the murder is wickedly imputed. They are prosecuted on the pretext of such fables ... they are deprived of trial and regular judgement; in mockery of all justice, they are stripped of their belongings, starved, imprisoned and tortured.'[72] A similar defence bull was issued in 1272 by Gregory X.

Blood Libel travelled like the wind and resurfaced time after time in any mixed community. Travelling monks were an important carrier of this virus. A leading Dominican, Giordano da Rivalto, in a sermon held on 9 November 1304, told his listeners that he was personally present and saw Jews stealing the Eucharistic Host in order to blaspheme it, as if they were attacking Jesus' body on the Cross. da Rivalto claimed that he saw how the 'boy Jesus miraculously appeared on the scene and rallied the Christian population to slaughter 24,000 Jews in punishment for their evil deed'. da Rivalto called for Jews who exhibited hostility towards Christianity to be exterminated. Like many other travelling monks, this Dominican friar was also instrumental in spreading the Blood Libel, which resulted in the murder by Christian communities of tens of thousands of Jews all over Europe.[73]

In her defence, one must stress that in the early days, the Church as an institution tried to repudiate accusations of ritual murder hurled at Jews and regularly called for Jews who were tried on such false charges to be released. In this context, popes would reissue *Sicut Judeis* papal bulls, which, based on the Augustine concept of keeping the Jews alive, demanded tolerance of the Jews. However, the Church's teaching and preaching of hatred and mistrust naturally produced Christian mistrust and acts of hatred. Moreover, spreading untrue stories about the Jews had its source in the Gospel depictions of the death of Christ. So violent were these mass-hysterical Blood Libels and the resulting attacks on Jews that their repudiation became a standard component of the papal *Sicut Judeis*. These papal bulls, issued at the behest and begging of Jewish communities, were often dependent on payment to the Church. In parallel with such defence bulls, the popes issued and reissued other bulls, such as *Turbato Corde*, which reminded their recipients that Judaism was a filthy ritual which Christians must always reject.

A derivative of Blood Libel were libels about Jews' attempting to kill not just one Christian child but whole Christian communities. Such charges made the rounds in the Christian world from the twelfth century onwards. In Bohemia in 1163, in Breslau in 1226, in Vienna in 1267 and in France in 1321, Jews were accused of conspiracies to poison wells. Such fantastic accusations, with all the ingredients to create anti-Semitic mass-hysteria, touched the most basic and raw nerves. Water, not only an essential source of life but also the ultimate cleanser – the ritual purifier – is contaminated by the Jews. For added mystery and tension, all such accusations included an element of conspiracy. The 1321 libel suggested that Jews conspired to poison no less than all the water wells of France. Five thousand Jews were burned alive in Guienne, France, accused of having incited villains to poison wells. The concept of a Jewish conspiracy to harm the Christian world, in one way or another, is still, even in the twenty-first century, a standard accusation born of two thousand years of hatred of Jews.

In a similar vein to the malignant well-poisoning slander, Jews were regularly blamed whenever plagues and epidemics struck. They were then executed, burned at the stake, or, if they were lucky, simply expelled in punishment for their culpability. Jews were considered responsible for the 1348–1349 Black Plague which caused havoc in Europe and which is estimated to have cost the lives of some thirty million. Jews were made to confess under torture at a trial in Chillon and, subsequently, pogroms wiped out hundreds of Jewish communities in Europe: in Basle all the Jews were gathered and burned alive; two thousand Jews were massacred in Strasbourg; twelve thousand in Mainz; and thousands were burned alive in Stuttgart, Speyer, Ulm and Dresden.

Blood Libel continued to crop up throughout the Middle Ages and for hundreds of years thereafter. Its symbols were frequently used by the Nazi propaganda machine to depict Jews and, of late, have appeared in extremist Islamic anti-Jewish publications. Blood Libel is a frightening example of incitement to hatred which has gone out of control. Jews were vilified, smeared and maligned by the Church and marginalised in society because of the Church. When catastrophes occurred, it was only simple and 'logical' to ascribe them to this rejected people. The people who killed God were 'obviously' capable of killing anyone. The sons of the devil must be behind the murder or the plague. It also suited local clergy and monastic orders, who were charged with developing the cohesion of their communities and increasing the numbers of the faithful, to blacken those who were outside the Christian community. Blood Libel was a means to that end. The *Sicut Judeis* bulls demonstrate that popes in general did not believe in these libellous accusations. They sometimes, but not always, objected to the unjust and cruel treatment of Jews who were falsely accused. And yet, over long periods of the nineteenth and twentieth centuries the Church clearly believed in the libel. Moreover, even when popes issued objections, these objections were not enough to prevent the virus-like spreading of the libel. It spread on the hotbed of well-prepared Church-induced and nurtured hatred.

Blood Libel was not just a phenomenon of the dark ages. It continued to hound Jews into the nineteenth century. When Father Tommaso, a Capuchin friar, went missing in Damascus in 1840, it did not take more than a day for the accusation to be formed that he had last been seen in the Jewish quarter of the city and that the Jews must have murdered him. The French Consul in Damascus, as Diplomatic Protector of the Catholic community, took charge of the investigation. To pressurise the Jewish community, more than sixty Jewish children were jailed and mishandled. The chief rabbi and several Jewish dignitaries were brought in for interrogation, as was a Jewish barber. Under the most terrible torture – flogged, thrown into ice water, genitals crushed, tourniquet placed around the head and ratcheted tightly – some of them 'confessed' to killing the friar, draining his blood and bottling it for the various synagogues in town. Old bones of a dead animal were produced as the remainders of Tommaso. Unlike the French consul, the Austrian consul maintained that the Jews were being framed for a murder they had not committed. The fact that no blood nor corpse had been found did not seem to stand in the way of the accusers. Ten Jews were sentenced to death by the Governor General, Sherif Pasha. The story quickly made the news all over Europe with full press coverage and international interest. Information about the forced confessions, the missing corpse, and lack of any real evidence created international pressure to free the accused Jews. The Austrian Ambassador for the Holy See approached the Secretary of State, Cardinal Lambruschini, requesting, on behalf of the Austrian Imperial Court, that the matter be reinvestigated as there seemed to be other explanations for the disappearance of the friar, reasons which were totally unconnected to the Jews. Lambruschini's response was negative. The Vatican had its own sources and did not doubt the truth of the accusation. Therefore, the Pope would not intervene. Damascus, at that time, came under the rule of the Egyptian viceroy of the Ottoman Empire, Mehemet Ali. It was Ali who at the last moment instructed Sherif Pasha in Damascus to drop the charges and free the Jews. By that time, two had already been hanged.

In 1869, Catholic scholar Henri Gougenot des Mousseaux published his book on ritual murder, *The Jew: Judaism and the Judaisation of Christian*

Peoples. In his book, the author claims that the Talmud 'not only permits the Jew but commands and urges him to cheat and kill the Christian whenever he finds an occasion to do so'. Pope Pius IX chose to praise the book and its author and awarded him the Cross Commander of the Papal Order. Fifty years later, the book would be printed in German under the sponsorship of Nazi ideologist, Alfred Rosenberg.[74]

At the end of the nineteenth century, Jews continued to be prosecuted in ritual murder trials. A spate of acquittals disturbed the Vatican. In an article published in 1892, *L'Osservatore Romano* explained why all recent trials had ended with acquittals:

> It only confirms the conviction that the Jews truly do murder Christians to use their blood in their detestable Talmudic and rabbinical rites, and that to help them conceal these crimes, as well as for others no less atrocious, the judiciary is entirely in the synagogue's control.[75]

With avid devotion the Catholic press covered every such trial giving minute details about the alleged crime which, in their reporting, was never alleged but was presented as the simple truth, regardless of the lack of any real evidence or of any subsequent acquittal. When an expert witness at a trial in Germany in 1892 testified that there was no basis in Judaism for ritual murder, *L'Osservatore Romano* explained that the professor had 'by his own confession not read the entire *Talmud*'. The Vatican manifestly knew better. Its paper concluded that: 'Unfortunately, although they tried to deny that the *Talmud*'s followers commit such an atrocious act, one cannot reasonably deny it.'[76]

As anti-Semitic agitation continued, the Vatican was approached by representatives of English Catholics (such as the Duke of Norfolk, Lord Russell, the Lord Chief Justice of England, and the Archbishop of Westminster) to publish a denial of ritual murder. The papal nuncio in Vienna considered it an outright temerity of 'the whole Judaic clique ... to invoke the Holy See's authority in support of the argument against ritual murder'. The nuncio need not have worried. In July 1900, the Vatican gave its ruling.

Monsignor Merry del Val, a future Secretary of State, was assigned by the cardinals as assessor on the matter. Chosen for the job because of his personal bias (an ancestor of his was, according to Catholic legend, crucified by Jews and venerated on church altars since), the Monsignor reported, with Pope Leo XIII's approval, that no such declaration of the Jews' innocence could be made. One of the Vatican documents on the matter added:

> Although nothing was found either in the Holy Office or at the Secretariat of State, where careful research was undertaken, bearing on this accusation

... ritual murder is a historical certainty. ...Such murder furthermore was charged and punished many times by lay courts in Austria, and recently another case of such murder, which took place in Polna, in Bohemia, was tried in court and brought to light, as the Vienna nuncio has written. Given all this, the Holy See cannot issue the statement that has been requested, which, while it may please a few dupes in England, would trigger widespread protests and scandal elsewhere.[77]

Thirteen years later in Kiev another ritual murder case shook Europe – the trial of Mendel Beilis. He was framed by the Russian authorities who, by raising anti-Jewish sentiments, hoped to divert anti-Tsarist tension. In the end, the Russian administration concluded that they had too much to lose in their international standing from a guilty verdict, and Beilis was found innocent. In this case too, the Vatican was approached to help. The request was made by Lord Leopold Rothschild with a covering letter from England's most senior Catholic aristocrat, the Duke of Norfolk. A limited letter of no great significance and in no way refuting the underlying allegation of ritual murder was sent by the Secretary of State, Cardinal Merry del Val, to Lord Rothschild. The Cardinal was, however, not willing to address his letter directly to the Russian court and it was thus not accepted by it. The Jesuit journal *Civiltà Cattolica* was, as usual, able to instruct the Catholic world of the Pope's and the Secretary of State's view: 'What in fact did the Jew Lord ask?', Father Paolo Silva wrote mockingly in articles which appeared in the spring of 1914:

> Among the authorities consulted ... to demonstrate the non-existence of ritual murder, there is one to which the synagogue attributes more value than all the rallies and all the newspapers in the world. It is one that merits our own special attention as well, for it is the authority of the Holy See. ... see the haste with which these eternal haters of the Christian name have sought to call on papal testimony to escape this capital charge.

> ... let us sum things up. A boy goes missing on the grounds of a Jewish factory and his body is found riddled with wounds. Science has established the time and the method; it has measured the systematic blows and the agony suffered by the victim. It has indicated the goal ... the murder was committed by people who wanted to extract the blood. Now of such people one race alone is known.[78]

The Catholic Church of 1914 still believed this. The Pope believed it, his hierarchy taught it and his media disseminated it. Therefore Jesuit Father Silva could write articles confirming that Jews actually drank blood all the time and that they must have ensured that the children they killed died in the most painful manner possible. It seems that those who read these articles would probably not have considered Nazi anti-Semitism extreme. Some, would not even have considered the Nazi solutions unjust!

It is, of course, understandable that a Church which is so engaged with the concept of the Eucharist in which the faithful drink the blood of Christ and partake in his flesh, should develop similar notions about the ritual use of blood in other religions. It is the centrality of the human sacrifice made by God, in offering his Son for the salvation of mankind, in the Catholic faith and the almost pagan notion in the Catholic ritual which demonstrate the Church's engrossment with blood. Unlike Judaism, which has totally forbidden human sacrifice and even the human consumption of animal blood, thereby removing it from the teaching, thinking, fantasy and ritual of the Jews, Christianity retained it, albeit in sublimated format.

The fact that it has been so difficult to stem the tide of blood libels is undoubtedly due to the pernicious effect of hundreds of years of hatred, mistrust and blame preached by the Church. Even when some popes spoke out in denial of the blood libel accusations, they never broke the spell of hatred, they never refuted the accusations of the Church Fathers and never condemned the revulsion stemming from the New Testament.

Rejection of Zionism

The Catholic Church's attitude to Zionism and later to the State of Israel was a direct consequence of her underlying anti-Judaism. The Church believed and taught that Jews, as unbelievers and rejecters of Jesus, were doomed to perpetual exile. Allowing Jews to return to the Holy Land, could, the Church feared, undermine this belief.

In 70AD, the Romans, who had conquered and ruled Judea, in reaction to a Jewish revolt against their rule, destroyed the Jewish Temple in Jerusalem and forced the Jewish leadership into exile. Sixty years later, according to some sources, another Jewish revolt in Judea resulted in up to one million Jews being killed. Many were sold into slavery and others were simply exiled. Some, however, managed to stay. Ever since, Jews have held on to their dream of a return to Zion. They prayed for it and educated their children to keep Zion always in their hearts. Some managed to reach it at the end of their lives, to die and be buried in the Holy Land. Others, a small number, lived in Judea, which the Romans renamed Palestine, throughout the long years in which Jews became dispersed all over the world. The Catholic Church's version is that Jews were exiled as a punishment for the rejection of Jesus and that they were doomed to live in exile. Zion, according to the Church, was no longer there for the Jews unless they converted to Christianity.

The nineteenth century saw an awakening of movements for national liberation in Europe. Zionism, the Jewish national movement, called for a homeland for the Jews to be established in Palestine. It was an attempt to bring an end to Jewish suffering. Not only were Jews discriminated against economically, limited in their choice of work, ownership of property and participation in civil society, they were also locked up in ghettos, forced to convert to Christianity, expelled from country after country and finally simply murdered – simply because they were Jews.

From the early days of Zionism, the Zionist leadership tried to gain papal blessing. In 1896, Zionist leader and visionary, Theodor Herzl, met Agliardi, the papal nuncio in Vienna and tried to interest the Church in his concept of a Jewish state in Palestine. A year later, the semi-official (Jesuit-edited) Vatican periodical *Civiltà Cattolica* made the following judgement on political Zionism:

> 1827 years have passed since the prediction of Jesus of Nazareth was fulfilled ... that [after the destruction of Jerusalem] the Jews would be led away to be slaves among all the nations and that they would remain in the dispersion [diaspora] until the end of the world ... According to the Sacred Scriptures, the Jewish people must always live dispersed and wandering among the other nations, so that they may render witness to Christ not only by the Scriptures ... but by their very existence.[79]

In 1904, Herzl had meetings with Cardinal Rafael Merry del Val, the Holy See's Secretary of State, and with Pope Pius X. He asked for papal support for the Zionist concept: Jews should be able to return to their roots and build a homeland in Palestine. The Pope left Herzl in no doubt – no ray of hope for the Jewish people would emanate from the Catholic Church:

> I know, it is disagreeable to see the Turks in possession of our Holy Places. We simply have to put up with it. But to sanction the Jewish wish to occupy these sites, that we cannot do. ... The Jews have not recognised our Lord and we cannot recognise the Jewish people ... The Jewish faith was the foundation of our own, but it has been superseded by the teachings of Christ ... Jerusalem is not to be placed in Jewish hands.[80]

At that time Palestine was still under Turkish rule; since 1517 it had been part of the Ottoman Empire. The Zionist movement tried, unsuccessfully, to lobby the Turks for recognition. As the First World War was coming to an end, the Turks lost control of their empire. In December 1917 the British army, under General Allenby, conquered Jerusalem. Where the Zionist movement failed with the Turks, it succeeded with the British government, which in November 1917 issued the *Balfour Declaration*. Lord Balfour, the British Foreign Secretary, wrote a letter to Lord Rothschild, which he asked to be brought to the knowledge of the Zionist Federation:

His Majesty's Government view with favour the establishment in Palestine of a national home for the Jewish people, and will use their best endeavours to facilitate the achievement of this object, it being clearly understood that nothing shall be done which may prejudice the civil and religious rights of existing non-Jewish communities in Palestine, or the rights and political status enjoyed by Jews in any other country.[81]

Benedict XV (1914–1922) continued the anti-Zionist policy of his predecessor, Pius X. The Zionist movement was informed that the Church objected to the Jews gaining control over the Holy Land. The Vatican Secretary of State, Cardinal Gasparri, mournfully spoke about the difficulty of taking 'back the part of our heart we have already given to the Turks, in order to hand it over to the Zionists'.[82] Gasparri was worried that the British might hand over the administration of Palestine to the Jews, which, of course, they never intended to do. In a meeting with the Belgian representative to the Holy See in 1919, Gasparri suggested that the Balfour declaration was the result of the influence of key British and American Jewish bankers. The British, according to Gasparri, did not understand the jeopardy, inherent in their policy, to Christian interests in the Holy Land.[83] A year later, the Cardinal, in a meeting with the French Cardinal Amette, spoke of Zionism which 'threatened to invade everywhere and take everything'. Gasparri said that the Holy See was not only opposed to the Zionist plans in Palestine, it was extremely worried about them. Gasparri, who embellished his points with anti-Semitic remarks, also undertook to influence Italian prime minister Orlando.[84]

Indeed, the Vatican used all of its political power to prevent the Zionist dream from materialising. To this end, the Vatican tried to interfere in the post-First World War restructuring of the Middle East even though it had no formal standing in the matter. The Church used her power, especially in Catholic countries, to attempt to exclude areas of Palestine from the mandate granted to Britain and to weaken the powers granted to Britain. It appears that the Church, as well as ensuring extra-territorial status for specific churches or holy sites, actually entertained hopes that she might gain territorial control over substantial areas in Palestine. In 1922, after lengthy negotiations, the newly established League of Nations granted Great Britain a mandate to administer Palestine. A similar mandate was granted to France to administer Syria and Lebanon.

Catholic and Orthodox Patriarchs instructed priests to preach against the selling of land to Jews by Christians. The Vatican's anti-Jewish and anti-Zionist message was also spread by the Catholic press. Articles warning of the danger of selling land in Palestine to the Jews appeared frequently. These articles were imbued with anti-Semitic bias toward Jews who take over businesses and trade and were 'well-known for their commercial acumen'. The Church was called upon to cooperate with missionaries of other Christian denominations and with Muslim clerics to convince farmers not to sell their land to Jews.[85] Although the Church tried to veil her anti-Zionist attitudes by maintaining that she was worried about the state of sites holy to Christianity, it was more than obvious that the Church knew that she had no reason to worry. Zionist leaders had always stressed this point; indeed they offered extra-territorial status for Christian holy sites. In 1921, Cardinal Gasparri confirmed that this was not an issue that worried the Church.[86] In the same year Ronald Storrs, the British governor of Jerusalem, met both Gasparri and Pope Benedict XV. The Pope complained that Jews had too much influence in the administration of Palestine, about the introduction of cinema performances in Jerusalem and about the government giving licences to prostitutes in Jerusalem.[87] Such underlying anti-Semitic concepts – connecting Jews with frivolity and immorality – were the basis for Vatican policy, propaganda and actions. In an interview given by a curial cardinal to *Il Secolo* in September 1921, the cardinal virtually attempted to blackmail the British government: 'England, which supports the one-sidedness of her High Commissioner in the Holy Land, with all her prestige and might, should not forget that the Holy See has at its disposal efficient means of retaliation. What impact – do you think – would a step by the pope in favour of the Irish Republic, have in the English speaking world?'[88] In England, Cardinal Francis Bourne, the Archbishop of Westminster, was supportive of anti-Jewish and pro-Arab policies and did his utmost to have the *Balfour Declaration* cancelled. He considered the idea of the Holy Land 'falling into the hands' of those who denied Jesus a 'grave affront to Christianity'.

Monsignor Luigi Barlassina, the Latin Patriarch of Jerusalem, also actively agitated against Zionism, spreading defamation wherever he went. He travelled around Europe attempting to blacken the Zionist movement with slurs and slander. In an interview he gave in 1922 to the paper *L'Italie*, Barlassina, who spoke of Zionism bringing moral disaster to Palestine, added that from the day Zionists became the lords of Palestine (which, of course, they were not) 'immoral acts – in the land which absorbed the blood of Jesus – had grown to distressing levels'. Titillating his audiences, the monsignor reported how this alleged Zionist control licensed the opening of brothels in Jerusalem, Jaffa, Nazareth and Haifa, bringing about a substantial increase in venereal diseases.[89]

The Catholic Church, which had failed in her attempts to keep the Holy Land from becoming a British mandate, tried hard to prevent a Jewish homeland from being established. The Vatican used its influence over Catholic countries such as Spain, Brazil, Italy, Belgium and France to further its anti-Zionist agenda. According to an Italian diplomat at the Council of the League of Nations, all clergy in France and in Italy were instructed to participate in an anti-Zionist crusade and to do their utmost to prevent the creation of Jewish hegemony anywhere in the world.[90]

Catholic Media

Professor David Kertzer demonstrates the use which the Vatican has made of the Catholic press to further its anti-Liberal, anti-secular and anti-Jewish drives.[91] In December 1880, *Civiltà Cattolica* started a series of thirty-six anti-Semitic articles, which were published over a period of three years. The articles could not have appeared without the pope's approval. Founded by the Jesuits in 1850, by order of Pope Pius IX (1846–1878), this publication received Vatican funding and its editors were appointed with the direct approval of the pope. Together with the Vatican daily *L'Osservatore Romano*, this bi-weekly publication was considered throughout the Catholic world to be representative of papal thinking, papal teaching and papal interests. Towards the end of the nineteenth century, the Catholic Church was producing language reminiscent, in its vilification of Jews, to that of the early Christian Church Fathers of fifteen hundred years earlier. More than that, the Church developed clearly racial concepts about the Jews, concepts which suggested that conversion did not change the Jews' negative traits and which led to Nazi racial ideology.[92]

The *Civiltà Cattolica* articles, which refer to the Jews as 'insolent children, obstinate, dirty, thieves, liars, ignoramuses and pests' craving 'absolute domination of the entire universe', were copied and quoted by Catholic media in Italy and in other European countries. Anti-Semitism spread. In 1882, the first international anti-Semitic congress was held in Dresden. More anti-Semitic articles followed. The articles directly fuelled political anti-Semitism. In 1892, Milan's *L'Osservatore Cattolico* furnished a German member of parliament with 'scientific material' for a parliamentary address on ritual murder. The anti-Semitic German Conservative Party had a hundred thousand copies of that speech distributed. In Austria a group of deputies, based on material received from *L'Osservatore Cattolico*, attempted to hold a public investigation of ritual murder by Jews. The President of the Assembly's failure to agree to the request was explained by the paper: 'As much as he feared retribution from the Jews, he loved their gold.'[93] In 1890, Father Raffaele Ballerini penned three long articles in *Civiltà Cattolica*, discussing 'The Jewish Question in Europe'. In 1893, Jesuit Father Saverio Rondina described the Jewish nation as one which 'does not work … has its stomach in the banks' and controls the stock market, freemasonry and the press.[94]

Catholic priest and theology professor Umberto Benigni was a protégé of Pius X, for whom he organised and ran the Sodality of St Pius V, an internal espionage ring which reported to the Pope on any clergy whose views were suspect. He was also violently anti-Semitic. In 1891, in *Picolo*

Monitore, he described Jews slitting Christian throats in preparation for Passover.[95]

Not only was it the fault of the Jews that the whole world hated them, according to *L'Osservatore Romano*, Jews actually organised pogroms to gain sympathy. In an article published in 1892, it was suggested the recent pogroms in Russia had been engineered by the Jews 'so that people sympathise with the victims and forget who their true persecutors are'. *L'Osservatore Romano* warned the Jews, less than fifty years before the Holocaust that they:

> had no one to blame but themselves ... As we have said on other occasions, take care what you are doing. Don't play with fire. The people's ire, although at the moment somewhat dampened by sentiments of Christian charity and by the tender influence of the Catholic clergy, may at any moment erupt like a volcano and strike like a thunderbolt ... A quarter-hour might be all it takes.[96]

Often these anti-Semitic articles in the Catholic press included a meaningless clause such as:

> We do not write with any intention of sparking or fomenting anti-Semitism in our country. Rather we seek to sound an alarm for Italians so that they defend themselves against those who, in order to impoverish them, dominate them, and make them their slaves, interfere with their faith, corrupt their morals, and suck their blood.

Such clauses are offered as proof that the Church did not espouse anti-Semitism. If you torch a house, whilst mumbling that you object to arson, you are still an arsonist. These articles were read by Catholic priests throughout the Church. Should they have doubted the truth as it appeared in the Jesuit journal, published in Rome, under the editorial control of the pope? Should they not have taught the members of their churches what they have repeatedly been taught by the Church? The Holocaust did not come out of the blue.

Unlike the Church herself, Church anti-Judaism was malleable. The hatred of Jews and its focus on their alleged killing of Jesus and rejection of Christianity were not dropped, but towards the end of the nineteenth and beginning of the twentieth century, a different kind of anti-Semitic Church propaganda started appearing. While constantly repeating that the Church objected to anti-Semitism, Jews were portrayed by Church organs with all the anti-Semitic terminology used by secular anti-Semites. In an article which appeared in 1928, the Jesuit journal *La Civiltà Cattolica* mourned the results of Liberalism's allowing Jews out of the ghetto. Jews had become powerful and had persecuted Catholics.[97]

Liberalism and modern society, were, of course, dangerous concepts in the Catholic mind. They are included in Pius IX's *Syllabus of Errors* (1864) and have been the subject of papal encyclicals. This article, which emphasises their role in the rise of Bolshevism, speaks of the Jews whose 'hidden meddling and the undue power thus acquired' were 'contrary ... to reason and the common good'. In a book review, which appeared in October 1936, a year after Germany had passed her race laws and three years into Hitler's rule, *La Civiltà Cattolica* spoke of Jewish involvement in both 'capitalist financial predominance and revolutionary Communism', concluding that 'if not all, still not a few Jews constitute a grave and permanent danger to society'.[98] Constantly repeating that the Church was against anti-Semitism, such articles and similar Church pronouncements, nevertheless, wrote the script for the rise to power of Fascism and anti-Semitism in Italy and Germany.

Chapter Six
The Holocaust

We Remember: A Reflection on the Shoah, the document issued by the Holy See's Commission for Religious Relations with the Jews in March 1998, states:

> This century has witnessed an unspeakable tragedy which can never be forgotten: the attempt by the Nazi regime to exterminate the Jewish people, with the consequent killing of millions of Jews. Women and men, old and young, children and infants, for the sole reason of their Jewish origin, were persecuted and deported. Some were killed immediately, while others were degraded, ill-treated, tortured, and utterly robbed of their human dignity, and then murdered. Very few of those who entered the camps survived, and those who did remained scarred for life. This was the *Shoah*. It is a major fact of the history of this century, a fact which still concerns us today.[1]

Until the Second Vatican Council (Vatican II, 1963–1965), the Church did not consider that she had to deal with her anti-Judaism, let alone with any guilt issues tainting the Church in respect of the Holocaust. Several Church documents, starting with *Nostra Aetate*[2] in 1965 and ending with *We Remember* in 1998, have attempted to handle this question. The Church is still unwilling to accept responsibility for her historical role, or for her conduct during the Third Reich.

Unlike the Nazis, most members of the Church hierarchy did not believe that Jews should be killed. However, certain bishops, archbishops and cardinals are on record as having uttered views that condone the ill-treatment of Jews (their being dragged to concentration camps and killed), seeing such treatment as their due punishment for killing and continuing to reject Christ. These were a minority, although the majority, did nothing about the fact that members of their own flock participated in such barbarous acts. The Church was led in her attitude by Pius XII, the pope in the years 1938 to 1958.

What did the Catholic Church – which maintains that she is the moral beacon of humanity – do in the light of growing and ever more menacing anti-Semitism, the coming to power of Hitler and the ensuing persecution of Jews in Germany? What did her leaders do in the light of information which reached them about the systematic killing of Europe's Jews?

Hitler's Rise to Power

The Nazi Party was established as the *Deutsche Arbeiterpartei* in 1919 and changed its name to *Nationalsozialistische Deutsche Arbeiterpartei* in 1920. In 1923, after Hitler's failed Beer Hall Putsch in Munich, he was jailed and the party and her uniformed Storm Group, the SA, were banned. A year later, Hitler – who had made use of his time in jail by writing his programmatic book, *Mein Kampf* – was released from jail. Ideologically the party and her senior activists were anti-religious. To them, the Nazi creed sufficed and there was no need for any other gods and most certainly not for any others who considered themselves to be representatives of another god. Both Hitler and Goebbels (Hitler's chief propagandist) came from Catholic backgrounds. They both understood the need to refrain from totally falling out with the Churches, because they recognised the power of religion. Although the Church would prove herself compliant, there was no question that in their plans, they would be 'dealing' with the Church, once the war had been won.

German Catholic leaders were concerned about the political successes of the National Socialists in the late 1920s and early 1930s. This concern was, however, not about the Nazis' anti-Semitism. Some Catholics, such as Franciscan father Erhard Schlund, considered the 'endeavour to maintain the purity of the German blood and German race', to be the Nazis' 'healthy core'. Moreover, he agreed with the Nazis' resolve to fight the Jewish 'hegemony in finance, the destructive influence of Jews in religion, morality, literature and art, and political and social life'.[3] The first reaction of members of the hierarchy of the German Catholic Church to the alarming growth in the popularity of the Nazis came in 1930. Although no joint policy was agreed by the German Bishops' Conference and bishoprics formulated their own views differently, the general line was that membership of the Nazi Party was not commensurate with being a Catholic. The Fulda Bishops' Conference had been a consultative body of German bishops for more than fifty years. It was, however, not a body whose decisions were binding. A decision in 1921 by the Bishops' Conference to prohibit membership of any organisation which was hostile to the faith was meant to ban membership of the Freemasons or any Socialist party. The rules were that if after a warning, members persisted in their membership in a proscribed organisation, they would be denied the sacraments. A specific decision, which was tabled at the 1931 Conference, to include the Nazi Party as a proscribed organisation as defined in the 1921 ruling, did not pass. Instead, the bishops passed a generally worded statement against radicalism. This covered extreme Nationalism, Socialism and Communism. The Church also went out of her way to state always how patriotic she was. Some of these statements, such as that made by the bishops of Paderborn, make, at least retrospectively, painful reading:

> We love the fatherland, the country of our cradle, the country of our language, the country of our forefathers, the country of our graves. ... Indeed, we consider the fulfilment of the citizen's duties towards the fatherland and his participation in the development of the individuality and greatness of our people a command of God.[4]

This statement was by no means unusual. The Church rarely issued a document without assuring the public and those in power of her loyalty to the state and with the ever growing nationalism, the Church would include the German *Volk*, the fatherland and, with time, the *Führer*, in her pledges of fidelity. The Church's perception that she had constantly to avow her allegiance stems from the *Kulturkampf* days of the 1870s. In those days, Bismarck seized upon the Catholic Church as a body whose allegiance was to Rome and to other Catholic countries, rather than to Germany.

Reichstag (federal parliament) elections in July 1932, gave the Nazi Party thirty-seven per cent of the votes, making them the largest party. At first, President Hindenburg refused to make Hitler Chancellor, but further elections and political wrangling gave Hitler the chancellorship in January 1933. On 27 February, the *Reichstag* was set on fire – a final backdrop for the very last *Reichstag* elections, to be held in March 1933. The arson attack was an opportunity for the Nazis to arrest thousands of Communists, Socialists and Liberals. The first concentration camps (Esterwegen and Dachau) were opened for the intake of these prisoners. Dachau was formally inaugurated by the Head of the SS, Heinrich Himmler, on 1 April 1933. Could one have expected the Catholic Church to have objected? They hated the Communists even more than the Nazis did. The elections in 1933 gave the Nazis forty-four per cent of the votes and with the aid of a few more nationalist delegates (the ultra conservative German National People's Party), Hitler now commanded a majority. Parliament immediately passed an Enabling Act which gave Hitler dictatorial powers for four years, thereby giving away its own powers and making itself redundant as a democratic institution.

The arrest and torture of political opponents in the newly established concentration camps did not bode well. On the other hand, many bishops who had been longing for a more authoritative running of the state, now, at long last, could see a strong hand which might save Germany from the mess and the unrest of the years following the First World War. Moreover, the Nazis, just like the Church, were ardent anti-Marxists. The bishops may not have been enamoured of some aspects of the Party but the main point is that the Nazis had won and the Church was eager to do a deal with the victors. These were the signals from Rome and this was the wish of the hierarchy. By the end of March 1933, a week after the Enabling Act was passed, the German bishops issued their declaration withdrawing their ban on membership of the Nazi Party. The clergy were issued with clear instructions: members of the Nazi Party were now entitled to receive holy sacraments, and should not be refused Church burial. At such burial services, it was permitted for secular organisations to parade their flags outside the church. Although the Church preferred flags not to be brought into churches, such situations should be handled with tact and without causing scandal. The clergy were further informed that there was no prohibition on members attending divine services in Nazi uniforms – regardless of their numbers – thereby opening the door to Nazi demonstrations inside churches.[5]

The German population was fully aware of the ever harsher steps taken by their Government against Jews. They were also eye-witnesses to the acting out of anti-Semitic sentiments by some of their fellow-citizens under a regime which not only condoned such activities but promoted them. In an atmosphere of growing anti-Semitism, the now formally anti-Semitic Government set out further to stir up the German people against the Jews. The first governmental act was to organise a one-day boycott of German Jewry on 1 April 1933. Posters, banners, radio broadcasts and newspapers called on the population to refrain from buying at Jewish shops. Uniformed SA men painted all the shops owned by Jews with a Star of David and a large sign: JUDE (JEW). They then stood menacingly in front of these shops.[6] A week later the government enacted a law to banish the Jews from the German civil service. In May, the Government organised the burning of books. All over Germany, students burned tens of thousands of books by Jewish authors. Other books deemed to be 'un-German' or 'anti-Nazi' were also burned. Culture was the first sphere in which the new Nazi regime tried to eradicate all Jews. The Historian Saul Friedländer makes the point that anti-Jewish measures were not only acts of terror but also symbolic declarations, reflecting the penetrative presence of ideology in the system.[7] Cardinal Bertram, the Presiding Bishop of the German Bishops' Conference, explained to his colleagues that the April boycott was an economic act which had nothing to do with the Church. Freiburg Archbishop Konrad Gröber was upset that it had also harmed Jews who had long ago converted to Catholicism. This point was also made by the Archbishop of München und Freising, Cardinal Faulhaber, in his letter to Pacelli. The boycott against the Jews was no problem – the fact that it ended quickly was proof of the Jews' ability to look after themselves – but the fact that loyal Catholics, and even those whose parents had already converted to Catholicism, should be harmed by the boycott and by the new employment laws was 'unfair and hurtful'.[8]

From the start, many were eager to participate in the anti-Jewish measures: sports organisations expelled their Jewish members, cities prohibited Jews from utilising municipal sports installations and public swimming pools, the use of Yiddish was prohibited in meat markets and Jewish artists were prevented from participating in cultural events. The city of Frankfurt removed a public sculpture of Heinrich Heine. Anti-Semites now had a license to demand anti-Jewish action and many local politicians succumbed to such demands. It spread everywhere; universities too, willingly participated in the purge of Jewish academics. In 1933 alone, one thousand two hundred Jewish academics were dismissed from German institutions of higher learning.[9]

Hitler met the chairman of the German Bishops' Conference, Bishop Wilhelm Berning on 26 April 1933. Hitler exploited the Church's own anti-Semitism and anti-liberalism to establish a common, almost communal, interest with the Church. At their meeting, Hitler said to Berning:

> I have been attacked because of my handling of the Jewish question. The Catholic Church considered the Jews pestilent for fifteen hundred years, put them in ghettos, etc., because it recognized the Jews for what they were. In the epoch of liberalism the danger was no longer recognized. I am moving back toward the time in which a fifteen- hundred-year tradition was implemented. I do not set race over religion, but I recognize the representatives of this race as pestilent for the state and for the Church, and perhaps I am thereby doing Christianity a great service by pushing them out of schools and public functions.[10]

Berning was truly taken with Hitler, who 'spoke with warmth and equanimity, here and there temperamentally. Not a word against the Church, for the bishops nothing but appreciation.' To convince the bishops that he would not do away with the Church schools, Hitler explained why they were important to him: 'Trouble with Poland is on the horizon. We need soldiers, devout soldiers. Devout soldiers are the most valuable, because they risk all. Therefore, we shall keep the confessional schools in order to bring up believers.'[11] Hitler was softening the German bishops' attitude to the newly elected Nazi Government, whilst making them party to his Poland campaign. Three weeks later, Berning and Konrad Gröber (the Bishop of Freiburg) went to the Vatican on their *ad limina* visit.[i] By July the *Reichsconcordat* would be signed.

A conference of all German Catholic bishops was convened in Fulda and sat for three days from 30 May to 1 June 1933. It produced the first

---

i   Once every five years, every bishop must present himself to the pope and render an account of the state of his diocese.

– of what turned out to be a flood – of Catholic documents hailing the Führer. The Fulda pastoral letter called for human liberty to be limited 'only as much as the common good demanded'. You might have expected the good people to demand freedom rather than suggest the most efficient level at which liberty should be curtailed. In fact, the bishops advised the Nazis that such policy would be most expedient. They should take care, not because it was morally wrong, but because abuse of authority weakened and damaged the state. This advice from one absolute power structure to another was followed by clear support for the concept of a strong dictatorship:

> The value and meaning of authority attain particular importance especially in our Holy, Catholic Church and have led to that complete determination and victorious strength of resistance which even our enemies admire. We Catholics, therefore, do not find it at all difficult to appreciate the new, strong stress on authority in the German state.
>
> … Our German nation, after years of bondage, disregard for our national rights, and shameful interference with them, must again receive that freedom and place of honour in the family of nations which is its due on account of its numerical size and its cultural ability and performance.[12]

This could have been penned by the Nazi ministry of propaganda. It was only the beginning. Bishop Franz Rudolf Bornewasser, bishop of Trier, declared before a gathering of Catholic youth inside the Cathedral of Trier: 'With raised heads and firm step we have entered the new Reich and we are prepared to serve it with all the might of our body and soul.'[13]

The *Reichsconcordat*, the infamous concordat with Nazi Germany, was signed in July 1933. Cardinal Pacelli was the Vatican's Secretary of State and former nuncio in Berlin. He was the man who had negotiated the Vatican concordat with Bavaria in 1924, that with Prussia in 1929, and that with Baden in 1932. He was not only a great believer in the power of contractual relations between the Vatican and various countries, but also a great admirer of everything German – language, culture and people. This would colour his attitude to Germany throughout the Third Reich years.

Chancellor Hitler, who was systematically dismantling all the civil structures in Germany and installing a regime of internal terror, was eager to attain the Vatican stamp of approval. By the time the new *Reichsconcordat* was signed, the following laws had already been passed in Germany: all Jewish staff in the civil service to be dismissed; all trade unions dissolved; all assets of the Communist Party seized; all parties except the Nazi Party dissolved. The concordat stipulated that Germans had the freedom to practice religion and that the Catholic Church had the freedom to administer herself. The legal status of the Church and the clergy was defined along with her role in education. The Church, on the other hand, undertook to stay out of politics. A clause confirmed that most diocesan clergy would be exempt from military service should general mobilisation take place. This clause was kept secret until the outbreak of the war. It is noteworthy that at a time when, according to the Versailles Treaty, Germany was not permitted to rearm or to build up an army, the Vatican included a (secret) annex to its concordat with Nazi Germany which ensured that clerics would be exempt from general conscription. Neither party wanted openly to reveal that it was making plans for the time when Germany would be going to war again.

Congratulatory letters and telegrams were sent to Hitler by individual bishops and cardinals as well as by the Fulda Bishops' Conference. They included jubilant declarations and patriotic pledges such as: 'diocese and Bishop will gladly participate in the building of the new Reich'. Munich's Cardinal Faulhaber congratulated Hitler on his statesmanship and on the boost to Germany's prestige which the 'handshake with the papacy' had brought.[14]

The Nazis ran the country and the Vatican – by signing the concordat – had given its approval. They were able to look away from the hundreds of Catholics who were incarcerated on trumped up charges, the interference by SA troops in religious services, not to speak of the terrorising of anyone who opposed the Nazis. In this mood of euphoria, Vicar General Steinmann from Berlin, at a public meeting of several thousand Catholic youths, said:

> What we all have longed and striven for has become reality: we have one Reich and one Führer and this leader we follow faithfully and conscientiously ... For us this is not a question of personality. We know that he who stands at the head is given us by God as our leader.[15]

What else should the young Catholics do than join the Nazi party, the SA, the SS, and take part in the building of a new Germany at the behest of their spiritual guides from the Catholic Church? What wonderful occasions these mass-gatherings of the faithful must have been for their Catholic attendees. For years the Church had preached about the danger of Bolshevism and Communism, as did Hitler. For almost two thousand years, the Church had taught about the 'perfidious' Jews, about the Jews who are forever to be punished, and the Jews who are not to be permitted the same rights as Christians. Hitler was in full agreement. Finally, the Nazis – who had undertaken to fight the Bolsheviks and Communism and to rid Germany of her Jews – and their beloved Church had come to an agreement. The Secretary General of the *Katholischer Gesselenverein* (Catholic Journeyman's Association) suggested that his members would turn into loyal SA and SS men. This enthusiasm did not help them. By early 1939, they too – just like the rest of the Catholic infrastructure in Germany, the Catholic Student Associations and Catholic Young Men's Associations – were closed down by the State and by the regime which they had done so much to support and to encourage.

The central service of thanksgiving for the signing of the *Reichsconcordat* was coordinated between the Nazi propaganda departments and the Church. The service was held on 10 September, some two months after the government passed a law which introduced the enforced sterilisation of handicapped persons, gypsies and blacks. At the Cathedral of St Hedwig in Berlin, uniformed formations of SA and SS men, holding Nazi flags and banners, attended the service jointly with Catholic organisations and the Papal Nuncio, Cesare Orsenigo. Before the Nazi hymn (the *Horst Wessel*) was sung, the preacher eulogised Hitler: 'a man of marked devotion to God and sincerely concerned for the well-being of the German people that will be governed in accordance with the will of the Divine Creator'.[16] The mood of Catholic collaboration with the Nazis infiltrated all levels and soon there were Catholic theologians available to explain the correlation between National-Socialism and Catholicism. In an article which is missing from the 1952 bibliography of his work to celebrate his seventy-fifth birthday, but which appeared in the 1933 *Theologische Quartalschrift*, the Catholic theologian from the University of Tübingen, Professor Karl Adam, wrote:

> Now he stands before us, he whom the voices of our poets and sages have summoned, the liberator of the German genius. He has removed the blindfolds from our eyes and, through all political, economic, social and confessional covers, has enabled us to see and love again the one essential thing: our unity of blood, our German self, the *homo Germanus*.[17]

Hitler, a strong believer in *Lebensraum* – 'living space', a concept of German expansionism dating back to before the First World War – felt that Germany was overpopulated and needed additional farmland. To this end, 'lesser' peoples such as the Poles should be removed. He explained, 'only thus can we gain the living space that we need'.[18] In his quest for *Lebensraum* too, Hitler had Catholic theological support. In his article entitled 'The moral right of the German People to colonies', published in *Theologische Quartalschrift* in 1934, Professor Otto Schilling defended the right of the German People to an enlarged *Lebensraum* and pleaded for the return of the colonies which were taken from Germany after the First World War.[19] The Catholic theologian did not call for the invasion of Poland, but he manifestly supported the concept that Germany needed and was entitled to more space, which could be had by taking other peoples' land.

1933 was a year in which pedestals for Hitler were built by Catholic theologians, and SS and SA units were sent volunteers by Catholic youth leaders. There was even a priest, Father Senn, who in 1934, hailed Hitler as 'the tool of God, called to overcome Judaism...'[20]

The Nazi Party objected to marriage or sexual relations between Jews and Aryans. In 1935, the Nürnberg Laws would make these a criminal offence, but this topic had occupied the Party propaganda machinery for years. Attempts were made by Nazis before 1933 to pass laws against such relations, which were defined by the Nazis as *Rassenverrat* (racial treason). This concept would not have been alien to the Catholic Church. For her own reasons, she did not allow such intermarriage and she definitely did not permit sexual relations without marriage. In April 1935, The SS magazine *Das Schwarze Korps* called for fifteen-year sentences to be imposed on Christian Germans who had sex with Jews. Harsher even was the punishment another paper demanded for the Jewish sex partners – these, according to the *Westdeutscher Beobachter*, on 19 February 1935, should be castrated.[21]

For some, the Nazis were not extreme enough in their anti-Jewish measures. Protestant theologian, Professor Adolf Schlatter of Tübingen University, wrote a pamphlet for Christmas, 'Will the Jew have victory over us?' (*Wird der Jude über uns siegen? Ein Wort für die Weihnacht*).

At the Nürnberg Rally of September 1935, the Nürnberg Laws were made public. These were a series of racial laws against Jews. The 'First Reich Law of Citizenship' differentiated between *Reichsbürger* and *Staatsangehörige*. *Reichsbürger* were citizens of pure German blood, all the others were no longer *Bürger*, that is citizens, but only subjects. A 'Law for the Protection of German Blood and Honour' forbade intermarriage between members of the two groups. Secondary decrees to the laws disenfranchised Jews and deprived them of most political rights.

It may have been too much to expect the Catholic Church, with her dismal record concerning human rights and her apparent sole interest in self-preservation, to object to the German government's brutal treatment of its population. Two and a half years into the new regime, the country was now dotted with government-established concentration camps in which anyone considered troublesome was incarcerated and tortured. Thousands of internal opponents were murdered. Jews were not only ostracised but also deprived of their right to work and to study and with the new Nürnberg Laws they were deprived of their citizenship. The Government defined a superior Aryan race and made Jews and others who were not purely German into lesser beings. In a speech to the Conference of Deans, on 28 October 1935, Bishop Clemens August Count von Galen told the deans of his diocese of Münster:

> It is not our job to pass judgements on political organisation and form of government of the German people, on measures and proceedings of the State, to mourn after past forms of government, to criticise present day policies.[22]

Galen changed his mind when the Nazi regime started its euthanasia programme and in 1941 spoke out against the killing of mentally handicapped people. This government programme was halted. It was a single protest: he never spoke out against the Government's treatment of the Jews, neither in the early days, nor when it came to the Final Solution.

Was it really not the bishops' job to defend the moral order? Should a bishop, such as Bishop Berning of Osnabrück, on visits to concentration camps have greeted their commanders with *Sieg Heil*? Having praised the camp guards for their work, should he have instructed the inmates of the camp in 'the duty of obedience and fidelity towards people and state that was demanded by their religious faith'?[23]

One cannot avoid the conclusion that the Catholic Church – which was anti-Communist and anti-Jewish, which was nervous about militancy in trade unions and which promised the fires of hell to homosexuals – had found a government with which she was in agreement. However, the rights which had been agreed in the *Reichsconcordat* were systematically eroded by the German government. The *Schriftleitergesetz*, a law which provided for the screening by Goebbels' *Pressekammer* of all newspapers' and periodicals' editors, had been introduced in 1933. At first the editors of many Catholic publications were exempt from this law. In 1935, Goebbels decided to turn the screw and cancelled that exemption. Additionally, all the daily papers were prohibited from publishing articles which had religious content. In 1933, there were some four hundred Catholic dailies in Germany. In 1935 they were all closed. Soon thereafter, additional restrictions meant that two-thirds of the Catholic weeklies had to close down. Continued limitations on Catholic life resulted, in March 1937, in the papal encyclical *Mit brennender Sorge*. The Pope, Pius XI, was worried.

Mit Brennender Sorge

The encyclical, which means 'With Deep Anxiety', was issued in March 1937. The Pope expresses his dissatisfaction with Nazi Germany's disregard for the terms of the concordat, agreed with Hitler only four years earlier. In January 1937, three cardinals and two bishops travelled to Rome to discuss the matter with the Pope. Cardinal Faulhaber drafted a suggested text which became the base for the encyclical. The final document condemned the German Government's treatment of the Church. Elaborate and secret arrangements were made to print it in Germany and to have it read from the pulpits of all Catholic churches on Passion Sunday, 14 March. To avoid postal censorship, bishops arranged for the encyclicals to be delivered to parishes by hand. The Church had proven that she was able to undertake a clandestine operation, although the twelve print plants which collaborated with the Church were immediately closed by the Nazis and many of their staff were imprisoned.

The publication and distribution of *Mit brennender Sorge* was a courageous feat. Unfortunately, it was wasted. When the Vicar of Christ spoke, he spoke like a lawyer dealing with a breach of contract. The terms of the *Reichsconcordat*, the Pope complained, were not adhered to by the Nazis. Although the Pope was proven wrong, as 'the other contracting party emasculated the terms of the treaty, distorted their meaning, and eventually considered its more or less official violation as a normal policy', he did not break the agreement.[24]

What could have been an opportunity to signal to Catholics worldwide that what Germany was doing was unacceptable and dangerous and that Nazi Germany must be fought with all means, was missed. Instead, the Vatican opted for: 'We shall continue without failing, to stand before the rulers of your people as the defender of violated rights, and in obedience to Our Conscience and Our pastoral mission, whether We be successful or not, to oppose the policy which seeks, by open or secret means, to strangle rights guaranteed by a treaty'. The only practical issue the encyclical dealt with was Catholic education.[25] If that was the most the Church would do to safeguard rights of the Church and of Catholics which had been agreed in the concordat, what – if anything – could one have expected from the Church with regard to the rights of Jews?

Racism was not defined as the main topic of the encyclical, and yet it did very clearly – without naming Nazism – condemn the Nazi racial concept. It also condemned the Fascist raising of the state to too high a level.[26]

The Pope condemned German governmental pressure on Catholics to leave the Church: 'If the oppressor offers one the Judas bargain of apostasy he can only, at the cost of every worldly sacrifice, answer with Our Lord: "Begone, Satan!"' He called on Catholics to withstand pressure suggesting 'that this infidelity to Christ the King constitutes a signal and meritorious act of loyalty to the modern State'. They were to withstand 'Secret and open measures of intimidation, the threat of economic and civic disabilities' and, as 'the highest interests are at stake, with the alternative of spiritual loss, there is but one alternative left, that of heroism'.

The encyclical, however, did not have a word to say about the hounding of Jews in Germany. The papal realm of pain is defined in the first paragraph of the encyclical, in which he speaks of the 'trials of the

Church' and those who have remained loyal to her.[27] The following forty-two paragraphs do not mention Jews overtly. Indirectly, Jews are referred to, in true Catholic style, as

> the chosen people, bearers of the Revelation and the Promise, repeatedly straying from God and turning to the world. Eyes not blinded by prejudice or passion will see in this prevarication, as reported by the Biblical history, the luminous splendour of the divine light revealing the saving plan which finally triumphs over every fault and sin.

Even in a period so difficult for Jews, the Vatican was unable to issue a document which did not remind its listeners that Jews were sinfully straying.

Five days after the publication of *Mit brennender Sorge*, in its vehement anti-Communist encyclical, *Divini redemptoris*, the Vatican showed that it was able to do better. Communism was clearly and substantially considered by the Catholic Church to be more evil than Nazism. Nazism was not even mentioned in *Mit brennender Sorge*, whereas *Divini redemptoris* is not only an anti-Communist propaganda tool, it is virtually a manual for the clergy on how to attack Communism. It explains Communist concepts and terminology and throws its own interpretations onto Communist activities in Russia, Mexico and Spain.[28]

Quoting his predecsssor, Leo XIII, who in his encyclical *Quod Apostolici Muneris* defined Communism as 'the fatal plague which insinuates itself into the very marrow of human society only to bring about its ruin', Pius XI, in his diatribe against the 'Communist plague ... the slippery path which will precipitate one and all to ruin and catastrophe', warns that 'entire peoples find themselves in danger of falling back into a barbarism'. Without holding back, the Vatican in its attack on Communism prepares an action plan against 'this all too imminent danger, ... bolshevistic and atheistic Communism', which 'strips man of his liberty, robs human personality of all its dignity, and removes all the moral restraints that check the eruptions of blind impulse.' Whereas *Mit brennender Sorge* did not refer to state terrorism in Germany, *Divini redemptoris* has no such compunction as it explains that 'it is terrorism that reigns today in Russia, where former comrades in revolution are exterminating each other'. This encyclical is a call to arms and a clear action plan, to 'defend Christ and Christian civilization from this pernicious enemy.' The Pope defines Communism as 'intrinsically wrong' and forbids collaboration 'with it in any undertaking whatsoever.' Priests are sent by the Pope to the poor and to 'the workingman', who he explains are more vulnerable to the 'wiles of agitators.' Priests are to rekindle their faith and specifically show the extent to which Christianity is a social religion, otherwise 'they will become an easy prey for the apostles of Communism.' *Divini redemptoris* is also a papal activation order for the lay movement *Catholic Action* and for 'auxiliary forces'. It is important that their members be trained, 'by study-circles, conferences, lecture-courses and the various other activities undertaken with a view to making known the Christian solution of the social problem.' The militant leaders of *Catholic Action* are called to action which 'is the means best calculated to save these, Our beloved children, from the snares of Communism.'

The Pope concludes by addressing the 'Catholic workingmen young and old… they are to bring back to the Church and to God those immense multitudes of their brother-workmen. .. this mission, which must be fulfilled in mines, in factories, in shops, wherever they may be labouring, should at times require great sacrifices.'

In *Divini redemptoris*, therefore, the Church had proven that she could speak in direct and clear language, attacking wrongs, attacking power and calling the people to combat what she considered to be evil.

Pro-German Vatican Secretary of State and future Pope Pius XII, Cardinal Pacelli, signalled to Germany that 'normal and friendly relations with [Germany] would be restored as soon as possible'.[29] Two months after *Mit brennender Sorge*, it was business as usual as regards Church anti-Semitism. German diplomats in Rome must have been relieved when they saw *La Civiltà Cattolica*'s series of three articles on the 'Jewish Question' in May 1937, in which they could read that:

> 'the Jews are a disruptive element because of their dominating spirit and their revolutionary tendency. Judaism is … a foreign body that irritates and provokes the reactions of the organism it has contaminated.

The whole question consists in finding the most appropriate way of getting rid of the irritation and re-establishing, on a durable basis, the social organism's equilibrium and tranquillity. There are only two possible solutions: elimination or segregation. Elimination can be achieved in three ways: in a clearly hostile manner, through destruction; in a hostile but less cruel manner, through expulsion; in an amicable and kindly manner, through absorption. The first two are contrary to Christian charity and natural law. The third one has proven impossible, historically.[30]

The articles, which discuss the 'disruptive Jewish dominance' and proceed to analyse the pros and cons of segregation, conclude with a 'Christian solution' based on 'charity and prudence'.[31] Hitler's 'remedies' were different from those of the Catholic Church, but their definition of the 'ailment' was very similar.

In 1936, three years before Germany invaded Poland, the Primate of Poland, Cardinal August Hlond, issued a pastoral letter which opposed violence against Jews whilst describing in detail how vile the Jews were. Jews, the Cardinal wrote, had a fatal influence on morals, disseminated pornography, and were embezzlers, usurers and white-slave traffickers. Having spread such poison, he then tries to prevent his flock from killing the first Jew they see on leaving the Church. 'One does well to avoid Jewish shops and Jewish stalls in the markets, but it is not permitted to demolish Jewish businesses. One should protect oneself against the influence of Jewish morals ... but it is inadmissible to assault, hit or injure Jews.' In this document, which was read from every pulpit in every Catholic church in Poland, Hlond adds, 'not all the Jews are, however, like that'. But,

> It is a fact that the Jews are fighting against the Catholic Church, persisting in free-thinking, and are the vanguard of godlessness, Bolshevism and subversion. It is a fact that the Jewish influence on morality is pernicious and that their publishing houses disseminate pornography. It is a fact that Jews deceive, levy interest, and are pimps. It is a fact that the religious and ethical influence of the Jewish young people on Polish young people is a negative one.[32]

Hlond was the most senior Catholic prelate in Poland. The preaching of other bishops was sometimes even worse. Why did Pope Pius XI – who was truly worried about growing anti-Semitism, and who, in 1938, would coin the phrase 'Spiritually, we are all Semites' – not reprimand Cardinal Hlond?

The *Anschluss*

On 12 March 1938, the German army crossed the Austrian border. The next day Germany announced that Austria had become a province of the German Reich. On 18 March, the Austrian Episcopate issued a declaration supporting the annexation. However, even the Vatican was not amused when Cardinal Innitzer, the Archbishop of Vienna and the most senior Austrian prelate, welcomed Hitler's triumphant entry into Vienna by ringing the bells of all the city's churches and adorning them with Nazi flags. Innitzer was called to Rome and reprimanded. Not only was Austria's Cardinal Innitzer glad to see Hitler, the whole country also appeared to welcome the annexation. The population seemed eager collaborators with their new anti-Jewish rulers. In fact, Simon Wiesenthal maintains that half of the Holocaust's crimes were committed by Austrians, despite the fact that they constituted under a tenth of the total population of the Greater German Reich.[33]

In the first few weeks there was an atmosphere of a free-for-all attack on and plundering of Jews. Jews on their hands and knees were made to clean the pavements with toothbrushes in Vienna. It is almost inconceivable that things were so bad that Reinhard Heydrich, Chief of the Reich Security Head Office, warned the newly established 'Commissar for the Unification of Austria with the Reich', Joseph Birkel, that unless he would control the mob, Heydrich would instruct the Gestapo to arrest them. For a few weeks, though, Jews were frightened into handing over money and jewellery and even their apartments to members of the SA and to many Austrian con-men who took advantage of the chaos to rob the Jews. Soon, the robbing of Austrian Jews would become an organised operation run by Adolf Eichmann, on behalf of the Gestapo. In addition to other 'aryanisation' measures to take over Jewish assets in Austria, the SS devised a system by which the Jews would have to buy their exit visas in order to leave the country.

The imposition of security measures under Himmler immediately followed the annexation and tens of thousands were arrested; seventy thousand in Vienna alone. Many were sent to Dachau and a special concentration camp, Mauthausen, was established outside Linz in Upper Austria, in which more than thirty-five thousand Jews were executed. Adolf Eichmann, the Gestapo expert on Jewish matters, was sent to deal with the Jews. He took great sadistic pleasure in humiliating and brutally debasing Vienna's Jews. His stated policy was to rid the town of all her Jews, whilst, at the same time, acquiring a hefty income from the issuing of exit visas. Jews were blackmailed for all their assets and even pressurised into appealing to friends and family abroad for money in return for exit visas.

Austria, a deeply Catholic country, was enthusiastically anti-Semitic and had a long record of anti-Semitism. For example, in 1871, Father August Rohling, Catholic priest and professor of theology, published his book *The Talmud Jew*. Rohling, who served as an 'expert' witness in ritual murder trials, developed the allegation that Jews murdered Christian children for their blood which they needed for Jewish ritual purposes. The Austrian government, worried about the impact of Rohling's anti-Semitic agitation, requested the local archbishop to rein him in. Fürst Cardinal Schwarzenberg refused on the grounds that: 'It would make the worst impression on the clergy and the people if the episcopate would protect and defend the Jews by censuring a Christian priest and scholar who is a distinguished authority on the *Talmud*.'[34]

By and large, the German bishops acquiesced with the demands put on them by the Nazi Minister for Ecclesiastical Affairs, Hanns Kerrl, to demonstrate their support for the *Anschluss*. Cardinal Bertram instructed the churches to ring their bells on 9 April, the day designated by the Government as 'The Day of the Greater German Reich', which was to be followed on 10 April by a plebiscite to confirm the *Anschluss*. Some bishops, such as Regensburg's Bishop Buchberger, disregarding the brutality of the Nazi subordination of Austria, jubilantly spoke of the ringing of church bells as an 'expression of joy over the return of our Austrian brothers to the Greater German Reich'.

In an article which appeared in *L'Osservatore Romano* on 10 June 1938, the Vatican daily appeared to condemn the Nazis' violence towards the Jews in Austria. The author, Jesuit priest Enrico Rosa, argued that 'it is an error to say ... that the hunt for Jews is a "holy enterprise"', and referred to it as a 'brutal process, without legal status'.[35] Then, however, the paper added that it had no quarrel with the Nazis as to their reasons for hunting the Jews, only about the way Jews should be dealt with.

In 1938, at the International Eucharistic Congress, which took place in Budapest, Cardinal Pacelli chose to give his spiritual support to the Fascist government of Hungary which at that very time was passing anti-Semitic legislation. Pacelli referred to Jews as those 'whose lips curse [Christ] and whose hearts reject him even today'. The slogan of that congress, which took place in May 1938, two months after Germany's annexation of Austria, was 'Eucharist the bond of Love'. The direction of Pacelli's love was apparent from his words, which could almost have been penned by Nazi Minister of Propaganda Goebbels, himself: 'In the concrete working out of its destiny and its potentialities, each people follows, within the framework of Creation and Redemption, its own particular way, promoting its unwritten laws and contingencies according as its forces, its inclinations, its characteristics, its general position, recommend and indeed, often compel.' The Jews, according to Pacelli, 'usurp the best position in every field, and not always by legitimate means'. The result was the 'suffering of the immense majority of the native populations.'[36]

In July 1938, the Jesuit journal *La Civiltà Cattolica* published an article entitled 'The Jewish Question in Hungary'. The author explained that Catholic anti-Judaism in Hungary should not be seen as vulgar fanaticism or racism but as 'a movement in defence of national traditions and of the true liberty and independence of the Magyar people'.[37]

Anti-Jewish Legislation

Mussolini's first racial laws were introduced in September 1938; they had the effect of excluding Jewish pupils and Jewish teachers from all public schools. In October, a 'Declaration on Race' was issued. This was followed in November by comprehensive anti-Jewish decrees. These included prohibition on marriage between Italian Aryans and other races. Jews were banned from employment in the public sector and from any positions in banks of national interest and insurance companies.

Jews were forbidden to employ Aryan domestic staff. Over time, Jewish property would be expropriated and Jews were excluded from most professions.

The first shock of the September decrees regarding education produced an immediate reaction from the Pope. In an audience with a group of pilgrims from the Belgian Catholic Radio, the Pope said:

> Listen carefully: Abraham is defined as our patriarch, our ancestor. Anti-Semitism is not compatible with the sublime thought and reality evoked in this text. Anti-Semitism is a hateful movement, with which we Christians must have nothing to do ... Through Christ and in Christ we are the spiritual descendants of Abraham. No, it is not licit for Christians to take part in manifestations of anti-Semitism. We recognise the right of all to defend themselves and to adopt measures against those who threaten their legitimate interests. But anti-Semitism is unacceptable. Spiritually, we are all Semites.[38]

The Pope's reference to 'the right of all to defend themselves' is a blot on an otherwise moving affirmation. It is notable that the Vatican *L'Osservatore Romano*, which reported the audience, did not mention these papal words of condemnation of anti-Semitism. It was, thus, not reported in Italy, the very country whose anti-Jewish laws had prompted the Pope's emotional statement. At the Pope's specific request, it was published in Belgium.

The Vatican's attempts to change the Italian government's anti-Jewish laws were focused on two points only: the prohibition of intermarriage, which contravened the concordat with Italy; and the inclusion of converts in the government's definition of Jews: 'It is necessary that converts to Catholicism not be confused with the Jews,' wrote the papal nuncio to Mussolini.[39]

There must have been a significant school of thought in the Vatican which supported the anti-Jewish legislation otherwise *L'Osservatore Romano* would not have published Bishop Giovanni Cazzani of Cremona's homily for Epiphany. The Vatican, in fact, should have rebuked the bishop for preaching such a homily, which was published in January 1939:

> The Church has always regarded living side by side with Jews, as long as they remain Jews, as dangerous to the faith and tranquillity of Christian people. It is for this reason that you find an old and long tradition of ecclesiastical legislation and discipline, intended to brake and limit the action and influence of the Jews in the midst of Christians, and the contact of Christians with them, isolating the Jews and not allowing them the exercise of those offices and professions in which they could dominate or influence the spirit, the education, the customs of Christians.

> ... Catholics, obedient to the directives of the Church at present do not take
> on or accept Jewish domestic servants, or put themselves in the service of
> Jews when they must live with the family; and still less do they entrust
> their babies to Jewish wet nurses, or their children to be instructed or
> educated by Jewish teachers. If in our schools, until recently, Jewish
> teachers were not few, it was not because of the work of the Church.[40]

On the night of 9 November 1938, the German government organised
a state-wide pogrom, known as *Reichskristallnacht*, against the Jews.
Reinhard Heydrich was in charge. Police stations throughout the
country were instructed to organise 'spontaneous' riots after the murder
of a German official by a Jewish refugee in Paris. Synagogues were to
be burned, as many Jews as possible arrested and the police were not
to interfere with the rioting. One hundred Jews were killed; thirty
thousand were arrested and taken to concentration camps; two hundred
and sixty seven synagogues were set on fire; hundreds of Jewish homes
and thousands of Jewish businesses were destroyed. Damage to Jewish
property was calculated to reach twenty-five million marks. Adding
insult to injury, the government 'fined' the Jews for the damage to their
own property. German Jews were levied a collective fine of one billion
marks for the damage caused by the government's agents. In addition,
the government confiscated all the insurance payments made to Jews for
the *Kristallnacht* damages.

The Church remained silent, keeping true to her stance that 'the
Jews can look after themselves'. Not one cardinal and not one bishop
had anything to say about the dead Jews, about the Jews taken to
concentration camps or about the burning synagogues. Only the provost
of Berlin's St Hedwig Cathedral, Bernhard Lichtenberg stated that the
'burned synagogue is also a house of God'.[41] Thousands of Germans who
had participated in the pogrom were not instructed by the Church in
the immorality of their acts, of the sinfulness of their deeds. So they
continued.

Humani Generis Unitas

Humani Generis Unitas was a last-minute attempt of Pius XI to speak out
against Nazi racism. He died before he was able to publish it and his
successor, Pius XII, buried it.

In May 1938, Pius XI instructed an American Jesuit, John LaFarge,
to prepare an encyclical condemning racism and anti-Semitism.
LaFarge's superior, the General of the Society of Jesus, Father Wladimir
Ledochowski, killed the project. He did so by appointing two other
Jesuits to assist him. Assistants who Ledochowski could rely upon to
ensure that the encyclical would not sway from the traditional Catholic
anti-Jewish teaching. One of them, Father Gustav Gundlach, was the

author of the entry on Anti-Semitism in the *Theology and Church Lexicon* of 1930. The text of this entry, in which Father Gundlach explains which type of anti-Semitism is permissible, is most revealing, considering that it is unlikely not to have had prior approval of the General of the Jesuit Order.[42] Gundlach, the author of this anti-Semitic entry, who speaks of people as 'vermin' which need to be fought, of Jews who 'operate within the camp of world plutocracy' and of the 'darker traits of the soul of the Jewish people', was the man appointed by the General of the Jesuits to 'help' LaFarge in writing the Pope's encyclical against anti-Semitism.

Although LaFarge was instructed directly by the Pope to 'say simply what you would say yourself if you were pope',[43] he delivered his draft to his superior. Ledochowski, to delay the encyclical further, and sensing that the Pope, already very old and very ill, was not likely to live long, had the draft sent to the extremely conservative editor of the Jesuit newspaper *Civilta Cattolica*, Enrico Rosa.

By the time the last draft was ready, it was no longer the 'say simply what you would say if you were pope' document, but a hard-line Jesuit product. In a mockery of what the purpose of such an encyclical should be, this draft encyclical of 1939 reminded those who were persecuting Jews that:

> the Jewish people put to death their Saviour and their King ... blinded by a vision of material domination and gain, the Israelites lost what they themselves had sought.

> ... this unhappy people, destroyers of their own nation, whose misguided leaders had called down upon their own heads a Divine malediction, doomed, as it were to perpetually wander over the face of the earth, were nonetheless never allowed to perish, but have been preserved through the ages into our own time.

> ... The lofty concept the Church has forever held relative to the vocation of the Jewish people as seen from their past history, and her ardent hope for their eventual salvation in the future, do not blind her to the spiritual dangers to which contact with Jews can expose souls, or make her unaware of the need to safeguard her children against spiritual contagion. Nor is this need diminished in our own time.[44]

The Church's teaching and practical attitude toward the Jews

> demonstrate the need for energetic measures to preserve both the faith and morals of her members and society against the corrupting influence of error, these same doctrines likewise show the utter unfitness and inefficacy of anti-Semitism as a means of achieving that end. They show anti-Semitism not only as pitifully inadequate, but also as defeating its own purpose, and producing in the end only greater obstacles to cope with.[45]

Were these words meant to persuade the Nazis to change their anti-Jewish programme? Or was it the encyclical's suggestion of the 'utter unfitness and inefficacy of anti-Semitism', which was to persuade Hitler to tackle the Jews the Church's way?

And yet, *Humani Generis Unitas* condemns racism as

> the struggle for racial purity ends by being uniquely the struggle against the Jews. Save for its systematic cruelty, this struggle is no different in true motives and methods from persecutions everywhere carried out against the Jews since antiquity. These persecutions have been censured by the Holy See on more than one occasion, but especially when they have worn the mantle of Christianity.
>
> As a result of such persecution, millions of persons are deprived of the most elementary rights and privileges of citizens in the very land of their birth. Denied legal protection against violence and robbery, exposed to every form of insult and public degradation, innocent people are treated as criminals.[46]

It was meant to be an encyclical against racism and a call to all Catholics to reject Nazism and Fascism. Even then, the Catholic Church was unable to speak out against anti-Semitism without giving a long list of reasons for being anti-Jewish and explaining that anti-Semitism was an inefficient method of fighting the Jews. Were Catholicism and Nazism simply two competing schools of thought offering the public different approaches to the containment of Jews?

Pius XI died before he was able to issue the encyclical and his successor, Pius XII, decided not to issue this last-minute protest against Nazism. The Catholic Church machinery had been at work to prevent an aging pope from issuing an encyclical which would condemn anti-Semitism. It succeeded. Moreover, the Vatican has for years tried to hide the existence of the suppressed encyclical. To that end, the Vatican and the Jesuit Order have strenuously attempted to block any investigation into *Humani Generis Unitas*.

Instead of an anti-Fascist message, four months into his papacy, in July 1939, the new Pope lifted the ban his predecessor had placed on the French Fascist group *Action Française*. He was attracted by any group which promised anti-Communist fervour, regardless of their other political baggage. *Action Française* was an anti-republican, monarchist, right-wing group which the new Pope considered worth supporting as the world was sliding into a war initiated by the Fascist Axis powers.

During the War

In 1939 Germany invaded Poland and immediately divided the country, annexing one part to Germany and establishing the *Generalgouvernement*, a civil administration, in the other. Hitler's instructions were to kill the Polish elites and use the ordinary Polish people as slave labour force. Before Germany began systematically to kill Jews in 1941, the main people who suffered in Poland were Polish gentiles. Millions held in concentration and annihilation camps died of starvation, ill-treatment and epidemics. Germany specifically targeted the Polish intelligentsia, including doctors, lawyers, teachers and Catholic clergy, for extermination. Hundreds of priests were imprisoned, thousands were killed. The Polish clergy appealed to the Pope to speak out against the atrocities carried out by the German army and by the Nazi authorities in Poland. To no avail. The Holy See was repeatedly asked by Polish bishops as well as by governments of the Allied countries to condemn Germany. The Pope, who still had fond memories from his years as papal nuncio in Berlin, kept silent. Pius explained that 'silence spared the Poles from greater atrocities'.[47] Surely, if the Polish bishops asked for the Pope's public intervention, they – more than the Pope – could assess the risk of even greater atrocities on their people? There are various explanations for Pius' silence but sparing the Poles is not one of them. The Pope was willing to pay with the lives of the Poles in order not to anger Germany, because, despite his dislike of Hitler, he continued to believe in the importance of a strong anti-Communist Germany. The Pope, also, hoped to be an eventual peacemaker and sought to maintain credentials of impartiality. Should the Pope's role have been that of international diplomat instead of moral leader? Some of the reactions of the papal aides were simply outrageous: Secretary of State, Cardinal Maglione, in response to a 1942 complaint by the Polish ambassador that the Pope had not condemned German actions, replied that it was impossible for the Vatican to document each atrocity. Maglione's assistant, Monsignor Tardini, explained that the Pope kept quiet about the murder and atrocities in Poland in order not to put at risk the Church's charitable work in Poland. (The Nazis did not allow this anyway.)

In April 1941, Germany occupied and partitioned Yugoslavia. A new state was established by Ante Pavelic, the Catholic leader of the Croat Fascist movement, the Ustasha. Under Pavelic Croatia became an anti-Serb, anti-Jewish, anti-Communist, pro-German Catholic state. Virtually all Jews under Croatian rule were either killed by the Ustasha or transferred to be killed by Germany. The killing of Jews and Serbs by the Catholic Croat government was not kept secret. The senior Catholic clergyman, archbishop Stepinac, who at first gladly collaborated with Pavelic's regime, began to distance himself from its atrocities. And yet, the Vatican, which was fully informed of the situation, chose not to reprimand the fledgling Catholic country. The attraction of a country which promised to be anti-Communist, the cause so important to Pius, was too great. It was important enough for him to overlook the killing of hundreds of thousands of non-Catholics. What is especially shocking in Croatia's genocide is the active participation of Catholic priests and members of religious orders in murder and torture. The Jasenovac concentration camp, in which Serbs and Jews, including many thousands of children, were killed, was, in fact, run by a Franciscan friar, Miroslav Filipovic-Majstorovic.

Unlike Nazi Germany, which was anti-clerical, Croatia was proudly Catholic and publicly proclaimed her loyalty to the Pope. This could have enabled the Pope unambiguously and openly to object to the barbaric killings. Moreover, this could have been an opportunity for the Pope to make clear that the Catholic Church considered such acts to be mortal sins, to call all Catholics to abstain from collaborating with these immoral activities and to excommunicate those who disobeyed. A clear papal instruction immediately to desist from these killings might even have had an impact on the ease with which Germany later murdered virtually all of Europe's Jews. Instead, the Church limited her activities to sporadic diplomatic efforts to help Jews who had converted to Catholicism and to lobby on their behalf with the Croatian government. The Church never publicly denounced the Catholic government of Croatia for its crimes, although she was aware of all that was going on. Timidly, Maglione instructed his representative in Croatia: 'If your eminence can find a suitable occasion, he should recommend in a discreet manner, that would not be interpreted as an official appeal.' This was the voice of the Catholic Church (see also chapter 4).

Slovakia, also newly established as an independent state in 1939, was led by a Catholic clergyman. Father Andre Hlinka had founded the Slovak People's Party in 1905 and his successor, Monsignor Josef Tiso became the President of Slovakia in 1939. This Catholic country immediately passed anti-Semitic laws and showed great willingness in deporting her Jews. Of Slovakia's ninety thousand Jews, fifty-two thousand were deported in the months March to June 1942. In their pastoral letter of 26 April 1942, Slovak Catholic bishops, astoundingly, gave their blessing:

> The greatest tragedy of the Jewish nation lies in the fact of not having recognised the Redeemer and of having prepared a terrible and ignominious death for Him on the cross.
>
> … Also in our eyes has the influence of the Jews been pernicious. In a short time they have taken control of almost all the economic and financial life of the country to the detriment of our people. Not only economically, but also in the cultural and moral spheres, they have harmed our people.

The Church cannot be opposed, therefore, if the state with[in] legal regulations hinders the dangerous influence of the Jews.[48]

The bishops, in their pastoral letter spoke about the need to act humanely and 'within legal regulations'. As requested by the Church, deportations were retroactively legalised by the Slovak parliament. On 15 May 1942, they passed a law depriving Jews of citizenship and expropriating their property. The papal representative to Slovakia, Monsignor Giuseppe Burzio, had, in 1941, passed to the Vatican information he had received of the extermination of Jews by the German army *Einsatzgruppen* in Russia. He regularly reported to the Vatican on the situation in Slovakia, including the deportation of Jews. The Vatican, which in Slovakia had a country run by clergy, was uncomfortable about the deportation of Jews but only energetically acted to save those who had converted. This was a country where the Vatican could have had much influence, had they wanted to act. An internal Vatican note, written by Monsignor Domenico Tardini, one of the two senior assistants of the Vatican's Secretary of State and head of the Section for Extraordinary Ecclesiastical Affairs on 7 April 1943, sets out the situation regarding Jewish policy:

The Jewish question is a question of humanity. The persecutions to which the Jews in Germany and in the occupied or conquered countries are subjected are an offence against justice, charity, humanity. The same brutal treatment is extended also to baptised Jews. Therefore, the Catholic Church has full reason to intervene whether in the name of divine law or natural law.

In Slovakia the head of state is a priest. Therefore the scandal is greater and greater also is the danger that the responsibility can be shifted to the Catholic Church itself. For these reasons it would appear opportune that the Holy See again issue a protest, repeating – in ever clearer form – what was already explained last year, in a diplomatic note to His Excellency, Sidor [the Slovak minister to the Holy See].

Since, especially recently, leaders of the Jews have turned to the Holy See to appeal for aid, it would not be out of place to discreetly make known to the public this diplomatic note of the Holy See (the fact of it being sent, the content of the document rather than the text). This will make known to the world that the Holy See fulfils its duty of charity rather than attracting the sympathy of the Jews in case they are among the victors (given the fact that the Jews – as much as can be foreseen – will never be too friendly to the Holy See and to the Catholic Church). But this will render more meritorious any charitable efforts.[49]

In April 1943, as was known to the Vatican, the German extermination machine was at work in all concentration and death camps. But the senior officials of the Church were not so much concerned about the saving of Jewish lives as they were about the public presentation of her position.

Not one member of the Slovak clergy was punished by the Church. Not one of them was excommunicated for being party to murder, not one of them was even defrocked. The Church did not consider any of their acts punishable. On the contrary, she tried to help them escape justice and when Tiso was imprisoned, the Church tried to have him moved to a convent instead of a normal prison. Evidently, the Church looks after her own.

The Final Solution

In June 1941 Germany attacked the Soviet Union. As the German army made its way, it was followed by the *Einsatzgruppen*, the SS killing squads sent in by Germany with the explicit purpose of rounding up and murdering Jews and Soviet political commissars. The SS troops would arrive in a town or village, round up all the Jews, transport them to a place of execution, where they were made to dig their own burial ditch, shot and thrown into the ditches. To speed up their work, Himmler ordered the supply of mobile gas chambers, vans with hermetically sealed chambers at the back, into which Jews were locked and into which the exhaust fumes of their diesel engines were pumped. They were dead within fifteen minutes.

When Göring instructed Heydrich, in July 1941, to prepare a 'Final Solution for the Jewish Problem', he was not in need of pastoral support from the Catholic Church. He would, however, have smiled had he read Freiburg's Archbishop Gröber's pastoral letter of 25 March 1941. At that point in history, the German archbishop saw fit to remind his flock that the Jews were guilty of the murder of Christ. He spoke of the self-imposed curse of the Jews which had come true: 'His blood be upon us and upon our children', the bishop pointed out 'has come true terribly until the present time, until today.'[50]

With the implementation of the Final Solution, the decision made in January 1942, ultimately to murder eleven million Jews, the big death camps were established. These camps had a killing potential of up to twenty-five thousand people a day.

The Vatican received reports early on of the systematic murder of Jews by Germans. Such reports came from the Vatican's own representatives, from Jewish organisations and from various governments and foreign diplomats. The historian Professor Michael Phayer lists twelve such reports in the period October 1941 to December 1942.[51] These include a report by the bishop of Lwow in Poland that in his small region more than two hundred thousand Jews had been murdered by the Germans and by the archbishop of Riga that most of the Jews of Riga in Latvia had been killed. The Vatican even received an eyewitness report by SS Colonel Kurt Gerstein describing in minute detail how the Jews were being exterminated in the death camp Belzec. The Catholic Church, her Pope and her cardinals remained silent. More reports followed. The Pope stuck to his policy. Monsignor Giuseppe Burzio was the Church representative in Slovakia who, as early as October 1941, reported to the Vatican of the massacres of Jews by German *Einsatzgruppen*.[52] On 12 May 1942, an Italian chaplain wrote directly to Pope Pius XII: 'The anti-Jewish struggle is inexorable and is becoming worse, with deportations and mass executions. ... The massacre of the Jews in the Ukraine is by this time complete. In Poland and in Germany, it is equally desired to bring it to completion, with a system of mass killings.'[53] In October of the same year, the same chaplain reported that 'over two million Jews have been killed', adding that Poles were moving into ghetto homes, 'which are day by day losing people because of the systematic slaughter of Jews'.[54] Two months later, at the end of 1942, a member of the Berlin Nunciature staff, Monsignor Giuseppe DiMeglio, delivered a detailed report on the situation of Jews in Germany to the Vatican.[55]

In May 1943, the Vatican's Secretariat of State prepared an internal memorandum entitled *Jews. Horrendous Situation*, which demonstrates how well informed it was about the killing of Jews in gas chambers:

> In Poland there were, before the war, about four and a half million Jews; it is calculated that now there remain only 100,000. At Warsaw a ghetto was formed which contained around 650,000: now there are 20–25,000.
>
> ... Special death camps [exist, where] ... they are locked up several hundred at a time in chambers where they are finished off with gas. Carried off in cattle wagons, hermetically sealed, with quicklime floors.[56]

The terrible plight of the Jews did not soften the Church's heart. The Jewish Agency, through its Istanbul office, had contact with Apostolic Nuncio, Archbishop Roncalli (the future Pope John XXIII). Roncalli had done much to help Jews escape Europe, and when asked, in early 1943, by a representative of the Jewish Agency to intervene with the Vatican to obtain assistance with the emigration to Palestine, he did so. And yet, Roncalli too was uncomfortable with the idea of Jews settling in Palestine. Roncalli wrote to Maglione in September 1943, referring to a messianic dream that the Jews might have of re-establishing Jewish reign in Palestine, a notion both visionary and utopian. Roncalli emphasised that the charitable activity of the Holy See should not be used to help with the realisation of such a Jewish dream.[57]

Cardinal Maglione, the Secretary of State, told Roncalli that he found 'insurmountable' difficulties with 'the transfer of Jews to Palestine, because one cannot prescind from the strict connection between this problem and that of the Holy Places, for whose liberty the Holy See is deeply concerned'. Later that year, in May 1943, Maglione wrote to Bishop William Godfrey, Apostolic Delegate in London, to confirm the Vatican's objection to a Jewish homeland in Palestine. It would, he wrote, offend the religious feelings of Catholics throughout the world.[58] In the same year, the Apostolic Delegate to the United States, Archbishop Amleto Cicognani, lobbied US President Roosevelt. Sandwiched between references to assistance it had given to save Jewish children from deportation to a German concentration camp and a general statement about 'charitable assistance non-Aryans [i.e. Jews] have received and will continue to receive at the hands of the Vatican', the Vatican lobbied against a '"Hebrew Home" in Palestine'. Whilst the Nazis were killing Jews in extermination camps, the Vatican was secretly trying to sway the United States against permitting a Jewish home to be established in Palestine, because 'this would be a severe blow to the real attachment of Catholics to this land'.[59]

Instead of speaking out publicly about the genocide, the Pope was busy lobbying the American president against US support for a homeland for Jews in Palestine, a move which would strike a 'severe blow to the real attachment of Catholics to this land' and which would greatly 'sadden the Holy See'.[60] Instead of calling on all Christian perpetrators to cease immediately, he pestered the Allied governments with requests not to bomb Rome. d'Arcy Osborne, the British ambassador to the Holy See, made the following entry in his diary on 13 December 1942:

> The more I think of it, the more I am revolted by Hitler's massacre of the Jewish race on the one hand, and, on the other, the Vatican's apparently exclusive preoccupation with the ... possibilities of the bombardment of Rome.[61]

Incidentally, the Pope, who did not condemn the Germans for bombing civilians in England in 1940 and 1941, was, all of a sudden, heard when the Allies gained aerial superiority. Now, the Pope spoke out publicly against the bombing of civilians. Myron Taylor, President Roosevelt's personal representative to the Vatican, had pointed out to Monsignor Montini that the Pope was in a weak position in his asking the Americans and British to refrain from bombing Rome: 'I am not clear whether the Holy See has condemned the bombing of London, Warsaw, Rotterdam, Belgrade, Coventry, Manila, Pearl Harbour, and places in the South Pacific.'[62]

Finally, under much pressure from the governments of the USA and Great Britain, the Pope gave way: in his twenty-six page radioed Christmas address in 1942, he hid twenty-seven words about the Holocaust. The Jews are not mentioned once. In a homily which deals with the problems of the individual in relation to the state, the Pope explained that the world's problems were brought about by the damaging economic policies by which everything had become subordinate to the profit motive. He did not mention the Nazis, he did not mention the fact that Germany had started a war, invaded country after country, killed millions and was systematically exterminating the whole of the Jewish population. All he said about the millions of Jews, who, by December 1942, had already been killed by German Christians, was:

> Humanity owes this vow to those hundreds of thousands who, without any fault of their own, sometimes only by reason of their nationality or race, are marked down for death or gradual extinction.[63]

The vow which the Pope refers to is his 'grand plan' to end the war; a vow which was to be made by men of good will to bring society back to its immovable centre of gravity. When asked why he had not mentioned the Nazis, the Pope retorted that he could not condemn the Nazis without also condemning the Communists. He spoke of 'hundreds of thousands' although he had been receiving report after report from various sources (including his own clergy) about millions of Jews killed, because according to Maglione 'the Holy See was unable to verify Allied reports as to the number of Jews exterminated'.[64] What exactly did the Church have in mind? A statistical report from SS headquarters, or did he want to send his priests to count the corpses? Did it not suffice that Hitler himself, in a radio broadcast in early February 1942, declared that 'the Jews will be liquidated for at least a thousand years!'?

This, unfortunately, was the *Weltanschauung* of the head of the Catholic Church and these few weak words, hidden in a long speech were, of course, totally ineffectual. Throughout the war, the Pope never again publicly touched on the Holocaust, mentioned the Jews or admonished the Nazis. He did not even act to stop the Germans from deporting Roman Jews in October 1943, nor did he warn them that 'resettlement' meant death. Several hundred, perhaps even thousands of Jews were allowed to find refuge in Church properties. A day after the train departed from Rome for Auschwitz, the Vatican confirmed in a public statement that it was satisfied with the correct and civil manner of the German military force occupying Rome. On the other hand the Pope was unhappy with the Allies for their bombardment of Rome. A morally bankrupt Catholic Church, which in a public statement paid compliments to the Nazis, thought nothing of asking the Germans to send more units to control Communists in and around Rome.

German bishops had shown that they were willing and able to come out fighting for issues they considered important, such as their objection to the 1940–41 Nazi euthanasia programme. The suffering and plight of Jews did not touch the Catholic Church; the Church certainly did not approve of their systematic murder but she did not come out fighting for them. The only people she attempted to defend in this context were former Jews who had converted to Catholicism and who had discovered that under the German race laws, conversion did not shield them from death. This attitude was not limited to German bishops. During the war, whilst the Jews were murdered in concentration camps in Poland, Prince Sapieha, the bishop of Krakow, who, after Hlond's departure for Rome, became senior Catholic prelate in Poland, spoke out for those Jews who had converted to Catholicism. He had nothing to say for those Jews who had not converted. The German Church issued a pastoral letter in August 1943, which was read out in Catholic churches. The bishops spoke of the ten commandments, stating that the killing of innocents was wrong even when carried out by the authorities and allegedly for the common good. The bishops spoke of 'men of foreign races and descent' and called for love of 'those innocent humans who are not of our people and blood', and of 'the resettled'. In other words, the bishops could not even bring themselves to mention the Jews by name nor refer to their murder. The pastoral letter made little impact: 'The population pays scant attention to such involved pronouncements burdened with stipulations', was the assessment of a senior Nazi official.[65]

Some Hungarian priests openly advocated annihilation of Jews, most were just happy to see the Jews go. On 19 March 1944, Germany occupied Hungary, a former ally, and two months later they started deportations to Auschwitz. Within two months, four hundred and forty thousand of the country's six hundred and seventy thousand Jews were deported. In Hungary, as in other countries, the Germans found happy and eager collaborators who helped them with the deportations. The message emanating from the Church concerning the extermination of Jews was not clear. A small number of bishops spoke out against the abandonment of Jews, whereas the cardinal was anti-Semitic. The papal nuncio was actively trying to help the Jews, although the Pope continued to be silent. On 6 July the Hungarian regent Miklos Horthy announced the cessation of deportations after warnings by the Allies that crimes against civilians would be punished after the war. The Pope too, at the behest of the American War Refugee Board, sent a telegram to Horthy, as did the King of Sweden and the International Red Cross. Of the two hundred and thirty thousand who were not deported, only one hundred and twenty thousand survived the slaughter in Budapest during the winter of 1944–1945.

A Pro-German Church

On certain issues the Pope clearly considered Nazi Germany's aims consistent with those of the Catholic Church – for example, the German attack on the Soviet Union in 1941 was undoubtedly attractive to a Pope who wished for the Soviet system to be crushed. The Pope even discussed with the German ambassador to the Holy See the possibility of reuniting Russian Orthodox Christians with Rome. The Russian Church had been in schism with Rome since 1054, and Pius XII was obviously looking forward to his very own spoils of war.

In 1939, Pius XII instructed his nuncio to congratulate Hitler warmly and publicly, on the occasion of his fiftieth birthday.[66] The pro-German Pope had a pro-Nazi nuncio in Berlin, Cesare Orsenigo, whose sympathies were so obvious that the priest he chose as his assistant was secretly a member of the Nazi party. Therefore it was not surprising that Orsenigo demanded that the German bishops support Hitler and support the war. As a direct result of the Vatican-led support, lower levels in the hierarchy toed the line.

The Pope's wish throughout this period was for Germany to come out of the war as a strong country. Cardinal Maglione's declaration, in September 1943, following Italy's extrication from the war, gives a good indication of the Vatican's priorities: 'the fate of Europe depends on the victorious resistance by Germany on the Russian front'.[67] As late as 1944, when it was obvious that Germany was losing, the Pope stated that Germany should not have to give up Austria and the Sudeten province of Czechoslovakia, both annexed by Hitler.[68] The Pope, hoping to be a mediator, was pushing for a negotiated peace, a concept which was totally unacceptable to the Allied governments. For the Catholic Church, Nazi Germany was preferable to the Soviet Union and the Pope preferred Hitler to Stalin as victor.

The Pope responded feebly to a *L'Osservatore Romano* reporter's question about why he would not protest against the extermination of the Jews: 'Dear friend, do not forget that millions of Catholics serve in the German armies. Shall I bring them into conflict of conscience?'[69] What then, is the role of the Church, if she dare not bring her members to consider their conscience?

The historian Guenther Lewy concludes that 'the Pope and his advisers – influenced by the long tradition of moderate anti-Semitism so widely accepted in Vatican circles – did not view the plight of the Jews with a real sense of urgency and moral outrage ... For this assertion no documentation is possible, but it is a conclusion difficult to avoid.'[70] Unfortunately, Pius XII was not only culturally and emotionally attached to Germany, there is anecdotal evidence to suggest that he was also personally anti-Semitic.[71] Language used by Pacelli while papal nuncio in Munich, in a letter to Vatican Secretary of State, Cardinal Gasparri, reveals Pacelli's underlying anti-Semitism. In this letter he describes a visit to the headquarters of the Communist revolutionaries who for several weeks in April 1919 had taken over power in Munich:

The confusion totally chaotic, the filth completely nauseating ... Absolute hell ... and in the midst of all this, a gang of young women, of dubious appearance, Jews like all the rest of them, hanging around in all the offices with lecherous demeanour and suggestive smiles. The boss of this female rabble was Levien's mistress, a young Russian woman, a Jew and a divorcée, who was in charge. ... This Levien ... also Russian and a Jew. Pale, dirty, with drugged eyes, hoarse voice, vulgar, repulsive, with a face that is both intelligent and sly.[72]

Pacelli's dread and hatred of the two groups which, in his thinking, were one (both Jews and Bolsheviks were out to destroy his world), was apparent as early as 1919. It never left him. His hatred of Communists was such that in 1949 he simply excommunicated all the Communists in the world. He did this after the Vatican had spent four years helping every Nazi murderer they could, flee from justice. Something must be terribly skewed in the morality of an organisation which acts this way.

There are many explanations for the Church's terrible silence during the Holocaust: the Pope's personal anti-Semitism; his love for Germany; his hatred of Communism; his hope eventually to act as mediator between the Allies and the Axis; and, finally, his fear of a possible bombardment of Rome. Whatever his motives, Pius XII was evidently willing to pay for them with the blood of millions of Jews. Pius XII's successors do not consider his behaviour to have been wrong, indeed attempts are being made to beatify him. The rest of the Church and especially his curial cardinals did not revolt and did not force him either to abdicate or change his policy.

The inability of the Catholic Church to rid herself of a hatred of Jews – hatred which first appears in the Gospels and was then expanded by the Church Fathers and put into practical anti-Jewish actions by one pope after another – has already been described. It is probably safe to say that most senior members of the Catholic clergy did not believe that the Jews – who they were taught to hate and who they believed were rightly suffering because of their rejection and murder of Christ – should be annihilated. Most of them did not consider Hitler to be part of the divine plan, but neither did they see it as part of the Church's duty to help the Jews. Gyula Czapik, the archbishop of Eger, the second-highest-ranking Catholic in Hungary, objected to a pastoral letter which was to inform the Hungarian population and protest about the deportation of Jews to Auschwitz. The Hungarian archbishop advised Cardinal Serédy that he should 'not make public what is happening to the Jews; what is happening to the Jews at the present time is nothing but appropriate punishment for their misdeeds in the past'.[73]

Except for Bishop Preysing in Berlin, the German Catholic hierarchy continued to support the Nazi war effort until the very end. In April 1945, the much feted Bishop von Galen, who led the successful opposition to Hitler's euthanasia programme, spoke about the fact that his heart had bled at 'the sight of the passing troops of our enemy'. Galen apparently was not relieved, happy, or grateful when he saw the American army liberate Germany and the world from Nazism. Instead, he was overcome with nationalistic emotions. Is that what one really expects of a bishop? The same Galen, in a sermon he gave in July 1941, explained:

> We Christians make no revolution. We will continue to do our duty in obedience to God, out of love for people and fatherland. Our soldiers will fight and die for Germany, but not for those who ... disgrace the German name before God and man. We will continue to fight against the external enemy: against the enemy in our midst who tortures and beats us, we cannot fight with arms and there remains only one weapon: strong tenacious, obstinate perseverance.[74]

These were a senior bishop's clear instructions to Germany's Catholics not to participate in any revolt against the Nazi regime. In July 1941, the Catholic Church was still exhorting her sons to fight and to die for *Vaterland* and for *Lebensraum*. Two years later, in October 1943, Cardinal Faulhaber made clear the Church's views as he wrote, 'nobody in his heart, can possibly wish an unsuccessful outcome of the war. Every reasonable person knows that in such a case the State and the Church, and organised society altogether, would be overturned by the Russian chaos.'[75]

Plainly, the Catholic Church considered the Hitler regime, the Nazi concentration camps, the extermination of Jews, the brutal occupation of substantial parts of Europe as 'organised society'. As late as January 1945, German bishops were still giving pep-talks to their flock urging them to fight against the Allies. Archbishop Lorenz Jäger called on Catholics fully to participate in the combat against 'liberalism and individualism on one side, collectivism on the other'.[76] If one considers what Jäger was really saying to the readers of the pastoral letter issued to mark the start of the New Year in 1945, he was encouraging them to kill more Americans, more Britons and more Russians. Sociologist and historian Gordon Zahn concludes that German bishops in the years of the Third Reich 'did call for martyrdom on the part of German Catholics – but it was a "martyrdom" for *Volk* and *Vaterland* and not for religious values ... Even in the midst of total military collapse, with the Third Reich in its death throes, bishops were raising their voices to inspire men to offer their last drop of blood for the national cause'.[77]

Upon hearing of the death of Hitler, on 2 May 1945, Cardinal Bertram instructed all the parish priests of his archdiocese 'to hold a solemn requiem in memory of the Führer and all those members of the *Wehrmacht* who have fallen in the struggle for our German Fatherland, along with the sincerest prayers for *Volk* and Fatherland and for the future of the Catholic Church in Germany'.[78] Hitler was evidently right when, in his meeting with Bishop Berning in 1933, he told him that 'devout soldiers are the most valuable, because they risk all'.

In a sermon delivered by Cardinal Faulhaber in February 1937, he praised the *Reichsconcordat* and the confidence which the Vatican had shown the new Nazi regime.[79] The Catholic Church chose to continue a 'working relationship' with Nazi Germany and not to annoy the German regime. Would this have been the Church's attitude, had the people who were being annihilated not been the same people for whom the Church had, for nineteen hundred years, been preaching contempt? The people whom the Church had tried, and continued to try to convert and whose rejection of Christianity she considered a terrible affront? It is a fact that some nuncios and curial hierarchy considered 'anti-Jewish legislation beneficial in minimising Jewish influence in countries where it was considered harmful to Christian society'.[80] Others, such as the nuncio in Romania, Archbishop Andrea Cassulo, a man who had done much to help Romanian Jews, was still 'not particularly concerned about the social aspects of the anti-Jewish legislation but only those areas in which the laws would be harmful to the baptised Jews'. Moreover, Cassulo seemed 'to sincerely believe that the increasing number of Jewish converts [referring to Jews who converted to Catholicism in haste during the War-years in order to save their lives], was part of God's plan'.[81]

The extent to which Nazi racial laws were linked to Church dogma and Church-induced legislation can be learned from the Vatican's reaction to the August 1941 enquiry by the Vichy government for an opinion on their anti-Jewish laws. The Vatican, which described the anti-Jewish laws as 'unfortunate', informed Vichy that it was not going to quarrel with them over the Jewish statute. The Vatican did not express objections to or disapproval of the Vichy press release, according to which 'From information obtained at the most authorised sources it results that nothing in the legislation designed to protect France from the Jewish influence is opposed to the doctrine of the Church.' Two years earlier, the Vatican paper *L'Osservatore Romano* carried an article by Bishop Giovanni Cazzani supporting the anti-Jewish laws newly introduced by Mussolini. When Mussolini fell, the Church did not want the anti-Jewish legislation introduced by Mussolini's Fascist regime to be abolished. A Jewish delegation begged the Vatican representative to act for the abolition of the law. The Vatican's representative, in a report to Cardinal Luigi Maglione, the Secretary of State, wrote:

> I took care not to call for the total abrogation of the law which, according to the principles and traditions of the Catholic Church, certainly has

some clauses that should be abolished, but which clearly contains others that have merit and should be confirmed.[82]

The only two clauses the Vatican representative, Father Tacchi Venturi, asked to have abolished were those which harmed Catholics who had converted or were in the process of converting from Judaism.

Conclusion

Some individual Catholic office-holders were truly sorry for the suffering of individual Jews, but not more than that. They were willing in some cases, when appealed to, to try and intercede on behalf of Jews, but not to object to the racial laws underlying their persecution. At the utmost this was charitable action, but never did they – as supposedly moral standard-bearers – challenge the immorality of the laws and the personal immorality of the perpetrators in the society in which they were operating. There can be no hiding from the terrible guilt of the higher echelons of the Church, specifically Pope Pius XII and his Secretary of State, Cardinal Maglione. They knew what was happening and decided not to act. There is no alternative but to consider the possibility that they felt that Jews had such a punishment coming to them – had the Church not taught this throughout her history? Whilst Germany systematically rounded up, deported to concentration camps, tortured and gassed to death millions of Jews, Monsignor Domenico Tardini of the Vatican Secretariat of State wrote memos objecting to the idea of a Jewish homeland in Palestine.[83] His boss, the Secretary of State Maglione, complained about unfriendly Jews who were ungrateful to the Church.[84] The Vatican was also aware of the public relations ramifications of its policy. It appears that in April 1943, the Vatican was troubled by its image in a post-War world, a world in which the Jews might – uncomfortably for the Church – be amongst the victors!

In 1980, John F. Morley, Catholic priest and Professor of Religion, published his thorough and well-documented book *Vatican Diplomacy and the Jews During the Holocaust 1939–1943*. His conclusions make stark reading. Morley, who questions their sincerity of commitment to humanitarian values, found 'little evidence that the nuncios manifested any consistent humanitarian concern about the sufferings of the Jews during the years 1939–1943'. Some nuncios

> felt that certain aspects of the anti-Jewish legislation would be beneficial in minimising Jewish influence in countries where it was considered harmful to Christian society. These diplomats viewed the Jewish badge, and regulations affecting Jewish professions, commerce, and education, as having merit in that they restrained Jewish activity in those areas.

Morley also concludes that Secretary of State, Cardinal Maglione,

> did not decide to use the full power of Vatican diplomacy in confronting the Jewish problem. In fact, he dealt with it only minimally. This point of view must be assumed to have reflected that of the Pope. Setting such a policy, without papal approval, was not entirely within Maglione's competence.
>
> ... It must be concluded that Vatican diplomacy failed the Jews during the Holocaust by not doing all that it was possible for it to do on their behalf.
> ... The nuncios, the secretary of state, and, most of all, the Pope share the responsibility for this ... failure.[85]

The Church asserted that it 'fulfils its duty of charity'. Their notion of Christian charity seems to be very limited indeed. So much could have been done. At the very least the Pope could have made it clear to all the Catholic participants and collaborators in the persecution of Jews that their actions constituted a mortal sin, with all the ramifications this has according to Catholic dogma. The Pope, who in 1949 excommunicated anyone who voted Communist in Italy, did not excommunicate a single Nazi, let alone anyone who voted Nazi. This is an important statement by the Church, which now is considering Pius XII's beatification. The clear message of the Catholic Church to any future pope, who might act similarly, is that he will be praised and not censured.

Chapter Seven
After the Holocaust

Senior Cardinal Eugène Tisserant tried, in vain, to convince the Pope to issue an encyclical on the duty of the individual to follow his own conscience, rather than blindly execute orders. In June 1940 he wrote to Cardinal Suhard, Archbishop of Paris:

> I fear that history will reproach the Holy See with having practiced a policy of selfish convenience and not much else. This is extremely sad, especially for those [of us] who have lived under Pius XI. Everyone [here] is confident that, after Rome has been declared an open city, members of the Curia will not have to suffer any harm; that is a disgrace.[1]

Indeed, Pius XII himself must have known that his pro-German policy was critically flawed. Cardinal Angelo Roncalli, the future Pope John XXIII, reports in his diary of an audience on 11 October 1941 with the Pope who asked whether his 'silence' concerning Nazism would be badly judged.[2]

Pius XII addressed the College of Cardinals at the end of the War and laid down the line which the Church was to take with regard to her conduct during the Holocaust. He strongly defended the concordat which the Church had signed with Hitler in 1933 and portrayed the Church as a victim. Moreover, fantasising or just lying, the Pope claimed that the Church had been a unified force of resistance to Nazi attacks: 'To resist such attacks millions of courageous Catholics, men and women, closed their ranks around their Bishops, whose valiant and severe pronouncements never failed to resound even in these last years of war.'[3]

The German bishops, who knew that the Pope was not telling the truth, chose to defend their docile conduct during the Nazi regime. A document reporting on a meeting which took place on 23 August 1947 between German Catholic Bishops and the US Military Government in Germany, gives a fascinating insight into their thinking. 'Who has the right to demand that the bishops should have chosen a form of fight that would have sent them to the gallows with infallible certainty, and which would have resulted in a campaign of extermination against the Church?'

asked Cardinal Frings, the titular head of the Church in Germany at the time.[4] Fellow Catholic and future German Chancellor, Konrad Adenauer, considered that this was exactly what the bishops should have done. Demonstrating very low regard for his flock, Archbishop Jäger of Paderborn was of the opinion that, had the Church challenged the Nazis, many of her members would have been 'driven into the arms of National Socialism by too sharp language'. Bishop Dietz of Fulda suggested that the German bishops had followed Christ's example when 'he was brought before the High Priests, before King Herod, and Pilate'.[5] The bishops – who in 1947 were busy resisting the Allies, taking an aggressive stand against the denazification programme and actively pursuing all avenues to release convicted Nazi war criminals from jail – all seemed to have 'good' reasons for not resisting their own Nazi government.

The Vatican systematically hid the truth about the extent of its awareness of the Holocaust. Many of the archives are still not available and incriminating documents were kept out of Vatican publications.[6] Munich's auxiliary bishop, Johannes Neuhäusler, published a 'study' for which – it was later discovered – he had falsified documents in order to cast the Church in a better light concerning her behaviour during the Nazi years.[7] The Pope went even further by issuing all German Catholics with a *Persilschein*, the popular term used for the denazification document that the Allied occupation authorities demanded from Germans. In it he stated that German Catholics had opposed Hitler with all their hearts.[8] Catholic Konrad Adenauer, post-War Germany's first chancellor, thought otherwise:

> I believe that if the bishops altogether had publicly taken a stance from the pulpit a lot could have been avoided. That didn't happen and there is no excuse for it. If the bishops had been taken to the concentration camps or to jail it wouldn't have hurt anything – on the contrary.[9]

This view, which Adenauer expressed in a letter that he wrote to the clergyman Bernhard Custodis in February 1946, was not shared by the post-War German bishops when they met at Fulda in August 1945. Adenauer considered that the 'German people, including to a large extent, bishops and priests, succumbed to Nazi agitation ... even with enthusiasm.' Cologne's Archbishop Frings, on the other hand, is on record stating that the Church was not a controlling body or supervisory agency of the state and that it was not the bishops' role to correct the state when it erred.[10] The defiant archbishop was, moreover, livid when, in July 1945, he was summoned to the British headquarters in Germany. Such disrespect, the archbishop maintained, did not happen under the Nazis, adding that he was, after all, due the rank and the respect of an army general. Frings expected the British commander to come to the bishop's palace; perhaps he also wanted the British commander to prostrate himself and kiss his ring. Less then a year later, the Pope elevated the proud archbishop to cardinal. In the following years, the German Catholic Church (as well as the German Protestant Churches) gave all her support to the Nazi war criminals.

The Church and Nazi War Criminals

The German Catholic hierarchy did its utmost to reduce the sentences of convicted Nazis. The Vatican went one step further: it ran an operation to smuggle senior Nazis to South American Fascist havens which were willing to open their countries and help mass-murderers such as Eichmann and Mengele escape justice. In her efforts, the German Catholic Church was often competing and sometimes collaborating with her great rival: the German Protestant Churches. In one such case, Protestant Adolf Eichmann was so grateful for the help he had received from the Catholic Church to flee justice that he registered himself as a Roman Catholic in his Argentinean passport. Eichmann wanted to 'honour the Catholic faith, by becoming an honorary member'.[11]

In June 1945, Bishop Albert Stohr of Mainz appealed to the Pope and asked for his intervention against the dismissal of Nazis from public service in Germany.[12] In July 1945, less than three months after the war had ended, Munich's Cardinal Faulhaber suggested to the American military authorities that neither membership of the Nazi party, nor of the SS, be considered a crime. He also wanted all industrialists and bankers who had been imprisoned to be released. The reason he gave was that it was too hard on these gentlemen, many of whom were not young, to be held in prison and that their families were suffering as a result.[13] The people Faulhaber was trying to free were the manufacturers of poison gas, the owners of weapon production lines which used slave labour and bankers who had laundered Nazi money. Many of them had from very early years funded Hitler and were the enablers who brought him to power. The Church attacked the Allied authorities as best they could, raising petty issues such as the sleeping hours of prisoners (a waking time of 5:30 am was apparently too early for the Nazis) to matters of substance in an outright denial that these Nazis were war criminals. Instead, the Church wanted them to be considered as prisoners of war. Some of their requests, such as Cardinal Faulhaber's plea in favour of Josef Tiso, showed amazing *chutzpah*.[14] Faulhaber called on the military governor to handle Tiso with respect, because Tiso 'according to Church law is member of the pope's family'. Faulhaber asked that Tiso not be held together with other political leaders of enemy countries, but in accordance with his Church status, possibly in a monastery. Tiso did, Faulhaber reminded the military governor, after all, 'in difficult conditions maintain religious life in his country'.[15]

Bishop Clemens August Graf von Galen, the 'Lion of Münster' who dared to challenge the Nazi euthanasia programme, never tried to save Jewish lives with a similar stand. Bishop Galen was, in reality, a proud nationalist. When, in 1935, Hitler sent his army into the demilitarised zone of the Rhineland in contravention of the Versailles peace accord, Bishop Galen applauded. He sent a telegram to Freiherr von Fritsch, supreme commander of the army, 'In the name of the staunchly German Catholics of the diocese of Münster and especially of the lower Rhine, I welcome the German armed forces, which from today on will again shield the German Rhine, as protectors and symbol of German honour and German justice.'[16] Ten year later, with tens of millions dead and a whole continent in tatters because of German warmongering, atrocities and genocide, the bishop had nothing better to occupy his mind than defending the Nazis and calling for a cessation of the International Military Tribunal (the Nürnberg trials). Bishop Galen wanted better conditions for Nazi prisoners of the Allies' occupational authority, as he worried that their conditions were worse than those in the Nazi concentration camps. Galen outrageously stated that the trials of Göring, Frank, Kaltenbrunner, Ribbentrop and others were not about justice but about the defamation of the German people.[17] Two years later, in 1948, Bishop Heinrich Wienken complained that the eight prisoners at *Spandau* prison in Berlin were being starved. Could the Catholic Church permit these men to be driven to death by hunger, he asked, especially as, except for Rudolf Hess, they all participated at divine service held by the prison vicar, and even Hess had recently asked to be given a Bible.[18]

Another Catholic prelate who was worried about the standard of living of incarcerated Nazis was the Benedictine friar, Professor Dr phil. Petrus Mayrhofer. In July 1947, in a sermon he gave at the Moosburg camp, which held SS and Gestapo officers, army generals and senior Nazi party functionaries, Mayrhofer maintained that inmates of the concentration camps were better fed, by a thousand calories a day, than free Germans under the Allies. The friar added:

If the gas chambers of Auschwitz were still in operation, they would become a place of pilgrimage. Millions of frightened people would make their way to Auschwitz to find a quick death and escape the stranglehold of the liberators, instead of, day after day, with innocent children, having to look hunger in the eyes.[19]

As already mentioned, the Churches not only competed but also joined forces. In 1949, Catholic–Protestant collaboration established a special office to deal with the inmates of the Landsberg prison. These included SS Major General Sepp Dietrich, the former commander of Hitler's SS bodyguard. He was personally involved in special executions (such as the 1934 Röhm purge). Other prisoners were doctors involved in human trials on inmates of Nazi concentration camps and doctors who ran the German euthanasia programme. Also held at Landsberg prison were General Hans Reinhardt, General Hans von Salmuth, General Otto Wöhler and other commanders of the *Einsatzgruppen*, the infamous SS killing squads which followed the regular army units rounding up Jews and Soviet political commissars and murdering them. The German Churches felt that these Nazis needed special help. When, in December 1948, the Landsberg prison director removed a Christmas wreath from the dining room, Munich auxiliary Bishop Neuhäusler immediately sent a protest to no less than General Lucius Clay, the US Military Governor of Germany. Not even in the Nazi concentration camps had he come across 'such disrespect and offence to both Christian Confessions'.[20] In May 1949, at offices made available by the Catholic *Caritas* organisation, with subsidies from the Protestant Churches, the joint effort was launched to commute the sentences of as many Landsberg prisoners as possible. The Churches' office was headed by Dr Rudolf Aschenauer, the defence lawyer of *Einsatzgruppen* commander, Otto Ohlendorf. The office director was former SS Obersturmbannführer, Dr Heinrich Malz. Another joint organisation was *Stille Hilfe*, informally established in 1947 by Prinzessin von Isenburg. In 1951, Isenburg, who signed her pamphlets and letters *Mutter Elisabeth* (Mother Elisabeth) or *Mutter der Landsberger* (Mother of the Landsberg prisoners), asked the Catholic and Protestant Churches to join in the formal establishment of *Stille Hilfe* as a registered organisation, which they did. *Stille Hilfe's* board included auxiliary Bishop Neuhäusler, *Caritas* director Father Augustinus Rösch and the Protestant bishop Theophil Wurm. In charge of the work were two former SS officers, former SS Obersturmführer, Gerhard Kittel (member of the Nazi Party since 1931) and Dr Heinrich Malz.

The bishops did not hesitate as they appealed for the reduction of the sentences of SS doctors that included characters such as Dr Hans Eisele, who injected Jewish inmates of concentration camps with poison and who carried out vivisections of Jews without anaesthesia.[21]

Other Nazis which the bishops were acting for included Waffen-SS general and SS Obergruppenführer Oswald Pohl who was in charge of the organisation of all Nazi death camps. To him these camps were businesses which produced slave labour from the living and clothes, shoes, glasses, hair and of course gold from the dead. In fact, his instructions were to carry out anal and vaginal searches of the incoming Jews to find hidden jewels and to pull the gold teeth out of the corpses of Jews who were murdered. Pohl ran the operation like a big industrial conglomerate, establishing companies, recruiting businessmen and enriching the SS. Unlike Eichmann who had only become an 'honorary Catholic', Pohl converted to Catholicism in February 1950. The man who is to be thanked for this conversion is Karl Morgenschweis, the Catholic priest at

War Crimes Prison Landsberg. Morgenschweis continued till the end of his days to boast of the help he had given the war criminals at Landsberg and especially to the Malmedy murderers (a German army unit which, between December 1944 and January 1945, murdered three hundred and fifty American prisoners of war and one hundred Belgian civilians). The priest carried papers to and fro and smuggled documents in and out of prison to help coordinate the accused's separate versions of events. He lobbied for them with Pope Pius XII, Vatican Secretary of State, Cardinal Montini, Cardinal Faulhaber, Bishop Neuhäusler and Chancellor Adenauer. Germany was especially grateful for his work: in 1952 he was awarded the highest public decoration, the *Bundesverdienstkreuz*. In 1959, the Church showed her approval and he was made Monsignor.

The Church tried to commute the sentences of all of the commanders of the notorious *Einsatzgruppen*. She also tried to help men such as SS Standartenführer Paul Blobel who, in September 1941, led the unit which murdered thirty-three thousand seven hundred and seventy-one Jewish men, women and children at Babi-Yar. At his trial, Blobel confirmed that he was in charge of these murders. In mitigation, he maintained that he did not believe they could have killed more than half that number, that is, no more than sixteen thousand eight hundred and eighty-five. This murderer, who to celebrate his own wedding anniversary announced that he wanted put his mark on the town of Lodz, at which his unit had just arrived, by having several thousand Jews shot, was not spared the death penalty, despite Bishop Neuhäusler's pleading.

The Pope also personally intervened to have sentences commuted. He tried to convince the Polish government to commute the death sentence of Arthur Greiser, the Nazi who was personally responsible for more than a hundred thousand murders in the Warthenau region. In 1948, the Pope urged President Truman to change the decision to lift a temporary ban which had been put on the execution of German war criminals. The ban had been in place whilst a special committee – set up because of the incessant pestering of religious lobbies – examined the trials to ensure that they were flawless and just.

These are just a few examples of the very many Nazi war criminals whom the German Church tried to help. The Church operation was extensive at both a national level, through the collective action of the Catholic Bishops' Conference, and a local level through individual appeals by local priests and bishops. At the national level, the Church was led by Cardinal Frings in an operation which was orchestrated in coordination with the Pope and the West German government (from 1949). They pressurised the occupying Allied forces and successfully caused the appointment of several review boards, postponing the execution of the verdicts. When this line of action was exhausted, the Church maintained that it was unfair on the convicted murderers, who had waited in limbo for so long, to be executed. With time, many of the death penalties were indeed commuted. At local levels, the clergy had no hesitation in falsifying records and confirming that members of the SS, the Gestapo and other war criminals, were personally known to them as honest and good citizens.

Brazenly, German bishops accused the occupational authority of playing God. All of a sudden, these German bishops found the civil courage which they had lacked earlier and which Cardinal Frings maintained was unnecessary during the Nazi period. The Church, which did not speak out during the pogroms, which did not forbid her members to participate in anti-Jewish activities rampant in Germany from the early 1930s, now regularly petitioned the US authorities to free the convicted Nazi criminals. What was this urgency? Does the Church regularly try to get convicted criminals out of jail? Where else does the Catholic Church systematically attempt to release murderers back into society as soon as they are convicted? Is there any explanation other than that deep in their heart the hierarchy of the Catholic Church did not feel that the German war criminals deserved to be punished.

In 1948, German bishops sent a joint memorandum to the highest-ranking US officer in Germany, General Lucius D. Clay, maintaining that the trials of German war criminals lacked both moral and legal foundations. Was it sheer stupidity or simple callousness which led the bishops to write this memorandum, the main argument of which was the bishops' assertion that Germans should not be tried 'under laws hitherto unknown in Germany'. The writer Ernst Klee rightly asks whether the bishops believed that there was no law against murdering Jews, denigrating, abusing and exterminating people in concentration camps, rounding up millions of people and using them as slave labour.[22]

Should the Pope, his cardinals and his bishops not have washed the feet of Jewish concentration camp survivors begging their forgiveness instead of campaigning for the quality of life of German mass-murderers? The Church, instead, moaned about how she had to suffer under Nazi rule. The enormity of the Holocaust and the six million Jews murdered by Christians was coming to light and the Church had the audacity to portray herself as the victim. The Austrian episcopacy issued a statement that 'no group had to make greater sacrifice in terms of property and wealth, of freedom and health, of life and blood as Christ's Church'.[23]

In line with his choice of nuncio before the war, the Pope chose an anti-Semite, bishop Aloysius Muench, as his Apostolic Visitator (a special envoy deputed by the pope for a transient mission in an emergency situation) to post-War zonal Germany. Extraordinarily, US President Truman also made Muench his Catholic Liaison to OMGUS (Occupational Military Government – United States). A fluent German speaker and the son of Bavarian immigrants to the USA, Muench considered Jews a basic nuisance. The bishop, later made cardinal, objected to the US occupational authority bringing in Jewish refugees, former German Jews who, as social scientists and historians, were implementing the US policy of establishing new democratic institutions in Germany. As anti-Semitism was spreading like wildfire in post-War Germany – a country full of perpetrators which was busy blaming everybody other than itself – the Pope's representative added his coal to the fire by blaming German anti-Semitism on the Jews. The Pope's choice of Muench proved just right. By choosing an American, his representative was in the very centre of the power structure of the US occupying force. However, not only was his representative above all a Catholic loyal to his Pope, he was also, in truth, culturally a German, whose sympathies lay – as did those of the Pope – with the Germans.[24]

The Vatican Ratlines

Whoever was able, tried to escape. Amongst Nazi war criminals, the word spread fast that help was at hand in Rome. You did not even need to be a Catholic to get help from the Vatican; you just needed to be a Nazi. According to the US State Department, the Vatican, in those post-War years, ran the most extensive of all illegal emigration networks. In fact, more than twenty Catholic agencies were busy spiriting perpetrators away. Of the many Church organisations which helped Nazis to flee, the two main operators were Bishop Alois Hudal and Father Krunoslav Draganović. Both used Vatican resources and ran their operations in Rome from Vatican properties.

Hudal, Rector of the *Pontificio Santa Maria dell'Anima* (a seminary for German priests in Rome), was a former professor of Old Testament Studies at the University of Graz. In 1923 he moved to Rome to assume his position at the German priests' seminary. From the very early days Hudal was a great Hitler supporter. He made no secret of his views, made public speeches in both Italy and Germany and after the Nazis came to power in 1933, he made the following statement in a speech he gave at the Anima, his seminary: 'In this hour of destiny all German Catholics living abroad welcome the new German Reich whose philosophies accord both with Christian and National values.'[25]

Hudal gave his speech in May and a month later, in June 1933, he was promoted by the Vatican to Titular Bishop. It was unusual for a Rector of the Anima seminary to be made bishop; this was a very clear message of approval from the Holy See. His closeness to power can also be gathered from his position as consultor to the *Holy Office*.[i] Then, as now, it was one of the most powerful of all Vatican bodies and it still is

---

[i]   The *Holy Office* was the name of the Vatican department which previously was called the *Holy Inquisition* and now is called the *Congregation for the Doctrine of the Faith*. Consultors are advisers to curial congregations.

in charge of enforcing religious discipline throughout the Catholic world. The work of this department is done in great secrecy and as a consultor Hudal would have been very close to the highest echelons of the Church. Hudal's views were evidently not detrimental to his career and his next step was to publish a book: *The Foundations of National Socialism*. The book, which he published in 1936, was given the official Church approval for publication, the *Imprimatur*, by the Primate of the Austrian Church, the pro-Nazi Cardinal Theodore Innitzer. In 1942 Hudal published *Europe's Religious Future*, in which he explained that Christianity had to get rid of Liberalism and Bolshevism, whose inspiring force was the Jews. To achieve its ends, Hudal maintained that Christianity had to use Nazis. However, things went wrong for the bishop: Germany lost the war. Hudal's heroes were now fugitives from justice. Supporters of Pius XII try to rebut any accusation of closeness between the Pope and Hudal. It is, however, unlikely that in an organisation which so closely scrutinises the behaviour of its members, Hudal would have been allowed to utter the sentiments he did without senior cardinals' knowledge and approval.

Early in 1944, the Allies landed in Sicily and by June they were in Rome. In August, the Vatican approached the Allied authorities for permission to visit German prisoners of war. In December, Monsignor Montini, the Under-Secretary of State for Ordinary Affairs (the future Pope Paul VI) asked that a Vatican representative be permitted to visit civilian German-speakers who were interned in Italy. Many of these were Nazis who, in their flight, dropped their uniforms and hid as civilian refugees. The Vatican then appointed none other than Bishop Alois Hudal, as the 'Spiritual Director of the German people resident in Italy'. This Vatican liaison officer diligently made contact with Nazi fugitives, establishing communication channels and promising them help. In his published diaries, Hudal reminisces:

> I thank God that He [allowed me] to visit and comfort many victims in their prisons and concentration camps and [to help] them escape with false identity papers.
>
> ... I felt duty bound after 1945 to devote my whole charitable work mainly to former National Socialists and Fascists especially to so called 'war criminals'.[26]

Bishop Hudal ran his operation together with SS colonel Walter Rauff, the man who invented the mobile gas van, who, as chief SS security officer for northwest Italy, had been based in Milan. After he was arrested by the Americans, Rauff apparently bought his freedom by selling American Counter Intelligence the lists he had of Fascists and Communists and his copy of Mussolini's secret police archives. Colonel Rauff became a money launderer who siphoned off substantial amounts from a money forging and laundering operation run by the SS during the war to help his colleagues resettle in South America. The third leg of the Catholic Church Nazi smuggling operation was Archbishop Siri of Genoa.

The Vatican Ratline sent war criminals first to Hudal in Rome, where they were hidden in Church properties while false documentation and travel papers were prepared, and then to Siri in Genoa. Siri arranged for them to be kept in hiding in monasteries and in other Church properties to await the ships on which they would travel (mainly) to South America.

Monsignor Karl Bayer was the Director of Caritas International, the Catholic relief agency, in Rome. Bayer confirmed to Gitta Sereny that the Pope provided money for Hudal's operation. He also admitted, albeit reluctantly, that Hudal probably did have batches of Red Cross passports for 'these particular people'.[27] Hudal, through Montini, had access to the Catholic relief agency and to the Pontifical Commission for Assistance. The former paid living and travel expenses to refugees and the latter helped them find jobs.

Some of the most notorious Nazis were helped by the Vatican through the Hudal operation, including the commander of Treblinka, Franz Stangl, who had killed nine-hundred thousand people, mostly Jews; Gustav Wagner, the deputy commander of Sobibor, who killed two-hundred-and-fifty thousand Jews; Alois Brunner, commander of an *Einsatzgruppe*; and Adolf Eichmann.[28]

In 1946, the Argentinean Cardinal Antonio Caggiano and Bishop Agustin Barrére travelled to the Vatican to meet with the French Cardinal Tisserant to organise the smuggling of French war criminals to the Argentine. It is therefore not surprising that fourteen years later, when Israel abducted Adolf Eichmann and brought him to trial in Jerusalem, the Cardinal objected. During their trip, Caggiano and Barrére informed Tisserant that 'the Government of the Argentine Republic was willing to receive French persons, whose political attitude during the recent war would expose them, should they return to France, to harsh measures and private revenge'.[29] They then worked out the details and procedures for the transfer of Nazi collaborators to the Argentine. At the same time, Cardinal Montini was discussing a possible immigration agreement between the Vatican and the Argentine with the Argentinean Ambassador to the Holy See.

Why were countries such as Argentina, Paraguay, Mexico, Brazil, Syria or Egypt happy to accommodate the Catholic Church which requested that Nazis be let in? Why were they importing Nazis? In some cases, it was pure empathy with the Nazis. Some countries were importing specific experts. Egypt and Syria wanted to utilise experts in the annihilation of

Jews for the same purpose: to kill Jews. The Argentine was interested in military and aviation industry experts and Nazi Germany had many such people on the run. In 1943, a military coup in the Argentine brought Juan Peron to power. In 1946, he was elected president. The new regime was highly Catholic, and even gave the Virgin Mary the rank of General in the Argentine army. The Catholic bishops supported the military dictatorship, a relationship which was ripe for a Vatican–Peron post-War co-production. The Nazis, shipped by the Vatican, brought expertise, security know-how (Croat leader Pavelic became security adviser to Peron) and substantial amounts of looted money, much of it laundered through the Vatican bank.

Whilst they were in Rome, the Argentinean clergymen signed visa requests for various war criminals before they moved to Madrid to do the same for Nazis who were in hiding in Spain. To ensure a smooth operation, the Argentinean clergymen provided the Croatian Father Krunoslav Draganović, who was in charge of the Vatican's main smuggling operation (mainly Croat war criminals and some of the stolen gold and money) with two hundred and fifty blank landing permits for the Argentine.

Draganović was formally Secretary of the *Confraternity of San Girolamo*, a Croat monastery in Rome which was founded in 1453. After studying in Rome, Draganoić returned to his country in 1935 and spent the next eight years as secretary to Bishop Ivan Saric of Sarajevo, a notorious butcher of Serbs. In 1943 he was returned to Rome as a representative of the Ustasha and the Croatian Red Cross. The Croatian Red Cross, not recognised by the International Red Cross, was a cover for the escape network that the Ustasha was planning. Vatican doors opened to the man who came to Rome with the support and letters of recommendation of Croatia's Archbishop, Aloysius Stepinac. He was in direct contact with Secretary of State Maglione and with the Pope himself, building the network which would eventually give cover and support to fleeing Croatian war criminals and provide money and travel documents to thousands of men who, thereby, avoided being brought to justice.

Draganović's smuggling operation, which was mainly manned by Catholic priests, is estimated to have smuggled some thirty thousand persons from Austria to Rome, via Genoa to North and South America and Australia.[30] It was a massive Church operation, which – among others – moved virtually the whole Ustasha leadership, Croat government ministers and military and police commanders of that Catholic stronghold in Croatia, to the Argentine.

A central figure in the Draganović network was Father Vilim Cecelja. This priest was the Deputy Military Vicar to the Ustasha militia, the militia which carried out the murders and under whose supervision Serbs were forcibly converted to Catholicism. Father Cecelja held the rank of Lieutenant Colonel. In 1944, he was moved by Pavelic to Vienna to prepare a possible escape route for the Croatian regime. In April 1945, Colonel Father Cecelja moved to Alt Aussee near Salzburg to welcome fleeing Ustasha members. He would visit refugee camps and supply Red Cross identity papers with assumed names to help his colleagues evade repatriation to Yugoslavia, where they would have been brought to justice. Cecelja's operation provided the fugitives with food and accommodation whilst they were in Austria and travel papers to enable their transfer to Italy. Such transfers to Rome for further handling were coordinated by Cecelja and Draganović, who once a week would let Cecelja know how many he was able to take in.

Many priests were active in this huge operation. Many Church properties were used to hide the Croatians and thousands of false documents were manufactured. In fact the Franciscans operated the printing press which produced all of the false San Girolamo documents for the Croatian fugitives. The Vatican allowed travel in its cars (which enjoyed diplomatic immunity) to shuttle these criminals between the Vatican and its properties outside its perimeter. The San Girolamo monastery was, according to a US Army Counter Intelligence Corps (CIC) report, run like a military fortress. Armed guards were placed inside the monastery and a password was required to move from one room to another.[31]

This was all taking place in a Catholic monastery in the centre of Rome. Did the Vatican really not know? At some point later, some of the senior Croats (Pavelic, some of his former ministers and heads of his air force) were moved to another Church property; this time it was a Vatican library. Most of those accommodated by the Church in her library were on the wanted lists of the Western powers. An operation of this magnitude did not go unnoticed. The British and US secret services knew what was happening. However, new political alliances were forming after the War and the Western powers found these fiercely anti-Communist Croatians useful for their attempts to destabilise Tito's regime in Yugoslavia. Investigative authors Mark Aarons and John Loftus conclude that 'Sections of the Allied authorities were in fact co-operating with the Vatican to ensure that many fugitives were allowed to slip quietly out of Genoa. ... the Vatican was cynically being used as a respectable cover for the West's own immoral conduct.'[32]

The Church did not forsake the Nazis. She may try to maintain that any action undertaken to help them flee justice was carried out by persons acting as individuals representing their own interests. However, the collective magnitude of these actions, the number of people involved, and the resources used in terms of money, properties and personnel, tell a different story. The ratlines were not a private operation of Bishop Hudal and Father Draganović, it was a Church operation. Monsignor Milan Simčić, who worked with Draganović – a fact which evidently did not hurt his career as he later became a senior Vatican official – has no qualms about their activity to help the perpetrators of such unbelievable atrocities. San Girolamo's role, according to the Monsignor, was not 'To make any moral judgements about the people we were helping. Our job was to make it possible for them to escape and history could judge them later.'[33]

Why only Nazis? One wonders why the Catholic Church has not extended her services to enable all the criminals of the world to escape. It would give the Church a truly universal mission. All the rapists and murderers, perhaps even minor burglars, could be given food, accommodation in Church properties, be supplied with false identity papers and have their travel to countries without extradition agreements paid for by the Catholic Church.

Impenitent

The Pope's lack of interest in the Jews and the post-War pro-German message was clear and in various Catholic countries of eastern Europe, post-War pogroms of Jews took place. The hatred of some of the senior Catholic hierarchy in Poland of all things Jewish did not save Catholic Poland from the Germans. Thousands of Polish Catholic priests were imprisoned by the Nazis and hundreds murdered in concentration camps. Polish Catholic anti-Semitism, however, did not abate. In July 1946, forty-one Jews were massacred in the Polish village of Kielce. Cardinal Hlond, the primate of the Polish Church, who had returned to Poland after the war, unashamedly blamed the Jews for their own deaths. Hlond 'explained' that the Jews who had survived the concentration camps 'were again holding important positions and they wanted to impose a regime alien to the Polish nation'. Hlond explained that the regrettable incident was the result of Jewish bureaucrats serving the Communist regime which was restructuring Polish life. Evidently, according to the Catholic Church, that was a rationale for murder. Fifteen hundred Jews are estimated to have been murdered by Poles in post-Holocaust Poland.[34] The Polish bishops considered issuing a condemnation of anti-Semitism but decided not to.

Growing anti-Semitism in Germany and other Catholic countries led some senior Catholics, such as Munich's Cardinal Michael Faulhaber and the French ambassador to the Holy See, Jacques Maritain, to plead with the Pope that he should act to stamp out anti-Semitism. In July 1946, Maritain wrote to the Vatican: 'When I think of the part Catholicism has played in the development of anti-Semitism in Germany, in Europe and in places like Argentina, I see how appropriate a word from the Pope would be.'[35] The Pope, clearly, did not agree. Instead, he continued with his energetic attempts to save the lives of Nazis.

Soon after the war, a Catholic circle headed by Gertrud Luckner and the theologian Karl Thieme, based in the southern German town of Freiburg, attempted to re-establish German–Jewish relations. One of their first efforts was instrumental in the removal of the term 'perfidious Jews' from the Good Friday liturgy. Thieme himself underwent a considerable evolution as a result of the atrocities of the Holocaust. This Catholic theologian expected Jews to have finally seen the light and for the survivors, who were not slaughtered, then to convert to Catholicism. By 1952, however, Thieme had concluded that Jews remained the people of God and stood in an ecumenical rather than missionary relationship to Christians. The Church did not like this. German Cardinal Frings and the Vatican were uncomfortable with the work of the Freiburg circle and warned them that their work was being monitored and scrutinised. A circular letter was sent to all German bishops warning about 'indifferentism', the belief that there is more than one 'true' religion and that different religions are equal.

When the Bavarian Bishops' Conference was appealed to by a retired Catholic priest in 1960 to abolish the commemoration in the Bavarian town Deggendorf of an old libellous story about Jews who in 1337 were said to have stolen and tortured a 'lovely little child', they said no. For centuries the people of Deggendorf had been celebrating the miraculous emergence of a child from a consecrated wafer. The citizens of the town, according to that story, killed all the local Jews 'out of legitimate zeal pleasing to God'. The week-long festival held by the local community to commemorate these wondrous events, drew some ten thousand guests every year. A play, written by a Benedictine monk, referring to Jews as 'poison mixers' and 'hordes of the devil' would be performed annually. Thanksgiving services were held at a church in which hung a picture of the massacre with the inscription 'God grant that our fatherland be forever free from this hellish scum'. And yet, in 1960, the Bavarian Bishops saw no reason to shut down such blatant anti-Semitic religion-based hatred in their very midst, until the national news magazine, *Der Spiegel*, picked up the story. The annual festival is now a call for forgiveness for the wrongs done to the Jews.[36]

Post-War Attitude to Zionism and to Israel

All the Church's efforts could not prevent the United Nations resolution for the partition of Palestine from being passed on 29 November 1947. Even though the UN resolution determined the establishment of two states, a Jewish state and an Arab state, and although it left Jerusalem as an internationally administered area, the Vatican was unhappy and a petition denouncing the partition was organised and signed by the leaders of all the Christian communities in the Holy Land in March 1948. On 14 May, Israel declared her independence and was promptly attacked by the armies of Egypt, Syria, Jordan, Lebanon and Iraq, whose leaders had repeatedly promised to drive the Jewish population into the sea and annihilate them. Needless to say, the Vatican did not recognise the newly established State of Israel.

For years, Arab countries and media refrained from calling Israel by its name and referred to Israel as the 'the Zionist state', whilst the Vatican spoke of 'the Holy Land'. The Jewish people, who had already lost six million in the Holocaust, now had new promises of annihilation. It is understandable that the Church should empathise with the suffering caused by war and with the plight of refugees. It is however, quite noticeable – if not glaring – that the Church did not call on the Arabs to quit arms and accept the UN resolution which would finally give a home to the survivors of Nazi concentration camps and which could signal an end to the suffering of the Jews. Instead, she issued an encyclical which focused exclusively on the Palestinian Question. *Multiciplibus Curis* was promulgated by Pius XII on 24 October 1948.

Papal sorrow for the suffering of the refugees would have had less anti-Jewish impact, if, in the past, the Pope had shown more interest in and empathy for Jewish suffering. Instead, he continued with his anti-Zionist stance and did not recognise the State of Israel. He issued another encyclical on 15 April 1949 (*Redemptoris Nostri*) voicing concern over damage done to sacred buildings and endeavouring to ensure the liberty of Catholic places of worship, Catholic rights and Catholic property. These did not cover only Christian holy sites, churches and monasteries but also other property which the Vatican owned in Palestine and for which it attempted to establish extra-territorial rights. Curiously it wished to have these extra-territorial rights without recognising Israel's right over the surrounding territory. Writer Livia Rokach confirms that the Vatican's steadfast opposition to Zionism and determined action to 'prevent the Zionist state from coming into being', were 'far greater than [those of] any other Western body'. More than that, she is of the opinion that

> had it not been for the Vatican's adamant opposition, ... those states that have extended diplomatic recognition to the state of Israel would probably have agreed to recognise Jerusalem as the Israeli capital as early as 1949–50. On the other hand the Catholic Church has had a much more positive attitude towards Arab national demands with regard to Palestine than it has shown towards other Third World liberation movements.[37]

In 1963, Pope Paul VI made a quick visit to the holy sites in Israel, whilst not uttering the word 'Israel' even once. It would take the Vatican another thirty years before it would recognise the State of Israel.

In 1974, the Greek Catholic patriarchal vicar in Jerusalem, Archbishop Hilarion Capucci, was found to be gun-running for the PLO, a terrorist organisation which was established in 1964 by Egypt, and had been run by Yasser Arafat since 1969. Undoubtedly, this was the Archbishop's personal decision. It was his religious conscience which enabled him to be comfortable helping Palestinians kill Israelis. He was tried and sentenced to twelve years in jail. The Vatican's reaction was, 'The Holy See has learned with profound pain and sorrow of the sentence passed on Monsignor Hilarion Capucci'.[38] Should they not instead have heard with pain and sorrow that a senior Catholic prelate operated as an arms smuggler for a terrorist organisation? Should they not have apologised for the abuse by their representative of the goodwill Israel had shown the Church? Unfortunately, the Vatican – rather than defrocking the Archbishop – chose to criticise Israel, commenting that the sentence could only increase tension 'in a territory where ... a just peace is still far away'. After intervention by the Pope, who considered that Capucci had endured his jail sentence 'for peace and reconciliation among the peoples of the Middle East', and on the understanding that he would not take part in political activity again, Capucci was released from jail in 1977. In a strange mode of defence, Capucci maintained that he had been blackmailed by the PLO into smuggling weapons. One would not expect an archbishop to have anything to be blackmailed for, but this one apparently did. Franciscan Fr David Maria Jeager, spokesperson for the Franciscan custodians of the holy sites in Jerusalem, shed light on the matter, saying that, in the 1960s, Capucci had developed 'personal interests, not at all compatible with the dignity of the priestly or episcopal office'.[39] Out of blackmailers' clutches and back in Rome, Capucci continued ceaselessly to promote Palestinian interests. He even served on the Palestinian National Council. He was recently quoted to have 'thank[ed] in the name of God the kamikazes who massacred Jews in pizzerias and supermarkets, calling them martyrs who go to their deaths as if to a party'.[40]

The Church has not excommunicated, defrocked or even condemned the Archbishop who was at first an accessory to murder and then a public promoter of combined murder and suicide. In fact, the Church intensified her relationship with the PLO. In 1982 and again in 1988, Pope John Paul II met Arafat. It is often necessary for politicians to talk to adversaries and enemies whose hands are not clean. But is this the role of the pope? Should the Pope really have met the head of an organisation which has as its goal the destruction of the Jewish state? Why was it necessary for the head of the Catholic Church to meet the head of a terrorist organisation who had so much Israeli and Jewish blood on his hands? A meeting with the pope cannot but be considered to be support, especially when the person met is neither a Catholic, nor a head of state.

The Pope's willingness to meet Arafat is especially significant as the Holy See, as a general policy avoids giving formal recognition to liberation movements, especially those professing armed struggle.[41]

Similar bad judgement and insensitivity was shown by Pope John Paul II in 1987 when he received Austrian President, Kurt Waldheim. Waldheim was considered *persona non grata* throughout the world. He was ostracised and not invited to visit any other country during his tenure as Austria's president because of his Nazi past. Yet, the Pope chose to break Waldheim's isolation. In the same year, the Pope enacted his own boycott: he forbade American Cardinal J. O'Connor from meeting the Israeli Prime Minister in the latter's official offices in Jerusalem. The Vatican, which had called for Jerusalem to be taken away from Israel as soon as the city was reunited in 1967, was still harbouring dreams about the internationalisation of the city.

The first time a pope made reference to the Jewish entitlement to a state was in 1975. In a Christmas message to the College of Cardinals, Pope Paul VI said:

> Although we are conscious of the still very recent tragedies which led the Jewish people to search for safe protection in a state of its own, sovereign and independent, and in fact precisely because we are aware of this, we would like to ask the sons of this people to recognize the rights and legitimate aspirations of another people, which have also suffered for a long time, the Palestinian people.[42]

The Church's growing interest in the Palestinian problem caused the Pope – by demanding that Israel recognise the Palestinians – to speak of the Jewish people who 'search[ed] for safe protection in a state of its own, sovereign and independent'. The Pope still did not say that the Vatican would like to recognise this sovereign Jewish state. That stage was only to be reached eighteen years later. The Fundamental Agreement between the Holy See and the State of Israel was signed on 30 December 1993. The recognition of Israel was, in the main, an agreement which assured the Church freedom and legal security in Israel. It is a sort of concordat covering the usual Church-sponsored schools, health care and media, Holy Places, Catholic institutions and it even deals with the promotion of pilgrimages. The agreement misses out on the opportunity, albeit belatedly, to redress the historical anti-Zionist policies of the Vatican.

Forty-five years are not a long time in the history of the Catholic Church. They were a very long time for the newly established Jewish state which was surrounded by enemies who continued to promise its annihilation. A clear message from the Christian world both after the War in 1945, and in 1948 when Israel gained independence, that the Jews were entitled to live in peace in their state would have been significant. It was not forthcoming. The Vatican – which had met PLO leaders as early as 1982 – concluded its agreement with Israel only in 1993 after the PLO itself had recognised Israel.

The Second Vatican Council

Pope John XXIII, Pius' successor, had a short papacy (1958–1963) in which he started to undo some of the evil Pius had done. Soon after his election, the Pope replaced all negative references to Jews in the Catholic liturgy with neutral or positive language. His main instrument for change was convening an ecumenical council, the first such council to take place since the First Vatican Council of 1870 (the Council which established the principle of papal infallibility). Unfortunately, the Pope died before the Council finished its deliberations. Had he still been the Pope in 1965, the Council would probably have concluded a stronger Jewish declaration. During the Holocaust, they did not speak out against the killings, and now they refrained from saying that they were wrong not to speak out. Shamefully, the Church let herself be lobbied and pressurised by conservative forces in the Catholic Church and by nationalistic Arab anti-Jewish interests.

John XXIII's successor, Paul VI, signalled his views to the Council by accusing the Jews of deicide in his Passion Sunday sermon. The accusation of deicide was a central issue which the Council Fathers had been debating for four years and which the more liberal Fathers had hoped finally to reject. Pope Paul VI chose to state that the Jewish people had refused to accept the Messiah whom they had awaited for thousands of years, and that when Christ revealed himself to them they 'derided, scorned and ridiculed him, and, finally, killed him'.[43] As late as 1965, the Pope did not want a Council declaration which would relieve the Jews of this accusation.

The document was originally envisaged as independent. But it first became chapter 4 of the Decree on Ecumenism, then an appendix to that decree, then an appendix to the Dogmatic Constitution on the Church, and finally ended as note 4 of the Declaration on the Relationship of the Church to Non-Christian Religions. As a result of considerable opposition, the final document, *Nostra Aetate*,[44] was a watered-down compromise: statements such as 'may Christians never present the Jewish people as one rejected, cursed or guilty of deicide' were considered too strong. It was replaced by 'the Jews should not be presented as repudiated or cursed by God, as if this followed from the holy Scriptures'. Deicide, in fact, is not mentioned. The document tried to exonerate the Church and blame the Nazis. There was so much opposition to a statement which would suggest that the Jews had, after all, not killed Jesus, that the compromise version did not admit any wrongdoing by the Church.

Yet, Vatican II's *Nostra Aetate* was a breakthrough in its statement that the death of Jesus 'cannot be blamed upon all the Jews then living, without distinction, nor upon the Jews of today'. The document also announced that 'The Church ... deplores the hatred, persecutions, and displays of anti-Semitism directed against the Jews at any time and from any source'. The Vatican itself considered the document to 'mark an important milestone in the history of Jewish–Christian relations'.[45]

Nostra Aetate, did not, however, deal with the Holocaust nor with Christian culpability. It made such sweeping statements as 'The Church repudiates all persecutions against any man' without mentioning that the Church had for a long time been the instigator, coordinator and ruler of such persecutions. *Nostra Aetate* fails to mention her direct and indirect role in persecutions in which Jews were marginalised, debased, tortured, expelled and killed. Moreover, *Nostra Aetate* repeats the Christian complaint that 'Jerusalem did not recognise the time of her visitation, nor did the Jews in large number accept the gospel; indeed, not a few opposed the spreading of it.' The very short document, which is meant to bring about 'mutual understanding and respect', reiterates the Church's teaching and declares 'True, authorities of the Jews and those who followed their lead pressed for the death of Christ.'

Nostra Aetate is theologically significant in that it repudiates the notion that present Jews are still to be blamed for the death of Christ. It is, however, not a *mea culpa*. Moreover, on the practical level, the document itself does not penetrate the anti-Semitic bias, so very much ingrained in Christianity. It did open up Jewish–Christian dialogues, which over the following thirty years produced three more Vatican documents and many documents issued by national congregations of bishops.

The first Vatican document that suggested practical steps to improve Jewish–Christian relations was *Guidelines and Suggestions for Implementing the Conciliar Declaration Nostra Aetate (no. 4)* (1 December 1974). *Nostra Aetate* called for dialogue between Jews and Catholics. *Guidelines and Suggestions* endeavours to suggest practical steps for such dialogue. It refers to the Holocaust, but without naming it. The reference is limited to a paragraph in the preamble in which it states that 'the step taken by the Council finds its historical setting in circumstances deeply affected by the memory of the persecution and massacre of Jews which took place in Europe just before and during the Second World War'. It almost sounds like a Christian charitable action to comfort the Jews instead of an attempt by the Church to deal with her role and Christianity's role in the extermination of millions of Jews in their very back yard, under their very windows.

In 1985, the Commission for Religious Relations with Jews issued a further document, *Notes on the correct way to present the Jews and Judaism in preaching and catechesis in the Roman Catholic Church* (24 June 1985). This document importantly states that the gospels may not necessarily be the truth, the whole truth and nothing but the truth. The Commission based itself on the Pontifical Biblical Commission which declared that the authors of the four Gospels which 'always ... told us the honest truth about Jesus', had selected material from the many things 'which had been handed on by word of mouth or in writing, reducing some of them to a synthesis, explicating some things in view of the situation of their Churches'. *Notes on the correct way to present the Jews and Judaism* states:

> Hence it cannot be ruled out that some references hostile or less than favourable to the Jews have their historical context in conflicts between the nascent Church and the Jewish community. Certain controversies reflect Christian–Jewish relations long after the time of Jesus.[46]

It is understandable that the Church could not doubt the veracity of the Gospels with regard to Jesus. This juggling act suggests that hatred towards Jews, which generations of Christians had been taught to believe originated from the days of Jesus, may have reflected later conflicts between Christians and Jews. The document *Notes on the correct way to present the Jews and Judaism* also makes the point that the Jews are a chosen people, and not as a didactic tool for Christianity: 'We must in any case rid ourselves of the traditional idea of a people *punished*, preserved as a *living argument* for Christian apologetic'. As important as these points are, the document still fails to grab the bull by the horns and to look at Christian culpability and Church culpability for the Holocaust.

National Conferences

In October 1995 the Dutch Bishops stated that they were 'filled with shame and dismay' when they recalled the *Shoah*, and added categorically that 'there is no doubt that Church institutions have made errors'. In their statement, the bishops confirmed:

> A tradition of theological and ecclesiastical anti-Judaism contributed to the climate that made the *Shoah* possible. What was known as the 'catechesis of vilification' taught that Jewry after Christ's death was rejected as a people. Partly due to these traditions, Catholics in our country sometimes were reserved toward Jews, and sometimes indifferent or ill-disposed. Just after the war this was still apparent on the return of those who had been hidden from or who had survived the concentration camps.
>
> We reject this tradition of ecclesiastical anti-Judaism and deeply regret its horrible results.[47]

In March 1997, the Swiss Bishops issued a statement which took responsibility for the teachings of the Church which gave rise to anti-Semitism and persecution:

for centuries, Christians and ecclesiastical teachings were guilty of persecuting and marginalising Jews, thus giving rise to anti-Semitic sentiments. Today, we shamefully declare that religious motivations, at that time, played a definite role in the process ... It is in reference to these past acts of churches for which we proclaim ourselves culpable and ask pardon of the descendants of the victims.[48]

In September 1997, the Catholic Bishops of France accused those who exercised authority in the Church of a 'loyalism and docility which went far beyond the obedience traditionally accorded to the civil authorities'. Referring to the silence of the Church in face of the anti-Semitic legislation enacted by the French government in 1940 and 1941, the declaration states, 'we are obliged to admit that the Bishops of France made no public statements, thereby acquiescing by their silence in the flagrant violation of human rights and leaving the way open to a death-bearing chain of events'.

The Bishops of France also admit that 'ecclesiastical interests, understood in an overly restrictive sense, took priority over the demands of conscience – and we must ask ourselves why'. They bring in 'historians' to introduce the connection between Catholic dogma and teaching and the 'venomous plant of hatred for the Jews', and thereby accept their judgement. Uniquely, they speak of the Church which has failed:

we recognise that the Church of France failed in her mission as teacher of consciences and that therefore she carries along with the Christian people the responsibility for failing to lend their aid ... This is the fact that we acknowledge today. For this failing of the Church of France and of her responsibility toward the Jewish people are part of our history. We confess this sin. We beg God's pardon, and we call upon the Jewish people to hear our words of repentance.[49]

The Polish Bishops also produced a declaration. One cannot avoid sensing the long history of anti-Semitism deep-rooted and entrenched in Catholic Poland making its mark on this document. *The Victims of Nazi Ideology* was issued by the Catholic Bishops in Poland to mark fifty years since the liberation of Auschwitz on 27 January 1945. It reminds the readers that Auschwitz was at first set up to imprison Polish intelligentsia and members of the resistance. It, naturally, yet repeatedly makes the point that Poland was occupied by the Germans and that these were German crimes. With regard to the relationship between Jews and non-Jews in Poland, the bishops say, 'It must be underlined that Poles and Jews have lived in this country for centuries, and although now and again conflicts did arise, they considered it their homeland.' For the Polish Bishops, with their track record of anti-Semitism, going back famously to Pope Benedict XIV's 1751, *A Quo Primum*, this is quite rich.

Evidently, as they juxtapose Poles and Jews, they still do not consider the Jews to be Poles. They point out that Jews considered Poland to be their homeland, suggesting that the non-Jews did not see it that way. According to the Polish Bishops, it was 'The loss of Polish independence ... [that] brought about ... a deterioration in Polish–Jewish relations.' Moreover, this deterioration, they maintain, was due to factors of 'psychological, economic, political and religious nature but never racist'. This sounds like, 'well, we had good reasons to hate the Jews'. During the Holocaust, we are informed by the bishops:

> many Poles reacted with heroic courage and sacrifice, risking their lives and that of their families. ... Many Poles lost their lives, ... because they dared to shelter Jews. ...
>
> Unfortunately, there were also those who were capable of actions unworthy of being called Christian. There were those who not only blackmailed, but also gave away Jews in hiding into German hands. Nothing can justify such an attitude, although the inhumane time of war and the cruelty of the Nazis led to Jews, themselves tormented by the occupier, being forced to hand over their brothers into the hands of the Germans.[50]

Having first made clear that 'many Poles' saved Jews and even died for them, they speak of those whose actions were un-Christian. It is not clear whether the purpose of including in this paragraph instances in which Jews were forced by the Nazis to hand over other Jews, is to lighten the deeds of the Polish non-Jews who collaborated with the Nazis, or just to besmirch the Jews. Whatever their purpose, it is outrageous and misleading. Poles who blackmailed Jews were not forced by the Nazis to do so. They simply took advantage of their plight. Similarly, Poles who made money by selling information about Jews in hiding, did so out of greed and out of anti-Semitism.

The Polish bishops do not fault the Church, do not fault the behaviour of the bishops during the holocaust, do not mention the role Catholic dogma, Church teaching and Church-induced hatred played in producing an anti-Semitic climate. It seems that the Polish bishops felt obliged by pressure from the Vatican and other countries to produce a statement and this forced document was the result.

Usurping the Holocaust

In 1984, Carmelite nuns established a convent in Auschwitz, the Nazi concentration and extermination camp area in which more than a million Jews and many non-Jews were murdered. Christian symbols and Christian prayer-sites at the camp where so many Jews were murdered, as a result of Christianity's long history of anti-Jewish preaching, caused unrest in the Jewish world. After much Jewish protesting, the Carmelite convent was moved. The nuns and their supporters did not go quietly, but finally left in 1993. However, they would not remove the very large (eight metres tall) cross which they had erected. Further to claim Auschwitz as a Christian site, right-wing and Catholic Polish groups erected dozens of small crosses, which were removed by the Polish government in 1999.

In his allocution to the College of Cardinals, on 2 June 1945, Pope Pius XII spoke only about the suffering of the Church under Nazism and her attempts to protest 'to the governing authorities in Germany'. He talked of the political prisoners who were coming out of the German camps and went into great detail about the priests who had been incarcerated. He even attempted to score points against the Protestant Church by proving that Catholics had suffered more. In his allocution, the Pope did not mention the Jews.[51]

The Church's attempt to usurp the Holocaust and prove that she was a victim too has at best shown insensitivity to Jewish feelings. At worst, it is a calculated attempt to mislead and deceive. If the Church could be considered a victim, people might not deem her to have been guilty of not speaking out against the Nazis. It might bring an end to the widespread accusations regarding the conduct of the Church, of many of her bishops, and above all of the Pope, during the Holocaust. One example is the canonisation of Edith Stein, who was a German philosopher who was born into a Jewish family and converted to Catholicism. She joined a monastic order and became a Carmelite nun. The Nazis deported her to Auschwitz and killed her, because, under German law, she was a Jew. The Church beatified her in 1987 and canonised her in 1998. It was necessary, according to the Church rules, for a miracle to have been performed and duly one was concocted by a Church which was eager to produce a Catholic martyr who had died in Auschwitz.[52] Edith Stein was not killed because of her Catholic faith; she would not have been killed in Auschwitz if her parents had not been Jews. This was a disingenuous attempt by the Church to be seen as a victim through Edith Stein's death.

It was not only in this case that the Church was willing to make shortcuts. Similar schemes were undertaken by the Church in the canonisation of Maximilian Kolbe, a Polish Franciscan priest who was imprisoned by the Nazis and who had volunteered to die to save the life of another prisoner. Understandably, the Church wanted to profile Father Kolbe and had him beatified and then commenced proceedings for his canonisation. It was, however, impossible to canonise him as a martyr (someone who has died for their faith), which is what his supporters, headed by Cardinal Wojtila, the future Pope John Paul II, had demanded. The Church professionals were unable, despite John Paul's pressure, to declare Kolbe a martyr, and suggested that Kolbe be canonised as a 'confessor' of the faith (someone who has lived an exemplary life of holiness). The Pope decided to disregard them. For the case he was building about the Catholic Church as victim, it was not enough to have Kolbe made a saint; he had to be shown as having died for his faith as a martyr – though it was not true. At Kolbe's canonisation in 1982, the Pope declared: 'And so, in virtue of my apostolic authority I have decreed that Maximilian Maria Kolbe, who, after his beatification was venerated as a confessor, shall henceforward be venerated also as a Martyr.'[53] The Pope continued beatifying and canonising Catholic clergy who were killed by the Nazis, always in a dishonest attempt to prove that they had died for their faith.

We Remember

In March 1998, the Vatican published its latest document, *We Remember: A Reflection on the Shoah*.[54] Having prevaricated for more than thirty years since Vatican II, it finally decided to examine the issue of guilt:

> [the Holocaust] calls for a 'moral and religious memory' and particularly among Christians, a very serious reflection on what gave rise to it.

> ... The fact that the Shoah took place in Europe, that is, in countries of long-standing Christian civilisation, raises the question of the relation[ship] between the Nazi persecution and the attitudes down the centuries of Christians toward the Jews.[55]

They do not speak of the relationship between Nazi persecution and the behaviour of the Church, or between Nazi persecution and Church teaching, scriptures or the Church Fathers, but rather the relationship between Nazi persecution and 'attitudes ... of Christians towards Jews'. The Vatican Commission took care not to touch on possible structural faults or on institutional culpability.

We Remember gives an eight-paragraph review of the 'Relations between Jews and Christians' confirming that 'the balance of these relations over 2,000 years has been quite negative'. It reminds the reader that Jewish leaders and others had 'in their devotion to the law, on occasion violently opposed the preachers of the Gospel and the first Christians'. On the other hand, 'Christian mobs who attacked pagan temples sometimes did the same to synagogues, not without being influenced by certain interpretations of the New Testament regarding the Jewish people as a whole.' It is interesting that Jewish violence, according to *We Remember*, stems from the 'Jewish leaders', whereas, apparently, Christian leaders were not involved in incitement against Jews. *We Remember* suggests that 'Christian mobs' 'sometimes' because of 'certain interpretations of the New Testament' attacked synagogues. Do the authors of *We Remember* include the Church Fathers in their definition of 'Christian mobs'?

In one paragraph of one-hundred-and-forty-nine words, *We Remember* covers the next fourteen hundred years, a period which includes the murder of hundreds of thousands of Jews by Christians in the crusades, both in Europe and in the Holy Land, and the massacres of Jews by Christians throughout the centuries in virtually every Christian country. In this one paragraph, this is all described thus: 'In a large part of the "Christian" world, until the end of the eighteenth century those who were not Christian did not always enjoy a fully guaranteed juridical status.' And 'In times of crisis such as famine, war, pestilence, or social tensions, the Jewish minority was sometimes taken as a scapegoat and became the victim of violence, looting, even massacres.' This quickly leads to 'By the end of the eighteenth century and the beginning of the nineteenth century, Jews generally had achieved an equal standing with other citizens in most states and a certain number of them held influential positions in society.' *We Remember* carefully omits the fact that in papal Rome, Jews had to wait until 1870 before achieving equality. It is quite outrageous that in 1998, the Church continue to mislead and deceive. In the mid-nineteenth century, Pius IX was fighting hard to keep Jews in ghettos and he put pressure on other rulers to revoke rights which Jews had been granted in the 1848 revolutions.

We Remember glosses over more than one thousand years of Church-induced hatred and dogmatic anti-Jewish teaching and preaching by priests, bishops and popes. A whole paragraph – one-hundred-fifty-one words – is dedicated to describing how wonderfully the Catholic Church in Germany had behaved during the Nazi years. Cardinals Bertram and Faulhaber are specifically mentioned among those who had condemned National Socialism in 1931. It is curious that *We Remember* chose to refer to Bertram, the cardinal who upon hearing of Hitler's death, instructed all the churches in his archdiocese to hold a special requiem mass in commemoration of the Führer. Faulhaber did indeed, in 1931, publish a pastoral letter against the Nazis. This, however, was before Hitler came to power and before the Vatican had signed its concordat with Hitler. After 1933, Faulhaber never came out against the Nazis' racial policies or their extermination of Jews. Other than the provost of Berlin's cathedral, Bernhard Lichtenberg, who was sent by the Nazis to Dachau, where he died, not one senior member of the German Catholic Church spoke out against the mass extermination of Europe's Jews.

The last paragraph in the Relations Between Christians and Jews is a section that describes Pius XI's *Mit brennender Sorge* and Pius XII's *Summi Pontificatus*, in which Pius XII spoke out against racism and against the deification of the state. Sister M. Christine Athans, a Catholic professor of Church history, argues that 'the historical overview is largely superficial and non-specific' and is also critical of the fact that 'the references to Pope Pius XII fail to give an historical account of his role or to acknowledge the ongoing research and controversy concerning his unwillingness to condemn the Nazis during World War II'.[56]

In the section entitled 'Nazi Anti-Semitism and the *Shoah*' the Vatican's Commission for Religious Relations with Jews attempts to distance the Church and Christianity from the Holocaust. It does so by defining anti-Semitism as 'based on theories contrary to the constant teaching of the Church on the unity of the human race', and referring to anti-Judaism as 'the long-standing sentiments of mistrust and hostility ... of which, unfortunately, Christians have also been guilty'. One almost wonders whether the authors of this document had access to their history books, in describing anti-Judaism as a 'sentiment ... of which Christians have *also* been guilty'. They overlook the fact that it was preached from the Church's pulpits and taught at Church schools.

Before asking the question whether 'Nazi persecution of the Jews was not made easier by the anti-Jewish prejudices imbedded in some Christian minds and hearts?', the document states that 'The *Shoah* was the work of a thoroughly modern neo-pagan regime. Its anti-Semitism had its roots outside of Christianity.' This important statement, probably the most important made in *We Remember*, is based on the fact that the Nazis were determined to 'remove the very existence of the Jewish people, a people called to witness to the one God and the law of the covenant'. As the Jews have a role to play in the grand plan of the Church, it is suggested that the liquidation of all Jews could not have had Christian roots. What about humiliating them, denigrating them, denying them any human rights, expelling them and massacring them? Do these have Christian roots? Are they not part of Christian history?

Professor Yehuda Bauer has no doubt: 'Without Christian anti-Semitism there would have been no Nazi anti-Semitism.'[57] The second point, which is designed to support the claim that the Holocaust had its roots outside Christianity, stems from the fact that some of the Nazi leaders rejected God and Christianity. Some Nazi leaders were, indeed, virulently anti-ecclesiastical. Yet only three members of Hitler's entourage had severed their connection with the Church.[58] Hitler, who grew up as a Catholic – as did Goebbels – took care not to aggravate relations too much. It is, of course, true that the regime wished to curtail the hold which any person or institution had over people under their rule and many members of the Church were persecuted too. Catholic theologian, Professor John T. Pawlikowski is quite clear in his view about the roots:

> *We Remember* leaves the strong impression that there was *no* inherent connection between Nazi ideology and classical Christian anti-Judaism and anti-Semitism. This is basically inaccurate. Among Europe's Christian population, Christian anti-Judaism and anti-Semitism had everything to do with widespread acquiescence and even collaboration with the Nazi

policy devoted to the destruction of the Jews. I like to speak of classical
Christian anti-Judaism and anti-Semitism as providing an indispensable
'seedbed' for Nazism.[59]

Before coming to the apology, the question 'Did Christians give every
possible assistance to those being persecuted and in particular to the
persecuted Jews?' is answered by We Remember with 'Many did not, but
others did.' The truth is different. Many Christians participated in the
persecutions and most did nothing to help the persecuted Jews. A few
gave some help, and only a very few gave 'every possible assistance'. It is
painful when such falsification finds a place in the document which is
meant to lead to a culminating apology. Since the deed has been watered
down, the apology commences with a 'Nevertheless, as Pope John Paul
II has recognised ... the spiritual resistance and concrete action of other
Christians was not that which might have been expected from Christ's
followers.'

'We deeply regret the errors and failures of those sons and daughters of
the Church.' Neither Christianity, nor the Catholic Church, the Vatican,
Pope Pius XI or Pope Pius XII seem to have had any responsibility. The
document had no trouble attributing guilt to others. The closing of the
borders by so many countries to fleeing Jews, for example, 'lays a heavy
burden of conscience on the authorities in question'. This document,
which failed to mention papal diplomatic efforts to keep Jews from being
allowed to settle in Palestine, should also have asked whether the Pope
had made the most of his influence in many Catholic countries, to urge
these countries to open their gates to fleeing Jewish immigrants.

Immediately after the short statement of regret, the Church assures
us that she 'condemns all forms of genocide', as if some Catholics were
still unsure about genocide and had to be instructed on the Church's
view! The Vatican's Reflection on the Shoah then lists other persecutions,
including the massacres of the Armenians, genocide of the Gypsies and
victims of totalitarian ideology in the Soviet Union, China and Cambodia.
In introducing other cases of genocide, massacres and atrocities, the
Church tried to subliminally suggest that the Holocaust was part of a
bigger picture unconnected to Christianity and Church teaching. The
next sentence also serves to muddy the waters, as it strikes an unclear
note of empathy: 'Nor can we forget the drama of the Middle East, the
elements of which are well known.'

We Remember, which begins its historical review by juxtaposing
violence on the part of Jewish leaders who opposed the first Christians
with Christian mobs who attacked synagogues, concludes with a prayer
for 'a new relationship with the Jewish people'. Unfortunately, in their
prayer, they resume their line of equating anti-Judaism among Christians
with anti-Christian sentiment among Jews: 'We wish to turn awareness

of past sins into a firm resolve to build a new future in which there will be no more anti-Judaism among Christians or anti-Christian sentiment among Jews.' Such deceptive balancing is offensive and harmful.

Rabbi James Rudin makes the point that '*We Remember* is rich with remembrance of past tragic history, it is abundant with calls for repentance, and it is eloquent in its resolve to improve future Catholic–Jewish relations. But the fourth 'r' responsibility, is inadequately and incompletely addressed in the document.'[60] In fact, *We Remember* has chosen to have a selective memory. Gary Wills, in his *Papal Sin: Structures of Deceit*, introduces his discussion of *We Remember* with the observation:

> The debilitating effect of intellectual dishonesty can be touching. Even when papal authority sincerely wants to perform a virtuous act, when it spends years screwing up its nerve to do it, when it actually thinks it has done it, when it releases a notice of having done it, when it expects to be congratulated on doing it – it has not done it.[61]

In extremely bad taste, the document which is meant to beg for forgiveness, takes advantage of its exalted platform to regurgitate the unproven legend that Pius XII 'personally or through his representatives [acted] to save hundreds of thousands of Jewish lives'. Heaping praise on the so-very-much disputed Pius XII and stressing that bishops and other clergy had opposed the Holocaust, *We Remember* conveniently fails to mention all those bishops and priests who supported the Nazis. This apparently never happened. It is, therefore, not necessary to ask forgiveness on their behalf. The only problem was Christians who had not given 'every possible assistance to those being persecuted and in particular to the persecuted Jews', Christians 'who were horrified … yet were not strong enough to raise their voices in protest'. It is in their name that *We Remember* calls for penitence.

It may have been too much to expect the Vatican to instigate an enquiry into the culpability of the Church and her hierarchy. The authors of the document – who conveniently make use of the passive voice in the paragraph on discrimination – were, indeed, under no duty to set themselves such questions. They therefore remain unanswered, at least unanswered by the Church. In reflecting on the Holocaust, *We Remember* not only 'did not contain the historical references, moral outrage and deep sense of contrition',[62] it deflected attention from the big issue.

Included in the extraordinary service held by Pope John Paul II on the first Sunday of the Church's Lenten Season in the new millennium (12 March 2000) was a special appeal for pardon for sins against the Jewish people. The president of the Vatican Commission for Religious Relations with Jews, Cardinal Edward Cassidy, commenced with 'Let us pray that, in recalling the suffering endured by the people of Israel throughout history, Christians will acknowledge the sins committed by not a few of their number against the people of the covenant and the blessings, and in this way purify their hearts.' The Pope continued,

> God of our fathers, you chose Abraham and his descendants to bring your name to the nations: We are deeply saddened by the behaviour of those who in the course of history have caused these children of yours to suffer, and asking your forgiveness, we wish to commit ourselves to genuine brotherhood with the people of the covenant.'[63]

At Yad Vashem, Israel's memorial to the victims of the Holocaust, which Pope John Paul II visited in 2000, the Pope attributed Nazi crimes to a 'godless ideology', adding that 'the Catholic Church ... is saddened by the hatred, acts of persecution and displays of anti-Semitism directed against the Jews by Christians at any time and in any place'.[64] There is no question about his feelings and his commitment, however, he did not apologise on behalf of the Church. The Church continues to claim that she is faultless.

When Pope John Paul II visited Syria in May 2001, he stood next to Bashar Assad, Syria's ruler, who in a barrage of anti-Israeli and anti-Jewish invective, said: 'They tried to kill the principles of all religions with the same mentality in which they betrayed Jesus Christ and the same way they tried to betray and kill the Prophet Muhammad.'[65] The Pope neither immediately nor later disassociated himself from Assad's rabidly anti-Semitic speech. Why the Pope should choose to visit a country which is considered to be one of the worst supporters of international terrorism is a riddle. Remarkably, even after the Church had acted to get rid of her anti-Jewish teaching and to cease preaching hatred of the Jews, a pope calmly stood by when such propaganda was aired, thereby giving it his tacit approval. Similarly, John Paul II, the same pope who engineered the Church's request for forgiveness from the Jews, a pope who manifestly is not anti-Semitic, has also beatified Pope Pius IX, a rabid anti-Semite, who famously referred to Jews as dogs. The act of beatification sends out clear signals to the Catholic world about the Church's values and priorities.

Vatican II moves to change Catholic attitudes and to remove blame for Christ's crucifixion from the Jews have not yet successfully reached all levels of the Catholic Church. Hence, a Catholic publication of 1998 thinks nothing of depicting the Jews as a people who 'Just as they crucified Christ ... try to do the same to Eugenio Pacelli today nearly forty years after the death of this quiet, but effective and holy Pope.

Have they forgotten the lessons of history?'[66] [ii] Elsewhere, senior Vatican official, Jesuit Father Peter Gumpel in an interview given to CBS News in March 2000, said 'Let us be frank and open about this as in all the things that I have said. It is a fact that the Jews have killed Christ. This is an undeniable historical fact.'[67]

[ii]   This referred to Jewish objections to the beatification of Pope Pius XII.

Part Three

The Church and Sex

Chapter Eight
Abused by Catholic Doctrine

In 1911, the Austrian Jesuit theologian Professor Hieronymus Noldin wrote that 'The Creator has infused human nature with sexual pleasure and the desire for it so as to entice people into something that is filthy in itself and burdensome in its consequences.'[1] The Catholic Church has a problem with sex. It is both a curse and a boon to her; a curse because the Church truly considers sex to be filthy and a boon because, by establishing herself as the controller of people's sexual lives, the Church has, for many years, managed to secure her powerful position in society.

> a good father, while discussing with his son a matter so delicate, should be well on his guard and not descend to details, nor refer to the various ways in which this deadly hydra destroys with its poison so large a portion of this world; otherwise it might happen that, instead of extinguishing this fire, he unwittingly stirs or kindles it in the simple and tender heart of the child. … Employ those remedies which produce the double effect of opening the door to the virtue of purity and closing the door on vice.[2]

According to instructions issued by the Catholic Church in England and Wales on how parents should discuss sex with their children, the young person who wanted to masturbate was, instead, to concentrate his mind on the Virgin Mary. The 'deadly hydra' referred to in this 1944 publication, *The Catholic Attitude to Sex Education* – a pastoral letter opposing sex education at schools – was not Nazi Germany, but sexual lust. The Church was in a state of panic and the Pope demanded world-wide action as, 'class or group instruction of children or of youth on the physiological aspect of sex would be fraught with grave dangers and would be against the traditional teaching of the Church'.[3] The Church's solution was to keep people in the dark. Instead of sex education, the British bishops suggested 'uninterrupted religious instruction', prayer and 'filial devotion to the Blessed Virgin'.[4] In 1944, at a time when, as a result of war-induced stress and increased mobility, people were having unprotected sex and there was a rising incidence of venereal disease, the Church considered 'the reason for the recent agitation in certain quarters for more general sex instruction … [is] not altogether clear'.

No other area of the human body and its functions has given the Church as much torment as sex. To understand the Catholic Church's extreme discomfort with anything connected to sex, one has to go back to Jesus. Two thousand years ago Jesus, as reported by the gospels, spoke vehemently against lust and ruled out divorce. One billion Catholics and many non-Catholics still suffer from the ramifications of his utterances.

> You have learned that they were told, 'Do not commit adultery.' But what I tell you is this: If a man looks on a woman with a lustful eye, he has already committed adultery with her in his heart.
>
> If your right eye leads you astray, tear it out and fling it away; it is better for you to lose one part of your body than for the whole of it to be thrown into hell. And if your right hand is your undoing, cut it off and fling it away; it is better for you to lose one part of your body than for the whole of it to go to hell.
>
> They were told. 'A man who divorces his wife must give her a note of dismissal.' But what I tell you is this: If a man divorces his wife for any cause other than unchastity he involves her in adultery; and anyone who marries a woman so divorced commits adultery.[5]

Moses, Jesus explained to his listeners, had only permitted divorce 'because you were so unteachable'. Jesus, however, had higher expectations from his followers. Jesus also dealt with celibacy when he spoke of those who 'renounced marriage for the sake of the kingdom of Heaven'. Celibacy was, in his eyes, a higher state which not everyone could achieve. Paul expanded on the value of celibacy: 'I should like you all to be as I am myself.' He accepted that not everyone could abstain as 'everyone has the gift God has granted him'. Moreover, Paul was aware of the power of sexual desire: 'To the unmarried and to widows I say this: it is a good thing if they stay as I am myself; but if they cannot control themselves, they should marry. Better be married than burn with vain desire.'[6]

The New Testament does not ascribe to Jesus any utterances concerning masturbation, homosexuality, contraception or other specific sexual activities. Paul, however, includes homosexuality as one of the depravities of the 'godless wickedness of men'.[7] Paul, who was a Jew and who preached to both Jews and pagans, considered the Mosaic Law as the relevant law by which people were judged. Considering the Old Testament's clear prohibition of homosexual acts, Paul's view is not surprising. Homosexuality was forbidden as 'such a thing is an abomination'.[8] It carried the death sentence: 'If a man lies with a male as with a woman, both of them shall be put to death for their abominable deed; they have forfeited their lives.'[9] In fact, the Old Testament established capital punishment for quite a few sexual and non-sexual 'crimes'.[i] Bestiality was forbidden: 'You shall not have carnal relations with an animal, defiling yourself with it; nor shall a woman set herself in front of an animal to mate with it; such things are abhorrent.'[10] What's more, 'Anyone who lies with an animal shall be put to death,' and 'the animal shall be slain'.[11] Very clear and detailed instructions also outlawed incest.[12] The punishment for incest depended on the degree of closeness and on the extent such incest was hurtful to a third party. For example, 'If a man disgraces his uncle by having intercourse with his uncle's wife, the man and his aunt shall pay the penalty by dying childless.' Whereas, 'If a man disgraces his father by lying with his father's wife, both the man and his stepmother shall be put to death.' Incest with siblings is unacceptable socially, but not punished by death.[13]

The Christian notion that sex was unclean goes back to the Old Testament. Before God's appearance on Mount Sinai, he told Moses to:

> go to the people and have them sanctify themselves today and tomorrow. … Then Moses came down from the mountain to the people and had them sanctify themselves and wash their garments. He warned them, 'Be ready for the third day. Have no intercourse with any woman.'[14]

The Old Testament rules give an indication of the importance of sexual 'cleanliness' for priests. They were not to marry prostitutes, not even divorcees, in fact they were only to marry virgins.[15] 'A priest's daughter who loses her honour by committing fornication and thereby dishonours her father also, shall be burned to death.' In an attitude, which in today's world would undoubtedly be considered politically incorrect, God also stipulated that disfigured and malformed people be kept out of the priesthood.[16]

Christianity, which has developed from Judaism, has dropped many Jewish rituals and customs and adopted others. Judaism's attitude to sex, is, in the main positive. Marriage is definitely seen as a positive thing: 'He who finds a wife finds a good thing, and obtains favour from the Lord.'[17] Neither masturbation nor contraception are mentioned in the Bible. However, the story of Onan, who practiced *coitus interruptus*,[ii] is regularly given as biblical proof of God's abhorrence of wasting semen. According to biblical custom, Onan was forced to have sex with the childless widow of his brother in order to impregnate her in his brother's stead:

> And Onan knew that the seed should not be his; and it came to pass, when he went in unto his brother's wife, that he spilled it on the ground, lest that he should give seed to his brother. And the thing which he did displeased the LORD: wherefore he slew him also.[18]

---

[i]   Such as cursing one's parents or acting as a medium or as a fortune-teller.
[ii]   Sexual intercourse in which the penis is withdrawn before ejaculation.

This is the only biblical 'justification' for two thousand years of Church harassment of masturbators and people practising contraception. Onan was indeed punished for spilling his semen outside his sister-in-law's body to prevent pregnancy, but he was punished for violating the law which decreed that he had to impregnate her. The text is quite clear, there is nothing to indicate that he was punished for wasting his semen, nor is there a suggestion that he had sex to satisfy his lust. He had sex because he was instructed to do so. The purpose of sex, according to Judaism, is procreation, but there is nothing to suggest that it may not be enjoyed. For some reason, Christianity introduced this notion – objecting to the joy of sex – which, even in the twenty-first century, still haunts the lives of millions of Catholics.

With Christianity came the image of Christ who died to atone for Adam's original sin and who has thereby opened the way for salvation of his followers.[iii] This idea, which was developed by Augustine, imbues the sexual act with sin. The unfortunate concept that original sin, itself considered by some as the sexual awakening of Adam and Eve, is passed genetically (that is through the semen and the egg to the unborn child) implies that every successful copulation produces further sin.

Judaism does not have such hang-ups about sex. The notion that married people are 'entitled' to get sex from their partners was consistent with the Jewish norms. Even Paul, who thought that it was 'a good thing for a man to have nothing to do with women', advised married couples 'do not deny yourselves to one another'.[19] The exaltation of celibacy had already been introduced by Jesus and has been promoted by the Church ever since.

In his First Letter to the Corinthians, Paul warns them that various sins of a sexual and non-sexual nature will prevent them from entering heaven. He develops the idea that our bodies are not just physical and that they are God's and not our property. 'Do you not know that your bodies are limbs and organs of Christ?', he asks. By describing our bodies as limbs of the Holy Christ and sex as dirty, Paul produces an explosive situation.[20]

Pope Paul IV (1555–1559) did not want married men to sing in the Sistine choir as he believed that they polluted the purity of the papal chapel. He also commissioned an artist to paint clothes onto the naked bodies of figures in Michelangelo's *Last Judgement*. The roots of the Church's discomfort with the human body and especially with human sexuality can be detected in her earliest history. An early Church Father who took this to an extreme was the Christian theologian and philosopher, Origen of Alexandria (185–254). Origen, who gave private tuition to women, was apparently worried about Jesus' warning regarding lust and that looking

---

iii   See also in Chapter 1.

at a woman could lead to committing adultery in one's heart. Matthew, 19:12 says: 'Some are incapable of marriage because they were born so; some, because they were made so by others; some, because they have renounced marriage for the sake of the kingdom of heaven. Whoever can accept this ought to accept it.'[21] Origen took Jesus' idea literally and castrated himself. He would later in his life regret his deed and criticised the literal understanding of this passage in Matthew.

The Church Fathers Strike Again

Nothing is known about the sexual activities or marital status of Jesus. The subject is simply not mentioned anywhere. Some of his disciples, however, were married and there is no indication that sexual activity in any way stood in the way of their devotion. Nor is it suggested anywhere that, polluted by coitus, they were impure when they were preaching. And yet, the Western Church has ever since the fourth century attempted to impose sexual abstinence on bishops and priests. Church councils instructed the married clergy to refrain from having sex with their wives, but found that such instructions were difficult to enforce.

Some cheating on the rules must have also existed from the very early days. St Jerome (341–420) thundered against cohabitation of supposed hermits. Jerome confessed: 'in my fear of hell, … I have often found myself surrounded by bands of dancing girls … The fires of lust kept bubbling up before me when my flesh was as good as dead.'[22] He therefore knew that cohabitation was but a sham: 'whence come these un-wedded wives, these new types of concubines, nay, I will go further, these one-man harlots? … They call us suspicious if we think that anything is wrong.' The practice has, of course, never died. Thousands of Catholic priests live in sin with their concubines, often conveniently defined as housekeepers.[iv]

Ambrose, Augustine and Jerome were the most prominent theologians of the Church in the fourth and fifth centuries. Ambrose (339–397), Bishop of Milan, when he was not inciting anti-Jewish hatred and defending the right of Christians to burn synagogues, wrote treatises extolling virginity and demanding that people have as little sex as possible. At the time, priests were still allowed to marry and Ambrose demanded that they should give up sex. They had, according to him, to refrain from intercourse with their own wives. The rest of the population should be reminded that the purpose of sex was procreation. Having sex with one's pregnant wife was unacceptable. In fact, Ambrose called for his congregation to 'either emulate the beasts or fear God'. Animals, he explained, are only 'animated by the urge to preserve their kind, not by the desire for sexual union. For, as soon as they perceive that the womb is gravid, they cease to indulge in sexual intercourse.' If his audience was

---

iv   See Chapter 9.

not convinced by the parallels to the animal kingdom, Ambrose exhorted them to 'Control your lust and look upon the hands of your Creator, who fashions a human being within the maternal body. If he be at work, will you profane the peaceful sanctuary of the maternal body with carnal desire?'[23] He also considered it shameful for older people to have sex.[24]

The Church's extreme discomfort with sex necessitated the creation of sex-free zones surrounding Jesus. Semen seemed especially dirty to her. In a letter to Bishop Anysius, Pope Siricius (384–399) wrote in 392, 'Jesus would not have chosen to be born of a virgin had he been compelled to regard her as so incontinent that the womb in which the body of the Lord took shape, that hall of the Everlasting King, would be defiled by the presence of male seed.'[25] Jovinian, a Catholic theologian, incurred the Church's wrath by disputing Mary's virginity; the Church continues to teach that Mary's hymen remained intact. Jovinian, who contended that married and celibate life were of equal merit, held that Mary retained her virginity at conception but that she lost it at child-birth. For publishing a book containing such heretical ideas, Jovinian was excommunicated by Pope Siricius. Furthermore, Ambrose got Emperor Theodosius to flog and then exile Jovinian.

St Jerome, in his treatise *Against Jovinianus*, also attacked the theologian. Jerome, who translated the Old Testament from Hebrew into Latin, the *Latin Vulgate Bible*, was an ascetic, who for thirty-four years lived as a hermit in a cave outside Bethlehem. That a Christian hermit who lived in the years 340 to 420 should be a misogamist and misogynist, suffering, in all likelihood, from repressed sexuality of one kind or another, would be of no significance, had he not also been an important influence over the Catholic Church. In his adamant belief that virginity was the preferred human state, Jerome even spun a story about Jesus' preference for John over Peter, allegedly because of John's virginity.[26]

Some later theologians developed the notion that the original sin for which Adam and Eve had been expelled from paradise was sex. Jerome likes the idea of a sexless paradise. According to him, coitus was not part of the prelapsarian world: 'And as regards Adam and Eve we must maintain that before the fall they were virgins in Paradise: but after they sinned, and were cast out of Paradise, they were immediately married.' Jerome was so disturbed by sex that he actually suggested that 'while Scripture on the first, third, fourth, fifth, and sixth days relates that, having finished the works of each, "God saw that it was good," on the second day it omitted this altogether, leaving us to understand that two is not a good number because it destroys unity, and prefigures the marriage compact.'[27]

In their decision to maintain the celibacy of the clergy, present-day popes carry the history, tradition and dogma which were developed by people of Jerome's ilk. Jerome taught that 'The truth is that, in view of the purity of the body of Christ, all sexual intercourse is unclean.'[28] Indeed, 'A layman, or any believer, cannot pray unless he abstain from sexual intercourse. Now a priest must always offer sacrifices for the people: he must therefore always pray. And if he must always pray, he must always be released from the duties of marriage.'[29]

Augustine was a fifth century Bishop of Hippo in North Africa and a prominent Church Father who had enjoyed a full and varied sex life before turning to God. He lived with one mistress for fifteen years with whom – through a glitch in contraception – he had one child, abandoned her, took on another mistress and finally became a Christian. At that stage, he 'discovered' how evil sex was and how offensive sexual acts were as even birth took place between the organs of defecation and urination. He was the man, according to the Catholic theologian Uta Ranke-Heinemann, who was responsible for welding Christianity and hostility to sexual pleasure into a systematic whole.[30] To Augustine, original sin was transmitted through the sexual act, thereby making copulation evil. Even when taking place within marriage, coitus was evil. It could only be redeemed by aiming the sexual act at procreation. Augustine interprets original sin as Adam and Eve's decision to have sex with lust, instead of choosing to copulate without lust. According to this theory, unless saved through God's grace, original sin condemns all human beings to eternal death and damnation.

The importance of Augustine's views cannot be overstated. His teaching continues to form part of Catholic dogma. Augustine accepted that 'The union ... of male and female for the purpose of procreation is the natural good of marriage. But he makes a bad use of this good who uses it bestially, so that his intention is on the gratification of lust.'[31] Adultery was, of course, out of the question but Augustine developed the concept that even sex with your husband or wife could be sinful: 'The married believer, therefore, must not only not use another man's vessel, which is what they do who lust after others' wives; but he must know that even his own vessel is not to be possessed in the disease of carnal concupiscence.' Devoured by self-torture over lust, Augustine tried to find a way of accepting biological facts whilst maintaining his belief in the sinfulness of lust. He explained, in his treatise *On Marriage and Concupiscence* that, 'cohabitation ... should not be a matter of will, but of necessity, without which, nevertheless, it would be impossible to attain to the fruition of the will itself in the procreation of children'. Even the begetting of children would not suffice, unless these children 'shall be born again in Christ, and remain in Him for evermore'.[32]

Augustine evidently found his own erections hard to come to terms with. He bemoaned the fact that unlike all other human organs, the penis had a mind of its own and would not obey the will. It was, according to him the direct result of Adam and Eve's transgression.[33] An obsessed Augustine continues that 'carnal concupiscence' is acceptable for procreation but 'in no case happens to nature except from sin. It is the daughter of sin, as it were; and whenever it yields assent to the commission of shameful deeds, it becomes also the mother of many sins.' Augustine explained how the 'seductive stimulus ... produced shame.'[34] This man, whose own carnality drove him crazy, feverishly agonised over Adam and Eve's sex life and developed his theory which delivered to the Church generation after generation of fresh recruits. Through the coital act, which, ever since the expulsion from paradise, is possible only with the aid of lust, the parental lust transmits the original sin from parents to offspring. Baptism, a service offered by the Church, was the mechanism which cleansed the baptised from this burden. The attraction of this theory to the Church was obvious. If people could be convinced that the only way to prevent their children from going to hell was Church baptism, the Church would collect the worried faithful – as a fisherman gathers fish in his net.

Augustine even found an explanation for polygamy. Men, in biblical times, were permitted to have many wives 'where the reason was for the multiplication of their offspring, not the desire of varying gratification'.[35] Women, on the other hand, were not allowed such luxury. As the plurality of husbands would not result in more pregnancies, 'but only a more frequent gratification of lust, she cannot possibly be a wife, but only a harlot'.[36] The beauty of marriage, in Augustine's eyes, was that it made the sinful lust necessary for the sexual act, pardonable. In fact, even sexual acts which served lust and not procreation – provided that nothing was done actively to impede procreation – were fine within the confines of marriage. Augustine was willing to forgive such coital acts; they are 'permitted, so far as to be within range of forgiveness, though not prescribed by way of commandment'. Human weakness, which could lead to lustful behaviour outside marriage, made Augustine accept such behaviour within marriage. They may 'be tolerated, that no lapse occur into damnable sins; that is, into fornications and adulteries. ... the married pair are enjoined not to defraud one the other, lest Satan should tempt them by reason of their incontinence'.[37]

Augustine drew the line when it came to contraception, which he defined as criminal, describing 'lustful cruelty, ... [which] resorts to ... poisonous drugs to secure barrenness'.[38] Knowledgeably, beautifully and attractively, Augustine describes lust[39] and then defines it as a venial sin within the confines of marriage and a mortal sin outside or if it involves contraceptive measures. Augustine became instrumental in fusing pleasure with sin, a notion which would trouble generations of Catholics.

Seneca (4BC–65AD) and other Stoic philosophers preached similar disparaging ideas regarding sexual pleasure and carnal desires. But unlike the Church which, two thousand years later, still aggressively tries to subjugate the world to these ideas, there was no imposing structure. Augustine developed and the Church propagated a concept in which sexual pleasure was deemed evil, which would have disastrous effects on mankind. In attempting to understand the Catholic Church's abhorrence of masturbation, one must also travel back to Augustine.

Solitary self-gratification, an act of pure lust, in which orgasm is sought in an environment which, by definition, cannot procure offspring, is, to Augustine, the essence of sin. Thus, one of the most natural human activities, which most children start when they are two or three years old, has been and still is vilified by the Church, because of a few sexually repressed Church Fathers who lived more than fifteen hundred years ago.

The Church Fathers' fascination with sex was hugely influential. Priests and monks who chose celibacy were evidently unable to get the subject off their minds and their way of dealing with it was to inflict sexual constraints on others. Not dissimilar to people who get sexual gratification through physical sadism, such as whipping another person, some Catholic clergy devoid of normal sexual relations, got their pleasure by torturing the faithful with their intimate questioning at confession and with the severe penitential regime they ran. Various penitentials which appeared between the sixth and the tenth centuries prescribed three years to life for intentional homicide as well as for oral intercourse. Penances for anal intercourse were three to fifteen years, whereas the time suggested for *coitus interruptus* was two to ten years. Anything from forty days up to seven years was apparently suitable for couples who had sex with the woman on top of the man.[40] The penalties normally included fasting in some form. This ranged from a reduction of the amount of food, through limitations on meat, butter and other luxuries, to omission of certain meals, reduction to only water and dry bread, or total fast.[41] It seems unlikely that long periods of seven, ten or even fifteen years of fast were actually enforced. Often, such penalties were commuted to shorter periods of prayer. Certain penitentials were fond of punishing the sinful by flogging.

Theodore of Tarsus, Archbishop of Canterbury (602–690) is credited with the organisation of the diocesan system of the Catholic Church in England. He is described by the Catholic Encyclopedia as 'inclined to be autocratic, but possessed of great ideas, remarkable powers of administration, and intellectual gifts of a high order, carefully cultivated. Practically his only literary remains are the collected decisions in disciplinary matters, well known as *The Penitential of Theodore*.'[42] Theodore ruled that boys who masturbate together should be whipped and male homosexuality was punishable by seven to fifteen years' penance, whereas manslaughter only received seven to ten years.[43]

One of the outcomes of the concerted anti-sex drive of the Church Fathers was a very wide restriction on the days on which sex was permitted by the Church. Restrictions on sex – only within marriage, ideally for procreation and thus under no circumstance in any form which precludes conception – did apparently not suffice. Sex was not to take place on Sundays, on all religious holidays, over the forty days of Lent and not on the days prior to Communion. As there was nothing in the scriptures on this matter, local bishops could go wild in their battle with the evil of lust. At a synod in 966, a bishop in Verona banned sex on Fridays. For a while, in Ireland, sex was banned by the Church on Wednesdays and Fridays in addition to Sundays and all the 'normal' off days. These were supplemented as a special top-up by the Irish Church with three forty-day periods each year.[44] Twenty to forty days of strict fasting on bread and water was the standard penance imposed in the middle ages for lapses. Whether because of difficulties in the policing of these restrictions, or just because there was actually nothing in the scriptures setting out coital exclusion dates, this slowly died out. The monk Regino, for a while Abbot of Prüm in Lorraine, compiled a collection of canonical regulations, *Of Synodical Cases and Ecclesiastical Discipline*, which appeared about 906. From Regino's book, which describes the procedure and dynamics of penitent management, it is possible to gauge the relative severity of crimes according to the Church. Cutting someone's hands or feet off or gouging out their eyes carried one year's penance, whereas intercourse with another's wife or with a nun was punishable by seven years' penance.[45]

The Augustine concept that sexual intercourse served mainly procreation but that it was tolerated to prevent fornication produced some violent Church teachings. Thus, a thirteenth-century Archbishop of Canterbury, Stephen Langton, considered a wife's life of lesser value than her husband's adultery-free life. If a man demanded sex from his wife, even in childbed, then 'Rather must the wife suffer herself to be killed than that her husband should sin'.[46] Rules in the Church were made by men who understood the fire in male loins but had no such empathy for the female need for sex. In the twelfth century, the chancellor of the University of Paris – in those days a Church institution – told men how to treat their wives if they demanded to have sex on a holy day. A husband was to 'quell her impudence with fasting and beating'.[47]

Theologians agonised over important issues such as whether monks and priests' wet dreams were sinful. Some were of the view that there could be no ejaculation of semen without sin. Others devised sliding scales, according to what they assumed were the reasons behind the wet dreams: too much food or drink; or, perhaps, erotic day dreaming which produced the nocturnal emission. Convoluted methods were devised by the Church to pinpoint exactly the aspects of sex that were sinful. Cardinal Robert Courson, who died as a Crusade preacher in 1219, explained that 'If a man know his wife for the purpose of procreation or in rendering her due, the first and last parts of that act, during which he strives after God, are meritorious, whereas the middle parts, during which the whole man is ruled by the flesh and becomes all flesh, are venially sinful.'[48] Whereas, others, such as Cardinal Huguccio of Ferara, tutor to Pope Innocent III, who considered pleasure the main criterion, had a different approach. Huguccio explained that coitus 'can never be without sin, for it always occurs and is exercised with a certain itching and a certain pleasure; for in the emission of the seed, there is always a certain excitement, a certain itching, a certain pleasure'.[49] Sin, according to Huguccio, was not in the act but, rather, in the pleasure derived from the act.

Books on sexual positions are not a modern-day invention; thirteenth-century Church theologians gave minute instructions as to the acceptability and sinfulness of non-missionary positions. It is not clear how much experience these Church dignitaries had and whether they permitted themselves any experimentation to perfect their research! The general view was that any other position, if indulged in for pleasure, was a mortal sin. Roland of Cremona allowed the exceptional 'doggie style' for the obese, who were unable to manage penetration in the missionary position. In his treatise *Summa de matrimonio solutio*, Roland recommended that the overweight change their lifestyle, undertake more manual work, sweat, and diet, eat only little meat, millet bread and drink vinegar. Where these measures did not suffice, Roland reluctantly allowed the obese 'to come together after the manner of the beast', but 'always with spiritual sorrow'.[50]

Saint Thomas Aquinas (1225–1274) is probably Christianity's foremost theologian. His major work, *Summa theologica*, is a complete scientifically arranged exposition of theology and a summary of Christian philosophy. Next to Augustine, Thomas is also the Church's highest authority on sexual matters. It is, therefore, of some importance to be aware of the language used by the man – whose teaching still influences the Catholic Church today in matters of sexual morality – when referring to marital intercourse. Thomas's deep-rooted disgust has defined and moulded the Catholic Church's attitude to sex and impregnated the minds of her faithful. In his writings, Thomas described marital sex as: filth (*immunditia*), a stain (*macula*), foulness (*foeditas*), vileness (*turpitude*), disgrace (*ignominia*), degeneracy (*deformitas*), a disease (*morbus*), a corruption of the inviolate (*corruptio integritatis*) and an object of disgust (*repugnantia*).[51] Thomas, therefore, considered 'The man who is too ardent a lover of his wife acts counter to the good of marriage if he use her indecently, although he be not unfaithful, he may in a sense be called an adulterer.'[52]

The Church created tortuous rules of what was and what was not permitted for two consenting adults in their own bedroom. But if one was clever enough, or at least experienced enough, one knew how to define one's intercourse so that it would pass through the loopholes of the confessional. Thomas suggested that to 'prevent fornication in his wife, it is no sin'.[53] This interesting notion of adultery with one's own wife has still not been abandoned by the Catholic Church. Pope John Paul II, gave it twentieth-century legitimisation at a general audience on 8 October 1980.[54]

This unnatural attitude of the Church has, from early on, driven her members to a life of deceit. Confessors were furnished with written manuals setting out the questions they were to ask in the confessional. The mid-thirteenth-century Dominican, Cardinal Hugh of St Cher, prescribed that penitents should be asked 'Have you known your wife only for delight? Because you ought to [come to] her only for the sake of generating, or avoiding fornication, or returning the debt.' On the question of sex in any position other than the missionary position, or contraception, the penitent should be told that 'The Lord gave one way which all men hold; wherefore, if you have done other than in that one way you have sinned mortally.'[55] If you were able to pass the buck, and maintain that you had sex because you believed that only sex would prevent your spouse from fornicating, you were in the clear. Thomas prepared a transgression table, ordering sexual transgressions by the severity of their sinfulness. Incest, rape or adultery were, according to Thomas, less sinful than masturbation, homosexuality or performing sex other than in the missionary position.[56]

The Church's preoccupation with sexual positions and the variety of the joys of sex, caused a new problem. Titillating questions by priests during confession often gave the sinning Catholics ideas which they hastened to try out in their bedrooms. Therefore, some manuals instructed confessors to speak in general terms and to refrain from suggesting sins to the faithful. In the fifteenth century, John Nider, in his *Manual for Confessors*, advised caution in asking about sins of the flesh and sins specifically against nature 'lest something be disclosed to the simple of which they were ignorant'.[57] Cardinal Hostiensis' instructions for the interrogation during confessional were:

> 'You have sinned against nature when you have known a woman other than as nature demands. ...You know well the way which is natural. Did a pollution ever happen to you otherwise?' If he says 'No' ask nothing further. If he says 'Yes' you may ask 'Sleeping or waking?'... If he says

'Waking', you may ask 'With a woman?'... If he says 'With a woman,' you
may ask, 'Outside the vessel, or within it, and how?'[58]

Similarly, Bartholomew of Exeter, in his *Penitential*, makes the point that
sexual sins should not be specified in the confession 'for we have heard
of both men and women by the express naming of crimes unknown to
them falling into sins they had not known'.[59]

The eighteenth-century theologian Alfonso de' Liguori did not concur
with the idea which some theologians had developed that a wife could
withhold sex in situations of dire poverty. The reason given by Liguori,
who was later canonised and in 1871 also made a Doctor of the Church,
was that withholding sex could lead the husband to fornication. Such
refusal, according to Liguori, was a grave sin. In this perverted morality,
the wife is being forced by the Church to have sex against her wishes, even
if the husband – who might otherwise go and seek his sexual pleasures
elsewhere – is unable to feed the children he produces with the Church's
assistance. The Church – led by men whose sex lives, if any, were furtive
– was besotted with male lust and, as a result, produced policies which
made it the wife's principal role to ensure that her husband's cup did
not overrun. If this meant that she would suffer, or endanger her health
or that of the children, so be it, as long as the husband was prevented
from going elsewhere for sex. The Church devised a system which did not
permit divorce and in which the wife could be forced by the husband to
have sex with him. Essentially, this was Church-authorised rape.

In January 1944, as Europe was burning, the Church's marriage
tribunal, the *Rota Romana*, stated that a man who had been compulsorily
sterilised by the German state was not permitted to get married. The
decision was based on *Cum frequenter* (1587), Pope Sixtus V's (1585–1590)
contribution to sexual issues. *Cum frequenter* was another vile offshoot
emanating from the Church's unhealthy interest in sex. According to
this decree, men who could not produce real semen were not permitted
to marry. It took the Church another thirty-three years, three hundred
and ninety years after the issuing of *Cum frequenter*, to rescind the decree.
Thirty-five popes did nothing about this absurd command of their
predecessor. In typical Church fashion, when it was finally rescinded, it
was done with a lie. The Church did not pronounce Sixtus' decree null and
void, instead they informed: 'The Sacred Congregation for the Doctrine
of the Faith has always taken the view that those who have undergone a
vasectomy or are in similar circumstances should not be prevented from
contracting marriages.'

The decision in 1977 stressed, however, that chronic impotence
continued to be an impediment to marriage. Indeed, in 1982, a Catholic
priest in Munich refused to marry a twenty-five-year-old man who
suffered from muscular dystrophy, without proof of his ability to have

children.[60] Two years later, in 1984, the diocesan marriage tribunal in Nottingham refused to grant permission for a former soldier to marry who was paralysed and therefore deemed impotent. It took a loophole according to which, if there was a chance that in future the marriage could be consummated, even if the chance was minimal, marriage could be valid. It was probably the Church's discomfort with the fact that the man in question was a former soldier that finally persuaded the bishop to agree and allow the church wedding to go ahead.

Marriage and Divorce

Until the fifth century, marriage had been a purely civil matter, dealt with by the secular authorities. Then the Church entered this domain and gave marriage ceremonies sacramental status. Appropriating this pivotal junction in people's lives helped the Church secure for herself an ever growing and indispensable role.

Marriage, according to the Church, is holy and therefore indissoluble. Although the Church accepts that 'It can seem difficult, even impossible, to bind oneself for life to another human being',[61] she does not consider ending marriage an acceptable solution. There is no divorce under Catholic (Canon) law. In certain cases, the Church will permit physical separation, for instance, when it can be shown that the welfare of children suffers during co-habitation. But the spouses continue to be married to each other and are forbidden to sleep with anyone else. Having sex with a third person, even for a separated person, is considered by the Church to be adultery and, thereby, a mortal sin. Worried about the ever growing number of Catholics who avail themselves of civil divorce procedures, the Catechism of the Catholic Church states that 'Divorce is a grave offence against the natural law. It claims to break the contract, to which the spouses freely consented, to live with each other till death.'[62] Thus, it is made clear that divorce does not break the marriage contract; all it does is *claim* to do so.

The Church creates a terrible dilemma for Catholics who wish to divorce and remarry. If they do go ahead with a civil divorce and civil marriage then the new marriage is not recognised by the Church. If, as is likely, they actually have sex with their new husband or wife, then this is considered to be adultery; if unabsolved, this sin will lead them to hell. But the door to confession is also closed to them. The Catechism states:

> If the divorced are remarried civilly, they find themselves in a situation that objectively contravenes God's law. Consequently, they cannot receive Eucharistic communion as long as this situation persists. ... Reconciliation through the sacrament of Penance can be granted only to those who have repented for having violated the sign of the covenant and of fidelity to Christ, and who are committed to living in complete continence.[63]

As every sexual act (of the civilly married couple) is considered by the Church to be a new act of adultery, the couple accumulate mortal sins which they are unable to confess and get absolution for. Their only way out is to separate from their new spouse and live alone, repent their sins of adultery and sincerely intend never to engage in 'adultery' in the future.

However, the Church does offer an escape route: Catholics can get married in Church, have children and then ask the Church to nullify the marriage. Although the popular term used is 'annulment', the Church speaks of 'nullification'. The difference being that the marriage which took place is defined as null, rather than annulled. Because it did not exist, it does not have to be annulled. Once nullified, they are free to remarry, or rather – as the first marriage is nullified – they do not remarry, but according to the Church, marry for the first time. It is as complicated and absurd as it sounds. In many cases, it is also as immoral as it seems. Although children of a nullified marriage are not considered by Canon Law to be illegitimate, it is difficult to explain to a child, whose parents have been granted this procedure, the bizarre concept that the marriage within which he or she was born had never existed.

Neither the absurdity nor the immorality and lies seem to matter to the Church. The trick is to find a fault in the original marriage. A physical, mental or even attitudinal defect is all that one needs. According to the Church, for marriage to be valid, the parties to it must freely express their consent. For consent to be 'free', it must not be given under constraint nor may it be impeded by any natural or ecclesiastical law. According to the Catechism, if such consent is lacking then there is no marriage.[64] The Archdiocese of Boston's document *How Can Marriage be Declared Null?* points the way: 'If it can be proven that the consent was defective, on the part of one or both of the parties, then marriage was NOT brought about.' An example which the Boston Archdiocese brings for consent not given under free will is a girl who got married when she found out that she was pregnant and was put under strong pressure by her parents to marry her boyfriend, although she did not want to marry him and wanted to bring up the child on her own. If it can be proven that she did indeed get married under the directives of her parents due to the fear of being abandoned with a child, the Church could declare the marriage null on the grounds of force and fear. The explanation is that 'The sacrament can only be brought about by a free act of the will. Therefore, there could not have been an exchange of the sacrament on the wedding day, as the faith community had presumed.'[65]

The Church has produced quite a few documents regarding marriage and sex in the twentieth century. In December 1930, with rampant anti-Semitism and Nazism at the door in Germany and just over two years before Hitler came to power, the Pope's concern was that 'the sanctity of marriage is trampled upon'.[66] The Church's way of dealing with divorce was to quote Jesus: 'Everyone that putteth away his wife and marrieth another, committeth adultery: and he that marrieth her that is put away from her husband committeth adultery.' *Casti connubii* sets out the evils which troubled the Church. The early twentieth century saw new trends of liberal thinking which questioned the Church's teachings and her role. Calls were heard for sex to be disconnected from marriage and from procreation. 'Modern subverters of society' outrageously – in the Church's mind – called for the removal of the Church from the whole realm of matrimony. These 'evil forces' wanted divorce to be permitted and, moreover, mixed marriages. The encyclical refers to those 'who rashly and heedlessly contract mixed marriages … with danger [it warns] to their eternal salvation'.[67]

In his encyclical the Pope informed the world of his grievance regarding 'the dignity of the chaste wedlock'. He explained that 'it is necessary, first of all, that men's minds be illuminated with the true doctrine of Christ regarding it'.[68] The view that matrimony was a man-made institution was false, the encyclical stated. It needed to 'be repeated as an immutable and inviolable fundamental doctrine that matrimony was not instituted or restored by man but by God'. As such, 'if one has once contracted matrimony he is thereby subject to its divinely made laws and its essential properties'. The Pope also considered it essential to declare that 'it is clear that legitimately constituted authority has the right and therefore the duty to restrict, to prevent, and to punish those base unions which are opposed to reason and to nature'. Pius goes back to Augustine's explanation regarding the blessings of matrimony, which in addition to begetting offspring and setting up an acceptable environment for sex, also is a sacrament and as such not to be broken. Pius reminds the world that 'the very natural process of generating life has become the way of death by which original sin is passed on to posterity'. He quotes Augustine in setting out a summary of the doctrine of Christian marriage.[69] There should be no doubt that 'The primary end of marriage is procreation and the education of children' and that 'Every use of the faculty given by God for the procreation of new life is the right and the privilege of the married state alone, by the law of God and of nature, and must be confined absolutely within the sacred limits of that state.'[70] To a world which had somewhat progressed since Augustine's days, the pope considered it timely to explain that, according to the Catholic Church:

> This order [of love] includes both the primacy of the husband with regard to the wife and children, the ready subjection of the wife and her willing obedience, which the Apostle commends in these words: 'Let women be subject to their husbands as to the Lord, because the husband is the head of the wife, and Christ is the head of the Church.'[71]

With token gestures to political correctness, such as 'this subjection, however, does not deny or take away the liberty which fully belongs to the woman', or by pointing out that women should not be 'put on a level with those persons who in law are called minors', the encyclical quickly adds that it forbids that exaggerated liberty, such as ideas of 'false teachers who try to dim the lustre of conjugal faith' with notions that 'the woman even without the knowledge and against the wish of her husband may be at liberty to conduct and administer her own affairs, giving her attention chiefly to these rather than to children, husband and family'.[72]

Pius had other ideas about family structures and power: 'For if the man is the head, the woman is the heart, and as he occupies the chief place in ruling, so she may and ought to claim for herself the chief place in love.'[73] Worried about change in society's structures, the Church kept repeating quotations from the Gospels and from Church Fathers' utterances, like sacred mantras. Women's liberation was considered dangerous, if for no other reason than that it attempted to change the existing structures. Once change was permissible, who knew where it might end? As is customary in papal documents, the encyclicals, bulls and so on of previous popes are also quoted in this encyclical. This demonstrates continuity and makes it difficult, if not impossible, to introduce change.

Pope Pius rants against those who 'suggest that the licence of a base fornicating woman should enjoy the same rights as the chaste motherhood of a lawfully wedded wife', and a society in which 'some men go so far as to concoct new species of unions, suited, as they say, to the present temper of men and the times, which various new forms of matrimony they presume to label "temporary," "experimental," and "companionate."' Some of these even 'desire and insist that these practices be legitimatized by the law'.[74] Fondly reminiscing about the 'good old days' when the popes had the use of government power for their Holy Inquisition, Pius calls for government assistance in disciplining the unruly masses, according to Catholic principles: 'Governments can assist the Church greatly in the execution of its important office, if, in laying down their ordinances, they take account of what is prescribed by divine and ecclesiastical law, and if penalties are fixed for offenders.'[75] This was in the past often achieved through bilateral treaties with willing countries.[76] The Church evidently doubted that it sufficed to bind her flock by sacramental means and she endeavoured to make use of state laws to enforce her religious doctrine.

Seventy years later, in January 2002, Pope John Paul II made it clear at a meeting with Vatican magistrates that Roman Catholic lawyers should refuse to handle divorce cases.[77] The Pope said that Catholic lawyers should not even try to help non-Catholics with a divorce. The unmarried head of a hierarchy of cardinals, archbishops and bishops – all of whom have never been married – insisted that marriage must be for life. Divorce was 'spreading like a plague' through society and lawyers should refuse to be part of the 'evil'.

On the basis of Jesus' few words, the Catholic Church has stopped the clock. It has destined millions of Catholics to a life of misery trapped in failed marriages. Arrogantly she claims that 'the Church has not erred and does not err' and even in the most heinous marital situations, she may permit separation but not divorce. Having once failed in the choice of a partner, a Catholic is not permitted ever again to remarry; unless one undergoes nullification – the Church's back entrance.

Homosexuality

According to the Church God does not particularly like homosexuals and really hates it when homosexuals actually have sex. The Roman Catholic Church is not alone in her attitude, which totally forbids homosexual relations. Most other religions do too. This attitude, employing the mystical power of religion and the political clout religious organisations have built up throughout history, has meant that for many years women, but especially men, who had same-sex relations were jailed and in some societies even sentenced to death. Thousands were driven to their death and many more were shunned and ostracised for behaviour which is now widely accepted to be both natural and legal. More and more countries have now decriminalised homosexual acts. There are, however, quite a few countries in which homosexual sex is still illegal. Indeed, some countries still use capital punishment against homosexuals. Islamic law is particularly harsh in this area. During the Taliban rule in Afghanistan, gays were crushed to death by having walls toppled on them. Saudi-Arabia still has the death penalty for gay sex.[78]

The following episodic evidence demonstrates the impact of the Catholic Church's teaching on homosexuality which can be found in virtually every Christian country. During the English Reformation powers of the Church courts were taken over by the King's Courts and in 1533 the 'Buggery Statute', the first British statute criminalising sodomy, was passed. Under this law, the Earl of Castlehaven was in 1631 convicted of sodomy with his male servants and he was beheaded. Britain continued to treat homosexuals ruthlessly. The 1533 Buggery Statute produced convictions and hangings until 1861, when the death penalty for buggery was abolished in England and Wales. It remained a criminal offence until 1967. The 1950s still saw many convictions of homosexuals, often on the basis of uncorroborated evidence.

The British law was exported to Britain's American colonies. Some of these colonies incorporated a quotation from Leviticus in their anti-sodomy laws: 'If a man also lie with mankind, as he lieth with a woman, both of them have committed an abomination: they shall surely be put to death.' Colony after colony introduced the death penalty for sodomy. Later, independence from Britain did not allow homosexuals in 'the home of the free' freely to have consensual sex, although, gradually, the death penalty was dropped and lower sentences were introduced. Anal sex was left as a criminal offence in many American states well into the twenty-first century.

Up to 1789, homosexual acts were a capital offence in France. As a consequence of the French revolution, France was the first European country to decriminalise homosexual acts. The libertarian principles of the revolution and the breaking of the power of the Roman Catholic Church brought about a new penal code that removed 'crimes against nature' and decriminalised all forms of consensual adult sexuality so long as it occurred in private. This new penal code came into force in 1791. But the long history of incitement by the Church against homosexuality could not be erased overnight by a new law. 'Homophobia' persisted in post-revolution France and pederasts – the French use the Greek term for homosexuals – continued to be harassed by the police.

In Holland, homosexual sex was punishable by death until 1811. In the 1730s an hysteria of convictions resulted in the public strangling and subsequent burning at the stake of dozens of men who were found guilty of having sex with men. By the time the law was changed in 1811, hundreds of Dutch men were legally murdered for their homosexuality.

In 1794 Prussia introduced more lenient punishment for homosexuals, who were no longer hanged. As a result, homosexuals in Prussia would 'only' suffer at least a year in prison, flogging at the beginning and again at the end of their prison terms, and finally banishment.[79] Unification in 1871 spread the Prussian attitude of criminalisation of homosexual acts to the whole of the new Germany. Up to then, many of the German Kingdoms had more liberal laws based on the French legal traditions. Paragraph 175 of the new penal code stated: 'An unnatural sex act committed between persons of male sex or by humans with animals is punishable by imprisonment; the loss of civil rights might also be imposed.'[80] Although the paragraph remained in the German penal code during the Weimar Republic (1919–1933), these were years in which gay life thrived in Germany and especially in Berlin. When the Nazis came to power, they enforced the paragraph with great vigour. Between 1933 and 1945, according to German documents, approximately one hundred thousand men were arrested for homosexuality. Roughly half were imprisoned and approximately ten to fifteen thousand were sent to concentration camps.[81] Post-War West Germany did not scrap paragraph 175. After all, virtually all other Western countries were still sending homosexuals to jail in those days. As a result, some homosexuals who were freed from concentration camps and Nazi jails at the end of the war, were rearrested to complete their jail sentences for their 'crimes'. This notorious paragraph 175 was finally removed from the German penal code in 1969.

In 1982, under the state's sodomy law, the police in Atlanta, Georgia, arrested two men having oral sex in the privacy of their own bedroom. One of the men, Michael Hardwick, attempted, several years later, to have the US Supreme Court declare the sodomy law unconstitutional. The Supreme Court of the United States, in its 1986 *Bowers vs. Hardwick* decision, concluded that nothing in the Constitution 'would extend a fundamental right to homosexuals to engage in acts of consensual sodomy'.[82] The Supreme Court's 2003 decision in *Lawrence vs. Texas*, repealed the *Bowers vs. Hardwick* decision and declared specifically that the relevant section in the Texas State Criminal Code was contrary to the Federal Constitution's guarantees of privacy and equal treatment under the law. In one blow, the anti-sodomy laws that still existed in fourteen states were struck down. And yet, to this very day some US politicians believe that they should have the right to legislate the sex lives of consenting adults.

So strong was the Catholic Church's influence in Ireland that many homosexuals emigrated to Britain or to the United States to escape the Irish 'homophobia' that was encouraged by the Church and given legal status by the state. The activist David Norris, a prominent leader of the Campaign for Homosexual Law Reform, challenged the Irish repressive and discriminatory laws. They were, however, upheld by the Irish Supreme Court as late as 1983. Norris did not give in and took Ireland to the European Commission on Human Rights. The Commission ruled in favour of Norris. Instead of accepting the ruling of the European Commission, Ireland fought on and contested the decision in the European Court. In 1988, the European Court found that Irish law violated Article 8 of the Convention on Human Rights. The Irish continued to prevaricate for five years until 1993 when the law was amended. Kicking and screaming, Catholic Ireland finally decriminalised homosexuality.

The Catholic Church, which – together with other religions – is responsible for the repugnance so many people have felt and still feel towards homosexuals, continues to consider homosexual sex sinful. Throughout the years in which homosexuals were hounded, harassed, hated, beaten, jailed and killed, the Catholic Church stood her ground and systematically tried to prevent changes in the laws under which homosexuals were being tried. This attitude made it easier for hate crimes to be perpetrated and for persecution of homosexuals to continue in dictatorships, such as Nazi Germany, as well as in liberal democracies, such as Britain.

The 1975 Vatican *Declaration on Certain Questions Concerning Sexual Ethics*, states 'homosexual relations are ... condemned as a serious depravity and even presented as the sad consequence of rejecting God ... homosexual acts are intrinsically disordered and can in no case be approved of'.[83] The Vatican made clear that it would not let 'observations in the psychological order' influence it. Those who 'have begun to judge indulgently, and even to excuse completely ... do [so] in opposition to the constant teaching of the Magisterium and to the moral sense of the Christian people'. Rather late in the day, the Vatican accepted that 'In the pastoral field, these homosexuals must certainly be treated with understanding and sustained in the hope of overcoming their personal difficulties and their inability to fit into society. Their culpability will be judged with prudence.' However, 'no pastoral method can be employed which would give moral justification to these acts on the grounds that they would be consonant with the condition of such people'. The Vatican spoke about culpability and about homosexuality being against the moral sense of Christian people. The Church did not reject homosexuals, as long as they refrained from having sex.

The Catechism of the Catholic Church, in its 1997 edition, is even clearer in its consideration: 'The number of men and women who have deep-seated homosexual tendencies is not negligible. This inclination, which is objectively disordered, constitutes for most of them a trial. They must be accepted with respect, compassion, and sensitivity. Every sign of unjust discrimination in their regard should be avoided.'[84] It is commendable that the Vatican is clear about the need for compassion. The Church's compassion is very limited and her objection to discrimination, qualified. Only 'unjust' discrimination should be avoided. This, of course, leaves the door open for 'just discrimination'. Homosexuals, according to the Church, 'are called to chastity. By the virtues of self-mastery that teach them inner freedom, at times by the support of disinterested friendship, by prayer and sacramental grace, they can and should gradually and resolutely approach Christian perfection.'[85] And lest there be any doubt, the Catechism reiterates:

> Basing itself on Sacred Scripture, which presents homosexual acts as acts of grave depravity, tradition has always declared that 'homosexual acts are intrinsically disordered.' They are contrary to the natural law. They close the sexual act to the gift of life. They do not proceed from a genuine affective and sexual complementarity. Under no circumstances can they be approved.[86]

In 1986, the Congregation for the Doctrine of the Faith told the Catholic bishops that science had its importance, but that Catholic ruling was based on 'the Catholic moral viewpoint [which] is founded on human reason illumined by faith and is consciously motivated by the desire to do the will of God our Father'.[87] Indeed, the Church's teaching today is tied and is unable to get away from the 'organic continuity with the Scriptural perspective and with her own constant Tradition'. As a result of religious indoctrination, homosexuality was not only illegal, but also considered by the majority of the population as sick, repugnant and sinful. Things have changed and in many countries most open-minded people no longer consider homosexuality an abomination. Pressure from within the Church to change her teaching with regard to homosexuality has failed up to now.

In 1993, Jesuit priest and psychotherapist, John McNeill, in the preface to his book *The Church and the Homosexual*, cried out: 'Through the centuries you have supported sodomy laws that have sent thousands of gays to their deaths. ... Enough! ... We cried out to you for bread, you gave us a scorpion instead!'[88] The reason for this anguish was the continued rejection by the Church of any debate which might lead to a revision of her teaching on homosexuality. Originally, McNeill's book received the Church's approval, the *Imprimi Potest*. This was removed in 1977, one year after it was granted. In addition, the Congregation for the Doctrine of the Faith forbade the Jesuit priest from discussing the issue of homosexuality and morality in public. For ten years McNeill observed the silence imposed on him, hoping that the Church would reconsider. The abundance of homophobic Vatican documents which followed made it obvious to McNeill that silence was not enough.

From the mid-1970s two Americans, Sister Jeannine Gramick and Father Robert Nugent, became active in catering for the spiritual needs of Catholic homosexuals. Gramick and Nugent were doing a job of immense importance for gay and lesbian Catholics who had nowhere else to go in a Church which shunned them. They established the 'New Ways Ministry' for Catholic gay men and lesbians and ran workshops, seminars and retreats. From 1981 onwards, as archbishop of Washington, Archbishop James Hickey fought Gramick and Nugent and did his utmost to prevent participation in their retreats, symposia and other activities. They did not give in and in 1999, after a long process of Roman Inquisition by the Congregation for the Doctrine of the Faith, the Vatican forced Gramick and Nugent out of their ministry and forbade them to teach. In 2000 they were informed that they were now prohibited from writing or speaking in public about homosexuality or about the whole ecclesiastical process which led to them being silenced. Archbishop Hickey, who had been so very instrumental in his hostility to Gramick and Nugent, was promoted by Pope John Paul II and made Cardinal.

The Vatican has demanded that those ministering to homosexuals should explain the full significance of the Church's 'truth' and ramification of homosexual acts. In referring to the Vatican's demand that homosexuals be emphatically told by their Catholic ministers of the immorality and evil of their acts, Nugent rightly says that this makes the pastoral task of reconciliation very difficult.[v] He equates such ministry to Jesus who, when confronted by a woman who was about to be stoned for adultery, did 'not take the occasion to deliver a sermon on the evils of extramarital sex'. And in bringing the argument to modern times, Nugent asks why the Vatican, which does not demand that military chaplains constantly proclaim the immorality of war or priests in the prison service constantly preach the immorality of criminal acts, expect a different norm from ministers to homosexuals.[89]

The Vatican was sufficiently worried by such pressures to hint at disloyalty or perhaps even treason. The bishops were informed that 'those within the Church who argue in this fashion often have close ties with those with similar views outside it. These latter groups are guided by a vision opposed to the truth about the human person.' In her letter of 1986, the Church instructed bishops that for homosexuals to 'live out' their tendency was unacceptable: 'Although the particular inclination of the homosexual person is not a sin, it is a more or less strong tendency ordered toward an intrinsic moral evil; and thus the inclination itself must be seen as an objective disorder.'[90] As the world was moving to make discrimination on the basis of sexuality illegal, the Church went into action in an attempt to keep discrimination going. In July 1992, the Congregation for the Doctrine of the Faith issued *Some Considerations Concerning the Response to Legislative Proposals on the Non-Discrimination of Homosexual Persons*.[91] In this document, bishops were reminded of the 1986 letter. Although the Church magnanimously agreed that 'all persons have the right to work, to housing, etc', she drew the line at homosexuals. Bishops were told by Cardinal Ratzinger who, at the time, was Prefect of the Congregation for the Doctrine of the Faith and who is now Pope, that 'rights are not absolute'. Homosexuals, the physically and the mentally ill are all groups for which the 'state may restrict the exercise of rights'.[92] The document, which speaks of those who seek the Church's approval for a change in discriminatory laws as people 'who seek to manipulate the Church', and which suggests that the best strategy for homosexuals to avoid discrimination in employment or in housing is to stay in the closet, also rouses the homophobes in society by suggesting that a change in legislation would 'encourage a person with a homosexual orientation to declare his homosexuality or even to seek a partner in order to exploit the provisions of the law'. The Church warns society of homosexuals who are no longer driven by lust but by sheer greed and the 'danger' that legislation 'would make homosexuality a basis for entitlements'. Bishops

---

[v]   Reconciliation of a Penitent, or Penance, is the rite in which those who repent of their sins may confess them to God in the presence of a priest, and receive the assurance of pardon and the grace of absolution.

are warned to pay strict attention to the single provisions of any new legislation that is being proposed.

The Catholic Church is not only a lawmaker for her one billion members, she also makes use of her political power to influence the lives of non-Catholics. A recent example is the Vatican's actions to stop laws being passed which would legalise gay marriage. In virtually all Western countries homosexuality is no longer illegal and moves abound to grant homosexuals equal rights to heterosexuals, including marriage. A small number of countries has already legalised same-sex marriage. Many more countries have gone part of the way by formally recognising same-sex unions without defining them as marriage. In June 2003, against this change in public attitude towards homosexuality, the Vatican issued its document *Considerations Regarding Proposals to give Legal Recognition to Unions Between Homosexual Persons.*[93] This homophobic document, which describes homosexuality as 'a troubling moral and social phenomenon', identifies marriage as a union that 'exists solely between a man and a woman, who ... cooperate with God in the procreation and upbringing of new human lives'. The Vatican proclaims: 'Marriage is holy, while homosexual acts go against the natural moral law.' The Church continues to expound her anti-gay ideology, repeating her assertions that 'the homosexual inclination is ... objectively disordered and homosexual practices are sins gravely contrary to chastity'. Catholic homosexuals have to listen to this barrage of hatred and accept it. They are told to live a life of chastity, whilst the Catholic priesthood, of which a very high percentage are thought to be homosexual, has to live with this torrent and deliver it, knowing that the Church's hierarchy is living a lie.

The Vatican document of 2003 resembles an agitator's handbook. Political tactics are suggested such as 'discreet and prudent actions can be effective'; these could include 'reminding the government of the need to contain the phenomenon within certain limits so as to safeguard public morality'. But if that does not suffice 'Those who would move from tolerance to the legitimization of specific rights for cohabiting homosexual persons need to be reminded that the approval or legalization of evil is something far different from the toleration of evil.' Homosexuality is evil and, as already suggested by the Vatican's letter of 1986, 'the practice of homosexuality may seriously threaten the lives and well-being of a large number of people'. Nonetheless, if the laws are passed, the Vatican calls for 'conscientious objection'. This is the Vatican at war. The Church continues to attack homosexuality with alarming claims suggesting that children brought up in gay households would be endangered. In her attempt to prevent the legalisation of adoption by gay couples, the Church made baseless statements, using language and terminology of incitement:

> Allowing children to be adopted by persons living in such unions would actually mean doing violence to these children, in the sense that their condition of dependency would be used to place them in an environment that is not conducive to their full human development.

Is it not outrageous that the Catholic Church, under whose roof so many children all over the world have been violated, by her own priests, with such abuses covered up by her own hierarchy, should speak of violence to children by merely being brought up by a same-sex couple? To round off this audacious tirade, the Vatican brings in the UN. Adoption by same-sex couples, it says 'is gravely immoral and in open contradiction to the principle, recognized also in the United Nations Convention on the Rights of the Child, that the best interests of the child, as the weaker and more vulnerable party, are to be the paramount consideration in every case'. How extraordinary that the Church came across the 1990 UN Convention on the Rights of the Child only in 2003, whilst she was apparently unaware of it during years in which instead of securing the best interests of the children she looked the other way when children were being buggered by her own clergy.

Masturbation

Masturbation has always been a hot topic for the Catholic Church. Eighteenth-century Catholic theologian, and moral authority during the nineteenth and twentieth centuries, Alfonso de' Liguori, who was canonised in 1839, instructed priests to question children at confession 'with whom they sleep and whether they have played with their fingers in bed'. Moreover, 'Even when the children say "no", it is often expedient to ask them leading questions.'[94] Dr Rudolph Geis, the director of the Archiepiscopal Seminary of Freiburg in Germany, who, in 1930, published *Principles of Catholic Sex Morality*, told his readers that 'Puberty to the Church is fraught with danger'. Geis urged those in charge of young adolescents to keep them from masturbating and to educate them in self denial.[95] The Catholic Church believes that the young should replace masturbation with a session with an 'earnest confessor'.

Virtually everybody masturbates, from childhood until old age. People masturbate on their own, during periods in which they do not have sexual partners, or to complement their sexual activity with their partners. Many also masturbate with their partners. The statistics are overwhelming – according to the 1950s Kinsey Report ninety-two per cent of men and fifty-eight per cent of women have masturbated. More recent research has shown that ninety-seven per cent of men and eighty-three per cent of women have masturbated at some point in their lives.[96] Moreover, it causes no harm. Some medical theories of the sixteenth and seventeenth centuries maintained that the human sperm contained a fully formed, miniature human body – the homunculus. This theory turned the female into a mere receptacle for the pregnancy and not a genetic co-producer of the child. Although sperm, which are constantly produced in the testicles, are automatically 'wasted' through nocturnal emissions during one's sleep, sperm wasted in masturbation was thought by some to be the killing of living humans.

As a result of religious condemnation including the prohibition of masturbation (such prohibition is also common in other religions), scores of myths abounded about the damage one causes oneself by masturbating. Famously, these included getting pimples, losing one's hair, becoming blind, growing hair on the palms of one's hands and the idea that the amount of semen produced is finite, meaning that one loses the ability to have sex in future through too much masturbation. Masturbation, it was claimed could even shorten one's life and bring on insanity. Time and the advance of medicine have proven these myths to be no more than myths. They did, however, suit the religions which found them to be convenient allies in their quest to control the people. In the eighteenth and nineteenth centuries some unscrupulous doctors made a name for themselves by spreading horrific science-fiction about masturbation. In 1710, an English physician by the name of Bekkers published his *Onania or the Heinous Sin of Self-Pollution and its Frightful Consequences in Both Sexes, Considered with Spiritual and Physical Advice.*[97] Half a century later, a Swiss physician, Dr Tissot came out with the assertion that masturbation desiccated the brain, which could actually be heard rattling in the skull. This was the kind of 'science' the Catholic Church heartily approved of. Unlike Galileo's heretical theories, this was science which served the Church. The doctors also provided the punishment for the sin defined by the Church. In 1842, J. C. Debreyne, physician and Trappist monk, described the consequences of masturbation as, 'palpitations, impaired eyesight, headaches, dizziness, tremors, painful cramps, epileptic convulsions, in many cases genuine epilepsy, general pains in the limbs or the back of the head, in the spine, in the chest, in the abdomen, severe renal debility, general symptoms of paralysis'. Debreyne's advice included sucking lumps of ice and sleeping on one's side. For girls, the doctor prescribed clitoridectomy; he saw no need for a clitoris, which only served to give pleasure to women. Such barbaric operations were, indeed, carried out not only in far-away Africa[vi] but by reputable and prominent surgeons in 'civilised' London in the second half of the nineteenth century. A special women's hostel, *The London Surgical Home,* was set up for clitoridectomies.[98]

This multi-pronged attack by the Catholic Church (and other Churches and religions) and by such irresponsible doctors, also produced

---

[vi]   Followers of various religions in Africa still subject their daughters to this outrage.

a multitude of recipes against male masturbation. Boy's trouser-pockets were removed, their hands tied at night to prevent them from playing with themselves and contraptions which pricked the penis when erect were connected to boys' bodies. The trend to circumcise boys in the USA and Britain also served the idea that without the foreskin, a boy would have less need to wash his penis and derive less pleasure from it.

Western medicine has fortunately progressed somewhat since these shameful doctors plied their trade. The Catholic Church has not. She continues to churn out documents about the sinfulness of masturbation. In our present society's not-very-successful endeavours to stop young people from causing harm to themselves through nicotine and stronger substances, it is instructive to learn that all the efforts by priests, doctors and teachers did not stop people from masturbating. Bob Geldof, the rock star who was knighted by the Queen for his services to charity, describes the predicament:

> Masturbation had become part of my daily life. And not just daily. It was a mortal sin, of course. At school during retreats one of the priests would go on about it. Your body was the temple of the Holy Ghost, and if you abused it, you abused God, because the Holy Ghost was in God. It was throwing your seed on fallow ground. You would tell that in confession to get rid of the sin, but when they told you to stop, you knew you couldn't.[99]

Although religious opposition to masturbation has softened greatly in recent years, Catholic doctrine continues to regard masturbation as a grave moral disorder. This was reconfirmed in December 1975, when the Church, worried about 'the corruption of morals [which] has increased', as most seriously indicated by 'the unbridled exaltation of sex', issued *Persona Humana – Declaration on Certain Questions Concerning Sexual Ethics*.[100] The Church tried to counter the criticism that she prohibited natural, harmless and, perhaps, even beneficial activity, and stated that, whatever the scientists said, masturbation was unacceptable. Moreover, as some Christian theologians had attacked Catholic doctrine by pointing out that there was no reference to masturbation in the New Testament, *Persona Humana* explained that 'Even if it cannot be proved that Scripture condemns this sin by name, the tradition of the Church has rightly understood it to be condemned in the New Testament when the latter speaks of "impurity", "unchasteness" and other vices contrary to chastity and continence.' The Church would not accept that activity which is practiced by virtually the whole of the world's population cannot be defined as a 'seriously disordered act' and claimed that masturbation was 'linked with a loss of a sense of God'.[101] The Church was willing to accept that 'psychological imbalance or habit can influence behaviour, diminishing the deliberate character of the act and bringing about a situation whereby subjectively there may not always be serious fault. But in general, the absence of serious responsibility must not be presumed.' Indeed, priests were called by *Persona Humana* to form a 'judgement in concrete cases' and consider 'the habitual behaviour of people'.

As is evident, masturbation continues to excite the heads of the Catholic Church. One cannot help wondering whether the statement included in *Persona Humana*, that masturbation was contradictory to 'pastoral practice', was meant as a pun. Although this document appears to permit masturbation, provided the sinner is able to convince his priest that he is trying to give it up, there can be no doubt that masturbation continues to be prohibited by the Church. In itself, masturbation is a mortal sin. It has been defined as a 'gravely disordered action' and provided there is also full knowledge of the gravity of the sin, of its offence against God, and full consent of the will, it is considered a mortal sin. It is through the narrow door of 'the full consent of the will', which may be impeded, that the Catholic Church enables her flock to masturbate. Having had scientific confirmation that virtually everybody masturbates, the Church now demands that all masturbators have in-depth discussions about their little joys with their confessing priests.

The Janus Report on Sexual Behavior (1993) shows that sixty-three per cent of Protestants, sixty-seven per cent of Catholics and seventy-five per cent of the Jewish faith agreed or strongly agreed with the statement: 'Masturbation is a natural part of life and continues on in marriage.'[102] The Church's teachings are, evidently, not taken seriously even by faithful Catholics. Masturbation is too strong an urge and now that it is no longer considered by the secular world to be wrong, has been proven to be harmless or even beneficial to one's health and peace of mind, the Vatican had to find a way out. The solution found was to continue defining masturbation as a 'gravely disordered action', whilst allowing the pastors leeway in minimising moral culpability. The fourth edition of the Catechism of the Catholic Church, published in 1997, argued that moral culpability might be reduced to a minimum due to 'immaturity, force of acquired habit, conditions of anxiety or other psychological or social factors'. So, the masturbating Catholic will be forgiven, but should definitely not continue to masturbate![103]

The Catholic Church has created a mechanism which has served her well for centuries. She defined a harmless and natural activity as a mortal sin. She also taught her members that dying without absolution for a mortal sin meant spending the whole of eternity in hell. What a price to pay. A fiery punishment for a moment's relief. It is likely that many of the preachers who promised the fires of hell to the masturbators, masturbated themselves. And yet the popes, cardinals and bishops would not let go. They knew that as long as Catholics believed that one of the most natural acts, pleasurable and satisfying and often necessary for one's peace of mind, was a mortal sin which demanded absolution, they ensured an automatic long line of clients who had to come and seek the services of the Church. Without the Church there is no absolution and the trembling wanking Catholic will burn in the fires of hell.

In her attitude to masturbation, the Catholic Church has over hundreds of years caused suffering, mainly to her own members. She has misled them, frightened them and continues to pressurise them. The Church has also historically (as have other religious organisations) used her political and public power to impose her views on masturbation to the detriment of society as a whole. Masturbation continues to be a 'controlled' activity by the Church. It is sinful unless fought against and it thus forms part of the relationship between the believer and the Church.

Contraception

Sex, the Catholic Church has been teaching for centuries, is solely for procreation and not for recreation. Sexual acts which prevent procreation are, therefore, not permitted. This concept itself is as difficult to understand as it is unnatural. Our sex drive is not extinguished when we cannot have children either because we are not married, because we are physically unable or because we are homosexual. As usual, principal theologians such as Augustine and Thomas are central to the Church's thinking. St Augustine condemned the 'cruel lust, [which] resorts to such extravagant methods as to use poisonous drugs to secure barrenness; or else, if unsuccessful in this, to destroy the conceived seed by some means previous to birth, preferring that its offspring should rather perish than receive vitality'.[104] Early penitentials prescribed two to ten years of penances to couples who practiced *coitus interruptus*.[105]

Thomas Aquinas considered any procreation-impeding acts to be sinful. It was, according to Thomas, worse than incest. An attempted solution which was for a while all the rage in the Catholic Church was *amplexus reservatus*,[vii] a sexual technique which entails sex in the missionary position without reaching orgasm. In *coitus interruptus*, a common contraceptive method, the penis is withdrawn at the penultimate moment and ejaculation takes place outside the vagina. This method has always and still is considered by the Church to be a mortal sin. In *amplexus reservatus*, withdrawal has to take place before the 'point of no return' has been reached, so that no ejaculation takes place. Huguccio (d. 1210), the twelfth-century cardinal and monk who considered himself an expert on human sexuality, believed that sex without ejaculation was free of pleasure and thus free of sin. Huguccio's solution for the married man who wanted to render his marital debt to his wife, without committing

---

vii   Latin for 'restrained embrace'.

the venial sin resulting from the pleasure of ejaculation, was to 'withdraw, not satisfying my pleasure, free of all sin, and not emitting my seed of propagation'.[106] Where the Catholic Cardinal got his sexual education and intimate knowledge of orgasms from is not clear. Huguccio, who evidently knew that many people used this method, which in his eyes had no sin attached to it, became an avid promoter of the restrained embrace technique. Other theologians objected as they were worried about too much pleasure which could still be had. In the fourteenth century, much was made of the pleasure that the wife was deriving when restrained embrace was practiced. Dominican monk Archbishop Petrus de Palude (1280–1342) defined the female orgasm as 'emission of semen' by the wife. Peter de Palude is not so easy on *amplexus reservatus* as Huguccio. Condemning *coitus interruptus* even in cases of economic hardship, when a husband does not want more children than he can feed, de Palude ruled that 'he does not seem to sin mortally; unless … the woman is provoked to semination', if 'he withdraws himself before completion of the act and does not emit seed'. de Palude apparently still considered this method to be a venial sin and in cases where the wife reached orgasm, even a mortal sin.[107] Over the following centuries, Catholic theologians filled volumes with their profound deliberations on this matter. These continued well into the twentieth century. Belgian Cardinal Suenens recommended the method as late as 1960.[108]

A renowned fifteenth-century preacher, Bernardino of Sienna, taught that 'Every time you came together in such a manner that you could not conceive and generate children, it was a sin.' His view about such intercourse was that whereas 'it is depraved for a man to have intercourse with his mother, [it is] far worse if he has unnatural intercourse with his wife'. Wives were instructed by Bernardino to 'die rather than consent' to such intercourse.[109]

The Belgian theologian Arthur Vermeersch (d. 1936) was the author of Pius XI's encyclical *Casti connubii*. Vermeersch instructed women whose husbands 'threatened' them with condom-clad members that notwithstanding the consequential 'domestic unhappiness, abandonment, divorce' they are to resist their husbands, as they would resist a rapist, until they were physically overpowered.[110]

The twentieth century was extremely difficult for the Catholic Church in the domain of birth control. Even before the contraceptive pill was introduced, this century saw dramatic developments in both contraceptive methods and mass communication. The breakthrough in the refinement of condoms as contraceptives took place in the middle of the nineteenth century. The scientific development of understanding of the monthly menstrual rhythm took place in the 1930s. A variety of other mechanisms such as inter-uterine devices, caps, coils and spermicidal creams, have been in use for a long time. In more primitive societies, anal intercourse and *coitus interruptus* were the main forms of contraception. This was also the case in Ireland, a Catholic state in which contraceptives were illegal and were not accessible to most people.[111]

Wider access to contraceptives together with the speed with which the written press and radio were able to report new developments and describe new life-styles, put pressure on the Church to deal with this matter which was and still is of such immense importance to Catholics world-wide. A Church which sends women to die rather than allow abortion or contraception, cannot be expected to permit contraception for economic, social or psychological reasons. Magnanimously, the gentlemen in Rome were 'deeply touched by the sufferings of those parents who, in extreme want, experience great difficulty in rearing their children'. However, we are informed that, whatever the hardship, contraception may not be considered, as 'No difficulty can arise that justifies the putting aside of the law of God.' The Church's response is based on the 1545–65 Council of Trent which has placed under anathema the assertion that 'there are precepts of God impossible for the just to observe'. People should stop complaining, procreate and 'pray for what you are not able that He may help you'.[112]

It appears that priests had been turning a blind eye or even advising the faithful, in certain cases, contrary to the teaching of the Church, to use contraception or to abort. Pope Pius XI warns both priests and governments of dire personal consequences.[113] In his 1930 encyclical, *Casti connubii*, the Pope, quoting Augustine on the immorality of contraception, spoke of 'this horrible crime [which God] at times has punished it with death'.[114] The idea that the crime in the biblical story of Onan, that Pope Pius XI referred to, was wasting seed and preventing conception has since been abandoned by biblical scholars. Future Vatican documents omit the Onan story as justification for the Church's prohibition of contraception.

In 1951, Pius XII in his *Allocution to Midwifes* accepted the rhythm method as an acceptable approach to birth regulation. In this method a couple would abstain from intercourse during the woman's fertile period whilst having sex only during the sterile period. This was a dramatic departure from all that the Church had been teaching up to that moment with regard to sex. Sex was no longer only meant for procreation. New explanations had to be developed. Sex had already been given multifarious interpretations over the past: according to the Church Fathers, ideally, sex was best avoided; sex was evil according to Augustine; the pleasure derived from the act was evil according to Gregory the Great; and, according to Thomas, sex was only meant by God as a way of insemination. Now, with papal permission, one could calculate the days on which a couple could have sex with a certainty that it would not produce a child. The fact that this method, which involves daily vaginal temperature taking and daily observations of the vaginal mucus, is uncomfortable and degrading for women, bothered the Church no more than the fact that, because of the complicated measurements involved, the rhythm method was not an efficient birth control mechanism. It was, however, a step forward, as it accepted that Catholic couples had a right to plan the size of their families and that marital sex was permitted for unmistakably non-procreative purposes. Especially absurd is the Church's thinking in permitting the rhythm method whilst prohibiting the use of other types of birth control.

In the 1960s the sexual revolution was started with the introduction of the contraceptive pill. It now became quite simple. None of the discomfort of inter-uterine devices was experienced and there was no need to overcome the (mainly male) reluctance to use condoms. The woman popped a pill and was free to engage in sexual intercourse without having to worry about possible pregnancy. In 1958, Pope Pius XII condemned the pill and prohibited its use. This revolution, which created behaviour in total contrast to the Church's teaching, fast gained acceptance. More and more pressure was put on the Vatican to reconsider its thinking on contraception. The Church was in a terrible dilemma. If she did not change her teaching, she would become irrelevant in this important area of human sexuality. If she did change her teaching, she would have to concede that all those who were sent to hell by her bishops and priests for the mortal sin of using contraception, were sent there in error.

The subject was next taken up by the Second Vatican Council convened by Pope John XXIII in 1962. The Pope wanted an open discussion with the Church's bishops and a conciliatory move towards the non-Catholic world. The Pope, who died during the second session, did not see the conclusion of his vision. He was succeeded by Pope Paul VI. The Roman Curia – the Vatican bureaucracy – did its utmost to ensure that Pope John's idea of an open Council in which all of the Church's bishops would openly discuss everything, should not come about. To that end, they prepared seventy draft resolutions for the bishops to vote on. The bishops were given more than two thousand pages of text, all in Latin, and were asked to vote. The bishops, much to the amazement of the Curial cardinals, revolted and decided to postpone the voting on the resolutions until they had had time to study them and come to their own conclusions. The schema (draft) on sexual matters was an ultra-conservative document entitled 'On Marriage, chastity and Virginity'. The Council fathers managed to soften this curial document, which included twenty-one condemnations and which the Curia originally expected to be approved as read. The Vatican old guard, however, powerfully acted to pull the Council their way. They wanted, among other things, a clear condemnation of contraceptive devices and that the document specifically refer to *Casti connubii*. To this end, they arranged for a letter from the Secretary of State to be read to the editing commission, listing certain amendments which the Pope had demanded. To add pressure, Cardinal Browne explained to the commission members 'This is Christ himself speaking'.[viii] Cardinal Ottaviani, who in 1966 would become pro-prefect of the Congregation for the Doctrine of the Faith, and who presided over the commission, demanded 'holy obedience' from the Council fathers. These, however, did not allow themselves to be gagged by Ottaviani and a compromise was reached. As a result, *Gaudium et Spes* became a somewhat ambiguous document on matters of birth control.[115]

Gaudium et Spes ('Joy and Hope'), a 'Pastoral Constitution on the Church in the Modern World', is one of the central documents approved by Vatican II. On questions regarding the family, *Gaudium et Spes* opened the door to an acceptance that the 'actions within marriage by which the couple are united intimately and chastely are noble and worthy ones'.[116] This would suggest that sex for non-procreative purposes has the Church's blessing. And yet the clause, which promisingly commences with 'Marriage to be sure is not instituted solely for procreation', turns out, importantly but solely, to comfort those cases in which 'despite the often intense desire of the couple, offspring are lacking'. Their marriage, the Vatican assures 'persists as a whole manner and communion of life, and maintains its value and indissolubility'. The Council decries the fact that the excellence of marriage and family 'is not everywhere reflected with equal brilliance, since polygamy, the plague of divorce, so-called free love and other disfigurements have an obscuring effect. In addition, married love is too often profaned by excessive self-love, the worship of pleasure and illicit practices against human generation.' The document maintains Church policy that 'Children are really the supreme gift of marriage.'[117]

Although *Gaudium et Spes* declared that procreative decisions were those of the parents, it added that 'they cannot proceed arbitrarily, but must always be governed according to a conscience dutifully conformed to the divine law itself, and should be submissive toward the Church's teaching office, which authentically interprets that law in the light of the Gospel'. Priests were no longer expected to demand a fresh baby per year from their Catholic flock. But the Church still considered that 'those merit special mention who with a gallant heart and with wise and common deliberation, undertake to bring up suitably even a relatively large family'. After all, 'married Christians glorify the Creator and strive toward fulfilment in Christ when ... they acquit themselves of the duty to procreate'.

---

viii   *Christus ipse locutus est.*

The Church accepted that 'certain modern conditions often keep couples from arranging their married lives harmoniously, and that they find themselves in circumstances where at least temporarily the size of their families should not be increased'. Lest there be any question, 'sons of the Church may not undertake methods of birth control which are found blameworthy by the teaching authority of the Church in its unfolding of the divine law'.[118]

There was so much disagreement between the Curial officials and the main body of bishops that the Pope decided to set up a special commission to study the issue of birth control. A small commission of six was first established. The commission was expanded several times and grew to more than fifty members. Its work was continued beyond Vatican II. Pope Paul VI decided – against the wish of the majority of the participants of Vatican II – to enforce the conservative view which prohibits contraception. The Vatican now did its utmost to ensure that the Papal Commission, which was looking into the issues of birth control, would produce a conclusion supporting the continued prohibition of any kind of artificial birth control. To that end, the membership of the commission was changed several times; 'safe' bishops were added to it by the then Secretary of State, Ottaviani. At the end, the Pope decided to disregard the Commission because it did not reach a unanimous decision. Nine out of twelve bishops, fifteen out of nineteen theologians and thirty out of thirty-five non-Episcopal members were apparently not enough.[119] Paul produced his own verdict in the 1968 encyclical *Humanae Vitae*, an encyclical which caused a revolt among laity and is generally disregarded, even by churchgoers. *Humanae Vitae* confirmed all of the old prohibitions. Contraception was still a mortal sin.

The Impact of AIDS

Nothing seems to have changed in the Catholic Church. Not even when the use of condoms could save lives. Jesuit Paul Laymann (d. 1635) was of the opinion that a woman may not take a medicine to prevent conception, even if she learns from her physician that the birth of a child may occasion her death.[120] Nowadays, the Church forbids the use of condoms even to those infected with the HIV virus. The extent to which an end justifies the means in the Catholic Church is epitomised in the Vatican's policy in respect of the use of condoms in light of the AIDS epidemic. In 1993, an anti-AIDS campaign in Italian high schools was blocked because it endorsed the use of condoms. In 1997, the Vatican's *L'Osservatore Romano* attacked the move to install condom dispensers in a high school in Italy, a step which according to surveys, had seventy-nine per cent support among the general population. A Brazilian archbishop was asked in an interview on British television whether a husband who was HIV positive, and was thus infected by the AIDS virus, was permitted to use condoms when he was having sex with his wife. His response was an adamant 'no', adding that the couple would have to abstain from sex; and if they were unable to abstain the wife's life would be in God's hands. One of his bishops warned a priest, who had been handing out condoms to halt the spread of AIDS, of punitive actions for his life-saving activity. Kenyan bishops warned their flock that many condoms were either perforated or laced with HIV, thus making them useless as protection against AIDS. In Indonesia Catholic clergy tell their people that condoms are actually porous to the AIDS virus.[121] In Mexico City Archbishop Norberto Rivera Carrera suggested that a warning label should be added to condoms to read 'Use of this product is harmful to health', whereas Fr Gerald Magera Iga ran a campaign urging condom sellers in Uganda to burn up their stocks using the slogan 'Every condom sold sends the buyer to acquire the AIDS virus.'[122] In July 2000, the Vatican's nuncio in Uganda, Archbishop Christophe Pierre, called Uganda's youth to ignore the government drive for use of condoms to contain the spread of AIDS, which affects ten per cent of the country's population.[123] These bishops and priests received their directives from Rome, where statements such as 'Using a condom to protect oneself against HIV amounts to playing Russian roulette', were issued by a member of the Vatican Council for the Family.[124] [ix]

The Church tries to force her views on the world using various means, including concordats, the bilateral contracts that she signs with civil governments. Pope Pius XI proudly mentioned this in his encyclical *Casti connubii*, in which he referred to the 1929 Lateran Treaty. The Pope explained that 'Governments can assist the Church greatly in the execution of its important office, if, in laying down their ordinances, they take account of what is prescribed by divine and ecclesiastical law, and if penalties are fixed for offenders.'[125] Indeed, Church lobbying ensured that Fascist legislation regarding contraception remained valid in Italy even after the fall of Benito Mussolini. Attempts to legalise birth control were thwarted and, as late as 1965, the Constitutional Court declared that disseminating detailed information about contraceptives should remain illegal because it offended public morality. Only in 1971 was this declared unconstitutional. Moreover, as a result of the strong Catholic influence in Italy, which prevented the distribution of contraceptives and contraceptive information and education, the Italian population is still practicing a high proportion of primitive *coitus interruptus*; a survey in 1997 showed this to be the most common method of contraception used by Italian women in a stable relationship.[126] Historically, the Italian upper classes, as those in many other countries, often found domestic servants and peasant women a useful tool to quieten their sexual needs. Here, no unpleasant condoms or nerve-wrecking withdrawal before

---

[ix]   See also Chapter 2.

ejaculation were necessary. If the girl got pregnant, she was sent away and despised by society. For the Catholic Church, this was preferable to contraception or to masturbation. Sex was enjoyed in a way which could lead to procreation. The Church was once again instrumental in the misery and wretchedness of those who most needed help.

The religion-infused anti-contraceptive culture took a while to overcome. In May 1960, the US Food and Drug administration (FDA) approved the first contraceptive pill. This did not stop many states from prohibiting their prescription. In those days, the use of contraceptive devices was punishable by jail. So in 1965, in some states, a married couple could be sent to jail for using a condom. The Vatican used its influence wherever it could to press for laws which would make contraceptives unavailable.

Catholic Ireland is a good case in point. Until 1979, the law prohibited the importation and sale of contraceptives. In November 1980, a new family planning act made it very difficult to obtain any form of contraception except through medical prescription. Not only the doctor, but the pharmacist could turn down a patient's request unless he or she was convinced that there was a serious medical reason for preventing pregnancy. Intra-uterine devices were labelled abortifacients and banned. Family planning clinics were ruled illegal. In 1985, the Family Planning Amendment Bill, which allowed anyone over eighteen to buy condoms and spermicides, was passed. Birth control pills remained available only to married couples on prescription. In a speech he gave in March 1999, Archbishop Desmond Connell of Dublin vehemently denounced contraception. He said that the 'contraceptive culture' led to 'insincerity' in the love between couples, and their 'planned' children were akin to 'technological products', whereas unplanned births were 'gifts' from God.[127]

Post-communist Poland, another country under strong Catholic influence, changed its laws regarding abortions, limited access to contraception and has made Catholic instruction compulsory in schools with virtually no sex education. Wherever the Catholic Church sees an opportunity to prevent the local population from having access to contraceptives and sex education she does so. Bishops admonish politicians about their duty and frighten them about the consequences if legislation with which they disagree is passed.

To combat an unusually low rate of contraceptive usage and high adolescent pregnancy, the Peruvian government implemented a national family planning programme which was immediately and harshly attacked by the Catholic bishops. The Peruvian President had to defend his programme with the words 'There's nothing terrible in not wanting more children eating trash in the streets.'

As a 'non-member-state permanent observer' since 1964, the Vatican, under the name of the Holy See, gets to take part in UN policy-setting conferences and influence their recommendations just like a member government. Other Christian denominations and major faiths such as Islam, Buddhism and Judaism, are represented at the UN by accredited nongovernmental organisations that have no such privileges. At the UN's 1994 International Conference on Population and Development in Cairo, one hundred and seventy-nine governments agreed to a new global 'programme of action' that stressed the empowerment of women. The Conference concluded that all women have the right to determine the size of their family and pledged to make voluntary contraceptive family planning available worldwide. The Vatican, which was short of allies for its conservative policies, enlisted the support of fundamentalist Muslim countries in the run up to the Conference, determined to oppose women's rights, sex education, contraception and abortion in the conference document. Much as it tried, the Vatican failed to prevent the Cairo accord.

Following the failure in Cairo, the Vatican initiated a programme of contacts with fundamentalist Muslim countries, to plan joint actions which would further their attitude to human rights. In 1999, a series of UN-sponsored conferences to assess progress after five years and to draft new actions and funding proposals for the UN General Assembly to vote on, was yet another opportunity for the Vatican to reopen the key issues of contraception, abortion and sex education. Suitably its partners in this were Catholic Argentina, Guatemala and Nicaragua, together with Muslim Libya and Sudan.

Yet, the Catholic Church's opposition to the use of contraception is fast losing impact in the developed world. A good indication is the fact that Catholic Italy and Spain have the lowest birth rates in Europe. In the very countries where condoms are most needed, the poor countries of the Third World, the Church continues to be influential and uses her influence to restrict or block the availability of contraception. So, whereas Western Catholics have concluded that the Church is totally out of touch on sexual matters and simply disregard the Pope and his teachings on sex, the population of poorer countries continues to be manipulated by the Church. Thanks to the Church plenty of poor, hungry and sick children continue to be born in Africa and in South America.

Abortion

Millions of Catholics have been propelled into misery by the Church, which forbids the use of contraceptives, regardless of the family's health, social and economic circumstances. Millions of poor women who found themselves with unwanted pregnancies because of the Church's influence, chose abortions, often performing the acts themselves or by accessing illegal, back-street abortionists. Daily, hundreds of women die in botched abortions in countries in which such operations are illegal.

Nobody in their right mind likes abortions. It is a surgical procedure which takes its toll both physically and psychologically on the woman who is having the abortion. It may cause complications and sometimes can be dangerous. Therefore, all women should have access to sex education, information about contraception and should have easily available contraception to ensure that those who should not, may not or do not wish to have a child do not find themselves with an unwanted pregnancy.[128] The Catholic Church has been instrumental, throughout the world, in preventing women from receiving such education, such information and such contraceptives. Their view is that women should not have sex outside marriage and that all sexual acts should be open to procreation. This includes incest and rape.

In *Casti connubii* Pope Pius XI joins the Bishop of Hippo in 'denouncing those wicked parents who seek to remain childless, ... or if [the offspring] already lives in the womb, to kill it before it is born'.[129] Lest the health of a mother be brought in as justification, this encyclical clarifies that 'Holy Mother Church very well understands and clearly appreciates all that is said regarding the health of the mother and the danger to her life. And who would not grieve to think of these things?' But as much as the gentlemen in Rome grieved for women who die at childbirth, or women whose lives could have been saved by aborting the foetus, the grief does not soften their hearts and ruthlessly they offer death to the 'mother risking her life with heroic fortitude, that she may preserve the life of the offspring which she has conceived'. Who needs science and medical help if the Catholic solution is at hand: 'God alone, all bountiful and all merciful as He is, can reward her for the fulfilment of the office allotted to her by nature, and will assuredly repay her in a measure full to overflowing.'[130] This papal 'go to heaven' sounds very much like 'go to hell'. Who knows how many tens of thousands of women have died as a result of this pressure put by the Catholic Church on women, their husbands, their doctors and the state to let women die rather than abort the foetus which endangers her life. Arrogantly, the Pope decides for the unborn foetus and against the living mother.[131]

Worldwide some fifty million abortions take place each year. Half of them are illegal and often in the most terrible, unhygienic conditions. History has proven that, regardless of the penalties, women have abortions in the direst conditions, paying extortionate prices, sometimes risking their lives in an abortionist's back-yard. Churches have frightened them with the fires of hell. State laws, often as a result of Church influence and pressure, have made abortions criminal offences. To no avail – abortions will continue to be performed as long as unwanted pregnancies exist.

The Church defines abortion as any method used to terminate a pregnancy from the moment of conception. Abortion, thus defined, is always illicit, is a grave sin according to the official discipline of the Catholic church, and can trigger excommunication for the parties involved. And yet, modern Catholics do not consider that they have to obey the pope on matters of abortion. A 1999 poll in the USA has shown eighty per cent of Catholics to consider abortion a personal issue.[132] This does not mean that they condone abortion, they simply do not feel that the Church should dictate to them on this issue. The issue is not the Church's opposition to abortion, it is the way the Church tries to prevent women from having abortions which should be examined and the question we must pose to ourselves is whether we should allow a body in our midst to use such violent tactics against women at their most vulnerable.

In her attempt to influence politicians, the Church threatens the Catholic ones with hell. In 1990, the Catholic New York Governor, Mario Cuomo, was warned by New York Bishop Austin Vaughan that the governor was running 'a serious risk of going to hell', as Cuomo had explained that as a public official he accepted 'the truth that to assure our freedom we must allow others the same freedom even if occasionally it produces conduct by them we would hold to be sinful'.[133] Bishop Vaughan was a prominent figure in the pro-life movement and the first American bishop to be arrested for blocking abortion clinic entrances.

In recent years, the Church has gone for an all-out war against the so called 'morning after' pill, which if taken within seventy-two hours of intercourse can prevent pregnancy. A document released by the Vatican's Pontifical Academy for Life misleadingly states that the morning-after pill is nothing other than a 'chemically induced abortion'.[134] The Church encourages health care workers throughout the world to practice 'conscientious objection' against the 'aggression' aimed at the 'human embryo'. Despite the Italian government's position that pharmacists would be breaking the law if they refused to supply the drug, the president of the Italian Bishops' Conference suggested that pharmacists should be allowed to claim conscientious objector status, a protection afforded to doctors and nurses who do not wish to participate in abortion.

It does not matter to the Catholic Church whether the woman who wishes to take the 'morning after' pill has been raped or is mentally or physically unable to have a child; the Church will not allow its use. In fact, the Vatican fought hard to deny thousands of women, who were raped in Kosovo and in Bosnia, emergency contraception which would alleviate some of their suffering and feeling of shame.[135] The use of rape as a weapon of war was widespread in the former Yugoslavia and used, among other things, as a tool of ethnic cleansing. Should we really allow the Vatican to interfere when Muslim women, who were raped by Christians, wish to have emergency contraception or even an abortion?

Ireland is a European country in which the Catholic Church has been extremely successful in pushing and holding on to its anti-abortion agenda. Until recently, Irish women were even denied information on abortion. In 1987, an anti-abortion group took two counselling centres to court to stop them from advising women where to obtain abortions in England. The Irish Supreme Court ruled against the centres. It actually took the European Court of Human Rights to void the Irish court ban on providing information to Irish women seeking abortions abroad. How far the ramifications of this dictatorial behaviour could go became evident in 1992 with the case of a fourteen-year-old Irish girl who was raped and wanted to have an abortion. As these were not legally available in Ireland, the girl and her family wanted to go elsewhere. The court decided to prevent the girl from travelling, a decision that caused a public uproar in Ireland (and around the world). The Supreme Court decided that, although the Irish law prohibits abortion without exception, the procedure is permissible when the pregnant woman's life is endangered by physical health conditions or threat of suicide. As a result of this case, a three-part referendum on abortion rights was held in November 1992. The Church campaigned to close this 'loophole'. If passed, they would have prevented a suicidal pregnant woman from qualifying for an abortion. The Church lost and the amendment was defeated. Against the wish of the Catholic Church, the voters decided that Irish women should be allowed access to abortion information and have the right to travel abroad for the procedure.

Ireland is not the only country in which Catholic pressure has resulted in an intolerant attitude towards women who find themselves in the traumatic situation of an unwanted pregnancy. Countries with strong Catholic influence often criminalise abortion: the Philippines attempted to introduce the death penalty for it; the strongly Catholic Andorra have banned it; and Poland, in a reversal of Communist policy, is making it more and more difficult to have access to it. In Portugal abortion is only permitted in the first twelve weeks of pregnancy in cases of foetal abnormality, rape or serious risk to the woman's physical or psychological health. The Portuguese government actively prosecutes doctors, nurses and women who have had abortions. In 2001, over forty women were charged with assisting in the provision of illegal abortions.

In 2004, a Dutch volunteer group, Women on Waves, which operates a boat on which doctors offer emergency contraception (the 'morning-after' pill), attempted to dock in Portugal. The Portuguese navy sent a warship to prevent the Dutch boat from crossing the twelve-mile line. The Portuguese court backed its government's barring of the boat from entering Portuguese waters.

Many South American countries which are under substantial Catholic influence, have laws banning abortion. In Argentina – where Roman Catholicism is the state religion and the constitution requires a Catholic president – abortion is illegal except in cases where there is a risk to the life of the pregnant woman and where the mentally handicapped have been raped. An estimated four hundred and fifty thousand women have illegal abortions in Argentina each year and botched abortions are the primary cause of maternal death. Doctors fear to become involved because they could lose their right to practice; but affluent women are able to pay and obtain safer abortions. Botched, illegal abortions are a leading cause of maternal death in Nicaragua, a deeply Catholic country in which abortion is a crime. One in three of the country's fifteen- to nineteen-year-old girls has a child, often as the result of rape. Thanks to the Church and to the Nicaraguan government an estimated fifteen thousand women are hospitalised each year with abortion-related complications.

The case of Rosa, a nine-year-old Nicaraguan girl who was raped by a twenty-year-old man, got pregnant and was infected with two venereal diseases, demonstrates the brutality of the Catholic Church. This did not happen in the Dark Ages, it happened in 2003. The girl's parents, risking the penal consequences, arranged for an abortion. The government decided not to prosecute because the operation had been carried out to save the girl's life. Cardinal Miguel Obando y Bravo, the Cardinal of Managua, declared the automatic excommunication of the parents and the doctors who performed the abortion. The Managua Archdiocese's newsletter explained that there is no difference 'between a bus full of passengers ripped apart by a car bomb and the impact of a metal instrument in the womb of a mother to suck out the foetus'. A Spanish internet campaign mustered the support of twenty-six thousand people world-wide who demanded to be excommunicated and signed a petition which read: 'I also want to be excommunicated in the face of the excommunication of Rosa's parents in Nicaragua because all of us have contributed actively in making the interruption of Rosa's pregnancy possible.' The Church caved in and the threat of excommunication was repealed.

Peru is a poor and Catholic country in which abortions are illegal unless there is no other way to save the pregnant woman's life or prevent serious and permanent injury to her health. Approximately, one in five pregnancies in this country ends in an illegal abortion and hospital expenditure for treating victims of botched abortions is higher than for delivering babies.[136] Some countries, such as Costa Rica or Columbia, where the Catholic Church is the established religion, are trying to limit the Church's power. When, in 2001, the Colombian Supreme Court ruled that abortion 'in those cases where the woman has been a victim of violence, rape, or non-consensual artificial insemination' is not punishable by prison, the bishops said they would take steps to have the new law declared unconstitutional. The Catholic Church in Colombia has warned doctors, medical practitioners and judges who participate in procuring abortion that they may face excommunication.

The impact of the Church in the area of abortion is threefold: direct impact on Church members through the condemnation of abortion; indirect impact through political clout which results in legislation criminalising abortion; and indirect impact by preventing Catholic physicians and nurses – especially in Church-run hospitals – from catering to the true needs of the pregnant woman and acting either according to their religious beliefs or simply as per the instructions of the Church. It is reported that in present-day Poland, women have difficulties even with abortions which are legal under the already strict laws; hospitals routinely refuse to carry them out.[137]

Taking advantage of its status at the United Nations, the Vatican actively opposed initiatives to define abortion as a human right and is widely credited for derailing the efforts for such a resolution at the 1995 UN-sponsored International conference in Beijing. Skilfully, the Church pulls the strings of Catholic politicians in various countries. Professor John Swomley described the anti-abortion activities of right-wing US Congressman and chairman of the House Judiciary Committee, Henry Hyde, who not only acted aggressively to prevent any public funding of abortion, but also associated himself with the *Pro Life Action Network* and the activist Joseph Scheidler, who was convicted of playing a role in coordinated assaults on abortion clinics. Congressman Hyde, a loyal soldier of the Vatican, was also a central player in the Republican move to have President Bill Clinton impeached in 1998. According to Vatican thinking, Clinton, who has defended family planning and abortion rights and vetoed anti-abortion legislation, had to be removed. The Vatican's footmen in the US Congress did their utmost to achieve this end.[138]

How much is the Church to blame for the actions of pro-life (anti-abortion) campaigners? What influence does the strong language used by the Church and her hierarchy, in describing abortions as murder, have on the violent acts of these campaigners? The Catholic Church, which does not excommunicate Catholic murderers and seems not to have had any qualms in enabling members of the IRA to celebrate the Eucharist and receive other sacraments, has an automatic sentence of excommunication for anyone connected with the practice of abortion. This, according to experts on canon law, includes doctors, nurses and family members involved in the decision to have an abortion.[139] The Church persistently calls abortion the murder of helpless unborn children. Cardinal Meissner, the Archbishop of Cologne, has compared the 'morning-after' pill to Zyklon-B, the gas used by Nazi Germany to exterminate Jews and other inmates of concentration camps.[140] Is it surprising that some people take the lead from their spiritual leaders and try to stop the 'perpetrators'?

Some of the anti-abortion campaigns have been extremely violent. In the US, 'pro-life' fanatics have used arson, shooting and bombing to terrorise and kill medical staff providing abortions. Such violent attacks have taken place over many years and the leadership of the Catholic Church, which coordinated many of the activities (albeit the non-violent ones), cannot but be aware of the impact of their aggressive stand on the behaviour of the fanatics pro-life activists.

Many clergymen and members of religious orders dedicate their lives to care for the sick and the needy. However, contrary to her claims, the Church is in her teaching often totally remote from human suffering and uncaring about her people. This is evident in many areas, but in no area are there so many millions affected by the Church's rigid dogma and her unwillingness to have any regard for the resultant distress, suffering, even death, as in her teaching and policing of contraception and abortion.

In the very countries in which children are forced into homelessness and prostitution and in which they lack the most basic nutrition and healthcare, the Church relentlessly pushes her rigid dogma. The poorer the population and the lower the level of education, the more successful the Church is in enveloping society in a contraceptiveless environment, one in which women are condemned to perpetual pregnancy and child-birth.

Some five hundred women are estimated by the WHO to die every day from botched attempts to end unwanted pregnancies. Five hundred women a day could be saved if they had sex and contraception education and access to contraceptives and to reliable and professional abortion clinics.

Conclusion

In their claim to occupy a central role in our lives, most religions have appropriated sex – a vital and fundamental force in our constitution – and have defined rules concerning sexual conduct. Undoubtedly, the Catholic Church is considered by many as fulfilling her role as a moral guide. But it must be clear that by defining a set of rules for sexual conduct and stipulating that contravention of her rules amounts to 'sinning', which unabsolved leads to hell, the Church has created the structure which can deliver her with clients. An essential component in the Catholic Church's teaching is the concept of original sin, which every child is born with and which can only be cleared through baptism. By defining as sinful many of the most natural, common and harmless sexual activities, the Church has ensured that as many as possible in need of absolution would fall into her net. To complete the Church's control of the population in sexual matters, she has also defined matrimony as a religious structure and ceremony. An important human and societal institution which is a crucial ingredient in many people's lives and happiness has thereby also been defined by the Church as hers to adjudicate on. The Church has set rules for the entirety of our sexual lives. These are not suggested norms, but strict rules with stiff penalties for any deviation. Moreover, the Church has used her influence to control people's conduct and to affect political secular structures to legislate in these matters as she ordains.

What the Church does in an area which is so central to our lives is of critical importance. Professional celibates, who consider virginity and celibacy the highest ideal, run the Catholic Church, define her dogma and develop her sexual ethic. As her attitude to sex goes back to her origins and as she has traditionally defined these sources to be unassailable truths, the Church has great difficulty in making any changes to her sexual codes. These are almost totally disregarded by many of her members and also by a substantial part of her own clergy.

The mystical power of religion over the population and the political clout religious organisations have built up throughout history have caused millions to be driven to their death and many to be jailed only because their behaviour went against the Church's dogma. Over centuries millions were tormented by the Church to believe that masturbation was sinful and required punishment. As a result of her (and other religions') indoctrination, homosexuality was not only illegal, but also considered by the majority of the population to be sick, repugnant and sinful. In most developed countries, it is now accepted to be natural and totally legal when performed by two consenting adults. The Church continues to lobby governments to limit the rights of homosexuals and homosexuals continue to suffer from the Church's ideology. Her rules against contraception and abortion have brought about endless misery of unwanted children, millions of botched abortions and millions who are condemned by the Church to death from AIDS. To complement her anti-contraception teaching, the Church also spreads lies, especially in poor countries and to vulnerable people. Would society permit any other public organisation to engage in such criminal deception? Do the Vatican's instructions, which forbid the use of condoms even by people who are infected with the AIDS virus, in effect make the pope a murderer? He knowingly prevents people from using a barrier to their own death. Moreover, if a child is born as a result of sex with an HIV positive person, the child is also very likely to be HIV positive and to die of AIDS. These deaths are the direct result of papal action. Should bishops and priests who propagate the Church's dogma in these matters, not be tried for murder?

The Church is responsible for the sexual abuse of millions through the imposition of her dogma. Underlying ignorance and erroneous theories which have formed the Church's attitude, blended with irrevocability, determination, autocracy, ruthlessness and effective political and psychological power over society, which typify the *modus operandi* of the Church, are the culprits in the Church's disastrous history in this area.

Chapter Nine
Do They Practice What They Preach?

The Catholic Church lays much importance on chastity, which she defines as: 'the successful integration of sexuality within the person and thus the inner unity of man in his bodily and spiritual being'.[1] The Church expects all the baptised to live in chastity

> in keeping with their particular states of life. Some profess virginity or consecrated celibacy which enables them to give themselves to God alone with an undivided heart in a remarkable manner. Others live in the way prescribed for all by the moral law, whether they are married or single. Married people are called to live in conjugal chastity; others practice chastity in continence.[2]

The Church also forbids and defines as grave sins 'masturbation, fornication, pornography, and homosexual practices'. Even to desire sexual pleasure is 'morally disordered when sought for itself, isolated from its procreative and unitive purposes'.[3] There is no doubt that priests are expected to abstain from sex.

The answer to the question 'do they practice what they preach?' should surprise hardly anyone. They do not. Some people, according to the Church, should not have sex at all – they have to remain celibate. In addition to anyone who is not married, all members of Catholic religious orders and the whole of the Catholic clergy are required to be celibate. However, there are several hundred married pastors originating from other Christian denominations who wished to convert to Catholicism and were given special dispensation from Rome. The requirement of priestly celibacy is unique to the Latin rite; Eastern rite Churches, which accept Rome's authority, have always allowed priests to marry. Although some Catholic priests who were accused of sexual abuse explained that they thought celibacy only meant that they were not allowed to get married, celibacy in fact means total abstinence from any sexual activity.

The apostles were not celibate, some of them were married. The earliest Canonical legislation on the matter of clerical celibacy stems from the fourth-century Council of Elvira. This Spanish synod decreed that 'bishops, priests, deacons and all clergy celebrating Mass are to be instructed to abstain from intercourse with their wives and beget no more children. All who act to the contrary are to be expelled from the priesthood.' This did not prevent Pope Hormisdas (514–523) from fathering a son who would eventually become a pope himself, Silverius (536–537). For a while the Church attempted to discourage sexual activity, whilst permitting her clergy to remain married. In 541, the Synod of Orléans decreed that 'Priests and deacons may not share the same bed and the same room with their wives, lest they be suspected of carnal intercourse.' Twenty-six years later, the Synod of Tours of 567 decided:

> A bishop may look upon his wife as a sister only. He must always, wherever he goes, be surrounded by clergy, and his own and his wife's apartments must be separated from each other so that the clergy attending him do not come into contact with the serving-women of the bishop's wife. ...
>
> Because, in the country, very many archpriests, and likewise deacons and subdeacons, are suspected of persisting in intercourse with their wives, the archpriest is always to have with him a cleric who accompanies him everywhere and must have his bed in the same room with him. ... Seven subdeacons, lectors, or laymen can take it in turn to do this.[4]

The phenomenon of Catholic clergy living a life of deceit and lies, to secure their sexual gratification whilst at the same time, retaining their status within the Church, is evidently not new. *Plus-ça-change*. Whether some of these archpriests found solace by taking a subdeacon or even a layman – their living chastity belts secured by the synod – into their own beds, we do not know. This would not have pleased the Council either. The Council was so worried about homosexuality that it ruled that monks might not sleep two in a bed.[i] Pope Pelagius II (579–590) had a more practical attitude. He overlooked his priests' sex lives, provided Church property was not handed over or inherited by their wives or children.

A priest should 'love his wife like a sister and shun her like an enemy', was Pope Gregory the Great's (590–604) instruction. However, implementation of celibacy has, throughout the Church's history, been difficult. The Western Church got stuck into this hard-line policy with regard to clerical celibacy, a policy which still continues to trouble her today. Various other popes have issued decrees concerning this matter, but the Catholic clergy continued to disregard them. Eighth-century St Boniface (c. 672–754) accused German clergy of promiscuity, rape and adultery. Priests, according to Boniface, slept with four or even five women a night and then got up to celebrate Mass. Their wish to celebrate

---

[i] At a time when it was common practice for people to share a bed when, for example, travelling.

Mass after such joyous nights and to thank God for all he has given them, should have been obvious to Boniface. He, however, saw it differently and wanted them all to be defrocked. St Boniface, also known as 'the Apostle of Germany', convened the first German Synod which took place in 742. Very strict regulations were decided upon to tackle carnal sins on the part of lecherous priests, monks and nuns. Priests guilty of lechery were to be publicly flogged and locked up in prison for two years. Monks and nuns were given only one year's imprisonment, but they too were to be publicly scourged.[5] The Church council of 836 at Aix-la-Chapelle admitted that monasteries were homosexual haunts and convents brothels where unwanted babies were killed and buried.[6]

The Lateran Council of 1059 threatened with loss of employment all the priests unwilling to give up their wives or concubines. However, having manifestly failed to stem the tide on the supply side, this Church council attempted to also work the demand side by ruling that 'No one shall hear mass from a priest who to his certain knowledge keeps a concubine or a secret wife.' Cardinal Humbert's critical observation of the unacceptable situation at the Eastern Church gives an interesting insight into the discomfort which the Church has with sex. Humbert, who headed the papal delegation to Constantinople in 1054, described a situation in that city where:

> Young married men, exhausted but lately by carnal lust, minister at the altar. And immediately thereafter they embrace their wives once more with hands sanctified by the undefiled body of Christ. That is no mark of true faith, but an invention of Satan.[7]

It was a tough battle. Catholic clergy did not want to accept these rules. There were mini-revolutions in various countries. When Archbishop Jean of Rouen, at a synod in 1074, threatened to excommunicate married priests, he was pelted with stones and driven from the church. In Germany, Bishop Altmann of Passau was physically assaulted for referring to priestly marriage as a vice deserving eternal damnation. Even a pope was physically attacked: Gregory VII (1073–1085) tried to be more successful in stamping out concubinage and enforcing priestly celibacy. The resistance to his edict was fierce. It included an occasion on which he was kidnapped by soldiers whilst he was performing midnight Mass on Christmas Eve 1075. He was beaten and tortured before he was released the next day. In 1076, a group of Italian bishops excommunicated Gregory for separating husbands and wives and thereby promoting licentiousness in the clergy. Four years later, the Council of Brixen condemned the Pope for 'sowing divorce among legitimate spouses'. Ultimately, Gregory gave up.

The Church was willing to go to great lengths to enforce her will. These included decrees making the wives of deacons slaves of the prince, or property of the bishop. In 1095, the Council of Piacenza took a drastic step to put an end to priestly marriage: it simply sold all the priests' wives into slavery. Pope Urban II (1088–1099), apparently decided that the income which could be derived from the priestly sex drive was preferable to prohibition. This Pope introduced the *cullagium*, an annual tax which was levied on clergyman who wanted to keep a concubine.

In 1139, Pope Innocent II decreed that priests would no longer be permitted to get married and the Second Lateran Council (1139) invalidated all priestly marriages. Between one day and the next, legal wives became concubines.[8] For the next four hundred years, clandestine marriages enabled priests to deceive the Church and enjoy both priesthood and a wife. The Council of Trent (1545–1563) put an end to this arrangement and decided that every marriage ceremony would, in future, have to be officiated by a priest, in front of witnesses. It was no longer possible to enter into clandestine marriages. The Church, in her ardour to have a sex-free clergy, found herself with priests and bishops who could no longer live in matrimony and kept concubines instead. Concubines were so common even before the Council of Trent that a fifteenth-century French bishop reported that the clergy of his diocese did not count concubinage a sin, and made no attempt to disguise their use of it.[9]

According to the Catholic Encyclopaedia, concubinage is 'the state – more or less permanent – of a man and woman living together in illicit intercourse. … it is immaterial whether the parties dwell together or not, the repetition or continuance of illicit relations between the same persons being the essential element'.[10] In the thirteenth and fourteenth centuries, Catholic synods throughout Europe passed resolutions condemning concubinage. In 1284, the Synod of St Pölten,[ii] decreed that priests should denounce each other. Slowly, but forcefully, the Catholic Church drove her clergy into deceit. The sex drive of the clergy has not gone away. The means had to be adapted. Priests' sex lives were pushed underground and everything had to be done clandestinely. Not surprisingly, this sex-with-one's-wife-hating culture became a convenient niche for homosexuals, who were able to conduct their sex lives with less suspicion than their heterosexual colleagues.

The continued flouting of Vatican rules by the Church's clergy was not limited to the lower hierarchy. Not all of the popes were corrupt, but much of the papacy's history is one of corruption. Scores of the popes who headed this Church which is so preoccupied with – and which has

---

ii   The Austrian town which is now infamous for the scandalous behaviour in her Priests' seminary. It was closed down in 2004, after dozens of seminarians were caught with pornographic material on their personal computers.

throughout her history agonised over and tormented her faithful on – issues of sex, sexuality and sexual mores, were definitely not practising what they preached. Many had mistresses and many were known to have fathered children; some of these papal children became popes themselves.[11]

Bisexual Pope John XII (955–964) was said to have run a brothel out of St Peter's. He died at the ripe age of twenty-four, from stab wounds inflicted by a jealous husband with whose wife he was found in bed. A twelve-year-old boy, Theophylact, became pope in 1032, Pope Benedict IX. He ran homosexual orgies in the Lateran Palace, sodomised animals and ordered murders. Benedict, who was also known to have run a brothel in the Lateran Palace which was said to have been the best in Rome, was ousted in 1047.

Twelfth- and thirteenth-century convents were often centres of debauched behaviour: nuns were having sex with bishops, priests and lay members, babies born as a result were brought up in the convents. Priests continued to have concubines and Church councils continued to forbid it. Gregory X (1271–1276) tried to convince the Bishop of Liege to mend his ways and repent. The bishop, who kept seventy concubines, some of whom were nuns, one a Benedictine Abbess, and who had fathered sixty-five illegitimate children, had no wish to repent and was finally defrocked in 1274 by the Council of Lyons 'for deflowering virgins and other mighty deeds'.

Boniface VIII (1294–1303) for a while kept a mother and her daughter as his mistresses. On the other hand he also had a string of male lovers. Boniface, who was charged and tried *in absentia* for sexual misconduct, heresy, tyranny and intercourse with the devil, never appeared before the court. Several years later, he lost his sanity and committed suicide.

Petrarch described the court of Pope Clement VI (1342–1352), which was 'home to wine, women, song and priests who cavorted as if their glory consisted not in Christ but in feasting and unchastity'.[12] He had various mistresses, and took special joy in picking women for his nightly pleasures from those attending special audiences he held for women alone, every evening. When this had become public, his confessor demanded that he live chastely, to which the Pope responded that he had become accustomed to sleeping with women in his younger days, and that he was only continuing now on doctors' advice. The Pope's court found the situation unacceptable and raised the subject at an audience at which Pope Clement vigorously defended his sexual activities, by bringing examples from the Church's history demonstrating that sexually active popes had ruled the Church better than sexually continent ones.

Sixtus IV (1471–1484), the builder of the Sistine Chapel and the pope whose bull of 1478 approved the introduction of the Spanish Inquisition, funded his war against the Turks from revenues of a brothel he established in Rome for both sexes. He created six 'nephews', the usual euphemism for illegitimate sons, cardinals. At least one of them was a son he had from his own sister, another, Giuliano della Rovere, who was also his lover, later became Pope Julius II (1503–1513). To set up his 'nephews' in the style he wished for them, Pope Sixtus plundered the coffers of the Church.

Rodrigo Borgia took the name Alexander VI (1492–1503). A libertine, whose total number of illegitimate children is unknown, Rodrigo Borgia fathered six alone during his youth in Spain. He had three children from a woman with whose mother and sister he also had affairs. He himself was probably the son of Pope Callistus III (1455–1458), through whom he collected Church appointments and offices which brought with them considerable income and which made Rodrigo a very wealthy man. This wealth enabled him in due course to buy the necessary votes of cardinals to secure his election as pope. His long-term mistress, Vannozza, was the mother of four of his children, including the notorious Cesare and Lucrezia Borgia. Rodrigo, in a letter to his mistress, instructed her to 'take particular care of the education of our children, because they are destined to govern nations and kings'.[13] At the time, Rodrigo was not yet pope and he explained to his mistress that one needs to have 'a little more patience and I shall have what they have called my uncle has left me for an inheritance, the See of St Peter'. At first, Rodrigo installed Vannozza in Venice and, to ensure her respectability, married her off to a harmless man. When he no longer felt the need for such discretion, he moved his mistress to Rome, where he bought her a palace, and stayed with her every night. In deals he made with the cardinals during the August 1492 conclave, some cardinals received money. One cardinal, a Venetian monk, did not demand much money, only five thousand crowns, but he also wanted to spend one night with Rodrigo's twelve-year-old daughter, Lucrecia. This was not too high a price for Rodrigo and the deal was done. As pope, Rodrigo moved his mistress and one of his daughters into the Vatican. He also made his son, Cesare, a cardinal. Well ensconced in his new seat, the Pope was ripe for a new mistress. Vanozza was no longer young, and the Pope fell for a ravishing beauty, Giulia Farnese. Her brother, Alessandro Farnese, received a pardon for a forgery and was later, at the ripe age of nineteen, given a cardinal's hat. Alessandro, who sold his fifteen-year-old sister as mistress to the Pope, would become Pope Paul III (1534–1549). Giulia, who was conveniently married to one-eyed Orsino Orsini, gave the Pope several children. Rodrigo's papacy proceeded with the same debauchery and corruption, as in his prior life.

Julius II (1503–1513), like Alexander VI, enjoyed his mistresses as well as his male lovers, fathered children and suffered from syphilis. In a papal bull issued in 1510, Pope Julius established a brothel in Rome.

Giovanni de Medici had already been made cardinal at the age of thirteen. Although predominantly homosexual, he too had several children. One of his first appointments as Pope Leo X (1513–1521) was to make his lover, Alfonso Petrucci, a cardinal. His attitude to the papacy was 'God has given us the papacy. Let us enjoy it.' This he did with alcohol, young boys and elaborate and extravagant balls and banquets. At one such banquet naked boys appeared from the puddings. Silver dishes were thrown into the Tiber after each course. A more lasting aspect of his extravagance was his patronage of Raphael and Michelangelo.

Alessandro Farnese, whose mistress bore him three sons and one daughter, and who reportedly poisoned his mother and his niece to lay his hands on the whole of the family's wealth, became Pope Paul III (1534–1549). He was accused of having incestuous relationships with his own daughter and with his niece. One of this pope's sources of income were thousands of prostitutes who all paid Pope Paul a monthly tribute.

Homosexual popes, such as Julius III (1550–1555), used their power give influential positions to their male lovers. Julius made his son Bertuccino, his 'adopted son', Innocente, a fifteen-year-old boy whom he had picked up in the street, as well as several other attractive teenage boys, cardinals.

After Julius, Cardinal Caraffa, who became Pope Paul IV (1555–1559), tried to clean up his house. There was much to be cleaned up. The sexual licentiousness was not limited to popes and cardinals, it enveloped the Church at all levels. Priests would seduce women during confession and the inquisition dealt with important theological questions such as whether touching hands could be considered soliciting, or whether it needed to include genital contact, the fondling of a confessing woman's breast, for instance. The Inquisition decreed that a priest who raped a woman, who had fainted during confession, was not considered soliciting. Priests would instruct women to undress and whip them. Some cases are recorded by the Inquisition of priests who joined the naked women and undressed too for the occasion. Flagellation was apparently fashionable and a priest in Ypres got nine nuns to strip and whip each other under his watchful eyes, after which he had sex with all of them.

When Henry VIII had the Catholic Church in England investigated, one of his men found the abbot at Langdon abbey in Kent in bed with his mistress and similar behaviour at scores of other monasteries and convents, in which nuns and monks were all sexually active. The Church, which preached the strictest sexual control and punished her members for any infringement of her often absurd rules, was infested by wantonness. It seems that in certain areas, things have really not changed much.

Father of three, Pope Pius V (1566–1572) tried to enforce clerical continence, but gave up when it turned out that sodomy soon replaced the heterosexual sex as the main sexual outlet of the clergy. His successor, Gregory XIII (1572–1585), lifted the ban on prostitutes in Rome which Pius V had introduced and the priests could again enjoy their nights in Roman brothels. He himself, had many children, one of whom he made cardinal. Things became tougher under Sixtus V (1585–1590). This Franciscan monk executed thousands, including monks and their mistresses. Things were more relaxed under his successors. Indeed, an early seventeenth-century Archbishop of Salzburg ruled that priests were allowed to keep concubines, as long as they were kept outside a six-mile exclusion zone around the city. Innocent X (1644–1655), who ordered all nudity in paintings and statues covered with fig leaves or tunics, ran his papacy aided by Donna Olimpia, his sister-in law, with whom he was intimate. Under his successor, the fig leaves were removed. These would be covered and uncovered by future popes, according to the level of their prudishness.

Nothing is known about the sexual activities of the popes of the last one hundred and fifty years. Considering all the information that has become public about the present state of sex and sexual abuse by Catholic clergy, it is more than likely that not all of these popes have been sexually continent.

Luther, in his successful attack on the Church, also attacked the issue of celibacy. The Protestant Church does not require celibacy from her clergy. In fact, the freedom to marry caused many Catholic clergy to cross the lines. In 1542, Archbishop Albrecht of Brandenburg confirmed, in a letter to the papal nuncio, that he was aware of the fact that all his priests had concubines, but claimed that if he were to discipline them, they would become Lutherans. Addressing the Council of Trent, Duke Albrecht of Bavaria's delegate to the Council stated that most of the Protestant German provinces would have remained Catholic, had Rome only been more accommodating in the matter of celibacy.

Some dioceses funded their activities by fining their own priests for contravening celibacy regulations. This, in turn, was another reason for Catholic priests to become Lutheran.[14] Not surprisingly, the strict rulings of the Council of Trent were not well received. The Council declared that, 'If anyone denies that it is better and more godly to abide in virginity or celibacy than to marry, he shall be excommunicated.' The clergy, in response, declared their wives to be their maidservants. Indeed, one vice-curate informed the Church in 1569 that he was unable to run his farm without the assistance of his maidservant and his four children.[15] One hundred years after Trent, the Church had to continue with her unyielding endeavours to uproot unchastity within the priesthood. In 1651, the Synod of Osnabrück decreed:

We shall ... visit the homes of suspects by day and night and have the
vile creatures publicly branded by the executioners; and, should the
authorities be lax or neglectful, they shall be punished by us.[16]

The suspects which the Synod of Osnabrück decided to valiantly
combat were priests living in concubinage. Further down in Bavaria, the
Archbishop Ferdinand had priests' wives imprisoned or deported, while
the Bishop of Bamberg, Gottfried von Aschhausen, demanded that
the civil authorities 'force their way into priests' houses, fetch out the
concubines, publicly flog them, and place them in custody'.[17]

There is constant pressure on the Vatican to allow priests to marry. Their
numbers have fallen sharply in the last forty years and some believe that
allowing marriage could help attract more people to the priesthood. It
would, of course, also change the ratio between gay and straight priests
and thereby ease the public concept of the Catholic Church as a breeding
ground of homosexual priests preying on young altar boys. The Church
has upheld and reiterated her stand on priestly celibacy, as documented
in Vatican II and in Pope Paul VI's encyclical, *Sacerdotalis Caelibatus – On
Priestly Celibacy* (1967).

Pope John Paul II has repeatedly and steadfastly reiterated his
opposition to any change in the celibacy for priests rule, rejecting calls for
such a change. Thousands of Catholic priests, however, maintain regular
sexual relationships with a female partner. Some find it convenient
not to be permitted to get married, others would have preferred to get
married than to succumb to a concubinal relationship. It is not a secret
and often the superiors of the priests are aware of the situation. In some
Third World countries priests and even bishops have mistresses with
the full knowledge of their community. 'Celibacy just runs against the
culture here', an Italian priest in central Africa explained, adding 'if we
find a priest who sticks to just one wife, we promote him to bishop'.[18]
This clearly is also known to the Vatican, which continues to produce
documents about clerical celibacy, perpetuating the lie its hierarchy is
living. Shockingly, the Vatican also kept quiet about the outrageous fact
that in certain African countries priests were regularly forcing young
nuns to have sex. It turned out that priests, who were used to having
mistresses, had concluded that young nuns were safer in the AIDS/HIV-
stricken countries. In certain cases, nuns who became pregnant were
forced by the priests to have abortions. In the US there is a support group
for women who were pressured by their priests-lovers to have abortions
in order to hush up their affair.[19]

A survey quoted in John Cornwell's book *Breaking Faith*, which covered
fifteen hundred priests in the USA and Germany, produced the following
results: forty per cent of the priests engaged in occasional sexual activity,

twenty-eight per cent were in a regular sexual relationship with a woman, ten per cent were in homosexual relationships and only ten per cent of the priests described themselves as completely chaste.[20]

It may have been difficult to have expected priests to abstain from the joys of sex when, contrary to Church teaching, many cardinals and popes had sexual partners, sometimes long-term mistresses who often also bore them children. This is no longer the case, however, in the context of 'do what you preach', there has always been and still is a wide gap between Catholic teaching on sexual morals and the behaviour of the clergy. As titillating as the papal and clerical stories may seem, this is not about titillation. It is about deceit. Throughout the Church's history, she has been obsessed by sex and has created rules the purpose of which is to take the pleasure out of sex, to define pleasure as sin and to allow sex only as a necessary evil for purposes of procreation. And yet, throughout all of this time, the Church from the bottom to top clergy lived a lie, fornicating wildly, whilst preaching abstinence to the rest of the world. The damage the Church has caused to her members in scaring them with the fires of hell and in creating environments in which natural and loving acts were banned, ostracised and criminalised cannot be overstated. The structure which made this possible has not changed. The sexual abuse scandals, which erupted towards the end of the twentieth century, in which it turned out that the hierarchy of the Catholic Church had for years covered up sexual abuse of tens of thousands of the young and vulnerable by the Catholic clergy, are a direct result of the Church's attitude to sex and her attitude to the truth.

Chapter Ten
Sexual Abuse

Saint Ignatius Loyola, the founder of the Jesuit Order, was a great believer in the power of education. He is quoted as having said 'Give me a boy of seven, and he will be mine for ever.' He did not mean it that way, but thousands of Catholic priests were unable to resist and went for those boys of seven. The widespread sexual abuse of children and other persons in positions of dependence by predatory Catholic priests and by members of Catholic orders has come to light in the last years of the twentieth century. It has shocked the entire world. It should not have come as a surprise, as rumours about such abuse had been in circulation for many years.

Such stories would regularly appear in different parts of the world only to be hushed up by the Catholic Church, using her position of power and influence to have the stories quashed and ensure that they did not trigger an investigation of the institution. A monumental scandal in the USA has forced the public to address a terrible truth; a truth which has been talked about for years in many Catholic countries. This story could no longer be contained.

A Scandal Breaks

The emerging stories are, of course, those of current victims, and even these go back more than sixty years. There is, however, no reason to believe that sexual abuse by Catholic clergy is a new phenomenon, that for some reason it only came into being in the twentieth century. Child abuse is not only a Church problem. It happens in all walks of life where children are entrusted to the care of others. The priests' positions of authority and trust – along with their supposed immaculate morality, or, more than that, having the advantage of being the very source of moral teaching – gave paedophiles and other sexual predators an almost free playground. Moreover, this playground was surrounded by the high walls of the Church which ensured that scandals were kept secret and were never reported to the authorities.

'Please join me … in continuing to pray for the priests' was Archbishop Renato Martino's, the Vatican's representative at the United Nations in New York, response to The Call to Accountability Campaign's request for a meeting to discuss the sexual abuse of nuns by priests in twenty-three countries.[1] Abusive priests have always been a problem. They are not a new phenomenon. St Peter Damian, who sought to have sodomites expelled from the clergy in the eleventh century, suggested the following in his *The Book of Gomorrah*:

> A cleric or monk who seduces youths or young boys or is found kissing or in any other impure situations is to be publicly flogged and he is to lose his tonsure. When his hair has been shaved off, his face is to be besmeared and he is to be bound in iron chains. For six months, he will languish in prison.[2]

The general state of morality of the clergy was such that Pope Leo IX (1049–1054) preferred to keep close control of his priests. He was losing his battle with the heterosexual ones, most of whom were married and were flouting the Church's laws on chastity. In those days, a priest who was to be consecrated as a bishop was reported to have had to answer the following questions: Have you sodomised a boy? Have you fornicated with a nun? Have you sodomised any four-legged animal? Have you committed adultery?[3]

The Inquisition Register kept by Jacques Fournier, an inquisitor who later became Pope Benedict XII (1334–1342), is full of his reports on clerical sexual transgression. One such report concerns a priest whose face swelled up after a visit to a prostitute. The priest vowed never to have sex with a woman again and started abusing boys. The priest was arrested after one of the boys in his charge complained that the priest came to his bed every night and inserted himself between the boy's thighs. Another is the report on the priest Pierre Clergue from Montbaillou. He regularly had sex with a dozen young girls – one reported having been deflowered by him in the haystack in the barn, whereas another, a widow, had sex with him in a bed he made up in the local church. To prevent conception, the curate brought a small bag of herbs he inserted in the woman's vagina and which he took with him after intercourse had taken place.

The Catholic Church, through her sexually predatory priests and with the connivance of her hierarchy to protect and to cover up their deeds, has abused both the children entrusted to her and to society at large. The scandal has been brewing for years. In the United States the Church has for more than two decades been party to private and confidential compensation deals, costing her huge amounts of money, to take care of claims made against her by victims of sexual abuse.

The report, *The Problem of Sexual Molestation by Roman Catholic Clergy: Meeting the Problem in a Comprehensive and Responsible Manner*, was co-authored by a member of the Vatican's Washington Embassy. It was distributed to US bishops at the meeting of the National Conference of Catholic Bishops[i] in May 1985 and pleaded with the bishops to take action; but it was largely ignored.[4] The report explained the psychological aspect of child abuse and the fact that there was an extremely high rate of recidivism with paedophilia. It called bishops immediately to suspend any priest accused of sexual abuse when 'the allegation has any possible merit or truth'. The report also analysed the legal and canonical framework and – possibly to try to prompt some action – the report calculated that the total projected cost to the Church for the coming decade could reach US $1 billion. This calculation was based on some of the settlements which Catholic dioceses had already agreed with victims of abuse. The report called the bishops to establish a national intervention team to respond to complaints in individual dioceses. The bishops rejected the proposal and, instead, decided that each diocese could handle such complicated, sensitive and devastating situations on its own.[5]

Some twenty years later, the Catholic bishops were fighting a rearguard war: 'The Review Board believes that the overwhelming majority of priests serving the Church in the United States fulfil their roles honourably and chastely.'[6] So deep is the crisis in the Church and so little faith is there in her moral standing, that the National Review Board for the Protection of Children and Young People, which was established by the United States Conference of Catholic Bishops, had to begin the summary of its *Report on the Crisis in the Catholic Church in the United States*, issued in February 2004, with those words. The next sentence, however, hits the nail on the head: 'According to Church records, however, there were credible allegations that several thousand priests, comprising four percent of priests in ministry over the last half-century, committed acts of sexual abuse of minors.'

God only knows how much unreported abuse there has been and what the real figures are. They bathed them, tucked them into their beds, gave them 'health checkups' to verify that their sexual development was in order. They fondled, masturbated and raped them. They preyed mainly on working class boys and those from broken homes by portraying themselves as father figures.

The term sexual abuse has been used so often in connection with the Catholic Church that we are almost de-sensitised to it. Sexual abuse has become an almost anodyne term that somehow removes the horror of what has actually taken place. It was convenient for the Church and for

---

[i]   Now known as the US Conference of Catholic Bishops.

the politicians to use this term, which does not hurt as much as the more graphic and concise term 'anal rape', for instance. These priests, fondled, masturbated, had oral sex with and raped pre-pubescent children and teenagers who were entrusted to them by their parents and by their Church. Several priests were found guilty of raping and having anal sex with altar boys, cheerleaders and others who were given alcohol and seduced in rectories, churches or in their own homes. Other priests took children to peep shows and sex clubs and showed them pornographic materials. The children would then be taken to motels for sex. Often children were seduced on camping trips and other outings organised by the Church. Court cases involving Catholic clergy have brought to light a long list of abusive acts (see Appendix 1).

At first, the Church tried deny it all, suggesting that these were caring priests who may have given a sixteen-year-old a congratulatory hug after winning a parish prize. Then the Church suggested that, in many instances, these were not cases of abuse, but of consensual sex with youngsters. Some of the abusive priests are paedophiles who are interested in young, pre-pubescent children, and others are interested in teenagers. Some of the teenagers may, indeed, have been willing consensual partners to the sexual activity. But even consensual sex, when it takes place with people under one's care, is illegal and highly immoral.

The venues chosen by the priests are also significant and just add to the outrage. A rape in a four-poster bed hurts as much as one by the church altar, but the contrast between the 'holy' role of the perpetrator and the deed is often heightened by the religious situation that the priest and the abused child are in. A vast number of cases took place in rectories and in the churches themselves, often only minutes after Mass and after the victims had finished their role as altar boys.

But perhaps the most abhorrent aspect of the abuse has been the Church's dishonesty. In 1992, when a scandal erupted concerning James Porter, the paedophile priest who had attacked more than a hundred children, Cardinal Law, head of the Boston Archdiocese, simply lied. It had been, according to Law, a case of one depraved man. Law called on God for help and dismissed the scandal, which he suggested was blown out of proportion by the anti-Catholic media, with which God was asked to deal: 'we call God's power on the media, particularly the *Globe*'.[7] God, however, was not asked to intervene in stopping the abuse, in healing the victims or in helping the Church to mend her ways.

The size of the USA and its population and the fact that the abuse scandals have recently come to light, have produced much more material about abuse by clergy and religious in the US than anywhere else. But this is not solely an American problem; it is a Catholic problem. Similar occurrences of sexual abuse by clergy, hushed up by the Catholic hierarchy, have been reported in many other countries. The following are only a small number of the very many cases to illustrate the widespread incidence of sexual abuse by Catholic clergy world-wide. They all follow a similar pattern of abuse; of the hiding and shuffling of abusive priests from parish to parish; denial and attempts to cover up with payments of hush money; and denial of complicity by the hierarchy. Cases only came to light when the media made them public.

For years a few brave Argentinean priests had demanded the resignation or removal of the Archbishop of Santa Fe, Argentina – Edgardo Storni – but to no avail. In 1994, the Vatican ordered an investigation into allegations of the sexual abuse of seminarians, but declined to publish the findings. Finally, he resigned. He did so only after the publication of Olga Wornat's book, *Nuestra Santa Madre*, in August 2002, in which the author claimed that the Archbishop had abused at least forty-seven seminarians.[8]

In Australia, Christian Brothers held raping competitions of their favourite boys in the orphanage that they ran. In another Catholic institution, members of *St John of God Brothers* sexually abused twenty-four mentally handicapped youngsters.[9] A UK parliamentary enquiry into the welfare of former British child migrants reported that 'the worst cases of criminal abuse in Australia appear to have occurred in institutions run by agencies of the Catholic Church'.[10] Newspaper advertisements placed across the country by Australia's Roman Catholic Church in June 2002, expressed regret over the Church's slowness in dealing with the issue of sexual abuse carried out by her priests. The advert, in the form of an open letter by Archbishop George Pell of Melbourne and Archbishop Denis Hart of Sydney, on behalf of the Church, apologised for the abusive priests but denied that the Church had tried to buy the victims' silence, insisting that offers of monetary compensation were not 'hush money'. However, this denial had to be reversed only days later, with the acknowledgment that the secrecy clauses in the compensation agreements effectively rendered any compensation 'hush money'.[11] Archbishop Pell, who in 2003 was made Cardinal, said that although it was unclear whether the scandal in Australia had reached the scale of that in the US, there was an 'evil' in Australia which had to be confronted.

In 1998, the former head of the Austrian Roman Catholic Church, Cardinal Hans Hermann Groer, was forced to resign as Prior of the Benedictine monastery, Maria Roggendorf, after allegations of sexual abuse. The seventy-eight-year-old cardinal had already, in 1995, been obliged to retire as Archbishop of Vienna when allegations were made that he had sexually molested minors and novice monks at a Catholic boarding school in the early 1970s. Neither Groer nor the Vatican admitted guilt and the Church never apologised for this most senior clergyman's criminal behaviour. When Groer died, Pope John Paul II sent a telegram of condolence saying that the Cardinal led the Archdiocese 'with great love for Christ and his church'. Several years later, another sex scandal erupted in Austria. Police uncovered some forty-thousand pornographic photos, including child pornography, and numerous videos at the Catholic seminary in St Pölten, about eighty kilometres west of Vienna. This latest sex scandal forced the Church to close down the seminary in August 2004.[12]

A Belgian court ruled that Cardinal Godfried Danneels and a local bishop were responsible for abuse by Father Andre van der Lijn, who was convicted of molesting three boys over a period of several decades. The Church resisted demands to pay damages to the victims of the abuse on the grounds that a bishop is not a parish priest's 'employer'. The court, however, ordered the Cardinal and Bishop to pay damages to one of the victims. Other cases of sexual abuse of minors by Belgian Catholic priests have also been dealt with by the police.

In 2002 Brazilian Father Paulo Segio Maya Barbosa was arrested after he was caught performing oral sex on a fourteen-year-old in a parked car. Photographs of children, condoms and pornography were also seized from the car. Father Jose Ari Degrandis was sentenced to twenty-four years in prison for the rape of two women, one of whom was sixteen at the time of the rape. Reverend Nilo Cezar Martins is accused of raping a twelve-year-old altar boy during an assignment in Philadelphia, PA, in 1985. He was arrested, admitted the abuse, and was imprisoned. However, after six weeks he was deported to his home in Brazil. His lawyer and the Philadelphia Archdiocese said they lost track of Martins, who was later found to have returned to active ministry in the diocese of Nova Iguacu. Nineteen girls between the ages of ten and sixteen reported some type of sexual contact with Father Sabastiao Luiz Tomaz in exchange for clothes and money. Later the same year, Bishop Aldo Pagotto was denounced by the Public Ministry of Ceara for attempting to coerce this priest's victims into changing their testimony. By July 2002, twenty-one victims had come forward, and nine claims had been supported by medical evidence. Dozens more cases have been reported in Brazil.

A report on abuse at St Joseph's and St John's Training School for Boys in Canada includes the following testimony:

> I saw many young children beaten up and strapped. I saw Brother A wake up young children and take them to a room to sexually assault them. I saw children handcuffed to a pillar in the basement. They would be pushed and kicked. I saw Brother B use a pool table stick to hit children if they would not have anal sex with him. Children were given cold showers then strapped. If I told any Brothers that another Brother tried to have sex with me, I would be strapped.[13]

More than three hundred pupils were sexually abused by Catholic brothers at the Mount Cashel Orphanage, Newfoundland, run by the *Congregation of Christian Brothers* order in Canada. Orphans as young as six were tormented with belts and leather bridle straps. They were regularly raped in their beds an night and in the showers in the morning. When allegations of physical and sexual abuse started to surface in the late 1980s, the government, police and Church cooperated in attempting a cover-up. As in many other countries, the status of the Church enabled her to get away with such crimes, and for a long time she did. This affair only came to light when the media publicised it, after which the orphanage was closed down. The courts decreed that the order's assets be sold in order to compensate the victims. In December 2000, a Canadian paper reported that senior leaders of the *Christian Brothers* in Rome had transferred ownership of millions of dollars of the teaching order's assets out of Canada to prevent courts from sequestering them to pay compensation to the victims. An internal memo, dated 1990, prepared by a lawyer for the *Christian Brothers*, set out that 'Within the last few years, in order to make C.B.I. less of a target in any suit for damages, we have been incorporating each school as a separate corporate entity ... and transferring title to the school from C.B.I'.[ii] The Catholic order's school in the Bronx, 'All Hallows High School', sold the school building, which is valued at between three and ten million US dollars, to a separate 'All Hallows Institute' for the princely amount of ten dollars.[14] There were also allegations that the Catholic hierarchy in Vancouver tried to help the Christian Brothers shield the largest asset held by the Brothers.[15]

When Chilean Father Victor Carrera Triviño was accused of raping a thirteen-year-old girl in 2001, a Church tribunal ordered him to undergo therapy and quickly sent him abroad, transferring him to Italy. At the family's appeal, the Supreme Court of Chile granted an extradition request to have him brought back to stand trial in Chile. In 2002, Father Jose Aguirre Ovalle was charged with abusing several children at his parish in Quilicura, thirty kilometres south of Santiago. Following the public outcry that accompanied this case the Church issued an apology to the victims of child sexual abuse by priests. The Father Aguirre case followed accusations against five other priests which had been concealed by the Church for years.

In 1996, Father Adrian McLeish of Durham was jailed for six years. He had abused four boys aged between the ages of ten and eighteen – the sons of parishioners – and boasted about it on the internet. Police seized more than eleven thousand images on computer discs from the collection of child pornography at his home. The pattern of priests and lay

---

[ii] The Christian Brothers Institute is the headquarters of the order which is based in New Rochelle, NY. The order operates twenty-two high schools and elementary schools as well as a college.

brothers raping and sexually molesting the most vulnerable children in orphanages, children who have no one to turn to for help or support, was also repeated in England. Father Eric Taylor received a seven-year prison sentence for sexual offences against eighteen children at an orphanage run by the Catholic charity *Father Hudson's Homes*. In July 2002, Father James Murphy pleaded guilty to eighteen charges of indecent assault against seven children at South London Parishes from 1976 to 1990. Some of the victims were assaulted inside the church itself.

Cormac Murphy-O'Connor, as Bishop of Arundel and Brighton, allowed Michael Hill, a known paedophile, to continue working as a priest. The priest, who is suspected of having abused more than thirty children during the 1980s and 1990s, pleaded guilty in November 2002 to six charges of molesting boys over an eighteen-year period. He was later convicted of abusing nine children. The Pope has since elevated Murphy-O'Connor to be the Cardinal Archbishop of Westminster, the leader of the Catholic Church in England and Wales.

Father John Lloyd, former press spokesman for Archbishop Ward, was jailed for eight years for eleven indecent assaults, one rape, and a serious sexual offence. The court heard that he had sexually abused two teenage altar boys and a woman in her twenties during a ten-year period, and had raped a girl of sixteen whom he had befriended at a church youth club. The four complainants came forward as a result of his conviction last February for abusing a girl of thirteen within hours of baptising her. He was acquitted of seven counts of indecently assaulting children and four counts of rape while a parish priest between 1970 and 1988. The jury was unable to reach verdicts on nine further counts of indecent assault. Lloyd's former boss, Archbishop Ward, a former papal adviser and the highest-ranking Roman Catholic cleric in Wales, was not prosecuted in connection with allegations that he had committed sexual assault on a seven-year-old girl nearly thirty years ago. Ward, who also allegedly ignored reports that two priests close to him were serial abusers, was asked by the Pope to resign.

In France, Abbot Jean-Lucien Maurel was sentenced to ten years in prison for raping and sexually abusing three boys, aged ten to thirteen. Reverend Rene Bissey was convicted of raping and molesting eleven minors between 1996 and 1998, and sentenced to eighteen years in prison. The court also found his bishop, Pierre Pican of Baycaux, guilty of failing to inform police that a priest in his diocese had admitted sexual abuse against minors. For covering up and concealing evidence, Bishop Pican was given a three-month suspended sentence. In various court cases which took place between 1995 and 2002 in France, thirty priests were convicted of sexual abuse of minors.

German Auxiliary Bishop Franziskus Eisenbach of Mainz resigned in April 2002, eighteen months after a female university professor accused him of molesting her while performing an exorcism. The Vatican said that his resignation was no admission of guilt. In 2004, a victims' association representing children abused in German children's homes from 1945 to 1985, was established. Jean-Pierre de Picco, chairman of the association, told reporters that of the cases of abuse reported thus far, ninety per cent happened in Catholic children's homes. Picco, who lived at the *Holy Hedwig Sisters* Catholic boarding school from 1963 to 1972, which has since been closed, described nine years of fear due to continual physical and psychological abuse, including beatings with thorny branches, immersions in hot water until his skin was red and burnt, and sexual abuse: 'We were beaten and whipped bloody by the nuns, even for the smallest of infractions.'[16]

Michael Lau was defrocked in 1995 after an internal Church investigation in Germany found that he had twice molested a fifteen-year-old altar boy in the early 1990s. The assaults took place in a monks' dormitory, whilst Lau was a trainee priest. The Church, however, did not report her findings to the police. Some years later, a German court sentenced Lau, who pleaded not guilty, to a four-and-a-half-year jail sentence for two counts of indecent assault, one of attempted sodomy and one of gross indecency.

At the beginning of 2003, numerous cases were reported in the German press, three alone in the diocese of Essen, which in 2003 sent into retirement a fifty-seven-year-old priest suspected of paedophilia twenty-two years before. The other two cases stem from 1992 and 1999. In the Mainz diocese, a priest was accused of having repeatedly abused a fourteen-year-old boy in his care in the late 1980s. Another priest was being investigated for sexually assaulting a thirteen-year-old boy in 1998. Two priests in the Paderborn district were suspended on paedophilia charges and another two were suspended in Bavaria. When in 1978 the mother of a nine-year-old altar boy in Bavaria complained to the Church that his priest had sexually molested him, all the Church did was to hush it up. The priest was transferred to another parish and, lo and behold, was accused of similar behaviour in the new parish. The Vicar General in Würzburg listened to the family but offered neither help nor compensation. The priest was shielded by the Church.

In Ireland, *The Christian Brothers*, the *Oblates of Mary Immaculate* and the *Sisters of Mercy* have all issued public apologies for abuse inflicted over the years in their institutions. The Irish government launched an inquiry into allegations of abuse and a special key to compensation was worked out, based on the severity of the case. Cases of sexual abuse were grouped into three levels: victims of violent anal or vaginal penetration; victims made to masturbate a member of staff or perform oral-genital acts, and victims subjected to sexual kissing or indecent touching of private parts over clothing.[17]

After receiving complaints that Fr Donal Collins had measured the length of some twenty boys' penises on the pretext of ascertaining whether or not they were growing normally, he was transferred by the Bishop of Ferns in Southeast Ireland, Bishop Herlihy, from the secondary school at which he was the science teacher to pastoral ministry in London for a period of two years. When he came back in 1968, he was reappointed to a teaching post in St Peter's College, at which, six years later, he was also placed in charge of swimming lessons. Bishop Herlihy's reply to his secretary's queries on the re-appointment was 'hadn't he done his penance?'[18] Fr Collins continued to abuse pupils at his school, of which he was appointed principal in 1988. In 1998 Collins was sentenced to four years imprisonment.[19]

Herlihy's successor, Bishop Brendan Comiskey, resigned in April 2002, after apologising for not stopping a priest's abuse. The accused paedophile priest was the Rev. Sean Fortune. The Church has acknowledged that Fortune molested dozens of boys in the 1980s and 1990s.[20] Comiskey had been informed about Fortune's behaviour, but did nothing for six years before sending him to London for psychological counselling. Fortune was later transferred to another parish, resulting in new allegations of sexual abuse. Fortune was arrested after his abuse was reported to the police in 1995, and he committed suicide in 1999 shortly before he was to stand trial. Comiskey resigned the day before a BBC documentary on Fortune's abuse and Comiskey's failure to stop it was expected to air.

Another case in which it is alleged that senior Church officials transferred an abusive priest from parish to parish to cover up known criminal behaviour, is that of Father Brendan Smyth. Smyth was jailed in 1997 after admitting guilt in seventy-four cases of abuse against male and female children from the 1960s to the 1990s. Also in Ireland: Father Eugene Greene received a twelve-year sentence for abusing altar boys and in April 2002, Fr Noel Reynolds admitted that he had abused a hundred children.[21] Reynolds had been appointed chaplain to a hospital in 1997 despite complaints in 1995 about his inappropriate behaviour with children. Archbishop Sean Brady said that the Church regretted the way that it handled cases of sexual abuse by the clergy. In March 2006, a year after an Irish government inquiry identified more than a hundred allegations of child sexual abuse against twenty-one priests in the Ferns diocese, the archdiocese of Dublin has confirmed that more than a hundred of its priests have faced paedophile accusations since 1940. A judicial committee of investigation is to examine the handling of complaints by the Church.[22]

Juliusz Paetz, the Archbishop of Poznan, was accused by fellow priests of paying night visits to the lodgings of seminarians, cuddling up to young clerics in public and using an underground tunnel to pay unannounced visits to his targets.[23]

The Catholic order of *The Salesians of Don Bosco* disputes allegations that it transferred priests of the order, who were accused of sexual abuse, to other countries in which they were able to continue to abuse. In one such case, Father Frank Klep, who was convicted of child molesting in Australia and was wanted there for additional child abuse charges, was placed by the Catholic order in Samoa. When the media found out about Klep and questioned him about it, his response was 'I'd prefer to just leave it ... if I felt I was still a risk to their children, then I'd think differently.'[24]

However, dozens of priests who were no longer eligible to work in the United States have found sanctuary abroad. It appears that hundreds of priests who had been accused of abuse have been moved by the Church from country to country, allowing them to start new lives in unsuspecting communities and to continue working in church ministries. Paedophiles are unlikely to be quite objective about the extent of the risk that they pose to society. Their superiors who moved them, even after the eruption of the abuse scandal in 2002, should have known better.

Conservatives in the Church blame liberals for the clerical sexual abuse. They suggest that Vatican II had been too open and had resulted in too much tolerance within the Church. This notion is as absurd as the first attempts of the Vatican to blame American sexual permissiveness for the behaviour of her priests. The fact is that throughout her entire history, the Catholic Church has had a problem with predatory priests, priests taking advantage of the confessional to seduce penitents, priests who kept catamites[iii] and priests who sexually abused the young and the vulnerable. It is neither a new phenomenon nor a specifically American one. In some Catholic families, more than one generation has suffered abuse.[25]

The perfidy of the Church also lies in the mind games she plays with the abused faithful: victims are made to feel guilty for being abused. Barbara Blaine, who was told by Father Chet Warren from Chicago 'you are holier than the other girls', and who from the age of thirteen until she was seventeen was this forty-year-old clergyman's sexual playmate, had for many years believed that she 'had caused a good holy priest to sin'.[26] In many cases, the Church's power is used to prevent litigation. Paul Ciaramitaro was fifteen when he was taken by Father Joseph Birmingham to his bedroom in the rectory and forced into sex. Several years later, at the age of nineteen, Paul decided to see a lawyer about his rights. As soon as the Boston Archdiocese found out about it, a bishop was sent to put pressure on Paul's mother. It worked, Bishop Mulcahy threatened to cut the mother off if her son would not retract and brought

---

iii   Boys kept for homosexual practices.

with him the legal waiver which he demanded Paul to sign. The release waived Paul's rights ever to sue the Church for any claim related to Father Birmingham. 'What if I don't sign?' he asked his mother, 'You're out of the family.'[27] This Catholic mother had been brainwashed to be more loyal to the diocese which covered up the abuse, than to her own son. In one seven-year period at St Michael's in Lowell, Massachussets, the man whose activities Bishop Mulcahy and the rest of the Archdiocese were so eager to conceal had molested one hundred and twenty-eight boys. Olan Horne described his ordeal:

> Let me explain something to you. You're grabbing an eleven-year-old kid. You pull him to the floor. You grab him by the back of the head and take your cock, and stick it down his fucking throat. Got him by the back of the head doing it. Kid's fucking having a panic attack. And then this guy puts me on the floor with his knee in my back, you know, the guy's ejaculating all over my back, he's beating the shit out of me because I'm trying to get away … That's rape.[28]

'Leave the Church alone', Mr Saviano warned his son. From the age of twelve, Phil Saviano was regularly forced by Father David Holley to perform oral sex on him. Phil and three other victims tried to get the diocese to open up their files to the public. Phil's homosexuality and his warfare with the Church embarrassed his father and stepmother, who were both active in Church affairs. Again, the loyalty to the Church was stronger than the loyalty to his own son, who was so badly abused by a priest and so criminally neglected by the Church. Holley, who abused more than a hundred boys, was sentenced to two hundred and seventy-five years in prison. Only much later would Phil's father see the light and tell his son that he was proud of his efforts.[29]

Before Robert P. Scamardo from Houston, Texas approached the Church for compensation for sexual abuse, he actually fought claimants like himself on behalf of the Church. That was the ultimate psychological suppression of his own past. A past in which, as a fifteen-year-old boy representing the Catholic Youth Organization of Austin at a Catholic Conference in San Antonio, he was jumped, in the middle of the night, by the Rev. Dan Delaney, director for youth ministry for the Austin Diocese. The boy awoke to find Father Delaney, with whom he shared a room, on top of him, masturbating him. Unfortunately, Scamardo chose the wrong person to confide in. James Reese, the lay youth minister at Sacred Heart Parish in Austin, listened sympathetically and then sexually abused him too.

For five years, Scamardo defended the Diocese of Galveston-Houston against claimants of sexual abuse. He was considered friendly yet unyielding. Accusers were resisted and sent away quietly with as little money as possible. Scamardo denies the yarn spun by many Church officials, that confidentiality clauses in the settlements were inserted due to the demand of the victims. It was always the church – never the victims – which insisted on this clause. After five years of representing the Church against his co-victims, he was unable to bottle up the internal conflict between his own abuse and his work any longer. For twenty-seven years he had told no one about the abuse. He was married and had three children but felt unable even to tell his wife. Not surprisingly, the Church employed against him tactics which Scamardo himself had used against others. They pointed out that the statute of limitations meant that he was unable to win any compensation through a court of law and offered money to cover one year's counselling. The Church then upped their offer to US $50,000 and finally settled at US $250,000.

Fourteen nuns, one priest, a staff member and Bishop Thomas V. Daily, the retired bishop of Brooklyn who had served in the Archdiocese of Boston, are named as defendants in an abuse case which allegedly took place at the Boston School for the Deaf in Randolph, a suburb of Boston. The deaf and mute plaintiffs, former students at the school run by the *Sisters of St. Joseph of Boston*, said that they were raped, fondled, beaten, stuffed into lockers and had their heads submerged in toilets by nuns. Many of the students had their hands tied behind their backs for trying to use sign language, which was discouraged at the school in favour of oral communication. The abuse, which is the subject of a lawsuit, took place between the years 1944 and 1977, and the plaintiffs were aged between four and eighteen at the time. Their lawyer said that he also represented twenty-two other students who were willing to sue the defendants.[30]

Episcopal Culpability

The abuse was performed by sick people driven by lust. This does not justify their behaviour, nor does it decriminalise it. However, as much as one is shocked by the widespread criminal sexual abuse by Catholic clergy and religious, the true outrage is the criminal behaviour of the Catholic Church's hierarchy: the cover-up which was carried out by calculating officials of the Church. For decades the Church kept victims silent and fostered a culture where priests would not report the crimes of their fellow priests who were sexual predators. As they had for centuries, bishops and priests regarded priests who molested not as criminals but merely sinners. Their attitude was, according to former priest, Paul E. Dinter, as follows: 'If a priest was having sex with a boy it meant he was weak and gave in, it meant he should go to confession and not be weak again'.[31] In response to a question in a deposition asking why he never investigated to see if a child molester had molested other children, Bishop Daily, who from 1975 to 1984 was the senior bishop in the Archdiocese of Boston, said, 'I'm not a policeman, I am a shepherd. I am a pastor who has to go after the Lord's sheep and find them and bring them back to the fold and give them the kind of guidance and discipline them in such a way that they will come back.'[32]

Central to this issue is how widespread the abuse has been. In the Boston diocese alone, more than five hundred members of the clergy have been accused over the past sixty years. More than seven hundred priests have been dismissed in the US over a three-year period as a result of disclosures of abuse.[33] The case of the Diocese of Palm Beach, Florida illustrates what a troubled Church this is. Within a period of four years, two bishops resigned after admitting that they had sexually molested minors.[34] These are not just a few rotten apples, or a few misguided bishops who overlooked or who were too weak to handle the abuse in their dioceses. According to an *Associated Press* report which appeared in 2004, twenty-one Roman Catholic bishops, ten of them Americans, have resigned since 1990 in the context of sex scandals (see Appendix 2). Indeed, these are not just one or two pockets of abuse. It was a worldwide Church phenomenon, in which, to quote the Massachusetts Attorney General Thomas Reilly, 'they sacrificed the children for many, many years'.[35]

This sacrifice, this cold-blooded cover-up, is the Church's unforgivable crime. But even those who are inclined to forgive must ask themselves whether such cover-ups are not inherent in the Church structure and therefore likely to be repeated. There is no end to the number of cases one can describe. The following pages give an idea of their magnitude and severity.

When Rev. Paul Aube, told Rev. Hector Lamontange, the head priest in his Claremont, New Hampshire parish, in 1972, that he was having sex with a seventeen-year-old boy, the reaction was: 'Well, Paul, we're all human, you know. We all have weaknesses.' Having received that response, Aube continued to have sex with adolescent boys in his rectory. In 1975, he was caught by the police in a car with a boy, both with their pants down. Aube turned to his bishop for help and asked to leave parish work. His bishop, Odore Gendron, instead of removing him from parish work, transferred Father Aube to a parish in Rochester, New Hampshire, where he sexually abused at least seven more boys. The bishop also arranged with the police to hush the matter up. In 1981 the mother of a fifteen-year-old boy complained to the bishop that Father Aube was having sex with her son in his room in the church rectory. The bishop still refrained from notifying the authorities, as New Hampshire law requires. As in many other dioceses, this was not a one-off case, but a pattern of behaviour. It is one of many cases detailed in a report of the New Hampshire (NH) Attorney General's office. The report shows a leadership of the NH Catholic diocese which has known of sexual abuse of minors by some of its priests for years and helped cover it up, violating the state's child endangerment law. The NH grand jury report, presented in March 2003, described 'wilfully blind' Church leaders who tolerated decades of child abuse by rogue priests. It describes the NH diocese as one in which a 'conscious course of deliberate ignorance' was the rule.[36]

> The Church in New Hampshire fully acknowledges and accepts responsibility for failures in our system that contributed to the endangerment of children. ... We commit ourselves in a public and binding way to address every weakness in our structure.

Thus spoke John B. McCormack, the bishop of Manchester, New Hampshire, whose diocese was on the verge of having criminal proceedings against it filed by the state. The Diocese of Manchester publicly acknowledged that it had failed to protect children from sexually abusive priests. The Attorney General's office explained:

> It's quite clear that in the decades we looked at, the diocese's priority was to protect the reputation of the diocese in these matters and to avoid public scandal ... The diocese put the victims second. There was a train wreck of bad decisions in this case that were made by a great number of people in the diocese over a great number of years. That made it clear that this was the problem collectively of the institution, the diocese as an entity, rather than any one of its officials or any one of its priests.

As such, the prosecutors considered an indictment of the diocese which was responsible for the institutional decisions and the pattern of behaviour of its officials. A settlement was signed between the diocese and the state Attorney General in December 2002. The canon lawyer and professor of Church law at Washington Theological Union, James A. Coriden, commented 'This really, it's mind-boggling to me ... The possibility of criminal action against a diocese, that's big-time stuff. I can't imagine what brought them to this admission.' The Manchester diocese has agreed to an annual audit by the Attorney General's office for the next five years to ensure it is complying with its obligation to protect children from abusive priests. All diocesan officials and employees would report allegations of sexual abuse to law enforcement authorities. Any accused priest would be removed from any post that might put him in contact with minors. Moreover, under the settlement the diocese has to disclose publicly its records on priests accused of abuse.[37]

'I'm not lying!' is not what you expect a bishop to say at a church when he is saying Mass. New Hampshire Bishop John McCormack found himself in that very situation as he was noisily urged by parishioners to step down and accused of lying about a sexually delinquent priest he assigned to their parish. Bishop McCormack, who lamented to the Vatican that a prison sentence dealt to one abusive priest seemed inappropriate because other felons were 'serving much shorter sentences for very serious crimes', was, up to 1998, a senior aide to Cardinal Law of Boston.[38] In this position McCormack repeatedly disputed complaints of abuse from parents and victims. In one such case in 1987, McCormack – at the time secretary for ministerial personnel in the Boston Archdiocese – met Peter Pollard, who reported that as a sixteen-year-old altar boy he had been sexually abused by Rev. George Rosenkranz. Pollard told McCormack that after the kissing and fondling, Rosenkrantz had asked the sixteen-year-old altar boy to masturbate. McCormack chose to protect Rosenkranz and give him cover. Although Rosenkranz's Church file had the 1981 police report of the incident in which Rosenkranz was discovered having sex with a young man in a Sears Roebuck toilet, McCormack told Pollard that his account lacked credibility, that 'there is no sign that Father Rosenkranz is a sexually deviant personality', and that the priest had every right to remain in his parish.[39] Reverend McCormack, had the audacity to defend his priest and said that the sex was in his view consensual. He also stated that 'some individuals growing up formed relationships with George Rosenkrantz in which [Rosenkrantz] might have expressed affection, and they might have interpreted these acts as sexual involvement.'[40] Evidently, consensual sex of a priest with a 16-year-old altar boy is just fine according to Bishop McCormack and kissing, fondling and masturbating are simply expressions of affection by the priest and no more should be said about it.[41]

Church officials knew about the paedophile priests and, to avoid scandal, shuttled them from parish to parish. Additionally, some bishops had begun, already in the 1970s, to refer priests to therapists. Very often these were in-house therapists, sometimes even other priests. An external therapist, Dr Stayton, described a case in which the bishop had prescribed six meetings with the therapist for a child-molesting priest. After the six meetings, 'they transferred him to a high school someplace outside of his diocese, and they didn't ask me. I never had to make a report, I just had to turn in a bill. I would never have recommended that he go to a high school.'[42]

Not only did the diocese officials know, other priests also knew.[43] This would be referred to as 'fooling around with the kids'.[44] When Rev. Francis Delaney was told by the housekeeper of the rectory he shared with Geoghan, that 'Father Geoghan had some urchins up there letting them use the shower', Delaney confronted Geoghan, got a denial and did nothing more about it. Moreover, when accusations against Geoghan came up in 1979, Delaney questioned the credibility of the accuser, describing his paedophile colleague as 'an outstanding dedicated priest … a zealous man of prayer who consistently gives of himself in furthering the cause of Christ'.[45] Indeed, he certainly gave of himself.

In the case of Father Porter, who had pleaded guilty to forty-one counts of sexual assault, there was evidence that at least two of his colleagues saw the abusing priest in action and did not do anything about it. How many other priests actually saw the abuse with their own eyes and just looked the other way?

Monsignor William McCarthy walked in on Rev. George Rosenkrantz as he was having sex with Peter Pollard, a sixteen year old altar boy, in the church basement on Easter Sunday of 1967. Ever alert, the Monsignor asked his colleague to 'please put out the light when you are finished.'[46]

Complaints that the Rev. Robert V. Gale was molesting young boys first reached the attention of the Roman Catholic Archdiocese of Boston in 1979. There were more reports in 1981, 1983 and 1987. It was not until 1991 that the Archdiocese removed Father Gale from parish ministry. Then, Father Gale was allowed to live at another church where, in 1994, more accusations were made. Cardinal Law arrived in Boston in 1984 and in September of that year he was informed that another of his priests, Father Geoghan, was a child molester. His reaction was to move Geoghan from St Brendan's in Boston to St Julia's in Weston, Massachussets. Many more children were molested by Geoghan in the nine years before Law finally decided, in 1993, to remove him.[47]

Church records concerning five priests from the Archdiocese of Boston, who had been accused of sexual abuse by some two hundred and fifty people, have revealed that in many cases the Archdiocese had received complaints and chose to ignore them. Thus when in 1981, the Rev. George Rosenkranz was arrested after a security guard in a Sears Roebuck store discovered him having sex with a young man in a toilet, the case came to Bishop Daily. According to Daily's notes, Rosenkranz denied the accusations and Daily accepted his denial. Father Rosenkranz was allowed to return to his parish. In fact, complaints were handled in Boston by some of the highest-ranking archdiocesan officials: Bishop Thomas V. Daily, who in 1990 was appointed Bishop of the Brooklyn diocese; the Rev. John B. McCormack, who in 1998 was appointed Bishop of New Hampshire; and Bishop Robert J. Banks, who in 1990 was appointed Bishop of Green Bay, Wisconsin.

Seventy-one-year-old Father Shanley was indicted on ten counts of child rape and six counts of indecent assault and battery. He was accused of repeatedly molesting six boys while at St Jean's parish in Newton, Massachussets, from 1979 to 1989. Shanley, who was given a twelve- to fifteen-year prison sentence, had pleaded not guilty. Bishop Daily has admitted to having known of complaints against Father Shanley years before he was placed in a parish. In fact, in the late 1960s, a priest reported to the Archdiocese that a boy had told him that he had been masturbated by Father Shanley in his woodland cabin. He also had names and addresses of other possible victims. The Archdiocese, which had the letter on file, did not show any evidence of any follow up.[48] Bishop Daily admitted that he had failed to act in response to complaints that Father Shanley was making speeches endorsing sex between men and boys and was attending meetings of the North American Man-Boy Love Association. In 1977, Daily received information that Shanley had said in a speech that 'the adult is not the seducer; the kid is the seducer'. Bishop Daily, in a deposition he gave, also acknowledged that as early as 1974, he knew that Shanley was a 'troubled priest' in need of help. He was aware of the fact that Shanley was neither sent to a psychiatrist nor given professional help. In 1979, after complaints that he was promoting homosexuality, Shanley was transferred from his work with alienated youths to a regular parish. The Archdiocese did not inform the parish of the problems with Shanley and he was not restricted in activities with children. In 1983, Bishop Daily promoted Shanley to acting pastor. A year later, Cardinal Law made the man – about whom Bishop Daily had testified that he could not recall another priest he had had to deal with more often – permanent pastor. Again, the Archdiocese of Boston had no qualms in recommending an abusive priest to other dioceses. In 1990, with Shanley's Church file full of details of his abusive behaviour, Bishop Robert Banks, the deputy of Cardinal Law, wrote a letter in which he confirmed that Shanley was a priest in good standing in Boston. In 1997, the Archdiocese – which had already made financial settlements with victims of Shanley – did not object to Shanley's applying to become director of Leo House, a guest house run by the Catholic Church in New York.[49]

In the case of Edward T. Kelley, who had been caught having sex with a teenager in a car, Daily convinced the police to release the priest and let the Church handle the matter. The Church, having undertaken to deal with the problem, simply did nothing.

In July 1982, Bishop Daily met a family which had come to him to complain that the Rev. John J. Geoghan, who had admitted abusing seven boys in their family two years earlier, had been seen with young boys at an ice cream parlour in their neighbourhood. Daily, according to his own notes, admitted imprudence in giving Geoghan a new assignment in a parish near their neighbourhood and told the family that he 'would act responsibly now'. His 'responsible' action was to let Geoghan go on a two-month trip to Italy, and then reinstall him in the same parish.[50] Daily even supplied Geoghan with a recommendation to a programme at the North American College in Rome, 'He enjoys adequate social adjustment … The applicant to my knowledge has no personal problems that the administration should be aware of.' Daily's response to the question of why he had recommended Geoghan, who had already been accused of sexual abuse, was: 'Because I felt that he had been through a traumatic experience because of the letters and the accusations.'[51]

Father Birmingham was transferred to Salem in 1964 after complaints of child abuse at his previous parish and then from Salem to Lowell in 1970 for similar reasons. When five Salem mothers came, in 1970, to tell the chancery of the Boston Archdiocese of Birmingham's abuse of their children, they were warned by Monsignor John Jennings 'You know, ladies, you have to be very careful of slander.'[52] What this means is, 'if you talk we (the Catholic Church) will sue you'. Tom Blanchette was abused from the age of eleven and over several years by the family priest, Joseph Birmingham. The priest had first tried to rape him when he was eleven and developed a pattern of mutual masturbation and other sexual activities on the boy. Birmingham, it appeared, did not limit himself to only one son of the Blanchette family; he abused the other four brothers too. Years later, after Birmingham had died, Tom Blanchette had sought out Cardinal Law to tell him about the abuse. Cardinal Law was so worried that Blanchette might talk to others about this abusive priest that he used the following technique: Law laid his hands on Blanchette's head for two or three minutes and then said 'I bind you by the power of the confessional never to speak about this to anyone else.'[53] Research carried out in Ireland indicates that 'when victims reported their abuse and received an inadequate response from church authorities, they experienced re-traumatisation'.[54]

> I did not, as a matter of policy, in 1984, '85, '86, '87, '88, '89, '90, '91, '92, '93, '94, '95, '96, '97, '98, '99, 2000, 2001, go to parishes on the occasion of dealing with a priest against whom an allegation of sexual abuse of a child had been made. ... I see now that that should have been done, but we did not do that.[55]

In a compelling deposition, which was broadcast by television stations almost in its entirety, Cardinal Law, the senior Roman Catholic prelate in the United States and head of the Archdiocese of Boston, confessed that he had allowed priests accused of sexual abuse – and even those who admitted the abuse – to return to parish ministry without informing parishioners of the accusations or admissions. Outrageously, Cardinal Law's defence of child molesting Rev. Shanley, in response to a specific accusation that Shanley had molested a six-year-old boy, was that both the six-year-old boy and his parents had contributed to the abuse by being negligent.[56]

Cardinal Law also confirmed that decisions about abusive priests were motivated by other considerations in addition to the protection of children. To the question 'There have been other focuses, have there not, Cardinal Law?' and 'One of those has been to avoid scandal in the Church?' Law responded 'That's correct.'[57]

323

In November 2002, Judge Constance M. Sweeney of Suffolk County Superior Court confirmed that

> archdiocesan records obtained through discovery reveal that some offending priests may well have been assigned to parishes, youth groups and the like, even though the cardinal or other archdiocesan personnel knew that the priests in question were at the least suspected of engaging in continuing sexual encounters with children.[58]

Massachusetts Attorney General, Thomas F. Reilly, described the behaviour of the Boston Archdiocese:

> There was an elaborate scheme to keep it away from law enforcement and to keep it quiet. ... The leadership – and this is a leadership problem, a management problem – felt it was more important to protect the Church than children. And as a result of that, countless numbers of children were harmed. ... It certainly is a cover-up. At the very least you would expect a different approach from a religious institution, and that's not the case here.[59]

Reilly said that Church officials had developed an 'elaborate scheme' to keep sexual abuse by priests away from the attention of law enforcement officials. The Attorney General and a grand jury explored ways of prosecuting Church officials for mishandling the cases of abusive priests. The grand jury subpoenaed Cardinal Bernard F. Law and seven bishops who worked for him. Reilly issued a report following his investigation of the sexual abuse scandal of the Roman Catholic Archdiocese of Boston, showing that nearly eight hundred people had complained of being sexually abused by clergy members and workers in the Archdiocese since 1940. These abuses involved two hundred and fifty priests and other Church workers in a sixty-year period. Reilly, who says 'I have absolutely no doubt that the number is far greater',[60] spoke of the responsibility of former administrators (i.e. cardinals, bishops and priests) of the Archdiocese who 'chose to protect their own priests and the reputation of the institution rather than protecting children'.

Despite these findings, the Attorney General, who spoke of 'deliberate, intentional choices, and the choice is pretty clear: It was between protecting children and protecting the Church, the reputation of the Church and the clergy who abused children', is unable to bring charges against the top hierarchy of the Boston Archdiocese. The law in Massachusetts that lists 'mandated reporters' of child sexual abuse, was not expanded to include priests until 2002. 'I believe they knew, they were aware they were under no legal obligation to report', Reilly said in the news conference, adding 'they took advantage of that exemption'.[61] The report detailing the roles of the top hierarchy of the Archdiocese considered Cardinal Law and two of the senior bishops as those mainly responsible. Bishop Daily, chief deputy to the cardinal from 1976 to 1984, who, like his fellow senior leaders in the Archdiocese, did not report abuses to the authorities, had a 'clear preference' for keeping abusers in ministry by quietly moving them to new parishes instead of banishing them, it said. Bishop Murphy, chief deputy to the Cardinal from 1993 to 2001, obviously understood the need to help the abusive priests and even established a supervised residence programme for abusive priests. However, according to the report, Murphy considered sexual abuse to be mainly a pastoral problem and not a criminal one. He, thus, 'continued to place a higher priority on preventing scandal and providing support to alleged abusers than on protecting children from sexual abuse'.

Sixteen years after Cardinal Roger M. Mahony had been told by one of his priests, Father Michael Stephen Baker, that he had molested young boys and only after the Los Angeles police had arrested Baker, did the Cardinal come out with his sentimental insight: 'My heart aches with the pain and suffering endured by victims of sexual abuse by clergy', he said. 'Sexual abuse is a crime as well as a terrible sin. As Pope John Paul II has said, "There is no place in the priesthood or religious life for those who would harm the young."' In 1986, when Baker had told his Cardinal of his crimes, Baker was sent for treatment and then was reassigned to another parish.[62] For sixteen years Mahony knew that one of his priests had orally raped a nine-year-old in the church rectory. Did this Cardinal not understand the gravity and depravity of such action? Did he have to wait for the Pope to instruct him that 'there is no place in the priesthood' for such a man?

Two retarded brothers who had lived for nearly thirty years at the *Sacred Heart Jesuit Center* – a retirement home for some sixty priests in Los Gatos – and worked there as dishwashers, were repeatedly subjected to sodomy, molestation and false imprisonment by some of the inmates for almost thirty years. As usual, the Catholic Church hushed it up. One of the perpetrators, Father Burke, was, in April 2000, relocated by his superiors at *Sacred Heart* after admitting to having had sexual contact with one of the victims. The law enforcement authorities were kept in the dark about the fact that priests at this home had sexually molested these two retarded brothers for years.

In Connecticut, Edward Egan, former Bishop of Bridgeport, regularly allowed priests who were accused of sexually abusing minors to remain in their positions. In a 1999 deposition, referring to a priest who had been accused by twelve former altar boys of rape, molestation and beating, he shamelessly and heartlessly said 'Allegations are allegations … Very few have even come close to having anyone prove anything.' When confronted by the lawyer with the admission of the priest that 'he had oral sex with this young boy and that he actually bit his penis and advised the boy to go to confession elsewhere', Egan cynically responded, 'Well, I think you are not exactly right … It seemed to me that the gentleman in question was an eighteen-year-old student at *Sacred Heart University*.'[63] As if that would make it right, acceptable, moral or legal. A year later, the Pope, always in need of those prepared to do ceaseless battle for the Church, promoted this arrogant man – who suggested that the abusive priest was but a figment of the imagination of his twelve accusers – to lead the Archdiocese of New York. Some get raped; others, who look the other way, are made cardinal. Three years later, in his Palm Sunday sermon of 2002, when the story of abuse and of massive cover-up by the Church hierarchy was already public knowledge, Cardinal Egan sought to belittle the matter with the following: 'With war and terrorism and sexual abuse on our mind, we all know that we are all sinners and we are all expected by our God to do penance.'[64] Under the Cardinal's broad brush all of his misdeeds and those of his fellow clergymen are covered by the general Catholic view of the world: we are all sinners from the moment we are born and when we grow up, some of us wage war or become terrorists and others become child molesting priests. Is, however, 'we are all sinners' an acceptable excuse for the Church's cover-up?

Role of Bishops Investigated

Twelve priests, one religious brother and the Diocese of Brooklyn were sued on behalf of forty-two adults, most of them former altar boys, who accused Roman Catholic clergy members in Brooklyn of groping, raping and abusing them when they were children. The abuse took place over decades in churches, rectories and on weekend retreats. However, the suit also asserted that Bishop Thomas V. Daily and his predecessors, going back at least fifty years, threatened and misled victims and their families, effectively preventing suits from being filed.[65] In their enquiries into whether Catholic bishops had endangered children by ignoring the crimes, district attorneys all over the USA introduced grand juries to obtain personnel and other records from Catholic dioceses and to compel bishops and priests to testify. The US political system, which, for years, has held the Catholic Church in reverence, has now, to some extent, gone to the other extreme, bringing about a very wide and intensive inquiry into the operations of the Catholic Church.

In Long Island, a Church official, in response to a question about an abused child, responded 'It's not my responsibility to worry about the boy. My job is to protect the bishop and the church.' At the same diocese, which had a team run by two lawyer-priests, one such lawyer-priest explained that meeting the victim was a waste of time because the statute of limitations on the abuse had expired. Monsignor John A. Alesandro, a member of the team, at a meeting with a victim who had come to talk about his abuse, started the meeting with the words 'You know, the statute of limitations has run out.'[66]

Unfortunately, the legislators had not foreseen the need for laws which would make it a criminal offence for a bishop to transfer child molesting priests from one parish to another. Bishops may be held for obstruction of justice, endangering child welfare or even conspiracy. In Westchester County, New York, a grand jury concluded an inquiry by accusing the Church of cover-ups and urging state lawmakers to eliminate the statute of limitations on child sexual abuse cases.

'The grand jury finds the actions of diocesan officials who were responsible for making and implementing policy reprehensible' is what the Suffolk County grand jury concluded. It spent nine months investigating the Diocese of Rockville Centre, a Long Island diocese – the sixth largest in the US – with 1.3 million Catholics in a hundred and thirty-four parishes in Nassau and Suffolk Counties. According to their one-hundred-and-eighty-page report, Church officials protected at least fifty-eight paedophile priests for decades. To that end they employed sham policies and a bogus 'intervention team' to trick and silence victims, cover up crimes, avoid scandals and minimise financial consequences. The report speaks of a Church that purported to help victims of sexual abuse but instead intimidated the victims to avoid lawsuits and publicity. In fact, the Catholic Church ran a deception programme.[67]

The sex-offending priests were shuffled from parish to parish and often allowed to minister to children. Abusive priests were protected under the guise of confidentiality and their histories were mired in secrecy. Thus, when an abusive priest was transferred to a new parish, his records did not go with him. Already in the mid-1980s, the diocese established an Office of Legal Affairs which was internally known as the 'intervention team'. Victims and their family members were immediately put in touch with a priest who, unbeknown to them, was also a lawyer. An internal memorandum of 1993 specifically instructed all diocesan officials referring victims not to divulge the fact that the priests were also lawyers. This team of three, of which two were high-ranking lawyer-priests, met with victims and their families supposedly to discuss possible avenues of action. 'In reality', the grand jury said, 'the office and the intervention team had one purpose, protecting the diocese'. The 'intervention team' treated crimes of priests as sins which were not to be reported to law enforcement officials. The team ignored any recommendations for psychiatric treatments. Their job was to suppress legal claims and to do this, the grand jury reported that the team employed

aggressive legal strategies ... [to] defeat and discourage lawsuits, even though diocesan officials knew they were meritorious. ... Victims were deceived, priests who were civil attorneys portrayed themselves as interested in the concerns of victims and pretended to be acting for their benefit while they acted only to protect the diocese.[68]

Of all cases investigated by the grand jury, they found only one in which a priest was defrocked. His crime? Having an affair with an adult woman! Suffolk County District Attorney, Thomas J. Spota, added,

> High-ranking prelates protected 58 colleagues from disgrace rather than protecting children from these predator priests. … Time after time, and despite overwhelming evidence that priests were committing crimes against children, they were willingly sacrificing the truth for fear of scandal and for monetary considerations.

Joanne C. Novarro, a spokeswoman for the Rockville Centre Diocese, called the grand jury report unfair.[69] William A. Donohue, president of the Catholic League for Religious and Civil Rights reacted 'Spota is atypical … I resent the fact that … Spota is being awarded medals for engaging in a wild goose chase.'[70]

Bishop Manuel D. Moreno of Tucson, Arizona retired three years before the age at which bishops tender their resignation. He had been in ill health for some time, but the true reason for his resignation and the Pope's acceptance of it was the state of his diocese. When he resigned in March 2003 the Tucson diocese was on the verge of bankruptcy.

In January 2002, the diocese paid US $14 million to settle eleven sexual abuse lawsuits involving several priests. One of the abusing priests was Monsignor Robert Trupia, who was accused of multiple abuses of young people and who was suspended by Moreno in 1992. Prior to that, Bishop Moreno had apparently been blackmailed by Monsignor Trupia to allow him to remain in ministry by threatening to reveal an affair Trupia had had with the late Bishop James S. Rausch of Phoenix.

Expert witness, Rev. Doyle, considered the cover-up by Bishop Moreno to be 'probably the most flagrant, well-documented, exasperating case of cover-up that I've ever seen, and I've seen a lot of them.' According to Doyle, if the cases had gone to trial, they would have been more damaging to the Church than the infamous cases in Boston. The documents in the case were so explosive that all parties were required to return them to ensure confidentiality.[71]

To avoid prosecution further to a grand jury investigation, the Bishop of Phoenix, Arizona, Thomas J. O'Brien, signed an agreement admitting that he knew of accusations of sexual abuse by priests and that he had transferred them without telling their new superiors or parishioners. At least fifty Church leaders in the diocese have been accused of inappropriate sexual contact with minors.

The Maricopa County prosecutor, Richard M. Romley explained: 'Why did I choose immunity in turn for an agreement? ... The No. 1 priority is to stop abuse and protect children in the future. Those who actually committed crimes were charged yesterday. In all likelihood, the bishop would have remained even if I had charged him.' The Bishop, who, according to Romley, only gave slow and grudging cooperation to the investigators, was granted immunity. 'Obstruction of justice is a low-level felony that more than likely would have meant probation', Romley said. 'We had been told that even if the bishop had wanted to resign, Rome would not allow it. That is, if he had been indicted, he would remain.'[72]

Reverence of the Law Enforcers

For years the Church enjoyed and took advantage of the respect and sometimes even the complicity of law enforcement agencies, politicians and the judiciary. The priesthood has over centuries been used to living in a very supportive culture. Dr Eugene Kennedy, a psychologist at Loyola University of America and a former priest explains: 'a fellow got a lot of cover just for wearing a Roman collar'.[73]

The following examples of cases already referred to, demonstrate the reverence with which the Church was treated by the police. In 1975, two Nashua, New Hampshire police officers caught Father Aube and a boy with their pants down in a car. Bishop Gendron 'contacted the Nashua police chief and asked him for a favour by making sure that there was no record of the incident'. The police chief agreed and there never was a police report.[74] In 1981, the Rev. George Rosenkranz was arrested after a security guard discovered him having sex with a young man in a restroom in a Sears Roebuck store. Bishop Daily, who dealt with the matter, added a comment in his notes that the police might not have arrested Rosenkranz had they known that he was a priest.[75] In a separate case Bishop Daily intervened in 1977 after police officers caught a priest, the Rev. Edward T. Kelley, having sex with a teenage boy in a car. The police called the Archdiocese, and Bishop Daily came to the police station and agreed with the police chief that the matter would be handled by the bishop. According to the testimony of a police officer, Bishop Daily undertook to have Father Kelley sent for treatment. This never happened and Father Kelley has been accused of molesting more boys from the 1960s to the 1980s.[76] In Ireland, the *Ferns Report* found that Cannon Clancy, who is alleged to have raped a great many girls between the ages of nine and fifteen over a thirty-year period, was able to do so when 'at various points in time during that period, members of the Gardai,[iv] the teaching profession, the medical profession and the Church were aware of rumours and suspicions concerning [him] but no action was ever taken against him'.[77]

[iv] Irish police.

Even the courts appear to have proffered deference and some US courts have held the Church immune from prosecution for the negligent hiring and supervision of priests who engage in sexual abuse. In a 1997 decision of the Wisconsin Supreme Court, it rejected a claim that the Church had negligently supervised a hospital chaplain accused of sexually assaulting a woman. The court said that it would 'excessively entangle the court in religious affairs, contrary to the First Amendment'.[78] When the lawyers for the plaintiffs in an abuse case in Rhode Island demanded that the Church turn over relevant documents, the diocese steadfastly refused to do so, citing First Amendment rights to religious freedom.

The Rhode Island courts upheld the Church's position until July 2002, when a Superior Court justice ruled that the First Amendment could not be construed as a blanket shield. It is noteworthy that the judge, Justice Robert D. Krause, felt the need to validate his ruling by pointing to the American bishops' own acknowledgment at their June meeting in Dallas that the Church and her flock had been hurt by a culture of secrecy. Moreover, he wrote: 'Insistence upon disclosure emanated not only from those not associated with the Church, but indeed from bishops within the Church as well.'[79] Did the US courts really believe that the religious freedom in the First Amendment to the Constitution of the USA was about granting freedom for Catholic clergy to molest and abuse without interference from the state? Or were these judges so awe-inspired by the mighty institution of the Church that they were prevented from thinking straight?

Martha Coakley, a district attorney from Massachusetts, referring to the deference that society – including politicians, police and prosecutors – showed the Catholic Church, said: 'There was an aura around priests that protected them, and that protection extended to sexual abusers.'[80] Many of these politicians, police officers and prosecutors were members of the Catholic Church themselves. Thus the Church contaminated her members and corrupted them, preventing them from acting morally and from carrying out their legal and professional duties. Massachusetts lawmakers refused to include clergy in the bill of 1983 which requires a very wide and inclusive list of professions (police officers, teachers, doctors, social workers etc.) to report suspected child abuse. At the time seventy-five per cent of them were members of the Catholic Church. And the Church wouldn't have it. In fact, she continued with the same dogged determination to fight any attempts to include clergy as mandatory reporters.[81]

In 1984, a judge in Massachusetts gave a priest, who had admitted to anally raping a thirteen-year-old altar boy, probation on the condition he not be allowed to work with children. It is not surprising that Cardinal Law – knowing that judges, like him, seemed unperturbed by priests who rape thirteen-year-old boys – disregarded the condition and posted the rapist priest to a new diocese. In 1991, a judge who was asked by state prosecutors to grant a search warrant for the home of a priest who was accused of child molesting, refused the request on the grounds that he considered it outrageous for police to search a home of a priest.

In fact, the report of 1985, *The Problem of Sexual Molestation by Roman Catholic Clergy*, admitted that, for many years, the Church had been used to receiving protection from Roman Catholic judges and district attorneys. It warned, however, that 'our dependence in the past on Roman Catholic judges and attorneys protecting the Diocese and clerics is GONE'. Bishops were warned by the report's authors that they could no longer rely on the justice system to miscarry justice in their favour. And yet, in Catholic areas such as Boston, as late as 1996, judges still impounded all the records in lawsuits involving sex-abusing priests to prevent the details from reaching the general public.[82]

Many raised the question of continued reverence for the Church when the Nassau County District Attorney, Denis E. Dillon, decided that, as all of the abuse allegations against the Diocese of Rockville Centre were past the criminal statute of limitations, nothing more was to be done (in contrast to his colleague the District Attorney of Suffolk County who had convened a grand jury to investigate that very diocese). Mr Dillon, it turned out, was for many years affiliated to the ultra conservative and extremely powerful Catholic lay group, Opus Dei.[83]

Legal Wrangling

Advice, which would not have been out of place at an organised crime conference, was given in a speech given by Bishop A. James Quinn, an attorney and auxiliary bishop of Cleveland, to the Midwest Canon Law Society. In his speech, entitled *NCCB Guidelines and Other Considerations in Pedophilia Cases*, he said: 'Standard personnel files should contain no documentation relating to possible criminal behaviour'[84] and added 'If there is something there you really don't want people to see, you might send it off to the Apostolic Delegate, because they have immunity to protect something that is potentially dangerous, or that you consider to be dangerous.' Quinn must have belatedly understood what a bombshell this advice was and set out to deny it, although he could not deny having said the words, as the speech was recorded and transcribed. Instead, he did the next best thing (other than perhaps sending himself to the safety of the Vatican Embassy). He denied that he suggested sending documents connecting a priest to allegations of sexual misconduct. 'The use of the word "dangerous" could be anything. It could be a confessional matter ... It could be a matter that doesn't belong in the file.' It is more likely that Bishop Quinn was reintroducing an idea, which the report *The Problem of Sexual Molestation by Roman Catholic Clergy* of 1985 had already ruled out as too risky: 'In all likelihood such action would ensure that the immunity of the Nunciature would be damaged or destroyed by the civil courts.'[85]

The Catholic Church is battling hard against the interference of the secular courts. To this end, the Church employs any instrument she can: from direct bullying of those abused by her priests up to formal arguments maintaining that the first amendment to the US constitution should prevent courts from gaining access to Church documents about child-molesting priests. In court cases, they have tried to claim that the Church was not responsible for the actions of her bishops and cardinals and when she agreed to pay compensation, she enforced confidentiality agreements on the abused.[86]

Should the Church really countersue a single mother whose two sons, aged seven and ten, were molested by a parish sacristan in Hawaii, charging that it was the mother, rather than the Church who was negligent? Should lawyers acting for the Church in Illinois in examining an abuse victim in court, not only ask him to describe the abuse in detail but also enquire whether he had perhaps enjoyed it?[87] Did the Church expect that the ejaculatory pleasure derived by a boy as he was fellated by a priest should quash the claim for compensation, or did the Church's legal advisors suggest that – as, after all, pleasure should be paid for – at least a discount might be agreed?

Boston's archdiocese claimed that it was not legally responsible for paying the Geoghan case because it was not specifically named as a defendant. The judge rejected the claim, explaining that as Boston's Cardinal Law was one of the defendants, the Archdiocese would be responsible. Even more outrageous was Cardinal Egan, who tried to convince a Connecticut court that the Church was not responsible for the actions of a priest, as priests were self-employed contractors working for autonomous parishes. 'Egan tried to present the Catholic Church as a McDonald's franchise' said the victim's lawyer. Taking a lead from the Cardinal's line, lawyers acting for the Church in yet another abuse case, argued that priests were not employees, but men called by God.[88]

Seeking another way out, the Archdiocese of Boston requested the court to dismiss all the sexual abuse lawsuits against it on religious freedom grounds. The First Amendment, the Archdiocese said, does not permit courts to tell churches how to conduct their internal affairs, including the questions of where to assign priests and how to discipline them.[89] The Archbishop of Los Angeles, Cardinal Mahony, or as referred to by the *New York Times* 'The Stonewalling Shepherd', vehemently resisted court orders to disclose Church personnel documents to criminal investigators. The Archdiocese claims that 'confidentiality between priest and bishop is paramount to the free exercise of religion'.[90]

More than sixty per cent of Rhode Island's population of about one million is Catholic. As such, it is the 'most' Catholic state in the USA. For some ten years the Church hindered a legal case in which eleven priests and one nun were accused by thirty-eight plaintiffs of sexual abuse. The diocese steadfastly refused to turn over documents in the case, citing First Amendment rights to religious freedom. The Rhode Island courts upheld the Church's position until they were overruled in July 2002.

Judge Constance M. Sweeney of Suffolk County Superior Court accused the Archdiocese of Boston of toying with the court. The Archdiocese's motion, for the court to seal eleven thousand documents of records on priests and not make them available to the public, according to the judge, 'appears designed to escape the full force of the court's multiple orders to produce documents and that these documents be opened to public inspection'. The judge also criticised the Archdiocese for the fact that the Church had seemingly produced the documents to opposing counsel only at the last minute and only under a warning of sanctions and contempt.

All in all, although she promised cooperation, the Church instead hired armies of lawyers who, according to Michael Allen (who was investigating the Archdiocese of Cincinnati), spent their time 'trying to come up with ways not to cooperate'.

Reaction of US Bishops' Conference

In early 2002, the US bishops knew that something had to be done to avoid total meltdown of the Catholic Church in America. Over the previous twenty years, more and more secret deals were done with victims who had sued their dioceses. The victims received financial compensation but all documentation was sealed and the victims were sworn to secrecy. The sexual abuse had already cost the Church hundreds of millions of dollars and there seemed to be no end to the claims which were unfolding all over America. Some of the compensation was covered by the Church's insurance, but not all, and they often had to sell Church properties to cover the payments.[91] A side-effect of the abuse scandal was an immediate drop in donations to the Catholic Church in America. The Archdiocese of Boston, for example, had to cut its budget by forty per cent in 2002. Not only have donations to the Cardinal's Appeal, the Archdiocese's annual fund-raising drive, dropped but their bank had also cut off their line of credit. In their plight, US archdioceses began investigating the possibility of declaring bankruptcy. By 2004, two had already filed for bankruptcy to bring to a halt the financial haemorrhaging resulting from the compensation deals that had been agreed.[92] Two additional dioceses followed suit in 2006.[93]

Across the country, Church leaders have been acknowledging their failure to take action against priests accused of sexually molesting children. In June 2002 the United States Conference of Catholic Bishops decided on a Charter for the Protection of Children and Young People, the national sexual abuse policy that calls for the removal from ministry of every priest who has committed even one confirmed act of sexual abuse. It was also agreed to report every abuse accusation against priests to government authorities, to conduct background checks on all Church employees who work with children, to establish abuse prevention programmes and to appoint special ministers to help abuse victims as well as lay committees, known as review boards, to assess accusations against priests. To oversee the bishops' compliance with the new policies it formed a sexual abuse review board composed of Catholic laypeople and headed by the Governor of Oklahoma, Frank Keating.

Members were chosen from those close and sympathetic to the Catholic Church. The only abuse victim on the board was a former priest who was working for the Church in the victim assistance ministry for the Archdiocese of Chicago. Governor Keating set off with an upbeat statement suggesting that the board could seek the prosecution of 'criminally sanctionable bishops'. He very quickly qualified that statement, saying such responsibility rested first with local diocesan review boards, but that if necessary, 'then yes, we will get involved'.[94] It did not take long for Governor Keating to be systematically censored by the very body which elected him. His comments that parishioners could withhold contributions or attend Mass in another diocese if bishops failed to comply with the new policy were not well received by some in the Catholic hierarchy. In Boston, where contributions had fallen dramatically, the Boston Archdiocese's newspaper, *The Pilot*, accused Keating of 'in effect calling all Catholics in a diocese to commit a mortal sin'. The bishops also revealed their hand with the choice of the one psychiatrist to the board; they chose a man who had testified on behalf of accused sexual abusers.[95]

And yet, even after the scandal had erupted, some of the bishops considered going to the police to be an unacceptable option. Bishop Doran, chairman-elect of the American bishops' canon law committee, said at that Dallas meeting, that his fellow bishops would be 'fools' if they voted to forward all accusations against priests to civil authorities. 'If we do this, we rat out our priests, and I'm not in favour of that.'[96] Nor did the situation seem grave enough for the Church administration and hierarchy to give up their summer holidays, as is evident from the response of the bishops' conference spokesman, Monsignor Francis J. Maniscalco, to the request of the review board to obtain reports on what had been done to implement the new policy within a month. Monsignor Maniscalco explained that it was unrealistic to expect a survey of one hundred and ninety-four dioceses so soon, given the August vacation slowdown.

The new buzzword was 'zero-tolerance'. This, in turn, created situations such as that of a fifty-five-year-old priest, who, over twenty years before, had sex with a sixteen-year-old, confessed to it four years ago, and was fired from his job. He was much loved by his community and appreciated by his Bishop, and some considered this to be too harsh. Some even went so far as to think that if the community wished to retain this priest they should have the power to do so. It is notable that the bishops who voted to remove from priestly duties a priest accused of even one act of sexual abuse took no steps to punish their colleagues, bishops and cardinals who had transferred sexual predators from parish to parish. They refrained from holding themselves and other Church leaders accountable for their failure to keep abusive priests from coming into contact with more children. In November 2002, the US bishops discussed and agreed their final policy document with regard to sexual abuse. Under Vatican pressure the zero-tolerance policy was shelved and it was decided that priests accused of abuse would be judged by Church tribunals. At the discussions, Archbishop Elden F. Curtiss of Omaha called for the bishops to censure the actions of bishops who had 'transferred priests accused of sexual abuse of minors from parish to parish'. The Bishops' Conference, however, would not go further than agreeing to regional groups of bishops which would provide one another 'fraternal support, fraternal challenge and fraternal correction'. Disciplining and demoting bishops is the sole prerogative of the pope, even at the price of molested children.

There were attempts to sabotage the Bishops' Conference anti-abuse moves. Rev. Canice Connors, as Franciscan president of The Conference of Major Superiors of Men, an umbrella organisation of the religious orders, was seemingly unable to understand the public interest in the Church scandal and attacked the media for making the clergy 'a legitimized target population for venomous language and violent action'. Connors considered it inappropriate for the Church to adopt the term 'zero tolerance', seeing it as a 'war slogan'.[97] Does Connors want tolerance for rapist priests? He criticised the media attention paid as a 'continuous graphic, public portrayal of abusive priest criminals, sometimes aided and abetted by Episcopal malfeasance'.[98]

In May 2003, the bishops of California, led by Cardinal Roger M. Mahony of Los Angeles, met in private and unanimously passed a resolution saying that they would not fill out the surveys for a study that the American bishops themselves had commissioned to assess the extent of the abuse problem in the church.[99] In reaction to this attitude of the Californian hierarchy, Governor Keating, as head of the national review board looking into the priest sexual abuse scandal, has said in an interview with the *Los Angeles Times* (June 2003) that members of the Church's hierarchy were acting like *La Cosa Nostra*. He named Cardinal Roger M. Mahony of Los Angeles as an example of a bishop who was resisting the panel's demands for complete information about the extent of the abuse in their dioceses. Mahony was not amused. His spokesman said 'Comparing the Church to an organization that kills people and deals drugs, that is just way out of line.'[100] Evidently, the Archdiocese of Los Angeles considered an organisation which has for decades run a cover-up of its officials' criminal sexual abuse of minors to be well in line. These remarks of the board's chairman, who had throughout his tenure been vocal in his criticism of the uncooperative attitude of intransigent bishops, did not go down well with his colleagues on the board. Keating was pushed to resign his post several days after he gave his interview to the *Los Angeles Times*. In his resignation letter, addressed to Bishop Wilton D. Gregory, president of the Bishops Conference, Keating pointed out that the Church:

> is not a criminal enterprise, ... It does not condone and cover up criminal activity. It does not follow a code of silence. My remarks, which some bishops found offensive, were deadly accurate. I make no apology. To resist grand jury subpoenas, to suppress the names of offending clerics, to deny, to obfuscate, to explain away; that is the model of a criminal organization, not my Church.[101]

Vatican Reaction

In 1998, nine ex-members of the priestly order, *The Legionnaires of Christ*, attempted to file a canon law suit with the Congregation for the Doctrine of the Faith (CDF) against Father Marcial Maciel Degollado, founder of that conservative order. Maciel had already been investigated by the Church for abuse and for a while he was suspended. The secretive CDF will not divulge the reasons for not proceeding with the case. One of his accusers, Felix Alarcon, wrote a letter which explained why he had remained silent for so long.[102] Another, Juan Vaca, told how at the age of twelve, he was called at night to Maciel's room, and

> In the bedroom, Maciel spoke of pains in his internal organs. He said, 'Rub me, rub me,' and made a circle on his stomach to show me, ... I was trembling. I was frightened, but I began rubbing. He said, 'Do it lower, lower.' Maciel got an erection. I didn't know anything about masturbation. I was on the verge of puberty. He moved my hand to his penis. I was terrified. Finally he was relieved and he faked being asleep.[103]

At a ceremony which took place in Rome in November 2003, the Vatican's Secretary of State, Cardinal Angelo Sodano, embraced Maciel and said 'Dear Father, I have seen the great work that you do.' Maciel, who is accused of abusing scores of youngsters in his institutions, not surprisingly thanked the Cardinal for the support he has shown the Legionnaires. Does the Church not continue to abuse these victims when her cardinals show public support for people accused of abuse? What really is the message regarding sexual abuse which emanates from the Vatican?

When, in August 2003, a secret Vatican document, *Crimen Sollicitationis*, came to light, Church spokesmen and canon lawyers hastened to emphasise that it was not a 'smoking gun', proof of a cover-up of sex abuse orchestrated by Rome. The document of 1962 may, however, explain the global uniform conduct of the senior Catholic hierarchy in keeping sexual abusers hidden in the Church's closet. The document, which was issued by the Church's Holy Office (the CDF), establishes a procedure for cases in which priests are accused of abusing the confessional to sexually proposition penitents. The document also includes four paragraphs concerning *crimen pessimum*, the worst crime. These are described as obscene acts perpetrated by a cleric with 'youths of either sex or with brute animals (bestiality)'.

So secret was the document, which was sent to all Catholic bishops, that it was never published in the official Vatican bulletin, *Acta Apostolicae* and bishops were instructed not to comment on it and to store it in the secret archives of their respective dioceses. The strictest form of Church secrecy, 'secret of the Holy Office', today known as pontifical secrecy, was imposed on all cases. Violation of this secrecy is punishable by excommunication. The Church expected even the victims to be sworn to secrecy at the time of making a complaint to Church officials.

Whatever explanation the Church may have for the procedures set out in this document, the fact is that bishops were instructed to keep cases of sexual abuse by priests secret at all costs. It may not be an 'instruction manual on how to deceive and how to protect paedophiles' as suggested by one of the lawyers acting for abuse victims.[104] It is, more likely, aimed at damage limitation for the Church, without much regard for the victims of abuse. If a bishop or cardinal had referred an abuse case to the police, he might, in fact, have violated the secrecy to which he was bound by Rome. Monsignor Francis Maniscaldo, spokesman for the US Conference of Catholic Bishops, said that the document was taken out of context and that 'it is not telling the bishops in any way about how to handle these crimes when they are considered as civil crimes'.[105] If that is so, why did not one of them report the crimes? Was Boston Cardinal Law not following the instructions of the Vatican, in *Crimen Sollicitationis*, when he met abuse victim Tom Blanchette and laid his hands on Blanchette's head for two or three minutes and then said 'I bind you by the power of the confessional never to speak about this to anyone else'[106]?

Moreover, not only in its instructions to bishops, but by direct action, or rather inaction, is the Vatican guilty of a cover-up. When the nun and physician Maura O'Donohue of the Roman Catholic Aid Agency, CAFOD, prepared a report on the rape of nuns by priests, she must have expected the shocking information contained in the report to trigger immediate papal action. In her report the author cites cases in which priests and missionaries forced nuns to have sex with them and in several instances not only raped but also obliged the nuns to have abortions. In one case a mother superior, who repeatedly complained to her local bishop that priests in his diocese had made twenty-nine of her nuns pregnant, was removed from her position by the bishop. The report, which was written and shown to the Vatican in 1994, covers cases in twenty-three countries in Africa, Asia, Europe, and North and South America. Four years later Marie MacDonald, head of the *Missionaries of Our Lady in Africa*, presented a similar study on *Sexual Abuse and Rape Committed by Priests* to the Vatican. It appears that, especially in AIDS infected areas, priests sought to replace the prostitutes with whom they had sex, with nuns. That was their version of safe sex. Pope John Paul II and his bishops and cardinals, who regularly exhort the Catholic faithful to keep chaste, prohibit the use of condoms even to save lives and do not yield to pressure to allow priests to marry, kept quiet. Seven years after receiving the CAFOD report, and only after the information about the report had been leaked to the media, the Vatican confirmed that such abuse had, indeed, been taking place. For years, nuns continued to be subjected to rape by their own 'brothers in Christ' and the Vatican kept quiet. The highest echelons of the Catholic Church, where no one seems ever to be accountable, sat on the information and did nothing.

Archbishop Pio Laghi was Apostolic Pro-Nuncio to Washington from 1980 to 1990. During those years the extent of the abuse started to become clear. In 1985, a member of his staff co-authored the report *The Problem of Sexual Molestation by Roman Catholic Clergy: Meeting the Problem in a Comprehensive and Responsible Manner*. And yet, the Church failed to act. The Pope, in total disregard of the negligence of his representative to ensure that the crisis was understood and dealt with, promoted Laghi to Cardinal in June 1991.

When the scandal erupted, the Church tried to defend herself by suggesting that most of the cases were not cases of paedophiles but rather ephebophiles.[v] By making this differentiation and by suggesting that most of the abusive priests were in actual fact ephebophiles, the Church had hoped to escape the image of being a haven for paedophiles, who are universally abhorred and feared. Her second goal was to suggest

---

[v] Paedophiles are sexually attracted to children, whereas ephebophiles are attracted to post-pubescent teenagers.

that much of the abuse was possibly consensual sex with teenagers. In a society in which many teenagers engage in sex, sole culpability of the priests for these acts – the Church hoped – could be questioned. However, priests have a position of immense emotional, spiritual and psychological power in relation to those they minister to. There can be no possible free consent in such relationships. More than that, case after case proved that priests systematically manipulated their victims.

Rome did not perceive it to be an immediate crisis. In fact, when the US bishops asked the Vatican for approval of the policy that they had agreed in June 2002, the Vatican took its time. When questioned as to why deliberations were taking so long, Rome answered that it was due to the summer vacations at the Vatican. Vatican officials considered the American bishops' policy too punitive and were worried that priests were not given the protection they required from the Church. One Vatican official told an interviewer 'The American bishops have made new laws and asked for a *recognitio*, which cannot be given. The pope – only the pope – can create new laws.'[107] Trying to explain why the Vatican appeared more concerned about priests' rights than victims' needs, a Vatican official said, 'it is important the concept of due process be there, not just for priests in this situation, but for all situations and the Church'.[108] Some critics in the Vatican spoke deprecatingly of US bishops panicking and giving in to secular pressure. The Church does not make her decisions under the influence of the painful stories of the victims of sexual abuse, they said, and certainly not in front of TV cameras. The US bishops, according to the Vatican, adopted a policy that contradicted the Code of Canon Law, the ecclesiastical law governing the Roman Catholic Church worldwide.

In October 2002, Rome spoke. The Vatican's response, signed by Cardinal Giovanni Battista Re, head of the Congregation of Bishops, rejected the American policy for dealing with sexually abusive priests, saying that elements in the new 'zero-tolerance' approach presented conflicts with established, universal Church law and needed to be changed. The Vatican criticised the American bishops' policy for defining child sexual abuse too broadly, for containing no statute of limitations and for not making certain that an accused priest received a full and fair hearing before he was punished.[109] The Vatican apparently considers removing a priest a punishment, rather than a security measure. The Vatican also objected to the decision by the American bishops to report all cases of sexual abuse to civil authorities as it would put at risk the pastoral relationship between a bishop and his priests.[110] The rejection, which deeply disappointed the abused, was received with relief by many bishops and priests. 'As a matter of fact, I've been hoping that there would be a refinement of the Dallas charter and the norms, and I welcome what's been called for today,' said Archbishop Thomas C. Kelley of Louisville, Kentucky, who said he had voted in favour of the policy but with 'enormous misgivings'.[111]

The Vatican's reaction was to try to remove the problem from the Church. Thus the rape and sexual abuse of hundreds of thousands of minors by thousands of members of the Catholic Church's clergy, which had been hidden, covered up and lied about, and thereby aggravated by Catholic bishops and cardinals, was not a Church issue, but, according to Pope John Paul II: 'The abuse of the young is a grave symptom of a crisis affecting not only the Church but society as a whole. It is a deep-seated crisis of sexual morality, even of human relationships, and its prime victims are the family and the young. In addressing the problem of abuse with clarity and determination, the Church will help society to understand and deal with the crisis in its midst.'[112] These are the Pope's words at a crisis meeting with the US cardinals which took place in April 2002. How remote and how arrogant, and what outright deceit. This line of manipulation was also adopted by Archbishop Sean O'Malley, the new Archbishop of Boston, in his installation speech on 30 July 2003, in which he said:

> Many Catholics feel that it is unfair that national concern on sexual abuse has focused so narrowly on the Catholic Church without a commensurate attempt to address the problem in our contemporary society at large. Yet we can only hope that the bitter medicine we have had to take to remedy our mismanagement of the problem of sexual abuse will prove beneficial to our whole country.[113]

A curious line, reminiscent of a naughty child who tries to justify his deed by telling his mother that the other kids had also misbehaved. Doubtlessly, sexual abuse is not confined to Catholic priests. The Catholic Church is, however, unique as an important and powerful global structure which has, for many years, acted to cover up the criminal behaviour of her clergy.

The Church prefers to protect her own and not to bow to public pressure. She is also worried about appearing to give in to the democratic requirement for accountability for her actions. Eventually Pope John Paul II understood that he had to give in to the popular demands for the removal of Cardinal Bernard Law. In December 2002, the Pope accepted Cardinal Law's resignation. In accepting it (which the Pope rejected when it was first offered in April 2002) the Vatican made it clear that he was neither fired nor asked to resign. The Vatican did not acknowledge that Cardinal Law had to go nor that there was any reason for this to be the beginning of a greater cull. Vatican sources spoke about a judgement made as to the Cardinal's potential effectiveness in governing the Archdiocese.[114] This probably also included the extremely important ability to raise funds. Law was the senior Roman Catholic prelate in the United States and one of the closest to the Vatican. The seventy-one-year-old Cardinal, who had been at the head of the Archdiocese of Boston since 1984, did not resign before fifty-eight priests in the Archdiocese of Boston endorsed a letter calling on him to step down. The Catholic lay group, the *Voice of the Faithful* which was formed in response to the abuse crisis, also called for him to resign.

The Boston Archdiocese's newspaper, *The Pilot*, which called out 'Mary, Mother of the Church, pray for us', suggested that 'The humiliation the Church in Boston is experiencing is a purification.'[115] The *New York Times*, in a leader entitled 'Boston's Negligent Cardinal' used rather stronger language:

> For too long Cardinal Bernard Law, the archbishop of Boston, abused his power in order to protect priests who had molested children. His belated resignation yesterday was a prerequisite for Boston's archdiocese to finally acknowledge and confront the scope of the child-molestation epidemic – and its disgraceful cover-up – that have roiled the community. Cardinal Law was so much a part of the problem that he could not have been part of any meaningful solution.[116]

Although experts do not consider homosexuality to be a factor increasing the risk to children,[117] the conservative Pope John Paul II took advantage of the sexual abuse crisis in the US – linking abuse with homosexuality – to push his homophobic agenda.[118] Talking to visiting Brazilian bishops he said in September 2002 that the Roman Catholic Church must be more careful not to let men with 'deviations in their affections' enter the priesthood. Such men 'can cause grave deviations in the consciences of the faithful, with obvious harm for the entire Church'.[119]

The undercurrent beneath Vatican concerns and a key to understanding its refusal to accept the policy of the American bishops is that the US bishops had gone beyond their authority in allowing the Church to be scrutinised by laypeople. The Catholic Church cannot permit the introduction of the idea that it is in need of external controls. This could have started an avalanche and this institution, which has managed to prevent outside controls (and for which transparency is a dirty word), which has been steadfast in preventing auditors from investigating her finances, was not going to give in now simply because of some sex scandals in America. She was and wants to continue to be a self-governing body. She has known scandals before and has outlived them.

Some remarkable statements were made to a *New York Times* reporter in explanation of the Vatican rejection. The Vatican is the master of Bishops and not laypeople. 'They're dealing with the matter as if they don't understand who they are,' said one Church official here, referring to the bishops. 'Don't make the mistake of putting the outside world's logic on the Church,' he continued, adding that the Vatican has the sense that its laws 'have a divine origin and a divine scope'. 'The Church is aware that it lost control over the last decade of its discipline', another Vatican official said. 'The major concern and business of Rome is the universal Church ... The concern for the universal Church always prevails over a problem that is passing through it.'[120]

Conclusion

An investigation into abuse revealed that more than sixty-three per cent of the victims had been abused more than once, and for some the assaults had continued for years. Nearly thirty per cent of the children had been reportedly abused by the same priests for two to four years; ten per cent had been abused over at least five and as many as nine years.[121] The US Conference of Catholic Bishops recognised that the response of some of the bishops to that abuse and the atmosphere of secrecy 'has inhibited the healing process and, in some cases, enabled sexually abusive behavior to be repeated'.[122] The National Review Board in their *Report on the Crisis in the Catholic Church in the United States*, issued on 27 February 2004, agreed that some Church leaders 'did not act effectively to preclude that abuse'; it spoke about the 'leniency afforded predator priests by some bishops' and about Church leaders 'placing the interests of the accused priests above those of the victims'.[123] The head of the Review Board said: 'We are stunned, sick, heartsick that these things could have occurred. ... There was a culture of acceptance of this dysfunctional and criminal behaviour that is inexplicable to me.'[124] Although the Vatican at first suggested that the abuse was due to a general social problem or that it was confined mainly to the United States, the reality is that criminal sexual abuse and criminal cover-up of such abuse have taken place within the Catholic Church all over the world.

It is deceitful, criminal and unfathomable, but unfortunately ingrained and inherent in the Catholic Church. In this organisation sick sex abusers did not find help, instead they found a playing field. Society-at-large and her own members were disregarded when the Church found out about sexual abuse and the matter was silenced. The police were not informed, the family of the abused was lied to and worst of all the offending priest was sent to a new parish. It is almost as if the bishops wanted to ensure that paedophiles regularly had a fresh assortment of children to pursue. The damage was multiplied by the Church's standing in the community that made law enforcement agencies and other figures in the public domain look the other way whenever a priest was caught offending. Not only that, but the Church is held in such awe by the faithful and members of the Church that for many years the sexually abused and their families participated in the hushing up of the abuse.

Contrary to the continued assertions of the Church, sexual molestation by paedophile and other clerics has been around for very many years, in fact since the earliest days of the Church. We also know that many of the non-abusive clergy were aware of the abuse which was taking place within their Church. They knew what their colleagues were up to and looked the other way. We know that bishops and cardinals, the hierarchy responsible for the Church, were aware of the abuse and covered it up, often enabling child-molesting priests to move from one parish to the next. Sometimes, but only sometimes, they were sent for treatment. As early as 1959 a treatment centre for priests with behavioural problems, including child sexual abuse, was established in England and in the US a treatment programme was established in 1976. The Church, which understood that she had a problem on her hands, might have attempted to treat some of the offenders but gave neither thought nor care to the victims of the abuse and to their families. In 1985, US bishops were confronted with a comprehensive report on abuse, its ramifications and suggested action to be taken. They neglected to act. It was also in the 1980s that protesters began picketing semi-annual Bishops' Conference meetings, demanding action on clergy sexual abuse. At the same time, insurance companies, which were being hit with claims, started excluding sexual abuse from group insurance cover that they were selling to Church organisations. In 1989, Survivors Network of those Abused by Priests (SNAP) was founded in Chicago and two years later, in 1991, Victims of Clergy Abuse Inc. (The Linkup) was established. And yet, when in 1992 the bishops finally agreed principles for handling abuse cases, they decided not to have a national policy, thus enabling more prevarication by dioceses. Only in 1993 did the bishops establish an Ad Hoc Committee on Sexual Abuse. The Dominican friar, Thomas Doyle, one of the authors of the 1985 report, explained the stubborn refusal of the bishops to act: 'To acknowledge the problem in its fullness would open the whole system to critique ... It would weaken the presumed power base and strength of the Hierarchy.'[125]

Throughout this period the hierarchy of the Church continued to give shelter to and to hide from justice the criminally abusive priests, often enabling them to continue with their deeds. Throughout this period, the hierarchy of the Church lied to the whole world about what was happening, about what it knew and about its culpability.

Information about what was happening and has been happening has unquestionably gone up to the level of the Pope. The Pope and the whole apparatus of the Vatican have themselves come to maturity within the Church and will themselves have come across cases of abuse and looked the other way. The issue of sexual abuse of minors by his priesthood around the world was not in any of his public speeches and written documents until 1993. It was very late in the day, many years after he most probably knew about the problem and eight years after a member of his own Washington embassy wrote a damning and frightening report about the situation. But even then the Pope did not use his power to address the failure of the Church to look after the victims of her clergy and to immediately stop the policy of secrecy and lying. The first time the Pope spoke about the victims and mentioned their suffering was in April 2002. At that very late stage, with grand juries across the US issuing subpoenas for Church documents and members of the hierarchy, the Vatican called all American cardinals to a meeting in Rome. At that meeting, the Pope expressed his 'profound sense of solidarity and concern' for the victims and their families.[126]

The same papal thinking – as is evident in various concordats – in which the Vatican attempted to secure the ex-territoriality of Church personnel to prevent their being subjected to state courts, can be observed in the Vatican's disregard for law and justice, as it ran its notorious ratlines smuggling Nazi war criminals to countries in which they could escape justice. With the same contempt for the rest of the world, the Catholic Church has whisked abusive priests across borders and brazenly lied and cheated, in her attempt to enable her criminally abusive clergy to avoid justice.

The Review Board states that 'These leadership failings have been shameful to the Church as both a central institution in the lives of the faithful and a moral force in the secular world, and have aggravated the harm suffered by victims and their families.' And yet, as late as October 2003, the Vatican demonstrated its remoteness when its Secretary of State, Cardinal Angelo Sodano, said in an interview: 'The scandals in the United States received disproportionate attention from the media. ... There are thieves in every country, but it's hard to say that everyone is a thief.'[127] It is, therefore, not surprising that theologian Tom Beaudoin described the perception of the Church by some of his fellow young Catholics, as 'often a place of self-deception, abusive silence and double talk'.[128]

The unfolding of the sexual abuse culture of the Catholic Church has exposed her as a dangerous institution which runs sophisticated cover-up operations to defend the criminal activities of her priests. This secret and authoritarian institution and its hierarchy have, by their conscious policy of hushing up and covering up, become accessories to sexual crimes perpetrated by their clergy. Intolerant and hypocritical, judgemental of everyone but herself, the Church excommunicates and dispatches her members to the fires of hell whilst covering up her own foul deeds and totally disregarding bleeding children raped by her own priests.

Conclusion

The Catholic Church has grown into a powerful institution by exploiting human frailty. Sigmund Freud speaks of the 'immense power, which overwhelms Reason and Science'[1] to describe the belief in a 'Divine Being'. Karl Marx famously suggested that 'religion was the opium of the masses'. As a purveyor of religion and religious services the Catholic Church fulfils a deep human need.[2] To some, religion explains the world; for others, it helps them to survive in the world. Religion is adept at exploiting human anxiety, human weaknesses and the centrality of the non-rational in human life. Religions thrive in the fertile soil of general uncertainty, man's existential anxieties and his fear of death. Most people are especially prone to religious experiences during periods of low self-esteem and when they feel helpless.[3] Indeed, people who feel vulnerable or anxious are more likely to seek shelter or emotional relief through the irrational. Into this morass religions enter and offer varied answers, but most importantly they offer certainty. To the unsure and susceptible, religions offer clear-cut answers and solutions. There are individuals who are more easily roused in situations of group excitement and some of the religious rituals have the effect of bringing about hyper-suggestibility, a state in which certain people are more open to external influences.

The Catholic Church offers her members a structured path to guide them to lead a virtuous life which the Church promises will land them in heaven. This, no doubt, has helped many Catholics who are grateful to the Church for being their moral beacon and for aiding them in coping with the difficulties of life. And yet, the soothing reassurance of religious authority comes with a risk tag attached to it. The preceding chapters have demonstrated the Catholic Church to have been morally wrong both in principle and in practice; to have and to exert a malignant influence; and to have caused great harm. In many aspects the very opposite of what the Church claims as her role in this world.

Should the Church have preached hatred of Jews, passed laws which closed various professions to them, had them locked up in ghettos and acted to systematically denigrate them? Should the Church prohibit the teaching of theories she does not approve of and should she have forbidden books, have them burned and their authors, printers and owners punished? Should the Church have run an inquisition and torture operation? Should she have enforced conversions? Should the Church have sent armies to conquer and kill? Should she have licensed colonial forays, permitted slavery and slave trading and even owned slaves herself? Should the Church have made 'unethical' investments, laundered illegal funds, including Nazi money and gold, and cooperated with the Mafia in her financial dealings? Should the Church have covered up sexual abuse by her clergy? Should she have attempted to blackmail victims of her clergy into silence? The answer to all the above is clear and yet time after time the Church made the wrong decision. She chose to act often illegally and always immorally. She continues to do so.

New York's former archbishop, Cardinal John J. O'Connor, in a homily he gave in 1998, suggested that corrupt clergy was not a reason to discard the Catholic Church. He accepted that the Church had 'experienced corruption ... [and] has at times demonstrated great arrogance through its bishops and priests and even through its popes'.[4] And yet, the Cardinal maintained that Catholics had no right to say 'enough is enough'; they had no right to say that they believed in Christ, in Christian values and that the institution of the Church was too corrupt and must go.

Catholics, the Cardinal added, must continue in total adherence to the institution. It is Christ's Church and if one believes in Christ one has to believe in and respect the Catholic Church, regardless of the fact that 'there have been so many sins in the Church, so much weakness in the Church, there have been so many corrupt popes in the Church, corrupt bishops, corrupt priests, corrupt Catholic lay persons'.

According to the Church's script the world needs Christ, Christ's only representative is the Catholic Church, and 'outside the Church there is no salvation'.[5] This notion of exclusivity has been softened in recent years but not abandoned. The Catechism allows for the possibility that 'Those who, through no fault of their own, do not know the Gospel of Christ or his Church, but who nevertheless seek God with a sincere heart ... – those too may achieve eternal salvation.' This, however, does not bring an end to her evangelism, as 'the Church still has the obligation and also the sacred right to evangelize all men'.[6] In an encyclical issued in 1975, Pope Paul VI confirmed the Church's claim that 'our religion effectively establishes with God an authentic and living relationship which the other religions do not succeed in doing, even though they have, as it were, their arms stretched out towards heaven'.[7]

The nature of religious organisations is that they promote what they believe to be God-given teaching and consequently cannot compromise. They do not have the authority to be flexible with the word of God. To this rigidity, the Catholic Church has added difficulty by giving the force of Tradition the same status as the written word.[8] In fact, the Church has added layer upon layer of rigidity, which make it very difficult for her to respond to an ever-changing world and ever-developing civilisation. By considering herself but a trusted guardian and not the author of her teaching, the Church leaves herself very little room for manoeuvre. Instead of being a source of values, the Church is a source of interpretation of a fixed set of God-given unchangeable texts. She does not make do with a claim that whatever Jesus is meant to have said and done corresponds with values which she considers worthy. She defines the words and the deeds as true and a set of early Christian interpretations as binding. Innumerable bulls and encyclicals which are based on quotations from the New Testament, sermons and writings of early Christian Church Fathers as well as later important Church figures such as St Augustine and Thomas Aquinas were issued by popes throughout the Church's history and were the basis of much of the suffering which the Church inflicted upon her members, her clergy and the rest of society. The Church finds it virtually impossible to rescind rulings made in the past. A Church document from 1815 makes this quite clear, as the then secretary of state, Cardinal Consalvi, stated 'it is equally repugnant to him to make any express, public innovations, different from what the large majority of his Holy predecessors, albeit in other times and circumstances, believed appropriate for the good of the Church and the state'.[9] This rigidity causes, for example, the Church's moral blindness as she is unable, when hundreds of thousands are contracting AIDS due to unsafe sex, to set the truly important value of conserving life above her anti-contraception dogma.

Democracy has established separation of powers: organising and balancing the legal powers of the executive, the legislative and the juridical branches of government and creating independent control bodies to prevent misuse of power. Above all, the need to be regularly approved by the electorate in democratic elections is a significant control mechanism. The Catholic Church is undemocratic and lacks any such mechanisms. It is a non-hereditary monarchy-like structure, in which the pope, its head, is elected for a life tenure by a forum of cardinals, all of whom were made cardinals by previous popes. Cardinals and bishops are created by popes and bishops, in turn, nominate priests. Members of the Church have no vote, power or say in these appointments. As the Church is not accountable to her members, she has never developed any mechanisms for openness. This lack of transparency regularly comes to the fore when Church scandals can no longer be kept out of the public domain. Corruption and money laundering by the Vatican Bank in the 1970s and 1980s, which caused the Vatican to lose hundreds of millions of dollars, is a case in point. Similarly, questions raised as a result of the many instances of sexual abuse by Catholic clergy have bounced off firmly closed doors. Although the Church has been unable to keep the scandals from the media, she has refused to open her archives and files to enable a full enquiry into the involvement of the Catholic hierarchy in these abuses and their cover up. Having harboured illegal and criminal activities, the Church has a good incentive to behave in this way.

The means the Church is willing to use and to condone are as forceful and ferocious as she can get away with under the circumstances. Historian George Sabine makes the point that 'The morality of the plain man, however much of the good will it may embody, is inevitably the morality of his time and place.'[10] But we do and we should expect more from a body which defines itself as the source and lighthouse of morality to mankind. As long as she was able to, the Church locked up Jews in ghettos. Not until 1965 did the Church begin to cease her vitriolic anti-Semitic propaganda. The Church is no longer able to run her Inquisition but whilst she was able to, she did. With the demise of colonialism, the Catholic Church lost her ability to enforce conversion. Pope John Paul II, in his message for the Millennium, in reference to the missionary tasks ahead for his Church in Asia, made it clear that the missionary zeal must not abate: 'the issue of the encounter of Christianity with ancient local cultures and religions is a pressing one. This is a great challenge for evangelization.'[11] The Church is not as powerful as she used to be and it has been a while since the personal corruption of popes produced one who castrated cardinals he disapproved of (Pope John XII) or one who organised prostitute copulating competitions at the Vatican (Pope Alexander VI). But senior Catholic hierarchy around the world until very recently have been willing to overlook rape and abuse by Catholic clergy, thereby abusing the very people with whose well-being they have been entrusted. This may not be personal corruption but is it not institutional corruption?

The Church no longer has an army or prisons at her disposal but wherever she can she continues to use her power to impose her dogma on society. As an autocratic structure, the Church never had any objections to dealing with dictatorships. On the contrary, the Church fought against liberal and democratic ideas and has only lately come to espouse democracy. Some papal encyclicals, as we have seen, have promoted social ideals which have a worrying affinity with those of Fascism, as opposed to those of either Liberalism or Socialism. Politically too, undemocratic Catholic ideas correspond with the Fascist conception of the functions of the 'leader' as head of a state. Historian Christopher Dawson wrote in 1936:

> Catholicism is by no means hostile to the authoritarian ideal of the
> State. Against the liberal doctrines of the divine right of majorities and

> unrestrained freedom of opinion the Church has always maintained
> the principles of authority and hierarchy and a high conception of the
> prerogatives of the State.[12]

Liberation theology, a Catholic movement which developed in Latin America in the 1960s and challenged the role of Christianity in perpetuating poverty, racism and sexism, was ruthlessly stifled by Pope John Paul II. More than a hundred years earlier, the philosopher and theologian Søren Kierkegaard already noted that 'The history of Christendom is the history of subtle disregarding of Christianity.'[13]

Importantly, the Church is unable to deal with and accept her own culpability. Many had hoped that the 1998 Vatican document *We Remember: A Reflection on the Shoah* would be the Catholic Church's *mea culpa* for the role she played in nurturing anti-Semitism and her guilt in neglecting to speak out against the Nazi persecution of the Jews. Instead the Church produced an *eiorum culpa*. Not my fault, but their fault. The Shoah, the Vatican points out 'was the work of a thoroughly modern neopagan regime. Its anti-Semitism had its roots outside of Christianity.' *We Remember* simply glosses over a long history of Church-induced hatred and dogmatic anti-Jewish teaching and preaching by priests, bishops and popes. The document does not touch on possible structural faults or on institutional culpability. Instead of apologising on her own behalf, the Church 'deeply regret[s] the errors and failures of those sons and daughters of the Church' who did not 'give every possible assistance to those being persecuted'.[14] Who is the Church trying to fool? Gary Wills makes the point that 'Even when papal authority sincerely wants to perform a virtuous act ... it has not done it. Not because it did not want to do it, or did not believe it did it. It was simply unable to do it, because that would have involved coming clean about the record of the papal institution. And that is all but unthinkable.'[15]

The recent internal investigation into the Galileo affair shows the same unwillingness or inability to accept responsibility. Pope Pius IX (1846–1878) declared that: 'In matters of religion it is the duty of philosophy ... not to scrutinize the depths of the mysteries of God, but to venerate them devoutly and humbly.' Like every power structure, the Church does not like her authority questioned or her deeds scrutinised. When forced to do so, by modern public opinion in a more democratic world, the Church grudgingly acquiesces. Pope John Paul II misleadingly referred to the interrogation by the Inquisition as a 'debate' and described the whole matter as a 'tragic mutual incomprehension'. He further pushed the blame on to Galileo and some theologians who 'did not know how' to examine their own criteria of scriptural interpretation.[16]

The Vatican's reaction to sexual abuse scandals demonstrates that here too the Church is unable to accept responsibility. 'The scandals in the United States received disproportionate attention from the media', Cardinal Angelo Sodano, the Vatican's secretary of state, said in October 2003 and added that 'there are thieves in every country, but it's hard to say that everyone is a thief.'[17] The Pope went even further in his attempt to remove the abuse issue from the Church. He claimed that abuse was a general societal problem and that 'the Church will help society to understand and deal with the crisis in its midst.'[18]

The Church's evident difficulty with true repentance is a significant indicator for the future. She has not shown any true repentance; she has in fact not accepted culpability. The various *mea culpae* delivered by the Church in recent years were all very limited and attempted to deflect from the Church's culpability instead of accepting her guilt.

Under an often misleading cloak suggesting a structure which is only dealing with love and salvation, the senior clergy of the Church are more loyal to the institution, or what they perceive the interest of the institution to be, than to the values espoused by the institution. Political scientist Professor Eric Hanson makes the point that 'Catholic Bishops perceive their loyalty to institutional unity as an integral part of their religious faith'. Hanson ascribes to the formative socialisation of seminary training and to priestly celibacy an important role in moulding this institutional loyalty. As a result, he writes: 'When faced with an attack with what are perceived to be essential features of the church, defence of the institution usually overrides all other goals.'[19] American philosopher Sidney Hook maintained that 'In any crucial situation, the behaviour of the Catholic Church may be more reliably predicted by reference to its concrete interests as a political organisation than by reference to its timeless dogmas.'[20]

Based on the hold which religion has over many and the specific devices of power integrated in Christian dogma and in Church tradition, the Catholic Church has been able to build up an extensive network of power bases worldwide. She has infiltrated political institutions and has for a long time been at the centre of power at first in most Western countries and later in many others. In recent history the Church has been able to take advantage of the sovereign status of Vatican City, the independence of her secretive financial institutions, her membership and observer status in almost all international organisations and her direct influence over the faithful to further her interests. The Church carries on in her attempts to use whatever means she has at her disposal to influence legislation in areas such as: opposition to divorce, discrimination against homosexuals, prohibition of same-sex marriage, prevention of legal abortion or availability of contraception and access to family-planning education. The Church continues to wield much influence, often with lethal effect. Her impact is most damaging in the poorer and needier societies, which have less access to more enlightened sources of information.

Dismantling the Structure

Theologian Tom Beaudoin describes the perception of the Church by some of his fellow young Catholics, as 'often a place of self-deception, abusive silence and double talk, especially about sexuality and about power'. Beaudoin compares the Catholic Church which 'can cover up its spiritual deficits' to 'WorldCom or Enron [which] can cover up their economic losses'.[21] Both companies are notorious for their accounting swindles. Both had to file for bankruptcy; WorldCom has been restructured and Enron wound up. Should the conclusion for the Catholic Church be similar? Is anyone accountable in the Catholic Church? Has a pope ever been fired? Have cardinals been fired? Should that really be out of the question? Should perhaps the whole organisation be closed down?

Because of the extreme importance of faith to so many people, it is imperative that organisations purporting to speak for God be rigorously scrutinised. The question should not be whether we have the right to scrutinise but whether we have the right not to scrutinise, to simply give the Church a waiver. We license organisations which handle our money; we do not allow anyone to practice medicine unless they have passed certain criteria and examinations; we do not even permit unlicensed people to handle our cars. Yet, we give great freedom to organisations which, under the guise of being loving spiritual guides, may play havoc with our lives.

Not all of the six problem areas (corruption, violence, truth, freedom of thought and speech, Jews, sex, cover-up of sexual abuse) dealt with by this book justify the dismantling of the Church. The Church's questionable financial ethics may be disappointing but they do not cause serious harm to anyone other than the Church herself. Fortunately the Church no longer is in a position to use violence against opponents, competitors or simply opportunistic targets. Nor can the Church effectively prevent the dissemination of ideas she disapproves of.

Her attitude to truth continues to be problematic. The Church continues to propagate lies to support her dogmas. I am not referring to matters of faith such as virgin birth or transubstantiation. I am talking about her willingness to spread false, supposedly scientific, information about the efficacy of condoms to prevent people from using them. This criminal conduct of the Church kills people.

The Church's attitude to Jews has changed dramatically since Vatican II. Tragically, these careful changes of nuance cannot undo two thousand years of the insemination of hatred. A real change in the attitude to Jews will probably necessitate an upheaval of traumatic magnitude. Breaking down the structure may drive home the message that everything Christianity has taught about Jews and Judaism is false.

Sexual abuse scandals have brought to light the criminal cover-up policy and practice of the Church. It has made clear that the Church – even in the twenty-first century – is willing to cause the most terrible injury to her members in order to protect her public image. The Irish writer Colm Tóibín thanks 'the Creator for small mercies' as 'No one is afraid of the priests anymore. ... Their years of fucking and fondling the more vulnerable members of the congregation have ended; their years of apologising sincerely and unctuously have begun.'[22] And yet, the motivation for the cover-up has not and most probably cannot be rooted out. *Time to Listen*, a document commissioned by The Irish Bishops' Committee on Child Abuse and published in 2003, reported that 'priests identified the hierarchical structure of the Church as an impediment to dealing effectively with the problem of clerical sexual abuse.'[23]

The Church's teaching on sex may have changed somewhat and heterosexuals are now permitted actually to enjoy sex provided it takes place within marriage and without the use of contraceptives. However, much harm continues to be caused by the Church, especially in the fields of abortion, contraception and homosexuality.

The previous chapters have revealed the modus operandi of the Church and the inherent faults in her structure and in some of her teaching which have led to the harm caused by her to many of her members, some of her clergy and to society at large. The actions of the Church are not random errors, nor are they occasional bad decisions soon rectified or just acts of corrupt members of the hierarchy; they reflect the well thought-out policy of the Church. The Church's history has proven her to have acted evilly throughout her existence and to have done so in virtually all realms. She has only ceased acting evilly when external forces forced her to do so. The Church herself accepts the legitimacy of punishment with 'the primary aim of redressing the disorder introduced by the offense.'[24] Dismantling the Church would be an act of redress, albeit a drastic one. However, this book has established that the Church's evil actions are the inevitable consequence of the fusion of her claim that all the popes form an uninterrupted line as Vicars of Christ going back to St. Peter, her undemocratic structure, her inability to compromise, the tendency of her hierarchy and those under her influence to be more loyal to the institution than to the purported values of the institution, and the formal and informal power base the Church has built. Judging by her past, the Church will, in all probability, re-offend.

What will happen if the structures of the Catholic Church were to be dismantled? The values often referred to as 'Judaeo-Christian' are not of the Church's making, nor does she have a monopoly over them. Dismantling the structures of the Catholic Church will not leave us without these values. As an organisation guided by rigid adherence to the original texts rather than the original values, the Church, judging by past experience, will not be at the forefront of progress. If at all, she will only traipse along belatedly and grudgingly. The good work carried out by priests, the religious and lay Catholics is their personal good work and not that of their super-structure.

On a practical level the dismantling of Church structures would involve the retirement of the pope, curial cardinals and other members of the curial bureaucracy and the removal of the sovereignty of the City of Vatican State. All Vatican and Church diplomatic and other representative offices would be closed and all ties between national Church structures and a governing body would cease to exist. This would also involve disbanding banking and all other economic enterprises and transferring all the assets to a trust. The realised assets, which would form the trust fund, could be applied to make reparations to victims of the Church's teaching and conduct. Additionally, all cultural assets could be transferred to a public cultural foundation.

Faithful Catholic liberals hope and believe that change can be effected within the Church. They hope for reform. Such reform, however, is unlikely to suffice. The shake-up which is necessary is beyond the scope of a reform.

Notes

Notes to Introduction

1. Küng, Hans, *The Catholic Church*, p.5, Weidenfeld and Nicholson, London, 2001.
2. Küng, p.5.
3. Wills, Gary, *Papal Sin: Structures of Deceit*, Darton, Longman and Todd, London, 2000.
4. Cornwell, John, *Breaking Faith*, p.8, Penguin Books, London, 2002.
5. Reagan, Ronald, *Speech given at the National Association of Evangelicals Convention*, Sheraton Twin Towers Hotel in Orlando, Florida on 8 March 1983.
6. Nietzsche, Friedrich, *Die Fröhliche Wissenschaft III*, p.130.
7. Paul clarified the Christian position that obedience should be due to those in authority in his letter to the Romans (13, 1–7). Some even consider Jesus' famous 'Render therefore unto Caesar the things which are Caesar's, and unto God the things that are God's' as proof that this concept goes back to him. This notion is negated by those who believe that this expression should be seen more as an expediency to avoid entrapment by the Pharisees, who tried to produce an anti-Roman rule. It was, not surprisingly, an attractive concept for the rulers; if they established a good relationship with God's representative, their power over the people would benefit from the added weighting of religion. Indeed, fourth-century Roman Emperor Constantine, who in 313 recognised Christianity and thereby brought it in from the cold, was the first ruler to understand the advantage in such collaboration. The Church, on the other hand, by developing a theory which asserted the independence of both the Church and State but which emphasised the shared divinity of their positions (both were divinely appointed), was guaranteed a superior status – as the body in charge of interpreting the rules and the divine wish. Such a status would induce the secular rulers to cooperate with her wishes. Church leaders did not have arbitrary power – this was subject to divine and natural law – but they had the power of interpretation.
8. When Albert Speer, Hitler's architect, was assigned the project to produce the 1934 Nuremberg Nazi Party Rally, he placed one hundred and thirty anti-aircraft searchlights around the marching field, sending individual light beams into the sky which merged into a great glow: 'It had the advantage of dramatising the spectacle while effectively drawing the veil over the not so attractive marching figures of paunchy party bureaucrats', Speer later explained. Sereny, Gitta, *Albert Speer: His Battle With Truth*, p.131, Picador, London, 1996. Torchlights, floodlights, speeches, parades, marches, flags and music were all made use of in this and subsequent rallies to produce nationalist fervour of adoration and loyalty to the Führer and his programme. The British Ambassador described 'The Cathedral of Light', Speer's light design, as a 'cathedral of ice'.
9. *Boston Globe, Betrayal: The Crisis in the Catholic Church*, p.134, Little, Brown, Boston, 2002.
10. Goldhagen, Jonah Daniel, *A Moral Reckoning*, pp.187–8, Little, Brown, London, 2002.
11. The Roman Index of Prohibited Books was established by Pope Paul IV in 1559. Over the years works considered 'dangerous' by the Church were added to it. By the time it was

last published in 1966, it had prohibited, among others, works by Hobbes, Descartes, Bacon, Locke, Hume, Rousseau, Kant and Mill.

[12] Pius IX, *A Syllabus containing the most important errors of our time, which have been condemned by our Holy Father Pius IX in Allocutions, at Consistories, in Encyclicals, and other Apostolic Letters*, para.80, issued by Cardinal Antonelli, Secretary of State, Vatican, 8 December 1864.

[13] Pallenberg, Corrado, *The Vatican Finances*, p.57, Peter Owen, London, 1971.

[14] Withholding tax is levied by the state on income such as dividends or interest, at source.

[15] Smallpox inoculations were objected to as an attempt to subvert God's will. Another 'medical' interference of the Church was her condemnation of anaesthesia for childbirth. This, the Church maintained, was wrong as according to the Bible women are supposed to have pain in childbirth, as punishment for Eve's sin in the Garden of Eden.

Notes to Chapter One

[1] Jesus himself had already referred to the concept of respect for the law of the land and the lawful authority in his response to the Pharisees, who tried to entrap him into speaking against the authority of Rome, when he said: 'Render therefore unto Caesar the things which are Caesar's, and unto God the things that are God's' (Luke, 20:25).

[2] In a letter to Emperor Anastasius in Constantinople, the first document to lay down the attitude of the Church refusing to accept any imperial authority over the Church, the pope wrote:

> There are, most august Emperor, two powers by which this world is chiefly ruled: the sacred authority of bishops and the royal power. Of these the priestly power is much more important, for it has to render account for the kings of men themselves at the judgement seat of God. For you know, most gracious son, that although you hold the chief place of dignity over the human race, yet you must submit yourself to those who have charge of divine things, and look to them for the means to your salvation.

Quoted by Duffy, Eamon, *Saints and Sinners*, p.50, Yale Nota Bene, New Haven, 2002.

[3] Quoted from a letter to the Bishop of Metz by Duffy, p.127.

[4] Quoted by Sabine, George H., *A History of Political Theory*, p.235, Harrap, London, 1966.

[5] Quoted by Duffy, p.147.

[6] Quoted by Carlyle, R.W. and Carlyle, A.J., *A History of Medieval Political Theory in the West*, Vol. V, p.323, Blackwood, London, 1922.

[7] Quoted by Bettenson, H., *Documents of the Christian Church*, p.157, Oxford University Press, Oxford, 1954.

[8]

	1378	1389	1394	1404	1406	1409	1410	1415	1417
Urban VI	[----------------]								
Clement VII	[--------------------------]								
Boniface IX			[----------------]						
Benedict XIII			[--]						
Innocent VII				[-----------]					
Gregory XII					[---------------------------]				
Alexander V						[------------]			
John XXIII							[------]		

This unbelievable situation, which started with Pope Urban VI who personally supervised the torture of his cardinals in the Vatican garden, only ended when the Council of Constance dismissed three reigning popes and elected Martin V (1417–1431) in their stead. The Catholic Church had known previous periods in which rival groups had elected contemporaneous popes, and the Church then had a pope and an anti-pope. The unique situation in this schism was that it was actually the same College of Cardinals, which six months after it had elected Urban, decided to elect a new pope, as Urban had turned out to be so violent a man. Later Clement would also prove to violent, when he ordered the bloodbath in Cesna. Throughout this period, there were separate papal courts and separate administrations. Each pope created cardinals and appointed bishops for the same sees. Not surprisingly, these competed for revenues from their constituencies, which had to decide where their loyalty lay and of course did not fail to preach war against the other. Only after the Schism ended, was the Church to decide who would be defined as the 'real' pope. In the case of Urban and Clement, the Church chose the pope who tortured six of his cardinals, five of whom disappeared, as the 'real' pope.

9   Quoted by Duffy, p.283. Gregory's successor, Pope Pius IX (1846–1878), in his 1870 *Syllabus of Errors* (para.80), condemned the idea that 'the Roman Pontiff can and should reconcile himself with progress, liberalism, and recent civilisation'.

10 In attempting to pacify France, Napoleon made advances to the Church. He made his observation about the power of the Pope in 1799, when he had funeral honours laid on for the body of Pope Pius VI, whilst it lay in Valence.

11 Quoted in Bernstein, Carl, and Politi, Marco, *His Holiness*, p.367, Bantam Books, London, 1997.

12 Pope Pius IX, *Nostis et nobiscu, Encyclical on the Church in the Pontifical States*, para.6, Naples, 8 December 1849.

13 *Quod Apostolici Muneris*, Encyclical of Pope Leo XIII on Socialism, Rome, 28 December 1878.

14 Quoted by Cornwell, John, *Hitler's Pope: The Secret History of Pius XII*, p.330, Viking, London, 1999.

15 Yallop, David A., *In God's Name: An Investigation into the Murder of Pope John Paul I*, p.312, Bantam Books, New York, 1984.

16 The concordat, which was signed by Pope Pius XI, was negotiated by Cardinal Pacelli, the Vatican's Secretary of State, who would later become Pope Pius XII. The subject is covered in greater detail in Chapter 6.

17 Lateran Accord, articles 5 and 8.

18 This was only deleted in 1972.

19 Quoted by Yallop, p.120.

20 The Truth Commission's report is considered 'unjust, inaccurate and politically biased' by Peruvian member of Congress and of Opus Dei Rafael Rey. Rey explained that 'the proper role of the Church as an institution is to cultivate souls and strengthen the dignity of the human person, not to try to solve all the problems of the world'. Sofia Macher, a member of the Commission, asserted: 'Cipriani's main relationship was with the political and military power structure, not the citizenry. He consistently downplayed the seriousness of the abuses and even refused to see relatives of the dead and disappeared.' Rohter, Larry, *Peru's Catholics Brace for Fissures in Their Church*, 8 May 2005, www.nytimes.com.

21 See Bernstein and Politi, p.240.

22 Bernstein and Politi, pp.516–7.

23 Catechism of the Catholic Church, 899.

24 Congregation for the Doctrine of the Faith, *Doctrinal Note on Some Questions Regarding the Participation of Catholics in Political Life*, Vatican, 2002.

25 Blumenthal, Sidney, *Holy Warriors*, in: www.salon.com/opinion/blumenthal/2005/04/21.

26 Catholic News Service, *Church morally obligated to play role in politics, archbishop says*, 8 October 2004, www.catholicnews.com/data/stories/cns.
    Archbishop Joseph Naumann of Kansas City asked voters 'What could be a proportionate reason to support the deaths of 40 million innocent children and 40-plus million

adults scarred by their involvement in abortion? Personally, I cannot conceive in our present circumstances what could qualify as a proportionate reason.' (Catholic News Service) Bishop Paul Loverde of Arlington defined 'material cooperation with evil' which he explained was where 'in certain circumstances, it is morally permissible to vote for a candidate who supports some immoral practices while opposing other immoral practices'. However, the Bishop added 'intrinsically evil acts such as abortion or research on stem cells taken from human embryos cannot be placed on the same level; as debates over war or capital; punishment, for example' (Catholic News Agency, 28 October 2004, www.catholicnewsagency.com).

27 www.vatican.va/news_services.

28 Amongst others, it is a member in: the International Atomic Energy Agency (IAEA), UN Conference on Trade and Development (UNCTAD), UN High Commissioner for Refugees (UNHCR), Council for Cultural Cooperation of the Council of Europe, Organisation for Security and Cooperation in Europe, World Intellectual Property Organisation (WIPO), International Grains Council, International Telecommunications Union, International Institute for the Unification of Private Law and the International Committee of Military Medicine. It is even a delegate in the Arab League in Cairo. It sits in as an observer in: the United Nations Organisation (UNO), Council of Europe (CE), Organisation of American States (OAS), Organisation of African Unity (OAU), UN Educational, Scientific and Cultural Organisation (UNESCO), World Trade Organisation (WTO), World Health Organisation (WHO), UN Food and Agriculture Organisation (FAO), International Labour Organisation (ILO), UN Environment Programme, UN International Drug Control Programme, UN Industrial Development Organisation and the Latin Union in Paris.

29 In a speech to the Italian Parliament which the Pope gave in November 2002, he urged Europe to 'maintain its Christian roots' (www.timesonline.co.uk, 6 February 2003). The Vatican's campaign was promoted by Italy and Poland, Portugal, Malta, Lithuania, the Czech Republic and Slovakia, and when they failed the Vatican made public its displeasure. The Vatican spokesman expressed 'disappointment at the opposition of certain governments to a specific acknowledgement of Europe's Christian roots'. These governments, the Vatican declared, 'failed to understand the historical evidence and the Christian identity of the peoples of Europe'(www.upi.com, 21 June 2004).

30 Heneghan, Tom, *Tripping over Europe's Religious Roots*, 14 June 2004, www.beliefenet. com.

31 'thou art Peter, and upon this rock I will build my church' (Matthew 16:18).

32 The Catechism states clearly that 'The college or body of bishops has no authority unless united with the Roman Pontiff, Peter's successor, as its head.' The line of succession leading back to Jesus is clear and the authority may not be queried. (Catechism of the Catholic Church, 882-3).

33 And I will give unto thee the keys of the kingdom of heaven: and whatsoever thou shalt bind on earth shall be bound in heaven: and whatsoever thou shalt loose on earth shall be loosed in heaven. (Matthew 16:19).

34 The Roman Pontiff, head of the college of bishops, enjoys this infallibility in virtue of his office, when, as supreme pastor and teacher of all the faithful – who confirms his brethren in the faith he proclaims by a definitive act a doctrine pertaining to faith or morals ... When the Church through its supreme Magisterium proposes a doctrine "for belief as being divinely revealed", and as the teaching of Christ, the definitions "must be adhered to with the obedience of faith". (Catechism of the Catholic Church, 891).

35 von Döllinger wrote to the Cardinal of Munich:

> The Pope's authority is unlimited, incalculable; it can strike ... wherever sin is; it can punish every one; it allows no appeal and is itself Sovereign Caprice; for the Pope carries ...all rights in the Shrine of his breast. As he has now become infallible, he can by the use of the little word, 'orbi,' (which means that he turns himself round to the whole Church) make every rule, every doctrine, every demand, into

a certain and incontestable article of Faith. No right can stand against him, no personal or corporate liberty; or as the [Roman Catholic] Canonists put it – 'The tribunal of God and of the pope is one and the same.' Quoted in MacDougall, Hugh, *The Acton-Newman Relations*, pp 119-120, Fordham University Press, New York, 1962.

[36] Catechism of the Catholic Church, 144.

[37] Catechism of the Catholic Church, 892.

[38] The Church's inability to accept errors, misbehaviour, immorality of her own and her hierarchy, is demonstrated in a Vatican document from 1815. It is a draft response for Cardinal Consalvi, the Secretary of State, to an appeal by an Austrian minister. The minister interceded on behalf of the Jews living in the area that in the 1815 peace conference, the Congress of Vienna, had been ceded to the Holy See. The Austrian minister wrote to Consalvi, stating that Jews should be allowed to live 'without fear of being sent back to that precarious, vilified state in which they found themselves near the end of the past century, leaving them instead in peace to enjoy that civil status which their civilisation and the liberal sentiments of the European courts have procured for them over the past twenty years'. The Pope, according to the Vatican document, was agreeable for Jews to 'remain in the state ... with modifications that can make such tolerance compatible with the doctrines of our Holy Religion'. Having found a way of not refusing Metternich's request and having opened the door for reinstating the constraints on the Jews, the document also states that the Pope found it:

> repugnant...to make any express, public innovations, different from what the large majority of his Holy predecessors, albeit in other times and circumstances, believed appropriate for the good of the Church and the state. (quoted by Kertzer, David I., *The Pope Against the Jews: The Vatican's Role in the Rise of Modern Anti-Semitism*, Alfred A. Knopf, New York, 2001, p.35).

[39] This system was introduced in the twelfth century. In the early Church, popes were elected by the clergy and people of Rome. This became impractical as the Church grew.

[40] Religious orders are a separate class within the Catholic Church. Their members do not form part of the clergy, nor are they considered as laity. They are 'consecrated religious'. Their members have taken vows of chastity, poverty and obedience. There are hundreds of religious orders and communities, each with different rules and regulations, which normally stem from the founder of the specific order or congregation. For most orders, obedience and loyalty to the order comes before obedience to the Church hierarchy. A notable exception to this is The Society of Jesus, which is more commonly known as the Jesuits. Formed in 1534 by the Spaniard Ignatius of Loyola, this order stipulates total obedience to the pope. Jesuits take a vow of obedience to the pope and are thereby available to serve the pope as he considers necessary.

[41] Reese, Thomas, *Inside the Vatican*, p.132, Harvard University Press, Cambridge, MA, 1996.

[42] According to Thomas Reese (p.199), 'some critics see Cardinal Ratzinger [the congregation's prefect at the time] as the "Grand Inquisitor" who is trying to suppress all dissent ... Others claim that [he] restrains the pope from issuing infallible declarations and from coming down even more strongly on dissident theologians'. In April 2005 Cardinal Ratzinger was elected pope.

[43] Such, for instance, was the case when the Vatican felt uncomfortable with Archbishop Emmanuel Milingo, who held public healing services and exorcisms in Africa. He was persuaded to move to Rome for the specially designed office of 'special delegate' of the *Council for Migrants and Travellers*. More stubborn bishops, especially when they take issue with matters of doctrine, are sometimes not so easy to control. When things get really out of hand a situation known as schism is reached. A well-known and recent schism has been caused by Archbishop Marcel Lefebvre's refusal to accept the reforms of Vatican II. He had a substantial following in France and ignored his suspension by

Pope Paul VI. Without the pope's approval Lefebvre ordained bishops who continue to ordain bishops and priests today, although Lefebvre himself has already died.

[44] Oxford University Press, *The Concise Oxford Dictionary*, 8th Edition, Oxford, 1990.

[45] Frazer, Sir James George, *The Golden Bough: A Study in Magic and Religion*, p.65, Macmillan, London, 1963.

[46] Smith, W.C., *The Meaning and End of Religion: A New Approach to the Religious Traditions of Mankind*, p.20, Macmillan, New York, 1963.

[47] Exodus 4:1–10.

[48] Exodus 7:1–12:33.

[49] Frazer, p.74.

[50] Eliade, Mircea, *The Sacred and the Profane: The Nature of Religion*, p.11, Harcourt Brace Jovanovich, Orlando, FL, 1987.

[51] A good example are the proceedings of the *semana santa*, as it is celebrated in some Catholic countries. Well managed, it can serve as an effective tool to further the impact and influence of the Church.

[52] Eliade, p.164.

[53] Otto, Rudolf, *The Idea of the Holy: An Inquiry into the Non-Rational Factor in the Idea of the Divine and Its Relation to the Rational*, Oxford University Press, London, 1950.

[54] Wulff, David M., *Psychology of Religion*, p. 82, John Wiley & Sons, New York, 1991.

[55] The Church must have either decided that Catholic souls are already so pure that one can lower the dosage of fasting and abstinence, or that the lower dosage suffices anyway. It could also be that this was just a bit of *realpolitik*. Rules which are so obviously disregarded, might as well be discarded.

[56] Daniélou, Alan, 'The Influence of Sound Phenomena on Human Consciousness', *The Psychedelic Review*, 1966, No. 7, 20–26.

[57] Luke, 6: 20–1,24.

[58] Luke, 18:24–5.

[59] Davies, Norman, *Europe*, p.280, Pimlico, London, 1997.

[60] John, 10:37.

[61] John, 5:9.

[62] John, 8:6–7.

[63] John, 8:3.

[64] John 20:30–1.

[65] Mark, 6:48.

[66] Mark, 6:41–2.

[67] Luke,5:10.

[68] Luke, 4:40.

[69] Mark,16:17–18.

[70] Luke, 10:8–9, 16.

[71] Matthew, 10:8.

[72] II Cor., 12:12.

[73] Acts, 10:40–42.

[74] I Cor., 15: 12–20.

[75] Catholic Encyclopaedia, *Miracle*, www.newadvent.org.

[76] Accordingly, the Catholic Church has saints who are, amongst others, patrons of rain and are worshipped by Catholics for their ability to make or end the rains. They include the sixth-century Bishop of Anastasiopolis, Galatia, Theodore of Sykeon, who also had the gift of healing; sister Scholastica, a sixth-century nun; the fifth-century Bishop Gratus of Aosta, whose patronage covers, amongst others, hail and lightning; and Eulalia, a third-century Spanish martyr who was tortured and burned alive during the persecutions under the Roman Emperor Diocletan.

77 It is not uncommon in the south of France for some – but not all – Catholic priests to be considered to have the power to avert storms. New priests would, in fact, be tested to ascertain whether they were in possession of that special *pouder*, as soon as the weather turned bad. Success in exorcising the clouds would bring about respect from the religious community.

78 Catholic Online, www.catholic.org/saints/isidore.shtml.

79 The Church refers to suffering without external marks as invisible stigmata. It is, of course, the suffering which is important to the Church: pity for Christ, participation in his sufferings and the ultimate penance for the sins committed in the world. Stigmata are not considered to be 'incontestable miracles', they do not suffice for canonisation. If science eventually proves them to have been fraudulent or to have a natural explanation, those made saints will not have to be de-canonised. And yet, the Church clearly promotes the idea of such stigmata and keeps these occurrences on the public agenda.

80 The Catholic Church, as a good event-manager, built a basilica over the grotto in 1876 and in 1958 an enormous church with a capacity of twenty thousand was erected.

81 Mary specifically asked, according to the faith, that Russia be consecrated to her Immaculate Heart by the pope and the Church's bishops. 'If My requests are not granted, Russia will spread its errors throughout the world, raising up wars and persecutions against the Church. The good will be martyred, the Holy Father will suffer much and various nations will be annihilated.' The last appearance of Mary in Fatima took place with an occurrence the believers call *Miracle of the Sun*, in which they say some eclipse of the sun, which scientists have not been able to explain, took place.

82 The Pope instigated the consecration in thanks for divine intervention when an attempt was made on his life on 13 May 1981. Fatima has gained much importance under the papacy of John Paul II who, on 13 May 2000, beatified two of the three children who had seen the apparition and who had died at the ages of ten and twelve, three years after the occurrences. Thus has the Pope made use of the date of the first appearance of the vision of Mary in Fatima and that of his escape from the assassin's bullet, charging it with significance and beatifying the two on the same date.

83 Catechism of the Catholic Church, 65.

84 Catechism of the Catholic Church, 65.

85 Catechism of the Catholic Church, 403.

86 Catechism of the Catholic Church, 404.

87 *A Catechism of Christian Doctrine*, 55–56, Catholic Church, England, 1921.

88 Catechism of the Catholic Church, 389.

89 Catechism of the Catholic Church, 95, 100.

90 Catechism of the Catholic Church, 977.

91 Catechism of the Catholic Church, 1263.

92 *A Catechism of Christian Doctrine*, para. 370, Catholic Church, England, 1921.

93 Catechism of the Catholic Church, 1407.

94 John 6:5, 54, 56.

95 Catechism of the Catholic Church, 1376.

96 US National Security Advisor, Richard Allen, described the Reagan–Vatican relationship as 'one of the greatest secret alliances of all times' (Bernstein and Politi, p.303).

Notes to Chapter Two

1 Catechism of the Catholic Church, Credo.

2 Catechism of the Catholic Church, 126.

3 *A Catechism of Christian Doctrine*, 63–5, Catholic Church, England, 1921.

4 Catechism of the Catholic Church, 65.

5   Catechism of the Catholic Church, 106.

6   Catechism of the Catholic Church, 81–2, 106–7.

7   Catechism of the Catholic Church, 88.

8   Catechism of the Catholic Church, 100.

9   Catechism of the Catholic Church, 85.

10 Catechism of the Catholic Church, 95.

11 Blackwell, Richard, 'Could there be another Galileo Case?', in Machamer, Peter (ed.), *The Cambridge Companion to Galileo*, p.351, Cambridge University Press, Cambridge, 1999.

12 McMullin, Ernan, 'Galileo on Science and Scripture', in Machamer, p.275.

13 Pope Pius X, *Pascendi dominici gregis* (On The Doctrine Of The Modernists), para.36, Rome, 8 September 1907.

14 Pope Pius X, *Pascendi*, para.28.

15 Pope John Paul II, *Allocution of the Holy Father John Paul II*, para.11, Proceedings of the Plenary Session of the Pontifical Academy of Sciences, 27–31 October 1992, Pontifical Academy of Sciences, Vatican City.

16 Dr Peter Hodgson, in a series of lectures offered by the International Catholic University, admits:

> The life and achievements of Galileo form a subject of enduring interest. He is certainly one of the greatest scientists of all time and indeed has been called the founder of modern science. He showed that natural phenomena obey mathematical laws and thus laid the foundations of quantitative dynamics and used it to give the first accurate account of the motions of falling bodies and of projectiles. He improved the telescope and used it to discover the moons of Jupiter, the mountains on the moon, the phases of Venus and the spots on the sun. All this combined to throw doubt on Aristotelian cosmology, and to support the heliocentric theory of Copernicus. More than any scientist, he was responsible for initiating the transition from the Aristotelian science of the Middle Ages to the mathematical science of the following centuries. (Hodgson, Peter, *Galileo and the Renaissance*, International Catholic University, http://home.comcast.net/c02902. htm , 3 March 2005)

17 Psalms, 104:5.

18 Davies, Norman, *Europe*, p.508, Pimlico, London, 1997.

19 Inquisition, *Admonition of Galileo*, 26 February 1616, http://www.law.umkc.edu/faculty/projects/ftrials/galileo/admonition.

20 Galilei, Galileo, Letter to Grand Duchess Christina, 1615, quoted in Finocchiaro, Maurice, *The Galileo Affair*, pp 93-96, University of California Press, Berkeley, 1989.

21 Holy Tribunal, *Papal condemnation*, 22 June 1633, www.law.umkc.edu/faculty/projects/ftrials/galileo/condemnation.

22 I, Galileo Galilei ... after an injunction had been judicially intimated to me by this Holy Office, to the effect that I must altogether abandon the false opinion that the sun is the centre of the world and immovable, and that the earth is not the centre of the world, and moves ... wrote and printed a book in which I discuss this doctrine already condemned, and adduce arguments of great cogency in its favour ... have been pronounced by the Holy Office to be vehemently suspected of heresy ...

> ... with sincere heart and unfeigned faith I abjure, curse, and detest the aforesaid errors and heresies, and generally every other error and sect whatsoever contrary to the said Holy Church; and I swear that in the future I will never again say or assert, verbally or in writing, anything that might furnish occasion for a similar suspicion regarding me; but should I know any heretic, or person suspected of heresy, I will denounce him to this Holy Office, or to the Inquisitor or Ordinary of the place where I may be. (Galilei, Galileo, *Recantation*, 22 June 1633, www.law. umkc.edu/faculty/projects/ftrials/galileo/recantation)

[23] Pope John Paul II, *Allocution of the Holy Father John Paul II*, Proceedings of the Plenary Session of the Pontifical Academy of Sciences, 27–31 October 1992, Pontifical Academy of Sciences, Vatican City.

[24] McMullin, p.275.

[25] Pope Pius X, *Pascendi*, para. 17.

[26] Pope John Paul II, *Discourse of His Holiness Pope John Paul II given on 10th November 1979 at the Plenary Academic Session to commemorate the centenary of the birth of Albert Einstein*, para. 6, www.ewtn.com/library/PAPALDOC/JP2ALEIN.HTM.

[27] Coyne, George V., *The Church's Most Recent Attempt to Dispel the Galileo Myth*, p.10, http://faculty.washington.edu/ewebb/Rome/Coyne.pdf, 2 March 2005.

[28] www.vatican.va/roman_curia/congregations/cfaith/, 2 March 2005.

[29] Congregation of the Index, Decree of the Index, 5 March 1616, quoted in Finocchiaro, pp.148–9.

[30] Pope Leo XIII, *Officiorum ac munerum*, Rome, 23 January 1897, quoted in Catholic Encylopedia, *Censorship of Books*, www.newadvent.org.

[31] Pope Pius X, *Pascendi*, paras 50, 52.

[32] Pope Pius X, *Sapienti consilio*, Rome, 29 June 1908, quoted in The Catholic Encyclopedia, www.newadvent.org.

[33] Catholic Encyclopedia, *Censorship*, 1907.

[34] Del Val, Cardinal Merry, *Index Librorum Prohibitorum*, Anno MDCCCCXL, quoted in Beacon for Freedom of Expression, www.beaconforfreedom.org, 12 March 2005.

[35] Blackwell, pp.361–5.

[36] Pope Pius X, *Pascendi*, paras 51, 54–5.

[37] Catholic World News, *Bishops Reject Government Decision To Curb Church's Freedom*, 20.6.1996, www.cwnews.com/news/, 15 March 2005.

[38] Congar, Yves, *Letter to the Holy Office*, National Catholic Reporter, 2 June 2000.

[39] Balasuriya, Tissa, 'Excommunication and Liberation', in Collins, Paul, *The Modern Inquisition*, pp 95-102, The Overlook Press, New York, 2002.

[40] Collins, Paul, *The Modern Inquisition*, p. 61, The Overlook Press, New York, 2002.

[41] Küng, Hans, in Collins, p.201.

[42] Miller, Patricia, *The Lesser Evil*, quoting Zenit News, 3 August 2001, www.condoms4life.org/facts/lesserEvil, 25 February 2005.

[43] Ibid.

[44] Ibid.

[45] Catholic News, *Church in Africa Continues AIDS fight without Condoms*, 10 October 2003, www.cathnews.com.

[46] Catholic Online, *Cardinal Lopez Trujillo on Ineffectiveness of Condoms to Curb AIDS*, 11 November 2003, www.catholic.org.

[47] BBC Panorama, *Sex and the Holy City*, 12 October 2003.

[48] Bradshaw, Steve, *Vatican: Condoms don't Stop AIDS*, in the Guardian, 9 October 2003, www.guardian.co.uk.

[49] MSNBC, *Spain's Catholics Reverse Condom Statement*, 20 January 2005, www.msnbc.msn.com.

[50] Medical News Today, *Los Angeles Times Examines Catholic Church Debate Over Use of Condoms To Prevent HIV Infection*, 6 February 2005, www.medicalnewstoday.com.

[51] Arie, Sophie, *Cardinal says Condoms could Help to Stop Aids*, The Guardian, 1 February 2005, www.guardian.co.uk.

[52] Blackwell, p.360.

Double Cross

Notes to Chapter Three

[1] Acts, 8:20.

[2] The Pope's arrogance, greed and power-lust eventually caused his downfall. The French king, Philip the Fair, sent an army to attack him in 1303. The Pope did not die during the attack, but the humiliation broke his resolve and he died a month later.

[3] To enable this transaction, the Pope transferred the income from Parma, Piacenza and Modena to Giuliano. Giuliano died only two years after his marriage and the papal dynastical plans were hampered. Not for long, as he shifted his energy to his nephew Lorenzo. Lorenzo was to become the Duke of Urbino. The unfortunate current duke was ousted. The Pope was aided by French troops who, not for the first time, obliged a pope in moving landowners to make space for papal relatives. As the incumbent duke, Francesco Maria della Rovere, did not go quietly, the Pope excommunicated him, raised substantial taxes and borrowed money to finance the war against della Rovere, which the Pope duly won.

[4] Catechism of the Catholic Church, 880, 882, 937.

[5] Yallop, David, *In God's Name*, pp.94, 98, Bantam Books, New York, 1984.

[6] Yallop, p.302.

[7] Pallenberg, Corrado, *The Vatican Finances*, p.85, Peter Owen, London, 1971.

[8] Pellegrini, Frank, *The Vatican Pipeline*, Time Magazine, 22 July 1997.

[9] Aarons, Mark and Loftus, John, *Unholy Trinity : The Vatican. The Nazis, and the Swiss Banks*, p.289, St. Martin's Press, New York, 1998.

[10] Yallop, p.31.

[11] Pallenberg, p.88.

[12] Ibid.

[13] Yallop, p.154.

[14] Reseau Voltaire, www.reseauvoltaire.net/article7600.html, 26 April 2003.

[15] Yallop, p.278.

[16] Williams, Paul L, *The Vatican Exposed*, p.100, Prometheus Books, New York, 2003.

[17] In 1969, the Italian government revoked the tax-exempt status of the Vatican on its investments. From then on, it would have to pay taxes like any other financial institution.

[18] Yallop, p.204.

[19] The Code of Canon Law defined enrolment in a Masonic association a 'serious sin', stating that Catholics who were Freemasons may not approach Holy Communion. A 1976 list of prominent Catholic freemasons included: Cardinal Bea, a former Vatican Secretary of State; Cardinal Baggio, prefect of the Sacred Congregation of Bishops; Cardinal Casaroli, later to become Secretary of State; Cardinal Lienart from France; Cardinal Macchi, Pope Paul VI's private secretary; Cardinal Pappalardo, archbishop of Palermo; Cardinal Pellefrino, archbishop of Turin; Cardinal Poletti, vicar of the Diocese of Rome; Cardinal Suenens; Cardinal Villot, Secretary of State; as well as scores of archbishops, bishops and other senior Churchmen.

[20] Calvi also established companies such as the Cisalpine Overseas Bank (to be renamed Banco Ambrosiano Overseas) in the Bahamas, a holding company in Luxembourg, Banco Ambrosiano Holding, the Swiss Ultrafin AG and the New York stockbroking firm Ultrafin International. In Latin America he created three banks: the Banco Ambrosiano Andino in Peru; Ambrosiano Group Banco Commercial in Nicaragua; and Banco Ambrosiano del America del Sud in the Argentine. In addition to these he established scores of Panamanian companies. The sole purpose of these and of the Latin American banks was to hide his illegal activities.

[21] Off-shore companies in tax havens are useful as, in return for a small annual payment to their jurisdiction, they are exempt from taxation and are not interfered with by the authorities. Typically, Calvi would establish such a company, more often than not in

Panama which was considered a convenient off-shore haven. He would then arrange for one of the banks he controlled, such as Banco Ambrosiano Andino in Peru, to make a loan to the Panamanian company, which would use most of the proceeds to buy shares in Banco Ambrosiano. Some of the money might be used for other purposes. As no supervisory authorities existed to scrutinise the activities of the Panamanian company, it was difficult and, in most cases, totally impossible to trace what would happen to the money once it was lent to the Panamanian company. This untraceability was one of the attractions of the set-up for Calvi and, as we shall see, to the Vatican. In such a transaction, in which the purchased shares in Banco Ambrosiano were mortgaged as security for Banco Ambrosiano Andino, there were three kinds of risk: a) more often than not, part of the loan would be used for payments to other parties and not only for Ambrosiano shares; b) the price of the shares could go down, thereby reducing their value as security for the loan; c) the shares in Ambrosiano were quoted in Italian Lire and many of the loans were nominated in US dollars so that any weakening of the Italian currency against the US dollar reduced the value of the security that Banco Ambrosiano Andino held.

Not only were substantial amounts siphoned off by the Panamanian company, as per Calvi's instructions, but both the share price of Banco Ambrosiano and the exchange rate of the Italian Lira dropped during the lifetime of these loans. As a result, Banco Ambrosiano Andino sat on a loss. Their main source of money was from direct and indirect loans from Banco Ambrosiano in Milan. When the crash came and Banco Ambrosiano in Milan demanded that the loans be repaid, Banco Ambrosiano Andino had no one to turn to for repayment. The Panamanian company was an empty shell and the security it had was worth much less than the money it owed. As there was not one but more than thirty off-shore companies, some owing US $500 million, others 'only' US $37 million, the magnitude of the problem was gigantic.

[22] This was confirmed in writing by the discovery of several 'letters of comfort' issued by the IOR in 1981. In those letters, which were written on the letterhead of the *Istituto per le Opere di Religione, Citta del Vaticano*, the IOR confirmed that it, directly or indirectly, controlled a named list of eleven off-shore companies and that it was aware of their borrowings(Yallop, p.293). The catch with 'letters of comfort' is that they give the semblance of security without giving real security. Too often, people fall into the trap of considering a 'letter of comfort' to be almost a guarantee. They should give a recipient very little comfort and they are definitely no guarantee. In our case, the fact that the Vatican owned a company, or even acknowledged its awareness of the company's borrowings, did not mean that it was responsible for its debts or any of its activities.

[23] When Banco Ambrosiano's representatives pulled out the 'letters of comfort', they realised that these letters were not guarantees of payment and that Calvi had given the IOR a written confirmation that the IOR would suffer no damage or loss as a result of the issuing of these letters (Williams, pp.173–4).

[24] The depth of the 'friendship' was demonstrated when in March 1982, eight months after Calvi had been sentenced to four years imprisonment and a US $13.7 million fine, Bishop Marcinkus gave an interview to the Italian weekly *Panorama* in which he said: 'Calvi merits our trust. This I have no reason to doubt'(Yallop, p.306).

[25] In a deal which was agreed in May 1984, the international banks, which were owed US $600 million by Calvi's Luxembourg holding company, got back approximately US $400 million, of which 250 million were paid by the Vatican, as a 'good-will' payment. The Vatican recognised its 'moral involvement' without accepting any culpability.

[26] Williams, p.175.

[27] Hammer, Richard, *The Vatican Connection*, p.197, Holt Rinehart and Winston, New York, 1982

[28] Hammer, p.275.

[29] *Il Mondo* article quoted in Yallop, pp.86–7

[30] Yallop, pp.211–13.

[31] Williams, p.175.

[32] Yallop pp.307, 312.

[33] O'Connor, Cardinal 'I'm a Catholic, But ...', New York, 21 June 1998, http://cny.org/archive/ch/ch062598.htm.

Notes to Chapter Four

[1] Catechism of the Catholic Church, 851.

[2] John Paul II, *Message of His Holiness Pope John Paul II for the Celebration of the World Day Of Peace 1 January 2000*, paras1–3, Rome, 8 December 1999.

[3] Quoted by Duffy, Eamon, *Saints and Sinners: A History of the Popes*, p.86, Yale Nota Bene, Yale, 2002.

[4] Concerted attempts to disqualify Pope Leo had been made by family and friends of the previous Pope Hadrian I. These included not only accusations of various crimes, including sexual misconduct, but also a physical attack, which took place in 799, at which his attackers endeavoured but failed to blind him and rip out his tongue.

[5] Duffy, p.167.

[6] Quoted by Duffy, p.138.

[7] Mark, 16:15.

[8] Paul VI, *Evangelii nuntiandi, Apostolic Exhortation of His Holiness Pope Paul VI to the Episcopate, to the Clergy and to all the Faithful of the Entire World*, para.15, Vatican, 8 December 1975.

[9] Paul VI, *Evangelii nuntiandi*, para.54.

[10] Hickey, Archbishop Barry, J, *How the New Catechism Can Impact on the Secular Culture*, www.ad2000.com.au/articles/1996, 10 November 2004.

[11] Paul VI, *Evangelii nuntiandi*, para.53.

[12] Paul VI, *Evangelii nuntiandi*, para.16.

[13] Paul VI, *Evangelii nuntiandi*, para.77.

[14] Catechism of the Catholic Church, 845–8, 618.

[15] Howe, Alan, *Evangelical Inclusivism. A Growing Threat to the Traditional View of the Destiny of the Unevangelized*, www.evangelical-times.org/Articles/May03.

[16] Paul VI, *Evangelii nuntiandi*, para.19.

[17] Davies, Norman, *Europe*, p.361, Pimlico, London, 1997.

[18] Code of Canon Law, 1364.

[19] These monastic orders – especially the Dominicans, nicknamed *Domini canes* ('the hounds of the Lord') and which considered itself to be the 'watchdog of Christianity' – took the lead in the Church drive to combat heresy, apostasy, magic and any deviation from Church policy.

[20] The Cathars, also known as Albigensians, believed that God could not have created both good and evil and that these were subject to two separate creations. Their sectarian movement taught that the world was created by a fallen angel, or Satan, who locked up our souls in human bodies which made them forget their heavenly origins. When a person dies, his soul is carried by demons and implanted in a pregnant woman, thus locking the heavenly soul for an additional lifetime. Jesus, according to the Cathars, was neither god, nor did he assume a human body or die on the cross, he was an angel sent by the good God to redeem our captive souls. This power to redeem, Jesus passed to his followers and in the central ceremony of the Cathars, baptism is conferred by the laying of hands. This baptism frees the souls from sin and enables them, when they die, to return to heaven. Waldensianism, inspired by the apostolic life of Christ, taught scriptural fundamentalism, which rejected extra-biblical concepts such as the existence of purgatory, the value of prayers for the dead, pilgrimages and veneration of images.

In demanding freedom to preach, Waldensians clashed with Canon law, according to which the right to preach had to be conferred by the local bishop.

21 Quoted by Given, James B., *Inquisition and Medieval Society*, p.71, Cornell University Press, Ithaca, 1997.

22 Quoted by Given, p.66.

23 The Inquisition made use of three main torture methods:

- tying a prisoner's wrists and ankles together with ropes and gradually squeezing them tighter and tighter (the rack);
- tying prisoners at their wrists, attaching weights to their feet and hanging them from a pulley (first the bodies were gradually raised and then abruptly dropped (the strappado);
- tying prisoners upside down to a sloped ladder, forcing their mouths open and forcing water into their mouths through a cloth.

A special inquisitorial torture was the 'Spanish chair' in which a prisoner was tied to an iron chair with burning coals placed beneath his feet. To prolong the agony, prisoners were regularly basted with lard as they were being roasted.

24 In 1858, a six-year-old Jewish boy from Bologna, Edgardo Mortara, who was secretly baptised by his Christian nanny, was kidnapped on Pope Pius IX's instructions, never to be returned to his parents. In the second half of the twentieth century, the Catholic Church was still at it. Jewish children who had been given to Catholic families or monasteries to be looked after in order to save them from being killed by the Germans, were often not returned to their families. The impact of the Inquisition and especially the Spanish and Portuguese Inquisitions on the fate of the Jews is covered in more depth in chapter 5.

25 Thomas Aquinas, *Quaestiones quodlibet* X, p.9. Thomas also believed that succubi, female devils, fellated men during their sleep and then, as they themselves were sterile, changed into incubi, male devils, and impregnated unmarried women during their sleep with the freshly farmed semen. In this theory, Thomas infused his disgust with sex, the total proscription of 'unnatural' sex and a belief in demons:

> Many persons affirm that they have had the experience, or have heard from such as have experienced it, that the Satyrs and Fauns, whom the common folk call incubi, have often presented themselves before women, and have sought and procured intercourse with them. Hence it is folly to deny it.
>
> … the demon assumes first the form of a woman, and afterwards of a man; … so that the person born is not the child of a demon, but of a man. (Thomas Aquinas, *Summa Theologica*, I, q.51, 3.)

26 Innocent was a man who knew the benefits of potency; he is known to have fathered at least one son, for whom he later arranged marriage to the daughter of Medici Lorenzo the Magnificent. In comparison to his successor, Pope Alexander VI (1492–1503), this was not that impressive: Alexander had at least nine illegitimate children.

27 Pope Innocent VIII, *Summis desiderantes*, Rome, 5 December 1484.

28 In their book, the inquisitors make the following instruction:

> … First, the jailers prepare the implements of torture, then they strip the prisoner… when the implements of torture have been prepared, the judge…tries to persuade the prisoner to confess the truth freely; but if he will not confess, he bid attendants make the prisoner fast to the strappado or some other implement of torture…. then, at the prayer of some of those present, the prisoner is loosed again and is taken aside and once more persuaded to confess, being led to believe that he will in that case not be put to death.
>
> … Some hold that even a witch of ill repute…may be assured her life. … Others hold, that for a time the promise made to the witch sentenced to imprisonment is to be kept, but after a time she should be burned. A third view is, that the judge

may safely promise witches to spare their lives, if only he will later excuse himself from pronouncing the sentence and will let another do this in his place....

But, if neither by threats nor by promises such as these, the witch can be induced to speak the truth, then the jailers must...torture the prisoner...and while he is being tortured, he must be questioned....while this is being done, the notary must write down everything. ...if he confesses under the torture, he must afterward be conducted to another place, that he may confirm it and certify that it was not due alone to the force of torture. (*Malleus Maleficarum*, www.fordham.edu/halsall/sbook.html.)

[29] Jučas, Mečislovas, *The Road of Christianity to Lithuania*, Society of Medieval Lithuania, www.viduramziu.lietuvos.net, 15 January 2005.

[30] Noonan, John T. Jr, *A Church that Can and Cannot Change*, pp.114–5, University of Notre Dame Press, Indiana, 2005.

[31] Noonan, pp.103–4, 109.

[32] Noonan, p.38.

[33] Quoted by Noonan, p.51.

[34] Noonan, pp.87, 92–3,

[35] Davies, p.453.

[36] Alexander VI, *Inter caetera*, Rome, 4 May 1493, www.catholic-forum.com/saints.

[37] Nicholas V, *Romanus pontifex*, Rome, January 1454, in Davenport, Frances Gardiner, *European Treaties bearing on the History of the United States and its Dependencies to 1648*, Carnegie Institution of Washington, Washington D.C., 1917.

[38] The Roman Pontiff, successor of the key-bearer of the heavenly kingdom and vicar of Jesus Christ, ... seeking and desiring the salvation of all, wholesomely ordains and disposes upon careful deliberation those things which he sees will be agreeable to the Divine Majesty...This we believe will more certainly come to pass, through the aid of the Lord, if we bestow suitable favours and special graces on those Catholic kings and princes who, like athletes and intrepid champions of the Christian faith, ...not only restrain the savage excesses of the Saracens and of other infidels, enemies of the Christian name, but also for the defence and increase of the faith vanquish them and their kingdoms and habitations, though situated in the remotest parts unknown to us, and subject them to their own temporal dominion...

And so it came to pass...they at length came to the province of Guinea, ...and war was waged for some years against the peoples of those parts in the name of the said King Alfonso and of the infante, and in it very many islands were subdued... many Guineamen and other negroes, taken by force, and some by barter...have been sent to the said kingdoms. A large number of these have been converted to the Catholic faith...

... fearing lest strangers induced by covetousness should sail to those parts, and desiring to usurp to themselves the perfection, fruit and praise of this work, or at least hinder it, should therefore, either for the sake of gain or through malice, carry or transmit iron, arms, wood used for construction... or should teach those infidels the art of navigation, whereby they would become more obstinate enemies to the king and infante... not without great offence to God...to prevent this and to conserve their right and possession, [the said king and infante] ...have prohibited and in general have ordained that none, unless with their sailors and ships and on payment of a certain tribute and with an express license previously obtained from the said king or infante, should presume to the said provinces or to trade in their ports or to fish in the sea.

... We [therefore] ...in order that King Alfonso...may be able the more zealously to pursue this most pious and noble work...by apostolic authority...decree and declare that the aforesaid letters of faculty...are extended...to the aforesaid acquisitions and all other acquisitions whatsoever, even those acquired before the date of the said letters of faculty. (Nicholas V, *Romanus pontifex*)

[39] This Christian Order was established in 1319 and endowed with most of the wealth of the dissolved Order of the Templars. The African expeditions of the Portuguese Prince were made under the banner of the Order of Christ, which thereby became even wealthier, benefiting from both ecclesiastical and other revenues emanating from the new lands.

[40] We have indeed learned that you ... chose our beloved son, Christopher Columbus ... whom you furnished with ships and men equipped for like designs, not without the greatest hardships, dangers, and expenses, to make diligent quest for these remote and unknown mainlands and islands ...and they at length, with divine aid and with the utmost diligence sailing in the ocean sea, discovered certain very remote islands and even mainlands that hitherto had not been discovered by others; wherein dwell very many peoples living in peace, and, as reported, going unclothed, and not eating flesh. Moreover, as your aforesaid envoys are of opinion, these very peoples living in the said islands and countries believe in one God, the Creator in heaven, and seem sufficiently disposed to embrace the Catholic faith and be trained in good morals. ....

In the islands and countries already discovered are found gold, spices, and very many other precious things of divers kinds and qualities. Wherefore, as becomes Catholic kings and princes,..., you have purposed with the favor of divine clemency to bring under your sway the said mainlands and islands with their residents and inhabitants and to bring them to the Catholic faith. ... And, in order that you may enter upon so great an undertaking with greater readiness and heartiness endowed with benefit of our apostolic favor, we...out of our own sole largess and certain knowledge and out of the fullness of our apostolic power, by the authority of Almighty God conferred upon us in blessed Peter and of the vicarship of Jesus Christ, which we hold on earth, do by tenor of these presents, should any of said islands have been found by your envoys and captains, give, grant, and assign to you and your heirs and successors, kings of Castile and Leon, forever, together with all their dominions, cities, camps, places, and villages, and all rights, jurisdictions, and appurtenances, all islands and mainlands found and to be found, discovered and to be discovered towards the west and south, by drawing and establishing a line from the Arctic pole, namely the north, to the Antarctic pole, namely the south, no matter whether the said mainlands and islands are found and to be found in the direction of India or towards any other quarter, the said line to be distant one hundred leagues towards the west and south from any of the islands commonly known as the Azores and Cape Verde. With this proviso however that none of the islands and mainlands, found and to be found ... be in the actual possession of any Christian king or prince up to the birthday of our Lord Jesus Christ just past from which the present year one thousand four hundred ninety-three begins. ...

Furthermore, under penalty of excommunication ... we strictly forbid all persons of whatsoever rank, even imperial and royal, or of whatsoever estate, degree, order, or condition, to dare without your special permit or that of your aforesaid heirs and successors, to go for the purpose of trade or any other reason to the islands or mainlands, found and to be found, discovered and to be discovered. (Alexander VI, *Inter caetera*)

[41] Todorov, Tzvetan, *The Conquest of America*, pp.43–4, 47, HarperPerennial, New York, 1992.

[42] Todorov, p.44.

[43] Clendinnen, Inga, *Ambivalent Conquest*, pp.73–4, Cambridge University Press, Cambridge, 1987.

[44] Clendinnen, p.79.

[45]   since the crude nature of the soil which they had to overcome, nor less the wealth of metals which had to be extracted by digging, required very hard work, unjust and inhuman plans were entered into. For a certain traffic was begun, slaves being transported for that purpose from Ethiopia. An oppression of the indigenous inhabitants (who are collectively called Indians), much the same as slavery, followed with a like maltreatment. (Pope Leo XIII, *In Plurimis*, Encyclical of Pope Leo XIII, para.15, Rome, 5 May 1888.)

[46]   Leo XIII, *In Plurimis*, para.9.

[47]   Leo XIII, *Quod apostolici muneris*, Encyclical of Pope Leo XIII on Socialism, para. 9, Rome, 28 December 1878.

[48]   Leo XIII, *In Plurimis*, paras9–10.

[49]   Pope Leo XIII, *Catholicae ecclesiae*, Encyclical of Pope Leo XIII to the Catholic Missionaries in Africa, para.2, Rome, 20 November 1890.

[50]   Catholic King Leopold II of Belgium (1835–1909) was resentful and envious of countries such as Spain, Portugal, England, Holland and France that had colonies which served as a vital source of their wealth. The Belgian king decided to colonise the Congo, which was relatively unexplored. He arranged for treaties to be signed with local chiefs, who probably did not understand what they were signing away, and set up a private army, the *Force Publique*, which turned the country into his private labour camp. As such it was run from 1885 until 1908, when the king sold 'his' Congo to his own government. The Congo was an important source of ivory, but the substantial wealth that Leopold extracted was due to natural rubber. To that end, the Congolese were systematically worked to death. It is estimated that eight to ten million lost their lives as a result of barbaric treatment by their noble European owner. The king's agents would arrive at the villages, lock up the women and children and hold them to ransom until the men delivered their assigned quota of rubber. Women and children of those who refused to deliver the rubber were slaughtered and chiefs who did not cooperate had their heads cut off. Rebellious villages were burned down, and soldiers of the *Force Publique* had to deliver the amputated right hands of rebels to prove to their officers that they had killed them. Known as the Congo Free State while it was the king's private possession, it was renamed the Belgian Congo when it became a Belgian colony. (Encyclopaedia Britannica, www.britannica.com/)

The world began to notice the Belgian king's scandalous behaviour when Joseph Conrad's novel *Heart of Darkness* (which describes his experiences as a seaman in the Congo) was published in 1902, and when the former shipping clerk Edmund Morel, who questioned why ships which came from the Congo laden with rubber sailed back with only guns and ammunition, established the Congo Reform Association. International pressure mounted until the Belgian parliament forced the King to establish an enquiry in 1905.

[51]   The exploit is in itself the highest and grandest which any age has ever seen accomplished by man; ... hundreds of thousands of mortals have, from a state of blindness, been raised to the common level of the human race, reclaimed from savagery to gentleness and humanity; and...recalled from destruction to eternal life. ...Through the constant interchange of business and ocean trade, an incredible addition was made to our knowledge of nature and to the commonwealth; while the prestige of the European name was marvellously increased.

... Columbus is ours...it is indubitable that the Catholic faith was the strongest motive for the inception and prosecution of the design; so that for this reason also the whole human race owes not a little to the Church. ... when he learned... that there were great tracts of land lying towards the West, beyond the limits of the known world, lands hitherto explored by no man, he saw in spirit a mighty multitude, cloaked in miserable darkness, given over to evil rites, and the superstitious worship of vain gods. Miserable it is to live in a barbarous state and with savage manners: but more miserable to lack the knowledge of that which is highest, and to dwell in the ignorance of the one true God. Considering these things, therefore, in his mind, he sought first of all to extend the Christian name and the benefits of Christian charity to the West, as is abundantly proved by the history of the whole undertaking. (Pope Leo XIII, *Quarto abeunte saeculo*, Encyclical of Pope Leo XIII, Rome, 16 July 1892.)

52 The Pope concedes that Columbus did not 'despise glory, which is a most engrossing ideal to great souls; nor did he altogether scorn a hope of advantages to himself'. Leo XIII, *Quarto abeunte saeculo*, para.3.

53 Pope Leo XIII, *Quarto abeunte saeculo*, para.5.

54 Pope Eugene IV, in *Sicut dudum*, quoted by Panzer, Fr Joel S., The Popes and Slavery: Setting the Record Straight, www.ewtn.com/library/.

55 Pope Paul III in *Sublimis Deus*, quoted by Panzer.

56 Pope Pius X, *Lacrimabili statu*, Encyclical of Pius X on the Indians of South America to the Archbishops and Bishops of Latin America, para.2, Rome, 7 June 1912.

57 Winter, Michael M., *Misguided Morality – Catholic Moral Teaching in the Contemporaary Church*, p. 46, Ashgate, Aldershot, 2002.

58 Hanson, Eric, *The Catholic Church in World Politics*, p. 20, Princeton University Press, Princeton, 1987.

59 Quoted by Kalibwami, Justin, *Le catholicisme et la sociètè rwandaise* 1900–1962, Presence Africaine, Paris, 1991.

60 Quoted by Kalibwami, p.169.

61 Mvuyekure, Augustin, 'Ideologie missionaire et classification ethnique en Afrique Centrale', in Chrétien, J.P. and Prunier, G., eds, *Les Ethnies ont une histoire*, p.319, Karthala, Paris, 1989.

62 Longman, Timothy, 'Christian Churches and Genocide in Rwanda', in *In God's Name*, p. 157, Berghahn Books, New York, 2001.

63 de Lespinay, Charles, 'The Churches and Genocide in East Africa', in *In God's Name*, Berghahn Books, New York, 2001.

64 de Lespinay, p.170.

65 Cornwell, John, *Hitler's Pope: The Secret History of Pius XII*, p. 253, Viking, London, 1999.

66 The poem appeared in various Croatian newspapers at Christmas in 1941. It is rather long, but some lines merit quotation. See Dedijer, Vladimir *The Yugoslav Auschwitz and the Vatican*, pp.97–102, Prometheus, New York, 1988.

> The poet saw you in the holy city
> In Saint Peter's Basilica.
> His presence was as dear to him
> As is our homeland.
> God himself, the almighty, be with you,
> So that you accomplish the sublime deed;
> … Against the greedy Jews with all their money,
> Who wanted to sell our souls,
> Betray our names,
> Those miserable ones.
> … Protect our lives from hell,
> From Marxism and Bolshevism.

67 Quoted by Manhattan, Avro, *The Vatican's Holocaust*, pp.37, 84, Ozark Books, Springfield, 1986.

68 Quoted by Manhattan, p.97.

69 Manhattan, p.101.

70 Less than a year into the Ustashe rule, the Gestapo chief and head of the German Security Service SD, Reinhard Heydrich, reported to SS Reichsführer Heinrich Himmler:

> The number of Slavs massacred by the Croats with the most sadistic of methods must be estimated at a count of 300,000. … The fact is that in Croatia, living

Serbs who have converted to the Catholic Church, are able to remain residing unharrassed ... From this it is clear that the Croat-Serbian state of tension is not least of all a struggle of the Catholic Church against the Orthodox Church. (Quoted by Deschner, Karlheinz, *Mit Gott und dem Führer*, p.282, Kiepenheuer & Witsch, Köln, 1988.)

71 Quoted by Dedijer, Vladimir *The Yugoslav Auschwitz and the Vatican*, p.142, Prometheus, New York, 1988.)

72 Quoted by Manhattan, pp.82, 92.

73 Quoted by Falconi, Carlo, *The Silence of Pius XII*, p. 298, Faber and Faber, London, 1970.

74 In one of the many barbaric killings 331 Serbs were rounded up and made to dig ditches. They were then bound and hacked to death with axes. The Serb priest and his son were kept to the end. 'The boy was cut to pieces under the eyes of his father who was forced to recite the prayers for the dying. When the priest had carried out this task, he was submitted to slow torture: first his hair was torn off, then his beard, then his skin; when they had dug out his eyes the show was still far from completion' (Falconi, p.278). Father Srecko Peric of the Gorica monastery instructed: 'Kill all Serbs, and when you have finished come here, to the church and I will confess you and free you from sin.' The immediate result was a massacre on 10 August 1941, in which 5,600 Orthodox Serbs in the district were killed (Manhattan, p.68).

75 Manhattan, p.87.

76 The choice of the apostolic legate is curious. Marcone was a Benedictine monk and philosophy teacher. The writer John Cornwell thinks that Marcone was chosen by the Pope for the very fact that he had no diplomatic experience: Marcone, according to John Cornwell, 'was an amateur who appeared to sleepwalk through the entire bloodthirsty era. ... His time in Croatia was largely spent in attending ceremonies, dinners, public parades and being photographed alongside Pavelic. He had clearly been selected to soothe and encourage' (Cornwell, pp.257–8).

77 In a meeting with a Croat representative on 6 March 1942, Tisserant said:

I know for a fact that it is the Franciscans themselves ... who have taken part in attacks against the Orthodox population so as to destroy the Orthodox Church. I know that the Franciscans in Bosnia and Herzegovina have acted abominably, ... and this pains me. Such acts should not be committed by educated, cultured, civilised people, let alone by priests.(Quoted by Falconi, p.382)

78 Quoted by Falconi, p.345.

79 Private letter to Cardinal Suhard in Paris, quoted by Cornwell, p.262.

80 Winter, p.45.

81 The Catechism of the Catholic Church states: 'The Lord made St. Peter the visible foundation of his Church. He entrusted the keys of the Church to him. The bishop of the Church of Rome, successor to St. Peter, is "head of the college of bishops, the Vicar of Christ and Pastor of the universal Church on earth".' (Catechism, 936).

Notes to Chapter Five

1 Philippians, 3:2.

2 Matthew, 23:33.

3 Romans, 11:7.

4 Acts, 7:51.

5 Matthew, 22:18.

6 John, 8:44.

7 Luke, 11:39–40, 44.

8 Matthew, 23:34.

9 Mark, 3:6.

10 Mark, 14:55–6.

[11] Thessalonians, 2:15–16.

[12] Saul grew more and more forceful, and silenced the Jews of Damascus with his cogent proofs that Jesus was the Messiah. As the days mounted up, the Jews hatched a plot against his life; ... He spoke out boldly and openly in the name of the Lord, talking and debating with the Greek-speaking Jews. But they planned to murder him. (Acts, 9:22–3, 29–30)

The Jews stirred up feeling among women of standing who were worshippers and among the leading men of the city; a persecution was started against Paul and Barnabas, and they were expelled from the district ... At Iconium similarly they went into the Jewish synagogue and spoke to such purpose that a large body both of Jews and Greeks became believers. But the unconverted Jews stirred up the Gentiles and poisoned their minds against the Christians. ... when a move was made by Gentiles and Jews together, with the connivance of the city authorities, to maltreat them and stone them, they got wind of it and made their escape. (Acts, 13:50, 14:1–6)

King Herod beheaded James, the brother of John, and then when he saw that the Jews approved, proceeded to arrest Peter also. (Acts, 12:2)

[13] Acts, 23:12, 14:19.

[14] Jesus, who according to the Gospel was expecting the betrayal, in his prayer accepted that it was God's will: 'My Father, if it is not possible for this cup to pass me by without my drinking it, thy will be done' (Matthew, 26:42). Indeed, when one of Jesus' followers tried to use his sword and protect Jesus from those who had come to seize him, Jesus said, 'Do you suppose that I cannot appeal to my Father, who would at once send to my aid more than twelve legions of angels? But how then could the scriptures be fulfilled, which say that this must be?' (Matthew, 26:53–4).

[15] Ruether, Rosemary Radford, *Faith and Fratricide: The Theological Roots of Anti-Semitism*, p.88, Seabury Press, New York, 1974.

[16] As people were evidently fickle and as preachers of various sects were doing the rounds, Paul in his Letter to the Galatians shows some exasperation:

I am astonished to find you turning so quickly away from him who called you by grace, and following a different gospel. ... only there are persons who unsettle your minds by trying to distort the gospel of Christ ... if anyone preaches a gospel at variance with the gospel which you have received, let him be outcast! (Galatians, 1:6–9)

[17] Matthew, 23:13.

[18] John, 8:43, 47.

[19] Romans, 10:3.

[20] Philippians, 3:2, 5–9.

[21] Romans, 11:17–20.

[22] Acts, 18:5–6.

[23] Matthew, 27:25.

[24] Goldhagen, Daniel Jonah, *A Moral Reckoning: The Role of the Catholic Church in the Holocaust and Its Unfulfilled Duty of Repair*, Little Brown, London, 2002.

[25] In Efroymson, David, 'Tertullian's Anti-Judaism and its Role in His Theology', as quoted by Michael, Robert, 'Antisemitism and the Church Fathers', in Perry, Marvin and Schweitzer, Frederick, *Jewish Christian Encounters over the Centuries*, p.15, Peter Lang, New York, 1994.

[26] Quoted by Flannery, Edward H, *The Anguish of the Jews: Twenty-Three Centuries of Anti-Semitism*, Macmillan, p.38, New York, 1965.

[27] See Flannery, p.37.

[28] Seaver, James Everett, *The Persecution of the Jews in the Roman Empire (300–428)*, University of Kansas Publications, Humanistic Studies No. 30, Lawrence, 1952.

[29] Quoted by Flannery, p.50.

[30] Quoted by Flannery, p.47.

[31] Chrysostom, Saint John, *Eight Homilies Against the Jews*, 1, II:5–6, Internet Medieval Sourcebook, www.fordham.edu.

[32] ...the Jews ... live for their bellies, they gape for the things of this world, their condition is not better than that of pigs or goats because of their wanton ways and excessive gluttony. They know but one thing: to fill their bellies and be drunk, to get all cut and bruised, to be hurt and wounded while fighting for their favourite charioteers. (Chrysostom, 1, IV.)

[33] Chrysostom, 1, III.

[34] Chrysostom, 1, VI:4.

[35] They sacrificed their own sons and daughters to demons. They refused to recognize nature, they forgot the pangs of birth, they trod underfoot the rearing of their children, they overturned from their foundations the laws of kingship, they became more savage than any wild beast. (Chrysostom, 5, VI:2.)

[36] Chrysostom, 1, VI:7.

[37] Chrysostom, 6, II:10.

[38] Chrysostom, 6, III:7.

[39] Ruether, p.180.

[40] Ibid.

[41] Quoted by Ruether, p. 193.

[42] Ambrose, Letter XL, in *Ökumenisches Heiligenlexikon*, www.heiligenlexikon.de/index.htm?Literatur/Online- Dokumente_Ambrosius_von_Mailand.html.

[43] Daily Catholic, www.dailycatholic.org/issue/2002May/may20doc.htm.

[44] Jerome, *The Homilies of Saint Jerome*, p.258, Catholic University of America Press, Washington, 1964.

[45] A fornicatress is a woman who has had intercourse with several men. An adulteress, one who, deserting her true spouse, joins herself to another. The Synagogue is both of these, and if she continues in fornication and adultery, God will strip off her clothes and remove the ornaments which He gave her. (Quoted by Seaver, part 7.)

[46] Quoted by Heer, Friedrich, *God's First Love*, p.37, Weybright & Talley, New York, 1970.

[47] Augustine, 'The Correction of the Donatists', in Schaff, *Nicene and Post-Nicene Fathers*, vol 6, 641, quoted by Carroll, James, *Constantine's Sword*, p.211, First Marine Books, New York, 2002.

[48] Quoted by Saperstein, Marc, *Moments of Crisis in Jewish-Christian Relations*, p.11, Trinity Press Internationals, Philadelphia, 1989.

[49] Augustine, *City of God*, book 18, ch. 46, pp.827–8, quoted by Carroll, *Constantine's Sword*, p.217.

[50] Carroll, *Constantine's Sword*, p.219.

[51] [it was prohibited to] cease being a Christian and adopt the abominable and disgusting name of the Jews [that is,] to adopt the Jewish perversity, which is alien to the Roman Empire which has now become Christianized. ...For it is an issue of life and death when someone rejects the Christian faith and replaces it with the disgusting Jewish form of perverse belief. (*Codex Theodosianus*, 16:8:19, www.hcacentre.org/CodexTheodosianos.)

[52] The wish to prevent Christians from mistakenly having sex with Jews or with Muslims would be the reason, given by the Fourth Lateran Council in 1215, for the rule that Jews and Muslims were to wear distinctive clothing.

[53] The Canons of the Fourth Lateran Council, 1215, canon 60, in *The Internet Medieval Sourcebook*, www.fordham.edu.

[54] Quoted in *The Jewish Encyclopedia.com*, Innocent III.

[55] Innocent III, Constitution for the Jews, in *The Internet Medieval Sourcebook*, www.fordham.edu.

[56] Ibid

[57] The Fourth Lateran Council, canon 70.

[58] Quoted by Young, Kimball, *Social Psychology: An Analysis of Social Behavior*, Alfred A. Knopf, New York, 1930, pp.478–502.

[59] Quoted by Kertzer, David I., *The Pope Against the Jews: The Vatican's Role in the Rise of Modern Anti-Semitism*, p.74, Alfred A. Knopf, New York, 2001.

[60] Quoted by Kertzer, p.75.

[61] Quoted by Carroll, p.375.

[62] The inscription, from Isaiah 65:2–3, speaks of 'a rebellious people, which walketh in a way which was not good, after their own thoughts; a people that provoketh Me to anger continually to My face'. In:Ellis, Richard S., 'A Jew in Rome: Christian Anti-Semitism and the Holocaust', www.math.umass.edu/~rsellis/jew-rome.html.

[63] Quoted by Kertzer pp.28–9.

[64] Luther, Martin, *The Jews and Their Lies*, Liberty Bell Publications, West Virginia, 1980.

[65] Cohen, Jeremy, *The Friars and the Jews: The Evolution of Medieval Anti-Judaism*, Cornell University Press, Ithaca, 1982, p.97.

[66] See Kertzer, p.302.

[67] Kertzer, David, I., *The Kidnapping of Edgardo Mortara*, p.159, Picador, London, 1997.

[68] Quoted by Pope Benedict XIV in *A Quo Primum*, New Advent, The Catholic Enyclopedia, www.newadvent.org/.

[69] Darring, Jerry, *A Catholic Timeline of Events Relating to Jews, Anti-Judaism, Anti-Semitism, and the Holocaust*, www.shc.edu/theolibrary/resources/timeline.

[70] Carroll, p.342.

[71] Carroll, p.361.

[72] Darring.

[73] See Cohen, pp.239, 241.

[74] Kertzer, p.128.

[75] Quoted by Kertzer, p.162.

[76] Ibid.

[77] Quoted by Kertzer, p.221.

[78] Quoted by Kertzer, p.235.

[79] Quoted by Stransky, Thomas F., *A Catholic Views Zionism and the State of Israel*, www.christusrex.org/www1/ofm/mag/MAen9901.

[80] Quoted by Lowenthal, Marvin, *The Diaries of Theodor Herzl*, pp 428-9, Victor Golancz, London, 1958.

[81] www.mfa.gov.il.

[82] Minerbi, Sergio Itzhak, *The Vatican, the Holy Land and Zionism*, p.142, Yad Izhak Ben Zvi Institute, Jerusalem, 1985.

[83] Minerbi, p.149.

[84] Minerbi, p.155.

[85] Minerbi, p.166.

[86] Minerbi, p.182.

[87] Storrs, R., *Orientations*, p. 508, Nicholson & Watson, London 1937.

[88] Minerbi, p.191.

[89] Minerbi, p.209.

[90] Minerbi, p.215.

[91] Kertzer, pp.133–52.

[92] Ibid.

[93] Quoted by Kertzer, p.164.

[94] Kertzer, p.145.

[95] Quoted by Kertzer, p.227.

[96] Quoted by Kertzer, p.147.

[97] Quoted by Zuccotti, Susan, *Under His Very Windows*, p.10, Yale University Press, New Haven, 2000.

[98] Quoted by Zuccoti, p.12.

Notes to Chapter Six

[1] Commission for Religious Relations with Jews, *We Remember: A Reflection on the Shoah*, Vatican, 1998.

[2] Ecumenical Council Vatican II, *Declaration on the Relationship of the Church to Non-Christian Religions, Nostra Aetate* (no.4) (28 October 1965), Vatican,1965.

[3] Quoted in Lewy, Guenter, *The Catholic Church and Nazi Germany*, p.271, Da Capo Press, 2000.

[4] Quoted in Lewy, p.14.

[5] Lewy, p.40.

[6] The SA (*Sturmabteilung*), was a voluntary association, established by Ernst Röhm in 1921, to protect Nazi speakers at public meetings. The SA recruited most of its members from the millions of post-First World War unemployed. As of 1924, they wore their brown shirt uniforms. Röhm originally also set up a special unit to guard the Nazi Party HQ, but this function was taken over by Heinrich Himmler and became the base for the foundation of the all-powerful SS. At the beginning of 1933, the SA numbered half a million members. The March 1933 elections brought in their train high hopes for the SA leadership, whose economic and social ideas were more radical and as such worrying to the conservative big-money supporters of Hitler. Indeed, Röhm, who considered that the SA was more important than the army, was also unpopular with the army generals. His recruiting seemed to have no limits. Soon, the organisation grew to four and a half million members. There was continuous competition between the SS and the SA, which only ended with the Röhm Purge of 1934, in which, under Hitler's instructions, Röhm together with a thousand others were killed.

[7] Friedländer, Saul, *Nazi Germany and the Jews, The Years of Persecution, 1933–1939*, p. 27, Weidenfeld and Nicolson, London, 1997.

[8] Friedländer, p.42.

[9] Physics professor at Göttingen University and Nobel Prize winner James Frank wrote in a letter published by the *Göttinger Zeitung* that 'we as Germans of Jewish origin are treated like aliens and as enemies of our country'. As a First World War veteran he was still permitted to work, but chose to resign. (The laws to dismiss all Jews regardless of their army track record were not yet in force.) The reaction of Frank's former colleagues at Göttingen University was a public condemnation of Frank's letter as an 'act of sabotage'. These academics called on the Government to 'hasten the necessary purging measures' (Friedländer, pp.67–8).

[10] Quoted by Friedländer, p.64.

[11] Quoted by Lewy, p.51.

[12] Quoted by Lewy, p.96.

[13] Quoted by Lewy, p.100.

[14] See Lewy, pp.104–5.

[15] Ibid.

[16] Quoted by Lewy, p.106.

[17] Quoted by Lewy, p.108.

[18] Phayer, Michael, *The Catholic Church and the Holocaust, 1930–1965*, p.21, Indiana University Press, Indiana, 2000.

[19] Lewy, p.165.

[20] Quoted by Lewy, p.279.

[21] Friedländer, p.146.

[22] Quoted by Lewy, p.169.

[23] Quoted by Lewy, p.173.

[24] Pius XI, *Mit brennender Sorge*, Vatican, 1937.

[25] Ibid.

[26] Ibid.

[27] Ibid.

[28] Pius XI, *Divini redemptoris*, Vatican, 1937.

[29] Quoted by Cornwell, John, *Hitler's Pope*, p.184, Viking, London, 1999.

[30] Quoted by Passelecq, Georges and Suchecky, Bernard, *The Hidden Encyclical of Pius XI*, pp.126-7, Harcourt and Brace, New York, 1997.

[31] Ibid.

[32] Quoted by Carroll, James, *Constantine's Sword: The Church and the Jews*, p.271, Mariner Books, New York, 2002.

[33] Kertzer, David I., *The Pope Against the Jews: The Vatican's Role in the Rise of Modern Anti-Semitism*, p.10, Alfred A. Knopf, New York, 2001.

[34] Quoted by Kertzer, p.158.

[35] Quoted by Zuccotti, Susan, *Under His Very Windows*, p.25, Yale University Press, New Haven, 2000.

[36] Quoted by Cornwell, p.185

[37] The two hundred and fifty thousand members of Catholic Action in Hungary who were demanding that Jewish immigration be halted and illegal immigrants be expelled, were given the full support of the Jesuit mouthpiece. Moreover, as to other laws which were being considered to restrict Jewish participation in the professions and public life, the author said, 'We do not enter into the particulars of this proposed legislation; we only note that it is inspired by the noble Magyar traditions of chivalrous and loyal hospitality, restricting itself only to what is absolutely necessary, which many believe to be sufficient' (quoted by Zuccotti, p.31). As the Jesuits themselves did not accept converted Jews, it is not surprising that this article did not object to the Hungarian definition of Jews, which rejected post-August 1919 conversions.

[38] Quoted by Zuccotti, p.45.

[39] Quoted by Zuccotti, p.51.

[40] Quoted by Zuccotti, p.54.

[41] Quoted by Lewy, p.284.

[42] Quoted by Passelecq and Suchecky, p.47.

[43] Quoted by Passelecq and Suchecky, p.36.

[44] *Humani Generis Unitas*, pp.133–43, quoted by Passelecq and Suchecky.

[45] *Humani Generis Unitas*, p.143.

[46] *Humani Generis Unitas*, pp.131–2.

[47] See Phayer, p.25.

[48] Quoted by Morley, John F., *Vatican Diplomacy and the Jews During the Holocaust 1939–1943*, p.85, Ktav, New York, 1980.

[49] Quoted by Morley, p.93.

[50] Quoted by Lewy, p.294.

[51] Phayer, pp.47-8.

[52] Morley, p.78.

[53] Quoted by Morley, p.117.

[54] Quoted by Morley, p.136.

[55] an Italian journalist, recently returned from Romania, gave me, some time ago, a long account concerning the brutal methods against the Jews, adopted in that country, above all through German instigation. He recounted to me that an

entire train was filled up with Jews; every opening was then carefully blocked up, in such a way that not even a breath of air could pass through. When the train reached a pre-established destination, the survivors were very few...(quoted by Morley, p.248.)

[56] Quoted by Morley, p.142.

[57] Morley, p.94.

[58] Morley, p.93.

[59] Letter to Myron Taylor, the Personal Representative of Roosevelt to the Vatican, from Archbishop Amleto Cicognani, quoted in Taylor, Myron C., 'Report by Myron C. Taylor, Personal Representative of the President of the U.S. to his Holiness Pope Pius XII', 1943, quoted in *American Catholics During the Holocaust* by Gershon Greenberg at http://motlc. wiesenthal.com/.

[60] Quoted by Greenberg, Gershon, *American Catholics During the Holocaust*, Simon Wiesenthal Center, Annual Volume No. 4, Los Angeles, 1997.

[61] Quoted by Cornwell, pp.290–1.

[62] Quoted by Phayer, p.62.

[63] Quoted by Cornwell, p.292.

[64] Quoted by Morley, p.118.

[65] Quoted by Lewy, p.292.

[66] Cornwell, p.209.

[67] Quoted by Lewy, p.249.

[68] Phayer, p.58.

[69] Quoted by Lewy, p.304.

[70] Lewy, p.305.

[71] In the late days of the First World War, Dr Werner, the Rabbi of Munich, on behalf of the 'Israelite Community of Germany', approached Pacelli, who was papal nuncio in Germany at the time. Could the Pope intervene in lifting an Italian embargo which was preventing the exportation of palm fronds to Germany? The palm fronds were needed for the coming Jewish Feast of Tabernacles. Pacelli told the Rabbi that he had sent an urgent report to the Pope and, due to 'wartime delays in communication, ... it was doubtful whether I shall get an answer in time'. Pacelli, instead of sending the request by enciphered telegram, chose to mail it in the diplomatic bag which took the slow overland route. Charitable Pacelli also instructed his superiors that such help went beyond 'the scope of practical, arms'-length, purely civil or natural rights common to all human beings, but in a positive and direct way ... assist[s] them in the exercise of their Jewish cult'. Cardinal Gasparri, the Vatican Secretary of State, responded by telegram commending Pacelli on his shrewdness in handling the matter. Gasparri 'approve[d] entirely in the way in which you have managed this delicate affair. The Holy See, evidently, cannot accede to the request of Professor Dr. Werner.'(quoted by Cornwell, p.70) In this unimportant episode, Pacelli reveals his manipulative qualities in achieving his goals. He was able to prevent the Jews from getting the help they had asked for by handling the practical aspects to make certain that his goal is achieved whilst lying to the Rabbi. To his grateful superiors Pacelli had offered a 'diplomatic' solution and it was to become a hallmark of his behaviour until his death: appear to help whilst in fact doing the opposite.

[72] Quoted by Cornwell, pp.74-5.

[73] Quoted by Phayer, p.106.

[74] Quoted by Lewy, p.311.

[75] Quoted by Lewy, p.232.

[76] Quoted by Lewy, p.232.

[77] Zahn, Gordon, C., *German Catholics and Hitler's Wars*, p.279, Sheed and Ward, London, 1963.

78 Quoted by Braham, Randolph, L., The Vatican: Remembering and Forgetting, in *The Vatican and The Holocaust*, edited by Randolph L Braham, p.26, Columbia U.P., New York, 2000.

79 Quoted by Lewy, p.90.

80 Quoted by Morley, p.198.

81 Quoted by Morley, p.46.

82 Quoted by Goldhagen, Daniel Jonah, *A Moral Reckoning*, p. 250, Little, Brown, London, 2002.

83 'The Holy See has never approved the project of making Palestine a Jewish home. But unfortunately, England does not yield ... Palestine is by this time more sacred for Catholics than ... for Jews' (quoted by Morley, p.92). This was his direct reaction to a request, made in March 1943, for help to enable one hundred Slovak Jewish children to emigrate to Palestine.

84 Morley, p.205.

85 Morley, pp.195–209.

Notes to Chapter Seven

1 Quoted by Lewy, Guenter, *The Catholic Church and Nazi Germany*, p.307, Da Capo Press, 2000.

2 JC Relations, *The Vatican and the Holocaust: A Preliminary Report*, October 2000, http://jcrelations.net/.

3 Quoted by Bernauer, James, *The Holocaust and the Catholic Church's Search for Forgiveness*, www.bc.edu/research/cjl/meta-elements/texts/articles/bernauer.

4 Ibid.

5 Quoted by Bernauer.

6 For example, in the eleven-volume Vatican collection *Actes et Documents du Saint Siège relatifs á la Seconde Guerre mondiale*, documents which put the Vatican in a bad light (such as a memo sent in March 1942 by the World Jewish Congress to the papal nuncio in Bern with information about the extermination of Jews) were simply omitted.

7 Phayer, Michael, *The Catholic Church and the Holocaust, 1930-1965*, p.142, Indiana University Press, Indiana, 2000.

8 Phayer, p.134.

9 Quoted by Phayer, p.136.

10 Phayer, p.135.

11 Quoted by Klee, Ernst, *Persilscheine und falsche Pässe*, p.25, Fischer, Frankfurt, 2002.

12 Klee, p.11.

13 Klee, p.14.

14 Monsignor Tiso, a Catholic priest, was President of Slovakia in the years 1930 to 1945. Slovakia, a highly Catholic country, was also highly anti-Semitic. It passed racial laws and eventually deported its Jewish population to be massacred in Poland. The Vatican's attempts to intervene were mainly to save Jews who had converted to Catholicism. Most of the country's ninety thousand Jews were murdered.

15 Quoted by Klee, p.10.

16 Quoted by Lewy, p.202.

17 Phayer, p.139.

18 Klee, p.66.

19 Quoted by Klee, p.22.

20 Quoted by Klee, p.77.

21 After persistent pestering, the bishops succeeded in having Eisele's death sentence commuted to life imprisonment. By 1952, the murderer was a free man, who with the help of Bavarian state aid opened up a clinic in Munich. He actually received DM 3,000

as a late-returning veteran. The 'new' post-Nazi Germany thus thanked the convicted killer and permitted him to practice medicine. In 1956, when Jewish survivors gave additional evidence against him which would have enabled a new trial to be opened, Eisele fled to Egypt.

22 Klee, p.66.

23 Quoted by Phayer, p.144.

24 Muench's priorities, as instructed by the Pope, were to ensure that the concordat of 1933 continued to be in force with whatever new government might be formed in Germany and to care for displaced Germans (eastern European *Volksdeutsch*). It would be a while before the US authorities noticed that the bishop was an obstacle rather than a help. Towards the end of 1947 General Clay tried to have him removed. However, the bishop had enough influence to weather that attempt. Clay failed and Muench stayed in his job.

25 Quoted by Aarons, Mark and Loftus, John, *Unholy Trinity – The Vatican, the Nazis, and the Swiss Banks*, p.14, St. Martin's Griffin, New York, 1998.

26 Aarons and Loftus, p.37, quoting from Hudal, Alois, *Römische Tagebücher: Lebenberichte eines Alten Bischofs*, Leopold Stocker, Graz/Stuttgart, 1976.

27 Aarons and Loftus, p.27.

28 Stangl was captured by the American army which handed him over to the Austrians from whose open prison in Linz he escaped and made his way into the open and waiting arms of Bishop Hudal. Hudal gave Stangl money, arranged secure lodging for him and after several weeks supplied him with a Red Cross passport, an entrance visa to Syria and a job in a textile mill in Damascus. Hudal also gave Stangl the ticket for the ship. Some time later, Stangl's family joined him in Damascus. In 1951, he moved with his family from Syria to Brazil, where he was located in 1967 and extradited to Germany. At his trial, he said 'My conscience is clear. I was simply doing my duty.'

Adolf Eichmann, head of the SS Department for Jewish Affairs was in charge of Germany's complete programme for the annihilation of Europe's Jews. His smooth operation delivered millions of Jews to the different concentration, labour and extermination camps. Hudal, according to Simon Wiesenthal, supplied Eichmann with the new identity papers under the name Richard Klement and sent him to Genoa where he was hidden in a monastery enjoying Archbishop Siri's hospitality until he was shipped to the Argentine. Caritas paid his ship fare. In 1960 Eichmann was caught by Israeli intelligence who brought him to Israel where he was tried and executed.

29 Quoted by Goni, Uki, *The Real Odessa – How Peron Brought the Nazi War Criminals to Argentina*, p.95, Granta Books, London, 2002.

30 Aarons and Loftus, p.87.

31 Aarons and Loftus, p.101.

32 Aarons and Loftus, p.109.

33 Quoted by Aarons and Loftus, p.115.

34 Goldhagen, Daniel Jonah, *A Moral Reckoning*, p. 37, Little, Brown, London, 2002, citing Irwin-Zarecka, Iwona, 'Poland After the Holocaust', in *Remembering for the Future: Working Papers and Addenda*, vol. I, p.143, Pergamon Press, Oxford, 1989.

35 Quoted by Phayer, p.182.

36 Lewy, pp. 272–3, 394–5.

37 Rokach, Livia, *The Catholic Church and the Question of Palestine*, pp. 30–1, Saqi books, London, 1987.

38 Rokach, p.114.

39 Allen, John, *National Catholic Reporter*, 21 February 2003.

40 Quoted by Fallaci, Oriana, *On Anti-Semitism Today*, Panorama, 15 April 2002, in www.tpi.umn.edu/shifman/fallaci.pdf.

41 Rokach, p.168.

[42] Quoted by Perko, F. Michael, *Toward a 'Sound and Lasting Basis': Relations between the Holy See, The Zionist Movement, and Israel, 1896–1996*, Israel Studies Volume 2, Number 1, http://iupjournals.org/israel/iss2-1.html#r12.

[43] Quoted by Phayer, p.213.

[44] Ecumenical Council Vatican II, *Declaration on the Relationship of the Church to Non-Christian Religions, Nostra Aetate* (no. 4) (28 October 28 1965), Vatican, 1965.

[45] Commission for Religious Relations with Jews, *Guidelines and Suggestions for Implementing the Conciliar Declaration Nostra Aetate (no. 4)* (1 December 1974), Vatican, 1974.

[46] Commission for Religious Relations with Jews, *Notes on the correct way to present the Jews and Judaism in preaching and catechesis in the Roman Catholic Church* (24 June 1985), Vatican, 1985.

[47] Catholic Bishops in the Netherlands, *Supported by One Root: Our Relationship to Judaism*, October 1995, www.bc.edu/research/cjl/meta-elements/texts/documents/catholic/dutch.

[48] Catholic Bishops' Conference in Switzerland, *Confronting the Debate About the Role of Switzerland During the Second World War*, March 1997, www.bc.edu/research/cjl/meta-elements/texts/documents/catholic/switzerland.

[49] Catholic Bishops of France, *Declaration of Repentance*, September 1997, www.bc.edu/research/cjl/meta-elements/texts/documents/catholic/french.

[50] Catholic Bishops in Poland, *The Victims of Nazi Ideology*, January 1995, www.bc.edu/research/cjl/meta-elements/texts/documents/catholic/poland.

[51] Pope Pius XII, *Allocution of His Holiness to the Sacred College of Cardinals on 2 June 1945*, The Avalon Project at Yale Law School, www.yale.edu/

[52] A child, whose parents had prayed to Edith Stein when she was very ill from a Tylenol overdose, recovered. This was enough for the Church to call it a miracle and the road was clear for the new Catholic saint. Doctors interviewed about the 'miracle' are on record confirming that 'ninety-nine per cent of children with Tylenol overdoses fully recover' (quoted by Wills, Gary, *Papal Sin: Structures of Deceit*, p.59, Darton, Longman and Todd, London, 2000.).

[53] Quoted by Woodward, Kenneth, L., *Making Saints: How the Catholic Church Determines Who Becomes a Saint, Who Doesn't and Why*, p.147, Simon and Schuster, New York, 1996.

[54] The Vatican has several levels at which it issues documents. This one was issued by the Commission for Religious Relations with Jews with a covering letter by Pope John Paul II. It is the third document promulgated by this Vatican commission, which was established by Pope Paul VI in 1974, and the first one to benefit from a papal covering letter. The Vatican could have chosen to issue the document as an encyclical or at least as a papal document signed by the pope himself, either of which would have given it more prestige.

[55] Commission for Religious Relations with Jews, *We Remember: A Reflection on the Shoah*, Vatican, 1998.

[56] Quoted by Morley, John, F., 'Reaction of a Catholic Theologian to the Vatican's "We Remember" Document', in *The Vatican and The Holocaust*, edited by Randolph L. Braham, p.50, Columbia University Press., New York, 2000.

[57] Morley, in Braham, p.53.

[58] Littell, Franklin, H., 'Reaction of a Protestant Theologian to the Vatican's *We Remember* Document', in *The Vatican and The Holocaust*, p.83.

[59] Quoted in Braham, Randolph L., 'The Vatican: Remembering and Forgetting', in *The Vatican and The Holocaust*, pp.18–19.

[60] Rudin, A., James, 'Reaction of a Jewish Theologian to the Vatican's *We Remember* Document', in *The Vatican and The Holocaust*, p.97.

[61] Wills, Gary, *Papal Sin: Structures of Deceit*, p.13, Darton, Longman and Todd, London, 2000.

[62] Morley, in Braham, p.54.

[63] Catholic Information Network, *Universal Prayer: Confession of Sins and Asking for Forgiveness*, www.cin.org/jp2/univpray.html.

[64] Eternal Word Television Network, *Remembrance:'To Ensure That Never Again Will Evil Prevail'*, www.ewtn.com/holyland2000/News/remembrance.

[65] Assad, Bashar, *Speech of President Bashar Al-Assad Welcoming His Holiness Pope John Paul II on his arrival in Damascus, Syria, May 5, 2001*, www.adl.org/Israel/al-assad_speech.asp.

[66] Daily Catholic, *Catholic PewPoint: Have they forgotten the lessons of history?*, 18 March 1998, www.dailycatholic.org.

[67] CBS News, *Vatican Advisor Offends Jews*, 17 March 2000, www.cbsnews.com.

Notes to Chapter Eight

[1] Quoted by Ranke-Heinemann, Uta, *Eunuchs for Heaven: The Catholic Church and Sexuality*, p.250, André Deutsch, London, 1990.

[2] Hierarchy of England and Wales, *The Catholic Attitude to Sex Education*, Joint Pastoral Letter, p.3, London, 1944.

[3] Hierarchy of England and Wales, p.5.

[4] ...care must be taken...to give a full, firm and uninterrupted religious instruction to youth of both sexes; that an esteem and desire for and love of the angelic virtue be instilled in them; that they shall be urged, especially, to be instant in prayer, assiduous in the reception of the sacraments of Penance and the Holy Eucharist; that they shall cultivate a filial devotion to the Blessed Virgin, Mother of holy purity, and place themselves under her protection; and that they shall carefully avoid dangerous reading, immodest shows, bad company, and all occasions of sin. (Hierarchy of England and Wales, p.5.)

[5] Matthew, 5:27-32.

[6] Corinthians, 7:7-8.

[7] God has given them up to shameful passions. Their women have exchanged natural intercourse for unnatural, and their men in turn, giving up natural relations with women, burn with lust for one another; males behave indecently with males, and are paid in their own persons the fitting wage of such perversion. (Romans, 1:26-7)

[8] Leviticus, 18:22.

[9] Leviticus, 20:13.

[10] Leviticus, 18:23.

[11] Exodus, 22:19; Leviticus, 20:15.

[12] Leviticus, 18:6-17.

[13] Leviticus, 20.

[14] Exodus, 19:10, 14, 15.

[15] Leviticus, 21: 13-15.

[16] Leviticus, 21:18-21.

[17] Proverbs, 18:22.

[18] Genesis, 38:9-10.

[19] It is a good thing for a man to have nothing to do with women; but because there is so much immorality, let each man have his own wife and each woman her own husband. The husband must give the wife what is due to her, and the wife equally must give the husband his due. The wife cannot claim her body as her own; it is her husband's. Equally, the husband cannot claim his body as his own; it is his wife's. Do not deny yourselves to one another, except when you agree upon a temporary abstinence in order to devote yourselves to prayer; afterwards you may come together again; otherwise, for lack of self-control, you may be tempted by Satan. (I Corinthians, 7:1-5.)

[20] Surely you know that the unjust will never come into possession of the kingdom of God. Make no mistake: no fornicator or idolater, none who are guilty either of adultery or of homosexual perversion, no thieves or grabbers or drunkards or slanderers or swindlers, will possess the kingdom of God. …

'I am free to do anything', you say. … But it is not true that the body is for lust; it is for the Lord – and the Lord for the body. …Do you not know that your bodies are limbs and organs of Christ? Shall I then take from Christ his bodily parts and make them over to a harlot? Never! You surely know that anyone who links himself with a harlot becomes physically one with her; …Shun fornication. Every other sin that a man can commit is outside the body; but the fornicator sins against his own body. Do you not know that your body is a shrine of the indwelling Holy Spirit, and the Spirit is God's gift to you?…Then honour God in your body. (I Corinthians, 6:9--20.)

[21] Matthew,19:12. The *New American Bible*, as it appears in the Holy See's website, has the following footnote:

Incapable of marriage: literally, eunuchs. Three classes are mentioned, eunuchs from birth, eunuchs by castration, and those who have voluntarily renounced marriage (literally, have made themselves eunuchs) for the sake of the kingdom, i.e., to devote themselves entirely to its service. Some scholars take the last class to be those who have been divorced by their spouses and have refused to enter another marriage. But it is more likely that it is rather those who have chosen never to marry, since that suits better the optional nature of the decision: whoever can … ought to accept it.

[22] Quoted by Parrinder, Geoffrey, *Sexual Morality in the World's Religions*, p.221, Oneworld Publications, Oxford, 1996.

[23] St Ambrose, *Expositio In Lucam*, 1.44, quoted by Ranke-Heinemann, pp.46–7.

[24] St Ambrose, *Expositio In Lucam*, 1.43, quoted by Ranke-Heinemann, pp.46–7.

[25] Quoted by Ranke-Heinemann, p.viii.

[26] We have read God's first command, 'Be fruitful, and multiply, and replenish the earth'; but while we honour marriage we prefer virginity which is the offspring of marriage. …Marriage replenishes the earth, virginity fills Paradise. …If virgins are first-fruits, it follows that widows and the continent in marriage, come after the first-fruits, that is, are in the second and third rank …

John, one of the disciples, who is related to have been the youngest of the Apostles, and who was a virgin when he embraced Christianity, remained a virgin, and on that account was more beloved by our Lord, and lay upon the breast of Jesus. And what Peter, who had had a wife, did not dare ask, he requested John to ask. And after the resurrection, when Mary Magdalene told them that the Lord had risen, they both ran to the sepulchre, but John outran Peter. And when they were fishing in the ship on the lake of Gennesaret, Jesus stood upon the shore, and the Apostles knew not who it was they saw; the virgin alone recognized a virgin, and said to Peter, 'It is the Lord.' … We have maintained that his virginity was the cause of the special love our Lord bore to him, … if he was not a virgin, why it was that he was loved more than the other Apostles.(Jerome, *Against Jovinianus*, 3, 16, 26, in Catholic Encyclopedia, www.newadvent.org/)

[27] Jerome, 16.

[28] Jerome, 20.

[29] Jerome, 34.

[30] Ranke-Heinemann, p.62.

[31] Augustine, *On Marriage and Concupiscence*, 1.5, Internet Medieval Sourcebook, www.fordham.edu.

[32] Augustine, *On Marriage*, 1.10.

33   When the first man transgressed the law of God, he began to have another law in his members which was repugnant to the law of his mind, and he felt the evil of his own disobedience when he experienced in the disobedience of his flesh a most righteous retribution recoiling on himself ... Well, then, how significant is the fact that the eyes, and lips, and tongue, and hands, and feet, and the bending of back, and neck, and sides, are all placed within our power – to be applied to such operations as are suitable to them, when we have a body free from impediments and in a sound state of health; but when it must come to man's great function of the procreation of children the members which were expressly created for this purpose will not obey the direction of the will, but lust has to be waited for to set these members in motion, as if it had legal right over them, and sometimes it refuses to act when the mind wills, while often it acts against its will! Must not this bring the blush of shame over the freedom of the human will, that by its contempt of God, its own Commander, it has lost all proper command for itself over its own members? (Augustine, *On Marriage*, 1.7.)

34   ..whenever it comes to the actual process of generation, the very embrace which is lawful and honourable cannot be effected without the ardour of lust, so as to be able to accomplish that which appertains to the use of reason and not of lust. Now, this ardour, whether following or preceding the will, does somehow, by a power of its own, move the members which cannot be moved simply by the will, and in this manner it shows itself not to be the servant of a will which commands it, but rather to be the punishment of a will which disobeys it. It shows, moreover, that it must be excited, not by a free choice, but by a certain seductive stimulus, and that on this very account it produces shame. This is the carnal concupiscence. Now from this concupiscence whatever comes into being by natural birth is bound by original sin, unless, indeed, it be born again in Him whom the Virgin conceived without this concupiscence.(Augustine, *On Marriage*, 1.27.)

35 Augustine, *On Marriage*, 1.9.

36 Augustine, *On Marriage*, 1.10.

37 Augustine, *On Marriage*, 1.16.

38   It is, however, one thing for married persons to have intercourse only for the wish to beget children, which is not sinful: it is another thing for them to desire carnal pleasure in cohabitation, but with the spouse only, which involves venial sin. For although propagation of offspring is not the motive of the intercourse, there is still no attempt to prevent such propagation, either by wrong desire or evil appliance. They who resort to these, although called by the name of spouses, are really not such; they retain no vestige of true matrimony, but pretend the honourable designation as a cloak for criminal conduct.

    ... Sometimes, indeed, this lustful cruelty, or; if you please, cruel lust, resorts to such extravagant methods as to use poisonous drugs to secure barrenness; or else, if unsuccessful in this, to destroy the conceived seed by some means previous to birth, preferring that its offspring should rather perish than receive vitality; or if it was advancing to life within the womb, should be slain before it was born. Well, if both parties alike are so flagitious, they are not husband and wife; and if such were their character from the beginning, they have not come together by wedlock but by debauchery. But if the two are not alike in such sin, I boldly declare either that the woman is, so to say, the husband's harlot; or the man the wife's adulterer. (Augustine, *On Marriage*, 1.17.)

39 Augustine, *City of God*, 14.16.

40 Noonan, John T, *Contraception: A History of Its Treatment by the Catholic Theologians and Canonists*, p.164, Harvard University Press, Cambridge, MA, 1966.

41 See Burchard of Worms (d. 1025) in McNeill, John T. and Gamer, Helena M., *Medieval Handbooks of Penance*, p.343, Columbia University Press, New York, 1990.

42 Catholic Encyclopedia, Theodore, Archbishop of Canterbury.

43 This collection of decisions, includes the following:

Penance for fornication was meted out as follows: Fornication with a virgin - one year; with a married woman - four years; a repetitive fornicator with other men or beasts - ten years. Two brothers who fornicate with each other – are prohibited form any sex for fifteen years. Just the desire to fornicate, if unfulfilled – 40 days, and sexual fantasies require penance until the 'libidinous imagination is overcome.'

Ejaculating semen in someone's mouth – between seven and twelve years' penance. Boys who mutually masturbate are to be whipped; if they are over twenty years old – fifteen years penance. A woman masturbating on her own or with another woman – three years penance. If the masturbator is a priest he will have to fast for three weeks. A priest who has a wet dream whilst asleep in church must do penance for three days, whereas if he is 'polluted through imagination' he shall fast for a week.

Husbands were not allowed to see their wives in the nude and after sleeping with their wives had to wash before going to church. 'Unnatural intercourse' with one's wife – forty days penance and intercourse 'at the improper season' – fast for forty days. (McNeill and Gamer, pp.184–214.

44 Ranke-Heinemann, p.12.

45 Quoted in McNeill and Gamer, 314–18.

46 Quoted by Ranke-Heinemann, p.134.

47 Ibid.

48 Quoted by Ranke-Heinemann, p.137.

49 Quoted by Price, Elizabeth, *Seeing Sin Where None Is*, www.womenpriests.org, 30 August 2004.

50 Quoted by Ranke-Heinemann, p.142.

51 Ranke-Heinemann, p.171.

52 Thomas Aquinas, *Summa Theologica*, II-II:154, 8, www.newadvent.org.

53 There are only two ways in which married persons can come together without any sin at all, namely in order to have offspring, and in order to pay the debt. Otherwise it is always at least a venial sin.

If a man intends by the marriage act to prevent fornication in his wife, it is no sin, because this is a kind of payment of the debt that comes under the good of 'faith.' But if he intends to avoid fornication in himself, then there is a certain superfluity, and accordingly there is a venial sin...(Thomas Aquinas, *Summa Theologica*, Supplement III, q. 49)

54 Ranke-Heinemann, p.50.

55 Quoted by Noonan, p.272.

56 ... Simple fornication, which is committed without injustice to another person, is the least grave among the species of lust. Then, it is a greater injustice to have intercourse with a woman who is subject to another's authority as regards the act of generation, than as regards merely her guardianship. Wherefore adultery is more grievous than seduction. And both of these are aggravated by the use of violence. Hence rape of a virgin is graver than seduction, and rape of a wife than adultery.

Wherever there occurs a special kind of deformity whereby the venereal act is rendered unbecoming, there is a determinate species of lust. This may occur in two ways: First, through being contrary to right reason, and this is common to all lustful vices; secondly, because, in addition, it is contrary to the natural order of the venereal act as becoming to the human race: and this is called 'the unnatural vice.' This may happen in several ways. First, by procuring pollution, without any copulation, for the sake of venereal pleasure: this pertains to the sin of 'uncleanness' which some call 'effeminacy.' Secondly, by copulation with a thing of undue species, and this is called 'bestiality.' Thirdly, by copulation with an undue sex, male with male, or female with female, as the Apostle states (Rm. 1:27): and this is called the 'vice of sodomy.' Fourthly, by not observing the natural manner of copulation, either as to undue means, or as to other monstrous and bestial manners of copulation. ...

Therefore, since by the unnatural vices man transgresses that which has been determined by nature with regard to the use of venereal actions, it follows that in this matter this sin is gravest of all. After it comes incest, which, ... is contrary to the natural respect which we owe persons related to us. ...(Thomas Aquinas, *Summa Theologica*, II-II: 154, 11)

[57] Quoted by Noonan, p.273.

[58] Quoted by Noonan, p.272.

[59] Quoted by Noonan, p.271.

[60] Ranke-Heinemann, pp.222–4.

[61] Catechism of the Catholic Church, 1648.

[62] Catechism of the Catholic Church, 2384.

[63] Catechism of the Catholic Church, 1650.

[64] Catechism of the Catholic Church, 1626–9.

[65] Archdiocese of Boston, *Can Marriage be Declared Null?*, www.rcab.org/marriage3.html, 19 September 2003.

[66] Pius XI, *Casti connubii: Encyclical of Pius XI on Christian Marriage*, 45–6, Vatican, 1930.

[67] Pius XI, *Casti connubii*, 79, 82, 85–6.

[68] Pius XI, *Casti connubii*, 2.

[69] Pius XI, *Casti connubii*, 10.

[70] Pius XI, *Casti connubii*, 17–18.

[71] Pius XI, *Casti connubii*, 26.

[72] Pius XI, *Casti connubii*, 74.

[73] Pius XI, *Casti connubii*, 29, 76.

[74] Pius XI, *Casti connubii*, 50–2.

[75] Pius XI, *Casti connubii*, 125.

[76] The Lateran Treaty, for example, which the Vatican signed with the Kingdom of Italy in 1929, declares: 'The Italian State, wishing to restore to the institution of matrimony, which is the foundation of the family, that dignity which is conformable with the Catholic traditions of its people, recognizes the civil effects of the Sacrament of matrimony regulated by Canon Law ... Causes concerning nullity of matrimony and dispensations from matrimony ratified but not consummated are reserved to the competence of the Ecclesiastical Tribunals and their departments.' Concordat between the Holy See and the Kingdom of Italy, 34, Rome, 1929.

[77] BBC News, 29 January 2002, http://news.bbc.co.uk/1/hi/world/europe/1787106.stm.

[78] Even after the 2001 ousting of the Taliban, homosexuality remained a crime in Afghanistan, punishable by lengthy prison terms with hard labour (www.sodomylaws. org/world/afghanistan/afnews012, 7 September 2004). In Saudi-Arabia, three men were beheaded in January 2002 for 'engaging in the extreme obscenity and ugly acts of homosexuality, marrying among themselves and molesting the young'. However, according to journalist Mubarak Dahir, there is an abundance of homosexual activity in Saudi Arabia and Saudi gay men believe that 'people are beheaded for murder, rape and drug smuggling, ... not for being gay'. Dahir, Mubarak, *Is Beheading Really the Punishment for Homosexuality in Saudi Arabia?*, www.sodomylaws.org/world/saudi_arabia/saudinews19.htm, 19 September 2004.

[79] www.gayhistory.com/rev2/events/1794.htm, 17 September 2004.

[80] www.fordham.edu/halsall/pwh/para175.

[81] www.tellingpictures.com/films/p175/p175_phis.html.

82 www.sodomylaws.org/bowers/bowers.htm, 18 September 2004.

83 Congregation for the Doctrine of the Faith, *Persona Humana: Declaration on Certain Questions Concerning Sexual Ethics*, Vatican, 1975.

84 Catechism of the Catholic Church, 2358.

85 Catechism of the Catholic Church, 2359.

86 Catechism of the Catholic Church, 2357.

87 Homosexual sex will not be permitted by the Catholic Church as:

> there is .. a clear consistency within the Scriptures themselves on the moral issue of homosexual behaviour. The Church's doctrine ...is based... on the solid foundation of a constant Biblical testimony. The community of faith today, in unbroken continuity with the Jewish and Christian communities within which the ancient Scriptures were written, continues to be nourished by those same Scriptures... (Congregation for the Doctrine of the Faith, *Letter to the Bishops of the Catholic Church on the Pastoral Care of Homosexual Persons*, Vatican, 1986.)

88 McNeill, John J., *The Church and the Homosexual*, Preface, www. Apollonetwork.com

89 Collins, Paul, *The Modern Inquisition, Seven Prominent Catholics and their Struggles with the Vatican*, pp.141–2, The Overlook Press, New York, 2002.

90 Congregation for the Doctrine of the Faith, *Letter to the Bishops of the Catholic Church on the Pastoral Care of Homosexual Persons*, Vatican, 1986.

91 Congregation for the Doctrine of the Faith, *Some Considerations Concerning the Response to Legislative Proposals on the Non-Discrimination of Homosexual Persons*, Vatican, 1992.

92
> Including 'homosexual orientation' among the considerations on the basis of which it is illegal to discriminate can easily lead to regarding homosexuality as a positive source of human rights, for example, in respect to so-called affirmative action or preferential treatment in hiring practices. This is all the more deleterious since there is no right to homosexuality which therefore should not form the basis for judicial claims. The passage from the recognition of homosexuality as a factor on which basis it is illegal to discriminate can easily lead, if not automatically, to the legislative protection and promotion of homosexuality.
>
> The 'sexual orientation' of a person is not comparable to race, sex, age, etc. also for another reason than that given above which warrants attention. An individual's sexual orientation is generally not known to others unless he publicly identifies himself as having this orientation or unless some overt behaviour manifests it. As a rule, the majority of homosexually oriented persons who seek to lead chaste lives do not publicize their sexual orientation. Hence the problem of discrimination in terms of employment, housing, etc., does not usually arise.
>
> Homosexual persons who assert their homosexuality tend to be precisely those who judge homosexual behaviour or lifestyle to be 'either completely harmless, if not an entirely good thing', and hence worthy of public approval. It is from this quarter that one is more likely to find those who seek to 'manipulate the church by gaining the often well-intentioned support of her pastors with a view to changing civil statutes and laws. ...(Congregation for the Doctrine of the Faith, *Some Considerations... non-Discrimination.*)

93 Congregation of the Doctrine of the Faith, *Considerations Regarding Proposals to give Legal Recognition to Unions Between Homosexual Persons*, Vatican, 2003.

94
> Children must be treated with the utmost love and gentleness. He [the confessor] shall cause them to recite all the sins they can remember. They may then be asked the following questions...Whether they have committed a nasty sin. The confessor must, however, question them very discreetly on this subject. ...Even when the children say 'no', it is often expedient to ask them leading questions, for example: 'And now tell me, how often you have done this? Five times, ten times? They shall then be asked with whom they sleep and whether they have played with their fingers in bed...(quoted by Ranke-Heinemann, p.247.)

[95] Geis, Dr Rudolph, *Principles of Catholic Sex Morality*, pp.76–8, Joseph F. Wagner, New York, 1930.

[96] Adding insult to injury, as in all other sexual teachings of the Catholic Church, preachers did not practice what they preached. According to the sexologist, Dr William Masters, a survey of two hundred Catholic priests revealed that one hundred and ninety-eight of them reported having masturbated at least once during the previous year. Sipe, A.W. Richard, *A Secret World: Sexuality and the Search for Celibacy*, Brunner/Mazel, New York, 1990.

[97] In his book, Bekkers warned that masturbation caused gastric disorders, dyspepsia, vomiting, wasting of the respiratory organs, coughing and hoarseness, palsy, impotence, lack of libido, back pain, impaired sight, impaired hearing, loss of energy, facial cysts, amnesia, dementia, epilepsy and paralysis. Some, he warned, were driven to suicide. His book was translated into many European languages, became a bestseller, and fomented public hysteria.

[98] Ranke-Heinemann, pp.282–6.

[99] Geldof, Bob, *Is That It?*, p.35, Sidgwick & Jackson, London, 1986.

[100] The traditional Catholic doctrine that masturbation constitutes a grave moral disorder is often called into doubt or expressly denied today. It is said that psychology and sociology show that it is a normal phenomenon of sexual development, especially among the young. ... This opinion is contradictory to the teaching and pastoral practice of the Catholic Church. Whatever the force of certain arguments of a biological and philosophical nature, ... the Magisterium of the Church – in the course of a constant tradition – and the moral sense of the faithful have declared without hesitation that masturbation is an intrinsically and seriously disordered act. (Congregation for the Doctrine of the Faith, *Persona Humana, Declaration on Certain Questions Concerning Sexual Ethics*, IX, Vatican, 1975.)

[101] ... The frequency of the phenomenon in question is certainly to be linked with man's innate weakness following original sin; but it is also linked with a loss of a sense of God. ...

Sociological surveys are able to show the frequency of this disorder according to the places, populations or circumstances studied. In this way facts are discovered, but facts do not constitute a criterion for judging the moral value of human acts.

... In the Pastoral ministry in order to form an adequate judgement in concrete cases, the habitual behaviour of people will be considered in its totality... In particular, one will have to examine whether the individual is using the necessary means, both natural and supernatural, which Christian asceticism from its long experience recommends for overcoming the passions and progressing in virtue. (Congregation for the Doctrine of the Faith, *Persona*, IX)

[102] Janus, Samuel S. and Janus, Cynthia L., *The Janus Report: Sexual Behaviour*, John Wiley and Sons, New York, 1993.

[103] Catechism of the Catholic Church, 2352.

[104] Augustine, *On Marriage*, 1.17.

[105] Noonan, p.164.

[106] One often renders the debt to his wife in such a way that he does not satisfy his pleasure, and conversely. Therefore, in the aforesaid case, I can so render the debt to the wife and wait in such a way until she satisfies her pleasure. Indeed, often in such cases a woman is accustomed to anticipate her husband, and when the pleasure of the wife in the carnal work is satisfied, I can, if I wish, withdraw, not satisfying my pleasure, free of all sin, and not emitting my seed of propagation. (Quoted in Noonan, pp.296–7)

[107] Noonan, p.298.

[108] Ranke-Heinemann, p.151.

[109] Quoted by Ranke-Heinemann, pp.182–5.

[110] Ranke-Heinemann, p.259.

[111] Cornwell, John, *Breaking Faith*, p.67, Penguin Books, London, 2002.

[112] Pius XI, *Casti connubii*, 60–1.

[113] Pius XI, *Casti connubii*, 57, 67.

[114] ... no reason, however grave, may be put forward by which anything intrinsically against nature may become conformable to nature and morally good. Since, therefore, the conjugal act is destined primarily by nature for the begetting of children, those who in exercising it deliberately frustrate its natural power and purpose sin against nature and commit a deed which is shameful and intrinsically vicious. .... Small wonder, therefore, if Holy Writ bears witness that the Divine Majesty regards with greatest detestation this horrible crime and at times has punished it with death. As St. Augustine notes, 'Intercourse even with one's legitimate wife is unlawful and wicked where the conception of the offspring is prevented. Onan, the son of Juda, did this and the Lord killed him for it'. (Pius XI, *Casti connubii*, 54–5)

[115] Wills, Gary, *Papal Sin: Structures of Deceit*, pp.83–5, Darton, Longman & Todd, London, 2000.

[116] Vatican Council II, *Gaudium et Spes, Pastoral Constitution on the Church in the Modern World*, 49, Vatican, 1965.

[117] Vatican Council, *Gaudium*, 47, 50.

[118] Vatican Council, *Gaudium*, 51.

[119] Wills, p.94.

[120] Ranke-Heinemann, p.244.

[121] Winter p.163, based on *The Tablet*, 8 March 1996.

[122] Catholics for a Free Choice, *Pros & Cons: Voices on the Church's Condom Policy*, www.condoms4life.org/facts/condomPolicy.htm, 21 September 2004.

[123] Cornwell, p.120.

[124] Catholics for a Free Choice, *Pros & Cons*.

[125] For as it is, there are those who think that whatever is permitted by the laws of the State, or at least is not punished by them, is allowed also in the moral order, and, because they neither fear God nor see any reason to fear the laws of man, they act even against their conscience, thus often bringing ruin upon themselves and upon many others..... .

To bring forward a recent and clear example of what is meant... in the solemn Convention happily entered into between the Holy See and the Kingdom of Italy, also in matrimonial affairs a peaceful settlement and friendly cooperation has been obtained... These decrees, are to be found in the Lateran Pact: 'The Italian State, desirous of restoring to the institution of matrimony, which is the basis of the family, that dignity conformable to the traditions of its people, assigns as civil effects of the sacrament of matrimony all that is attributed to it in Canon Law.' (Pius XI, *Casti connubii*, 125–6.)

[126] Wanrooij, Bruno P. F., *Contraception, Abortion, and Population Planning*, www2.hu-berlin. de/sexology/ 21 September 2004.

[127] Call to Action, Church Watch, *Vatican contraception views obstruct U.N. population talks*, www.cta-usa.org/watch5-99/vatican.html, 21 September 2003.

[128] A case in point is the Czech Republic, in which there has been increased availability of the birth control pill and other types of contraception, and where abortions dropped from one hundred and seven thousand in 1990 to thirty-two thousand five hundred in 2000. BBC News, *Europe's Terms for Terminations*, 2 June 2002, http://news.bbc.co.uk.

[129] Pius XI, *Casti connubii*, 65.

[130] Pius XI, *Casti connubii*, 58.

[131] Pius XI, *Casti connubii*, 64.

[132] Cornwell, p.123.

[133] *Time* Magazine, 19 February 1990.

[134] http://www.vatican.va/roman_curia/pontifical_academies/acdlife/documents/rc_pa_acdlife_doc_20001031_pillola-giorno-dopo_en.html

[135] The vice-president of the Vatican's Academy for Life, Elio Sgreccia, criticised United Nations refugee workers for providing rape victims from Kosovo with such pills and the Catholic Church withdrew her contribution to the United Nations children's fund UNICEF following use of the pill for rape victims during the war in Bosnia-Herzegovina in 1992–95. BBC News, http://news.bbc.co.uk/1/hi/world/europe/, 13 April 1999.

[136] Childbirth by Choice Trust, www.cbctrust.com/abortion.html#15, 1995.

[137] BBC News, 2002.

[138] Swomley, John M., *The Two Faces of Mr. Hyde: Vatican Puppets in American Politics*, Humanist, January 1999.

[139] Cardinal Dionigi Tettamanzi of Milan explained the Church's excommunication laws pertaining to abortion: 'Excommunication for procured abortion constitutes a gesture of maternal love. It expresses and puts into action the love of Mother Church, who comes to the defence of the defenceless unborn child, and who recalls and supports the one who has erred so that it doesn't happen again.' Allen, John L. Jr, *Under Vatican ruling, abortion triggers automatic excommunication*, National Catholic Reporter, 17 January 2003, www.natcath.com.

[140] Westdeutsche Allgemeine Zeitung, 7 December 1998, 22 December 1998, www.schmidt-salomon.de/ir_199.htm.

Notes to Chapter Nine

[1] Catechism of the Catholic Church, 2337.

[2] Catechism of the Catholic Church, 2349.

[3] Catechism of the Catholic Church, 2396, 2351.

[4] Quoted by Ranke-Heinemann, Uta, *Eunuchs for Heaven: The Catholic Church and Sexuality*, p.87, André Deutsch, London, 1990.

[5] Ranke-Heinemann, p.90.

[6] Cawthorne, Nigel, *Sex Lives of the Popes*, p.44, Prion, London, 2004.

[7] Quoted by Ranke-Heinemann, p.91.

[8] Ranke-Heinemann, p.93.

[9] Durant, Will, *The Reformation*, p.21, Simon and Schuster, New York, 1980.

[10] Catholic Encyclopedia, Volume IV, Concubinage, www.neadvent.org.

[11] Popes who are known to have fathered children include Anastasius I (399–401), Sergius III (90–-911), Benedict VIII (1012–1024), Anacletus II (1130–1138), John XXII (1316–1334), Pius II (1458–1464), Sixtus IV (1471–1484), Innocent VIII (1484–1492), Callistus III (1455–1458), Alexander VI (1492–1503), Julius II (1503–1513), Paul III (1534–1549), Julius III (1550–1555). Innocent I was the son of Anastasius I and John XI was the son of Sergius III. Julius II was the son of Sixtus IV and Alexander VI was probably the son of Callistus III. Many more examples can be found in Nigel Cawthorne's *Sex Lives of the Popes*, Prion, London, 2004.

[12] Cawthorne, p.125.

[13] Cawthorne, p.176.

[14] For example, Catholic priest, Samuel Frick of Maienfeld, who had fathered seven children and paid Episcopal dues on account of his trespasses between the years 1515 and 1521, decided that he had had enough and changed over to the Lutheran Church.

[15] Ranke-Heinemann, p.98.

[16] Ibid.

[17] Ibid.

[18] *New York Times*, 10 April 2005.

[19] Sipe, A. W. Richard, *A Secret World: Sexuality and the Search for Celibacy*, p.124, Brunner/ Mazel , New York, 1990.

[20] Cornwell, John, *Breaking Faith*, p.157, Penguin Books, London, 2002.

Notes to Chapter Ten

[1] Bonavoglia, Angela, *Groups target abuses by clergy*, Chicago *Tribune*, 18 July 2001.

[2] Cawthorne, Nigel, *Sex Lives of the Popes*, p.85, Prion, London, 2004.

[3] Cawthorne, p.85.

[4] *Boston Globe*, The Investigative Staff of, *Betrayal: The Crisis in the Catholic Church*, p.36, Little, Brown and Company, Boston, 2002.

[5] Fox, Thomas, *National Catholic Reporter*, 17 May 2002.

[6] The National Review Board for the Protection of Children and Young People Established by the United States Conference of Catholic Bishops, *A Report on the Crisis in the Catholic Church in the United States*, 27 February 2004.

[7] *Boston Globe*, p.7.

[8] Wornat, Olga, *Nuestra Santa Madre : Historia Publica y Privada de La Iglesia Catolica Argentina*, Ediciones B, Barcelona, 2002.

Also in the Argentine: in January 2001 a priest was arrested following allegations that he raped residents of a home for adolescent boys. Another priest accused of molesting several young girls was moved to a parish in another city.

[9] The mentally handicapped men were teenagers at the time and were abused by some twenty brothers in three institutions run by the Roman Catholic order, the *St. John of God Brothers*, in Melbourne, Australia. A statement from the order, which has agreed to pay a A $3.64 milion out of court settlement, said: 'The order acknowledges that some of the residents under its care were sexually abused by some brothers.' *St. John of God* has previously settled other cases out of court. The Catholic order of nuns, *The Poor Sisters of Nazareth*, made payments of A$75,000 (US$41,400) to 13 women who claimed they were sexually and physically abused in an orphanage in the 1940s and 1950s. The payments were made without acknowledgement of guilt.

[10] A UK parliamentary report on the welfare of former British child migrants found that:

The worst cases of criminal abuse in Australia appear to have occurred in institutions run by agencies of the Catholic Church, in particular the Christian Brothers (especially the 'Boys' Town' at Bindoon, north of Perth, although we heard grim stories about Clontarf, Tardun and Castledare as well) and the Sisters of Mercy (especially the orphanage at Neerkol in Queensland, and also Goodwood Orphanage in South Australia). The Sisters of Mercy were frequently described to us as the 'Sisters without mercy', just as the Christian Brothers were often described as the 'Christian buggers'.

... It is hard to convey the sheer weight of the testimony we have received. It is impossible to resist the conclusion that some of what was done there was of a quite exceptional depravity, so that terms like 'sexual abuse' are too weak to convey it. For example, those of us who heard the account of a man who as a boy was a particular favourite of some Christian Brothers at Tardun who competed as to who could rape him 100 times first, his account of being in terrible pain, bleeding, and bewildered, trying to beat his own eyes so they would cease to be blue as the Brothers liked his blue eyes, or being forced to masturbate animals, or being held upside down over a well and threatened in case he ever told, will never forget it. But if it were one account it could perhaps be dismissed as exceptional— unfortunately adult after adult described their suffering as children. We heard of being told that 'whatever a priest did was the Will of God, but if a boy told what a priest did he would commit a mortal sin'. As well as such depravity, which was not suffered to the same extent by all, the boys were treated as slave labour.

At Bindoon they actually constructed a large building, which one witness has described as having boys' blood embedded in it.

...We also noted that when giving evidence to us in Perth, the Christian Brothers were very insistent that the abuses were not known to those who controlled these institutions. We cannot accept this. We believe that there is more to learn about the circumstances of child migrants at Christian Brothers institutions (and possibly some other Catholic institutions) in Australia, and that in some cases criminal investigation may be called for. (UK Parliament, Select Committee on Health, Session 1997–98, Third Report, *The Welfare of Former British Child Migrants*, Paras 49,51,55, www.parliament.

[11] BBC, http://news.bbc.co.uk/1/hi/world/asia-pacific/2035823.stm

[12] Other photos showed candidates for the priesthood kissing and fondling each other and their older instructors and engaging in sex games. The rector and vice-rector of the seminary, photographs of whom, kissing and fondling seminarians at a Christmas party, were published worldwide when the affair came to light in July 2004, protest their innocence, although they admit the photos are genuine. Sixty-eight year-old Bishop Kurt Krenn, in whose diocese the seminary is located, dismissed the photos as part of a 'schoolboy prank', and refused to step down. Ultra-conservative Krenn, who publicly defended Cardinal Groer, was a favourite of Pope John Paul II, who appointed him bishop of St Pölten in 1991. The Pope, who chose to include Krenn's diocese in his 1998 trip to Austria, signifying his support for the bishop, had to endure symbolic rebuke, as he arrived in St Pölten. Liberal Austrian Catholics angry with their arch-conservative bishop stood waving around a thousand black balloons in protest. In September 2004, at the Pope's request, Bishop Krenn resigned.

[13] Religious Tolerance Org., *Sexual Abuse by Catholic Clergy – The Canadian Situation*, www.religioustolerance.org/clergy_sex3.htm, 3 October 2004.

[14] *New York Times*, 3 November 2005.

[15] In the winter of 1991, a Church-appointed commission criticised Archbishop Alphonsus Penney for his handling of reports of sex abuse by priests. Under Penney's leadership, the diocese had received more than twenty complaints of sexual abuse of children between 1989 and 1991. The commission accused Penney of failing to take the proper steps to respond to the reports. Penney resigned from his position. Investigations came up with similar sexual abuse cases in schools which the *Christian Brothers* ran in other Canadian provinces. Another Canadian Catholic order, *The Missionary Oblates of Mary Immaculate*, faced about two thousand lawsuits on sexual abuse.

[16] Deutsche Welle, www.dw-world.de/dw/article/0,2144,1220276,00.html

[17] Fifty-two 'industrial schools' – schools where children were detained if their parents were deemed too poor to look after them, or if they stole or played truant – were run by Catholic religious orders and backed by the Irish government. They closed in the 1970s. Campaigners say that the priests and nuns subjected most children to physical or sexual attacks. In a deal to help out Catholic religious orders in Ireland, these orders paid the Irish government €127 million in cash and land, in return for which the government undertook to underwrite all claims for abuse compensation. The Irish government has, in 2002, set up its Residential Institutions Redress Board of Ireland, which handles claims and makes awards to people who, as children, were abused while resident in various institutions in Ireland.

[18] The Ferns Inquiry, *The Ferns Report*, p.124, Dublin, 2005.

[19] His custodial sentence was reviewed after one year on grounds of ill health and Collins was indeed released after one year. According to the *Ferns Report* one of the complainants alleged that during the 1980s, whilst he was at boarding school, Collins called him to his room and told him 'to take off his shirt and jumper, using a measuring tape, measured his chest and waist and the inside of his legs. Fr. Collins then unzipped his trousers and measured his penis with the measuring tape. Fr. Collins fondled Darren's testicles and penis while talking to Darren about the size of his penis and what size

it could be. The abuse continued on a regular basis throughout Darren's remaining period at St. Peter's College. Fr. Collins performed oral sex on him, gave him alcohol and showed him two pornographic films.' (Ferns Report, p. 75)

20 Allegations about Fr Fortune include, according to *The Ferns Report*, the most horrific tales of abuse, such as: Ian, a sixteen-year-old boy who was working when 'Fr. Fortune bent over him to show him how to do something and pressed down on him. He then fumbled with his belt and Ian shouted '*no no*', struggling for breath. He said that Fr. Fortune took down his trousers, fondled his genitals and buggered him. He said this was brutal and painful and occurred despite struggles to get away. Ian says that Fr. Fortune left him '*in a mess on the floor, bleeding heavily*'. The same clergyman, another boy, Patrick alleged, picked him up in his car 'spoke to him about relationships and sexual preferences...masturbated himself throughout the journey and then smeared his face with semen telling Patrick that it would heal [the scarring on his] face. ...Patrick was raped and abused by Fr. Fortune approximately three times a week for two to three years.' Another boy, Colin, alleged that when he was twelve years old, Fortune pushed him into a cubicle of a public toilet in Wexford, bolted the door and raped him. Years later, Fortune successfully blackmailed Colin to perform oral sex on him, lest he would tell Colin's wife and other people of his rape. (The Ferns Report, pp.91, 93, 99.)

21 When he was not rejecting pleas for annulment, in his capacity as head of the Dublin diocese Marriage Tribunal, Father Ivan Payne abused boys. He was jailed for six years for abusing altar boys and patients in *Our Lady's Hospital for Sick Children*. To help him buy the silence of an alleged abuse victim, Archbishop Desmond Connell of Dublin, who regularly denounced contraception, divorce, abortion and homosexual relationships, gave him a loan. Conservative Connell was made Cardinal by the Pope in 2001. After the Irish television documentary in October 2002, which investigated the scope of abuse cases in Dublin and which accused the Cardinal of demonstrating little sympathy for abuse victims, pressure had been mounting on Connell to resign. He finally did so and was replaced in April 2004.

22 *The Guardian*, 9 March 2006.

23 'Not everyone understood my genuine openness and spontaneity toward people', the Polish Catholic news agency, KAI, quoted the Archbishop as saying; the same Archbishop who is alleged to have been abusing young priests and who finally was forced to resign. 'There was a misinterpretation of my words and gestures.' These allegations had been known within the Church for a number of years, but action was only seen to be taken after it became headline news in the Polish press. A front-page article, accompanied by a large photo of the Archbishop, called on the episcopate to acknowledge the truth which was being concealed by the archbishop's palace in Poznan. Local priests waged a long campaign to have him removed from office. Paetz submitted his resignation after the Vatican began investigations into the allegations.

24 *New York Times*, 21 June 2004.

25 One of the cases described by David France in his *Our Fathers: The Secret Life of the Catholic Church in An Age of Scandal*, is of two brothers Gary and Edward Bergeron who were abused by a priest, and whose father Joseph had already been abused by his priest in the 1920s, almost forty years before Vatican II. When a thirty-nine-year-old Gary told his father about the abuse, his father broke down:

> I might as well tell you now, because I have never told anybody. You kids need to know that I know you are suffering. I know you have suffered all of your life. *Because of my sins!* Because what you went through, I went through. You see? I went through the same thing. When I was eight years old. ..I never even told your mother. Never told nobody. And because I never said anything to anybody, it kept happening, don't you see? Those are my sins. And there is nothing I can do about it now, because it is too late. (France, David, *Our Fathers: The Secret Life of the Catholic Church in An Age of Scandal*, p.424, Broadway Books, New York, 2004.)

When the father and son, one in his eighties, the other in his forties, went to Rome asking for an audience with the Pope, the Pope had no time for them. This 'episode' demonstrates not only that this is not a new phenomenon of the swinging-sixties, but also the long-term psychological damage this un-dealt with abuse has caused its victims.

[26] *New York Times*, 2 May 2004, quoting Berry, Jason and Renner, Gerald, *Vows of Silence: The Abuse of Power in the Papacy of John Paul II*, Free Press, New York, 2004.

[27] France, p.204.

[28] France, p.332.

[29] France, pp. 230, 593.

[30] *New York Times*, 12 May 2004.

[31] *New York Times*, 12 January 2003.

[32] *New York Times*, 23 March 2002.

[33] *New York Times*, 12 and 14 October 2005.

[34] Bishop Joseph Keith Symons resigned in 1998 after admitting that he had molested five boys earlier in his career. Bishop Anthony J. O'Connell, who had succeeded Symons, had to leave in February 2002, after a former student at a Missouri seminary disclosed abuse by him. *New York Times*, 4 September 2002.

[35] *New York Times*, 24 July 2003.

[36] *New York Times*, 6 March 2003.

[37] *New York Times*, 11 December 2002.

[38] *New York Times*, 6 March 2003.

[39] *New York Times*, 22 October 2002.

[40] *Boston Globe*, p.79.

[41] The priests Edward Booth and Armando Annunziato had, on separate occasions, walked-in when Father Porter was molesting a boy in the rectory office in St. Mary's parish, North Attleboro, Mass. The boy recalled 'Father Booth looked at Father Porter and then back at me, and then at Father Porter, who was zipping his fly. Then Father Booth shook his head and walked out of the door. He didn't say a word.' When Annunziato walked-in on a similar situation with a different boy, all he did was to say 'It's getting late. It's time for everyone to go home.'(*Boston Globe*, p.44) That was the pastoral care Father Annunziato gave to an eleven-year-old, who had just been molested by one of his colleagues.

[42] *New York Times*, 12 January 2003.

[43] A fifteen-year-old boy in Ireland told an inquiry how when he reported to a priest that he saw another priest abusing a younger teenager 'the priest asked him for a detailed account of the abuse and a demonstration of how the abuse occurred'. Moreover, the boy said, this priest then 'put his hand on [his] penis ... he hit his hand away'. *The Ferns Report*, p.97.

[44] *Boston Globe*, p.23.

[45] *Boston Globe*, p.24.

[46] *Boston Globe*, p.79.

[47] *Boston Globe*, p.35.

[48] *Boston Globe*, p.69.

[49] *Boston Globe*, p.71.

[50] *New York Times*, 23 March 2002.

[51] *New York Times*, 15 February 2003.

[52] *Boston Globe*, p.58.

[53] *Boston Globe*, p.96.

[54] *The Ferns Report*, p.19.

[55] *New York Times*, 14 August 2002.

[56] *Boston Globe*, p.162.

[57] *New York Times*, 14 August 2002.

58 *New York Times*, 26 November 2002.

59 *New York Times*, 13 December 2002.

60 Indeed, the number exceeds five hundred. *New York Times*, 12 December 2005.

61 *New York Times*, 23 July 2003.

62 *New York Times*, 27 September 2002.

63 *Boston Globe*, p.111.

64 Ibid.

65 *New York Times*, 16 October 2002.

66 *New York Times*, 12 February 2003.

67 *Ibid.*

68 *New York Times*, 11 February 2003.

69 Ibid.

70 *New York Times*, 15 February 2003.

71 The Arizona bishop, Manuel D. Moreno, ran one of the most outrageous concealment operations uncovered up to now. He actively discouraged priests from reporting sexual abuse to him. When, in 1988, a Tucson priest reported to him that Monsignor Robert Trupia regularly took children to his bedroom, Moreno 'got hostile'. Perhaps he did not want to face the fact that he had already been warned about Trupia by an archbishop at a California seminary in 1982 and again in 1988. When eventually the abuse came to the attention of the police, the Church actually refused to give the police the address of Trupia, who, at that time, was already suspended by the Church for his sexual molestations (*Boston Globe*, p.77). Lynne M. Cadigan, a lawyer who has handled many of the lawsuits against this man, who as bishop, allowed abusers to continue in ministry, 'I don't think Bishop Moreno was deliberately evil or deliberately trying to inflict harm, but unfortunately with the medieval power structure of the church, an ineffectual administrator can have the same effect' (*New York Times*, 8 March 2003).

72 *New York Times*, 3 June 2003.

73 *New York Times*, 12 January 2003.

74 *New York Times*, 4 March 2003.

75 *New York Times*, 13 September 2002.

76 *New York Times*, 29 October 2002.

77 *The Ferns Report*, p.187.

78 *New York Times*, 24 December 2002.

79 *New York Times*, 10 September 2002.

80 *Boston Globe*, p.123.

81 *Boston Globe*, p.134.

82 *Boston Globe*, pp.125–6.

83 *New York Times*, 15 February 2003.

84 *Washington Post*, 13 May 2002.

85 *Boston Globe*, p.40.

86 Between 1992 and 2001 the Archdiocese of Boston settled claims against more than seventy child-molesting priests. They all had confidentiality agreements imposed by the Church. This ensured that the story remained hidden and prevented other victims from coming forward by keeping them in the dark, both emotionally and financially. It also resulted in continued child abuse. *Boston Globe*, p.49.

87 *Washington Post*, 13 May 2002.

88 *Ibid.*

89 *New York Times*, 24 December 2002.

90 *New York Times*, 14 October 2005.

[91] When in 1998, former Archbishop Rembert G. Weakland of Milwaukee paid US $450,000 to a man who had accused him of sexual abuse, the money came from an account that contained nearly US $1 million from the sale of an office building previously donated to the archdiocese by a foundation endowed by Ms Erica John. Ms John was one of fifty wealthy Catholic donors who, in June 2002, wrote to Bishop Gregory, the president of the US Conference of Catholic Bishops, asking the conference to hire an external auditor to prepare a survey of monies paid by the Church over two decades for abuse settlements, lawyers' fees and other costs resulting from sexual misconduct by clergymen. The American Roman Catholic bishops, who are uncomfortable with the idea of an external audit, rejected this demand.

[92] The first one to actually do so was the Archdiocese of Portland, Oregon, which had paid more than US $53 million to settle about a hundred abuse claims, and more claims were pending at the time it filed for bankruptcy. Bankruptcy proceedings stop any ongoing litigation and thereby also save substantial legal costs involved in the lawsuits. Importantly, it prevents a public airing of the cover-up of child-abuse crimes by the Church's local hierarchy and officials. This is of paramount importance to the Church, which has done her utmost to prevent cases from going to court. The Church has found that court proceedings not only broadcast her shame, but also that juries often determine punitive compensation to victims of abuse, at rates much higher than those her lawyers negotiate in out-of-court settlements. The case which triggered Portland archdiocese's decision to go for bankruptcy was that of a priest accused of molesting boys in his car, in the rectory, on camping trips and even during what he called confessions, and who explained that he bore no responsibility because children would 'throw themselves' at him (*New York Times*, 7 July 2004). When the next diocese, that of Tucson, filed for bankruptcy, a lawyer for the plaintiffs said that the Church 'is using this bankruptcy as a public relations tool to make the victims appear to be the predators of the diocese' (*New York Times*, 21 September 2004).

[93] CBS News, www.cbsnews.com/stories/2006/10/10/national/main2079538.shtml

[94] *New York Times*, 25 July 2002.

[95] Dr Paul R. McHugh has been one of the strongest critics of psychiatric therapy based on the theory that traumatic experiences can be subconsciously repressed for years. He has testified on behalf of accused sexual abusers, including at least one priest, who faced the statements of adults who said they had repressed memories of molestation for years before recovering them. In one case Dr McHugh testified that the accusers' memories of abuse were false. Dr Gartner, the president of the National Organization on Male Sexual Victimization, had the following reaction: 'This reveals the mindset of how the church intends to deal with this problem. ... Up until now, people have not been questioning the veracity of the victims' stories' (*New York Times*, 26 July 2002).

[96] *New York Times*, 24 October 2002.

[97] *New York Times*, 10 August 2002.

[98] *New York Times*, 21 July 2002.

[99] Eventually, they agreed to release the information. For this survey, which was conducted by academic researchers at the John Jay College of Criminal Justice in Manhattan, every bishop in the country was mailed an extensive questionnaire requesting information in relation to abusive priests in their diocese. The priests and victims are not identified by name and the results of the study would be cumulative and would not offer a breakdown of the results by diocese. Robert S. Bennett, a lawyer who led the Review Board's task force evaluating the causes of the crisis, used strong language to describe the uncooperative bishops who were acting like 'risk assessment officers of insurance companies', and suggested they:

> start acting like pastors and shepherds of their flock ... In the Church there has been a culture of secrecy, and it has gotten them in a lot of trouble. And the time has come where they have got to understand that it will not work anymore, and that they must be open, they must be transparent and they must be accountable. (*New York Times*, 13 June 2003)

[100] *New York Times*, 14 June 2003.

[101] *New York Times*, 17 June 2003.

[102] I frankly believed that in my years with all of you it was me who had to endure the experience worse than anyone else. I regret that in my innocence and isolation I was not in a position to help anybody else. I did not know the abuse reached so many of you. ... I admire your courage and integrity. As far as I am concerned, I should have preferred to remain silent, but it is clear now that my only choice is to make common cause with our suffering. Our lives may be considered little or insignificant, but we are telling the truth, without hatred, without seeking gain, embracing the Cross of our Lord Jesus, in whose faith we want to live and die. I hope a reborn Church might emerge from all this turmoil, more coherently sensible, humbler, less arrogant. (Berry, Jason and Renner, Gerald, *Vows of Silence: The Abuse of Power in the Pacacy of John Paul II*, p.177, Free Press, New York, 2004)

[103] Berry, Jason and Renner, Gerald, p.14

[104] *Catholic News*, 8 August 2003, www.cathnews.com/news/308/42.php

[105] CBS News, *Sex Crimes Cover-Up by Vatican?*, 6 August 2003, www.cbsnews.com.

[106] *Boston Globe*, p.96.

[107] *New York Times*, 28 September 2002.

[108] Ibid.

[109] *New York Times*, 18 October 2002.

[110] *New York Times*, 19 October 2002.

[111] *Ibid.*

[112] *Boston Globe*, p.200.

[113] *New York Times*, 31 July 2003.

[114] *New York Times*, 15 December 2002.

[115] *New York Times*, 13 December 2002.

[116] *New York Times*, 14 December 2002.

[117] *The Ferns Report*, p.22: 'It would be seen as a factor in increasing the risk to adolescent boys but no more than a heterosexual priest would be a risk to adolescent girls.'

[118] *Boston Globe*, p.170.

[119] *New York Times*, 7 September 2002.

[120] *New York Times*, 20 October 2002.

[121] The investigation was undertaken by the National Review Board for the Protection of Children and Young People which was established by the US Conference of Catholic Bishops into abuse by Catholic clergy in the United States. The Review Board was chaired by Robert S. Bennett, a former federal prosecutor. It included two judges, a law school dean, a psychologist, a psychiatrist and Leon E. Panetta, former chief of staff to President Bill Clinton.

[122] The National Review Board for the Protection of Children and Young People Established by the United States Conference of Catholic Bishops, *A Report on the Crisis in the Catholic Church in the United States*, 27 February 2004.

[123] The report further concluded that:

This is a failing not simply on the part of the priests who sexually abused minors but also on the part of those bishops and other Church leaders who did not act effectively to preclude that abuse in the first instance or respond appropriately when it occurred.

... As a result, priests who had engaged in sexual abuse of minors were, with distressing frequency, allowed to remain where they had abused, reassigned to other parishes within the same dioceses, or allowed to live in other dioceses where they posed a further threat to children that predictably materialized into additional incidents of abuse.

The leniency afforded predator priests by some bishops may in some instances have been a misguided act of forgiveness. Nevertheless, the failure of some bishops to temper forgiveness with responsible actions to insulate minors from additional acts of abuse has seriously undermined the confidence of the laity in the leadership of the Church as a whole.

... Perhaps even more troubling than the criminal and sinful acts of priests who engaged in abuse of minors was the failure of some bishops to respond to the abuse in an effective manner, consistent with their positions as leaders of the flock with a duty to protect the most vulnerable among us from possible predators. Sexual abuse of minors is an evil and, as one priest told the Board, knowingly allowing evil conduct to continue is 'cooperation with evil.'

Among the causes, the Review Board suggested that:

- Some bishops and other Church leaders often put what they erroneously believed to be the institutional concerns of the local Church above the concerns of the universal Church. The fear of scandal caused them to practice secrecy and concealment.

- The threat of litigation caused some bishops to disregard their pastoral role and adopt an adversarial stance not worthy of the Church.

- Some bishops and other Church leaders failed to comprehend fully the extent and magnitude of the harm suffered by victims of sexual abuse by priests.

- Bishops and other Church leaders did not do enough in the way of 'fraternal correction' to ensure that their brethren dealt with the problem in an effective manner.

- Some bishops and other Church leaders placed the interests of the accused priests above those of the victims and too often declined to hear from victims directly, relying instead on denials and assurances from those accused of abuse.

- Canon law and canonical procedures made it too difficult to remove a predator priest from ministry, and bishops did not make sufficient use of what canonical authority they did have to take action against such priests and protect the children and young people of the Church.

[124] *New York Times*, 5 October 2002.

[125] Fox, Thomas, *National Catholic Reporter*, 17 May 2002.

[126] *Boston Globe*, p.5.

[127] *New York Times*, 11 October 2003.

[128] Quoted by Appleby, R. Scott, 'Unheavenly Days for the Catholic Church', *New York Times*, 7 September, 2003.

Notes to Conclusion

[1] Freud, Sigmund, *Moses and Monotheism*, p.157, Vintage Books, New York, 1955.

[2] Religion is defined by the Blackwell Dictionary of Sociology as a 'social arrangement designed to provide a shared, collective way of dealing with the unknown and unknowable aspects of human life, death and existence, and the difficult dilemmas that arise in the process of making moral decisions. As such, religion not only provides responses to enduring human problems and questions but also forms a basis for social cohesion and solidarity.' Allan G. Johnson, *The Blackwell Dictionary of Sociology*, Blackwell, Oxford, 2000.

[3] Wulff, David M., *Psychology of Religion*, p.82, John Wiley & Sons, New York, 1991.

[4] O'Connor, Cardinal 'I'm a Catholic, But ...', New York, 21 June 1998, http://cny.org/archive/ch/ch062598.htm.

[5] Catechism of the Catholic Church, 845.

[6] Catechism of the Catholic Church, 847–8.

7   Paul VI, *Evangelii nuntiandi, Apostolic Exhortation of His Holiness Pope Paul VI to the Episcopate, to the Clergy and to all the Faithful of the Entire World*, para.53, Vatican, 8 December 1975.

8   Paragraph 95 of the Catechism of the Catholic Church states:

> It is clear therefore that, in the supremely wise arrangement of God, sacred Tradition, Sacred Scripture and the Magisterium of the Church are so connected and associated that one of them cannot stand without the others. Working together, each in its own way, under the action of the one Holy Spirit, they all contribute effectively to the salvation of souls.

9   Quoted by Kertzer, David I., *The Popes Against the Jews*, pp.35–6, Alfred A. Knopf, New York, 2001. This was in response to a plea to the Pope by an Austrian government minister who objected to the bringing back of old restrictions on Jews in territories which were returned to the Pope in the framework of the 1815 Congress of Vienna.

10 Sabine, George, *A History of Political Theory*, p.579, George Harrap & Co., London, 1966.

11 John Paul II, *Tertio Millennio Adveniente, Apostolic Letter of His Holiness Pope John Paul II to the Bishops, Clergy and Lay Faithful on Preparation for the Jubilee Of The Year 2000*, para.38, Rome, 1994.

12 Dawson, Christopher, *Religion and the Modern State*, pp.135–6, Sheed and Ward, New York, 1936, quoted in Lewy, p.329.

13 Quoted by Davies, Norman, *Europe*, p.796, Pimlico, London, 1997.

14 Commission for Religious Relations with Jews, *We Remember: A Reflection on the Shoah*, Vatican, 1998.

15 Wills, Gary, *Papal Sin: Structures of Deceit*, p.13, Darton, Longman and Todd, London, 2000.

16 Pope John Paul II, *Discourse of His Holiness Pope John Paul II given on 10 November 1979 at the Plenary Academic Session to commemorate the centenary of the birth of Albert Einstein*, www.ewtn.com/library/.

17 *New York Times*, 11 October 2003.

18 *Boston Globe*, The Investigative Staff of, *Betrayal: The Crisis in the Catholic Church*, p.200, Little, Brown and Company, Boston, 2002.

19 Hanson, Eric, *The Catholic Church in World Politics*, p.356, Princeton University Press, Princeton, 1987.

20 Hook, Sidney, *'Integral Humanism' Reason, Social Myths and Democracy*, New York, 1940. p.91, quoted in Lewy, Guenter, *The Catholic Church and Nazi Germany*, p.326, Da Capo Press, 2000.

21 Quoted by Appelby, R. Scott, 'Unheavenly Days for the Catholic Church', *New York Times*, 7 September 2003.

22 Tóibín, Colm, 'At St. Peter's', in *London Review of Books*, vol. 27, no. 23, 2005.

23 The Ferns Inquiry, *The Ferns Report*, p.26, Dublin, 2005.

24 Catechism of the Catholic Church, 2266-7. Indeed, the Church even says that 'Assuming that the guilty party's identity and responsibility have been fully determined, the traditional teaching of the Church does not exclude recourse to the death penalty, if this is the only possible way of effectively defending human lives against the unjust aggressor.'

Appendix One

The following are but a few examples, which emerged from court cases involving Catholic clergy:

- MH, a British priest, was found guilty of sexually assaulting children, among them two disabled youths, between 1969 and 1987.
- Between September 1993 and September 1994 Father B performed fellatio on (sucked the penis of) an eleven-year-old altar boy and then forced the boy to touch the priest's genitals. The priest then warned the boy that his parents would be harmed if he told anyone of the incidents.
- The same priest grabbed the buttocks of an altar-boy and masturbated in front of him.
- A priest in Lawrence, Mass. told a boy that if he wanted to 'get closer to God' he should undress and get closer to the priest.
- Father P pleaded guilty to three counts of child rape involving an altar boy between 1990 and 1992.
- Rev. K, sexually assaulted a seventeen-year-old girl while counselling her about a previous sexual assault. Upon hearing of the girl's complaint, the pastor of the church, Rev. W, in an interview with a local paper, referred to the girl as 'a tramp'.
- Father K is accused of repeatedly groping a boy.
- Father S and Father C raped altar boys.
- Rev. H pleaded guilty to two counts of sodomy for abusing a fourteen-year-old boy from November 1999 through to January 2001.
- Father N was convicted in Brooklyn of molesting a twelve-year-old girl at her home in 1999. Father N entered the girl's home on the pretext of visiting her sick grandmother. With her terminally ill grandmother in her wheelchair a few feet away, Father N pulled her onto his lap and pressed himself against her buttocks through their clothing. When the girl tried to get away, he pulled her onto his lap again, this time

putting his hand up her shirt and touching her breast. Then, Father N said, 'Let's pray'.

- Father M was convicted of raping a fifteen-year-old boy during 'pastoral counselling' sessions in 1983 at the rectory of St B.

- Father K tied up and molested two boys, ages eleven and twelve, in a rectory in Union City, San Francisco.

- A New Jersey priest initiated wrestling sessions at social gatherings, during which he used to fondle a fourteen-year-old boy's crotch. The sessions took place at the boy's mother's house.

- A nurse was raped by the priest whose advice she sought with regard to an annulment of her marriage to her abusive husband. On the couch in a Brooklyn rectory she was raped and sodomised by the priest. It was New Year's morning and the priest pulled her down onto his lap on the couch, and said, 'I want you to be my baby.' He flipped her onto her back on the couch, tore her jeans, panties and sneakers off in one yank, performed oral sex on her and then raped her while holding her down.

- Father S paid children for sex and drove them to having sex with other adults, including priests, while he watched. The same priest sent a boy and his cousin out to work as prostitutes at a bus station in Boston and allowed them to keep the money they earned as long as they recounted the details to him. Father S told his victims that he was a 'worker of God', warning the boys not to report the molesting, saying that no one would believe them.

- Father S pulled fourteen to seventeen year olds out of religious education classes, sexually assaulted them and made them perform oral sex on him in various locations at churches, including the rectory and the confessional. He also organised groups of older men and then played spin the bottle with the boys, pairing the 'winner' off with one of the older men for the purpose of sex.

- A fourteen-year-old boy was taken to meet Father S by a man in his church who gave him $50 each time he had sex with the priest.

- A seventeen-year-old boy was taken by a priest to gay bars.

- A priest asked an eleven-year-old boy whether he masturbated, then asked him to demonstrate.

- One boy was handed his train fare home by his priest after he had raped him and left him bleeding.

- A seven-year-old boy was anally raped so viciously that he had to be hospitalised.

- Rev. G of Louisiana took pornographic photos of his victims.

- Father Joseph E B molested children during confession.

- Father B played with the penis of a twelve-year-old boy in the sacristy, just off the altar at Our Lady of Fatima parish, Sudbury, Mass. This came out during a father-son sexual education talk, during which the boy told his father 'Jeez, dad, Father B played with my penis'.'

- Father S masturbated a child at a cabin in a woodland reservation south of Boston to which he would routinely take teenagers.

- A twelve-year-old boy was abused by a Dublin priest in the bathroom at a pub reception after his father's funeral, which the priest had attended.

- A Milford, New Jersey, priest had just finished saying Mass and he and an eleven-year-old, who had served as his altar boy, were changing clothes in a small changing room near the main altar where he sucked the boy's penis.

- On every night of a three-week cross-country trip, a priest sexually molested a boy in his care.

- Father L took thirteen- and fourteen-year-old boys from his parish on camping trips and had sex with them.

- Father A performed sexual acts on adolescent boys in the rectory in his New Hampshire church.

- Canon M in the south-east of Ireland, regularly came to the house of a twelve-year-old girl and inserted his finger in her vagina while questioning her about her development. The same priest also raped various other young girls in his parish.

- Father G came to the house of an eighteen-year-old married woman who was pregnant and offered to give her a 'maternity blessing'. He brought one hand underneath her bra … he was feeling her breasts for a few seconds and then brought the same hand from her breast over her stomach down to her genital area. He fondled with his fingers around her genital area for a few seconds. He then took away his hands and stopped praying and went to the kitchen to speak to the woman's mother.

- The same priest while preparing an eight-year-old girl for her First Holy Communion regularly stroked the back of her legs and would bring his hand directly up her legs to her private parts. The girl had presumed that this was the test for Holy Communion. On various occasions Father G actually penetrated the child's vagina with his fingers during confession.

Appendix 2

Roman Catholic bishops who have resigned since 1990 in the context of sex scandals (www.nhcatholics.org/whatsnew.htm#14jan2004, accessed 2 October 2004):

- The late Archbishop Eugene Marino of Atlanta, Georgia, in 1990, upon admitting involvement with a woman parishioner.
- Archbishop Robert Sanchez of Santa Fe, New Mexico, in 1993, after confessing relationships with adult women.
- Bishop J. Keith Symons of Palm Beach, Florida, in 1998, after admitting past molestation of five boys in three parishes.
- Bishop G. Patrick Ziemann of Santa Rosa, California, in 1999, when a priest claimed sexual coercion after Ziemann learned he had stolen parish funds. Ziemann said their relationship was consensual.
- Bishop Anthony O'Connell, Symons' successor in Palm Beach, in March 2002, after admitting repeated abuse of an underage student at the Missouri seminary he led. Others filed later suits.
- Archbishop Rembert Weakland of Milwaukee in May 2002, following news that his archdiocese paid US $450,000 to a man claiming Weakland attempted to sexually assault him. Weakland admitted an 'inappropriate relationship' but denied abuse.
- Auxiliary Bishop James McCarthy of New York, on 11 June 2002, after apologising for affairs with adult women.
- Bishop J. Kendrick Williams of Lexington, Kentucky., on 11 June 2002, following allegations he abused two minors and an eighteen-year-old decades before, which Williams denied.
- Cardinal Bernard Law, Archbishop of Boston, on 13 December 2002, following months of criticism for his mishandling of sex abuse claims against priests.
- Bishop Thomas J. O'Brien of Phoenix, on 18 June, 2003, after he was charged with leaving the scene of a fatal accident. He had recently

struck a deal to avoid indictment for allegedly sheltering molesters in the clergy.

- Archbishop Alphonsus Penney of Canada, in 1990, after a church commission criticised him for failing to prevent extensive abuse of orphanage boys.
- Bishop Eamonn Casey of Ireland, in 1992, upon admitting he fathered a child and used church offerings to pay the mother secret child support.
- Bishop Hubert O'Connor of Canada, charged in 1992 and imprisoned in 1996 for sexually assaulting two teenage girls as principal of a boarding school.
- The late Cardinal Hans Hermann Groer of Austria, sent into exile in 1995 following molestation claims from former high school boys. Neither Groer nor the Vatican directly admitted guilt.
- Bishop Hansjoerg Vogel of Switzerland, in 1995, after admitting he had impregnated a woman following his appointment to the hierarchy the preceding year.
- Bishop Roderick Wright of Scotland, in 1996, a week after he disappeared with a woman parishioner.
- Archbishop John Aloysius Ward of Wales, in 2001, after charges he ignored warnings about two priestly molesters.
- Archbishop Juliusz Paetz of Poland, in March 2002, amid allegations he had sexually harassed several priests, which he denied.
- Bishop Brendan Comiskey of Ireland, in April 2002, after apologizing for not preventing a priest's serial abuse.
- Auxiliary Bishop Franziskus Eisenbach of Germany, in April 2002, after a woman accused him of sexual abuse and injuries during an exorcism. The Vatican said resignation was no admission of guilt.
- Archbishop Edgardo Storni of Argentina, on 1 October, 2002, after a book said he abused at least forty-seven seminarians, although a Vatican investigation in 1944 found insufficient evidence to act. Storni said his resignation did not signify guilt.

Index

Index

Peron, Juan 136, 227
Perpignan 170
Perry, Marvin 373
Persona Humana 275-276, 387-388
Perth 108, 392
Peru 21, 118, 284, 289, 364
Pesaro 102
Petain, Henri 21
Peter's Pence 33, 84, 88-89
Petrarch, Francesco Petrarca 299
Pforzheim 170
Phayer, Michael 206, 376-81
Philadelphia 310
Philip IV (the Fair), King 15, 364
Philippines 74, 288
Phoenix 98, 328, 405
Piacenza 364
Pican, Pierre, Bishop of Baycaux 312
Picco, Jean-Pierre de 313
Piccolomini, Aeneas Silvio 83
Picolo Monitore 180, 181
Pierre, Archbishop Christophe 283
Pilot, The 334, 341
Pinochet, General Augusto 22
Pio of Pietreicina 45, 51
Pius II, Pope 83, 107, 390
Pius IV, Pope 86, 170
Pius V, Pope 163, 301-302
Pius VI, Pope 87, 108, 161, 357
Pius VII, Pope 117, 161
Pius IX, Pope 7, 18, 25, 27, 56, 161,
    165, 174, 180, 182, 241, 245, 349,
    356, 357, 367
Pius X, Pope 55, 65, 126, 147, 177,
    180, 362, 363, 371
Pius XI, Pope 20, 131, 178, 192, 194,
    196, 200, 202, 241, 243, 278-279,
    283, 286, 357, 377, 386, 389
Pius XII, Pope 80, 89, 132, 134-36,
    183, 195, 200, 202, 207, 211-212,
    215-17, 222, 225, 231, 234, 239,
    241, 243-244, 246, 279, 280, 357,
    378, 381
    See also Pacelli, Cardinal Eugenio
Place de Grève 66, 169
PLO 232, 234
Pohl, Oswald 221
Poitiers 102
Poland 18, 20, 52, 96, 98, 137, 187,

190, 196, 203, 206-207, 210, 229,
    237-238, 284, 288, 290, 358, 379,
    381, 406
Politi, Marco 357, 361
Political Life, Doctrinal Note on 23, 357
Pollard, Peter 320, 321
Polna 175
Pontifical Academy of Sciences 57,
    62, 67
Pontifical Council for Family 74
Pontoise 170
Poor Sisters of Nazareth 391
Porter, Fr James 308, 321, 394
Portugal 7, 16-17, 21, 45, 114, 117,
    119-121, 123, 169, 288, 358, 370
Poznan 314, 393
Practica inquisitionis 111
Preysing, Bishop Konrad Count von
    212
Price, Elizabeth 385
*Problem of Sexual Molestation by Roman
    Catholic Clergy* 307, 331, 338
Provence 167
Prunier, G. 371
Prussia 188, 267
Ptolemy, Claudius 57, 58
Puebla 22

Quarto abeunte saeculo 125, 371
Quijada, Diego 122
Quinn, Bishop A. James 331
Quod Apostolici Muneris 194, 357, 370

Rabelais, François 64
Radio Vatican 26, 74
Rahner, Karl 109
Ranke-Heimemann, Uta 255, 383,
    385-90
Raphael 301
Ratzinger, Cardinal Joseph 24, 71,
    271, 359
    see Benedict XVI, Pope
Rauff, Walter 225
Rausch, Bishop James S. 328
Ravenna 102, 104
Raymond VI, Count 155
Re, Cardinal Giovanni Battista 339
Reagan, President Ronald 2, 18, 355
Redemptoris Nostri 231

Printed in the United States
149360LV00002B/1/A